INQUIRY *into the*
NEW TESTAMENT

Ancient Context to
Contemporary Significance

DAVID T. LANDRY *with* JOHN W. MARTENS

ANSELM
ACADEMIC

Created by the publishing team of Anselm Academic.

The scriptural quotations contained herein are from the New Revised Standard Version of the Bible (unless otherwise noted). Copyright © 1993 and 1989 by the Division of Christian Education of the National Council of the Churches of Christ in the United States of America. All rights reserved.

Cover image: © Sant'Apollinare Nuovo, Ravenna, Italy/Bridgeman Images

Printed in the United States of America

7063

ISBN 978-1-59982-174-0

CONTENTS

INTRODUCTION

At one point, the working title of this book was *Academic Introduction to the New Testament*. Although the title did not survive, the concept did. What is an "academic" introduction to the New Testament? How is this book different from the numerous other books that are available to students and teachers of the New Testament?

To answer these questions, we must first make a distinction between the venues in which the Bible is studied. People read and discuss or think about the meaning of the Bible most commonly during church services, in church-sponsored Bible study groups, in religious education classes, on retreats, as part of individual quests for guidance and spiritual development, and in college classrooms. Usually there are no classes on the Bible in public school classrooms prior to the college level. Courses on the Bible are offered in both religiously-affiliated and secular schools, although the orientation of these classes might be somewhat different. This book is designed for academic use in the college or university classroom.

One of the things that is characteristic of the academic study of the Bible at the college level is that the teacher and the teaching materials usually strive to be neutral and objective in their approach, rather than favoring the interpretation of a particular religious tradition. Or, if neutrality and objectivity are abandoned, the teacher and the materials will at least be open and intentional when they are engaged in reading the Bible from a particular ideological perspective or social location. The academic study of the Bible seeks to avoid bias (or at least hidden or unstated bias), and to prevent presuppositions from determining the outcome of an inquiry with regard to, for example, whether a given historical event referenced in the Bible actually occurred, what the theological significance of this event was, or what a particular biblical author intended to communicate to his readers in a controversial passage. The effort to avoid bias is especially important and especially difficult when it comes to the Bible.

I often begin my undergraduate course introducing the New Testament by saying that the Bible is the most misread and most misunderstood book of all time. This is an opinion, of course, but one that I try to back up with evidence, namely with historical examples of blatant misreadings of the Bible. There is, for example, the theory espoused by the "Christian Identity" organization and other neo-fascist groups that Jesus was a Nazi. Most students immediately (and rightly) recognize this as a terrible misreading of the text. The only way that one could conclude that Jesus was an authoritarian and a white supremacist who hated Jews and racial minorities is by taking a small subset of Jesus' teachings wildly out of context, twisting the meaning of his words almost beyond recognition, and ignoring a massive body of evidence that contradicts the central claim. What these neo-fascists are doing, I explain, is what biblical scholars call *eisegesis*. This refers to "reading into" a text what one wants to see there. Its opposite is *exegesis*, which means getting out of a text that which it actually says. Now it is obvious to most students that the "Jesus-as-Nazi" theory is a particularly egregious example of eisegesis. But my point to them is that this happens *all the time*. It is not often quite so blatant, but people read into the Bible what they want to see there with amazing frequency. It is because of this that people with diametrically opposed viewpoints can nonetheless sincerely claim that the Bible agrees with them and disagrees with their opponents. Both feminists and men's rights activists argue strenuously that the Bible is on their side. Both capitalists and communists claim the Bible as an ally.

Why does this happen so often with respect to the Bible? Perhaps because many readers ascribe tremendous importance to the Bible *prior to their ever reading it*. Now it is certainly true that many people misrepresent what the Bible says because they never read it at all; they simply assume that they know what it says.[1] But the problem of eisegesis is not illustrated by these people, but rather by those who do read the Bible—with laser focus on proving that the Bible agrees with all of their preconceived notions. What is at work in their thought process, almost certainly unconsciously, is a syllogism something like this:

> P[1] The Bible contains the truth.
>
> P[2] What I believe is the truth.
>
> ∴ The Bible contains what I believe.

The first premise would be accepted by the overwhelming majority of those who were raised Christian, even (and perhaps especially) by those with little or no direct knowledge of the Bible's contents. The second premise is difficult to deny. People might be more or less certain that their beliefs are true, but they do not believe things that they know to be false. Each of these premises seems innocuous on its own, but when one combines them the result is rather dangerous: "The Bible contains what I believe." This suggests that people will tend to interpret the Bible in such a way as to confirm and verify everything they have always been taught. One can easily see how this thought process works in the "Jesus-as-Nazi" example. A modern neo-Nazi is convinced, for whatever reasons, that Aryans are the master race and that Jews and other racial groups are inferior and suitable only for enslavement or extermination. They are very certain that this is true. But they have also been raised to believe that the Bible contains the truth, and that Jesus preached the truth. Hence, they reason, Jesus *must have* been an advocate of white supremacy and vicious anti-Semitism. Jesus was all-knowing, so goes their logic, so there is simply no way that he would not have known the "truth" about the races. Therefore, whatever interpretive moves one needs to make in order to force Jesus into the mold of Nazi orthodoxy are justified. Taking quotes out of context, twisting the meaning of words, ignoring countervailing evidence or treating it as a later corruption of Jesus' actual teaching—all of these practices come to seem legitimate because they are deployed in the pursuit of a "higher truth" they believe they already know.

The Critical Interpretation of the Bible

The interpretive moves just mentioned are all part of what biblical scholars would call the "uncritical" use of scripture. Some principles of the critical use of the Bible, then, can be deduced by deriving their opposites. Hence, the critical study of the Bible includes (at least) the ideas that one should interpret passages in context, base one's conclusions on evidence, and avoid "special rules" for interpreting the Bible.

Context Is Crucial

Critical interpretations of the Bible will take into account both the literary and historical context of the verse, passage, and book under examination. *Literary context* refers to a consideration of both

---

1. An example of this I often cite is the result of a poll showing that a large majority of Americans believe that the saying "The Lord helps those that help themselves" comes from the Bible. It does not. The aphorism is attributed to Benjamin Franklin.

the genre of the text in question and of a verse or passage's place in the larger work of which it is a part. Bible verses and passages should not be taken out of context. To say that I claim in the pages above that "Jesus was a Nazi" would be an example of taking a quote badly out of context. Those four words did appear in a sentence, but in no sense did I indicate that I support this view; in fact, I made it very clear that I think the "Jesus-as-Nazi" theory has no merit whatsoever.

An example of taking something out of *historical context* might be claiming that Jesus was a Democrat (or a Republican). There were no Democrats or Republicans at the time of Jesus, and even the idea of a political spectrum running from liberal to conservative has little applicability in the time of Jesus. Jesus did express some views that have political implications, but to understand his political stance one would need to consider the political groups and ideologies *that were available at the time and place* of Jesus' ministry.

Evidence-Based Conclusions

Critical interpretations of the Bible base their conclusions on the weight of evidence, rather than on personal preference, conformity with tradition, or the guidance of religious authorities. In deciding a question such as Jesus' stance on homosexuality, for example, it should not matter whether the reader personally supports acceptance of homosexuality or opposes it, nor whether the interpreter's church leaders have voiced opposition or support for the LGBTQ

Prooftexting

Resolving not to take biblical verses and passages out of context would cause a large amount of contemporary biblical interpretation to disappear. When one reads popular books on the Bible or collections of sermons from famous preachers, so often it appears to be the case that a supposed expert on the Bible will take a pre-determined idea or conclusion, and then go looking for a biblical passage that will "prove" that the Bible supports it. The search for a verse or text that proves the author's point is supported by, or derived from, scripture gives this practice its name: prooftexting. Within critical biblical studies, prooftexting has a bad name, because (1) it often takes the quotes it uses out of context and hence distorts their meaning, and (2) it does not consider the *entirety* of what a particular biblical book says on a topic, or what the Bible as a whole has to say. If I wanted to argue that the Bible supports binge drinking, I might cite the fact that Jesus changes somewhere in the neighborhood of *150 gallons* of water into wine at the Wedding at Cana (John 2:1-12). That is a great deal of wine, and one could imagine its consumption leading to a festival of drunkenness. But in truth this fact means little unless one assumes that this large quantity of alcohol will be consumed by a small number of people over a short period of time. This is almost certainly not a safe assumption with respect to first-century Jewish wedding feasts, which were large affairs that often lasted several days. Moreover, one would need to balance whatever conclusion one might draw about Jesus' position on alcohol consumption from this one passage in the Gospel of John with any other statements Jesus might have made about drunkenness elsewhere in John and in other books of the New Testament (for example Luke 12:45 and 21:34). This example illustrates the problem with prooftexting: the Bible can be made to say virtually anything if one is willing to take its words and statements out of context.

community. The only thing that matters is identifying those passages from the Gospels that are relevant to the topic, interpreting those passages in context, reading them as fairly and accurately as possible, and then weighing the evidence on each side. Interpreters are then free, of course, to disagree with this teaching of the Bible, or of one of its authors, but at least this will be an honest disagreement rather than a manufactured consensus.

No "Special Rules" for Interpreting the Bible

Critical interpretations of the Bible use the exact same methods to determine the meaning of biblical texts that would be used to determine the meaning of any other work of literature. Critical interpretations draw historical conclusions about events referenced in the Bible by using the exact same methods one would apply in evaluating any other account of a historical event.

Uncritical biblical interpretation frequently insists that "special rules" must be used when it comes to the Bible, that its authors must be accorded special deference and authority, or that words and phrases that would almost certainly mean one thing in any other context mean something else when they are found in the Bible. For example, in 1 Corinthians 9:5, Paul mentions that the other apostles frequently bring their wives along with them when they travel. The Catholic Church, however, has often maintained that the apostles were unmarried and celibate, and that their celibacy is part of the reason that ordained priests should not be married. Many Catholic authorities have insisted that the Greek word *gynaika* that Paul uses here for the apostles' companions, a word that usually refers to "wives," in this context refers instead to "female servants."

Non-Catholic biblical scholars, as well as Catholics who engage in critical biblical scholarship, would regard this as an example of special pleading. The word *gynaika* almost certainly refers to wives when Paul uses it in 1 Corinthians 9:5. From the standpoint of critical biblical scholarship, the fact that this creates a bit of a problem for the Catholic policy on priestly celibacy is entirely beside the point.[2]

The rigorous use of the various critical methods of biblical interpretation is one way to limit the tendency to see in the Bible what we want to see there, rather than what the text actually says. However, it must be acknowledged that, since the advent of postmodernism, there has been a growing skepticism about whether anyone's interpretation of the Bible or any other text can be truly objective, neutral, or unbiased. Many would argue that bias is inevitable, and that people will invariably be influenced either consciously or unconsciously by their presuppositions. Rather than claiming an objectivity that is based on a lie, would it not be better, they argue, to acknowledge one's biases and admit that the interpretations of any individual are controlled by gender, class, sexual orientation, race, and other factors? All interpretations are relative to the perspective of the reader, and hence no single interpretation is any better than another.

This debate is similar to the dispute that has arisen in recent years involving television news. When Fox News Channel was created, its basic claim was that the other news outlets, although claiming to offer objective, fact-based journalism, were in fact all guilty of liberal bias. Fox, by contrast, would offer news and analysis that was genuinely "fair and balanced." It would include the conservative point of view rather than marginalizing or excluding it. Fox's critics from the beginning argued that instead of being fair and

---

2. Of course, the value of a celibate priesthood does not stand or fall with the interpretation of this one verse. Many Catholic theologians have made a strong case for priestly celibacy while acknowledging that Jesus' apostles were probably married.

balanced, the network was offering an explicitly right-wing perspective on the news and utilizing more bias than any of the so-called "liberal" news organizations it claimed to be counterbalancing. To combat the boost given to conservatives by Fox News, a number of unabashedly liberal news outlets emerged, both online and over the air.

One of the results of the intense polarization of the news business in the Fox News era is that we seem at times to be living in a "post-truth" society. Once it was commonly thought that both sides on any particular issue would have to agree on the facts, given their objective character, and they would disagree only about the interpretation of the facts. Now the facts themselves are in dispute. Whether the climate is changing, whether vaccines prevent or cause childhood illness, whether tax cuts produce surges in economic growth, whether the earth is round or flat, whether twenty children were shot and killed at Sandy Hook elementary school in 2012, are items about which there would once have been a wide consensus, because they are all questions of fact, not of opinion. Now it seems as if there are no subjects on which there are an agreed-upon set of facts.

This state of affairs is both lamentable and unnecessary. The truth is that facts are as stubborn as they have always been, despite the delusions of partisans and conspiracy-theorists on both sides. It is true that there is no such thing as a purely objective, unbiased interpretation of scripture, but that does not mean that all interpretations are equally valid, or that no interpretation is any better than another. There might not be a single, correct interpretation of a controversial biblical text, but it does not follow from this that there are no objective standards by which one might evaluate the relative merit of divergent interpretations. The great Hebrew Bible scholar Jon Levinson was once asked about the inevitability of biased interpretation and the corresponding need to admit that objective reading

was a fiction. Levinson responded with an analogy: one might not be able to achieve perfect antisepsis (a germ-free environment) in the operating room, but that did not mean that he would advocate performing surgery in a sewer. His point was that all interpretations are biased, but some are more biased than others. One might not be able to avoid the presence of all germs in the operating room, but it is both possible and preferable to have as few as possible. The chaos of a "post-truth" society is not the inevitable outcome of the acknowledgement of the biased character of all interpretation. It is worth the effort to distinguish between those interpretations that are supported by more evidence and those that lack such backing. Reasonable application of the critical method should help us make this distinction.

A Nod to Predecessors

I began this introduction by reflecting on the question of how this book is different from other introductions to the New Testament, and in answering it I placed heavy emphasis on the word "academic" and distinguished between the study of the Bible in a university setting as opposed to a non-academic setting. Of course, this is hardly the first book written to accompany the study of the New Testament in an academic context.

I have used several very good introductions to the New Testament in my three decades as a teacher. I started with Norman Perrin's classic *The New Testament: Proclamation and Parenesis, Myth and History* (1974), a project that was taken over very capably by Dennis Duling after Perrin's death in 1976 and revised into several new editions. I also briefly used Stephen Harris's fine textbook, *The New Testament: A Student's Introduction*. But since its first appearance in 2003, I have used Bart Ehrman's immensely popular *The New Testament: A Historical Introduction to the Early Christian Writings*. Now in its sixth edition, this textbook has dominated the market in recent years.

This book resembles Ehrman's in several ways. In two instances—when introducing the formation of the New Testament canon and the characteristics of pagan religions—I use an organizational schema drawn from Ehrman. Other similarities between my work and Ehrman's are coincidental. For example, Ehrman's work is admirably free of sectarian or denominational bias, and I strive for this as well. Also, from my first years of teaching the New Testament, I was a proponent of introducing the various methods of biblical criticism inductively. So was Ehrman, which is one of the reasons I chose his textbook for my class; it fit very well with what I was already doing. Ehrman does not teach the methods of biblical criticism in the abstract but introduces them in connection to their practical application. He introduces each method in connection with a single New Testament text: literary criticism with Mark, redaction criticism with Matthew, etc. I follow the same strategy in this book.

Although there are many similarities, there are differences as well. Ehrman's book is quite long. It is too long—or so it seemed to me—to work very well in a one-semester introduction to the New Testament. Ehrman also spends a fair amount of time interpreting second- and third-century Christian literature and showing how the trajectory of New Testament texts continued into the post-apostolic period of early Christianity. This is interesting and valuable information, but I found that I never had the time to include it in my sections of Introduction to the New Testament. I do see the value in going past the New Testament era to examine noncanonical gospels, but I confine that examination to a single chapter and otherwise stick almost exclusively to the Christian literature produced in the first century CE.

Lastly, my own teaching is characterized by frequent digressions from the strictly historical examination of the meaning of the New Testament into what I call the "so what?" question. Perhaps this is because I teach exclusively at the undergraduate level and my students are taking the course to fulfill a general requirement—in other words, they are there because they *have to* be there, not always because they *want to* be there—but I feel compelled to explain how and why the debates over the meaning of various biblical texts is relevant to modern people. Very often this relevance is confined to people of faith, and thus questions of theology are among the most frequently addressed in these digressions. But I am also at pains to point out that even people with no particular faith commitment can profit from the study of the New Testament and that there are times when such people will be affected by the outcomes of debates over the meaning of the New Testament whether they like it or not. Hence I have sprinkled every chapter with sidebars, many of which address the "so what?" question, and I have also dedicated an entire final chapter to exploring the role of the New Testament in the modern world. These kinds of discussions are almost invariably more controversial than conversations that restrict themselves to the meaning and role of the New Testament in the distant past. But people who wish to avoid controversy are well-advised not to talk about the Bible. Passionate disagreement comes with the territory.

The Formation of the New Testament

Neither the New Testament nor early Christianity dropped from the sky fully formed. Scholars who seek to understand early Christianity in an academic context look at its history and literature as a *process* rather than as a *product*. They also examine the variety of expressions of early Christianity rather than imagining early Christianity as a single, monolithic entity. Christianity eventually developed in such a way that certain views became unacceptable and the religion generally united under a single set of beliefs. But this was not always the case.

Early Christianity was a highly diverse phenomenon. There were a large number of groups calling themselves Christian that had some radically different views on issues that were far from trivial, such as the number of gods that existed and the humanity and divinity of Christ. Many modern Christians might be more comfortable if the truths of early Christianity were immediately and manifestly obvious to all the faithful, such that there were no significant disagreements among them that might raise later doubts about the facts of the matter. However, that which is comforting is not always that which is true.

Evidence of the diversity of early Christianity can be found within the New Testament itself. Leaders of a particular branch of the early Christian church—the **proto-orthodox**[1] branch—chose the books of the New Testament at least in part because they reflected the distinctive views of that group and refuted the views of their Christian rivals, but even these texts exhibit a range of opinion. The Gospel of Mark, for example, presents a very human Jesus, while the Gospel of John places much more emphasis on his divinity. Although the books of the New Testament reflect a broad consensus and came to represent the views of a single group, the authors of the books of the New Testament do not always agree with each other. Indeed, scholarly study of the New Testament involves identifying the points of agreement and disagreement, seeing how Christianity turned one way and then another, what different possibilities were explored, which options were embraced or rejected, and how things could have turned out quite differently.

Scholars know even more about the diversity of early Christianity from the books that did not make it into the New Testament. Numerous ancient gospels were written besides the four found in the New Testament. Many early histories in addition to the New Testament's Acts of the Apostles purport to recount the deeds and teachings of Jesus' disciples. Far more letters were

---

1. The terminology as well as the classification scheme for the major groups of early Christianity are taken from chapter 1 of Bart Ehrman, *The New Testament: A Historical Introduction to the Early Christian Writings*, 6th ed. (New York: Oxford University Press, 2016).

The Books of the New Testament

The books of the New Testament fall into four categories:

1. Gospels, which are quasi-biographical accounts of the life and teaching of Jesus

2. Acts, comprising stories about the words and deeds of a special class of Jesus' followers, namely the apostles who spread the message of Christ after his death

3. Letters (or "epistles"), which purport to be the direct communications of Jesus' apostles to churches or particular groups of Christians

4. Apocalypses, books written by seers or visionaries to whom the secrets about the end of the world have been revealed

supposedly written by apostles than those found in the New Testament. Moreover, the book of Revelation is one of a number of apocalypses written by early Christians.

Why do Christians know the Gospel of Matthew and Gospel of Luke but not the *Gospel of Peter* and *Gospel of Thomas*? The short answer is that Matthew and Luke are included in the Bible, while *Peter* and *Thomas* are not. But this begs the question: How did it come to be that some books were included in the New Testament while others were not? The answer to this deeper question lies in the history of the formation of the canon.

A **canon** is a collection of books regarded as authoritative by a given religious community. Usually these books are regarded as inspired by the gods or revealed from above. In some way they are thought to have some kind of divine origin that guarantees their reliability. Most religions practiced by literate people have a set of sacred texts that are authoritative to various

degrees. Hindus venerate the books of the Vedas, Buddhists have their sutras, and Muslims revere the Qur'an. The Christian canon is known simply as the Bible (or the Holy Bible). It consists of two major divisions: the Old Testament and the New Testament. The word **testament** (Latin, *testamentum*) comes from the Latin translation of the Bible, where it means "covenant"; it reflects the Christian view that God originally made a covenant with the Jewish people that entailed practicing circumcision and following the Law of Moses, and that God made a new covenant with those who believe in Jesus Christ.

The existence of the Old Testament, then, reflects the fact that Christianity has a mother religion. Christianity emerged from ancient Judaism, first as a sect of the older religion and then as a distinct religion separate from its progenitor. Ancient Judaism already had a canon, a collection of sacred texts, now commonly known as the Hebrew Bible. While the makeup of that canon was still in flux at the time of Jesus, certain books—such as the five books of the **Torah** (Hebrew, "Law") or **Pentateuch** (Greek, "five scrolls")—were canonical for all Jews. One of the decisions, then, that early Christian leaders faced was whether to keep or discard the Jewish scriptures when forming their own canon. Many advocated dispensing with these books, believing that the new religion represented a basic rupture from the old. The proto-orthodox Christians, however, who emerged as the dominant group, advocated retaining the Jewish scriptures. In their estimation, the Jewish scriptures included not just the Torah but also the **Nevi'im** ("Prophets," including such historical books as Joshua, Judges, Samuel, Kings, and books by or about ancient Israelite prophets such as Jeremiah, Ezekiel, and Isaiah) and the **Ketuvim** ("Writings," including such books of wisdom as the Psalms, Proverbs, Job, and Ecclesiastes). With the triumph of proto-orthodox Christians over their rivals, this decision was cemented in place for all modern forms of Christianity. Every

Biblical Inspiration

Believers and nonbelievers take different approaches to any text for which inspired status is claimed. Such claims are, by their very nature, impossible to prove.

Even among believers, however, "**inspiration**" can be taken to mean different things. Some claim that the very words of a sacred text are inspired by God. This is known as "verbal inspiration," and it is characteristic of most (but not all) evangelical denominations of Christianity, especially those that embrace the "fundamentalist" label. This view holds that while human authors played a role, the real author of the Bible is God. As a result, they maintain that the Bible is inerrant, containing no mistakes whatsoever, and generally argue that the Bible should be interpreted literally.

The Southern Baptist Convention is an example of a denomination that is not reluctant to state its belief in biblical inerrancy: "The Holy Bible was written by men divinely inspired and is God's revelation of Himself to man. It is a perfect treasure of divine instruction. It has God for its author, salvation for its end, and truth, without any mixture of error, for its matter. Therefore, all Scripture is totally true and trustworthy."[2]

Many people find it difficult to hold such a view because of the many seeming contradictions within and between the books of the Bible, apparent mistakes by biblical writers on matters of fact, and the difficulty of reconciling the findings of modern science with a literal reading of some parts of scripture. In view of these difficulties, more moderate and progressive Christian denominations have developed a more nuanced notion of inspiration. The Catholic Church and the mainline Protestant denominations do not insist that every

Public domain

Caravaggio's "Inspiration of Saint Matthew" (1602) illustrates the concept of verbal inspiration; Saint Matthew, writing his Gospel, takes dictation from an angel.

statement in the Bible is literally true, nor do they maintain that God directly authored the texts. Instead, they assert that God inspired the biblical authors in a more general way, such that there is a divine assurance that the Bible as a whole includes those truths essential for human salvation. They also believe the human authors of the Bible were given the freedom to express these truths in genres as

continued

---

2. "Basic Beliefs," Southern Baptist Convention, *www.sbc.net/aboutus/basicbeliefs.asp.*

they saw fit (including myth as well as history), and in ways that were appropriate for their time and culture.[3] These denominations allow for the possibility of errors, but deny that the scriptures as a whole could ever lead a person astray on essential matters of salvation. They also insist that scripture must be interpreted according to its genre and historical context, and that not every biblical statement represents a timeless and literal truth.

denomination of Christianity today has a canon that includes the Old Testament.

When it came to the formation of the New Testament, early Christians engaged in a sometimes-bitter debate over which books were reliable and trustworthy. Indeed, the canon of the New Testament formed as a result of a competition among rival early Christian groups.[4] Each group sought to maximize its influence and garner the largest number of supporters. One way to argue that a group's beliefs and practices were superior to those of its rivals was to assert that the sacred texts of that group were older, better, and more reliable.

Early Christian Groups and Their Sacred Texts

Christianity began as a small religious movement founded by an itinerant preacher known as Jesus of Nazareth, who lived in the beginning of the first century CE. Jesus left no writings, but his followers eventually began writing down sayings and stories by and about Jesus that had circulated orally for decades. The problem with these written records—the canonical and noncanonical gospels—is that, taken together, they provide an incomplete, confusing, and wildly contradictory account of the life and teachings of Jesus. The earliest surviving gospel—the canonical Gospel of Mark—was written some forty years after the death of Jesus. Moreover, Christians continued to write gospels for centuries thereafter. Each of these gospels implicitly claims to contain the truth about Jesus Christ, and carries the corresponding but unstated claim that any gospel speaking to the contrary about Jesus is perpetrating falsehood. Given the amount of contradiction, there is no chance all these accounts can be 100 percent accurate. Some are almost certainly the inventions of later generations of Christians who developed their own views about Jesus and then created stories that justified and confirmed those views. For example, as the rivalry between Christianity and Judaism became more bitter, some Christian groups came to believe that Jesus was completely opposed to Judaism, and wrote gospels[5] in which the Jewish authorities' hatred of Jesus and responsibility for his death were seriously exaggerated, and in which Jesus' criticisms of Judaism are especially pointed and damning.

---

3. Catholics can consult official church documents such as the papal encyclical *Divino afflante spiritu* (1943), the Vatican II document *Dei verbum* (1965), and the Pontifical Biblical Commission's "The Interpretation of the Bible in the Church" (1994) for further information. The Protestant world is too diverse to enable a listing of various mainline denominations' statements on biblical inspiration, but curious students can usually find such statements on each denomination's web site.

4. This is not to say that if early Christianity had been a completely unified phenomenon, a canon would not have emerged. However, the reality was that several rival groups claimed to be the true inheritors of the tradition of Jesus and used a variety of sacred books to buttress their claims. This fact created a certain urgency and forced groups to define themselves, at least in part, in comparison to their opponents.

5. An example of such a gospel, discussed in chapter 2, is the noncanonical *Gospel of Peter*.

Year Markings

At the time of Jesus, there was no widespread system for determining what year it was. In the absence of such a system, authors used well-known events or figures to establish a relative time frame. Roman writers often used the identity of the consuls of Rome or the regnal year of an emperor to establish the timing of an event.

To apply an absolute number to a given year, one needs a starting point. The idea of dating events using the birth of Jesus as the linchpin was conceived by a Christian monk named Dionysius Exiguus in the sixth century and became popular in Christian Europe within a few centuries. The supposed date of the birth of Jesus was assigned the designation of AD 1 (Latin, *anno Domini*, "year of the Lord"), while the previous year became known as 1 BC (based on the English phrase "before Christ").

This system is widely used in the Christian West but is not universal. Jews have a dating system that starts with the supposed year of creation, and by their reckoning most of the year AD 2000 was the year AM 5761 (Latin, *anno mundi*, "year of the world"). The Muslim calendar begins with the *hijra* ("flight") of Muhammad and his followers to escape persecution in Mecca and the establishment of the first Muslim community in Medina, which made AD 2000 the year 1421 AH (Latin, *anno hegirae*).

Most biblical scholars continue to use the Christian practice of dating events from the birth of Christ, although the designations of AD and BC have been largely replaced by **CE** (the Common Era) and **BCE** (before the Common Era). Some see this as a nod to political correctness, but for most it is an easy enough adjustment to make to avoid giving the impression that the whole world revolves around Christianity.

It is impossible to establish the "truth" of these matters to everyone's satisfaction. This does not mean, however, that it is impossible to adjudicate any of the competing claims about Jesus. Was he really anti-Jewish, or was he a Jewish reformer? Was he a human prophet or an all-powerful divine visitor? Arguments could be mounted to assert that some accounts are more probable than others, and it is precisely this claim that each of the rival groups of Christianity made for their sacred texts vis-à-vis those of their competitors.

Marcionite Christians

The first real canon was apparently created by a prominent Christian leader of the mid-second century, **Marcion** of Synope.[6] Marcion believed that the apostle Paul was the one true follower of Christ, the one who correctly and accurately transmitted the teachings and significance of Jesus. In particular, Marcion attached tremendous importance to Paul's letters, and argued that Christianity needed to change course and return to Paul's vision. Paul, at least as Marcion interpreted him, taught that salvation cannot be found in the observance of the Law of Moses and is granted only to those who have faith in Christ. Marcion appears to have taken this as a blanket condemnation of the Old Testament; he came to believe that the God he saw represented there—demanding, vengeful, impossibly strict—was irreconcilable with the merciful, compassionate, forgiving God spoken of by Paul. Marcion concluded that there were two different Gods,

---

6. Three of the most prominent New Testament scholars of the canon—Metzger, Grant, and Ehrman—all grant Marcion the honor of having been first.

and that the God of Christianity was infinitely preferable to the creator-god of the Old Testament (whom he called the "Demiurge"). Marcion began to preach that Christians should utterly reject Judaism, its scriptures, and all of its ways.[7]

In effect, Marcion rested his claims on a canon of scripture. His canon consisted of ten letters of Paul, which he grouped under the heading "Apostle," and one (unattributed) written account of the life and teachings of Jesus, which he termed "Gospel." While Marcion enjoyed a brief popularity, his movement was eventually consigned to the dustbin of history. During his lifetime he was declared a heretic by the proto-orthodox group to which he had once belonged (as a bishop, no less), and his writings were suppressed.

While there are no extant copies of Marcion's writings or of his version of the gospel and epistles he held sacred, scholars do know something of their contents from books written by his opponents. Marcion's gospel, for example, reflected his view that Jesus was not really human but was strictly a divine spirit. The idea that Jesus merely "appeared" to be human is known as **Docetism** (from the Greek word *dokeō*, "to appear"). This gospel contained, then, no account of the birth of Jesus—birth to a human mother apparently being impossible for a being who is fully divine. In addition, Marcion's version of Paul's letters emphasized the strict discontinuity between Judaism and Christianity.

The gospel used by Marcion is essentially the one that would eventually be known as the Gospel of Luke, although the canonical version of this gospel clearly differs in some important respects from Marcion's gospel. Which version is

the more authentic? Did Marcion take the Gospel of Luke and edit out parts he did not like (such as the virgin birth)? This is what his leading orthodox opponent, the late-second-century bishop Tertullian, claimed. Or did proto-orthodox Christians take Marcion's gospel, add some non-Marcionite elements, and then rechristen it as the Gospel of Luke? The original of the gospel (known as the **autograph**) or a very early copy could decide this question, but no such manuscripts survive, which leaves this as something of a "he said–she said" issue. The same debate rages over the letters of Paul in Marcion's canon. All ten of these letters are also in the proto-orthodox canon, but the canonical versions are not nearly as anti-Jewish as the Marcionite versions.[8]

What these discrepancies tell us is that rival groups not only selected different sacred texts to justify their beliefs but also that when two groups chose the same book, it was not uncommon for one or both groups to edit the book to better reflect their views. Attempting to determine the original version of these books is the aim of much scholarly work (see especially chapter 7).

Jewish-Christian Adoptionists

At the other end of the spectrum from the anti-Jewish and docetic Marcionites was a pro-Jewish group of Christians who saw Jesus as just a man—a great man, to be sure, but still a man and not a god. These **Jewish-Christian adoptionists** looked to Peter and James, "the brother of the Lord," rather than Paul as their apostolic ancestors. Apparently the strictness of the monotheism they inherited from Judaism led them to deny the divinity of Christ. If there

---

7. This summary of Marcion's thought is based mostly on Tertullian's five-volume *Adversus Marcionem* ("Against Marcion"). Given that Tertullian hated everything about Marcionite Christianity, scholars have had to sift through his report of Marcionite beliefs for signs that Tertullian exaggerated or caricatured them. See Bart Ehrman, *Lost Christianities: The Battles for Scripture and the Faiths We Never Knew* (New York: Oxford University Press, 2003), 104–9, for a fuller account of Marcionite Christianity and its sacred texts.

8. See Tertullian, *Adversus Marcionem* 2.643–46, for examples of "pro-Jewish" passages allegedly purged by Marcion.

Digital image courtesy of the Getty's Open Content Program

The Gospels declare that the Holy Spirit descended upon Jesus at his baptism and a heavenly voice declared him to be God's "Son." Adoptionist Christians sometimes cited this event as the point at which God adopted Jesus.

is only one God—all-powerful, eternal, and indivisible—then it would not make sense to say that Jesus was a god. In their view, if there is God the father (Yahweh) and God the son (Jesus), then there would be two gods. They did not see any way around this dilemma, other than to say that Jesus was not God but was a creature, that is, a being created by God.

In what sense, then, could this group be termed *Christian*? Like other groups of Christians, they claimed salvation was found in Jesus.

Jesus may have been a creature, but he was the best and most perfect of God's creatures. His righteousness, in their view, led God to choose him above all other creatures to be the Messiah. When God elected Jesus as the Messiah, he adopted Jesus as his son. This was a ceremonial rather than literal description, but it had power nonetheless. Because Jesus had been chosen, he was endowed with special powers (like the ability to perform miracles) and his life and death took on a special significance. Because he was God's adopted son, Jesus' death on the cross was not like an ordinary human death but functioned as a sacrifice that brought about the forgiveness of sin.[9]

Jewish-Christian adoptionists thought the sacrifice of Jesus on the cross meant there was no longer any need to perform animal sacrifices like those Jews had performed for centuries at the Temple in Jerusalem. But the other requirements of Judaism remained: subjecting males to circumcision, observing the commandments found in the Law of Moses, and observing ritual purity (including "keeping kosher," the Jewish system of dietary restrictions).

Unlike the Marcionites, who rejected the Old Testament and revered Paul as the one true apostle, Jewish-Christian adoptionists continued to think of the Jewish scriptures as their own and had no regard for the letters of Paul, whom they regarded as a traitor to Judaism. They kept the Law, Prophets, and Writings and simply supplemented them with some gospels that reflected their distinctive point of view. Their eventual designation as heretics led to the suppression of their sacred texts, and so there are no surviving copies of their gospels. Descriptions[10] of them written by their opponents, however, reveal that adoptionists used at least three gospels: the *Gospel of the Ebionites*, the *Gospel of the Nazareans*,

---

9. This summary of Jewish-Christian adoptionist thought is based in part on Ehrman, *Lost Christianities*, 99–103.

10. References to the Jewish-Christian gospels are found in the writings of Clement, Origen, Jerome, and Cyril of Alexandria.

and the *Gospel of the Hebrews*. One of these (*Nazareans*) is thought to have been very similar to the canonical Gospel of Matthew, but without Matthew's infancy narrative. These gospels did not include the story of Jesus' birth to a virgin named Mary, because Jewish-Christians believed Jesus had two human parents. Adoptionists also saw Jesus' baptism as the moment at which God chose Jesus and "begat" him as his son. The wording of the Gospel of Mark with respect to Jesus' baptism seems to have resonated with Jewish-Christian adoptionists: "You are my son, my beloved son, with whom I am well pleased" (Mark 1:11; author's translation). Their view would have been that God was not acknowledging a preexisting situation, but that God was *making* Jesus his son at that very moment. He was also explaining why he had chosen Jesus for the role: because he was "well pleased" with him.

Gnostic Christians

The sacred texts of the Marcionites and the Jewish-Christians are lost to us, but history has been kinder to another group that was eventually condemned as heretical and eclipsed by proto-orthodox Christianity: the **Gnostics**. Some copies of Gnostic gospels were known to scholars prior to the twentieth century, but the study of Gnostic Christianity received a huge boost with an incredible archeological find in 1945. Two brothers were supposedly digging for fertilizer—others say they were grave robbing— outside of a town named Nag Hammadi in upper Egypt when they found an earthenware vessel containing thirteen ancient books written on papyrus. They brought the codex-form[11]

manuscripts home and began to sell them individually to antiquities dealers in Cairo, although their mother is alleged to have burned some of the priceless artifacts as well. The texts turned out to be a trove of Gnostic Christian literature written in the third and fourth centuries and buried shortly thereafter, probably for safekeeping during a persecution. Included were the only complete copy of the *Gospel of Thomas* and the only partial copy of the *Gospel of Philip*, among other treasures. Eventually, the significance of the find was recognized, and it became known as the **Nag Hammadi library**.[12]

While the library and other evidence uncovered about Gnosticism before and after 1945 reveals this was the most internally diverse group of ancient Christians, there are some common elements to Gnostic Christianity. One of the Nag Hammadi texts, the *Apocryphon* (Greek, "secret book") *of John*, contains a reasonably clear statement of the foundational myth of Gnosticism.

According to this version of the Gnostic myth, in the beginning there was only one being: a purely spiritual, all-powerful, perfect, and eternal god known as the **Monad**. The Monad eventually spawned a second generation of divine beings called the **Aeons**, and one of the Aeons in turn produced the first of a third generation of beings—the **Archons**. This third generation is an inferior class of demonic beings and comes to operate independently of the higher gods. Their leader, an arrogant god called Yaltabaoth (or Ialdebaoth) fashions a world for them to inhabit, a world "below" the heavenly realm occupied by the Monad and the Aeons. This is the physical world as we know it, an evil world created by a malevolent being out of inferior materials,

---

11. A codex has a form like that of today's books, with pages or leaves bound on one side so that pages can be flipped or turned. This form supplanted the older kind of manuscript, the scroll, which had no binding and needed to be turned in order to advance or go back.

12. The story of the discovery of the Nag Hammadi codices is recounted in James M. Robinson's "The Discovery of the Nag Hammadi Codices," *Biblical Archaeologist* 42, no. 4, "The Nag Hammadi Library and Its Archeological Context" (Autumn 1979): 206–24. Some elements of this story have since been disputed.

physical elements that by their nature are corruptible and not eternal.

Yaltabaoth is also responsible for the creation of human beings, but these creatures are unique because they contain a "spark" of light or spirit that was captured by the Archons. This causes the Archons to become jealous of humans, and they seek to keep them trapped below and to prevent them from ascending to the heavenly world of spirit from which their "sparks" originated. Their method for doing so includes keeping humans ignorant of their true nature and luring them into sins of the flesh that prevent them from awakening to their spiritual nature. Foremost among the sins of the flesh is sex.

As a result, following their creation, human beings become mired in the world of the flesh, a world of sin, evil, and suffering. This is caused by their ignorance of their true (divine) nature and potential. The solution to this is for the Monad to send someone from the heavenly realm, a **revealer**, who can provide ignorant humans with the knowledge (Greek, *gnōsis*) they need to escape the shackles of earthly misery and realize their divine potential. According to Gnostic Christians, Jesus is this revealer.

Jesus' heavenly origin meant that, for Gnostics just as much as for Marcionites, Jesus was strictly divine and not at all human. Some Gnostics embraced the previously mentioned notion of Docetism, whereby Jesus merely pretended to be human. According to this theory, despite Jesus' fleshly appearance, he was purely spirit. And because he did not have a human body, he could not suffer or die. Other Gnostics embraced an alternate theory in which there was a human being named Jesus of Nazareth whose body was temporarily occupied (or "possessed") by a divine being called the Logos. The Logos then used Jesus as a human mouthpiece to communicate the wisdom and knowledge essential for salvation. This divine being is thought to have entered Jesus' body at the time of his baptism and to have departed it just prior to his death on the cross. A Gnostic version of Jesus' famous cry on the cross reads, "My power, my power! Why have you abandoned me?" (*Gospel of Peter* 5.19).[13]

Regardless of which explanation was embraced, it is clear Gnostics did not believe Jesus saved humanity by suffering and dying on the cross. His salvific activity consisted of providing knowledge, and so in Gnostic gospels the emphasis is not on Jesus as miracle worker or martyr, but Jesus as teacher.

The denial of Jesus' humanity and of his sacrificial death, combined with the unabashed polytheism of Gnostics, led to their being condemned as heretics by the proto-orthodox Christians. Their works were suppressed just as were those of Marcion and the Jewish-Christian adoptionists, but their popularity and longevity—along with some good fortune—meant their books have not completely disappeared. In fact, most of the noncanonical gospels that survive are Gnostic gospels, and they provide the best illustration of just how different the Christian canon would have been if some other group had won the battle for dominance in early Christianity.

Proto-Orthodox Christians

The competition between rival groups of early Christians was won by a group that would eventually be known as the "holy catholic and apostolic church." However, it was not known as such in its earliest days, and the titles that it gave itself (such as *catholic*, which means "universal," and *apostolic*, which implies that this is the only version of Christianity that can properly trace its ancestry back to Jesus' apostles) were

---

13. As quoted in Bruce M. Metzger, *The Canon of the New Testament: Its Origin, Development, and Significance* (Oxford: Clarendon, 1987), 172.

The Lefke Gate, shown here, was part of the ancient city wall of Nicaea, cite of the church council in 325. The Nicene Creed, which resulted from this council, would become the standard of faith for most Christians.

either not yet true or a matter of considerable dispute. Hence scholars refer to the members of this group as "proto-orthodox" Christians. This term indicates this was the version of Christianity that eventually achieved dominance over all other forms, a dominance reflected in the fact that it was declared the official religion of the Roman Empire in the late fourth century. The term *orthodoxy* literally means "true (or straight) opinion/belief," and its opposite is *heresy*, which means "opinion, system of thought" and came to be synonymous with "false teaching." Members of rival Christian churches would not have ceded the title "orthodox" to this group, nor would those rival groups have accepted the pejorative "heretic" for themselves. History is written by the winners, as the cliché goes, which is why the proto-orthodox group was able to claim the "orthodox" label for themselves and to brand their opponents as "heretics."

The beliefs of the dominant group are well-known to members of Christian denominations today, because most modern forms of Christianity derive from the "orthodox" Christianity that was summed up in the Nicene

Creed of 325 CE (revised and expanded at Constantinople in 381 CE), a creed still recited in many Christian churches. The polytheism of Gnosticism and the bitheism (belief in two gods) of Marcion are rejected in the creed's opening statement, "We believe in one God." The creed further rejects the Gnostic and Marcionite belief that the physical world is an evil place created by an evil god, while heaven is a good place inhabited by a good god (or gods). This is evident in the second half of the creed's first line: "We believe in one God . . . maker of heaven and earth."

The section on Jesus shows that the proto-orthodox did not share the Jewish-Christian adoptionists' denial of Christ's divinity: "We believe in one Lord, Jesus Christ, the only Son of God, eternally begotten of the Father, God from God, Light from Light, true God from true God, begotten, not made, of one Being with the Father." However, neither did they accept the Gnostic and Marcionite view that Jesus was strictly divine and did not share our human nature. Against the docetic view of Gnostics and Marcionites, that Jesus was a pure spirit who had merely pretended to be human and who could not suffer or die, the creed states that Jesus "became man," "suffered," and "died."

The proto-orthodox group also rejected the extreme anti-Jewishness of Marcion and the corresponding dismissal of the Old Testament. This is clear from the statement that Jesus rose again "in accordance with the scriptures" and the reference to the Holy Spirit as having "spoken through the prophets."

The proto-orthodox canon included the Old Testament and the collection of Christian writings now known as the New Testament. The

The Nicene-Constantinopolitan Creed

We believe in one God,
the Father, the Almighty,
maker of heaven and earth,
of all that is, seen and unseen.
We believe in one Lord, Jesus Christ,
the only Son of God,
eternally begotten of the Father,
God from God, Light from Light,
true God from true God,
begotten, not made,
of one Being with the Father.
Through him all things were made.
For us and for our salvation
he came down from heaven:
by the power of the Holy Spirit
he became incarnate from the Virgin Mary,
and was made man.
For our sake he was crucified under
    Pontius Pilate;
he suffered death and was buried.
On the third day he rose again

in accordance with the Scriptures;
he ascended into heaven
and is seated at the right hand of
    the Father.
He will come again in glory to judge the
    living and the dead,
and his kingdom will have no end.
We believe in the Holy Spirit, the Lord,
    the giver of life,
who proceeds from the Father and
    the Son.[14]
With the Father and the Son he is
    worshiped and glorified.
He has spoken through the Prophets.
We believe in one holy catholic and
    apostolic Church.
We acknowledge one baptism for the
    forgiveness of sins.
We look for the resurrection of the dead,
and the life of the world to come.
    Amen.[15]

books chosen for the New Testament reflect the views of the proto-orthodox group. Nonetheless, the views found in each canonical text do not all agree perfectly with those of fourth-century orthodoxy. Part of the reason for this is that the beliefs found in the fourth-century Nicene-Constantinopolitan Creed represent the mature and considered views of proto-orthodox Christianity, whereas the first-century Gospels and letters represent the earliest, most primitive attempts to articulate that faith. For example, orthodox theologians eventually formed the idea of the Trinity to explain how there could be one God in three persons. Yet the New Testament does not use the word *trinity* and contains only one or two passages in which one can detect even a hint of the concept (see Matt. 28:18–19 and 2 Cor. 13:13).[16]

---

14. The phrase "and the Son" is historically controversial, as it was not originally part of the creed, but was added to the form of the creed used in Western churches in the eleventh century.

15. The preceding is the 1975 English translation of the Nicene-Constantinopolitan Creed produced by the ICET (International Consultation on English Texts), published in a booklet entitled *Prayers We Have in Common*, and adopted for use in the Catholic and Episcopal Churches for several decades thereafter.

16. This list does not include 1 John 5:7–8, because the Trinitarian version of these verses—which reads, "For there are three that bear record in heaven, the Father, the Word, and the Holy Ghost: and these three are one" (KJV)—was not originally part of the text of 1 John, but was a later addition. Note that the NRSV translation of these verses—"There are three that testify: the Spirit and the water and the blood, and these three agree"—does not have the same Trinitarian overtones.

The Development of the Proto-Orthodox Canon

When the leaders of the proto-orthodox church identified texts to be included in the canon of the New Testament, they did not do so thinking that each and every book reflected and agreed with the final views of proto-orthodox doctrine, but rather that the books *taken as a whole* did so. For example, the definitive, orthodox position on the humanity and divinity of Christ was that Jesus is fully divine and fully human, like us in all things except for sin. No book in the New Testament exactly articulates this view, and some books emphasize Jesus' humanity (like Mark, and sometimes Luke and Acts) while others emphasize Jesus' divinity (like John and Paul). Taken together, however, these books emphasize both humanity and divinity, just as the proto-orthodox group believed.

Eventually, the rivals were vanquished and the proto-orthodox Christians prevailed. Nonetheless, the canon of the New Testament developed only gradually, and not without controversy.

Canon Lists

Some early proto-orthodox leaders listed books they regarded as canonical. In the case of other leaders, who did not make such lists, it is possible to infer which books they considered authoritative by reading their works and noting which books they quoted as scripture.

Several patterns are apparent in comparing these lists. First, from at least the late second century, there was consensus about many of the books that would eventually make it into the New Testament, including all of the most important works. Each canon list contains four and only four Gospels: Matthew, Mark, Luke, and John. The Acts of the Apostles also appears on every list, as well as thirteen letters of Paul and the first letter of John. Precisely when this consensus emerged will never be known, as there is little evidence from the late first to mid-second centuries, but once agreement formed it was solid. Nineteen books are included in every proto-orthodox canon that survives.

Some books made it into the canon only with difficulty. The two letters of Peter, the letters of James and Jude, and 2 and 3 John were regarded with some suspicion but ultimately accepted. The book that had the most difficulty making it into the New Testament was clearly the book of Revelation (also known as the Apocalypse of John). As late as the middle of the fourth century, prominent Christian leaders such as Eusebius and Cyril of Jerusalem were publishing canon lists that did not even mention Revelation.

Other books were considered for inclusion but ultimately rejected. Foremost among these are the *Shepherd* of Hermas, the *Acts of Paul (and Thecla)*, the *Epistle of Barnabas*, *1 Clement*, and the *Didache (Teaching of the Twelve Apostles)*.

The canon that became the New Testament has twenty-seven books: four Gospels (Matthew, Mark, Luke, and John), the Acts of the Apostles, twenty-one letters or "epistles" (*epistolē* is the Greek word for "letter"), and one apocalypse (the book of Revelation). The first known publication of the proposed canon dates to 367 CE, when Bishop Athanasius issued a festal letter containing the list. In the 390s, Jerome used Athanasius's list in his production of the Latin Vulgate version of the Bible. The Vulgate became the definitive edition of the Bible in Western Christianity for the next thousand years (even longer in the Catholic Church), effectively ending all debate over the canon.

Criteria for Inclusion and Exclusion

The appearance or nonappearance of certain books on these lists provides important hints about

Development of the Proto-Orthodox Canon

Muratorian Canon (late 2nd century)	Tertullian (early 3rd cent)	Origen (middle 3rd cent)	Eusebius (early 4th century)	Athanasius (367 CE)	Jerome (390 CE)
Matthew	Matthew	"Uncontested" Matthew	"Accepted" Matthew	Matthew	Matthew
Mark	Mark	Mark	Mark	Mark	Mark
Luke	Luke	Luke	Luke	Luke	Luke
John	John	John	John	John	John
Acts	Acts	Acts	Acts	Acts	Acts
13 letters of Paul	13 letters of Paul	14 letters of Paul	14 letters of Paul	14 letters of Paul	14 letters of Paul
Jude	Jude	1 John	1 John	3 letters of John	3 letters of John
1 & 2 John	1 John	Revelation	1 Peter	2 letters of Peter	2 letters of Peter
Wis. Solomon	Revelation	1 Peter		James	James
Revelation	1 Peter			Jude	Jude
Apocalypse of Peter		"Doubtful" or "Disputed"	"Disputed"	Revelation	Revelation
		2 & 3 John	2 & 3 John		
		2 Peter	2 Peter		
		James	James		
		Jude	Jude		
		"False"			
		Gos. Egyptians			
		Gos. Thomas			
		Gos. Matthias			
		Gos. Basilides			
24 books total, including 2 that were later excluded, and excluding 5 that were later included	22 books total, excluding 5 that were later included	22 books are accepted; 5 books are disputed	21 books are accepted; 5 books are disputed; 1 book that would ultimately be included (Revelation) is not even mentioned	27 books total	27 books total

the criteria used to select books for the proto-orthodox canon, criteria that were also explicitly identified and debated by prominent leaders and theologians. Foremost among these criteria were authorship, antiquity (the age of the text), and conformity with proto-orthodox doctrine.

The thirty-ninth festal letter of Bishop Athanasius of Alexandria, written in 367, included the first canon list to contain all the New Testament books now accepted as canonical and no others.

Authorship

The letter to the Hebrews provides an interesting example of the first of these criteria. The letter is not included in the earliest proto-orthodox canons, but is eventually accepted. The debate shows the reason for its early exclusion was entirely related to the question of authorship, not to the contents of the book. Unlike the thirteen letters of Paul that are included on every list, the letter to the Hebrews does not explicitly claim to have been written by Paul. Paul's name is attached to the first line of all of the other letters, but Hebrews is anonymous. Some believed Paul was its author, while others claimed its contents and style are dissimilar to the other Pauline letters and therefore he could not have written it. Eventually the proto-orthodox would agree that the letter was written by Paul and

it was therefore included. Questions about authorship also dogged books such as 1 and 2 Peter, 2 and 3 John, James, Jude, and Revelation, which explains why these books were sometimes excluded or identified as "disputed."

Why was the question of authorship a vital criterion? As already noted, wildly contradictory things were being said about Jesus. To whom could one look for the authentic teachings of the master, and for accurate and reliable information about his life? One would assume that those who were closest to Jesus, and who had been specifically chosen and trained for the task of carrying on his ministry, would be the best sources. It was understood in virtually all varieties of early Christianity that Jesus had many followers, for whom the broad term *disciple* was used (Greek, *mathētēs*, "learner," or "disciple"). Of these, only a few had been hand-selected for the task of missionary work and commissioned as Jesus' official representatives after his death. These select few are known as *apostles* from the Greek *apostellō*, which means "to send out."

Many gospels speak of Jesus having an inner circle of disciples known as "**the Twelve**," who were also commissioned as apostles. Included on this list were Peter, James, John, Andrew, Thomas, Matthew (or Levi), and Philip, to whom many canonical and noncanonical books are attributed. It was generally acknowledged among all groups of early Christians that the Twelve were apostles, and that a book actually written by one of them should be included in the canon. However, these men were not the only apostles. One Gospel mentions a larger group of seventy (some manuscripts have seventy-two), who were apostles sent out by Jesus as missionaries (Luke 10:1–20). Four men known as Jesus' brothers, including James and Jude, were also usually acknowledged as apostles. In addition, many others were sometimes regarded as apostles in the early church, itinerant preachers who claimed to have been called by Christ. The foremost of such apostles is Paul. Paul never knew Jesus, and because of this some denied him the status of apostle. But Paul argued that Jesus had appeared to him in a post-resurrection revelation (or a series of revelations), naming him the apostle to the Gentiles and instructing him in the gospel. Paul clearly had some difficulty gaining acceptance as an apostle during his lifetime, and he was often compared negatively to the apostles in Jerusalem who had been personal associates of Jesus. But he was vigorous and persistent in his claim to apostleship, and most Christian groups eventually accepted that designation. In his letters, Paul also refers to many other colleagues as apostles.

The debate among proto-orthodox shapers of the canon[17] reveals that they came to believe that for a book to be included in the canon, it must have been written by an apostle or an associate of an apostle (an "apostolic man").[18] It was believed that some of Jesus' apostles were illiterate, therefore it was acceptable if one of their followers wrote down the stories and traditions that had come from the apostle, even if that follower had not personally been acquainted with Jesus or otherwise qualified as an apostle. For example, the Gospel of Mark is alleged to have been written by an associate of Peter, who came to know the apostle in Rome and wrote down Peter's preaching.[19] In this view, the real source of the Gospel is Peter and not Mark, so the Gospel was regarded as apostolic. Similarly, the Gospel of Luke (and its companion volume, the Acts of the Apostles) is said to have been written by an associate and colleague of Paul.

In this way all twenty-seven books of the New Testament were thought to have been written by apostles or associates of apostles. The Gospel of Matthew, the two letters of Peter, and the Johannine literature (the Gospel of John, the three letters of John, and the book of Revelation) were written by apostles who were among the Twelve. The fourteen letters of Paul were written by an apostle commissioned in a post-resurrection revelation. The letters of James and Jude were written by brothers of Jesus, and the Gospel of Mark, the Gospel of Luke, and the Acts of the Apostles were written by associates of apostles. There are, however, several kinds of problems associated with proto-orthodox claims for the apostolic origin of these documents.

1. *Anonymity.* Some books were **anonymous**, originally written with no name attached to them. The Letter to the Hebrews was one such: the letter was eventually attributed to Paul, but this was basically a guess made decades or even centuries after it was written. Most modern scholars believe the attribution to Paul is mistaken because the writing style and theology of Hebrews is thoroughly un-Pauline.

The same problem of anonymity applies to all four Gospels and the Acts of the Apostles. All of these books originally circulated anonymously; none of the earliest quotations of these books name the authors. The earliest source claiming to identify the authors of some of the Gospels (Mark, Matthew, and John) is Papias (around 125–140 CE). However, the relevant section of Papias's work survives only as a quotation in Eusebius (around 324 CE), raising questions about the reliability of this tradition. The first

---

17. The use of this criterion is attested as early as the writings of Papias (ca. 140 CE) and Irenaeus (ca. 180 CE). See below for the problems associated with this evidence.

18. Justin Martyr writes, "For in the memoirs which I say were drawn up by His apostles *and those who followed them*" (*Dialogue with Trypho* 103). Tertullian states, "The evangelical Testament has apostles for its authors, to whom was assigned by the Lord Himself this office of publishing the gospel. . . . Therefore, John and Matthew first instil faith into us; while of apostolic men, Luke and Mark renew it afterwards" (*Against Marcion* 4.2.2; 4.5.3).

19. Papias, Irenaeus, Origen, Tertullian, and Clement of Alexandria all assert Mark's association with Peter.

undisputed reference to the identity of the four evangelists is found in Irenaeus's *Against Heresies* (around 180 CE). Most modern scholars do not believe any of the four Gospels were actually written by the authors to whom they are traditionally attributed.[20]

2. *Pseudonymity*. While some books were written with no name attached, others had a false name—a **pseudonym**—appended to them. It was common in ancient religious literature for an author to attach the name of a famous predecessor to a book. Jewish literature, for instance, contains abundant examples of books attributed to Adam, Enoch, Abraham, and Moses that were written centuries or even millennia after the death of their purported authors. The fact that many proto-orthodox leaders and theologians expressed reservations about the authorship of 1 and 2 Peter, 2 and 3 John, James, and Jude shows they were aware of the phenomenon of pseudonymity.[21] All of these books were eventually judged authentic and included in the canon, but modern scholars believe early suspicions about authorship were well founded. In fact, modern biblical scholarship suggests far more books are likely to be pseudonymous than ancient Christians suspected. Of the thirteen letters of Paul, only seven are universally thought to have been written by Paul.[22] The other six are usually designated as "deutero-Pauline" (*deutero* meaning "secondary"), having been written by Paul's followers in his name after his death. The same judgment has been rendered with respect to 1 John.

3. *Mistaken Identity*. The book of Revelation identifies its author as "John" of Patmos. There is no reason to doubt this is the real name of the author. But was this the same John as the apostle, the son of Zebedee and brother of James, or another person who shared this common name? Ancient scholars were divided on this question, the skeptics pointing out that the theology of the book of Revelation and that of the Gospel of John and letters of John are incompatible, and the writing less polished.[23] The final verdict was that John the apostle and John of Patmos were the same person, but modern scholars think this highly unlikely.

In sum, probably only seven of the twenty-seven books of the New Testament were actually written by an apostle, or by the person to whom the book was traditionally attributed. While this seems like a low percentage, it is helpful to keep in mind two facts. First, no other group of early Christians could make a legitimate claim to have even one book that was written by an apostle or an associate of an apostle. All of their books bearing the names of apostles are pseudonymous. Second, because a book was not actually written by an apostle does not mean it cannot be "apostolic" in a more fundamental sense. The Gospel of Mark, for example, was written by an anonymous second-generation Christian in 70 CE, but this author was relying on oral traditions that were far older, many of which undoubtedly originated with Jesus' apostles.

---

20. The most vigorous defense has been mounted for the authorship of the Fourth Gospel by the apostle John. Richard Bauckham, *Jesus and the Eyewitnesses* (Grand Rapids: Eerdmans, 2006), claims as many as three or four of the Gospels were written by those to whom they are traditionally attributed, but Bauckham's work has been heavily criticized.

21. Origen, for example, says about 2 and 3 John that "not all say that these are genuine," and about the apostle Peter, that he left "one acknowledged epistle; and possibly also a second, but this is disputed" (quoted in Eusebius, *Ecclesiasticl History* 6.25.8–10).

22. This issue will be explored in greater detail—with arguments for and against the claim that these six books are pseudonymous—in chapter 18.

23. See Eusebius, *Ecclesiasticl History* 7.25. Eusebius is summarizing the arguments of Dionysius, bishop of Alexandria (mid-third century).

Antiquity

A second criterion for inclusion in the proto-orthodox canon is **antiquity**. To be included, a book needed to be judged "ancient," which meant it must have been written during the apostolic age and not later. The "apostolic age" refers to the time when the apostles might still have been alive. This criterion seems to reflect a view that as long as there were still apostles alive, they would have acted as a check on the development of legends about Jesus and embellishments of his words or deeds. Given that Jesus died around the year thirty CE, the longest an apostle could possibly have lived would have been another seventy years or so; thus a rough estimate for the close of the apostolic age would be the end of the first century CE. A book that was clearly written after this point would not have a credible claim to be "apostolic" in origin. It was on this basis that some early Christian leaders excluded the *Shepherd* of Hermas from the canon, a book with an otherwise strong case.[24] Some of the other books possibly excluded on this basis include *1 Clement* and the epistles of Ignatius of Antioch.

Estimated Dates of Composition for the Books of the New Testament

The challenges of dating the composition of ancient texts will be discussed later (see chapter 6), but the following list represents the main contenders for canonical status in early Christianity, according to scholars.

Genuine letters of Paul (Romans, 1 & 2 Corinthians, Galatians, Philippians, 1 Thessalonians, and Philemon)	50–60 CE
Deutero-Pauline Letters (2 Thessalonians, Colossians, Ephesians)	60–80 CE
Gospel of Mark	70 CE
Gospel of Matthew	80–90 CE
Gospel of Luke	80–135 CE
Acts of the Apostles	80–125 CE
Pastoral Epistles (1 & 2 Timothy, Titus), James, and Hebrews	80–100 CE
Gospel of John, Letter of Jude	90–100 CE
Johannine Epistles (1, 2, 3 John)	95–105 CE
Revelation	95–100 CE
2 Peter	110–115 CE

24. The author of the Muratorian Fragment, for example, speaks highly of the *Shepherd* of Hermas, but cannot admit it to the canon because it was not written in the apostolic age. "But Hermas wrote the Shepherd *quite lately in our time*," he says, so it "ought indeed to be read, but it cannot be read publicly in the Church to the other people either among the prophets, whose number is settled, or among the apostles to the end of time."

Broad Conformity with Proto-Orthodox Doctrine

The third and final criterion[25] for admission to the New Testament canon involved whether the book was generally accepted throughout the proto-orthodox world, which meant the book broadly conformed with proto-orthodox doctrine (or at least did not clearly contradict it). It is true some positions were deemed heretical because they were too extreme. Any book claiming that Jesus was strictly divine but did not share our human nature, or claiming that Jesus merely pretended to be human but was in fact only a divine spirit, would have been excluded on this basis. A popular gospel such as the *Infancy Gospel of Thomas* (see below) would have been deemed unacceptable because it portrayed the boy Jesus as disobedient and reckless in the use of his power.

The final result of the application of these criteria was the inclusion of twenty-seven books in the canon of the New Testament. While the issue of the contents of the canon was hotly disputed within and between rival groups of early Christians, that controversy ended with the emergence of a single, dominant strain of orthodoxy from which virtually all modern denominations of Christianity derive. Every Christian New Testament published today includes the same books: the four Gospels, Acts of the Apostles, the letters of Paul, the catholic epistles, and the book of Revelation.

Key Terms

canon	Docetism	revealer
testament	autograph	orthodoxy
inspiration	Jewish-Christian adoptionists	heresy
Torah	Gnostics	disciple
Pentateuch	Nag Hammadi library	apostle
Nevi'im	Monad	the Twelve
Ketuvim	Aeons	anonymous
BCE and CE	Yaltabaoth	pseudonym
Marcion	Archons	antiquity

Review Questions

1. What is the difference between the fundamentalist/evangelical understanding of biblical inspiration and that of the Catholic Church and the mainline Protestant churches?

2. How did the various early Christian communities differ with regard to the number and nature of god(s), the status and significance of Jesus, and the orientation of Christianity toward Judaism? How did the stance of each group affect that group's acceptance of certain books as canonical?

3. What criteria were used by proto-orthodox Christians for inclusion in their canon? What problems are associated with their claims? How did the process of forming the proto-orthodox canon unfold?

---

25. These criteria were never officially promulgated, nor is it the case that no other criteria were ever utilized by the proto-orthodox leaders who compiled canon lists. Another factor that figured prominently in the thinking of some of these leaders is whether the books were generally accepted—and thus being used liturgically—in the proto-orthodox churches, or whether they may have been popular only in a few areas.

Discussion Questions

1. Is the use of CE and BCE in place of AD and BC a pointless exercise in political correctness or an easy and appropriate adjustment in a diverse, pluralistic world?

2. Might knowledge of the formation of the canon have an effect upon the way Christians view the New Testament? Does such knowledge undermine Christian confidence in the reliability of these texts?

3. To the degree that most Christians know about the multiple varieties of early Christianity, they tend to assume that the "right" version emerged as the dominant one, and that the others were properly rejected. Some scholars have questioned this, and have argued that there is truth and beauty in some of the lost versions of Christianity, and perhaps some flaws in what became orthodox Christianity. Do you agree or disagree with this view?

4. In choosing books for a canon, Christian leaders tended to assert that their beliefs had been shaped by the books they knew were reliable, rather than admitting that they chose books based on their preexisting beliefs. Does this make a difference? Do you tend to believe this claim or are you skeptical of it?

Bibliography and Suggestions for Further Study

(Books and websites that are accessible for general undergraduates are marked with an asterisk; other sources listed are appropriate for advanced students.)

Bauckham, Richard. *Jesus and the Eyewitnesses: The Gospels as Eyewitness Testimony.* Grand Rapids: Eerdmans, 2006.

*Davis, Glenn. The Development of the Canon of the New Testament. *www.ntcanon.org.*

*Ehrman, Bart. *Lost Christianities: The Battles for Scripture and the Faiths We Never Knew.* New York: Oxford University Press, 2003.

*Ehrman, Bart. *The New Testament: A Historical Introduction to the Early Christian Writings.* New York: Oxford University Press, 2012.

Grant, Robert M. *The Formation of the New Testament.* New York: Harper & Row, 1965.

*Kirby, Peter. Early Christian Writings. *www.earlychristianwritings.com.*

Metzger, Bruce. *The Canon of the New Testament: Its Origin, Development, and Significance.* Oxford: Clarendon, 1987.

*Pagels, Elaine. *The Gnostic Gospels.* New York: Vintage Books, 1989.

Tertullian. *Adversus Marcionem.* Edited and translated by Ernest Evans. Oxford: Clarendon, 1972.

Some Prominent Noncanonical Gospels[1]

It is impossible to know exactly how many gospels were written by early Christians. While hundreds of ancient copies of the canonical gospels have been preserved, copies of noncanonical gospels are rare. In some cases only a single copy survives. In other cases only a few fragments of the text of a gospel are available. There are also noncanonical gospels that survive only in the form of quotations in the works of orthodox opponents, who considered the noncanonical gospel heretical. Such opponents were not always careful to quote the noncanonical gospels accurately, and some may have deliberately misquoted or cited nonexistent sources, in order to attribute ridiculous and outlandish claims to the groups they opposed. Finally, there may have been gospels for which no evidence remains, not even a quotation or reference mentioning the gospel by name. One possible example of such a gospel is known as "Q," which will be discussed at length in chapter 9. Q's existence is hypothesized by many scholars but disputed by others because of a lack of hard evidence.

Of the noncanonical gospels whose existence is certain and of which we have complete copies or substantial portions, some are regarded as more significant than others. Among the factors that make noncanonical gospels of more or less interest to scholars are the date of authorship, the potential for historical accuracy, and the originality of the ideas expressed in the text. Some of these gospels were simply written too late to be of interest to students of earliest Christianity, while others date from a very early period and help flesh out the portrait of the development of Christianity in its crucial formative stages. Similarly, some noncanonical gospels consist mainly of legends about Jesus—stories with no basis in fact—while others may contain authentic teachings and traditions. Finally, even late gospels of dubious historical value can provide interesting glimpses into the distinctive belief systems of nonorthodox groups of early Christians. The noncanonical gospels deemed worthy of individual attention below each fit one or more of these descriptions.

The *Gospel of Thomas*

The noncanonical gospel that has garnered the most attention from scholars and the general public is the ***Gospel of Thomas***.[2] Most scholars date the final composition of *Thomas* to between

---

1. Some parts of this chapter appeared in David Landry, "Noncanonical Texts: *The Da Vinci Code* and Beyond," *Word and World* 29 (2009): 367–79. Used with permission.

2. This is not the only noncanonical gospel attributed to Thomas, so to distinguish it from other Thomas gospels it is often referred to as the *Coptic Gospel of Thomas*. Coptic is the ancient Egyptian dialect in which the gospel is written.

90–150 CE, although a primitive version could have been written as early as the fifties. If *Thomas* was written in the nineties, this would place it roughly in the same time frame as the canonical gospels. *Thomas* is probably the only noncanonical gospel to rival the canonical gospels in terms of antiquity, which is one of the reasons historians are so interested in it (see chapter 21 for a discussion of the prominence of *Thomas* in the so-called Quest for the Historical Jesus).

Thomas was notorious among the orthodox heresy-hunters of early Christianity, but it eventually faded from history. Scholars did not possess a complete copy of the gospel until the discoveries at Nag Hammadi, Egypt, in 1945 and the eventual publication of the trove of Gnostic texts that were found there.

Examination of its contents reveals just how vast the gap was between the orthodox understanding of the significance of Christ and that of the Gnostics. The gospel consists of 114 sayings of Jesus, presented consecutively and without any intervening narrative. Almost all of the sayings are given utterly without context. The following is a sample run of sayings:

> Jesus said, "No prophet is accepted in his own village; no physician heals those who know him." (31)
>
> Jesus said, "A city being built on a high mountain and fortified cannot fall, nor can it be hidden." (32)
>
> Jesus said, "Preach from your housetops that which you will hear in your ear. For no one lights a lamp and puts it under a bushel, nor does he put it in a hidden place, but rather he sets it on a lampstand so that everyone who enters and leaves will see its light." (33)[3]

The *Gospel of Thomas* contains no mention of a virgin birth, no healing or nature miracles, no

Public domain

Of the gospel texts that were not accepted as scripture, the *Gospel of Thomas*, shown in this Coptic manuscript, is the most likely to preserve at least some actual teachings of Jesus.

descriptions of Jesus' movements or relationships, and (most interestingly) no passion narrative. The absence of the story of Jesus' arrest, trials, crucifixion, and resurrection is consistent with the Gnostic view that Jesus was a pure spirit who was not really human and hence could not suffer, bleed, or die. The emphasis upon Jesus' teaching, as opposed to his acts, is also consistent with the Gnostic understanding of Jesus as a divine revealer who is sent from heaven to provide humans with the knowledge (*gnōsis*) they need to gain salvation. The first lines of *Thomas*

---

3. Quotations from *Thomas* are taken from *The Gospel of Thomas*, ed. and trans. Thomas O. Lambdin, in *The Nag Hammadi Library in English*, ed. James Robinson, 4th rev. ed. (New York: Brill, 1996).

express this view clearly: "These are the secret sayings which the living Jesus spoke and Didymus Judas Thomas[4] wrote down. And he [Jesus] said, 'Whoever *finds the interpretation of these sayings* will not experience death'" (1, italics added). Another saying reads, "When you come to know yourselves, then you will become known, and you will realize that it is you who are the sons of the living father. But if you will not know yourselves, you dwell in poverty and it is you who are that poverty" (3). This voices the Gnostic belief that the basic human problem is ignorance. Because of this, great importance is placed on (1) knowing one's true nature, that humans have a "spark" of the divine in them, and (2) knowing one's destiny, that with guidance humans can return to the heavenly realm.

Some sayings in *Thomas* are highly esoteric and difficult to interpret, such as the following:

> Jesus said, "Blessed is he who came into being before he came into being. If you become my disciples and listen to my words, these stones will minister to you. For there are five trees for you in Paradise which remain undisturbed summer and winter and whose leaves do not fall. Whoever becomes acquainted with them will not experience death." (19)
>
> Jesus said, "Where there are three gods, they are gods. Where there are two or one, I am with him." (30)
>
> Jesus said, "Become passers-by." (42)

It is possible sayings that appear bizarre and incomprehensible make perfect sense if one understands their ancient, Gnostic context.

A classic example is found in the final lines in *Thomas*: "Simon Peter said to him, 'Let Mary leave us, for women are not worthy of life.' Jesus said, 'I myself shall lead her in order to make her

male, so that she too may become a living spirit resembling you males. For every woman who will make herself male will enter the kingdom of heaven'" (114). Gnostics maintained a strict dualism between two parts of the human person: the body, which is transitory and evil, and the soul or spirit, which is real and lasting. Both men and women had bodies and souls, but in the ancient world gender stereotypes suggested that women were more fleshly (oriented toward and governed by the body) and men were more spiritual (oriented toward reason and the intellect). For example, texts from the early Christian era often suggested that women were more sexually aggressive than men and had stronger sexual appetites. This passage, in which Simon Peter urges that Mary Magdalene be banished, seems to buy into these gender stereotypes.

Thomas 114, then, appears to be hopelessly sexist, but the truth is more complicated. Simon Peter suggests that Mary Magdalene be left behind, because as a fleshly, emotional, highly sexual woman, she is "not worthy of life," that is, eternal, spiritual life. But Jesus says he will guide her so that he will make her male, that is, more rational and more focused on the spiritual dimension of life. In this way, Mary will become a "living spirit" like Jesus' male disciples, and in the process become worthy of salvation. Thus, while the saying does rely on sexist assumptions, its basic message is one of equality: that women can be saved as well as men.

The *Infancy Gospel of Thomas*

One reason Christians continued to write gospels even after the four canonical Gospels had become firmly entrenched is that Mark, Matthew, Luke, and John leave significant gaps in the story of

---

4. The names *Didymus* and *Thomas* are rooted in the Greek and Aramaic terms for "twin," respectively. There is considerable speculation that the gospel implies that its author was Jesus' twin brother, but the near-certainty that the gospel is pseudonymous renders the question moot.

According to Luke 2:41–52, Jesus taught in the Jerusalem Temple at age twelve, as depicted in this sculpture from the church of Our Lady in Mechelen, Belgium; apart from this episode, the canonical Gospels say nothing of Jesus' boyhood. The *Infancy Gospel of Thomas* attempts to fill this gap.

Jesus and his family. Only two Gospels—Matthew and Luke—say anything about Jesus' birth. Only one (Luke) says anything about Jesus' childhood, and that Gospel contains only a single account of Jesus as a twelve-year-old boy (the so-called finding in the Temple, Luke 2:41–52). Many early Christians were curious about Jesus' parents and about other exploits he may have had as a boy, and gospels were written to satisfy that curiosity.

The *Infancy Gospel of Thomas*, written probably in the late second century, tells tales of Jesus' life from the ages of five to twelve. The early chapters of this gospel are shocking to orthodox Christians, because they present the young Jesus as a naughty, ill-tempered, and vindictive child. As the gospel begins, Jesus is seen gathering pools of water and then making sparrows out of clay on the Sabbath. When Jesus is reported for apparently violating the Sabbath, he turns the clay sparrows into real birds and orders them to fly away, thus destroying the evidence. Another boy scatters the pools of water Jesus was using, and Jesus curses him for his interference, causing

his flesh to wither and become like that of an old man. Later a boy bangs into Jesus' shoulder when they are playing and Jesus impulsively causes the boy to fall down dead. When the parents of Jesus' victims ask Joseph to intercede, begging him to teach Jesus "to bless rather than to curse," Jesus rebukes his father and causes the complaining parents to go blind.

The author of this gospel seems to be imagining what it would be like for a young boy with a typical child's developmental arc to wield all the power of God. As the gospel progresses, Jesus gradually learns to control his temper and his emotions and to channel his power in more positive directions. He saves his brother James from a deadly snakebite, heals a man who has cut off his foot and is bleeding to death, and raises several people from the dead (although some of them were people he himself had killed). Ultimately, Jesus restores to life all those he killed and restores to health all those he maimed, and he becomes a perfect, obedient child, growing in wisdom and holiness.

Biblical scholars do not lend any credence to these stories. They appear too late to have any historical plausibility and there is no corroboration of the gospel's claims anywhere in the historical record. They are classified as legends about Jesus, stories invented by believers because they thought such stories served some good purpose. The good purpose in this case was to help parents teach their children the importance of developing emotional maturity, humility, and self-control, using Jesus as a role model.

The gospel seems to have been written with good intentions, but its "all's well that ends well" stance with respect to Jesus' youthful indiscretions was not satisfactory to orthodox leaders like Irenaeus, who branded the gospel heretical.[5] That Jesus regrets his outbursts of temper and fixes the damage he has done cannot, according to Irenaeus and others, make up for the fact that he did these deeds in the first place, deeds that seem unworthy of a sinless man.

The *Protoevangelium of James*

The ideals of purity and sinlessness are also the focus of the ***Protoevangelium of James*** (also known as the *Infancy Gospel of James*), although in this gospel it is not Jesus whose spotless record is defended, but that of his mother, Mary. Surprisingly little is said about Mary in the canonical New Testament. In the Gospel of Mark, Mary has no speaking role and does not seem to be among Jesus' supporters. In Matthew, she is the virgin "betrothed" of Joseph who gives birth to Jesus, but again does not say a word and is not counted among Jesus' supporters during his ministry or at his death. The letters of Paul do not mention her at all, nor do any of the other apostolic letters. Only Luke-Acts and John record the words of Jesus' mother, although in Luke these words are concentrated entirely in chapters 1 and 2 and in neither Luke nor John does Mary appear in more than a few episodes.

As Christianity developed, however, Marian spirituality became an important part of the religion for some people, and numerous noncanonical texts attest to their devotion to her. The aspect of Mary that fascinated many Christians was her virginity. While orthodox Christianity never adopted the extreme body/spirit dualism of Gnosticism, nonetheless a strong line of thinking took hold in some orthodox circles that insisted the body and its desires were the source of all sin, and that discipline, self-mastery, and denial of bodily appetites (a lifestyle known as **asceticism**) were the key to holiness. Since sexual desire is one of the strongest bodily desires, and since lust and the desire for pleasure were considered the source of all manner of sins, ascetics came to prize celibacy and virginity. The best way to lead a life pleasing to God, they came to believe, was never to engage in sex, or if one had already indulged, to cease having sex immediately and forevermore. They would admit that it was only through marriage and sex that children could be produced (legitimately), and lip service was always paid to the notion that sex within marriage was not evil as long as it was done for the purpose of procreation. However, it is nonetheless clear in the writings of many champions of asceticism that the celibate life was seen as superior to the married life.

When ascetics looked to the Bible for role models, they found almost nothing in the Old Testament. Jews believed it was every person's religious obligation to get married and procreate (cf. God's command in Gen. 1 that humans "be fruitful and multiply") and abstinence was recommended only in certain very limited contexts

---

5. See Irenaeus, *Against Heresies* 1.20.1. Irenaeus does not refer to the *Infancy Gospel of Thomas* by name, but the context of the passage makes it clear that he can only be speaking of this gospel.

and for limited periods of time. But in the New Testament, Christian men could find role models in John the Baptist, Jesus, and Paul, all of whom were allegedly or avowedly unmarried and celibate. On the female side, advocates of celibacy and virginity gravitated naturally to Mary, who, according to two Gospels, was a virgin when she gave birth to Jesus.

But for ascetics, it was not enough for Mary to have abstained from sex prior to Jesus' birth. To be the kind of example they wanted, and for her to have embodied the kind of purity they idealized, she needed to be a model of lifelong virginity. Whether these ascetics invented stories that posited lifelong virginity for Mary or whether they simply drew upon existing traditions about the perpetual virginity of Mary is unknown. But the stories eventually went even further than claiming Mary was a lifelong virgin. Some even began to say she must have been a virgin in every sense of the word, including the narrow, biological sense of a woman or girl whose hymen is intact.[6]

There is no evidence for these claims in the Gospels that the proto-orthodox were already promoting as the only reliable, apostolic sources. The canonical texts say nothing at all about Mary's "physical" virginity or an intact hymen. Moreover, numerous New Testament texts (including all four Gospels and Paul's letters) speak of the "brothers and sisters" of Jesus, and these texts seem to presume these siblings are children of Mary and Joseph born after Jesus. No one was claiming Mary conceived as a virgin multiple times, so these "brothers and sisters" present a substantial obstacle to the claim that Mary remained a virgin throughout her life.

Only two Gospels mention the idea that Mary was a virgin when Jesus was conceived in her womb, and one of them (Matthew) does so

rather ambiguously. The earliest New Testament texts—the genuine letters of Paul and the Gospel of Mark—say nothing about a virgin birth. A pagan critic of Christianity named Celsus claimed Mary had been impregnated by a Roman soldier named Panthera and had then claimed to have conceived as a virgin to avoid the shame of having been raped or seduced.

The *Protoevangelium of James* attempts to address all of these problems. It retells the story of Jesus' birth and adds huge swaths of text on the circumstances of Mary's childhood, Joseph's marriage to her, and Jesus' birth, all of which seem designed to promote belief in the threefold virginity of Mary. This involves the belief that Mary was a virgin (1) before Jesus' birth (known in Latin as *virginitas ante partum*, usually rendered in English as **virginal conception**), (2) after Jesus' birth and for the rest of her life (*virginitas post partum*, also known as **perpetual virginity**), and (3) during Jesus' birth (*virginitas in partu*, **virginity during birth**, the notion that God miraculously intervened during Mary's delivery of the baby Jesus' so that her hymen was not torn and she remained a physical virgin).

The story begins with Mary as a young girl, vowing to dedicate her life to the service of the Lord and hence eschewing marriage and children. She goes to live in the Temple, where the priests are able to raise her in holiness and safeguard her virginity until she reaches puberty. When she begins menstruating, she must leave the Temple lest her blood profane this sacred precinct. How would she be able to continue her life of celibacy and service to the Lord without the oversight of the Temple priesthood? The decision is made to enlist one of the elderly widowers of Israel—a man who had already been married and had children—to enter into a sham marriage with Mary that would enable him

---

6. This was, and is, a popular belief despite its inaccuracy. Anyone wishing to be enlightened on this point could see the "hymen" portion of "The Truth about Hymens and Sex," *Adam Ruins Everything, https://www.youtube.com/watch?v=1ikXim4wevc.*

to protect her and permit her to proceed unhindered with her life of holiness and purity. Lots are cast, and the duty falls on a carpenter named Joseph. As an old man with grown sons, he is reluctant to wed this young girl, but after being persuaded that this is the will of the Lord he agrees under the conditions stipulated—that they will never consummate this marriage but will live more as brother and sister.

Drawing on the account in Luke, the *Protoevangelium of James* proceeds to show how Mary is visited by an angel and informed that she will give birth to the Son of God without the involvement of a human father. She becomes pregnant, and when Joseph realizes this, he is distraught. He believes he has failed in his duty to protect the virgin entrusted to him and that he will be accused of having impregnated her. His fears are realized when a priest of the Temple visits Joseph's house and realizes Mary is pregnant. Joseph is vilified for having broken the agreement he made and violated the young virgin under his care. He swears he is innocent, and Mary for her part claims Joseph has not touched her, nor has any other man.

The skeptical priests then conduct what is known as a **trial by ordeal**. This is where the accused is forced to undergo a test wherein some usually harmful process is inflicted. If a defendant is innocent, then it is understood that God will not allow him or her to come to harm but will provide protection. The guilty, on the other hand, will suffer the consequences of the ordeal. In ancient Judaism, such trials involved the ingestion of the "waters of bitterness," an apparently poisonous concoction that would ordinarily produce severe gastrointestinal distress or even death. First Joseph and then Mary drink the waters of bitterness, go off into the hill country, and then return unharmed. Thus it is proven, according to the *Protoevangelium of James*, that Joseph was not lying when he claimed not to have impregnated Mary, nor was Mary lying

when she said that neither had she been with any other man.

Perhaps more important to the author of the *Protoevangelium of James*, however, are a variety of claims that support both Mary's perpetual virginity and virginity during birth and explain any countervailing evidence that seems to be present in the canonical texts. After Mary and Joseph pass the test involving the "waters of bitterness," they leave Nazareth and journey to Bethlehem to be enrolled in a Roman census (as in Luke 2). When they arrive, Mary is ready to deliver, and Joseph finds a midwife and a cave that provides her with some privacy. A bright cloud and then a blinding light obscure events in the cave, until the baby Jesus "appears" and then takes the breast of his mother. The midwife runs from the cave and cries that something unprecedented has occurred: "A virgin has brought forth" (*Protoevangelium of James* 19.18). A woman named Salome doubts this claim and insists she will not believe it until she sees for herself. She enters the cave and gives Mary a manual gynecological exam that confirms her hymen is intact. In fact, Salome's hand is burned away as a consequence of her doubt and affront.

The belief in Mary's perpetual virginity is buttressed, first, by claiming that Mary had made a vow from childhood to serve the Lord and remain a lifelong virgin and, second, by offering an alternate explanation for Jesus' siblings. They are not children of Mary and Joseph born subsequent to Jesus, as one might conclude from the canonical evidence alone, but children of Joseph from his previous marriage. They are not true siblings of Jesus but rather half-brothers and half-sisters, sharing one parent (the father, legal if not biological) but having a different mother.

The Catholic Church ended up embracing the **threefold virginity of Mary** as dogma, although only Mary's *virginitas ante partum* is supported by canonical texts. The sixteenth-century Protestant Reformers, however, insisted that only doctrines explicitly affirmed in the Bible should be accepted. Consequently, they rejected the doctrines of *virginitas in partu* and *virginitas post partum* because of the lack of scriptural evidence.

The *Gospel of Peter*

The *Gospel of Peter* is one of the few Gnostic texts to survive independently from the Nag Hammadi library. A partial copy was discovered in the late nineteenth century, missing both the beginning and the end. The section that survives, however, includes the trial, crucifixion, and resurrection of Jesus. The account has noteworthy Gnostic overtones. At one point Jesus is said to have endured the crucifixion as if he was not in pain, and at the end he is not said to have died but to have been "taken up."

The gospel clearly attempts to place the blame for Jesus' crucifixion squarely on the Jews, and to deflect the blame from the more obvious culprits, the Romans. This is accomplished in part by building on the Gospel of Matthew, in which the Roman governor, Pontius Pilate, literally washed his hands of the death of Jesus while the Jewish authorities happily claimed full responsibility. *Peter* adds that the Jews who called for his crucifixion "did not wish to wash" (*Peter* 1),[7] and that as Jesus was killed, the Jews gave Jesus "gall mixed with vinegar" and thereby fulfilled scripture and "completed all their sins on their heads" (*Peter* 17). When Jesus died, the Jews "were glad" (*Peter* 23), and after the news of his resurrection came from the guards posted at the tomb (see Matt. 28:11–15), Pilate reiterates that the responsibility for his death lay entirely with the Jewish authorities: "I am clean of the blood of the Son of God; you decided to do this" (*Peter* 46).

The Metropolitan Museum of Art, Purchase, Gift of J. Pierpont Morgan and Bequest of Helena W. Charlton, by exchange, Gwynne Andrews, Marquand, Rogers, Victor Wilbour Memorial, and The Alfred N. Punnett Endowment Funds, and funds given or bequeathed by friends of the Museum, 1978

Mattia Preti's painting depicts Pilate washing his hands (Matt. 27:24), symbolically divesting himself of responsibility for Jesus' death. The apocryphal *Gospel of Peter* elaborates on this scene.

The overt anti-Jewish tone of the *Gospel of Peter* was not at all uncommon in post-second-century Christian literature, when Christianity broke from Judaism and relations deteriorated between the two religions. Even in the first century, the canonical Gospels make clear efforts to shift the blame for Jesus' unjust murder away from the Romans and toward the Jews. The *Gospel of Peter* merely exaggerates this tendency.

The anti-Jewish character of both (some) canonical and noncanonical gospels had tragic consequences for the history of Judaism. Eventually Christianity gained the upper hand over Judaism, and the record of Christian persecution of Jews is horrifying, to say the least. The early Christians who preached hostility toward Jews

---

7. Quotations are from *The Gospel of Peter*, in Bart Ehrman and Zlatko Plese, *The Apocryphal Gospels: Texts and Translations* (New York: Oxford University Press, 2011).

for their alleged mistreatment of Jesus may not have anticipated the degree to which future generations of Christians would punish the Jewish people for this supposed transgression, but there is little question that the seeds of hatred were sown in Christianity's earliest literature.

The *Gospel of Philip*

The *Gospel of Philip* became instantly famous with the 2003 publication of Dan Brown's novel *The Da Vinci Code*, which was made into a successful motion picture in 2006. The story revolves around the search for the Holy Grail, which Brown asserts is not the chalice used at the Last Supper but the "receptacle" for Jesus' holy and royal bloodline—namely, his wife Mary Magdalene, the child she bore to him, and subsequent generations of Jesus' descendants. Brown argues in his book that the noncanonical gospels that contain this explosive information are actually earlier and more reliable than their canonical counterparts, and the gospel to which he refers primarily is the *Gospel of Philip*, another of the Gnostic texts found at Nag Hammadi in 1945.

Anyone familiar with *The Da Vinci Code* knows that Brown presents a radical alternative to the standard narrative of the origins of Christianity. He indicates that Jesus was originally understood as a prophet who was married and fathered a child. This human side of Jesus was preserved in the earlier, unaltered noncanonical gospels but covered up by the orthodox church, which altered the four Gospels of Matthew, Mark, Luke, and John to reflect a fully divine Jesus and then enshrined their trumped-up Gospels in the canon. This version of events has

come under attack, not only by Christian apologists but also by scholars and historians of a more neutral persuasion.

Brown's book also misrepresents the text of the *Gospel of Philip*. He claims that proof of Jesus' relationship with Mary Magdalene is found in this quote from the *Gospel of Philip*: "And the Companion of the Savior is Mary Magdalene. Christ loved her more than all the disciples and used to kiss her often on her mouth." Brown's interpretation centers on the significance of the kissing, the greater love Jesus has for Mary Magdalene, and the interchangeability of the word "companion" with the word "spouse" in the Aramaic language Jesus spoke. Brown's interpretation of the *Gospel of Philip* here[8] leaves out two key elements of the passage: (1) the disciples' jealous reaction to the fact that Jesus loves Mary more than them, and (2) Jesus' explanation that his preference for her is based on her spiritual superiority, not physical love. Moreover, Brown adds at least one key word to his quotation that is not found in the original text: the word "mouth." In the sole surviving copy of the *Gospel of Philip*, there are a number of gaps in the text due to damage; the word indicating where Jesus often kissed Mary Magdalene is missing. Most responsible translations then present this verse in the following fashion: "And the companion of the [. . .] Mary Magdalene [. . . loved] her more than [all] the disciples [and used to] kiss her [often] on her [. . .]" (*Philip* 63.34).[9] Brown essentially had to supply the word "mouth" in order to guarantee that people will draw the desired conclusion— namely, that the verse suggests a romantic and sexual relationship between the two. In other words, the verse does not conclusively state one way or the other the nature of Jesus' relationship

---

8. Brown derived many of these ideas from a group of British television producers (Michael Biagent, Richard Leigh, and Henry Lincoln) and a book of pseudo-scholarship written by them, *Holy Blood, Holy Grail* (New York: Dell, 1983).

9. Translation by Wesley W. Isenberg, in *The Nag Hammadi Library in English*, ed. James M. Robinson, 4th rev. ed. (New York: Brill, 1996), 148.

with Mary Magdalene; one would need evidence from elsewhere to draw a definitive conclusion. Such evidence is lacking, however.

Indeed, even if Jesus did kiss Mary Magdalene on the mouth, this would not necessarily mean that the author wished to imply a sexual relationship. In the best scholarly discussion of this passage in the *Gospel of Philip*, Antti Marjanen points out that kissing can have both sexual and nonsexual implications, but there are several reasons why the sexual interpretation of kissing is unlikely in the context of the *Gospel of Philip*.

> First, in the only other passage [in the *Gospel of Philip*] where kissing is referred to (58,30–59,6) it is used without concrete sexual implications as a metaphor of spiritual nourishment which leads to spiritual procreation. Second, in other contemporary religious writings, there are plenty of examples where kissing functions as a metaphor for transmitting a special spiritual power. . . . Third, the altercation between the disciples and the Savior in Gos. Phil. 63,37–64,9 suggests that kissing is not to be understood as an expression of sexual love.[10]

To restate this last point, a sexual interpretation of the kissing of Mary Magdalene would require us to believe the jealous disciples are expressing their desire that Jesus would make sexual overtures toward them rather than Mary Magdalene.

Moreover, kissing—even between a man and a woman—did not always have erotic implications in the ancient world, especially in the context of Judaism and Christianity. Kisses could indicate kinship and were also used as an outward sign of reconciliation. In one Gospel, Jesus complains that Simon the Pharisee gave him a rude welcome at his home, saying, "You gave me no kiss" (Luke 7: 45). The apostle Paul enjoins Christians on numerous occasions (e.g., 1 Cor. 16:20) to "greet one another with a holy kiss," and there are instances where it is clear the addressees would be kissing members of the opposite sex as well as of the same sex (Rom. 16:16).

Furthermore, the author of the *Gospel of Philip*, like many other Gnostics, seems to advocate *encratism*, which involves a rejection of marriage, procreation, and sexual activity of any sort. It is the ultimate irony that Brown's interpretation of Jesus' relationship with Mary Magdalene, which he hopes will promote a healthy, positive view of human sexuality, rests upon a text that in truth advocates the exact opposite view.

Finally, with respect to Brown's comment that, "as any Aramaic scholar will tell you, the word *companion*, in those days, literally meant *spouse*," one need only note that the *Gospel of Philip* was not written in Aramaic. The only surviving manuscript is written in Coptic, and the term "companion" does not mean "spouse" in Coptic.[11]

The *Greater Questions of Mary* and the *Secret Gospel of Mark*

Forgery was epidemic in ancient Christianity. All pseudonymous texts are technically forgeries in that they falsely claim authorship by an important and well-known figure from the past to increase the reader's sense of the antiquity, authority, and reliability of the text. Most noncanonical gospels are pseudonymous; the only ones that are not are those that do not identify their author. Even some canonical texts (such as the deutero-Pauline letters and most if not all of the non-Pauline epistles) are pseudonymous as well.

---

10. Antti Marjanen, *The Woman Jesus Loved: Mary Magdalene in the Nag Hammadi Library and Related Documents* (Leiden: Brill, 1996), 158–59.

11. Ibid., 151–52.

Some cases of forgery are more egregious than others. The deutero-Pauline letters may not have been written by Paul, but they were probably written by close associates of his who were intimately familiar with his teaching. They may not tell us exactly what Paul himself thought about a given issue, but they reveal the thinking of the Pauline "school" and thus have some connection with the purported author. Other kinds of forgeries are far more objectionable. In this category one must place (1) ancient forgeries that do not reflect the true thinking of the group with which they are associated but are written by that group's opponents in an attempt to discredit them, and (2) modern forgeries that attempt to pass off as ancient and authoritative the words and opinions of the forger himself.

An example of the first type of forgery involves the **Greater Questions of Mary**. This gospel is known to us only through the writings of a fourth-century heresy-hunter by the name of Epiphanius. Epiphanius indicates that this book, which he claims to have read, belonged to a group of Gnostics called the Phibionites. He reveals that he had personal knowledge of the Phibionites' cannibalism and deviant sexual practices. These so-called Christians, Epiphanius assures his readers, would worship by having sex with each other's spouses. In each case the man would withdraw prior to climax, and the couple would collect the semen and ingest it as "the body of Christ." If the woman was menstruating, then they would also collect the blood and ingest it as "the blood of Christ." If by some accident a child was conceived, they would abort the fetus and then consume the remains as a special Eucharistic meal. If the men in the group wanted to consume the body of Christ in the privacy of

their rooms, they would engage in sacred masturbation. Supposedly they defended this practice by appealing to a verse from Paul in which he urges his readers to "work with [their] own hands" (1 Thess 4:11).[12]

Just as the orthodox practice of consuming bread and wine in the Eucharist is justified by the story of the Last Supper, so too for this group of Gnostics their gospel speaks of a foundational event. In the *Greater Questions of Mary*, Epiphanius tells us, Jesus takes Mary Magdalene to the top of a mountain and then pulls a woman out of his side and begins having sexual intercourse with her. When he reaches his climax, he withdraws from her and consumes his own semen, telling Mary, "Thus must we do, that we may live."[13]

If all of this is true, then the Phibionites (and by association, other Gnostics) probably deserved all of the scorn and contempt that Epiphanius heaped upon them. The problem is that all indications point to Epiphanius having fabricated this gospel and exaggerated what little he knew about the Phibionites to scare orthodox Christians away from this heretical group. There is no evidence apart from Epiphanius that there really was a gospel called the *Greater Questions of Mary*, or that the Phibionites (or any other Gnostics) ever engaged in cannibalism or these bizarre sexual practices. Indeed, the Gnostics were known for their aversion to sex, which was part of their general commitment to asceticism. Epiphanius, despite his "orthodoxy," is not known as a particularly reliable source. As Bart Ehrman points out, "He constantly exaggerates, he invents connections between historical events that we otherwise know are unrelated, and he explicitly claims that his horrific accounts (there are others) are

---

12. On the *Greater Questions of Mary*, see Bart Ehrman, *Lost Christianities: The Battles for Scripture and the Faiths We Never Knew* (New York: Oxford University Press, 2003), 198–200.

13. See Bart Ehrman, *The Lost Gospel of Judas Iscariot: A New Look at Betrayer and Betrayed* (New York: Oxford University Press, 2006), 54.

designed to repulse his readers from the heresies he describes."[14]

An example of the second kind of forgery, at least according to some recent scholarship, is the **Secret Gospel of Mark**. This previously-unknown version of the gospel of Mark, with "secret" passages not found in the canonical text, was allegedly discovered in 1958 by Columbia University professor Morton Smith. While cataloging the contents of the library of the ancient monastery at Mar Saba, Smith said that he found a seventeenth-century book that had some Greek text handwritten on its blank end pages. The Greek writing turned out to be a copy of a fragment of a previously unknown letter by the well-known church father Clement of Alexandria to a certain Theodore. The letter mentions a heretical group called the Carpocratians who had been boasting of knowledge of a *Secret Gospel of Mark*. Clement tells Theodore their claims about the gospel's contents are false, but that the *Secret Gospel* does exist. Clement's letter indicates that this secret version was written by Mark, the same author who wrote the public version of the Gospel, for those in Alexandria who were advanced enough to have been initiated into the great mysteries.

To correct his opponents, Clement's letter to Theodore quotes two passages from the *Secret Gospel*. One of the passages describes the raising of a young man from the dead (reminiscent of the raising of Lazarus in the Gospel of John). After his resurrection, the youth becomes a follower of Jesus and Jesus stays at his house. Clement quotes the Secret Gospel as follows: "And after six days Jesus told him what to do and in the evening the youth comes to him, wearing a linen cloth over his naked body. And he remained with him that night, for Jesus taught him the mystery of the kingdom of God." There are some rather obvious homoerotic overtones to this passage. Later, Clement indicates, the Secret Gospel reveals that "the sister of the youth whom Jesus loved and his mother and Salome were there, and Jesus did not receive them," apparently indicating his preference for the company of men. Needless to say, the *Secret Gospel of Mark* caused something of a sensation.

From the beginning there were doubts about the authenticity of both the *Secret Gospel of Mark* and the supposed letter to Theodore in which the existence of the *Secret Gospel* was revealed. Morton Smith claimed that he took photographs of the text and left the book in the Mar Saba library. He then sent copies of the photographs to various colleagues, asking them to authenticate the text. With some reservations, they agreed that the Greek handwriting appeared to date from the eighteenth century, which suggested at least that Smith himself did not write it. However, generally speaking a document can only be said to have been truly authenticated if the original is produced, not a photograph, so that the ink and the fiber of the paper can be examined as well as the handwriting. The book, however, was subsequently moved from the Mar Saba monastery to a library in Jerusalem and then lost, so no physical examination was ever carried out.

Despite this problem, many scholars accepted the *Letter to Theodore* as a genuine letter of Clement. Philological and literary analyses were done comparing this letter to the known writings of Clement, and the writing and thinking proved to be very "Clementine." To some, however, the letter appeared to be a little *too* Clementine for their comfort. The letter uses an exceptionally high number of Clement's favorite words, as if the author may have been using a modern tool such as a concordance to help him imitate Clement's style.

---

14. Ehrman, *Lost Christianities*, 200.

Other scholars pointed to suspicious parallels between Smith's discovery and work on *Theodore* and some other famous scholarly hoaxes. But such parallels are not proof of forgery. Smith's doubters lacked a "smoking gun," and so the authenticity of *Secret Mark* was grudgingly accepted for several decades.

The stalemate was broken in 2005 with the publication of a brilliant little book by Stephen Carlson, entitled *The Gospel Hoax: Morton Smith's Invention of Secret Mark*. At the time Carlson was a practicing attorney who dabbled in serious biblical scholarship, and he used his forensic expertise and facility with biblical scholarship to build a solid case against the authenticity of *Theodore* and *Secret Mark*. Carlson concluded the forger in all likelihood was Smith himself. Familiar with the techniques used by law enforcement to identify forged signatures on checks, Carlson found many telltale signs of forgery in the handwriting of *Theodore*.[15]

Carlson provides close-up photographs of the Mar Saba manuscript that reveal a number of characteristics of a forgery.[16] Carlson also shows that the forger apparently became fatigued as he wrote the manuscript and started forming his letters less and less in the fashion one would find in an authentic manuscript and unconsciously lapses into writing that is more and more like his own Greek handwriting. Carlson finds examples of these more unconsciously formed letters and compares them to Morton Smith's own Greek handwriting. Not surprisingly, there are striking resemblances. *Theodore* appears to be a modern forgery, invented by none other than Morton Smith.

Carlson provides numerous additional pieces of evidence in favor of Smith's invention of *Theodore* and the *Secret Gospel of Mark*. Besides the handwriting, there are numerous indications in the content of the letter that the author was a modern person and not an ancient one. For example, one of the statements in *Theodore* speaks of salt as if it were a free-flowing substance that can be mixed with an adulterant and thus lose its flavor. But free-flowing salt was not invented until the twentieth century; prior to that time salt was clumpy and could not be mixed with an adulterant in this way. There are also a number of indications that Smith may have hidden in the forged document several subtle clues that he himself was the author, perhaps to amuse himself or to leave traces of his cleverness to any later scholar who finally uncovered his fake.

Carlson's case against *Secret Mark* is compelling. The final verdict is not yet in, but *Secret Mark* appears to have fewer and fewer defenders.

This type of forgery is not unique. In 2012 another "new" gospel fragment was allegedly discovered, one that includes the phrase, "Jesus said to them, 'My wife. . . .'" The fragment was authenticated by prominent Harvard University New Testament scholar Karen King. It caused a brief sensation, with television stations and newspapers broadcasting the discovery of "The Gospel of Jesus' Wife." However, as scholars voiced their doubts, further investigations began to unravel the story behind the discovery of this gospel. A brilliant article by investigative journalist Ariel Sabar in *The Atlantic* magazine[17] exposed the fraud in vivid detail, and by 2016 even King was forced to admit that it was probably a modern forgery.

---

15. Stephen Carlson, *The Gospel Hoax: Morton Smith's Invention of Secret Mark* (Waco: Baylor University Press, 2005), 13–22.

16. These include "forger's tremor," "pen lifts," the absence of "flying ends" at the ends of words, and retouching.

17. Ariel Sabar, "The Unbelievable Tale of Jesus' Wife," *The Atlantic*, July/August 2016, *www.theatlantic.com/magazine /archive/2016/07/the-unbelievable-tale-of-jesus-wife/485573*.

The *Gospel of Judas Iscariot*

The *Gospel of Judas Iscariot* was revealed to the world with great fanfare in 2006. The group of scholars that initially examined, translated, and interpreted the *Gospel of Judas* were part of a "dream team" put together by National Geographic, among whom were Bart Ehrman, Elaine Pagels, and Marvin Meyer. Their translation and interpretation suggested the text presented a shocking new perspective on an infamous historical figure.

The team's consensus was that the gospel presented Judas as the only disciple who truly understood the (Gnostic) teachings of Jesus, and that as a consequence Judas became Jesus' trusted friend and confidante. The gospel records numerous dialogues in which Judas' superiority to the other disciples is emphasized—in some cases by his more accurate understanding of Jesus' divine origin and identity—and also includes conversations between Jesus and Judas to which the other disciples are not privy. In the end Judas is not blamed for betraying Jesus; rather he is entrusted with handing Jesus over so that, following common Gnostic teaching, Jesus can escape his mortal body and return to his heavenly home. In this line of interpretation, the *Gospel of Judas Iscariot* becomes an important and valuable text, because it says something that no other ancient gospel does—that Judas was a hero—and in this way contributes to the understanding of the incredible diversity of early Christianity.[18]

This view has come under sharp criticism, however, most notably from Rice University biblical scholar April DeConick. DeConick argues that the National Geographic consensus was a

© jorisvo / Shutterstock.com

The canonical Gospels depict Judas as Jesus' betrayer, as in this fourteenth century Italian fresco. Does the *Gospel of Judas* take a more positive view, as some have claimed?

result of sloppy translation, selective interpretation, and wishful thinking. The claim that Judas's betrayal of Jesus is praiseworthy is clearly undercut, she notes, by the fact that Judas's motive in the text is not to release Jesus' spirit to the heavenly realm but to sacrifice him to the demon god Saklas. Nor is Jesus always complimentary toward Judas. In fact, Judas is frequently singled out as the worst of an ignorant group of disciples whose members are all clearly excluded from salvation. At one point in the text, Jesus refers to Judas as the "thirteenth *daimōn*." The National Geographic team (clearly led in matters of translation by Marvin Meyer) translates *daimōn* as "spirit" and sees this as a compliment. But DeConick points out a puzzling mistake here. In Christian literature the word *daimōn* almost always has a negative connotation and is translated

---

18. See Ehrman, *The Lost Gospel of Judas Iscariot,* for one version of the early consensus view of this newly discovered text.

as "demon." Moreover, the number thirteen in Gnostic literature almost unmistakably refers to the realm ruled over by the evil god Yaltabaoth. The identification of Judas as a demon also mitigates any credit he might be given for knowing Jesus' true, divine identity. In the Gospel of Mark, the demons know who Jesus is, but that does not make them heroes.[19]

In another passage, DeConick points out that the National Geographic team leaves out a negative, so that instead of reading Judas "would ascend to the holy generation," the full text reads, he "would not ascend to the holy generation." Meyer also argues that Jesus has "separated [Judas] for the holy generation," but DeConick clarifies that the Coptic necessitates the sense of "separated from" rather than "separated for." Bart Ehrman argues that the key line in the entire gospel is Jesus' final verdict on Judas, "But you will exceed all of them [the other disciples]. For you will sacrifice the man that clothes me."[20] DeConick insists the proper translation is, "But you will do worse than all of them. For the man that clothes me, you will sacrifice him." Although Ehrman's interpretation is reasonable in one respect, in that the release of Jesus' spirit from the prison of his body might be cause for rejoicing in Gnosticism, he overlooks the fact that the whole notion of sacrifice is anathema to Gnostics. Gnosticism understood sacrifice as a form of worship demanded by the bloodthirsty, wicked gods of the physical universe, those who were responsible for the creation of the evil, material world. In point of fact, by his betrayal, Judas was serving the evil god Yaltabaoth by ridding the world of the saving *gnōsis* provided by Jesus, *gnōsis* that would have led the wise to abandon the worship of Yaltabaoth and his ilk.

How could a National Geographic project, overseen by a select team of prominent scholars, go so terribly wrong? In a *New York Times* op-ed, DeConick raises the question of whether the biblical scholars were so eager to help produce a sensational *National Geographic* special—and to cash in with their own books exploiting the resulting publicity—that they blinded themselves to gaping flaws in their translation and interpretation. Some of the errors are so egregious that DeConick wonders if they were, in fact, accidental.[21]

This accusation brought howls of protest, especially from Marvin Meyer, and the ensuing drama played out on the pages of the *New York Times* and the *Chronicle of Higher Education*, as well as in tension-filled scholarly meetings. Seldom has the guild of biblical scholars seen such a public squabble, especially among such prominent figures and featuring such high stakes.

The weight of scholarly opinion has come down clearly on the side of the underdog, April DeConick. Meyer has tried to defend his translation, for example by using a much later Christian text that uses the word *daimōn* as he believes the *Gospel of Judas* does, but the response of John D. Turner in the *Chronicle*—"That's a bunch of crap"—was shared by many. Some other members of the National Geographic team have retracted some of their earlier statements (e.g., Elaine Pagels) or expressed regret that they were misled by Meyer (e.g., Craig A. Evans). Bart Ehrman has said little but has been among the small minority voicing support for Meyer's defense against DeConick's criticism. Ehrman also denied that he was the leading cheerleader for the now-discredited theory of Judas as Gnostic hero, claiming this is a small

---

19. See April De Conick, *The Thirteenth Apostle: What the Gospel of Judas Really Says* (London: Continuum, 2007).

20. Ehrman, *Lost Gospel of Judas Iscariot*, 96.

21. April DeConick, "Gospel Truth," *New York Times*, Dec. 1, 2007, *www.nytimes.com/2007/12/01/opinion/01deconink.html*.

part of his assessment of the gospel.[22] But his book provides a wealth of ammunition for critics. Ehrman refers to Judas as Jesus' "beloved" disciple and even claims the document's title (the *Gospel of Judas* rather than the *Gospel according to Judas*) is a deliberate indication that it does not concern the good news about Jesus but rather the good news about Judas himself. "Judas," Ehrman states, "even more than Jesus, is the hero of this account."[23] In the face of this evidence, Ehrman's denials ring somewhat hollow. The last word on this riveting scholarly controversy has not yet been heard, but some scholarly reputations will probably emerge permanently damaged.

More Gospels to Come?

Will more gospels be rediscovered in the future? The chances are fairly good. The number of gospels that are still "lost" remains substantial. Scholars know these gospels once existed because other ancient authors quote from them or refer to them. There are at least thirteen more gospels whose existence is well-attested in the ancient literature,[24] and many more whose existence is at least hinted at.

Philip Jenkins believes the most likely next discovery would be the *Gospel of Matthias*, judging from the frequency of ancient references to it. "Foretelling such discoveries," he argues, "is not a matter of mystical or apocalyptic prophecy, but rather a logical extrapolation from the history of archaeology and New Testament research over the last century or so. Major finds have occurred quite regularly, and there is no reason to believe that the two most famous manuscript hoards [Qumran and Nag Hammadi] were the only ones of their kind."[25] Whether the next find will have earth-shattering significance, as will probably be claimed for it, is another matter. Hopefully, scholars will learn from past mistakes and avoid making overblown claims about the import of the new discovery, at least until the dust has had time to settle. The damage caused by some of biblical scholarship's recent missteps has been substantial, and will likely take some time to undo.

Key Terms

[Coptic] Gospel of Thomas
Infancy Gospel of Thomas
Protoevangelium of James
asceticism
virginal conception

perpetual virginity
virginity during birth
trial by ordeal
threefold virginity of Mary
Gospel of Peter

Gospel of Philip
forgery
Greater Questions of Mary
Secret Gospel of Mark
Gospel of Judas Iscariot

Review Questions

1. In what ways does the *[Coptic] Gospel of Thomas* reflect a distinctively Gnostic perspective?

2. How does the *Infancy Gospel of Thomas* portray Jesus as a five- to six-year old boy? What is the purpose of this gospel?

---

22. For details about the aftermath of DeConick's critique of the National Geographic translation and interpretation, see Thomas Bartlett, "The Betrayal of Judas," *Chronicle of Higher Education* 54 (May 30, 2008), B6.

23. Ehrman, *Lost Gospel of Judas Iscariot*, 98.

24. For information on these still-lost gospels, including evidence of their existence, see J. K. Elliott, ed., *The Apocryphal New Testament: A Collection of Apocryphal Christian Literature in an English Translation based on M. R. James* (Oxford: Clarendon, 1993), 3–25.

25. Philip Jenkins, *Hidden Gospels: How the Search for Jesus Lost Its Way* (New York: Oxford University Press, 2001), 215.

3. How does the *Protoevangelium of James* reflect belief in the threefold virginity of Mary? What details does it provide to support the claims that Mary was a virgin when Jesus was conceived in her womb, remained a virgin throughout her life, and retained her biological virginity despite giving birth?

4. How does the *Gospel of Peter* attempt to deflect blame for Jesus' crucifixion away from the Romans and place it entirely on the Jews?

5. Does the *Gospel of Philip* suggest Jesus was married, as Dan Brown and others claim?

6. How does Epiphanius's forgery of the *Greater Questions of Mary* attempt to discredit his Gnostic opponents as sexual deviants?

7. Why do an increasing number of scholars regard the *Secret Gospel of Mark* as a modern forgery?

8. What are the arguments for and against the claim that the recently discovered *Gospel of Judas Iscariot* presents Judas as a hero rather than a villain?

Discussion Questions

1. Do you think that the discovery of the complete text of the *Gospel of Thomas* and other noncanonical gospels really makes a difference to our understanding of early Christianity, or do these gospels represent marginal voices that were rightly consigned to the dustbin of history? How would you defend your answer?

2. Would it make a huge difference to you if Jesus was married? Why or why not?

Consider the same question with respect to some of the other key assertions of noncanonical texts about Jesus, Mary, and Judas.

3. Given the frequency with which accusations of forgery and fraud have surrounded some recent "discoveries" of ancient gospel texts, will you be inclined to be skeptical or credulous the next time a major network or magazine announces a major discovery? Why?

Bibliography and Suggestions for Further Study

(Books and websites that are accessible for general undergraduates are marked with an asterisk; other sources listed are appropriate for advanced students.)

*Carlson, Stephen C. *The Gospel Hoax: Morton Smith's Invention of Secret Mark.* Waco: Baylor University Press, 2005

DeConick, April D. *The Thirteenth Apostle: What the Gospel of Judas Really Says.* London: Continuum, 2007.

*Ehrman, Bart. *Lost Christianities: The Battles for Scripture and the Faiths We Never Knew.* New York: Oxford University Press, 2003.

*Ehrman, Bart. *The Lost Gospel of Judas Iscariot: A New Look at Betrayer and Betrayed.* New York: Oxford University Press, 2006.

Elliott, J. K., ed. *The Apocryphal New Testament: A Collection of Apocryphal Christian Literature in an English Translation based on M. R. James.* Oxford: Clarendon, 1993.

Marjanen, Antti. *The Woman Jesus Loved: Mary Magdalene in the Nag Hammadi Library and Related Documents.* Leiden: Brill, 1996.

*Miller, Robert J., ed. *The Complete Gospels: Annotated Scholars Version.* Rev. and expanded ed. Santa Rosa, CA: Polebridge, 1994.

*Sabar, Ariel. "The Unbelievable Tale of Jesus' Wife." *The Atlantic.* July/August 2016. *www.theatlantic.com/magazine/archive/2016/07/the-unbelievable-tale-of-jesus-wife/485573.*

Greco-Roman Religions: Alternatives to Christianity

Despite some of its own later claims, Christianity was not an overnight success. Even as late as the turn of the fourth century, Christianity was an unlikely candidate to become the dominant religion in the Roman Empire. Most Roman subjects continued to participate in one or more of a group of cults that Christians eventually came to refer to collectively as **pagan religions**. These ancient religions had significant differences but also much in common.[1]

For one thing, all pagan religions were **polytheistic**. Even those that acknowledged a single, supreme deity affirmed subordinate deities or emanations of the one god, which led to the worship of a multiplicity of figures. Pagans devoted to one god generally acknowledged the existence of other gods.

Another shared characteristic was that, although pagans did worship at home, the real centers of worship were **temples** devoted to particular gods where **priests** sacrificed animals brought to them by worshippers. **Sacrifices** were conducted throughout the year, but the entire community would come together for annual **festivals.**

In general, pagan religions all focused on life in the present, putting little emphasis on seeking rewards in the afterlife. Most pagans did not believe that the afterlife involved heavenly perfection or eternal torment. Most held that all people—whether good or evil, faithful or not—went down to the "land of the dead" after their earthly lives ended. This place, known by the Greeks as Hades, was characterized by

© Doc-wood / Pixabay

The ancient Greek temple of Poseidon at Sounion was surrounded by water on three sides. Poseidon, god of the sea, was naturally a favorite deity among seafaring people.

---

1. Much of the following list of commonalities draws upon Bart Ehrman, *The New Testament: A Historical Introduction to the Early Christian Writings*, 6th ed. (New York: Oxford University Press, 2016), 41–57.

neither pain nor bliss. Hades was a land of mist and gloom, where one's senses were dulled and memories were dim, It was not a place of happiness. Happiness could only be experienced in life. One maximized happiness in the present by undertaking actions that pleased the gods, thereby earning blessings such as longevity, good health, many children, fulfilling love lives, fertile land, and wealth.

Pagan religions aimed to please the gods through correct **ritual** practice rather than through ethical living or faith. Adherents developed **cults** devoted to gods and goddesses. "Cult," here, is not used in the modern sense of a fringe religious group that uses coercive techniques. The Latin word *cultus* means "care," so in the ancient context the term simply meant that those with faith "took care of" the god or

goddess by carrying out proper public and external rituals. Sacrifice and prayer were the most important of these rituals, but they also included votive offerings (objects "donated" to a sacred place), games, processions, and the construction of monuments.

Finally, pagan religions tended to be concerned about the forces of nature, and the gods and goddesses they worshiped reflect this. Most pagan religions included a sun god, a sky or thunder god, a god of the sea, and an earth goddess. The forces of nature were key to determining the fertility of the land, upon which the agricultural economy of the ancient world depended. The gods were also thought to be responsible for the fertility of livestock and human beings. Most couples wanted to have as many children as possible, especially sons who would grow up

Greek Gods	Roman Gods	
Zeus	Jupiter	King of the gods, champion of justice, lawful order, and cosmic harmony, a sky-god associated with both daylight and storm
Poseidon	Neptune	Lord of the sea and earthquakes
Helios/Apollo	Sol	God of the sun
Hades	Pluto	Lord of the underworld, the subterranean world that housed the dead
Hera	Juno	Queen of heaven and guardian of marriage and domesticity
Demeter/Gaia	Ceres	Goddess of the fertility of the earth
Athena	Minerva	Goddess of wisdom
Apollo	Apollo	God of self-discipline, health, male beauty, and the creative arts
Artemis	Diana	Goddess of wildlife and hunting
Hermes	Mercury	Messenger of the gods and guide of souls to the underworld
Ares	Mars	God of war and aggression
Aphrodite	Venus	Goddess of love, female beauty, and sexual allure
Dionysus	Bacchus	God of wine and ecstasy

and work the land; the key to fertility was **piety** (religious observance).

One can see some of the characteristics of pagan religions by examining the pantheon of Greek and Roman mythology. The Greeks learned about the gods through the telling and retelling of myths (such as those found in Hesiod's *Theogony*), and of other stories (such as the epic poems of Homer, the *Iliad* and the *Odyssey*) in which the gods interacted with human characters. Some of the major gods of the Greek pantheon are listed in the preceding table, along with their Roman counterparts.

Noteworthy from this listing is how similar the Greek and Roman systems were; some of the Greek and Romans gods even shared the same name. The Romans were generally great admirers of Greek culture, and this led them to copy some aspects of their religion and mythology. However, any nature-based, polytheistic religion is likely to have a sky god, a sea god, a god of war, a goddess of love, and so on. Hence a direct influence need not be posited in every case.

Greco-Roman Religions

A complete survey of all religions practiced in the ancient Greco-Roman world would neither be possible in a single chapter nor desirable in an introduction to the New Testament. However, examining specific examples of major pagan ideas—both from earlier times and from the Hellenistic age—is useful. Such an examination aids in understanding the religious milieu in which early Christianity developed.

Patriotism, the Gods of Rome, and the Imperial Cult

Religion and the state were closely tied in the Roman Empire and among its Mediterranean predecessors. There was no formally-declared, empire-wide state religion, but the worship of certain gods was mandatory for Roman subjects. The temples and priesthoods of officially recognized gods were supported at public expense. Their festivals were declared public holidays during which most people were not required to work, according to law and custom. In the city of Rome, most of the gods whose festivals filled the religious calendar were native and traditional, and only a few foreign deities were honored.[2] In the provinces, the Romans tried to respect local sentiments and usually allowed conquered peoples to continue their traditional patterns of worship. Nevertheless, a provincial city would often develop cults to Roman deities, in part because the city could gain imperial favor by building temples to Roman gods and emperors. Moreover, certain aspects of Roman religion, especially the veneration of the emperor as a god, became mandatory throughout the empire. Thus Roman subjects enjoyed a religious freedom that fell short of absolute: they were (usually) free to worship the gods and goddesses of their choice, in addition to fulfilling certain obligations to the gods and emperor of Rome.

Rarely did the Roman Empire actually ban a religion or persecute its practitioners.[3] The persecution of Christians was an exception (see below and chapter 5). The Romans did disapprove of

---

2. However, many foreign deities were incorporated into the official Roman religion. From the Greeks, for example, the Romans "borrowed" Apollo, Dionysus, and Asclepius. Egyptian gods like Isis and Osiris, or Persian deities such as Mithras, also found a home in Rome.

3. Even the suppression of the Bacchanalia in Rome in 186 BCE did not involve a total ban on the Dionysian cult, since the Greek god Bacchus/Dionysus had already been officially accepted into the Roman pantheon. Instead, after reports of Bacchanalians seeking ecstasy through drunkenness and sexual orgies, the Senate simply restricted their activity by requiring government permission for any communal ritual and restricting the total number of participants in each group to five. See Luther Martin, *Hellenistic Religions: An Introduction* (New York: Oxford University Press, 1987), 96–98.

certain religions, however; they termed such cults "**superstitions**." Legitimate religions were traditional—having long pedigrees—and their observance was associated with the past successes and present welfare of the state. Superstitions were considered strange, innovative, foreign, and divisive. People who subscribed to superstitions, then, were not "religious" in the proper sense; they were deemed "atheists." Even though they worshipped gods, they refused to worship traditional Roman gods.[4] Judaism was sometimes referred to as a superstition because Jews scorned the worship of pagan gods and had practices (circumcision, the Sabbath) that the Romans regarded as strange or barbaric. However, Judaism was an ancient faith with a long tradition, and because the Romans respected antiquity, Judaism was tolerated as a legitimate religion.[5] Christianity, on the other hand, was definitely considered a superstition, and its adherents were regarded as atheists (see Justin Martyr, *1 Apology* 6; Suetonius, *Domitian* 15).

The Roman view of superstitions as divisive is key to understanding the empire's treatment of religious deviants and newcomers like the Christians. One of the main purposes of legitimate religion was to unify the empire. Indeed, the historian Polybius regarded religion as "the very thing which keeps the Roman commonwealth together" (*Histories* 6.56).[6] Religion was seen as the key to both the founding of

Rome and its current and future success. The great Roman orator Cicero voiced the popular Roman view that the founding of the Roman state and its long history of victories and prosperity was due to the piety of its people. In Virgil's famous epic poem, *The Aeneid,* the Roman Empire gains recognition from Jupiter precisely because Aeneas is so religiously observant. Propertius declared that "the gods founded the walls" of Rome "and the gods protect them" (*Elegies* 3.11).[7]

Because of these Roman beliefs, the refusal of Jews and Christians to worship the gods of Rome was taken as an offense and seen as dangerous to the unity and welfare of the state. The Christian apologist Marcus Minucius Felix quotes a Roman who complained that Christian refusals were as much a civic as a religious violation: "You do not go to our shows, you take no part in our processions, you are not present at our public banquets, you shrink in horror from our sacred games, from food ritually dedicated by our priests, from drink hallowed by libation poured upon our altars" (*Octavius* 12).[8]

The phenomenon that came to most clearly illustrate the civic and unifying purpose of Roman state religion was the cult of the emperor. By the time of **Pliny the Younger** (112 CE), a willingness to make offerings to the emperor had become the litmus test for patriotism and

---

4. Many provincial cults did not worship traditional Roman gods either; but they did worship many gods whom the Romans could easily see as versions of their own gods. The Romans frequently substituted Roman names for these gods and assimilated them into the Roman pantheon. In fact, many Romans simply accepted that their gods and the Greek gods were identical. This combination of once independent religious traditions into a merged unity is known as *syncretism*, and Roman religion was highly syncretistic. See Arnaldo Momigliano, "The Disadvantages of Monotheism for a Universal State," *Classical Philology* 81 (1986): 286.

5. See Helmut Koester, *Introduction to the New Testament*, vol. 1, *History, Culture, and Religion of the Hellenistic Age* (Philadelphia: Fortress, 1982), 365, on the status of Judaism as a religion that was not technically sanctioned by the state but that enjoyed many of the privileges of a *religio licita* because of its long tradition.

6. Translation from Polybius, *The Histories of Polybius*, trans. from the text of F. Hultsch by Evelyn S. Shuckburgh, with a new introduction by F. W. Walbank (Westport, CN: Greenwood, 1974).

7. Translation from Sextus Propertius, *Propertius in Love: The Elegies*, trans. David R. Slavitt, foreword by Matthew S. Santirocco (Berkeley: University of California Press, 2002).

8. Translation from Minucius Felix, *The Octavius of Marcus Minucius Felix*, trans. and annotated by G. W. Clarke, Ancient Christian Writers 39 (New York: Newman, 1974).

loyalty to the state. The imperial cult developed slowly in Rome. In Greece and throughout the eastern Mediterranean world, it had been common to view the king as the epiphany of a particular god. The Romans, however, traditionally saw their gods in more transcendent and abstract terms and not as beings who made "appearances" in human form, no matter how noble that form. Nonetheless, the Romans believed transcendent powers could become active in exceptional human beings, so it was considered appropriate to worship the "genius" of the emperor. In Roman religious thinking, all people and things had a **genius**—an element of the divine, a kind of personal guardian deity. When an individual accomplished extraordinary things, the credit belonged—at least in part—to his genius. After Octavian (later Caesar Augustus) won the civil war and established the *Pax Romana* (the "peace of Rome," an era of unusual stability and prosperity) the Senate voted that all feasts include a libation to his genius.

Eventually the Romans lost their reluctance to follow the Greek model and began thinking of emperors as gods, dedicating temples to them and worshipping them as the other gods. Julius Caesar was the first emperor to be raised to divine status, although this occurred only after his assassination. Following Caesar's murder by Roman aristocrats who feared he would declare himself both god and king, the people of Rome clamored for their supposed champion to be divinized, and the Senate voted to make it official. Later it became common for the Senate to vote emperors into godhood posthumously, although some of the worst emperors were denied this honor.

Some emperors, such as Caligula, began to demand they be worshipped as gods during their lifetimes. Caligula even insisted his statue be raised in temples dedicated to other gods, a highly controversial move. Other emperors, though, discouraged the cult of the living emperor and attempted to return to the practice of the time of Caesar Augustus.

The Correspondence between Pliny the Younger and the Emperor Trajan

A fascinating glimpse into the relationship between Roman state religion and the persecution of Christians is provided by surviving letters between Pliny the Younger, the governor of the province of Bithynia, and the Emperor Trajan, dating from 112 CE.[9] Pliny writes to Trajan (*Epistulae* 96) asking his advice about what to do with persons accused of being Christians. The initial accusations seem to have been made by local merchants, most likely butchers who were finding it difficult to sell meat because Christians refused to consume animals that had been slaughtered as part of a religious sacrifice to pagan gods. Such meat would have comprised the lion's share of the butchers' inventory.

Pliny's language shows that he presumes Christians are criminals and deserving of punishment, although he is unclear whether they should be presumed guilty simply by virtue of being Christian or whether evidence of specific crimes would need to be presented. Pliny certainly would have known of Nero's persecution of Christians after the Great Fire

continued

9. The following account of Pliny's persecution of the Christians of Bithynia draws upon Robert Wilken, *The Christians as the Romans Saw Them* (New Haven: Yale University Press, 1984), 15–30.

The Correspondence between Pliny the Younger and the Emperor Trajan *continued*

in Rome in 64 CE as well as the period of persecution under the emperor Domitian (81–96 CE). There is later documentation of rumors that Christians engaged in gross sexual immorality and even the ritual murder of children and the consumption of their flesh, but it is unclear whether Pliny had heard (or believed) that Christians engaged in such behavior. Pliny tells Trajan, though, that his inquiries revealed that Christians "took food of an ordinary, harmless kind" and that he found no evidence of Christians having committed other crimes.

Nonetheless, Pliny did not hesitate to take action against those who admitted to being Christians. He summoned the accused, proceeded to ask them if they were Christians, and warned them they would be executed if they said yes. If a Christian admitted his or her faith, then Pliny would ask them a second time and a third to be absolutely sure. Those who "confessed" were then immediately killed. "Whatever the nature of their admission," Pliny wrote, "I am convinced that their stubbornness and unshakeable obstinacy ought not go unpunished."[10]

If a person accused of being a Christian denied the charge, Pliny set up a "test"

to make sure he was not being deceived. He brought in statues of the emperor and of the three "Capitoline" Roman gods (Jupiter, Juno, and Minerva) and demanded that the defendant repeat an invocation to the gods and make an offering of wine and incense to the emperor. Pliny also insisted that the accused "revile the name of Christ." He believed no true Christian could do such things, so only those who were not Christian or had renounced their former Christian faith would obey and hence exonerate themselves.

Once Pliny began punishing Christians, a host of new accusations erupted. Apparently, Christians were extremely unpopular with their neighbors, who took the opportunity afforded by Pliny's presence to rid themselves of those Christians who either confessed or failed his test and were thus executed. Trajan assured Pliny that he was proceeding as his emperor would have wished, although he specified that Pliny should not allow accusers to remain anonymous. Pliny's correspondence with Trajan documents a pattern of Christian persecution that also occurred before and after Pliny's time.

Worship of the emperor most often involved offerings of wine and incense in the presence of a statue of the emperor in a temple or other public building. While such offerings were made regularly, in truth there were few occasions when a person would have been forced to worship the emperor. The Romans might never have known there were increasing numbers of people who would refuse to do so had it not been for informants who called attention to this apparent disloyalty. Those accused were almost always Christians.

Divination

Almost as important as prayer and sacrifice in Greco-Roman religion was "the observation of signs (*omina*) from which one could learn what the gods intended to do."[11] Greco-Roman religions maintained that a finite, ordered world existed and that the universe was not as arbitrary as it appeared. One way to understand the order of the universe and how to act in accord with it was through the application of reason, which is

---

10. Pliny the Younger, *Letters and Panegyricus*, trans. Betty Radice, Loeb Classical Library 55, 59 (Cambridge, MA: Harvard University Press, 1969).

11. Koester, *History, Culture, and Religion of the Hellenistic Age*, 363.

the concern of philosophy. Another approach was the practice of **divination**. Divination involved reading signs offered by the universe and its governing powers to predict the future.

Two main kinds of divination marked Greco-Roman religion: natural and artificial. Artificial divination observed natural phenomena and detected patterns that revealed the cosmic order, aided by reason or deduction. Natural divination did not use reason or deduction, and did not observe or record signs, but depended on individuals who spoke under some kind of "inspiration."

Artificial divination took many forms, including the observation of the instinctual patterns of animals (theriomancy), the migratory patterns, characteristic calls, and flight patterns of birds (ornithomancy), or the patterns exhibited in the brightness of configurations of flame and smoke (pyromancy).[12] In each case there were experts who understood what the patterns portended about the future actions of the gods. One well-known example in Rome involved the **augurs**, priests who could interpret the will of the gods by studying the flight of birds. This was known as "taking the **auspices**." All of Rome's successes were attributed to the fact that prior to taking action the auspices were taken and the action "augured well." Of course, the effectiveness of augury could only be judged in retrospect. When Rome suffered a setback, it was thought that something had gone wrong with the process of taking the auspices. Romans like Cicero were aware that certain types of auspices could easily be used fraudulently. It was rumored that some wealthy Romans could bribe the augurs to guarantee a favorable "verdict" or that the augurs would develop tricks to ensure that Rome was not paralyzed into inaction by persistently negative omens.

By far the most widespread and influential type of artificial divination was **astrology**. Because the sun and moon had indisputable effects on earthly life, it seemed only natural that the stars and other planets would have similar influences. Hence astrology was considered the most scientific and rational of the ancient methods of divination. The Babylonians were the first to develop the idea that the regular and predictable movement of the heavenly bodies reflected an otherwise unseen order and predictability in both cosmic and earthly affairs. The Greeks and Egyptians further developed Babylonian astrology by applying advanced principles of logic and mathematics, although astrology also had a nonscientific, religious component in that the planets were named after gods and the characteristics of the planets were thought to derive from those of their namesakes. Astrology gained great popularity. Both rich and poor commonly consulted an astrologer prior to taking any significant action.

The realm of natural divination included **oracles** and dreams. The predecessor of such verbal signs was divination by lot or chance (cleromancy), a concept found not only in the Greco-Roman world but the Jewish as well. For example, Old Testament passages show the use of a sort of sacred dice, the *urim* and *thummim*, to divine guilt or innocence, also referred to as the casting of "lots" (Lev. 16:8; Josh. 18; Neh. 11:1; Job 6:27).

If the gods revealed their will and the future through such things as the tossing of sticks or dice, then it stood to reason they might also speak directly through human beings. The most famous example in the Greco-Roman world was the oracle of Apollo at Delphi. At Delphi there was a chasm that was thought to be sacred in the sense that a crevasse was thought to give access to the gods and goddesses of the earth. One who approached would enter a trance and become inspired. Eventually the oracle was institutionalized. Instead of a frenzy of disorganized seekers shouting random prophecies, a single earth-goddess priestess was chosen to enter into a trance on behalf of supplicants seeking to know the future. The oracle could only be

---

12. On the various types of artificial and natural divination, see Martin, *Hellenistic Religions*, 40–50.

consulted one day a month, and the supplicant had to pay a fee by means of a preliminary offering, which gained one the right to make a blood sacrifice of sheep or goats on the altar at the sacred site itself. The god would thus be summoned to the site, and the priestess would purify herself with a ritual bath, enter the shrine, mount a tripod, and provide inspired answers to the questions posed to her.

Although ancient Judaism included the casting of lots and the patriarch Joseph was a noted practitioner of divination, the general opinion of divination in the Old Testament/Hebrew Bible is decidedly negative. There are condemnations of divination and various warnings against its practice (Deut. 18:10; Josh. 13:22; 1 Sam. 15:23). Perhaps for this reason, divination is one of the elements of Greco-Roman religion for which there is little or no parallel in early Christianity.

Sickness, Disease, and the Cult of Asclepius

Healing was a significant part of ancient religions. Unsanitary conditions and the poor quality of ancient medicine meant only the lucky few maintained good health throughout life and died of old age. Given that the onset of illness seemed to be as arbitrary and inexplicable as the weather, it is not surprising that many ancient people associated sickness with the work of malevolent forces of supernatural origin (demons) and linked healing with deities who were benevolent, compassionate, and humane. As a result there were hundreds of local temples and shrines throughout the Mediterranean world dedicated to healing.

Healing was associated not only with sacred places but also with individuals. Many philosophers were thought to have the ability to heal.

Two of the more noteworthy are Pythagoras and his disciple **Apollonius of Tyana**. Pythagoras (sixth century BCE) is popularly remembered as a mathematician and author of the Pythagorean theorem, but he was also a philosopher and founder of a popular religious movement. His followers used poultices, music, and even the reading of Homeric poetry as part of their healing arts. The neo-Pythagorean philosopher Apollonius (first century CE) was even more renowned as a miracle-worker, owing to the popularity of his biography *The Life of Apollonius of Tyana* by Philostratus, written in the early third century. Apollonius is best known today for the many parallels between his alleged biography and that of Jesus. He is said to have had a miraculous birth, frequently dispensed wise teachings and sage advice, predicted the future, bravely faced conflict with secular authorities, and appeared to his followers after death. Apollonius was also reputed to have had the ability to heal the sick, cast out demons, and raise the dead.[13] It was almost expected that an itinerant preacher and philosopher like Apollonius would have healing in his repertoire.

The most famous, popular healing cult, however, was associated with the Greek god **Asclepius**. Archaeologists have found traces of more than three hundred temples to Asclepius scattered throughout the Greco-Roman world. Asclepius is said to have been born a demigod, the mortal son of Apollo and a human woman, who inherited from his divine father the gift of healing. Following an exemplary life, he was said to have attained divine status, and Asclepius became the supreme patron of medicine.

The "sons of Asclepius," the healing priests of his temples, were skilled in self-promotion. Each temple advertised its effectiveness by publicizing

---

13. The strong parallels between claims regarding the life of Apollonius and that of Jesus has led to many controversies over whether the Gospel writers borrowed motifs from stories about Apollonius or whether Philostratus appropriated patterns from the Gospels in writing his life of Apollonius. Certainly Philostratus was writing more than a hundred years later than the evangelists; however, it is possible the evangelists and Philostratus independently drew upon a common pool of ideas about elements in the life of a divine-human savior.

its most spectacular healings. Records of alleged cures, originally written on wooden votive tablets, were eventually "published" in the form of stone inscriptions. Larger temples employed professionals (aretalogists) whose primary job was to tell of the great healing deeds of the gods on special occasions.

Sacred sites dedicated to Asclepius were usually entire complexes, not single buildings. In addition to one or two temples to Asclepius himself, there would be additional temples for Apollo, Artemis, and the daughter of Asclepius, Hygieia (from which the English word "hygiene" derives). There were also baths, a library, a theater, a gymnasium, a stadium, rooms for medical treatment, a special room in which the god Asclepius appeared to the patient in a healing dream, and a guest house with as many as 160 rooms.[14] The complex operated more like a health spa than a simple doctor's office. Because of all the tight organization, comprehensive facilities, badly-needed services, and effective publicity machine, the cult of Asclepius became one of the most popular and respected in the Greco-Roman world.

This collection of votive objects comes from the site of the temple of Asclepius in Corinth. These statues of afflicted body parts were offered to the god by grateful worshippers who believed they had been healed by Asclepius.

Wisdom and the Popular Philosophies

While the majority of religions of the Greco-Roman world cared most about rituals and did not concern themselves so much with ethics, there were groups whose main message involved the proper way to live. These groups used reason to develop their wisdom about the human condition and the optimal path to happiness and fulfillment. Known as the **popular philosophies**, they include the Cynics, Stoics, and Epicureans.

While it is not necessary to review the precise teachings of each of these groups and the fine distinctions between them in order to read and understand the New Testament, a single example will suffice to show how these groups shared with Christianity a deep concern for ethics and virtue but were very different from Christianity in many other respects.

The **Epicureans** sought to escape the world of fortune by withdrawing from public life and retreating into the life of the mind. The followers of Epicurus (341–270 BCE) pursued a reflective and prudent existence according to the dictates of human reason. True happiness, they preached, came from the pursuit of "pleasure" and the cultivation of friendship. While they are often associated with hedonism in the sense of "wine, women, and song," originally the Epicureans meant something else by pleasure: the absence of physical suffering and mental turmoil. Epicurus explains, "By pleasure we mean

14. See Koester, *History, Culture, and Religion of the Hellenistic Age*, 174.

Epicurean Quotes

A number of famous quotes are attributed to Epicurus or his followers, although not all of them are authentic. One of the most famous is the so-called Epicurean paradox, which questions the existence of God (or gods) based on the reality of evil and suffering:

> Is God willing to prevent evil, but not able?
> Then he is not omnipotent.
> Is he able, but not willing?
> Then he is malevolent.
> Is he both able and willing?
> Then whence cometh evil?
> Is he neither able nor willing?
> Then why call him God?

However, this argument (known as a *trilemma*) is not Epicurean in origin. Although they are sometimes classified as atheists, the Epicureans did not deny the existence of the gods. They simply held that the universe was governed by natural laws and that the gods played no part in the affairs of human beings. Therefore, it was pointless to worship them.

One reason later thinkers, especially Christians, were likely to think of Epicureans as atheists and to attribute to them skeptical arguments like the one mentioned above is that they did not believe in an afterlife or the immortality of the soul. Written on the tombs or gravestones of many ancient Romans was the Epicurean epitaph: *Non fui, fui, non sum, non curo* ("I was not; I was; I am not; I do not care"). This shows that while many Greeks and Romans believed in the traditional pagan view that all who die go to the same, shadowy existence in the "land of the dead," others thought there is no afterlife at all. After death, the Epicureans thought, there is nothing. So there is no point to putting off the pleasures of today in the hope of a happy afterlife. One must live for the moment.

the absence of pain in the body and of trouble in the soul. . . . It is sober reasoning, searching out the grounds of every choice and avoidance, and banishing those beliefs through which the great tumults take possession of the soul."[15] Although happiness is defined in a highly individualistic way, Epicureans believed that the individual flourished in a community of friends who took meals together and supported one another in times of need.

While Epicureanism and its rivals Stoicism and Cynicism are referred to as "popular" philosophies, their popularity was mostly restricted to the educated upper classes. Their importance lies not so much in being actual competitors with Christianity and paganism for large numbers of adherents, but in the influence they had on other belief systems. The nonconformist, antiestablishment, and ascetic ethos of the itinerant philosopher Zeno (490–430 BCE) and his Cynic followers has strong affinities with both Jesus and John the Baptist. The Stoic idea of a divine animating principle, called the *Logos*, which pervades the universe and provides its order, has clear connections to the Logos-Christology of the Gospel of John: "In the beginning was the Word [*Logos*]" (John 1:1); John's Christology, in turn, became the basis for the orthodox Christian understanding of Jesus. Although studied mostly by the elite, Greek philosophy contributed a great deal to the religious thinking of the Hellenistic age.

---

15. Translation from Diogenes Laertius, *Lives of Eminent Philosophers*, trans. R. D. Hicks, Loeb Classical Library 184, 185 (Cambridge, MA: Harvard University Press, 1959), x. All quotations of Epicurus are from this edition.

The Mystery Cults

A group of diverse Greco-Roman religions are collectively termed "**mystery religions**" because, in contrast to most pagan religions, their rituals were not carried out in public and did not involve the whole community, but took place in private gatherings at which only initiates were welcome. The most widespread and popular of these were the cult of **Isis** (of Egyptian origin); the **Eleusinian mysteries** devoted to the harvest mother-goddess **Demeter** (native to Greece); the cult of Dionysus (also known as Bacchus), the god of wine and ecstasy; the cult of Cybele (or Magna Mater, "Great Mother"); and the cult of Mithras (of Persian origin).

Because of their secretive nature and the paucity of surviving textual evidence, a great deal about the beliefs and practices of the mystery cults remains elusive. The picture is further complicated by the **syncretistic** tendencies of Greco-Roman religion. The cult of Serapis was originally an independent religion that deliberately sought to combine elements of Greek and Egyptian religious thought and practice to help unite these peoples under a single Hellenistic ruler. However, this once-independent religion eventually became entwined with a more traditional Egyptian cult when the god Serapis grew in popularity to the point where he often replaced Osiris as the consort of Isis. Similarly, the Orphic mysteries, whose initiates worshipped Dionysus and Persephone, are in many ways indistinguishable from the two other mystery cults that revered these divinities.

The Myth of Demeter and Persephone

The beautiful goddess **Persephone**, daughter of Zeus and the harvest mother-goddess Demeter, was found irresistibly attractive by many of the male Greek gods. Apollo, Hermes, and Hades were all in love with her, but her mother refused to allow any of them to win her. Zeus eventually decided to give her to Hades, but did so without Demeter's knowledge or permission. Persephone was in a meadow gathering flowers when Hades, god of the underworld, sprang out from his subterranean realm and dragged her away to the land of the dead. Demeter was heartbroken over her daughter's disappearance, and began wandering the earth in a fruitless search for Persephone. Demeter's sorrow led to an extended period of fasting, because her neglect meant the grain would not grow. Not only did the people begin to starve, but the gods were deprived of their sacrificial offerings. During this period, the people of Eleusis gave shelter and support to the grieving Demeter. Finally Zeus intervened and ordered Hades to return Persephone to her mother. But Hades tricked her into eating some pomegranate seeds before her departure, and because she had tasted food in the underworld she was obliged to return to Hades every year. Hades was able to keep Persephone in the underworld for one-third of the year, but she would be reunited with her mother for the remaining two-thirds of the year. Demeter rejoiced when Persephone was restored to her; she in turn restored the fertility of the earth and revealed her "mysteries" to the loyal people of Eleusis.

The agricultural origins of this myth are apparent. The period of Persephone's absence and Demeter's sorrow corresponded with the unfruitful seasons, when no grain would grow. In Greece, these were the hot, drought-ridden summer months. The return of Persephone in October marked the beginning of the planting season, and in the spring the people gave thanks to Demeter for the harvest.

In addition to the secret rituals and initiation requirement, the mystery religions differed from traditional paganism in other significant ways. For example, some of these religions taught that adherents were not necessarily doomed to a shadowy afterlife in the land of the dead but could hope for eternal bliss in a peaceful paradise where they indulged in whatever activities they had enjoyed in life. Among the religions that made such promises were the cult of Isis and Osiris[16] and the Eleusinian mysteries. The Greek term for this heavenly afterlife was **Elysium** (or the "Elysian fields"). Traditional Greek religion (as expressed in Homer) held that this reward was for a select few, such as mortals of divine parentage, or the great heroes. Some mystery religions, however, held out the possibility that the gods might bestow a happy afterlife on humans outside of their family circle. Naturally, the possibility of hell also occurred to the architects of mystery religions: Orphism, for example, warned adherents about postmortem punishments for certain transgressions. Hence the Christian understanding of eternal reward and punishment was not entirely without precedent in Greco-Roman religion.

The pantheons of every ancient polytheistic religion included goddesses, but often they were understood as the wives or consorts of male gods, whose importance was greater. In the mystery religions, however, the goddess was often the most significant object of worship. Demeter and Cybele/Magna Mater were usually worshipped without reference to a consort. Isis was paired with Osiris or Serapis, but it was clear that Isis was the more important deity. Perhaps by design, some of these cults appealed more to women than did other, male-dominated religions. The autumn rituals associated with Demeter were restricted to women, although the spring celebrations were

The Metropolitan Museum of Art, Gift of J. Pierpont Morgan, 1917

In this ancient Egyptian statue, the goddess Isis nurses her infant son, Osiris. Did such images inspire later Christian depictions of the Virgin Mary and the infant Jesus?

open to men and women. Many men seemed to prefer a feminine deity as well, or at least a balance between male and female when it came to the gods. In Christianity, the development of the cult of the Virgin Mary could be seen as an attempt to fulfill this popular desire, although Mary was never accorded divine status.

The motif of the dying and resurrected god in paganism has perhaps been overemphasized by some early history of religions scholars, who claimed it was found in dozens of ancient religions. The real number is perhaps two or three.[17] However, the motif is no less significant for that.

---

16. The possibility of a happy afterlife (at least for some) was not new in Egyptian religious thinking; the Egyptians had long been held this exceptional belief.

17. The number is reduced if one counts only *gods* who actually died and then were restored to life in something resembling their former physical manifestation.

Dionysus was thought to have been born from a human mother (Semele) and a divine father (Zeus). Zeus's wife Hera became jealous over his infidelity and arranged for Dionysus to be torn apart by the Titans. There are various versions of his subsequent "resurrection." In one, the only part of Dionysus's body left by the Titans was his heart. The heart is rescued by Rhea (mother of both Zeus and Hera) and Zeus is able to remake Dionysus from it. This makes sense in light of Dionysus's status as the god of wine. His dismemberment by the Titans is analogous to the sharp pruning back of grapevines after the harvest, after which they become dormant in winter (death) and come back to life in the spring (rebirth).

A similar pattern is seen in the story of **Osiris**, the Egyptian god who brought civilization to the people by teaching them how to cultivate grain. Osiris is killed by his twin brother Set, and his body is floated down the Nile River entombed in a chest. Later, Set takes the body, chops it into fourteen pieces, and scatters them around the world. His grief-stricken wife, Isis, wanders the land seeking Osiris, and is eventually able to recover all but one piece of her husband's body (the phallus). Isis makes a replica of this crucial part and the restoration of his body is complete. Eventually he returns from the land of the dead to help his son Horus defeat Set once and for all. The symbolism of Osiris's death and rebirth is again agrarian: he "was known to Egyptians as the corn-god, who, like the corn, annually was threshed—dismembered by Set— only to return from the dead in a new crop."[18]

Defenders of Paganism, Critics of Christianity

Though Christianity survived persecution to become the dominant religion in the Roman Empire, paganism did not go down without a fight, either literally or figuratively. Christians were strongly disliked by many of their fellow Roman subjects for most of the first three hundred years of Christianity's existence. Many of the persecutions that took place were not "top-down" affairs ordered by a few powerful Christian-hating leaders, but rather resulted from spontaneous mob uprisings against Christians or from other kinds of popular pressure. However, the battle between paganism and Christianity took place not just in the streets but also in the academies and forums where intellectual debates replaced shoving and the screaming of accusations.

Unfortunately, scholars know of the defenders of paganism usually through the works of their opponents, those Christians who responded to pagan attacks—and may not have represented their opponents' positions fairly. A pagan named **Celsus** wrote the first known major work attacking Christian beliefs and practices in a systematic fashion around 177 CE. Unfortunately, this work has not survived; however, in 248 CE the great Christian author **Origen** wrote a response to Celsus titled *Contra Celsum* (*Against Celsus*), and in it he preserves many quotes from Celsus and summarizes his arguments. In the late third century, **Porphyry** wrote an even more detailed and expert refutation of Christianity called *Adversus Christianos* (*Against the Christians*), but only fragments of this work survive, along with quotations in works generally hostile to Porphyry. To the degree that scholars can reconstruct these works, they are valuable to the study of the New Testament. The criticisms made by these later pagans were not very different from the criticisms articulated even during the New Testament period; thus the later writings indirectly shed light on the attitudes that contributed to Roman persecution of Christianity.

These reconstructions reveal that only some of the pagan objections to Christianity concerned

---

18. Martin, *Hellenistic Religions*, 75.

strictly religious issues. The more general social and political reasons for Roman persecution of Christians are covered in chapter 5. Here, the ways in which Christianity offended pagans' theological sensibilities are considered.

A key complaint was that Christianity emphasized faith to the exclusion of reason. Christianity was known as a religion that demanded a blind, irrational faith and discouraged people from asking too many questions.[19] Christians believed things based on hearsay and were unable to give reasons for their beliefs (see Origen, *Contra Celsum* 1.9).[20] The anti-Christian Roman emperor **Julian**[21] (361–363 CE) slammed the Christian reliance on faith rather than reason, exclaiming, "There is nothing in your philosophy beyond the one word 'Believe!'" (quoted in Gregory of Nazianzus, *Orations* 4.102).[22] It was thought Christians showed their fear of rational debate of their views by avoiding dialogue with educated Romans and operating primarily among the uneducated lower classes, targeting women and children particularly.

Many other pagan objections to Christianity involved the unworthiness of the emerging religion's founder, Jesus. Certainly, aspects of Jesus' wonder-working biography were disputed; however, pagans also argued that even if many of these claims about Jesus were true, he still did not measure up to Orpheus, Heracles, or Asclepius

(see Origen, *Contra Celsum* 7.53). Jesus' miracles were equaled or exceeded by many other ancient figures. As early Christian historian Robert Wilkin explains it, many pagans believed that "Jesus was a low-grade magician, not a great hero like the men of old."[23]

The charge that Jesus was a magician reflects a common pagan suspicion about Jesus. Pagan critics of Christianity did not generally deny that Christ performed miracles, but they thought his supernatural abilities stemmed from dark magic. Celsus was apparently the first to record this accusation: "It was by magic that he [Jesus] was able to do the miracles which he appeared to have done" (*Contra Celsum* 1.6). Although belief in magic was common enough in the ancient world, it was never respectable; indeed, its practice was a criminal offense. Not only was Jesus a magician, pagan critics charged, but his disciples followed in his footsteps. Many tales circulated about the apostles performing miracles, and later Christians continued to use the name of Jesus in what appeared to be spells and incantations. "Christians get the power which they seem to possess by pronouncing the names of certain daemons and incantations," Celsus charged (*Contra Celsum* 1.6).[24]

Moreover, pagans refused to admit that all of the stories Christians told about Jesus were true. The fact that all of the sources involved were

---

19. This picture began to change with the appearance of learned Christian defenders of the faith, known as "apologists," in the third century CE.

20. No one denied that the followers of many religions besides Christianity, including paganism, were also unable to give a strong, rational account of the basis of their beliefs. The specific charge against Christianity was that while paganism did have at least some articulate, well-educated defenders who could give solid reasons for pagan beliefs and practices, Christianity had none.

21. Usually referred to as "Julian the Apostate," because he departed from the pattern of post-Constantine emperors by rejecting Christianity and advocating a return to paganism.

22. As quoted by Gregory of Nazianzus, *Orations*, trans. Martha Vinson, Fathers of the Church 107 (Washington, DC: Catholic University of America Press, 2003).

23. Wilken, *The Christians as the Romans Saw Them*, 105.

24. All quotations from *Contra Celsum* are from Origen, *Contra Celsum*, trans. with an introduction and notes by Henry Chadwick (Cambridge: University Press, 1953).

written by Christians, presumed to be biased in favor of Christianity, led to a certain degree of suspicion.[25] According to Celsus, Jesus himself had fabricated the story of his birth from a virgin, because the truth was too embarrassing. In Celsus's version, Mary was a poor married woman who became pregnant by another man, a Roman soldier named Panthera, after which she was convicted of adultery and driven away in disgrace (*Contra Celsum* 1.28, 32). Other stories, Celsus claimed, were invented by Jesus' disciples to promote their claim that he was the Son of God.[26] In some cases the lack of credible witnesses who could verify Christian stories about Jesus seemed suspicious to Celsus. If the baptism of Jesus took place as the Gospels indicate, for example, should not large numbers of people have heard the voice of God thundering from heaven and seen the Holy Spirit descend like a dove on Jesus (*Contra Celsum* 1.41)? In Origen's telling, Celsus reserves some of his most pointed comments for the resurrection:

> While he was alive he did not help himself, but after death he rose again and showed the marks of his punishment and how his hands had been pierced. But who says this? A hysterical female, as you say, and perhaps some other one of those who were deluded by the same sorcery, who either dreamt in a certain state of mind and through wishful thinking had a hallucination due to some mistaken notion (an experience which has happened to thousands), or which is more likely, wanted to impress the others by telling this fantastic tale, and so by this cock-and-bull story to provide a chance for other beggars. (*Contra Celsum* 2.55)

Other objections to Christianity were theoretical rather than factual. In particular, the concepts of an incarnated god and the resurrection of the body were seen as nonsensical by many pagans. Similarly incredible was the Christian claim that the potential for salvation was introduced into history at a particular moment (Christ's death and resurrection), implying that, before that moment, no one could be saved. Many of the most educated pagans had come around to the idea of a single, supreme deity, although they continued (usually) to believe in the existence of subordinate divine beings, such as Olympian gods, *daimones*, heroes, and demigods, who pointed to and were ruled over by the one high God. This supreme god was thought to be incorporeal, immoveable, impassible, and in need of nothing external to himself (Porphyry, *On Abstinence from Animal Food* 2.37). **Anthropomorphic** notions of this god (assigning "human" traits and characteristics to him) were seen as vulgar.[27] Pagans also contended the Christian belief that God underwent change and "became human" was nonsense. Classical scholar E. R. Dodds put it this way: "That such a God should take human shape and suffer earthly humiliation is naturally incomprehensible to the pagans."[28] Origen quotes Celsus to this effect:

---

25. On this point, see Wilken, *The Christians as the Romans Saw Them*, 110, 147. Wilken attributes this position to Celsus: "The Gospels are based only on hearsay. Why should one give greater credibility to what is written in them than to other stories about Jesus? The accounts in the Gospels were written solely by Christians and passed on in Christian circles. Should the legends there be taken with greater seriousness than the many legends in Greek literature?"

26. Some pagans credited Jesus with being a good and wise man who never claimed the divine status his followers later attributed to him.

27. On this point Christians seemed to agree, at least when referring to God the Father, whom they regarded as impassible and immutable.

28. E. R. Dodds, *Pagan and Christian in an Age of Anxiety: Some Aspects of Religious Experience from Marcus Aurelius to Constantine* (New York: Norton, 1965), 118–19.

God is good and beautiful and happy, and exists in a most beautiful state. If then he comes down to men, he must undergo a change, a change from good to bad, from beautiful to shameful, from happiness to misfortune, and from what is best to what is most wicked. . . . It is the nature only of a mortal being to undergo change and remolding, whereas it is the nature of an immortal being to remain the same without alteration. Accordingly God could not be capable of undergoing this change. (*Contra Celsum* 4.14)

Similarly, the idea that a body that had rotted could be restored again—which Christians claimed had happened to Jesus and believed would happen to all those who died before Jesus' second coming—made no sense to pagan thinkers. "For what sort of body," Celsus asked, "after being entirely corrupted, could return to its original nature and that same condition which it had before it was dissolved?" The answer he received from Christians, that "all things are possible for God," was profoundly unsatisfying to him. Celsus, like many other pagan thinkers, believed that even God could not do the impossible. God was subject to the laws of nature and reason. It is in the nature of flesh to be mortal and corruptible. "God would neither desire nor be able to make it [flesh] everlasting contrary to reason. For he himself is the reason of everything that exists; therefore He is not able to do anything contrary to reason, or to his own character" (*Contra Celsum* 5.14).

It would also be irrational of God, charged Celsus and Porphyry, to make salvation available only to those who were lucky enough to live in the right historical era. Christians claimed only explicit faith in Christ could lead to salvation. So what about the countless generations who lived prior to the time of Christ? "Is it only now after

such a long age that God has remembered to judge the human race? Did he not care before?" (*Contra Celsum* 4.8).

Some pagans were also bothered by the rupture between Christianity and Judaism. That the overwhelming majority of Jews rejected Jesus as the Messiah did not speak well of the new faith, which claimed to be the fulfillment of all the hopes of the Jews. Would not the Jews best judge whether Jesus was the Messiah foretold in their scriptures? After investigating some of the Jewish criticisms of the time, the pagan Porphyry found the Christian arguments for Jesus as the fulfillment of messianic prophecy weak. Christian apologists relied heavily on reading the Old Testament book of Daniel as a work of prophecy written in the sixth century BCE. Porphyry was able to show rather convincingly that the book was actually written during the second century BCE and thus many of the events that it purported to have foretold had already taken place.[29]

Moreover, Wilkin notes, "It perplexed pagans that Christians claimed to be inheritors of the Jewish tradition while at the same time rejecting the Jewish community and its customs and laws."[30] Following Paul, Christians appeared to have abandoned the Jewish law (if not the Jewish scriptures) and split with their former Jewish brethren. Jesus himself had taught many things contradictory to Jewish tradition and disputed by his Jewish contemporaries. Why, asks Celsus, did God "give contradictory laws to this man from Nazareth, his son?" When Jesus taught things that were different from what Moses taught, "Who is wrong? Moses or Jesus? Or when the Father sent Jesus had he forgotten what commands he gave to Moses? Or did he condemn his own laws and change his mind, and send his messenger for quite the opposite purposes?" (*Contra Celsum* 7.18).

---

29. Porphyry's arguments about the book of Daniel are cited in *Jerome's Commentary on Daniel*, trans. Gleason Archer (Grand Rapids, MI: Baker Book House, 1958), 15, 128–34. See Wilken, *The Christians as the Romans Saw Them*, 138–42, for further information.

30. Wilken, *The Christians as the Romans Saw Them*, 114.

In Celsus and Porphyry, Christianity faced formidable foes. Both men were thorough, well-informed, highly educated, and intelligent. They identified precisely those points on which Christianity appeared to be most vulnerable. That Christianity was able to withstand these attacks and ultimately prevail is a testament to the religion's innate strengths and the ability of its leaders and seminal thinkers to respond to the challenges of paganism. Although the attacks of Celsus and Porphyry date from the second and third centuries, Christians were responding to early versions of these criticisms almost from the beginning, as can be seen in the books of the New Testament. In the mid-first century Paul was already at work devising strategies for dealing with Roman persecution—which was then, as later, more local and "popular" than official—and encouraging peaceful coexistence between Christians and pagans. Similarly, one of the major themes of Luke-Acts is that Christianity does not represent a rupture with Judaism but a continuation and fulfillment of it. The authors of the Gospels, although not as well-educated as the learned defenders of Christianity that emerged later, nonetheless make a case for Christianity that goes far beyond a simple command to believe without question. In short, not all of the pagan criticisms of Christianity were fair or true, and they were certainly not fatal.

Key Terms

pagan religions	divination	Demeter
polytheistic	augurs	Persephone
temple	auspices	syncretistic
priests	astrology	Elysium
sacrifice	oracle	Dionysus
festival	Apollonius of Tyana	Osiris
ritual	Asclepius	Celsus
cult	popular philosophy	Origen
piety	Epicureans	Porphyry
superstition	mystery religions	Julian (the Apostate)
Pliny the Younger	Isis	anthropomorphic
genius	Eleusinian mysteries	

Review Questions

1. What are the common features of traditional paganism? What kinds of gods did pagans worship, and what forms did this worship take?

2. What was the difference, according to the ancient Romans, between a superstition and a legitimate religion? Why were Judaism (sometimes) and Christianity (always) classified as superstitions?

3. What does the correspondence between Pliny the Younger and the Emperor Trajan reveal about the nature and extent of Roman persecution of Christianity in the early second century CE?

4. What were the elements of the Roman "state religion"? How and why did the refusal to participate in these practices create problems for Christians?

5. What is the difference between artificial divination and natural divination? What are the main examples of each type in the Hellenistic age?

6. Which god did people turn to more than any other for healing in the Hellenistic age? How did this god's cult work?

7. Describe the beliefs and practices of the Epicureans. In what way were they typical of Greco-Roman popular philosophies?

8. What religious innovations were developed by the Greco-Roman mystery religions? Which of these have parallels in Christianity and which do not?

9. Why did pagan critics regard Jesus as unworthy of the divine status his followers accorded him? Why were others regarded as more worthy of such a distinction?

10. What Christian theological concepts were the most nonsensical to pagans and why?

11. What objections did pagans raise about Christianity's split from Judaism?

Discussion Questions

1. Would you be willing to risk persecution for your religion in the way that early Christians did? Why do you think so many were willing to take this risk in antiquity? Are there any parallels in modern American history to the dangers faced by early Christians under Roman rule?

2. The First Amendment of the Constitution of the United States of America prohibits the establishment of a state religion and is the basis for the concept of a "wall of separation" between church and state. But many countries, like ancient Rome, have a state religion. What do you see as the advantages and disadvantages of each system?

3. Some modern people—especially the more environmentally-conscious—have praised paganism's close connection to nature and respect for the natural world. Are there any aspects of pagan religions, either individually or collectively, that you regard as perhaps superior to the prevailing religious beliefs in the modern world? What would those advantages be? By contrast, are there elements of paganism that are repugnant to modern thinking? If so, why?

4. Which of paganism's criticisms of Christianity seem to be the most valid to you? How do you think defenders of Christianity might respond to them?

Bibliography and Suggestions for Further Study

(Books and websites that are accessible for general undergraduates are marked with an asterisk; other sources listed are appropriate for advanced students.)

Dodds, E. R. *Pagan and Christian in an Age of Anxiety: Some Aspects of Religious Experience from Marcus Aurelius to Constantine.* New York: Norton, 1965.

Koester, Helmut. *Introduction to the New Testament.* Vol. 1, *History, Culture, and Religion of the Hellenistic Age.* Philadelphia: Fortress, 1982.

*Martin, Luther H. *Hellenistic Religions: An Introduction.* New York: Oxford University Press, 1987.

Momigliano, Armondo, "The Disadvantages of Monotheism for a Universal State." *Classical Philogy* 81 (1986): 285–97.

*Wilken, Robert L. *The Christians as the Romans Saw Them.* New Haven: Yale University Press, 1984.

Ancient Judaism: Christianity's Mother Religion

Christianity began as a sect of Judaism. Its first members distinguished themselves from other Jews by claiming that the Messiah had come in the person of Jesus of Nazareth. This belief—which most other Jews did not share—by itself might have led Christianity to develop into a separate religion, but in the sect's early decades still other disagreements developed between believers in Christ and their fellow Jews, and the two groups eventually split apart.

The story of Christianity's separation from Judaism has its own complications, as noted in chapter 1. The diverse groups of early Christians held radically different views on Judaism, ranging from an insistence on continuity with Judaism in every possible way (Jewish-Christian adoptionists) to outright hostility to all things Jewish (Marcionites). What became orthodox Christianity took a more moderate approach; they retained the Jewish scriptures and they accepted the belief that God had made a covenant with Israel even as they asserted that this old covenant was now surpassed by the new.

To appreciate why and how different groups of early Christians rejected some aspects of Judaism while maintaining others, one needs to understand Judaism, a religion that was already ancient by the time of Jesus.

The Covenant between YHWH and Israel

In the book of Genesis, the Jewish people trace their origins to Abraham, their ancestor with whom God first forged a covenantal relationship.

The Names of the Parties to the Covenant

The Hebrew Bible describes a covenant between a particular group of people and their god, both of which have a variety of names. Abraham's people are referred to as the Hebrews or Israelites, the latter term deriving from Abraham's grandson, Israel (also known as Jacob). Jacob/Israel had twelve sons, the progenitors of the Twelve Tribes of Israel. One of these sons was Judah, and the tribe named after him settled eventually in the southern part of the Promised Land. Judah's territory later became an independent kingdom. The terms *Jew* and *Judaism* refer to the people of Judah and their religious beliefs and practices.

The god these people worshipped was known as "Elohim" or by a name represented by four Hebrew consonants: "**YHWH**." While

continued

> **The Names** *continued*
>
> non-Jews will often spell and vocalize this name as "Yahweh" (or "Jehovah"), devout Jews believe that the name is too sacred to be pronounced, so they use a substitute expression, namely "Adonai," which means "the Lord."

A **covenant** is a kind of contract, an agreement between two parties whereby each has certain rights and responsibilities. A covenant, though, has unique qualities that separate it from other types of pacts. Covenants deal with major issues, not trivial ones. Covenants are not temporary arrangements; they involve (at least in theory) permanent states of affairs. Entering into a covenant is so momentous that the agreement is often accompanied by a formal ceremony, and often one or both parties will display or carry with them a sign of their commitment and fidelity to their covenant partner. Marriage, as traditionally conceived, is a covenantal relationship. Each party has the responsibility to love, honor, and respect the other, and has the right to expect the same treatment from the other party. The formal ceremony is the wedding, and the sign of fidelity is the wedding ring worn by each spouse. Corresponding features are present in the covenant forged between God and Abraham and his descendants. Genesis 15 describes the covenant ceremony, and the sign of the covenant is circumcision. The basic terms of the covenant—each side's rights and responsibilities—are revealed to Abraham, although they are extended and refined when the covenant is renewed through Moses (see Exod. 24).

God's Promises to Abraham

The part of the covenant that outlines the benefits that will accrue to Israel for their faith and obedience is found in Genesis 11–15, where God makes a threefold promise to Abraham and his descendants. The first promise is that they will possess a land. Originally, this was known as the land of Canaan, although it was later known as Israel, and still later a part of this land was called Judah. The Romans would call it **Palestine**.

God also promises Abraham that he will have many descendants, who will form a "great nation," as numerous as the grains of sand on the seashore or the stars in the sky. It appears that early Judaism did not believe in an eternal heavenly reward after death, so a person experienced immortality of a sort through one's descendants. For Abraham, this is a promise of immeasurable value.

Finally, God promises to bless Abraham and his people. This blessing would be threefold, encompassing (1) military victories, (2) material prosperity, and (3) health and longevity. "Success in battle against foreign enemies, good health, and an abundance of all good things were proffered to those who followed God's commandments, and their opposites to those who did not."[1]

The prospect of military victories made sense because the Israelites thought of YHWH as a warrior who fought on their side in battle. When Abraham defeats an alliance of kings who had raided his territory and kidnapped his nephew, a local priest proclaims, "Blessed be Abram [Abraham] by God Most High, maker of heaven and earth; and blessed be God Most High, who has delivered your enemies into your hand!" (Gen. 14:19). Later Israelites would attribute their triumph over the Egyptians during the Exodus to the mighty intervention of God (see Exod. 15:21), as well as their conquest of the Canaanites who stood in the way of their taking possession of the Promised Land.

Material prosperity was also a blessing from God. Abraham becomes wealthy as a consequence of his alliance with the Lord (Gen.

---

1. Shaye Cohen, *From the Maccabees to the Mishnah* (Philadelphia: Westminster, 1987), 88.

13:2). Job is another faithful servant of God who prospers exceedingly as a result (Job 1:3, 10; 42:10–12). The Israelites thought of their God as providential, a God who provided for them abundantly, as long as they kept the faith.

The blessing of a long and healthy earthly life was especially important because the ancient Jews believed that, in the afterlife, all were doomed to a shadowy existence in the land of the dead, Sheol (Ps. 6:5). Moses is said to have lived 120 years, the maximum Jews believed God allowed for a human life (Gen. 6:3), and at the end "his sight was not impaired and his [sexual] vigor had not abated" (Deut. 34:7). In the Ten Commandments, Israelites are told, "Honor your father and your mother, so that your days may be long in the land that the Lord your God is giving you" (Exod. 20:12).

Israel's Religious Obligations

The other side of the covenant required the people of Israel to meet God's demands. The first of these was the mechanism by which a person became part of the covenant people: **circumcision**. Circumcision was first and foremost a rite of initiation in which a person indicated his[2] acceptance of the terms of the covenant.[3] Thereupon the agreement went into effect. Under no circumstances could an uncircumcised male become the beneficiary of the promises made by God to the people of Israel.[4] One must remember that a covenant is essentially a contract. In today's written contracts, a person indicates acceptance of the terms by autographing the contract's signature line, but in ancient Judaism there was no written version of the covenant for a person to sign. God was offering a covenantal relationship, but people still needed to agree to it; circumcision was the means by which they did so.

Circumcision also functioned as a marker of group identity. It distinguished the Jews from other groups of people in a permanent, physical way,[5] and was sufficiently distinctive[6] that they could refer to themselves as "the circumcised" and everyone else as "the uncircumcised."

Once a person becomes a part of the covenant people, the other rules of the covenant go into effect. These religious obligations can be

---

2. Only males are circumcised in Judaism. There is no corresponding rite by which women can enter into a covenant relationship with God by themselves. Through the first century CE, a woman could only become a part of the covenant people by means of her relationship with a Jewish male (usually her father or husband). "Rabbinic texts of the second and third centuries are the earliest references for conversion rituals for women." See Cohen, *From the Maccabees to the Mishnah*, 54.

3. In most cases it is more accurate to say that in circumcision the parents of a boy indicate his acceptance of the terms of the covenant, since the ceremony is usually performed on eight-day-old infants, except in cases of adult conversion to Judaism. Jews eventually developed a secondary ritual in which the boys would be allowed their own say in whether they wanted to be part of the covenant people: the bar mitzvah.

4. Shaye Cohen (in *From the Maccabees to the Mishnah*, 52–53) suggests that circumcision did not become "the essential mark of Jewish identity or the sine qua non for membership in the Jewish polity" until the Maccabean period (second century BCE). However, passages such as Exodus 4:24–26, where Moses' wife Zipporah saves him from death at the hands of God by performing a timely circumcision, are regarded as among the most ancient traditions in the Hebrew Bible.

5. The use of a permanent, physical marker of group identity is not unique to the Jews. Youth gangs often have distinctive tattoos, with the permanence of the ink signifying the depth of the gang member's commitment and the impossibility of quitting. Some African tribes use facial scars to distinguish themselves from other tribes. Some college fraternities go to the extreme of branding their members with a hot iron. The idea of body modification to signal one's commitment and belonging to a particular group is not unusual.

6. E. P. Sanders acknowledges that "Jews were not the only circumcised males in the Mediterranean world," but says that despite this "both insiders and outsiders regarded circumcision as distinctively Jewish." See E. P. Sanders, *Judaism: Practice and Belief, 63 BCE– 66 CE* (London: SCM; Philadelphia: Trinity, 1992), 213.

grouped under three main headings: observance of religious and ethical commandments in the Law of Moses, maintenance of ritual purity, and performance of sacrifice.

Observing the Torah

The foundation of the Jewish Law, or Torah, is the Ten Commandments, believed to have been given by God to Moses on Mount Sinai. The first and most important of these commandments is "I am the LORD your God, who brought you out of the land of Egypt, out of the house of slavery; you shall have no other gods before me" (Exod. 20:2–3). The earliest traditions recorded in the Hebrew Bible suggest the Israelites did not always practice pure monotheism. They believed other gods existed, but they thought that YHWH was the best, most powerful god. This had been demonstrated by YHWH's defeat of the Egyptian gods and their representatives during the ten plagues inflicted on the Egyptian enslavers of Israel, and in the parting of the Red Sea that lead to the destruction of the Egyptian army. Moreover, the Israelites believed YHWH was *their* god, a god that had shown his preference for them by his miraculous actions on their behalf. YHWH was Israel's national deity, and in return for his benefactions he expected Israel's exclusive and unwavering loyalty. YHWH describes himself as a "jealous" god (Exod. 20:5; 34:14).

Traces of the view that other gods existed but were inferior to YHWH can still be found in the Hebrew Bible (for example, Exod. 15:11), although Judaism eventually evolved to the point that followers believed YHWH was the only god who existed and all other gods were false. In the Hebrew Bible, the prophets were the leading defenders of monotheism in a nation that was constantly tempted to worship other gods. By the time of Jesus, however, a strict monotheism had long since taken hold of the Jewish religious imagination. Idolatry had become the worst sin a Jew could commit.

The Torah, also known as the Pentateuch or the Law, is the heart of the Hebrew Scriptures. In traditional Judaism, copies of the Torah for use in synagogues are still meticulously hand-copied.

Several of the Ten Commandments specify additional obligations toward God. The commandments require that Jews not only worship no other gods but also that they refrain from making any kind of image or representation of YHWH. This second commandment marks Judaism as an **aniconic** (opposed to "icons," or images) religion, and expresses the belief that God is too great and unfathomable to be adequately represented in a mere statue. The commandment that they never make wrongful use of the name of the Lord was originally understood as a prohibition against using the name of YHWH in a magical curse or incantation.

The commandment to keep the Sabbath holy is one of the most distinctive of Jewish practices. The **Sabbath** was designated as a day of rest, on which no work was permitted. Jews celebrated the Sabbath on what they regarded as the seventh day of the week, which began on sundown Friday and ended on sundown Saturday. This religious observance not only allowed humans (including slaves) and animals a much-needed respite from a hard week of toil but also carved out space for family, worship, and celebration. Exactly what counted as work was a source of potential disagreement. According to the Gospels, Jesus' comparatively lenient interpretation of the Sabbath restriction led to major opposition from some of his contemporary Jews.

The remaining commandments concerned obligations toward others. Again, Judaism was quite different from other ancient religions in connecting religion with ethical behavior, maintaining that God cares not only about rituals and worship but about how a person treats his fellow human beings. Some religion scholars describe Judaism as **ethical monotheism**, because of the centrality of the ideas that there is only one God and that this God cares about human behavior. The Israelites believed in a God who cares about human beings and feels compassion for them, and felt that they, in turn, were called by God to demonstrate care and compassion to others.

Concretely, this meant that faithful observers of the covenant were prohibited from murder, stealing, bearing false witness (akin to perjury), committing adultery, or coveting another person's property, and that they were required to honor their mothers and fathers. "Honor" involved respect and obedience, but most crucially it meant providing for parents financially in their old age. **Coveting** involved more than simple mental desire—for example, fantasizing about another man's wife. Coveting meant actually taking steps to acquire the coveted object. A

The Evolving Meaning of the Ten Commandments

The ancient Israelites did not always understand or interpret the commandments in the same way modern believers are taught to do. For example, the common definition of adultery in our culture is "sexual relations between a married person and someone other than his or her spouse." However, ancient Judaism defined adultery as "sexual relations between a married woman and someone other than her husband."[7] The obvious difference is that in ancient Judaism married men were free to explore extramarital sexual encounters without the taint of adultery, as long as their partners were not themselves married women. This reflects the understanding of women as property, a view evident in many other ancient Jewish practices, such as polygamy and the right of fathers to sell their daughters into slavery (Exod. 21:7). As women came to be seen as full human beings with equal rights, the definition of adultery evolved so that married men were required to be as faithful as their wives. There are, however, still laws on the books in some places that reflect the earlier understanding of adultery. A Minnesota state law says, "When a married woman has sexual intercourse with a man other than her husband, whether married or not, both are guilty of adultery and may be sentenced to imprisonment for not more than one year or to payment of a fine of not more than $3,000, or both" (Minnesota Statute 609.36). There is no similar provision for married men.

---

7. It is true that Lev. 20:10 suggests that married men who sleep with unmarried women have committed adultery, but the majority of the passages in the Hebrew Bible are like Deut. 22:22, which speaks of adultery only when "a man is found lying with another man's wife."

man who propositioned another man's wife was guilty of coveting even if she refused him. A person who hired a third party to murder his wife, or to steal from his neighbor, was guilty of coveting even if the crime never came to pass.

Although the Ten Commandments are the foundation of the Law of Moses, they are by no means the only orders included in the Torah. The Pentateuch speaks of additional commandments, ordinances, and statutes given by God through Moses. In traditional Jewish reckoning, they total 613 commandments. That number may seem excessive, but Torah was the only set of laws governing Israelite society, so it was not beyond the capacity of people to be familiar with most if not all of the commandments. Most modern people know far more than 613 laws, if one includes traffic laws, tax laws, criminal laws, civil laws, property laws, and other categories of law.

Ritual Purity

The Torah requirements regarding **ritual purity** deserve special attention. These requirements rest upon a distinction between **clean and unclean** that has largely disappeared from modern culture. The Israelites believed God had created the universe with a distinct sense of order, according to which there was a place for everything and everything should be in its place. A person who lived in harmony with this order was "clean" or "pure" in the eyes of God. When things violated this sense of order and humans were part of that violation, they became "unclean" or "polluted," and this state was displeasing to God. It was inevitable that persons became unclean at times; women, for example, became unclean every month when they menstruated. This did not mean that they had done

something wrong. The ritual impurity of persons did not result from sin,[8] but it did prevent the person from accessing holy places or contacting others who were not unclean. There is another kind of impurity—moral impurity—that resulted from the commission of sins, but this kind of impurity differed in important respects from ritual impurity. For example, it was not *contagious* (see below).

The best-known application of the principles of clean and unclean involves the special set of Jewish dietary restrictions known as **keeping kosher**. The word *kosher* means "fit" for human consumption. Certain foods and animals are designated as unclean and cannot be consumed at all. Included on the list of unclean animals are pigs, shellfish, birds of prey, horses, camels, and snakes. Some parts of the cow are clean, but others are not. Moreover, even clean foods must be butchered, prepared, and served in particular ways. For example, an observant Jew can eat meats and cheeses, but these two things (meat and dairy) can never be served on the same plate. Kosher meats are butchered and processed in such a way as to drain as much of the blood as possible from the flesh.

No one explanation can account for all of the kosher restrictions. One view is that certain animals were considered unclean because they somehow violated a sense of order; they were out of place. For example, most sea animals have scales and swim through the water by means of their fins. These common characteristics establish a sense of "normal" for sea creatures. Shellfish, by contrast, violate this sense of normal because they have hard shells and crawl on of the floor of the sea with their legs. Crawling on legs is normal for land animals, but not for sea creatures. Therefore, the crab and the lobster violate a set of boundaries established by God between

---

8. See Hyam Maccoby, *Ritual and Morality: The Ritual Purity System and Its Place in Judaism* (Cambridge: Cambridge University Press, 1999).

land and sea animals and are thus considered unclean. Pigs are said to be unclean because they do not chew their own cud in the same way that do cows, sheep, and goats.[9]

This sense of a violation of boundaries also accounts for the prohibition of garments made of mixed textiles. A piece of clothing made of wool or linen is permissible, but not one of wool and linen woven together (Deut. 22:11). Similarly, the place for blood is in the body, not outside of it. A bleeding person was considered unclean, and this included women who were menstruating.

Uncleanness was seen as communicable as well, not physically but spiritually. A man who had contact with a woman during her period would not, clearly, begin menstruating, but he became unclean as a result of such contact. If he touched a menstruating woman or she touched him, he became unclean for a day. If a man had sex with a menstruating woman, then he became unclean for a week. For this reason the Torah dictated that menstruating women needed to "separate" themselves for the duration of their monthly period, a length of seven days. During this time, a woman could not pass an item to her husband or sleep in the same bed with him. After the seven-day "separation," the woman was obliged to undergo a ritual bath with its own special requirements. All of these rules are still followed today by Orthodox Jews.

Another physical state that caused uncleanness was leprosy. People with leprosy were shunned and had to live outside the confines of the community. They were required to tear their clothes like those in mourning and were not allowed to cut their hair, apparently so they could be more easily identified and avoided. They even needed to cry out "Unclean! Unclean!" to warn others to keep their distance (Lev. 13:45). This naturally raises the question of whether this system was cruel or unjust in some of its applications, a sentiment with which Jesus seems to have agreed (see chapter 8).

Temple Sacrifice

Animal sacrifice appears to have been an important part of Israelite religion from the start, as it was for most ancient religions. Sacrifice served a number of religious purposes. One was *thanksgiving*. It was believed God had provided everything the Israelites had—including their crops, their livestock, and their children—and that it was appropriate to acknowledge the debt of gratitude they owed God by offering a portion of these things back to God in return. Children could be "redeemed" (or bought back from God) for a price, a substitute offering. A second purpose of sacrifice was *atonement*. If a person had offended God through some insult or misdeed, he or she could make up for the wrong and repair the damage done to their

Tamarah / Wikimedia Commons / Altar from Tel Be'er-Sheva. JPG / CC BY SA 3.0

Archeologists have uncovered numerous ancient Israelite altars, such as this one from Beer-Sheba. Eventually the offering of sacrifices would be limited to the Jerusalem Temple, but it is clear that this restriction was a comparatively late development in the history of Israel.

---

9. On this understanding of the distinction between clean and unclean animals, see Frederick J. Murphy, *The Religious World of Jesus: An Introduction to Second Temple Palestinian Judaism* (Nashville: Abingdon, 1991), 84.

relationship with God by doing something right. A sacrifice was just the kind of good deed that was thought to engender forgiveness from God. Finally, some sacrifices were understood as *gifts*, in that they were freely offered to God for no particular reason, but were designed simply to maintain good relations.[10]

After the Israelites settled in the Promised Land, the Twelve Tribes erected a number of altars and shrines. When Israel became a united monarchy, King David established his capital in Jerusalem. David's son Solomon later erected a magnificent Temple there. The Jerusalem priestly establishment eventually decreed that sacrifices should be offered only in the Jerusalem Temple, and all other altars and shrines were to be torn down. Although the process was long and hardfought, eventually Jews came to accept that the only legitimate site for sacrifice was the Temple in Jerusalem. As a result, the people were expected to make **pilgrimages** (journeys made for religious purposes) to the Holy City in order to arrange for sacrifices to be offered during the major festivals.

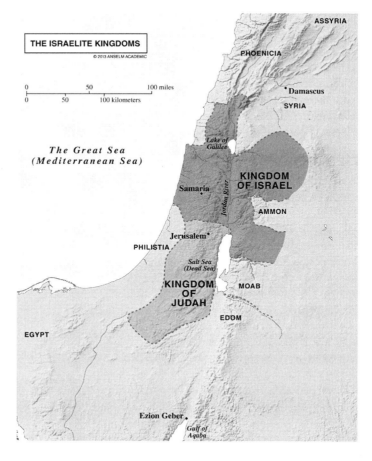

THE ISRAELITE KINGDOMS
© 2013 ANSELM ACADEMIC

Jerusalem was in the land controlled by the tribe of Judah, David's tribe, in the southern part of the Promised Land. The ancestral shrines of the northern tribes, in Bethel, Shiloh, and Shechem, were eclipsed by the new Jerusalem Temple. Jerusalem would now experience a huge financial windfall from all of the pilgrims who would travel there during major religious holidays, needing food, lodging, and animals for sacrifice. The northern tribes and their shrines would experience a corresponding loss. Eventually this resentment helped lead to a rebellion, and ten of the northern tribes split off from Judah to form an independent kingdom known as Israel, or Ephraim (the name of the dominant northern tribe). The northern tribes established their own capital, complete with a temple, in the city of Samaria.

The northern kingdom was short-lived, however. The Assyrian Empire conquered Ephraim in

10. On the purposes of sacrifice, see ibid., 82–87.

721 BCE and utterly destroyed it in the process. Many Israelites were deported and the land was colonized by Assyrian settlers. The intermingling of Israelite and Assyrian blood, cult, and religion eventually led to the creation of a new "mixed-race" group of people that came to be known as the **Samaritans**. Residents of the southern kingdom of Judah ("Jews") survived the Assyrian onslaught—with help from God, according to the Bible. The Jews took these events as evidence of divine approval of their religious practices and their Temple, and divine disapproval of the religious practices and shrines of the Northern Kingdom.

In Judaism, several rules had to be followed if an offering was to have any chance of swaying God. First, sacrifices had to be offered in the *right place*, the Jerusalem Temple. Second, sacrifices had to be made by the *right person*, a **priest**. The priesthood was hereditary. The Pentateuch indicates the tribe of Levi was set aside for religious service, but only one branch of that tribe—the descendants of Moses' brother Aaron—could actually serve as priests. The other **Levites** provided more menial kinds of religious service, such as maintenance of the Temple, gatekeeping, and singing at services.

Third, sacrifices needed to be made at the *right time*. The right time for offering a sacrifice could be any of a number of occasions, the most important being the three major religious holidays, referred to as "pilgrimage" festivals because each required an Israelite to travel to Jerusalem. These three festivals were **Passover** (early spring, conjoined with the preceding Feast of Unleavened Bread), **Weeks** (late spring), and **Tabernacles** (early fall). Each corresponded with the harvest season for one of Israel's staple crops. The Temple became a beehive of activity during Passover, Weeks, and Tabernacles. E. P. Sanders estimates that Passover drew between

three and five hundred thousand attendees every year.[11]

In addition to these holidays, there was **Yom Kippur**, the Day of Atonement, in which the high priest would enter the Holy of Holies in the innermost part of the Temple to make a sacrifice on behalf of all the people, to atone for the sins of the nation. Other sacrifices were conducted year-round, especially if people had something special to atone for or to feel grateful about, such as the birth of a child.

Fourth and finally, a person had to make the *right offering*. Grain and incense were sometimes offered to God, but most sacrifices involved animals. When grain was offered, there was a preference for the "first fruits" of the crop (and similarly, for "firstborn" animals) because the first symbolizes the whole. In the case of animals, the offering additionally had to be of a (ritually) clean animal and it had to be "unblemished." The animal could not have any obvious defect or flaw. This last requirement goes hand in hand with the understanding that the more valuable an animal was, the more efficacious the sacrifice would be. An imperfect animal, one with a leg missing or with hoof-and-mouth disease, was not a particularly valuable animal and would not make a very good gift for YHWH. Likewise, a pigeon or a turtledove would not be as effective an offering as a goat or a lamb because of the relative value of these animals. Allowances were made, though, for different social classes. People who were poor were not expected to sacrifice animals whose purchase was beyond their means or whose loss would cause financial hardship. Those who could afford more generous sacrifices were expected to offer them.

This system of sacrifice was honed and perfected in the centuries after the building of the

---

11. Sanders, *Judaism: Practice and Belief, 63 BCE– 66 CE*, 126–28.

The Assyrians commemorated their successful siege of the Judean city of Lachish in 701 BCE with this highly detailed bas-relief. The siege of Jerusalem by the Babylonians in 586 BCE would have looked much like this.

Temple in Jerusalem by Solomon in the tenth century BCE. This sacrificial regime came to an abrupt end, however, when the forces of the Babylonian Empire, which had conquered the small kingdom of Judah in 597 BCE, decided to punish a Jewish rebellion by exiling many of the Jews back to Babylon and destroying the Jerusalem Temple in 586 BCE. These tragic, catastrophic events led to a great deal of sadness and soul-searching, much of which is documented in the pages of the Hebrew Bible. A frequent refrain among the exiles was the desire to return to Judah and rebuild the Temple.

Second Temple Judaism

The exile of the Jews ended some seventy years after it began, when the Persians defeated the Babylonians and took over their empire. Jews were so grateful to the Persian king Cyrus that they actually referred to him as the Lord's anointed one (or "messiah"; Isa. 45:1). Persian rule was not nearly as harsh and restrictive as Babylonian, and Jews were given the option of returning to the Promised Land. Those who did return set about the task of rebuilding the Temple and restoring a sense of normalcy to Judaism. The rebuilt Temple, dedicated in 516 BCE, was not as magnificent as the structure built by Solomon, but would be restored to world-class status by the major renovation started by Herod the Great (reigned 39–4 BCE). This Second Temple would stand until it was destroyed by the Romans in 70 CE. The Second Temple period of Judaism saw a continued emphasis on the covenant, the Torah, circumcision, ritual purity, and animal sacrifice, but there were some innovations as well.

The Synagogue

When Cyrus allowed the exiled Jews to return to Palestine, some chose to remain in Babylon. The phenomenon of Jews living outside the Promised Land is termed the **Diaspora** (meaning "dispersion," referring to Jews who were "dispersed" to foreign lands). The faith and practice of Palestinian Jews and Diaspora Jews developed in somewhat different ways. For example, Diaspora Judaism centered more on the Torah and the **synagogue**[12] than on the Temple and its sacrifices. Synagogues were places[13] where Jews gathered to read their scriptures and discuss their interpretation and application

---

12. See Shaye Cohen, *From the Maccabees to the Mishnah*, 111–15.

13. Whether the early synagogues were all or even mostly separate buildings is doubtful, but eventually separate structures did become the norm. The earliest stand-alone synagogue for which there is clear evidence (Modiin) dates from the second century BCE.

to daily life. The increasing importance placed on the ethical and ritual requirements involved in adhering to the Law of Moses gradually led to the establishment of a synagogue in every locale with a significant Jewish population. Synagogues came to function as multifaceted community centers that served vital social and economic functions as well as religious ones. Jesus is said to have preached often in the synagogues of Galilee. Early Christian missionaries regularly began their quest for converts in the synagogue of every new town they visited, and many Jewish converts to Christianity maintained their ties to the synagogues in which they had grown up and been nurtured. Eventually, Jews would expel these Christians from the synagogue as Christianity began to separate from Judaism and relations between the two religions began to sour.

Concepts of the Messiah

The Jews believed they had a covenant relationship with God whereby if they followed the Torah, maintained ritual purity, and performed their sacrifices, God would fulfill his promises to them and they would prosper in the land he had given them. For most of their history, however, it appears these promises did not come true for the Jews. Only during David's rule did the Israelites enjoy something close to the military success, economic prosperity, and religious unity envisioned by the covenant. After David, the kingdom was eventually split in two. The Northern Kingdom (Israel) was destroyed by the Assyrians (721 BCE), and the Southern Kingdom (Judah) was taken over by the Babylonians (from 597 to 539 BCE), the Persians (539–333 BCE), the Greeks (333–164 BCE), and the Romans, who took partial control of Judah in 63 BCE and full control in 6 CE. The Jews suffered terribly under the rule of these foreign powers.

The prophets believed that these disasters were punishments from God; that the Jews must have sinned against the Lord and broken the covenant. They had worshipped false gods, violated God's commands to treat widows, orphans, and resident aliens with justice, and practiced sexual immorality. All of these transgressions caused God to withdraw his protection and expose them to their enemies. The Jews almost always blamed themselves, not God, for breakdowns in the proper functioning of the covenant. The way to regain God's favor and release themselves from bondage, therefore, was to repent of their sins and adhere more precisely to the terms of the covenant.

During these difficult times some Jewish prophets began to predict God would send someone to rescue the Jews from oppression, just as God had sent Moses to deliver them from slavery and the judges to rescue them from the Moabites and Philistines. Sometimes Jewish hopes coalesced around a figure they called the **messiah**, meaning "anointed one" (Greek, *christos*). The great leaders of Israel's past succeeded, Jews believed, because they had been chosen by God, and God's election of them was symbolized by the process of anointing with oil. By using the term *messiah*, the Jews simply expressed their belief that God would raise up a chosen leader from among the people to save them.

Exactly how this was going to happen, though, was a matter of some disagreement. Many Jews hoped for a messiah who would deliver them in the political realm. Such deliverance would, it seemed, necessarily involve a military conflict. Proponents of the **military/political messiah**, reflecting on 2 Samuel 7, believed that God would raise up a descendant of King David and reestablish him on the throne of Israel. They believed this "son of David" would raise an army, lead it to victory, restore the independence of the Jewish kingdom, and become its ideal ruler. The first-century Jewish historian Josephus mentions several leaders near the time of Jesus who claimed to be this messiah, declared their kingship, and attracted significant numbers of followers. Those who rejected these claims, Josephus included, referred to such leaders as "bandits."

The most famous of these messianic claimants was a man named **Simon bar Kokhba**, the leader of a Jewish rebellion against Rome in 132–135 CE. Despite some initial successes this rebellion was crushed and bar Kokhba was killed in battle. Because of this failure he is known to history not as the messiah but as a "**messianic pretender.**" Whether Jesus ever made similar political claims is hotly disputed. The Gospels suggest Jesus never raised an army or advocated violence, but marched peacefully to his death. However, the Romans executed Jesus for treason—for claiming to be a king and implicitly advocating the overthrow of the Roman regime. This suggests they viewed him as a political threat, much the same as they did the bandits who styled themselves "kings."

Other Jews thought Israel's suffering was rooted less in political setbacks and more in social injustices or spiritual maladies; as a result they thought more in terms of a **prophetic messiah**. The prophets of Israel had a tradition of feeding the hungry, healing the sick, calling sinners to repentance, defending the poor and downtrodden, championing monotheism, and seeking a renewal of Israel's commitment to following God's law. Some Jews hoped the messiah would be like one of the great prophets of old—Moses and Elijah in particular were often identified as the greatest of God's representatives—and would fulfill some or all of the traditional prophetic functions.

Still other Jews anticipated an **apocalyptic messiah**. Various Jewish apocalyptic groups (see below) believed God would soon bring an end to this evil world, destroying the wicked and establishing a new paradise for the righteous. Some thought the messiah would be God's appointed agent to bring this about. The book of Daniel in particular supports the idea that God would send a heavenly emissary called the **Son of Man** to purge the world of evildoers and rescue the righteous in a battle of cosmic proportions.

As I watched in the night visions
I saw one like a son of man coming with
    the clouds of heaven.
And he came to the Ancient One and was
    presented before him.
To him was given dominion and glory and
    kingship,
that all peoples, nations, and languages
    should serve him.
His dominion is an everlasting dominion
    that shall not pass away,
and his kingship is one that shall never be
    destroyed. (Dan. 7:13–14)

Finally, some Jews rejected the idea of a messiah altogether, apparently because the concept is absent from the earliest and most authoritative Jewish texts. Thus the concept of the messiah was hugely important to some Jews and not at all important to others. Only twice was there a serious, credible claim that the messiah had come, and each time the messianic claimant was killed by the Romans. For one man—Simon bar Kokhba—that was the end of his story. For the other—Jesus of Nazareth—it was only the beginning.

Apocalypticism

Although the traditional Jewish framework allowed for the possibility of human suffering as a consequence of divine wrath, it retained a fundamentally optimistic religious outlook. A person who observed the terms of the covenant could expect good things to happen. During the Second Temple period, Jewish religious thought turned more pessimistic. Centuries of war, famine, disease, poverty, and political oppression had taken their toll, and many Jews began to believe darker forces were at work in the universe.

The idea that the universe is the site of **spiritual warfare** between cosmic forces of good (God and his angels) and cosmic forces of evil (Satan and his demons) began to take root in some corners of Judaism. **Satan** is mentioned in the Hebrew Bible as a heavenly being whose primary task is to catch human beings in the act of sin and call their misdeeds to God's attention (see Job 1–2). The Hebrew *ha-Satan* literally means "the Accuser" and reflects the early Jewish view that this angel was not pure evil but simply a prosecutor for the heavenly court of judgment. From this origin, Satan evolved to an angel who actively tried to lure people into sin so he could accuse them before God. Eventually, and possibly influenced by Zoroastrian dualism, some Jews began to believe that this Satan fell from heaven after leading a failed rebellion against God. He and his allies (fallen angels, that is, demons) were cast out of heaven. Together they created and ruled over the realm of hell. From that base they continued their war against God and his angels, in part by seeking human allies whom they lured to sin and converted to the cause of evil. Satan, now also termed "the Devil," had been transformed from accusing angel into the supreme manifestation of evil.[14]

Among those Jews whose thought took this direction, it was also commonly believed that in the battle between the forces of good and the forces of evil, Satan and his demons currently had the upper hand. If good human outcomes could be attributed to God and human suffering to Satan, every indication was that Satan was winning. However, faithful Jews were convinced that this was a temporary situation. Ultimately, God was more powerful than Satan, and there was no question eventually he would defeat the forces of evil in a final, decisive battle that would bring an end to this "evil age" and restore justice and

righteousness to the universe. The question was when this would happen and how.

The literary genre of the **apocalypse** was developed to answer this question. In an apocalypse, a human seer is given a vision not accessible to humans through the ordinary channels of reason or even revelation. This vision lays out the sweep of human history and explains the cosmic forces at work in the universe. The vision itself is usually obscure and impenetrable, but an angelic guide provides the seer with the proper interpretation of the symbolic meaning of the various elements of his vision.[15] A common theme of apocalyptic literature, such as the book of Daniel, is that human history is rapidly approaching its conclusion and the end of the world is near at hand. How long would the all-powerful God permit Satan and his demons to inflict suffering on his people? Not long, answered the authors of Jewish apocalyptic literature. The final battle between good and evil was imminent, and the time for humans to declare their allegiance to one side or the other was now. The message to God's allies was to hang on despite all the persecution and hardships they were experiencing, because help was on its way and all of their sorrows would be turned to joy.

Heaven, Hell, and the Resurrection of the Body

Another development within the Second Temple period involved a departure from the traditional view that everyone who died went to the same destination, the land of the dead known as Sheol.[16] More progressive Jewish groups like

---

14. See Shaye Cohen, *From the Maccabees to the Mishnah*, 90–91, for further information.

15. On the apocalyptic genre and worldview, see Murphy, *The Religious World of Jesus*, 163–65.

16. This understanding of the afterlife is reflected in a variety of texts from the Hebrew Bible. The dead congregate in the underworld of Sheol, but they are "shades" (or shadows) without energy (Job 3:17), bereft of pleasure (Sir. 14:16), and without knowledge or memory (Eccles. 9:5, 10; Ps. 31:17; 88:12), where sleep is the norm (Jer. 51:39). It is a place of pure silence (Ps. 31:18; 94:17; Eccles. 9:10), gloom, and darkness (Job 10:21–22). It has gates (Isa. 38:10) or "bars" (Jon. 2:6) that keep its inhabitants imprisoned (Ps. 88:8).

the Pharisees began to argue that after death a person entered a state of sleep from which they would be awakened at the end of time to face the final judgment. The **resurrection of the body** that would take place was something that might require a lengthy wait, but it held out the possibility of something that ancient Judaism did not envision: eternal life with God in heaven. The other possibility was eternal damnation, but faithful Jews did not need to fear such an outcome.

The reasons for the shift in Judaism from a single-destination view of the afterlife to the notion of eternal reward and punishment are not clear, but many scholars trace this change to the Maccabean Revolt.[17] Traditionally, it had been thought that YHWH dispensed rewards and punishments in this life, and that those who were righteous would be compensated with prosperity and a long, healthy life. During the Maccabean Revolt, there were many stories of Jews who stood up to Greek persecution and refused to worship the Greek gods or abandon their devotion to YHWH despite the threat of death. However, the immediate consequence of such behavior was usually a quick death at the hand of Greek executioners. The Jews who suffered this fate came to be regarded as **martyrs**, and the idea that such faith and courage would be followed by the drab, shadowy existence of Sheol was hard to accept. Surely the martyrs would be welcomed by God into heaven. But if this was true of the martyrs, why would it not be true of other faithful Jews, some of whom would never get the opportunity to demonstrate their devotion to YHWH by making the ultimate sacrifice? Thus the gates of heaven were swung open, and faithful, obedient servants of God of all stripes were thought to be welcome.

Formation of Jewish Sects

The sects that developed within Judaism during the Second Temple period are perhaps best compared to the denominations within modern Christianity. Each sect thought of itself as the truest expression of Judaism, but in most cases they would not have denied that members of the other sects were Jews or that they continued to be their coreligionists. They tended not to differ with each other over the fundamentals of the religion—monotheism, the covenant, the central importance of the Temple and the Torah—but they disagreed on some secondary issues. Josephus referred to these sects as "philosophies" within Judaism, of which he identified four: Pharisees, Sadducees, Essenes, and members of the "Fourth Philosophy."

Pharisees

The word *Pharisees*, meaning "separated ones," refers to the desire of this group to lead lives of elevated purity and holiness in all aspects of life.[18] This meant they would have to separate themselves from those who did not observe such rigorous standards. Their religious devotion was expressed in the form of personal **piety**, according to which they practiced religious good deeds such as frequent prayer, fasting twice a week, and giving a tenth of their income (tithing) for widows and the poor. While the Pharisees did not degrade the importance of the Temple and its sacrifices, their emphasis was on observing the requirements of the Torah in one's daily life and even going above and beyond those requirements.

The dissemination of knowledge about the Torah and its application took place in the synagogue, an institution controlled largely by the Pharisees. Exceptionally learned Pharisees became

---

17. Shaye Cohen, for example, in *From the Maccabees to the Mishnah*, 92.

18. Most of what is known about the Pharisees is based on texts written after the first century CE by the Pharisees' successors in rabbinic Judaism. While it is possible the rabbis represented their Pharisaic ancestors in terms that are largely fair and accurate, there is no guarantee of this and historical claims about the Pharisees must be made with caution.

Scribes and Pharisees

Scribes were people who were literate, who could read and write, and made their living by means of their literacy. The ability to read and write was rare enough that scribes could command a fee for their services, which included public recitations, the writing of contracts, the copying of texts, and acting as experts or authorities on all manner of issues, especially religious ones. Each sect of Judaism had its scribes, but the New Testament suggests scribes were especially associated with the Pharisees, which makes sense given the emphasis that sect placed on scholarship. Indeed, in the Gospels, the "scribes and Pharisees" are sometimes lumped together as if they are one group (see Mark 2:16; 7:1, 5).

known as **rabbis** (meaning "teacher" or "master"), and rabbis became trusted leaders of local religious communities who oversaw the workings of the synagogues and whose advice about the Torah and religious life was sought out and followed.

The Pharisees were the most progressive sect of Judaism in the sense that they embraced the more recent innovations in the religion. They accepted the messiah, resurrection of the body, and heaven and hell. They included the Law, the Prophets, and the Writings within the Jewish canon, and even supplemented these texts further with what was known at the time of Jesus as the **Oral Torah** or the "Tradition of the Elders." For the Pharisees, the Oral Torah was necessitated because the Law of Moses was already several centuries old and did not address all the situations and circumstances of contemporary life. In matters where the Torah was not completely clear or comprehensive, Pharisees began to cite the teachings of the great rabbis. When a question arose, the first thing one should do is to look for

a solution in the Law of Moses. If none presented itself, then the next best thing was to consult the opinions of great rabbis such as Hillel or Shammai, men whose knowledge, wisdom, and holiness had become legendary among the Pharisees.

In the centuries after Jesus, Jews would write down these teachings. The first collection of such teachings and interpretations is known as the **Mishnah**. Eventually more teachings and commentary were added to the Mishnah; the resulting compilation became known as the **Talmud**. The Talmud is still revered and studied by most Jews of today. It is one of the great legacies of Pharisaic Judaism.

Sadducees

The **Sadducees** were the party of the upper classes: the priests (especially those of higher rank, known as "chief priests") and the landed aristocracy. They represented the religious and political establishment in the part of Roman Palestine known as Judea. Sadducees occupied most of the positions of leadership after the Roman takeover of Judea. The Romans often sought to secure control of a conquered territory by finding local collaborators among the former ruling elite, and the Sadducees were apparently willing to accommodate them in this regard and help them govern the Jewish people. In particular, the Romans entrusted the lesser functions of government to local elites, such as the police, lower judicial courts, and other more mundane layers of bureaucracy. When Jesus was arrested in the Garden of Gethsemane, it was a Jewish police force that detained him. When he was initially put on trial, it was a Jewish council dominated by Sadducees that heard the case and convicted him of blasphemy.

The Sadducees could justify this cooperation on pragmatic grounds: a close relationship with the Romans enabled the Jews to negotiate terms that allowed the religion to continue to function. Not only were the Jews exempt from military

PALESTINE AT THE TIME OF JESUS
© 2013 ANSELM ACADEMIC

The Great Sea
(Mediterranean Sea)

PHOENICIA

Sidon

Damascus

SYRIA

Mt. Hermon

Tyre

Caesarea Philippi

GAULANITIS

GALILEE

BATANEA   TRACHONITIS

Capernaum   Bethsaida

Cana   Magdala   Lake of Galilee

Mt. Carmel

Sepphoris   Tiberias

AURANITIS

Nazareth   Mt. Tabor

CARMEL

Caesarea Maritima

SAMARIA

DECAPOLIS

Mt. Gerizim   Sychar

Gerasa

Joppa

Arimathea?

PEREA

Lydda

JUDEA   Jericho

Philadelphia

Emmaus?

Jerusalem   Mt. Olives

Bethany   Qumran

Medeba

Hebron

Salt Sea (Dead Sea)

En Gedi

Greatest extent of Herod's Kingdom

Beersheba

IDUMEA

0   20   40 miles
0   20   40 kilometers

The Sadducees were religious conservatives. Unlike the Pharisees, who accepted the Law, the Prophets, and the Writings as scripture and had even begun to supplement these with the Oral Torah, the Sadducees accepted only the Law as scripture.[20] Consequently, the Sadducees did not accept any religious ideas not expressed in the five books of the Pentateuch, such as the resurrection of the body, heaven and hell, and the messiah. It seems unlikely the concept of a messiah would have appealed to the Sadducees in any event. Given their wealth and privilege, the Sadducees probably did not see themselves as in need of a messiah to rescue them.

The source of the Sadducees' wealth, power, and political connections was the Temple. All Jews were required to pay a Temple tax of one-half shekel yearly to support the institution and its operations. In addition, Jews were supposed to tithe one-tenth of their produce to the priests and the Levites. The apocryphal book of Tobit describes the procedure as fulfilled by one observant Jew:

service, the Romans also did not require the Jews to worship the gods and goddesses of the Roman state or to acknowledge the divinity of the emperor. Instead, Jews were only required to make sacrifices for the well-being of "Caesar and the Roman nation."[19] However, the Sadducees' close ties with the Romans earned them the enmity of many of their fellow Jews. Many Jews sought a more confrontational stance toward the Romans.

I would often go by myself to Jerusalem on religious holidays, as the Law commanded for every Israelite for all time. I would hurry off to Jerusalem and take with me the early produce of my crops, a tenth of my flocks, and the first portion

19. On special privileges the Romans granted to the Jews, see Norman Perrin, Dennis Duling, and Robert L. Ferm, *The New Testament: An Introduction*, 2nd ed. under the general editorship of Robert Ferm (New York: Harcourt Brace Jovanovich, 1982), 19.

20. This claim is not uncontroversial, as the evidence regarding the actual views of the Sadducees is scant. Early church writers such as Origen asserted that the Sadducees accepted only the five books of the Torah, but this may have been based on a misreading of Josephus. Still, many scholars maintain that the New Testament's claim that the Sadducees rejected the concept of the resurrection of the dead (Mark 12:18; Acts 23:8) means that they could not have accepted the Prophets, which speak several times of resurrection (Isa. 25:7; 26:19; Ezek. 37:1–14; Dan. 12:2).

of the wool cut from my sheep. I would present these things at the altar to the priests, the descendants of Aaron. I would give the first tenth of my grain, wine, olive oil, pomegranates, figs, and other fruit to the Levites who served in Jerusalem. (Tob. 1:6–7, CEB)

The priests also benefitted from the sacrifices. One of the most common kinds of sacrifices required that an animal be killed and its blood drained into sacred vessels, after which it was splashed on the altar in the Temple. This left the entire carcass of the animal. Following the sacrifice, therefore, part of the meat was given to the family sponsoring the sacrifice, and part was given to the priests for their consumption. In a society with significant food scarcity, easy access to a rich and varied diet is wealth, and the priests had this in abundance.

Given that the priests were largely responsible for the sacred texts that mandated sacrifices, from which they benefitted personally, modern readers may wonder whether the entire system was created by the priests for their own benefit. Whether any ancient Jews shared that view is uncertain, but some Christian texts suggest that there were Jews who had their doubts about the Temple system. The Gospels claim that when Jesus drove out the money-changers and merchants from the Temple precincts, accusing the religious establishment of corruption, his actions were well-received by the people (Mark 11:15–19).

Essenes

Josephus includes the **Essenes** among the three main "philosophies" to which first-century Jews adhered. Josephus describes them as a monastic group whose religious fervor bordered on the fanatical. The Essenes, Josephus reports, practiced a strict form of **asceticism**, whereby they avoided the pleasures of the body and sought to impose discipline on their passions and appetites. Many Essenes practiced celibacy, a truly exceptional phenomenon in a culture that believed getting married and having children was a religious obligation. The Essenes gave all their wealth and property to their monastic community, after which it was distributed equally among its members. They passed their days with a highly regimented schedule of work, prayer, meals, and purifying baths. They demanded that members observe a strict set of ethics; any violation could result in expulsion from the community.

Very little else was known about this group until a startling archaeological discovery was made in 1947 when a Bedouin goat herder on the cliffs near the Dead Sea fell into a cave and found some ancient manuscripts. The manuscripts were eventually brought to an antiquities dealer and sold.[21] Once these texts, which came to be known as the **Dead Sea Scrolls**, came to the attention of scholars and governments, a full-scale excavation of the site, near Qumran, was undertaken. The search would eventually yield fragments or complete copies of some eight hundred manuscripts. Many of these were copies of books from the Hebrew Bible, while others were copies of books that were regarded as sacred by some Jews but that did not make it into the canon of scripture. These books are collectively known as the **pseudepigrapha** (literally "false writings") because many of them are falsely attributed to ancient biblical figures, such as Enoch.

The manuscripts also included the distinctive literature of a sectarian Jewish group, such as the *War Scroll*, the *Damascus Document*, and the *Community Rule*. Most scholars have concluded that the authors of the Dead Sea Scrolls were the Essenes, due to some strong similarities between the beliefs and practices of this group and the description of the Essenes in Josephus, as well as the testimony of Pliny the Elder that the Essenes

21. John C. Trever, *The Dead Sea Scrolls: A Personal Account* (Piscataway, NJ: Gorgias, 2003).

had a major monastery in this area. Recently some scholars have disputed this identification,[22] but a solid majority continues to believe the Essenes wrote the Dead Sea Scrolls.[23]

These documents reveal that the Essenes were founded shortly after the Maccabean Revolt (167–164 BCE) restored political independence to the Jews for the first time in centuries. As part of their consolidation of power, the Maccabees—the family that led the rebellion—decided to replace the high priest with a member of their own family. Under the leadership of the ousted high priest, who came to be known as the "Teacher of Righteousness," a group of Jews concluded from this alarming development that the sacrifices done in the Temple were no longer legitimate or effective. Without sacrifices to assuage his anger about human sin, God's wrath would grow until it reached a boiling point. This could only mean the end of the world was nigh. The Essenes withdrew from the world and went off to live in the desert in order to lead pure and holy lives in anticipation of the imminent arrival of the final battle between good and evil. The Essenes, then, were the most apocalyptic of the first-century sects of Judaism.

Because early Christianity also was highly apocalyptic and because both Jesus and John the Baptist are thought to have practiced celibacy, some scholars initially thought that one or both men may have spent some time in an Essene monastery and picked up some of their teachings. This now appears unlikely. While it is not impossible that there was some cross-fertilization between Christians and Essenes, the evidence for direct Essene influence on either Jesus or John the Baptist is exceedingly slim.

The Fourth Philosophy

Another group within first-century Judaism was comprised of Jews who advocated violent revolution against Rome and engaged in guerilla campaigns and open warfare against the Romans. Josephus does not have a single name for this group (hence the term "**Fourth Philosophy**") because there were a variety of factions who took up arms against the Romans and urged their fellow Jews to do the same. In the wake of Herod the Great's death (4 BCE) and throughout the reign of his son Archelaus (4 BCE–6 CE), a number of revolts sprang up in Judea led by commoners who had been proclaimed king by their peasant followers.[24] The Romans possibly saw Jesus as following this model when they heard him termed the "King of the Jews," and executed him. Still another messiah/king with a peasant army surfaced during the Jewish Revolt of 66–70 CE: Simon bar Giora. He fought the Romans in Jerusalem until the bitter end, and when his escape was thwarted he was taken captive, marched in chains in Rome as part of a "triumph" (a spectacular victorious parade), and executed.

Two revolutionary groups that played a prominent role in the Jewish Revolt of 66–70 CE were the **Zealots** and the **Sicarii**. The Zealots took their name and their inspiration from the Maccabean Revolt of 167–164 BCE, a revolt started when a Jewish man named Mattathias resisted attempts by Greek rulers to force Jews to forsake YHWH and worship Greek gods. Mattathias raised a rebellion against the Greeks, crying, "Let every one who is *zealous* for the law and supports

---

22. See, for example, Steve Mason, "Did the Essenes Write the Dead Sea Scrolls? Don't Rely on Josephus," *Biblical Archaeaology Review* (November/December 2008).

23. See Murphy, *The Religious World of Jesus*, 187; Sanders, *Judaism: Practice and Belief, 63 BCE– 66 CE*, 341–45; Cohen, *From the Maccabees to the Mishnah*, 152. Many scholars cite Yigael Yadin and Geza Vermes as the most influential advocates of the hypothesis that the Dead Sea Scrolls were written by the Essenes.

24. Josephus mentions three: Judas the son of the "brigand-chief" Ezekias, Simon the former servant of King Herod, and the shepherd Athronges (*Antiquities* 17.271–85). For full details see Richard Horsley and John S. Hanson, *Bandits, Prophets, and Messiahs: Popular Movements in the Time of Jesus* (Minneapolis: Winston, 1985), 110–17.

the covenant come out with me!" (1 Macc. 2:27). Mattathias and his family came to be known as the Maccabees, and their successful rebellion against the mighty Seleucid (Greek) Empire inspired Jews of Jesus' time to imagine they too could overthrow a powerful foreign empire.

The Sicarii took their name from *sicarius*, Latin for "daggerman" or "murderer." They were known to carry hidden weapons such as the dagger in order to surprise Roman soldiers and civilian government officials with sudden, deadly attacks. Their tactics probably amounted to terrorism in some cases, but they believed such methods were justified by the righteousness of their cause and the impracticability of employing conventional warfare. Their goal was to provoke a Roman response so violent that it would prompt the Jews as a whole to take up arms and join the revolution.

Roman soldiers carry spoils from the Jerusalem Temple in this scene from the Arch of Titus in Rome, constructed a mere eleven years after the fall of Jerusalem. The Temple's sacred menorah and trumpets are clearly seen.

These and other revolutionary groups succeeded in starting three major armed rebellions (in 66–70 CE, 115–117 CE, and 132–135 CE), along with numerous smaller uprisings. Each one led to ruin and disaster for the Jewish people.

Religious tensions between Jews and Gentiles in Jerusalem were the proximate cause of the discontent in 66 CE, which fed long-simmering resentments and grew into anti-taxation protests and the slaying of Roman citizens. The Romans responded by killing an estimated six thousand Jews as punishment and looting the Temple treasury. This reaction led to a countrywide revolution.

At first the Jewish forces experienced surprising success. The shocked Romans put together a massive force of four legions under the general Vespasian to put down the rebellion. Vespasian, assisted by his son and second-in-command Titus, invaded Galilee and defeated a Jewish force under the command of a man who would later defect to the Roman side and become known as the Jewish historian Flavius Josephus. The Jewish resistance was weakened by infighting among the Sicarii, Zealots, Sadducees, and the followers of the messiah-king Simon bar Giora.

In 69 CE, Vespasian was recalled to Rome, and ended up becoming emperor. His son Titus took command of the army as it laid siege to Jerusalem. After a brutal seven-month campaign, Jewish resistance was crushed. The rebels made their last stand on the Temple Mount itself. During the intense fighting, the Romans set the Temple on fire and it was destroyed. Tens of thousands of Jews were slaughtered during the final battle. Those who survived were captured and sold into slavery. The city was put to the torch and destroyed.

The subsequent rebellions followed the same pattern: early successes followed by ultimate failure and severe punishment. After the defeat of the bar Kokhba rebellion in 135 CE, Jews were expelled from the city in perpetuity and the Roman emperor Hadrian decided to raze the city of Jerusalem and rebuild a Roman city, named Aelia Capitolina, on the former site of the holiest city in Judaism. The Jews would not regain control of any part of Jerusalem for eighteen hundred years.

The Fate of Second Temple Judaism

With the destruction of the Temple and the souring of relations with the Romans, the Sadducees lost the basis of their wealth and power, their political influence, and their religious *raison d'être*. Many priests may have survived, but the fall of the Temple meant that any authority they had was gone.

The Essenes also fared badly. Many scholars believe that their major monastery at Qumran was wiped out by the Romans and its population massacred. In fact, the Dead Sea Scrolls were probably hidden in the caves near Qumran by Essenes who saw the Romans coming for them and decided to hide their sacred texts until the danger had passed. When no one survived to retrieve the scrolls, they remained in the caves for nearly nineteen hundred years until they were discovered by Bedouin goat herders.

The Zealots, the Sicarii, and other groups who formed the "Fourth Philosophy" lost all of the wars they fought. After the permanent expulsion of the Jews from Palestine in 135 CE, there was no more reason and no more people to fight for Jewish nationalism. The "Fourth Philosophy" was gone.

Given their focus on the synagogue and the Torah, the Pharisees were in an excellent position to reform Judaism after the Jewish War and preserve it for future generations. Yavne (or Jamnia) on the Israeli coast became the new center of Jewish religious life after the fall of Jerusalem, and the Pharisaic brand of Judaism—subsequently known as **rabbinic Judaism**—survived and flourished. All modern branches of Judaism descend from rabbinic Judaism.

Key Terms

YHWH	Weeks	Pharisees
covenant	Tabernacles	piety
Palestine	Yom Kippur	rabbis
circumcision	Diaspora	scribes
aniconic	synagogue	Oral Torah
Sabbath	messiah	Mishnah
ethical monotheism	military/political messiah	Talmud
coveting	Simon bar Kokhba	Sadducees
ritual purity	messianic pretender	Essenes
clean and unclean	prophetic messiah	asceticism
keeping kosher	apocalyptic messiah	Dead Sea Scrolls
pilgrimage	spiritual warfare	pseudepigrapha
Samaritans	Satan	Fourth Philosophy
priest	apocalypse	Zealots
Levite	resurrection of the body	Sicarii
Passover	martyrs	rabbinic Judaism

Review Questions

1. What makes a covenant different from other kinds of contracts or agreements?
2. What are the terms of the covenant between YHWH and Israel? What promises does YHWH make to Abraham and his descendants? What are the four main religious obligations of Israel toward God?

3. How did ancient Israelites interpret or understand each of the Ten Commandments?

4. What were the two main purposes of circumcision in Judaism?

5. For what purposes did Jews perform sacrifices? What were the rules for sacrifice in ancient Judaism?

6. What did Jews have to do, or avoid doing, to maintain ritual purity?

7. What innovations developed in Judaism during the Second Temple period?

8. What different concepts of the messiah were held by various groups of Jews in the Second Temple period? What were the sources of the disagreement over the messiah?

9. What are the major differences between the Pharisees, Sadducees, and Essenes?

10. What was the result of the wars of rebellion against the Romans advocated by members of the "Fourth Philosophy"?

Discussion Questions

1. The previous chapter discussed Greco-Roman pagan religions and philosophies. How does ancient Judaism compare to these other belief systems? What are the major points of agreement and disagreement?

2. Christianity is now a religion that is distinct and separate from Judaism. This chapter suggests that one needs to know quite a bit about ancient Judaism in order to properly understand the emergence of Christianity. After reading it, do you agree or disagree with this? What parts of ancient Jewish belief and practice seem especially relevant to you? What parts seem unimportant?

3. Judaism at the time of Jesus was characterized by considerable diversity, evidenced by the various sects of Judaism (Pharisees, Sadducees, Essenes, and the Fourth Philosophy) active at the time. How and why did one sect emerge as the dominant one?

Bibliography and Suggestions for Further Study

(Books and websites that are accessible for general undergraduates are marked with an asterisk; other sources listed are appropriate for advanced students.)

*Anderson, Bernhard W. *Understanding the Old Testament*. Englewood Cliffs, NJ: Prentice-Hall, 1986.

*Cohen, Shaye. *From the Maccabees to the Mishnah*. Philadelphia: Westminster, 1987.

Horsley, Richard A., and John S. Hanson. *Bandits, Prophets, and Messiahs: Popular Movements in the Time of Jesus*. Minneapolis: Winston, 1985.

Josephus, Flavius. *Jewish Antiquities*. Edited and translated by H. St. J. Thackeray. Cambridge, MA: Harvard University Press, 1998.

Josephus, Flavius. *The Jewish War*. Edited and translated by Gaalyahu Cornfeld, Benjamin Mazar, and Paul L. Maier. Grand Rapids: Zondervan, 1982.

Josephus, Flavius. *The Works of Josephus*. Edited and translated by William Whiston. Nashville: Nelson, 1998.

*Murphy, Frederick. *The Religious World of Jesus: An Introduction to Second Temple Palestinian Judaism*. Nashville: Abingdon, 1991.

Neusner, Jacob. *From Politics to Piety: The Emergence of Pharisaic Judaism*. New York: Ktav, 1978.

Sanders, E. P. *Judaism: Practice and Belief, 63 BCE–66 CE*. London: SCM; Philadelphia: Trinity, 1992.

The Roman Empire

The world into which Jesus and his first followers were born, and in which early Christianity spread, was dominated by the Roman Empire, a political juggernaut whose like has never been seen before or since. Other empires may have been larger (at least for brief periods of time), but none had the longevity and impact of the Roman Empire. The early Christians had to deal with the realities of imperial rule every day of their lives, and this was an unhappy situation for most of them. While conditions were especially difficult for Christians because of religious persecution, all who lived under Roman rule suffered under the yoke of oppression. Roman rule was harsh and tyrannical. The empire as a whole was fairly prosperous, but this great wealth was concentrated in the hands of an elite few, while the vast majority of people struggled to survive. The Romans brought an advanced technological culture epitomized by bridges, aqueducts, and dams, and imposed a semblance of law and order. But the evils of slavery, food scarcity, disease, rampant corruption, and warfare went unchecked. Life for most people was miserable, and there was little hope for change. The anxiety and despair characteristic of daily life in the Roman Empire played a considerable role in the rising and falling fortunes of the religions that competed for the allegiance of the common people. For this reason, the study of early Christianity demands that these conditions receive further consideration.

History and Administration of the Roman Empire

While the successors of Alexander the Great divided up the remains of his empire in the wake of his sudden death in 323 BCE and continued the Greek dominance of the eastern half of the Mediterranean world, the powerful city-states of Rome and Carthage were engaged in a death struggle for dominance of the western Mediterranean. Following a series of bitter wars (264–146 BCE), Rome emerged as the unquestioned master of Italy, Spain, and North Africa. Moreover, just as Rome's power was rising in the West, the various Greek empires in the East were beginning to decline. When Rome set its sights on additional conquests, the Greeks proved to be easy targets. By the end of the reign of Caesar Augustus (14 CE), Rome had added the formerly Greek-controlled territories of Greece, Macedonia, Asia Minor, Palestine, Syria, Egypt, and Libya to its lands, and had expanded northward into Gaul (France) and the Balkans. By the time of Jesus, Rome controlled every inch of land that touched the Mediterranean Sea.

Key Dates in the History of Rome Related to Early Christianity

753 BCE	Founding of the city of Rome
509–27 BCE	Roman Republic
333–323 BCE	Conquests of Alexander the Great; establishment of Greek Empire
323–31 BCE	Hellenistic kingdoms dominate eastern Mediterranean
264–146 BCE	Punic Wars between Rome and Carthage
214–146 BCE	Wars between Rome and Hellenistic kingdoms
241 BCE	First Roman province established in Sicily
197 BCE	Provinces in Spain established
147–146 BCE	Provinces of Africa and Macedonia established
63 BCE	Jerusalem falls to Roman general Pompey; Roman province of Syria established
58–50 BCE	Roman conquest of Gaul
44 BCE	Assassination of Julius Caesar
42–30 BCE	Roman Civil War
30 BCE	Province of Egypt established
27 BCE–14 CE	Reign of Caesar Augustus
12 BCE	Roman invasion of Germania
6 CE	Roman province of Judea established
30 CE	Death of Jesus
43 CE	Roman province of Brittania established
50 CE–115 CE	New Testament written
54–68 CE	Nero is Emperor of Rome
64 CE	Great Fire of Rome; first state-sponsored persecution of Christians
66–70 CE	Jewish Revolt against Rome
132–135 CE	Bar Kokhba Rebellion of Jews against Rome
250 CE	Measures passed by Roman Emperor Decius lead to first empire-wide persecution of Christians
303–313 CE	Great Persecution under Roman Emperor Diocletian
313 CE	Edict of Milan issued by Constantine and other Roman leaders, proclaiming religious toleration of Christianity
380 CE	Emperor Theodosius proclaims Nicene Christianity as the state religion of Rome, ends state sponsorship of pagan cults

Conquest and Military Occupation

While some Roman leaders may have had high-minded ideals for their military interventions in foreign countries, the primary motive for empire-building is typically the extraction of resources, which took place in a variety of ways. There was the initial infusion of cash known as the "spoils of war," wherein soldiers looted houses and stole the valuables of individuals, and officers raided the city treasury and procured bribes from high-ranking citizens for protection. After the conquest, considerable wealth was transferred to the victorious side in the form of confiscated land and the taking of slaves. Surviving soldiers on the losing side were usually enslaved, as well as many noncombatants. Often, victorious soldiers were given a bonus, proportionate to their rank and demonstrated merit on the battlefield, of a number of slaves that they could then sell in Rome.[1] Natural resources were targeted by the conquering Romans as well. The Italian countryside could not feed the burgeoning urban population of Rome, for example, so the city relied on grain imports from fertile lands like Egypt. When Egypt was sovereign, it could extract a heavy price for its grain, but once it fell under Roman control the terms of trade were much more favorable to Rome.

---

1. See, for example, Livy, *Ab urbe condita* 4.34.4, describing the aftermath of the sack of Fidenae in 504 BCE: "The following day the cavalry and centurions each received one prisoner, selected by lot, as their slave, those who had shown conspicuous gallantry, two." Translation from Livy, *History of Rome*, trans. William M. Roberts (New York: Dutton, 1912).

However, the primary means of extracting resources involved the imposition of taxes. After conquering a new territory, the Romans transformed it into a province by registering the cities, conducting a census, and surveying the land. Once the Romans knew who lived in a province and what kinds of businesses they conducted, they would impose taxes on individuals, certain industries, certain kinds of transactions, and the transportation of goods. Individuals paid taxes on any land they owned and also a poll tax or head tax, a tax on each individual in a household. Taxes on the transportation of goods were known as tolls. Some of these taxes were collected directly by the Romans, and some were collected by private contractors (tax farmers) on behalf of the government. Tax collectors were notoriously corrupt, often greedily overcharging people to enrich themselves, and as a result these collectors acquired a terrible reputation. This explains why, in the Gospels, Jesus' association with tax collectors created such a scandal (see Mark 2:15–17).

The Romans gained control of once-sovereign territories by assorted means. The standard route was through invasion and conquest. The Roman military was a well-oiled machine that seldom lost a battle and almost never lost a war during Rome's golden age. The Roman military enjoyed several advantages over most of their opponents. The Romans were famous for their building of roads and bridges. Their advanced transportation system not only aided commerce but helped the Roman army supply their troops and deploy them effectively. Roman military technology was second to none, noted especially for the development of deadly and effective infantry weapons (like the *gladius*, a short sword that could be employed to great effect in fighting at close quarters, unlike the long spears favored

by many other armies), powerful siege weapons, and strong fortifications and other defensive apparatus. The Roman army also usually enjoyed a tactical superiority over their opponents, having developed fighting formations that exceeded the famous Greek phalanx in flexibility and maneuverability. Roman soldiers were extremely well-trained and disciplined. During the imperial period, conscription was rare and most soldiers were career professionals. Soldiers volunteered for twenty-five-year terms of service and were fairly well-paid. Roman officers were well-educated in military history and tactics. The Romans had a powerful navy that ensured they always controlled the seas and waterways, and their army made the best use of cavalry of any force in the West. This combination of advantages meant that the Romans were virtually unbeatable.

It was not always necessary to use force to conquer a territory and bring it under Roman control. Some cities or states surrendered to the Romans rather than have their property destroyed and their people killed, raped, or enslaved. Quite commonly the Romans were able to take advantage of internal divisions within a targeted population. The Romans would agree to back one faction over the other and guarantee its ascendance in return for a degree of Roman influence. Herod the Great, king of Judea (reigned 37–4 BCE), came to power with the help of his Roman allies; his kingdom was semi-independent while he lived. The Romans made the Jewish homeland part of their province of Judea in 6 CE.[2]

Combined with the natural resistance of any people to foreign domination, the common people's unhappiness with Roman rule generated a constant feeling of unrest that could easily turn into revolution. This led the Romans to post

---

2. It should be noted that the northern Jewish region of Galilee—the birthplace of the Jesus movement—was less fully integrated into the Roman imperial system than the southern region of Judea at this time and may not have had to deal with the Roman authorities as often or as directly.

large numbers of soldiers in each of the provinces to prevent and put down rebellions. The Romans maintained a standing army of 300,000–400,000 soldiers in addition to provincial auxiliary forces of about 125,000. A large force (the Praetorian Guard) was stationed in Rome to protect the emperor and enforce his will, but most soldiers were garrisoned in the provinces. This meant that the majority of people in the Roman Empire lived under military occupation. Their political behavior was closely watched, and the slightest hint of dissent or resistance to Roman rule was met with brutal suppression. The soldiers of the Roman garrisons were often hated by the local populations, and this resentment was often exacerbated when the soldiers would extort money or services from locals by means of threats or false charges (see Luke 3:14).

Empire Management

The genius of Rome was not just that the Romans carved out such a tremendous empire, but that they were able to maintain control of it for so long. Hitler, Napoleon, and Genghis Khan each conquered vast territories, but their empires did not last even a generation. Once the Roman Empire achieved its height it was able to maintain control over most of its territory for four hundred years, and in some places for far longer This was because the Romans had mastered techniques of empire management, the primary objective of which was to secure borders and prevent or suppress internal rebellions.

Preventing rebellions was hugely preferable to squelching them, so the Romans used every opportunity to instill fear in their subjects. The presence of the military occupation forces accomplished this goal to a large extent, as did the prospect of overwhelming forces being deployed from elsewhere in the empire to the site of a rebellion. In addition to this, the Romans discouraged rebellion by imposing a reign of terror, according

to which slights and insults against Rome or the emperor were punished severely and potential rebel leaders were killed mercilessly.

The Romans' most famous method of execution, **crucifixion**, was borrowed from the Greeks and Carthaginians. Not all capital crimes were punished with crucifixion, only the offenses of slaves, foreigners, and insurgents of whom the Romans wished to make an example. Josephus reports that the Romans tried to quell the uprising that became the Jewish War of 66–70 CE by crucifying *en masse* the city leaders of Jerusalem, as well as a number of "quiet people" who happened to fall into the path of marauding Roman soldiers (*Jewish War* 2.14.9). The purpose of crucifixion was to kill an enemy of the state in the slowest, most painful, and most humiliating fashion.

Despite the enormous strength of the Roman military and the fear instilled in the hearts of Roman subjects, the Romans could never have maintained control of such a vast empire without some cooperation from the local population. Hence collaboration with local elites was an essential aspect of Roman empire management. The Romans would essentially agree to provide the indigenous leaders of a province with riches, power, and influence in exchange for their help in controlling the native population. One kind of collaboration involved the appointment of a **client king**. Frequently this was someone who had been part of the royal dynasty prior to the Roman conquest, whom the Romans appointed or allowed to continue as ruler as long as he obeyed the commands of his Roman superiors. This had the advantage of giving people the sense they were still being ruled by one of their own, instead of a foreigner. Client kings are sometimes referred to as puppet rulers, because they had no real power but simply danced on the strings pulled by their Roman masters. The Jewish kings mentioned in the New Testament, such as Herod the Great, Herod Antipas (reigned

Crucifixion

Although the process of crucifixion varied, there were some shared elements. The condemned person, usually male but not always, was beaten with a whip or scourge and then was forced to carry the cross to the site of execution. The victim often wore a placard or *titulus* around the neck, stating the crime of which he had been convicted, and part of the humiliation was the "parading" of the bloody criminal through public thoroughfares. Another humiliating feature was that the victim was stripped naked prior to being affixed to the apparatus, which could be a wooden stake, a true cross, or, most commonly, a T-shaped device, on top of which the placard stating the person's crime was nailed. The condemned could be tied or nailed to the cross, or some combination thereof. The nails were usually pounded through the wrists and ankles of the victim, to secure him as firmly as possible to the cross.[3] These wounds were not fatal, however, as no vital organ was affected. The person would hang on the cross, often for several days before finally expiring. While on the cross, the victim felt hunger and thirst in addition to the pain of the nails and the whipping, was unable to care for bodily functions, was helpless against animal predators such as birds pecking at the eyes or dogs chewing on the feet, and was subjected to the jeers of the crowd of onlookers that invariably gathered at such spectacles. Death might result ultimately from dehydration, exhaustion, blood loss, or some combination of these, but asphyxiation was often the final cause, as the victim eventually grew too weak to gather breath. Executioners seeking to prolong the process used a "saddle" (or *sedile*) on which the victim could rest part of his weight. By contrast, those seeking to hasten death would break the legs of the victim, depriving him of the strength to draw breath. Finally, the dead bodies were usually denied a decent burial, being left on the cross to rot or tossed into a pile where the bones would be picked clean by scavengers. Crucifixion was, as the Roman statesman Cicero admitted, a cruel and revolting practice (*Pro Rabirio Perduellionis* 5.16).

4 BCE–39 CE), and Agrippa (37–44 CE), all were Roman clients. If a client king failed to control his people, the empire would terminate his reign and institute direct Roman rule. This was the fate of Herod the Great's son Herod Archelaus, whose reign over Judea was ended in 6 CE after he failed to prevent a rebellion. After Archelaus's ouster, Judea was ruled by a series of Roman **prefects** (sometimes also referred to as procurators), one of whom was **Pontius Pilate** (governed 26–36 CE), at whose command Jesus was crucified.

In addition to the appointment of a monarch with local ties, the Romans also farmed out many of the bureaucratic tasks of local government to native elites. For example, in Judea the wealthy Sadducees were entrusted by the Romans with many of the judicial and law enforcement functions of government.

The granting of local control in certain areas indicates the Romans were just as interested in placating conquered populations as they were in frightening them into submission. This motive also contributed to a general strategy on the part

---

3. This claim is based partially on the discovery of the bones of a crucified man in 1968. The initial analysis of his crucifixion was made by Nicu Haas, in "Anthropological Observations on the Skeletal Remains from Giv'at ha-Mivtar," *Israel Exploration Journal* 20 (1970): 38–59.

of the Romans to intrude on the lives of conquered peoples as little as possible. The Greeks under Alexander the Great pursued a policy of Hellenization, which involved pressuring conquered peoples to speak the Greek language, adopt Greek dress and customs, and embrace Greek culture and religion. The Romans took the opposite approach, believing that if subjugated people were left alone to worship their traditional gods and continue the practices of their ancestors, they would be less likely to rebel. As a result, the Roman government adopted a policy of general religious freedom and toleration. The Romans did require that their subjects worship the gods and goddesses of the state, as well as the divine emperor, but this was seen as minimal and did not present a problem to the polytheists who populated much of the empire. The point was that people were free to worship whatever gods and goddesses they liked *in addition to* the Roman state deities. The Jews, who were monotheists, did have an objection to worshipping deities they viewed as "false gods," and the Romans attempted to accommodate their unique religious sensibility, albeit inconsistently. Roman and Jewish leaders negotiated a deal whereby the Jews were exempt from most kinds of worship of the Roman gods, and in Jewish territory the currency used was often *aniconic* (without an image of a Roman god or emperor, in deference to the Jewish observance of the commandment against "graven images").[4] The Jews were only required to make offerings for the health and well-being of the emperor; they were not required to place Roman statues or idols in their sacred precincts nor were they required

to acknowledge the divinity of the emperor.[5] Although some Jewish hardliners saw even this compromise as a sell-out, most Jews were resigned to the situation and only became rebellious when these religious boundaries were transgressed by insensitive or overzealous local Roman officials.

The Roman Emperors

Rome had been a republic for five hundred years prior to morphing into an empire. During the republic, instead of having a hereditary monarch, governing power was in the hands of two elected consuls who were advised by the Senate, which was composed of Rome's wealthiest citizens. The consuls served for a limited term (one year), so there was no risk a single person could assume absolute power and become a tyrant. The republic came to an end when Julius Caesar assumed dictatorial powers in 44 BCE. When a cabal of senators assassinated Caesar, a devastating civil war erupted that would not end until Caesar's nephew and adopted son **Octavian** defeated the last of his rivals in 31 BCE. Octavian consolidated his power in Rome and adopted the name **Augustus** in 27 BCE as a sign of his status as the undisputed ruler of Rome. The Senate conferred upon Caesar Augustus the title of "emperor" and allowed that he would rule for life and would be able to choose his successor (subject to the approval of the Senate, at least in theory). Augustus reigned from 27 BCE to 14 CE, and inaugurated a two hundred–year era of relative internal peace and prosperity known as the **Pax Romana** ("Peace of Rome"). During Augustus's

---

4. See E. Mary Smallwood, *The Jews under Roman Rule: From Pompey to Diocletian* (Boston: Brill, 2001), 148: "The bronze coins struck by the Roman governors for local use did not show the emperor's head but bore designs of inanimate objects such as a cornucopiae, a wreath, a flower and a palm-branch."

5. Smallwood, again, citing Philo's *Legatium ad Gaium* and Josephus's *Jewish Wars* and *Against Apion*, says that "a substitute for the direct worship of the emperor as a deity was devised for the Jews: in accordance with their Law, which countenanced prayer and sacrifice for temporal overlords, sacrifices of two lambs and a bull were to be offered daily in the Temple to God for the emperor's well-being, to replace the offering of sacrifices to the emperor himself normal in other provinces"; see *The Jews under Roman Rule*, 148.

Yale University Art Gallery, The Ernest Collection in memory of Israel Myers / Photo credit: Christopher Gardner

In Matthew 22:15-22, Jesus looks at a denarius and asks, "Whose head is this, and whose title?" Most likely, the image was that of Tiberius, with an inscription that read, "Augustus Ti[berius], son of the divine Aug[ustus], chief priest."

reign the imperial cult was born. After death a Roman emperor could be honored by the Senate as a god; Caesar Augustus was the first emperor deified in this manner. The more popular emperors had temples dedicated to their worship after death, while the worst emperors were never granted divine status.

Caesar Augustus was succeeded by his adopted son Tiberius, who reigned from 14–37 CE. It was during Tiberius's administration that Jesus conducted his ministry and was executed by order of one of the emperor's appointees, Pontius Pilate. Tiberius was in turn succeeded by his great nephew and adopted grandson Caligula. As emperor, Caligula was known for unorthodox sexual proclivities (including incestuous relations with several of his sisters and the sponsorship of orgies), wanton cruelty toward those who displeased him, an insatiable appetite for personal power, lavish spending, and a luxurious lifestyle. Caligula seemed to justify the earlier republican reluctance to invest so much power in a single man. He was assassinated by the Praetorian Guard after less than four years as emperor and succeeded by his uncle Claudius (reigned 41–54 CE). It was during Claudius's reign that Paul's early letters were written, one of which contains the first hint of Roman persecution of Christians (1 Thess. 2:14). After the death of Claudius (probably poisoned by his

wife), the infamous **Nero** (reigned 54–68 CE) assumed power.

The few ancient historians whose works survive, especially Tacitus, Suetonius, and Dio Cassius, all condemn Nero as a brutal tyrant and a madman. He is reputed to have executed hundreds or even thousands of people, including his own mother and brother. He is also suspected of being the arsonist who torched a huge portion of the city of Rome in the Great Fire of 64 CE, allegedly to clear space so he could build an enormous palace complex complete with a giant statue of himself. Tacitus asserts that Nero attempted to deflect blame by accusing the wildly unpopular Christians of starting the fire and then engaging in a vicious persecution of them. Later Christian historians would claim Nero took the lives of the apostles Peter and Paul during this reign of terror. He was the first emperor to be deposed by a revolt, started by Roman generals whose legions—allegedly unhappy with Nero's severe taxes—wanted to replace Nero with their commanders. That so many senators and leaders of the Praetorian Guard quickly joined this rebellion seems a strong sign of his unpopularity. Even the story of his suicide reveals him as an abject coward. He intended to fall on his sword but found himself unable to do so. Then he asked one of his freedmen to kill himself first to set an example, and even then could not summon the courage to take his own life. Ultimately, he ordered one of his servants to draw his sword and deliver the death blow.

Josephus, however, suggests the portrayal of Nero as a tyrant was a fiction perpetrated by biased historians, and it is possible that Nero's reputation as a crazed tyrant could be overblown. Although Nero certainly had powerful enemies and committed many political murders, he is thought to have been popular with the lower classes of Rome, who were often the beneficiaries of his lavish spending.

In the eastern provinces, where Nero's popularity was strongest, there was a widespread belief that Nero was not dead and would somehow return. Many scholars believe the author of the book of Revelation alludes to this belief in a revived Nero in his description of the "beast" with the number 666 (Rev. 13; see chapter 20).

After Nero, four different Roman generals proclaimed themselves emperor, with each one using his loyal legions to defeat and kill the previous claimant and his supporters. The last of these was Vespasian (reigned 69–79 CE), who restored stability to the empire and was succeeded as emperor by two of his sons. When the latter son (Domitian) was assassinated in 96 CE, the Senate appointed a new emperor (Nerva) who began a new dynasty that would produce some of Rome's greatest emperors, including Trajan (98–117 CE), Hadrian (117–138 CE), and Marcus Aurelius (161–180 CE).

Most people were less affected by political intrigues in Rome than the sheer fact of Roman domination. Imperial policies, however, did affect the average Roman subject in regard to the kinds of taxes imposed, the quality of local officials appointed by the emperor, and the degree of political and religious repression. Christians certainly saw their fortunes rise and fall depending on who was on the throne, with some emperors who hated and persecuted Christians (such as Domitian in 81–96 CE, Decius in 250 CE, and Diocletian in 303–313 CE) and others who were indifferent to the new faith. The conversion of the emperor **Constantine** (reigned 306–337 CE) to Christianity was a huge turning point in the history of the religion, and its eventual adoption as the official state religion by Theodosius (379–395 CE) guaranteed not just the survival of Christianity but its eventual ascendance as the dominant religion in the West.

The Roman Economy

The Roman Empire was notorious for the gulf between the haves and the have-nots. Perhaps 2–3 percent of the population were spectacularly rich,[6] while more than 80 percent of the people were desperately poor. The ancient world was never an egalitarian paradise, but the coming of the Roman Empire exacerbated the wealth gap.

Most ancient societies were agrarian, Rome included. In the centuries prior to the Roman conquest, most Jews would have lived in rural rather than urban areas, in villages or near small towns like Nazareth, with an estimated population of four hundred people at the time of Jesus. Even the great city of Jerusalem had a population of only about fifty thousand.

The city of Rome supported a population of one million, and a few other cities like Alexandria or Antioch also had large populations, but they were exceptional. The life of ordinary people in the Roman Empire is difficult to reconstruct because surviving accounts come almost exclusively from the urban upper classes. Only about 3–5 percent of the population was able to read and write, and most of these literate people came from wealthy families who could afford a private education—the only kind of education available at the time. These accounts are full of the stories of members of the senatorial and equestrian classes, people with large villas constructed of carved stone and fine woodwork, frescoes adorning the walls, performances of music and poetry, and a rich and varied diet including beef, pork, fish, and fowl cooked and served by large numbers of household slaves.

We have few written records of the life of average people because average people did not write books. However, scholars have been able to piece together a picture of life in the provinces

---

6. Warren Carter, *The Roman Empire and the New Testament: An Essential Guide* (Nashville: Abingdon, 2006), 3. Carter uses the 2–3 percent figure for the elite and estimates that they consumed 65 percent of the empire's resources.

and among the lower classes through archaeology and the discovery of several troves of **papyri**, that is, texts written on papyrus. The papyri generally record elements of daily life—such as transactions—rather than literary texts.

As in Rome, the wealthier members of Palestinian society were somehow connected to the government or the religious establishment (and hence received tax revenue) or had large landholdings that produced cash crops or were mined for valuable metals. Approximately 75 percent of the population consisted of **peasants**, that is, people who worked the land.

There were four main types of peasants. **Freeholders** owned small tracts of land, usually property that had been in the family for generations. Prior to the coming of Rome, most people would have fallen into this category. Freeholders would have engaged in subsistence farming, growing a variety of crops and some livestock. They produced enough for their own needs, with a little surplus to sell or barter for those necessities they could not produce. In Galilee, however, the reign of Herod Antipas saw huge resources being poured into the development of cities like Sepphoris and Tiberias, with public buildings and amenities funded by taxes on farmers and with large populations in need of increasing amounts of grain. More and more farmland was cultivated—it is estimated that only 3 percent of arable land was not under cultivation under Antipas—and more and more of it was devoted to a single crop, either barley or wheat. Increasing taxes put pressure on freeholders to sell their land; this land was snapped up by wealthy aristocrats, whose estates grew ever larger. Quite often the peasant who sold his land then rented it back from the new owner, most often an absentee landlord from Rome or a provincial city.[7] Thus the second class of peasants, **tenant farmers**, grew precisely as the number of freeholders declined. These tenant farmers paid about one-third of the value of their produce in rent, and about one-third in taxes, leaving about a third for themselves. Rent and taxes, of course, were due regardless of whether the crops had been abundant or paltry. Poor harvests often caused farmers to go into debt or to see their status decline even further.

Peasants who did not own or rent farms usually hired themselves out for seasonal work—such as planting or harvesting—on a daily basis. Such peasants were known as **day laborers**. These workers would gather in the village square each morning, hoping to be hired by the manager or overseer of a local orchard, vineyard, or farm who needed extra hands. The usual wage for a day laborer was one **denarius**, enough to feed a worker for a day (four loaves). Thus the pay for a day laborer was barely a living wage, and this meant not only that day laborers were themselves "food insecure," but that any dependents they had (wives, parents, and children) were at risk of malnutrition and even starvation.

Other agricultural workers did not receive any wages at all, because they were **slaves**. People entered slavery as captives of war, or were born into slavery, or sold themselves into bondage out of economic necessity. In the countryside around Rome, slaves made up about 15–25 percent of the population.[8] Free workers had so much trouble competing with this cheap labor that occasionally emperors passed laws limiting the total number of slaves who could be employed, to prevent mass unemployment within the free population

---

7. The notion that the reign of Herod Antipas saw a fundamental realignment of the economy in ways that were especially detrimental to the peasantry is associated primarily with John Dominic Crossan, *Jesus: A Revolutionary Biography* (New York: HarperOne, 1994).

8. See Walter Scheidel, "The Roman Slave Supply," in *The Cambridge World History of Slavery*, vol. 1, *The Ancient Mediterranean World*, ed. K. Bradley and P. Cartledge (Cambridge: Cambridge University Press, 2011), 287–310.

and corresponding social instability. Slavery in ancient Rome was not based on race. Slaves had some legal rights and were sometimes set free by their masters. Many slave owners protected their investment by giving their slaves adequate food, clothing, and shelter. However, slaves were often abused, killed, subjected to cruel and unusual punishment, or worked to death.

Certain rungs of Jewish society were below even that of slavery. Approximately 10 percent of the population would have been seen as **unclean and degraded** or **expendable**. Expendable people included beggars, prostitutes and other criminals, those with severe physical or mental disabilities, and the homeless; such people were expendable in the sense that society did not care whether they lived or died. Unclean or degraded people included those who did jobs so disgusting that no one with any other options would do them. Butchers, tanners, street sweepers, latrine cleaners, and the like fell into this category.

Many of these people would have lived in the cities rather than the countryside, and living alongside them were merchants, artisans, and retainers (employees of the elite). The small middle class of Roman society—about 10 percent of the population—consisted of such people. Upward social mobility was not impossible for such people in the Roman Empire, but it was extremely rare. A person's political connections counted for everything, while personal merit or virtue counted for little or nothing. As a whole, the economic situation was as hopeless as the political.

Life and Death in the Roman Empire

Most of the empire's poor people lived in small houses or apartments with walls made from uncarved stones held together by mud or animal dung, roofs made of reeds, and floors of packed dirt. Windows were located high on the walls to allow for privacy and minimize the stench wafting in from the garbage, animal dung, and human waste that covered the streets and alleyways. In these squalid conditions, peasants tried to carve out a living, of which the first and most important task was the acquisition and preparation of food.

The staples of the ancient Mediterranean diet were olive oil, wine, and grains that were ground into flour to produce bread. Bread was the foundation of most meals, especially among the lower classes. Wealthy tables would have featured meat, poultry, fresh fish (in coastal areas), and a variety of seasonal fruits and vegetables. Poorer people seldom ate meat, except perhaps during feasts celebrating religious festivals, and their diets had significantly less variety. Those who lived near fisheries might have had fresh fish, but most had to content themselves with dried fish or a fermented fish sauce into which people dipped their pita bread. In Palestine, the poor supplemented their diet with locally grown fruits such as figs, grapes, and dates, legumes such as chickpeas or lentils, wine, honey, and dairy products, including milk and cheese.[9]

In the Roman Empire, lack of food, especially during times of famine, was a main contributor to an average life expectancy of less than thirty years. Another major factor was the high rate of **infant mortality**. Many children (and mothers) died during childbirth, while others succumbed to malnutrition or disease. An estimated 20 percent of children did not survive infancy, and almost 50 percent of all children born at the time of Jesus died before the age of ten.[10]

Given the high infant mortality rate and the labor-intensive nature of agriculture, families

---

9. See E. P. Sanders, *Judaism: Practice and Belief, 63 BCE– 66 CE* (London: SCM; Philadelphia: Trinity, 1992), 119–20.

10. See Carter, *The Roman Empire and the New Testament*, 10.

generally sought to produce as many babies as possible. Male children were preferred, in part because they would grow up to work the land, while girls would marry into another family and would require a dowry. The desire to maximize the production of offspring is one reason females tended to marry as soon as they were sexually mature, sometimes as young as twelve or thirteen. Marriage was typically arranged, and almost universal, especially in Judaism, where getting married and having children was generally considered a religious obligation.

The low life expectancy was also related to frequent epidemics, coupled with poor medical care. Urbanization contributed to the prevalence of disease, given the close quarters in which people lived and the difficulties with sanitation and hygiene created by primitive or nonexistent sewage systems and inadequate water supplies. Another factor was that Romans who occupied or colonized the provinces brought with them lethal diseases to which the local populations had no natural immunity, including malaria, tuberculosis, typhoid fever, and dysentery. There were no antibiotics, so even a small infection could lead to sepsis and death.

Violent death was common as well. Casualty rates from ancient battles were high, especially because even minor wounds could lead to death. Indeed, more soldiers succumbed to disease than perished in battle. People could also be killed by criminals, and in turn criminals were often killed by the state. The Roman Empire did not have a real prison system, so most criminals were punished with whippings, fines, or execution.

An **ossuary** or "bone box" from the time of Jesus discovered in Jerusalem in 1968 provides an interesting illustration of the causes of death. The box contained the remains of several generations of a Jewish family, thirty-five people in all. The discovery became famous largely because it included the only known skeleton of a person who had been crucified, a young man identified as Yehochanan. The nature of the find suggested Yehochanan's family was relatively wealthy, so the other remains found in the ossuary may not be typical, but they are nonetheless instructive. New Testament historian J. D. Crossan describes what the bones revealed: "Of those thirty-five, one woman and her infant had died together in childbirth for lack of a midwife's help; three children, one of six to eight months, one of three to four years, and another of seven to eight years, had died of starvation; and five individuals had met violent deaths: a female and a male by burning, a female by a macelike blow, and a child of three to four years by an arrow wound,"[11] and Yehochanan by crucifixion. If starvation, infant mortality, capital punishment, and murder caused the deaths of so many members of one relatively wealthy Jewish family, one can only imagine how much worse the poor fared.

Roman Persecution of Christianity

The Romans were tolerant of almost every religion practiced by their subjects save one: Christianity. Christians were singled out by the Romans for persecution almost from the beginning. The degree of this persecution varied, depending on the circumstances and whether a particular emperor or local Roman official had an especially passionate hatred for the religion. Prior to 250 CE, it is thought most persecutions were small and local. The severest persecution took place from 303–313 CE during the reign of Diocletian, when an estimated three thousand Christians lost their lives. Accused Christians were called upon to recant by making a sacrifice to the

---

11. Crossan, *Jesus: A Revolutionary Biography*, 125.

A condemned malefactor is thrown to the wild beasts in this second-century mosaic. Many early Christians suffered the same fate.

Roman gods and to the "genius" (divine element) of the emperor; those who refused could be deprived of property, exiled, tortured, imprisoned, or executed. Sometimes the killing of Christians was regarded as a form of public entertainment, and at times elaborate spectacles were arranged, such as putting Christians in an arena to be torn apart by wild beasts. The following paragraphs describe the major reasons for Roman persecution of Christians.

Christian rejection of the state religion. Christians refused to worship the Roman emperor or the gods of the state because they, unlike their pagan neighbors, believed their God required exclusive loyalty. This made them seem impious (or irreligious), selfish, and unpatriotic. The sacrifices and ceremonies of the Roman state religion were one of the few things that united Roman subjects in a common endeavor. Everyone else, it seemed, was willing to participate in the rites expected by the state, but the Christians, like the Jews, refused. Not only did this insistence on following their personal beliefs seem to Romans like religious zealotry, it also jeopardized the welfare of society as a whole. The prosperity and security of the state depended on keeping the gods happy, and when their festivals were poorly attended and their offerings meager, the gods were not happy. Surely disaster would follow, and if it did—in the form of an epidemic, an earthquake, a military defeat, or the like—the Romans knew who to blame: those wretched Christians who had mocked the gods.[12]

Christianity as a new religion. Romans had some of the same problems with Judaism as with Christianity, in that Jews too refused to worship the Roman gods and claimed to have the only path to salvation. Judaism, however, had one crucial quality that Christianity did not: **antiquity**. Judaism was an ancient religion with well-established traditions and several million adherents. The Romans respected any religion with such venerable credentials. Christianity, however, was a brand-new religion, and so was not regarded as a legitimate faith but as a **superstition**.[13] In the modern world, new religions tend to be regarded with suspicion; if anything, this tendency was more marked in the ancient world. It took decades or even centuries for new religions to gain wide social acceptance.

---

12. Tertullian expresses this view as follows: "If the Tiber rises as high as the city walls, if the Nile does not send its waters up over the fields, if the heavens give no rain, if there is an earthquake, if there is famine or pestilence, straightway the cry is, 'Away with the Christians to the lion!'" (*Apologeticus* 40); translation from Tertullian, *Apologeticus*, in *The Ante-Nicene Fathers: Translations of the Writings of the Fathers down to A.D. 325*, vol. 3, *Tertullian*, ed. Alexander Roberts and James Donaldson, trans. Sidney Thelwall (Grand Rapids: Eerdmans, 1956). Augustine quotes a popular saying in times of drought: "No rain; blame the Christians" (*Civitas Dei* 2.3); translation from Augustine, *The City of God, Against the Pagans*, trans. R. W. Dyson (Cambridge: University Press, 1998).

13. See Wilken, *The Christians as the Romans Saw Them*, 50–62.

The criminal status of the founder of Christianity. Christians worshipped as a god a man who had been executed by the state as a criminal, Jesus Christ. Moreover, the crime of which he was convicted was treason, a most heinous offense in the eyes of patriotic Romans. Jesus allegedly claimed to be the "King of the Jews," implicitly advocating the overthrow of Roman rule. Romans were familiar with the idea that great men could be gods or could be deified after their passing. This was claimed for great kings like Caesar Augustus or great philosophers like Pythagoras. But in Roman eyes a traitor like Jesus, who had died the humiliating death of a vicious criminal, did not qualify as a great man.

Perception of Christians as arrogant and intolerant. Pagan religions did not require an exclusive commitment, nor did they claim to have a monopoly on religious truth. However, Christians asserted that only through Christ could one gain salvation, and that all other religions were false. This claim seemed like the height of arrogance to many Romans. Robert Wilkin notes, "How presumptuous, thought the Romans, that the Christians considered themselves alone religious. As a Roman official aptly remarked at the trial of the Scillitan martyrs, 'We too are a religious people.'"[14]

Christian commitment to nonviolence. Early Christians were pacifists; their commitment to nonviolence resulted in a refusal to serve in the military. Many Romans regarded their empire as an island of civilization surrounded by an ocean of barbarism. Romans thought that, given half a chance, the barbarians would surely destroy the highly advanced culture they had built (see Origen, *Contra Celsum* 8.67–75). The Christian refusal to even defend the borders of the empire seemed dangerously naïve, disloyal, and possibly traitorous.[15]

Strange beliefs and practices. One example of a Christian practice that was considered weird is the Eucharist. The idea of eating the body and drinking the blood of Jesus Christ sounded to many outsiders like ritual cannibalism. Justin Martyr (*1 Apology* 26; *2 Apology* 12), Origen (*Contra Celsum* 6.27), and Minucius Felix (*Octavius* 9) all defended Christianity against this charge.

Overemphasis on a threatening afterlife. Pagan religions did not place much emphasis on the afterlife (see chapter 3). For Christians, however, the afterlife meant everything. One would either gain eternal life in heaven with God or face everlasting torment in hell. The promise of a blissful afterlife would surely lure many who were attracted by this hope, but many Roman thinkers found the threat of damnation repellant. It seemed to them that Christianity based its appeal on fear, and that Christian preachers with their lurid tales of the tortures of hell were trying to scare people into converting.[16] This simply did not seem like a valid argument for practicing a religion, especially to the exclusion of all others.

Christianity as a subversive private association. Christianity was something of a secret organization; its rituals were only open to initiates who had undergone a regimen of instruction. The state viewed any kind of private, unsanctioned

---

14. Quoted in ibid., 63.

15. This accusation against Christians is more likely to have been made in the third century CE than in the New Testament era. The presence of a pacifist group in a country that maintains a large military is not a problem when that group is a tiny minority, as was Christianity in the first century. The problem arises when that minority comes to represent a more significant percentage of the population.

16. Plutarch charged that superstitious people such as Christians do not use their intelligence in their religious thinking and as a result conjure fearful and horrible apparitions. They compel themselves and their coreligionists to be faithful, "for they are afraid not to believe" (Plutarch, *On Superstition* 167d); translation from Plutarch, *Moralia*, trans. F. C. Babbitt (Cambridge, MA: Harvard University Press, 1962).

association as a potential threat. People might grumble about the government to their families or close friends, but organization is the key to turning political dissent into a potent movement. Roman rulers sought to deprive their opponents of the opportunity to organize. Pliny the Younger (see chapter 3) was apparently sent to Bithynia with orders from the emperor Trajan to discourage and suppress associations, clubs, guilds, and burial societies that could become hotbeds of rebellion. He may have persecuted Christianity, at least in part, because he viewed it as an association.

Allegations of sexual misconduct. Terrible rumors circulated about Christianity involving promiscuous or deviant sexual activities, the ritual murder of babies, and the consumption of the flesh of infant sacrificial victims.[17] Such rumors are easily dismissed as the kind of lies that often attach themselves to new and unpopular fringe religious movements, and there is no doubt the overwhelming majority of Christians never engaged in any such activities. However, Christians themselves sometimes charged that members of other "heretical" Christian sects engaged in incestuous sex and bizarre rituals. For example, proto-orthodox Christians accused Gnostic Christians of engaging in bacchanalian forms of frenzied, drunken, and orgiastic worship. This made it all too easy for average Romans to believe all Christians did these things, and worse.[18]

These factors, most of them exclusive to Christianity, contributed to the strong antipathy that developed toward Christians. Indeed, some persecutions, like the one in Lyons in 177 CE, were not dictated from above but arose from local mob violence against Christians. The momentum of Christianity was slowed, but never stopped, by such outbreaks. Many believers, when they were accused and put to the test, chose to save their lives rather than sacrifice them, committing **apostasy** by denying Christ and sacrificing to the Roman gods. Later, when apostates sought forgiveness and readmission to the Christian church, the church had to decide whether to allow their return.

Those brave Christians who did stand up for their faith in the face of death or torture were celebrated as heroes. Those killed became **martyrs**, and the Christians who revered them began to celebrate their birthdays or death days, and to make pilgrimages to the sites of their relics (bones or possessions). The cult of the saints grew out of the veneration of the martyrs. The idea that these holy men and women could "intercede" with God on behalf of believers who petitioned them became the basis of an important strain of Christian prayer and spirituality.

Attacks on Christianity by pagan critics also led Christian theologians to respond with increasingly articulate, persuasive defenses of the faith. Such a defense is called an **apology**, and among the early practitioners of apologetics were some of the most enduring and influential writers in Christian history: Justin Martyr, Origen, Tertullian, and Augustine of Hippo.

The fierce resistance of Christians to persecution eventually resulted in a dramatic reversal of fortunes. Immediately following the worst persecution of Christians ever recorded, the Roman

---

17. See Wilken, *The Christians as the Romans Saw Them*, 17–21.

18. Much of the information about Roman reasons for persecuting Christians comes from sources that postdate the New Testament period. However, the persecution began very early on, apparently, as the earliest book of the New Testament (1 Thessalonians, ca. 51 CE) speaks of persecution from non-Jewish sources, as do many other New Testament texts. Several of these texts speak of Christians being subject to the death penalty (the Gospel of John, the book of Revelation). The earliest evidence from a Roman source involves the correspondence between the Roman provincial governor Pliny the Younger and the Emperor Trajan dating from the years 111–112 CE. Pliny's letters confirm many of the items on this list and suggest most if not all of these accusations against Christians circulated during the New Testament period.

emperors Constantine and Licinius signed the Edict of Milan in 313 CE, legalizing Christianity throughout the empire. By the end of the fourth century, Christianity had become the official state religion of the Roman Empire. The days of Christian persecution ended, and the era of Christian domination began. One can see only the earliest traces of the history of Roman persecution and the Christian response in the New Testament. Many of its texts suggest persecution was a key issue facing Christianity, even though it was true that persecution was inflicted more often by the Jews than the Romans in the New Testament period. Nonetheless, Roman persecution of Christians was on the rise as Christianity began to spread throughout the empire, and this grave threat caught the attention of a number of New Testament writers.

Key Terms

crucifixion	papyri	expendables
client king	peasants	infant mortality
prefect	freeholders	ossuary
Pontius Pilate	tenant farmers	antiquity
Octavian/Caesar Augustus	day laborers	superstition
Pax Romana	denarius	apostasy
Nero	slaves	martyr
Constantine	unclean or degraded	apology

Review Questions

1. How did the Romans acquire territory for their empire? What was the main purpose of their empire-building, and how did they accomplish that purpose?

2. What features of the Roman management of their empire enabled it to last longer than other empires?

3. Which Roman emperors were seen as the best and worst of their kind, and why? Which Roman emperors were the most significant in terms of their stance with respect to Christianity?

4. How was the lifestyle of the rich different from that of the poor in the Roman Empire? Given the huge gap between rich and poor, why did more Roman subjects not rebel against their oppressors?

5. What was the purpose of crucifixion? How were crucifixions normally carried out?

6. Why was the average life expectancy so low during the Roman Empire?

7. What were the main reasons that Christianity was singled out for persecution by the Romans during the first three centuries of the Common Era? How did Christianity cope with this persecution? Why did the persecution end in the fourth century CE?

Discussion Questions

1. The "foreign policy" of Rome was imperialism, and its thirst for empire claimed many victims. However, for all the criticism that could be justly directed at the Roman empire, the fall of Rome helped usher in the Dark Ages, a time of ignorance, economic

stagnation, and savage conflict. In your view, was Rome and its empire mainly a force for good or for evil in the sweep of human history? What specific features of life during Roman rule would you point to in this regard?

2. Although the stated goal of many Roman persecutors of Christianity was the eradication of a pestilential religion, Rome also provided the incubator in which Christianity developed into the largest religion

in the world. How did that happen? Were there features of Roman life and governance that may have helped Christianity gain a foothold and then thrive, however unintentionally?

3. Did the Romans have any good reasons for their opposition to Christianity, or did their opposition to Christianity stem from their aversion to anything new and the persistence of stubborn myths?

Bibliography and Suggestions for Further Study

(Books and websites that are accessible for general undergraduates are marked with an asterisk; other sources listed are appropriate for advanced students.)

Ando, Clifford. "The Administration of the Provinces." In *A Companion to the Roman Empire*, edited by David S. Potter, 177–92. Malden, MA: Blackwell, 2010.

*Carter, Warren. *The Roman Empire and the New Testament: An Essential Guide*. Nashville: Abingdon, 2006.

Crossan, John Dominic. *Jesus: A Revolutionary Biography*. New York: Harper-One, 1994.

*Dupont, Florence. *Daily Life in Ancient Rome*. Translated by Christopher Woodall. Cambridge, MA: Blackwell, 1993.

*Koester, Helmut. *Introduction to the New Testament*. Vol. 1, *History, Culture and Religion of the Hellenistic Age*. Philadelphia: Fortress, 1982.

*Smallwood, E. Mary. *The Jews under Roman Rule: From Pompey to Diocletian*. Boston: Brill, 2001.

Suetonius. *Lives of the Twelve Caesars*. Translated by Robert Graves. New York: Penguin, 1957.

Tacitus. *Annals*. Translated by Cynthia Damon. New York: Penguin, 2012.

*Wilkin, Robert Louis. *The Christians as the Romans Saw Them*. New Haven: Yale University Press, 2003.

Introduction to the Gospels

In the beginning, there were no Gospels. Jesus apparently left no writings, and his followers did not begin to write down his teachings and deeds until many years had passed. Jesus came from a culture with a high rate of illiteracy, where oral tradition was the norm. Many ancient cultures touted the superiority of the spoken word to the written text, for persons speaking can interact with their audience, gauging their reactions and explaining themselves further as need be.[1]

The question of how long after the death of Jesus the Gospels were written is one of several issues that are standard introductory fare. Besides date of composition, New Testament introductions typically discuss a work's authorship, **provenance** (where the work was written), audience, sources, and genre. In the case of the Gospels, some of these issues are more easily dealt with than others. For example, the question of authorship remains unsolved. As noted in chapter 1, the Gospels originally circulated anonymously, and only decades after their writing were the names of apostles and apostolic associates assigned to these texts. Most scholars agree that the identity of the authors of the four Gospels simply cannot be determined.

The questions of provenance and audience are also probably unanswerable, although scholars once offered answers with confidence: Mark was supposedly written in Rome, Matthew and Luke in Antioch (Syria), and John in Ephesus (Asia Minor). Mark was thought to have targeted a Roman audience, while Matthew and John were written for Jews and Jewish Christians, and Luke for a broadly Gentile readership. Recent scholarship, however, has shown that little evidence exists to decisively link any Gospel to a particular city of origin. Moreover, a number of scholars now think that all four of the Gospels were written with a general or universal audience in view.[2]

By contrast, the questions of genre and date are very much alive in Gospel studies, and these questions must be considered in tandem with an understanding of the process by which the Gospels came into existence. This process began with the development of **oral traditions** about the teaching and deeds of Jesus. These traditions eventually served as the main source of the earliest Gospels and a significant source for the later ones as well. How long did these oral traditions circulate before they were written down in the Gospels?

---

1. This is allegedly why Socrates never wrote anything, and it was left to his pupil Plato to preserve his wisdom (and even then in a dialogue form that mimics spoken conversation).

2. See, for example, Richard Bauckham, "Introduction" and "For Whom Were the Gospels Written?," and Loveday Alexander, "Ancient Book Production and the Circulation of the Gospels," in *The Gospels for All Christians: Rethinking the Gospel Audiences*, ed. Richard Bauckham (Grand Rapids: Eerdmans, 1998).

Dating the Gospels and Other New Testament Texts

Most ancient works include no direct reference to the time of their composition. Scholars, therefore, must estimate the date of composition by establishing a **terminus a quo**, the earliest possible date of composition, and a **terminus ad quem**, the latest possible date of composition. Five kinds of data are brought to bear: the use of chronologically significant words or phrases, the use of ideas characteristic of a particular period, direct or indirect reference to historical events, the date of actual manuscripts, and evidence of literary dependence (both by and of the Gospel in question).

Five Types of Dateable Data

Words or Phrases. The first kind of evidence is a text's use of dateable vocabulary, that is, words or phrases that were coined at a known point in time, or that became archaic at a known point in time. American English speakers of a certain age know, for example, that a text using the word "groovy" to mean "excellent" or "wonderful" suggests it was written between 1945 and 1980. A reference to "World War I" would make sense only post-1940, as prior to that date the conflict was known simply as the World War, or the Great War. Similarly, many scholars argue that the *terminus a quo* of the Gospel of John is 85–90 CE, because it uses the Greek word *aposynagōgos* ("cast out of the synagogue"). This is a word that would not have come into use prior to about 85–90 CE, at which time the definitive decision was allegedly made by rabbinic leaders to excommunicate Jewish-Christians.

Ideas. Another important consideration involves the constellation of ideas found in the text and their consonance or dissonance with a particular historical context. New Testament scholar J. C. O'Neill provides one version of the logic behind this method: "If it can be shown that two writers shared a whole range of presuppositions and were concerned about many of the same questions, then we may conclude that they belonged to the same generation, provided that one did not employ the other's writings."[3] One of the main reasons for scholarly consensus that certain letters attributed to Paul were not actually written by Paul but by his associates in the decades after his death is that the ideas they contain and the concerns they address are more characteristic of the late first century (several decades after Paul's death) than of the mid-first century (when Paul was writing). The Gospel of Mark's rapid pace and ominous tone seem appropriate for the days immediately preceding or closely following the year 70 CE, which brought news of the final defeat of the Jews at the hands of the Romans and destruction of the Temple, a time when apocalyptic fervor appears to have run high. The evidence in the Gospel of Matthew appears to many scholars to reflect a slightly later time, when apocalyptic expectations had not been met and when tensions between Judaism and Christianity were running higher. Biblical scholar J. C. Fenton provides a representative summary of this argument:

> Matthew's Gospel contains a strongly anti-Jewish note running through it, from the teaching not to do *as the hypocrites do* in Chapter 6, to the Woes on the *scribes and Pharisees* in Chapter 23; and this may point to a date after c. A.D. 85 when the Christians were excluded from the Jewish synagogues. It is worth noting here that Matthew often speaks of *their synagogues* (4:23, 9:35, 10:17, 12:9, 13:54), as if to distinguish Christian meetings and meeting places from those of the Jews, from which the Christians had now been turned out.[4]

---

3. John C. O'Neill, *The Theology of Acts in Its Historical Setting* (London: SPCK, 1970), 5.

4. John C. Fenton, *The Gospel of St. Matthew* (Harmondsworth, UK: Penguin, 1963), 11.

Historical Events. A third kind of evidence, namely reference to historical events, is the most easily understood criterion for dating a Gospel, particularly with respect to its *terminus a quo*. Any historical event clearly mentioned in a Gospel indicates the Gospel was written after the date of that event. Thus an author's knowledge (or lack of knowledge) of the Jewish War, the sack of Jerusalem, and the destruction of the Temple (70 CE) provides an important dividing line. Even here, however, the evidence is not always as clear as scholars would like. The Gospel of Mark is vague about the destruction of the Temple and betrays no specific knowledge of the sack of Jerusalem, which has led many to argue that it was written prior to 70 CE. Other scholars date Mark to 70 CE or shortly thereafter, on the principle that, in Mark, Jesus foretells the downfall of the Temple, and Mark highlights this prediction because the Temple is in ruins when Mark is writing. In the case of Matthew, it is widely accepted that the author knew of the sack of Jerusalem, as is evident from his version of the Parable of the Great Banquet: "The king was enraged. He sent his troops, destroyed those murderers, and burned their city" (Matt. 22:7).[5] Hence Matthew must have been written post–70 CE.

Existence of an Early Manuscript. The existence of a very early manuscript can help determine the *terminus ad quem*. For example, the fragment of the Gospel of John known as 𝔓52 has been dated paleographically to circa 125 CE. Plainly, then, John must have been written prior to 125 CE.

Estimating the Date of an Ancient Manuscript

Establishing the date of the earliest surviving manuscript of a New Testament book does not tell us when the book was originally written, only when *this particular copy* was made. Nonetheless, the existence of early copies broadly establishes the book's antiquity and forces scholars to date the composition of a text no later than the time of the earliest copy's production. There are two main techniques used to date a manuscript.

Radiocarbon dating, a scientific technique developed in 1949, can determine when the organic material of plants and animals essentially "died" and were turned into manufactured products like the papyrus and parchment on which early New Testament manuscripts were written.

While radiocarbon dates are indisputable, they are not necessarily precise. For a more precise estimate of a manuscript's composition date, scholars use an older technique called **paleography**. Paleography is the study of the history of handwriting in manuscripts. Anyone who has ever studied a handwritten document from an earlier age, such as the American Declaration of Independence, can see many differences from the standard handwriting of today. The "correct" way to form letters that is typically taught in school does not remain constant over time; it evolves. One clear example in English is the now-obsolete long s, a letter resembling the letter *f* that was used when the letter *s* occurred in the middle or beginning of a word; formerly the word *lost* would have been written *loſt*. The standard formation of most letters has changed repeatedly over time. Thus each era has an identifiable handwriting style. This is especially true of people who earn their living by means of handwriting–namely, professional scribes such as those who produced most of

continued

---

5. Ibid.

Estimating the Date of an Ancient Manuscript *continued*

the manuscripts of the New Testament. This applies not only to letter formation but also to other features of the text, such as the use of punctuation, spaces between words, line breaks, and so forth.

In the accompanying images, the older manuscript uses block printing with all capital letters (known as **uncial** script), ends each line at the same point regardless of whether the scribe is in the middle of a word or not, and includes no punctuation. The newer manuscript uses **miniscule** script, a form of cursive that was more efficient than block printing because the pen does not leave the paper for every letter. It also employs both upper-case and lower-case letters, uses spaces between words, and has some punctuation. These features of the text, along with the handwriting style, allow scholars to determine that one manuscript was written earlier than the other and to provide a narrow range of dates in which both manuscripts were likely to have been produced.

Jose Francisco Del Valle Mojica / Flickr / John Ryland's Library / CC BY-2.0

𝔓52, containing a portion of the Gospel of John, has been dated to approximately 125 CE. If the date is correct, this copy was made only about thirty years after John's Gospel was composed.

Evidence of Literary Dependence. Finally, there are instances when a clear reference to a Gospel appears in the work of a later writer. This could take the form of a direct quotation, a paraphrasing that is so close as to indicate literary dependence, an allusion to its content, or an explicit external notice. An example of an external notice occurs when Irenaeus (180 CE) speaks about the Fourth Gospel and refers to it as the Gospel of John. From this it follows that the Gospel of John must have been written prior to 180 CE. In the case of Matthew, there is compelling evidence that this Gospel was used by Ignatius of Antioch, whose letters date to the first decade of the second century, even though Ignatius does not refer to Matthew by name, or to the Gospel by title. Once again J. C. Fenton summarizes the argument well:

The earliest surviving writings which quote this Gospel are probably the letters of Ignatius, the Bishop of Antioch, who, while being taken as prisoner from the East to Rome about A.D. 110, wrote to various churches in Asia in Asia Minor and to the church at Rome. Ignatius refers to the star which appeared at the time of the birth of Jesus, the answer of Jesus to John the Baptist, when he was baptized, and several sayings

Left side: Public Domain. Right side: British Library, Leipzig University Library, St Catherine's Monaster at Sinai and the National Library of Russia

Differences between miniscule script and the older uncial script are evident in this comparison. The uncial manuscript on the right, Codex Sinaiticus, contains the oldest surviving complete New Testament and originally contained a complete Old Testament as well.

of Jesus which are recorded only in this Gospel (12:33, 15:13, 19:12). It seems almost certain that Ignatius, and possibly the recipients of his letters also, knew this Gospel, and thus that it was written before A.D. 110.[6]

Conversely, the *terminus a quo* is circumscribed by any use a Gospel writer made of a previously written source. If Mark's Gospel was written first and used as a source by both Matthew and Luke, as most scholars believe (see chapter 9), neither Matthew nor Luke can be dated before Mark was written (probably ca. 70 CE). Indeed, most scholars reason that one would need to allow for a certain period of time for Mark to have circulated before it would likely have been found, revised, and developed by authors such as Matthew or Luke. Prominent New Testament scholar Werner Kümmel points to Matthew's use of Mark and Ignatius's use of Matthew to establish the window in which Matthew could have been written as 80–100 CE.

> Even if, indeed, Mark and Matthew originated in different regions, precisely in his reworking of Mark, Matthew shows so clear a development of community relationships and theological reflection (see, e.g., 18:15 ff and 28:19) that a date of writing shortly after Mark seems less likely than a time between 80 and 100. A date of origin after 100 is excluded by Matthew having been used by Ignatius.[7]

The use of these five techniques, then, has led to the near consensus that Mark was written in 70 CE or just prior, that Matthew was written between 80 and 100 CE, and that John was written between 90 and 100 CE. The Gospel about which there is the least agreement is Luke. While most scholars accept the longtime consensus that Luke was written in the same window as Matthew (80–100 CE), there are a number of scholars who hold that Luke was written much later, perhaps as late as 115–135 CE. The first undisputed reference to Luke does not come until 180 CE, when Irenaeus refers to it as the Third Gospel. Justin Martyr (ca. 150 CE) and Marcion (ca. 125–140) might have referred to Luke, but this is uncertain. Even if they did, Luke still could have been written as late as about 120 CE. The famous passage from Papias[8] that is the first to identify any of the Gospel writers by name mentions Mark and Matthew but not Luke. Papias, whose writing is dated to 115–140 CE, does not seem to have been aware of the existence of Luke's Gospel, perhaps because it had not yet been written or was not in wide circulation.

It is widely believed that Luke knew Mark's Gospel and used it as a source but was not aware of the contents of Matthew and John. If Luke was written as late as 115–125 CE, then it is highly unlikely he would have been ignorant of the Gospels of Matthew and John. However, as discussed in chapter 9, some scholars think Luke knew Matthew, and some think he knew John as well; if true, it becomes highly unlikely that Luke was written in the late first century.

The Process of Oral Tradition

The earliest Gospel, Mark, was written perhaps forty years after the death of Jesus; other Gospels may have been written as many as seventy to

---

6. Ibid., 11.

7. Werner G. Kümmel and Paul Feine, *Introduction to the New Testament* (Nashville: Abingdon, 1975), 119–20.

8. Papias's work *Exposition of the Sayings of the Lord* did not survive, but he is quoted by the fourth-century Christian historian Eusebius in *Ecclesiastical History* 3.39.15–16. The quotes identify Mark, Matthew, and John as authors of Gospels, and are often said to provide the earliest attribution of canonical Gospels to particular individuals. Many believe that the Papias quotation provides strong evidence regarding the authorship of these Gospels. However, scholars question whether Eusebius has accurately quoted Papias, whether Papias is a reliable source in any event, and whether Papias actually wrote as early as is claimed.

ninety-five years after his death. Before the writing of the Gospels, stories about Jesus' sayings and deeds circulated orally.[9]

The nature of the oral tradition shaped the Gospels. First, oral tradition tends to circulate in small and simple rather than large and complex units. Stories with too much detail and intricacy would be difficult to pass along. Hence the earliest Christians tended to preserve brief accounts of Jesus' teaching and deeds: short miracle stories, parables, pronouncements, wisdom sayings (or *apothegms*), and controversy stories, in which Jesus sparred verbally with his opponents.

Second, these stories would have been largely independent of each other. Christians who preserved these oral traditions probably did not view them as having any particular sequence. Plainly, they knew the story of Jesus' death and resurrection belonged at the end, but other than this there was probably little sense that certain sayings or deeds date to early in Jesus' career, while others occurred later.

Third, oral traditions tend to be preserved because they have a particular utility in the life of the believing community. One example is the story of the Last Supper and of Jesus' passion, which would have been repeated when Christians gathered to celebrate the Eucharist. The "situation in life" (German, *Sitz im Leben*)[10] that led to the preservation of some stories and the disappearance of others was often one of worship. Parables, pronouncements, and wisdom saying likely provided fodder for sermons, for example. Other kinds of stories were useful for proselytizing (seeking converts to the faith), debating with opponents, or instructing the faithful in norms of behavior and belief. In most cases, however, the oral traditions would have simply provided the bare bones of the teller's message. The context of Jesus' words and deeds and their applicability to a current situation would almost certainly have been provided by the speaker.

The Gospel Writers as Theologians and Authors

When the anonymous author of the Gospel of Mark set out to turn his oral traditions into a written account, he had a monumental task ahead of him. Producing a coherent narrative with such brief, disconnected units of material would require ingenuity and a certain amount of creativity, qualities associated with the "author" of a text.

Previously, the Gospel writers (or "evangelists") were not considered authors. Rather, they were thought of as mere compilers of oral tradition who employed a cut-and-paste technique while adding a bare minimum of transitions to produce a semblance of a story line. The individual episodes (also known as **pericopes**) were thought to be essentially independent of each other, having been simply placed one after another with no sense of each being a part of a greater whole.

It is certainly possible to take episodes from the Gospels out of the context into which they were placed by the evangelists and to understand them as distinct and separate entities. This is exactly what churches have been doing for millennia when they select a Gospel reading for a particular Sunday and ask their preachers to construct a sermon on that passage alone. More recent Gospel scholarship, however, successfully argues the cut-and-paste perception of the evangelists and the

---

9. More will be said about what can and cannot be known about the period of oral tradition in chapter 7 (see the section "Form Criticism").

10. The German biblical critics who developed form criticism (see chapter 7) coined this phrase. Herman Gunkel pioneered the method in the study of the Old Testament, and Rudolf Bultmann, Martin Dibelius, and others applied it to the New Testament. See Rudolf Bultmann and John Marsh, *The History of the Synoptic Tradition*, rev. ed. (New York: Harper & Row, 1976), for the classic explication of the theory of oral tradition and its application to the Gospels.

episodic understanding of the Gospels seriously underestimates both the evangelists and the narratives they constructed. The Gospels are works of considerable artistry and sophistication, and this complexity was supplied by their authors.

Consider the example of the beginning of the Gospel of Mark. After an opening line that almost certainly is meant to function as the title of the book, the author includes a quote from scripture and then a summary of the ministry of John the Baptist before ending the episode with a quotation from John's preaching.

> The beginning of the good news of Jesus Christ, the Son of God. As it is written in the prophet Isaiah, "See, I am sending my messenger ahead of you, who will prepare your way; the voice of one crying out in the wilderness: 'Prepare the way of the Lord, make his paths straight,'" John the baptizer appeared in the wilderness, proclaiming a baptism of repentance for the forgiveness of sins. And people from the whole Judean countryside and all the people of Jerusalem were going out to him, and were baptized by him in the river Jordan, confessing their sins. Now John was clothed with camel's hair, with a leather belt around his waist, and he ate locusts and wild honey. He proclaimed, "The one who is more powerful than I is coming after me; I am not worthy to stoop down and untie the thong of his sandals. I have baptized you with water; but he will baptize you with the Holy Spirit." (Mark 1:1–8)

While the words of John and the quotation from Isaiah may have come from oral tradition, most of the words in the rest of this episode likely came from the evangelist. Verse 6 includes the seemingly unnecessary description of John's clothing and diet: "Now John was clothed with camel's hair, with a leather belt around his waist, and he ate locusts and wild honey." Far from being superfluous, though, this description is an allusion to a passage in the Old Testament in which the prophet Elijah is described in similar fashion (2 Kings 1:8).

The importance for Mark of making a connection between John and Elijah is made clear when one understands it was widely believed in ancient Judaism that the prophet Elijah would reappear just before the coming of the Messiah and the Day of Judgment, to warn people and to prepare them. This expectation is based on the well-known prophecy in Malachi 4:5, "Lo, I will send you the prophet Elijah before the great and terrible day of the Lord comes." By means of the clothing allusion and the fact that John the Baptist fulfills exactly Elijah's expected role of warning and preparing, Mark is suggesting that John the Baptist *is* Elijah, and that the ancient prophet's reappearance is a sign that people should look next for the coming of the Messiah. When Mark introduces Jesus in the next episode, having already identified him as the Messiah in 1:1, this expectation is met. Without saying so directly, Mark leads his reader to the desired conclusion: if John the Baptist is Elijah, then Jesus must be the Messiah.

It is unlikely this subtle argument in favor of Jesus as the Messiah was present in the oral tradition, and it is even less likely that Mark inherited the series of interconnections within the Gospel that confirm John's identity as Elijah for both the disciples and any readers who may have missed the meaning of 1:2–8. Having prepared the way for Jesus, John the Baptist/Elijah's job is finished. He is arrested in 1:14 and the author eventually tells the story of his beheading by Herod Antipas in 6:14–29. Still later, Jesus' disciples question whether Jesus' coming as Messiah should not have been preceded by the reappearance of Elijah: "Why do the scribes say that Elijah must come first?" (9:11). Jesus answers, "I tell you that Elijah has come, and they did to him whatever they pleased" (9:13). Although Jesus does not say explicitly that John was Elijah, his meaning cannot be otherwise. There is no one else to whom Jesus could have been referring when he says that "Elijah has come," and the reference to the prophet's having been mistreated ("they did to him whatever they pleased") can only be understood as a reference to the arrest of John in 1:14 and his subsequent beheading in 6:14–29.

Thus the beginning of the Gospel of Mark in 1:1–8 not only quotes or alludes to passages in Isaiah, 2 Kings, and Malachi, it foreshadows Jesus' later confirmation of John's identity as Elijah in 9:11–13, a passage that also requires readers to recall an earlier passage in 6:14–29 to be understood. These interconnections show the Gospel was not slapped together but was carefully and cleverly constructed as a coherent narrative in which the whole is much greater than the sum of its parts. The episodes in the Gospels are placed in a dramatic structure in which one event leads to another. This structure is basic—increasing conflict between Jesus and his opponents leads to death (apparent defeat) and resurrection (ultimate victory)—but it could only have been supplied by the evangelists.

The evangelists' contribution to the process that produced the Gospels was not just literary but theological. The Gospels are not theology in the strict sense; a true work of theology is expository rather than narrative, and it treats its topics (such as God, Christ, the Holy Spirit, the church, and ethics) explicitly and systematically rather than implicitly or in the process of accomplishing other aims. The evangelists were theologians in the sense that their theological vision led them to shape the Gospels in the way they did. Consider the case of Matthew and Luke, who used Mark as a source and chose to retain some stories and omit others. Studying these choices reveals that Matthew and Luke retained stories that they found theologically appealing and were consistent with their theological vision. The same process is doubtless true for Mark and John, each of whom would have selected material to include in their Gospels from a larger body of stories available to them. Each Gospel has theological themes that are both distinctive and consistent, and hence must have their source in their respective authors. These themes will be discussed in the chapters devoted to each Gospel.

The Genre of the Gospels

Identifying the genre of a work dramatically affects the way in which its meaning is perceived. Filmgoers, for example, anticipate very different things depending on whether they have been led to believe they are watching a drama, comedy, fantasy, action film, horror movie, or science-fiction.

There are several ancient genres to which the Gospels might belong, although the two most commonly proposed are those of **ancient history** and **ancient biography**. Numerous scholars note similarities between the Gospels and the biographies of great men written in the ancient world.[11] Many such biographies focused on generals and statesmen, but there were biographies of philosophers and teachers as well. The latter kind of biography tended to mix public incidents with private anecdotes, quotations, and speeches in much the same way the Gospels do. The purpose in both the Gospels and the biographies of philosophers and teachers is to promote morality and religion by eulogizing and commending the great teacher in his message and example. The method common to each was to recount the life in a general, chronological order from birth to death. In both Gospels and the ancient biographies of wise men, the words and deeds of the teacher were intermingled in a narrative form. Another common motif was to include the miracles of the teacher. Authors of these biographies were usually not immediate disciples but admirers who wrote a generation or so after the master's death, just as was true for the evangelists.

---

11. See, for example, Charles Talbert, *What Is a Gospel? The Genre of the Canonical Gospels* (Philadelphia: Fortress, 1977), and Richard Burridge, *What Are the Gospels? A Comparison with Greco-Roman Biography* (Cambridge: Cambridge University Press, 1992).

Ancient versus Modern History and Biography

Most readers of the New Testament are not concerned about whether the Gospels are histories or biographies. They tend to worry more about whether these genres qualify as nonfiction and assure the historical reliability of the Gospels. Unfortunately, the standards of neither ancient biography nor ancient history could provide this sort of assurance. Modern biographers and historians strive for objectivity in describing their subjects, tend to be skeptical of reports unless they can be confirmed by multiple sources, do not put quotation marks around a person's statements unless they can be reasonably sure the words quoted represent exactly what the person said, and generally seek to be historically accurate. Ancient biographers and historians did not have access to the wealth of sources that most modern writers do, and there was no tradition of neutrality or objectivity toward their subjects. Historians and biographers had a definite point of view about their subject matter, and it was not seen as unprofessional to allow that point of view to influence their writing. Moreover, although ancient writers of history and biography did not accept everything they heard or read as true, they were far more trusting toward their sources than their modern counterparts. Also, precise accounts of speeches made by great men or historical figures were almost never preserved; hence, historians or biographers were expected to invent speeches that would have been appropriate for their subjects to have given on particular occasions. Consider the following description by a professional ancient historian named Arrian of his method in writing about Alexander the Great:

> Whenever Ptolemy the son of Lagos and Aristoboulos the son of Aristoboulos [two of Alexander's generals] have both written the same things concerning Alexander the son of Philip, these I have written as being completely true. But those things (they wrote) that are not the same, I chose (from one or the other) those things which seemed to me more believable and at the same time more interesting.
>
> Many other writers have written things about Alexander, nor is there anyone about whom more discordant things are written. But to me Ptolemy and Aristoboulos seem more credible to use in my own account because Aristoboulos fought beside King Alexander while Ptolemy besides fighting with him, was king later on, and for him to lie were even more shameful than for Aristoboulos. . . . There are still other writings I have used, which contain things that seemed to me to be worth telling, and are not completely incredible. These I included as "rumors about Alexander."[12]

While Arrian expresses concern for the credibility of his sources, a modern historian would never assume a source is reliable simply because he is powerful and it would be "shameful" for him to lie, nor would he prefer one account over another because it was "more interesting."

Believers sometimes argue that the Gospel writers would never have shown as little concern for precise, historical accuracy as was characteristic of other ancient historians and biographers. In fact, the opposite is probably true. As low as the bar was, it is not clear that the Gospel writers were even trying to meet or exceed the standards of ancient history and biography—standards of which they may not have been aware. Clearly, the Gospel writers were not attempting to write objectively, but instead had a pro-Christian agenda. Whether the evangelists applied skepticism toward their sources, sought to verify facts, or felt any compunction about editing the oral traditions they inherited simply cannot be known or assumed. The Gospels may indeed be largely historically accurate. This question will be discussed in Chapter 21. However, the accuracy of the Gospels is not guaranteed by their belonging to a certain genre.

---

12. Arrian's preface to *The Expedition of Alexander*, as translated by David Cartlidge and David Dungan, *Documents for the Study of the Gospels* (Minneapolis: Fortress, 1994), 125–26.

Other scholars believe some or all of the Gospels belong to the genre of ancient history rather than ancient biography. The Gospel that is most commonly singled out as history rather than biography is Luke, because Luke follows his Gospel with a companion volume (the Acts of the Apostles) that is clearly not a biography.[13] The combined work is known to scholars as "Luke-Acts." The presence of biographical elements does not disqualify Luke (or Acts) from the genre of history. Many ancient histories dwelt on biographical details fully as much as the author of Luke-Acts. Both Hebrew and Greco-Roman history have a strong bias toward focusing on individuals. As in Luke-Acts, the narratives of ancient history were often told as events carried forward by the careers of successive individuals. John-Jesus-Peter-Paul (Luke's series) is similar to Eli-Samuel-Saul-David in the Old Testament or Sulla-Pompey-Caesar-Antony-Augustus in Roman histories.

Luke in particular frequently uses the techniques of the ancient historian. His treatment of his sources generally follows the historian's dictum: one source at a time. The insertion of speeches written by the author is another historical convention: Paul's speeches in Acts 20, 22, and 24 are almost certainly Lukan compositions. The prefaces to both Luke and Acts follow several conventions of ancient historiography, as does the precise citation of dates with synchronisms, such as Luke 3:1–2. Luke's stylistic improvements on Mark—turning direct discourse into indirect, historical present into past tense, simple verbs into compound ones—also follow the standard practices of historians reworking their raw source material.

New Testament scholar David Aune points out that there is a subgenre of ancient history known as "general history" to which Luke-Acts bears special affinities.[14] This kind of history is *mimetic*—that is, it dramatizes and interprets the memorable actions of people in time rather than simply collecting and reporting such data without explanation or dramatization. The mimetic historian created the illusion he was an observer of the events he depicts. General history narrated the key historical experiences of a national group from their origin to the recent past, usually reflecting a national consciousness, and written so as to communicate their achievements and superiority to a dominant culture. This well describes the apparent purpose of Luke-Acts with respect to the dominant culture of Rome.

The Metropolitan Museum of Art, Rogers Fund, Transferred from the Library, 1941

The modern genre of history, which strives to be objectively factual, did not exist in ancient times. The *History of Rome*, by Titus Livius (ca. 64 BCE–ca. 12 CE), whose bust is shown here, openly promoted Caesar Augustus and the Roman Empire.

13. See Henry J. Cadbury, *The Making of Luke-Acts* (New York: Macmillan, 1927; London: SPCK, 1968) for the classic version of this argument. Scholars who disagree with Cadbury and his allies, maintaining that the Gospel of Luke is a biography, include Charles H. Talbert, *Literary Patterns, Theological Themes, and the Genre of Luke-Acts* (Missoula, MT: Scholars Press, 1975), 125–34, and David L. Barr and Judith Wentling, "The Conventions of Classical Biography and the Genre of Luke-Acts: A Preliminary Study," in *Luke-Acts: New Perspectives from the Society of Biblical Literature Seminar*, ed. Charles H. Talbert (New York: Crossroad, 1984), 63–88.

14. David Aune, *The New Testament in Its Literary Environment* (Philadelphia: Westminster, 1987), 77–140.

By late first to early second century CE, the Christian movement needed definition, identity, and legitimation. Definition was needed because the first generations of Christians exhibited a broad spectrum of beliefs and practices, sometimes manifested in splinter groups making exclusive claims. An identity problem arose because, unlike other ancient Mediterranean religions, Christianity had ceased to remain tied to a particular ethnic group. Christianity moved away from Judaism and the social and religious identity that the connection had provided. Further, Christian congregations were fully comparable neither to religious groups nor to philosophical schools. Most religious groups focused on distinctive ritual practices with little or no concern for ethics or theology, while most philosophical schools did the opposite. Christianity focused on both. Finally, Christianity had a legitimacy problem because no religious movement or philosophical sect was considered credible unless it was rooted in antiquity. Luke-Acts sought to provide legitimation by demonstrating the Jewish origin of Christianity and by emphasizing the divine providence that was reflected in every aspect of the development and expansion of the early church.

That Luke-Acts seems to fit the description of general history, and the other canonical Gospels that of ancient biography, does not mean scholars universally agree that the Gospels belong to these genres. Many scholars also point out differences between the Gospels and their supposed generic peers. Some offer alternate theories about the genre of the Gospels, while still others claim the Gospels represent a hybrid genre or a unique development in ancient literature. The lingering controversy cautions against assuming that a Gospel's meaning is determined by the genre to which it is supposed to belong. That said, the genres to which the canonical Gospels are compared all have one element in common: they use a narrative form. Hence one cannot err too far in examining the canonical Gospels as narratives, even if scholars are uncertain whether that classification could be narrowed further to biography, history, or something else.

Key Terms

provenance	*terminus ad quem*	miniscule
oral tradition	radiocarbon dating	pericope
Sitz im Leben	paleography	ancient history
terminus a quo	uncial	ancient biography

Review Questions

1. What are the five techniques scholars use to estimate the date of composition for an ancient text? How have these techniques been applied to the Gospels to estimate the date of their composition?

2. What is the difference between dating an ancient manuscript and estimating the date of composition for an ancient text? What techniques are used specifically for the dating of manuscripts?

3. What are some likely characteristics of the oral traditions on which the Gospels were probably based? Why do these characteristics seem to suggest an important authorial role on the part of the evangelists?

4. How does the example of Mark's presentation of John the Baptist as Elijah demonstrate the artistry, creativity, and imagination of the author in turning oral tradition into a coherent, narrative Gospel?

5. What evidence suggests that the Gospels belong to the genre of ancient biography? Why do some scholars believe the Gospel of Luke and the Acts of the Apostles (Luke-Acts) belong to the genre of history rather than biography?

6. How concerned were ancient historians and biographers about accuracy and objectivity?

Discussion Questions

1. The canonical gospels were written later than most Christians know. To what degree do you think knowledge of their true dates of composition can or should affect one's understanding of the reliability of these texts?

2. Some scholars—mostly from a conservative Christian background—insist that the Gospels were written much earlier than this chapter suggests. Does it seem to you that there is sufficient uncertainty about the dating of the Gospels that this is a real possibility? Or is there enough evidence for late dating to convince you that these conservative scholars are engaged in wishful thinking?

3. Given what you have learned about ancient standards for writing history and biography, if you came across an ancient text that included a tale that seemed to you to be far-fetched or highly improbable, would you be more inclined to be skeptical about that story or to give the author the benefit of the doubt and accept it as true?

Bibliography and Suggestions for Further Study

(Books and websites that are accessible for general undergraduates are marked with an asterisk; other sources listed are appropriate for advanced students.)

*Aune, David. *The New Testament in Its Literary Environment*. Philadelphia: Westminster, 1987.

Barr, David, and Judith Wentling. "The Conventions of Classical Biography and the Genre of Luke-Acts: A Preliminary Study." In *Luke-Acts: New Perspectives from the Society of Biblical Literature Seminar*, edited by Charles H. Talbert, 63–88. New York: Crossroad, 1984.

Bauckham, Richard. *The Gospels for All Christians: Rethinking the Gospel Audiences*. Grand Rapids: Eerdmans, 1998.

Bultmann, Rudolf, and John Marsh. *The History of the Synoptic Tradition*. Rev. ed. New York: Harper & Row, 1976.

Cadbury, Henry J. *The Making of Luke-Acts*. New York: Macmillan, 1927; London: SPCK, 1968.

*Cartlidge, David R., and David L. Dungan. *Documents for the Study of the Gospels*. Minneapolis: Fortress, 1994.

Fenton, John C. *The Gospel of St. Matthew*. Harmondsworth, UK: Penguin, 1963.

Gregory, Andrew. *The Reception of Luke and Acts in the Period before Irenaeus: Looking for Luke in the Second Century*. WUNT 2.169. Tubingen: Mohr Siebeck, 2003.

*Kümmel, Werner G., and Paul Feine. *Introduction to the New Testament*. Nashville: Abingdon, 1975.

O'Neill, John C. *The Theology of Acts in Its Historical Setting*. London: SPCK, 1970.

*Schweizer, Eduard. *The Good News according to Matthew*. Atlanta: John Knox, 1975.

Talbert, Charles. *Literary Patterns, Theological Themes, and the Genre of Luke-Acts*. Missoula, MT: Scholars Press, 1975.

Methods of Biblical Criticism

Each critical method of studying the books of the New Testament asks different questions and yields different results. One set of methods involves determining the exact words of the biblical text. Included among these methods are textual criticism and the theory and practice of translation. A second cluster of methods asks whether the events that the New Testament purports to record actually occurred. These methods fall under the general heading of historical criticism. A third set of methods seeks to determine whether one can detect behind the final written versions of New Testament texts earlier sources and traditions. Source criticism and form criticism fall into this category. Other methods take the final form of the text and attempt to determine what it means. Among these methods are literary criticism, redaction criticism, and ideological criticism. Each method of biblical criticism has its place, and the full spectrum of approaches is necessary to provide the most complete picture of the meaning of the New Testament.

Establishing the Text to Be Interpreted

Before one can begin reading and interpreting the Bible, one must choose which translation of the text to use. The books of the Old Testament were originally written almost entirely in ancient Hebrew. The books of the New Testament were written entirely in a dialect of ancient Greek called Koine. Those who do not know these languages must read the Bible in translation. However, there are many different translations, and some are more accurate or accessible than others.

Even a person who is able to read ancient Greek, however, will need to come to grips with the fact that the Greek text of the New Testament is uncertain. In the ancient world there were no printing presses, so books were copied by hand, often by professionals known as **scribes**, sometimes working in a manuscript-copying shop called a scriptorium. Even the most professional scribes made mistakes when copying. It is almost impossible to copy a book-length manuscript without a single error, however hard one tries. Sometimes these accidental mistakes were caught by other scribes, who would make corrections in the text or in the margins of a manuscript. If the alteration was not caught, the manuscript with the error might then be copied by numerous later scribes who dutifully repeat the mistake. Then multiple copies of the text would exist, some with the mistake and some without it. At times it is easy to see where the mistake was introduced and what the original reading was, but other times it is not so easy.

Sometimes, instead of simply copying a text, ancient scribes made intentional alterations designed to improve the text in some way. For example, if a scribe found something that he thought was a mistake, he would often correct it.

If the original used awkward grammar or phrasing, a scribe might rearrange the wording, perhaps telling himself that some previous scribe must have copied it down wrong. Sometimes scribes would seek to create consistency between the different books of the New Testament. If three Gospels portray a certain event one way, and the other Gospel portrays it differently, then a scribe might introduce changes in the odd version to bring it into harmony with the others. Theological considerations also clearly played a part in some scribal alterations. A scribe might read a passage in which Jesus says something that seems out of place for the Son of God to say. The scribe may conclude this must be a mistake because Jesus could not possibly have said such a thing, and might alter the text to show Jesus speaking in a more acceptable way.[1] Some of these modifications are easy to detect, while others are more difficult. In some cases there are dozens of manuscripts that present a given passage in one way, and dozens of others that portray the passage in a completely different way. These differences are termed **variant readings**, or simply *variants* or *readings*. How do scholars decide which reading is more likely to have been part of the original text, and which one represents a later scribal alteration?

Textual Criticism

Textual criticism examines the surviving ancient manuscripts and attempts to reconstruct, as closely as possible, the original wording of a given book or passage.[2] The original text (or **autograph**) has not survived for any New Testament book, nor

has any of the first generation of copies. Most of the books of the New Testament were written during the first century CE. However, there are no known copies or fragments of the New Testament that can be dated to the first century. A few fragments exist, however, that can be dated to the second century CE. The earliest complete copies of the New Testament known to biblical scholars date from the fourth century CE. Most of the hundreds of other manuscripts that are extant date from the fifth to ninth centuries CE. This means that during the decades and centuries between the writing of the original texts and the production of the earliest extant copies, many other copies were produced that are now lost. The copies available to scholars today have thousands of textual variants. The textual critic considers both external and internal evidence to deduce which variant is most likely to represent what the biblical author wrote.

External Evidence

Consideration of **external evidence** involves looking at the manuscripts that support each variant and determining (1) the dates the different manuscripts were produced, (2) the quality of the manuscripts, which in large measure is determined by the reliability of the scribes, and (3) the geographic distribution of the manuscripts. The logic in each criterion is largely self-evident. First, older manuscripts tend to be more reliable than later ones, simply because there was less time for alterations to creep in. Consequently, a reading supported by the most ancient manuscripts is usually accepted over one that is supported by

---

1. For example, in Mark 13:32 Jesus speaks of the timing of the coming of the Son of Man at the end of time: "But about that day or hour no one knows, neither the angels in heaven, nor the Son, but only the Father." Some ancient scribe apparently found it incredible that Jesus would not know what God the Father knows, and omitted the phrase "nor the Son." Many of the later manuscripts have this omission.

2. The classic introduction to textual criticism was written by Bruce Metzger, *The Text of the New Testament: Its Transmission, Corruption, and Restoration,* 3rd enlarged ed. (New York: Oxford University Press, 1968; 1992), although Bart Ehrman, *The Orthodox Corruption of Scripture: The Effect of Early Christological Controversies on the Text of the New Testament,* updated and with a new afterword (New York: Oxford University Press, 2011), has become nearly as influential.

textual evidence from a much later period. Second, a manuscript that can be shown to be reliable in some sections is usually reliable throughout.[3] Some scribes were very professional, while others tended to be sloppy or inclined to use their own judgment in making supposed improvements to the text. Finally, if the manuscripts supporting a given reading are concentrated in a particular geographical region, while the other reading is found in manuscripts produced in a wide variety of places, it is easier to imagine that the variant reading began as a mistake by a copyist in that one location.

Sometimes these criteria all support a single variant, making for an easy call by the textual critics. However, there are difficult cases where the evidence is divided.

Internal Evidence

Internal evidence involves looking at the variant readings themselves and deducing which is more likely to have been the original version and which is more probably a later alteration. In other words, the critic attempts to determine the most persuasive account for how the alternate readings arose. An example can be seen when two words or lines are repeated in a manuscript. Such repetition is far more likely to have been caused by a tired scribe failing to notice that he had already copied the word or line rather than the original author having written the same word or line twice. Similarly, if one manuscript includes an entire line that is missing in another manuscript, it is most likely that the latter copyist simply skipped a line, a phenomenon that is most common when two consecutive lines end with the same sequence of letters.

The **principle of the more difficult reading** articulates the common-sense view that scribes were more likely to solve problems than to create them—or, that is, more likely to solve what

looks like a problem to the scribe. If a scribe found an awkward or troublesome verse, he would be tempted to make some kind of improvement. It is far less likely that a smooth and trouble-free passage would be altered by a scribe to make it more awkward. The ending of the Gospel of Mark at Mark 16:8 provides a perfect illustration; this ending, which lacks resurrection appearances and reconciliation between Jesus and his disciples, is by far the more difficult reading. It is abrupt, deflating, and totally out of sync with the other three canonical Gospels. It is easy to picture scribes encountering this ending and being inclined to alter it. On the other hand, it is almost impossible to imagine that the Gospel originally included the longer endings found in many manuscripts and that the scribes whose manuscripts lack this ending somehow decided to delete this ending in favor of ending the Gospel at 16:8. Such a decision is so improbable that scholars are confident it did not happen this way. Many modern versions of the Bible include annotations, footnotes, or markings within the text (such as the passage being encased in double brackets) to indicate that the longer endings of Mark are unlikely to have been part of the original version of the Gospel.

Translating the New Testament

The many different English versions of the Bible currently available are usually known by a three- or four-letter acronym. The King James Version of the early 1600s is the KJV. The Revised Standard Version of the 1950s is the RSV; a newer version of this translation, the New Revised Standard Version (or NRSV), is a favorite among biblical scholars, and for this reason it is the default translation used in this textbook. Another excellent translation, and the most popular among Roman

---

3. Imagine that a textual critic compares ten different readings between manuscript A and manuscript B and concludes that, in each case, manuscript A had the better reading. Manuscript A is thus more reliable than manuscript B, and will probably have better readings than manuscript B for any other variants encountered.

Catholics, is the New American Bible (NAB), while many evangelical Protestant denominations prefer the New International Version (NIV).

Two factors account for most of the differences between these translations. One is the date the translation was made. Older translations tend to use *archaic* English, like "thee" and "he giveth." More recent translations use modern English.

The second factor making one translation different from another is the philosophy of translation used. Some translations attempt to preserve the cadence and form of the original Greek text, even if that does not always make for the most elegant English. Other translations do not seek to replicate the wording and structure of the original language but instead try to get across the gist or underlying meaning of the text in the most modern, conversational, or elegant fashion possible. In the latter case, the translator is essentially paraphrasing the text rather than translating it strictly. These kinds of translations, although sometimes possessing greater clarity, are less appropriate for academic study. Included on this list would be the Good News Translation (GNT, also known as Today's English Version or TEV), the Living Bible, and the New English Bible (NEB).

Evaluating the Accuracy of the Claims Made in the Text: Historical Criticism of the New Testament

Scholars use **historical criticism**[4] to determine whether the scriptural texts are historically accurate or not. Did the events described in the Gospels really happen? Were the words attributed to Jesus really spoken by him? The task of the historian is to compile the available sources and rigorously examine them to discover what actually happened, or at least what version of events is most probable. Each source is examined objectively and with a certain degree of skepticism. It is assumed, for example, that sources will be biased in some direction. The historian must detect that bias and account for it when reconstructing events.

There are particular reasons for suspecting that the New Testament accounts of the life of Jesus are not entirely accurate and objective. First, a strictly factual account was probably not the primary concern of the authors of the Gospels and other early Christian texts. If these authors knew of unflattering traditions regarding Jesus Christ, they would probably not include them in their accounts.

Moreover, the Gospels were not written by eyewitnesses to the ministry of Jesus, but rather by second-generation Christians who were relying on **oral traditions**, not personal reminiscences. The canonical Gospels were probably written between 70 and 100 CE, some forty to seventy years after Jesus' death. Given the average life expectancy at the time (less than thirty years), it is doubtful many of Jesus' original followers were alive when the Gospels were written.

In addition, the Gospels do not have the characteristics of eyewitness testimony. No Gospel contains a first-person narrative that suggests the author was present at the events recounted. Only John's Gospel makes a vague claim to be based on eyewitness testimony (John 21:24), which is curious inasmuch as John's is probably the latest Gospel to be written (between 90–100 CE). The author of Luke's Gospel freely admits he is not an eyewitness and is relying on the

---

4. The term *historical criticism* sometimes refers more broadly to the study of a scriptural passage in light of its original historical context, in which case the questions raised involve the authorship, date, and provenance of the text rather than its historical accuracy. The question of the historical accuracy of the Gospels is more commonly referred to as "historical Jesus research" or "the Quest for the Historical Jesus." However, questions of historical accuracy can be applied to texts other than the Gospels, hence the need for a broader term to describe all such research.

testimony of others (Luke 1:1–4). The Gospel of Matthew was once thought to be an eyewitness account, but this is unlikely given that much of it was virtually copied from the Gospel of Mark. Although Mark is the earliest Gospel, it has every appearance of having been stitched together from short, unrelated sayings and stories such as would have circulated in the oral tradition.

If the stories about Jesus circulated for as much as seventy years before being written down, they are unlikely to have been preserved with perfect accuracy. Almost certainly some things were forgotten, while others were added; some stories were probably embellished or exaggerated. Moreover, the evangelists themselves did not simply transcribe the oral traditions they received, but subjected them to editing.

These and other factors led to the development of the so-called Quest for the Historical Jesus.[5] This scholarly endeavor seeks to sift through the available data and to determine which stories and traditions found in the early Christian texts are most likely to be authentic. See chapter 21 for a complete treatment of this important but controversial topic.

Looking behind the Text to Its Prehistory

The Gospels and Acts, at least, are unquestionably based on previously existing material, either oral tradition or written sources. Is it possible, then, to take apart these texts and identify their oral or written predecessors? Two branches of biblical criticism seek to do exactly that. Source

criticism focuses on the written sources used by the biblical authors. Form criticism focuses on the oral traditions used by the biblical authors. At first form and source critics were motivated by historical concerns: if one could find an earlier version of a given story, that version was thought to be closer to the truth. Later scholars tended to be more skeptical of the historical value of these methods, but many continue to believe that understanding the prehistory of canonical biblical texts can be useful for a variety of purposes.

Source Criticism

One of the most famous applications of source criticism to the Bible was the great nineteenth-century German scholar Julius Wellhausen's work on the Old Testament. Wellhausen and others used the techniques of source criticism to determine that the Pentateuch (the first five books of the Old Testament/Hebrew Bible) had not been written by a single author but rather wove together the writings of four different authors (designated J, E, D, and P). This became known as the Documentary Hypothesis.[6]

The development of the Documentary Hypothesis illustrates many of the techniques of **source criticism**. Wellhausen and his colleagues looked for seams in the text of the Pentateuch, abrupt transitions where two different written traditions appeared to have been "stitched" together. An obvious example occurs when the same story is told twice, with significant variations in detail. The two creation stories in Genesis (1:1–2:4a and 2:4b–3:24) suggest that the work of two authors has been combined. Sometimes

5. Some of the more famous books in this area include Albert Schweitzer, *The Quest of the Historical Jesus,* ed. John Bowden, 1st complete ed., 1st Fortress Press ed. (Minneapolis: Fortress, 2001); Norman Perrin, *Rediscovering the Teaching of Jesus* (New York: Harper & Row, 1967); John Dominic Crossan, *The Historical Jesus: The Life of a Mediterranean Jewish Peasant* (San Francisco: HarperCollins, 1991); and John P. Meier, *A Marginal Jew: Rethinking the Historical Jesus,* 5 vols., Anchor Bible Reference Library (New Haven: Yale University Press, 1991–2016).

6. See, among other works, Julius Wellhausen, *Prolegomena to the History of Ancient Israel* (New York: Meridian Books, 1957).

such stories are placed next to each other; sometimes they are combined into one story. For example, there is only one story about Noah and the flood in Genesis, but it clearly combines elements from what were once two independent written versions of the tale. The final combined version of the flood in Genesis contains contradictions, at one point claiming the great deluge prevailed for forty days, at another claiming the flooding continued for 150 days. This suggests that multiple sources were combined but not perfectly harmonized.

Old Testament source critics, studying the different units they had identified, saw that many shared certain characteristics and concluded from this that they were written by the same author. One author preferred the name "Yahweh" for God, while another used the name "Elohim." This and other identifying characteristics led to the identification of portions of the story contributed by the Yahwist (the J writer) and the Elohist (the E writer). Another set of stories seem to have been written by an individual who cared a great deal about priestly matters, such as animal sacrifices or matters of ritual cleanliness: this author became known as the Priestly writer (P).

The same techniques of source criticism have been applied to the New Testament. The most fruitful and controversial research has concerned the sources of the Gospels of Mark, Matthew, and Luke, and will be discussed in detail in chapter 9. However, there are other applications of source criticism to the New Testament that can serve as brief illustrations of the method at work. For example, the Gospel of John contains seven miracle stories. Some scholars claim these stories exhibit a uniformity of style that differs from that found in the rest of the Gospel. For example, Jesus' miracles are referred to as "signs" (Greek, *sēmeia*) rather than the more common "miracles" (Greek, *dynameis*). The famous German biblical scholar Rudolf Bultmann posited that these miracle stories were once part of an independent written text, a collection of Jesus' miracles he called the Signs Gospel.[7] Both Bultmann and the prominent American Catholic biblical scholar Raymond Brown[8] argued further that the author of the Signs Gospel was the Beloved Disciple (see chapter 13) himself. This theory, if true, would bring part of the Gospel of John much closer to Jesus, having been written by a follower and eyewitness to Jesus' ministry, unlike most other parts of the canonical Gospels.

Source criticism has also been applied to Paul's letters. While some letters appear to be unified and well-preserved, other letters contain seams, such as abrupt shifts in topic or tone, that suggest the surviving text has been pieced together from several originally separate letters. Second Corinthians especially is seen by most scholars as an amalgam of several letters (see chapter 17).

Form Criticism

The realization that oral sources lay behind much of the Gospels led to the development of **form criticism**.[9] This method derives from the study of folklore, which also has oral transmission as its basis. Form critics believe that understanding how folk traditions are passed from one community to another, and from one generation to another, can help scholars reconstruct how the oral traditions that became the Gospels were likely created, preserved, and altered. Form critics claim these oral

---

7. Rudolf Bultmann, *The Gospel of John: A Commentary*, ed. R. W. N. Hoare and J. K. Riches, trans. G. R. Beasley-Murray (Oxford: Blackwell, 1971).

8. Raymond E. Brown, *The Community of the Beloved Disciple* (New York: Paulist Press, 1979).

9. A good introduction to the particulars of this method can be found in Edgar V. McKnight, *What Is Form Criticism?* (Eugene, OR: Wipf and Stock, 1997).

traditions most likely had certain genres that were determined by their function in the believing community (their *Sitz im Leben* or "situation in life"), such as worship, evangelization, moral instruction, or disputes with unbelievers. The building blocks of the Gospels, then, could be classified as parables, apothegms (wisdom sayings), controversy stories, miracles, and so on, each of which had a specific function in one of these settings. If a Gospel episode did not appear to have such a function, then it was deemed not part of the oral tradition. Once a Gospel episode had been boiled down to its likely oral version, then a distinction could be made between **tradition** (the original oral form of the story) and **redaction** (the elements that were added later by the evangelist to produce the final, written version). The redaction could then be discarded, along with those episodes having no likely viability in the oral tradition, leaving only the pure, unvarnished oral tradition, which would be much closer to the historical Jesus. Although form criticism was among the dominant methods of biblical criticism in the late nineteenth and early twentieth centuries, it has since fallen from favor. Strong doubts were raised about (1) the method's ability to separate tradition from redaction with any degree of confidence unless written sources were available for comparison, (2) the applicability of studies of modern folklore to ancient biblical material, and (3) the authenticity of a passage resting so completely on its alleged *Sitz im Leben* or lack thereof.

The Meaning of the Text

While the question of historical accuracy is central to historical, form, and source criticism, determining the *meaning* of the biblical texts is the core of numerous other methods of biblical criticism. What messages were the evangelists trying to communicate to their readers? The different methods in this category vary according to how they conceive the authors of the Gospels and what

they see as key to determining the text's meaning. Redaction criticism views the evangelists primarily as editors of existing oral and written materials, and identifies their editorial changes and insertions as key in determining each evangelist's purpose in writing, with this purpose usually being understood in theological terms. Literary criticism views the evangelists not as editors but as authors who took existing traditions and artfully shaped them into narratives that communicate through plot and character. New Testament theology views the evangelists as proto-theologians, whose message can be broken down into categories of systematic theology. Each Gospel, then, is thought to have its own doctrine of God (theology), understanding of Jesus (Christology), code of morality (ethics), notion of the church (ecclesiology), teaching about the end of the world (eschatology), and so on. Finally, ideological criticism views the evangelists as promoters of particular cultural values on issues such as gender, race, or class, among others. A specific example would be feminist biblical criticism, which focuses on each text's portrayal of women and understanding of gender roles.

Redaction Criticism

The early form critics separated Gospel material into tradition and redaction, then discarded the redaction and studied the tradition, which they hoped would provide access to the historical Jesus. **Redaction criticism** also separates tradition from redaction, but focuses on the input of the evangelist, that is, his editing of the material. The word *redact* means "to edit"; hence redaction criticism views the evangelists as editors who (1) selected previous oral and written traditions for inclusion in their Gospels while discarding others; (2) polished, altered, and reshaped the traditions they selected to reflect a particular theological stance; and (3) added material, such as transitions between stories or perhaps entire episodes, to produce finished Gospels that communicated their vision of Christianity.

If this is how the Gospels were written, then each evangelist's purpose would be revealed by their handling of their source material, in the process of which they made deliberate omissions, major additions, and significant alterations. In some cases, scholars can only speculate about what the source material originally looked like, but in other cases they know exactly because the source also survives. This is the case with the Gospels of Matthew and Luke, each of which used the Gospel of Mark as a source (a conclusion that is explained in detail in chapter 9).[10] The method of redaction criticism will be illustrated primarily in chapter 10, on the Gospel of Matthew.

Literary Criticism

Biblical **literary criticism** examines the Gospels as literature, envisioning the evangelists as true authors who shaped their stories to communicate particular messages to their readers. This method is often justified by reference to the basic choice made by the evangelists themselves to communicate their views about Jesus Christ in the form of a story, or a **narrative**. Other early Christian authors wrote letters, compiled sayings of Jesus, or composed sermons. But the writers of the canonical Gospels chose to take the oral traditions (and, in some cases, written sources) and shape them into a coherent story that flows logically from beginning to middle to end, and to populate the story with consistent characters. In other words, the canonical Gospels exhibit the unmistakable signs of narrative literary works: they are built around a plot and a set of characters. Hence, literary critics argue, they may be subjected to the same kind of analysis as short stories, novellas, novels, and other literary works.

The techniques that are available to an author to communicate meaning to an audience are familiar: plot, character, themes, motifs, setting, narration, point of view, anticipation or foreshadowing, retrojection, and allusion, among others. This method of biblical criticism will be illustrated in chapter 8, on the Gospel of Mark.

New Testament Theology

The authors of the New Testament were all in a sense theologians. However, none of the books of the New Testament presents a proper systematic theology. A systematic theology examines each issue in a particular religion, coming up with an understanding of the religion that is complete and internally consistent. In Christianity, for example, a systematic theology must have a section on God, a section on Jesus (Christology), and a section on the Holy Spirit (pneumatology), and must in addition explain how these three "persons" of the Trinity are part of the same Godhead. In addition, a Christian systematic theology would have a section on the church (ecclesiology), a section on morality (ethics), a section on the end times (eschatology), a section on how to obtain salvation (soteriology), a section on human nature (anthropology), and so on. No book of the New Testament is organized in this fashion, but some scholars have attempted to deduce from the narratives of the evangelists and the letters of the apostles how they might fill in such a work.

The German scholar Rudolf Bultmann, who wrote the most influential work of New Testament theology in the modern era, thought only two New Testament authors provided sufficient information in their writings to determine their theologies systematically: Paul and John.[11] Other scholars have written monographs about

---

10. For an excellent illustration of this method in action, see Norman Perrin, *The Resurrection according to Matthew, Mark, and Luke* (Philadelphia: Fortress, 1977).

11. Rudolf Bultmann, *Theology of the New Testament* (New York: Scribner, 1965).

the theology of a particular author,[12] the collected teaching of various authors on a single theological topic,[13] or even about one particular aspect of the theology of a single New Testament author.[14]

One can illustrate the results of this method by comparing one Gospel to another with respect to a particular theological issue. **Christology** refers to one's understanding of the status and significance of Jesus within the Christian religion. An important facet of Christology involves whether one sees Jesus as more human or more divine. A work that emphasizes Jesus' humanity more than his divinity is said to have a **low Christology**, while one that shows a more powerful, Godlike Jesus has a **high Christology**. The Gospel of Mark exhibits a low Christology, while the Christology of the Gospel of John is much higher.

There are a number of ways in which this claim can be proven. One involves how each author refers to Jesus. The Gospel of Mark never calls Jesus "God." The most common term applied to Jesus in Mark is "Son of Man," although occasionally "Christ" or "Son of God" is used. By contrast, the Gospel of John asserts that Jesus is God in numerous passages. The prologue to the Gospel begins by saying, "In the beginning was the Word, and the Word was with God, *and the Word was God*" (John 1:1). Later, Jesus asserts, "the Father and I are one" (10:30). The disciple Thomas, after seeing the risen Jesus, proclaims, "My Lord and my God!" (20:28).

This carving from Notre Dame in Paris illustrates John 20:28, in which Thomas observes the wounds of the risen Christ and exclaims, "My Lord and my God." A "high" Christology, like that of John's Gospel, emphasizes Jesus' divine nature.

Jesus exhibits all of the qualities of divinity in John as well. He is both all-powerful (omnipotent) and all-knowing (omniscient). There are no passages in which Jesus does not know something or cannot do something. In Mark, however, Jesus twice indicates he does not know something (Mark 5:24–34; 13:32). In Mark, Jesus is also said to be unable to do something (6:1–6), hence he lacks omnipotence.

Christology will be a focus of each of the chapters dedicated to the canonical Gospels. However, the method of New Testament theology more broadly will be specifically illustrated in chapter 11, on the Gospel of Luke.

Ideological Criticism

Interpretation is always influenced by the identity and perspective of the reader. The reader's

---

12. For example, Joseph Fitzmyer, *Luke the Theologian: Aspects of His Teaching* (New York: Paulist Press, 1989).

13. For example, Frank Matera, *New Testament Ethics: The Legacies of Jesus and Paul* (Louisville: Westminster John Knox, 1989).

14. For example, Jack Dean Kingsbury, *Matthew: Structure, Christology, Kingdom* (Minneapolis: Fortress, 1989).

historical, cultural, and social location determine to a significant degree what she is able to see in the text. For example, an ancient Palestinian Jewish reader would likely have a different reaction to Jesus' cursing of the rich in Luke 6:24 ("Woe to you who are rich") than would a modern American Christian. In the ancient world, most people were desperately poor, and the vast wealth concentrated among the relatively few Roman elite was a cause for resentment. Wealth was more often a consequence of one's birth than a result of hard work and personal merit. The super-wealthy in the Roman Empire were strongly associated with selfishness, greed, and unscrupulous business practices. It would not surprise an ancient person that Jesus condemns the rich.

The assumptions readers bring with them are often referred to as presuppositions. Presuppositions can taint the reading process and lead to misreading. For example, neo-Nazi readers of the New Testament such as the members of the Christian Identity sect often (wrongly) assume that ancient people understood racial distinctions as modern people do, that Jesus was white, and that he supported a platform of white supremacy.

Because of the potential for misreading, some scholars attempt to bracket their presuppositions as much as possible and approach the text in a neutral, objective way. Others embrace the fact that their particular identity allows them to see aspects of the text's meaning that others do not. A reader's social identity—their race, gender, class, ethnicity, and so on—can be seen as a lens through which certain aspects of the text's meaning can come alive. A female reader (or a male reader who is attuned to women's issues), for example, might become aware of aspects of a biblical text's portrayal of women that are often missed in a male-dominated society. **Feminist biblical criticism**[15] evaluates the text from a particular perspective—namely, that women are equal to men and should not be discriminated against or limited to certain social roles. Some biblical authors are praised because their books contain passages, ideas, or characters that are "liberating" for women or assert women's equality to men. Other biblical texts are critiqued for ignoring women, constraining their freedom, or insisting they remain subordinate to men.

The Gospel of Luke, for example, is a favorite of many feminist biblical critics because it shows Jesus having women followers who played crucial roles in his ministry (Luke 8:1–3), as well as defending a woman's right to receive an education and insisting women are not limited to servile, domestic roles (Luke 10:38–42). By contrast, Paul has been disparaged by many feminist critics for asserting that women must be silent in church and are not allowed to address or have authority over men (1 Cor. 14:33b–35). Feminist biblical criticism will be explored at greater length and applied to particular New Testament texts in chapters 11, 17, 18, and 22.

The conviction that women are equal to men and every effort should be made to help women realize their potential is an ideological perspective, although the term "ideological" is not used pejoratively here. Hence feminist biblical criticism is a kind of **ideological criticism**. Other common ideological approaches include examining the Bible through the lens of Marxism, black liberation theology, and postcolonial theory.[16] These approaches are discussed in greater detail in chapter 22.

---

15. The earliest attempt at feminist biblical criticism, although it was not called that at the time, involved the work of famous suffragist Elizabeth Cady Stanton and her committee of commenters in *The Woman's Bible* (1895 and 1898). Prominent recent practitioners of this method include Phyllis Trible, Elisabeth Schüssler Fiorenza, Mary Ann Tolbert, Elizabeth Struthers Malbon, and Janice Capel Anderson.

16. For a good demonstration of the variety of ideological criticisms, see Janice Capel Anderson and Stephen Moore, eds., *Mark and Method: New Approaches in Biblical Studies* (Minneapolis: Fortress, 2008), and Fernando F. Segovia and Mary Ann Tolbert, *Reading from This Place* (Minneapolis: Fortress, 1995).

Key Terms

scribes
variant readings
textual criticism
autograph
internal evidence
principle of the more difficult
   reading

historical criticism
oral tradition
source criticism
form criticism
tradition
redaction
redaction criticism

literary criticism
narrative
Christology
low Christology
high Christology
feminist biblical criticism
ideological criticism

Review Questions

1. What basic question or questions is each cluster of methods of biblical criticism attempting to answer?

2. Why do English translations of the Bible differ so much from one another?

3. How does the controversy over the ending of the Gospel of Mark illustrate the theory and practice of textual criticism?

4. What reasons have been given for undertaking historical investigations of the events recounted in biblical texts? Why might some readers *not* assume that these accounts are 100 percent reliable?

5. Source criticism and form criticism each attempt to discover earlier versions of the stories found in the Gospels. What motivates scholars to undertake this work? How do these two methods differ even as they attempt to achieve the same overarching goal?

6. Those methods that focus on determining the meaning of the Gospels differ from one another in (1) how they conceptualize the evangelists, and (2) what they identify as the keys to unlocking the meaning of the text. Explain in turn how (a) redaction criticism, (b) literary criticism, (c) New Testament theology, and (d) ideological criticism address these issues. How does each method justify its particular focus?

Discussion Questions

1. What questions does the uncertainty about the text and translation of the New Testament raise for people who profess that the Bible is the inerrant word of God?

2. Each of the methods described in this chapter are extremely important to somebody, whether that group includes only a small number of scholars or general readers with all kinds of perspectives. However, do any of the methods presented in this chapter seem to you to be illegitimate or not worth pursuing? If so, why?

Bibliography and Suggestions for Further Study

(Books and websites that are accessible for general undergraduates are marked with an asterisk; other sources listed are appropriate for advanced students.)

Anderson, Janice Capel, and Stephen Moore, eds. *Mark and Method: New Approaches in Biblical Studies*. Minneapolis: Fortress, 2008.

Bultmann, Rudolf. *Theology of the New Testament.* New York: Scribner, 1965.

Ehrman, Bart. *The Orthodox Corruption of Scripture: The Effect of Early Christological Controversies on the Text of the New Testament.* Updated and with a new afterword. New York: Oxford University Press, 2011.

*McKnight, Edgar V. *What Is Form Criticism?* Eugene, OR: Wipf and Stock, 1997.

Metzger, Bruce. *The Text of the New Testament: Its Transmission, Corruption, and Restoration.* New York: Oxford University Press, 1968; 1992.

*Perrin, Norman. *What Is Redaction Criticism?* Philadelphia: Fortress, 1969.

*Perrin, Norman, Dennis C. Duling, and Robert L. Ferm. *The New Testament: An Introduction.* New York: Harcourt Brace Jovanovich, 1982.

Segovia, Fernando F., and Mary Ann Tolbert. *Reading from This Place.* Minneapolis: Fortress, 1995.

Tolbert, Mary Ann. *Sowing the Gospel: Mark's World in Literary-Historical Perspective.* Minneapolis: Fortress, 1989.

The Gospel of Mark

The Gospel of Mark, is widely believed to be the oldest of the four Gospels (late 60s to 70 CE). In this chapter **literary criticism** (introduced in chapter 7) will be used to study the Gospel of Mark. Literary criticism examines the Gospels as narratives, in much the same way that literary critics analyze short stories, novels, and other kinds of nonreligious literature with a narrative structure. The technique basically asks what the author was trying to communicate to his audience by telling the story as he did. Determining what a Gospel means as a narrative involves understanding its plot structure, characterization, and use of allusion, foreshadowing, and other literary techniques.

Aristotle argued that all plots have three parts: the beginning, the middle, and the end. The terms that literary critics use for these three essential parts are the exposition, the complication, and the climax. The **exposition**, or beginning of a story, introduces the main characters and establishes their identities, furnishes the setting, and generally lays out the assumptions from which the story will proceed. In the **complication**, an element of conflict is introduced. This conflict creates dramatic tension, which increases as the story progresses. One common type of plot is the "quest of the hero"; in the complication of such a plot the hero encounters obstacles and seeks to overcome them. The **climax** is the moment of highest tension, where the conflict is resolved in some decisive way.

Understanding a story, then, means being able to locate the exposition, identifying who the major characters are and how their identities are established. It means knowing what conflict drives the plot forward, who the conflict involves, and how it develops through the middle of the story. And it means knowing how the conflict is resolved in the climax of the story. In the Gospel of Mark, the main conflict is between Jesus and the Jewish authorities who oppose him. Their opposition grows as the Gospel progresses and culminates in the crucifixion, which comes during the climax of the Gospel.

This chapter's analysis of the Gospel of Mark follows the three-part structure of the story: the beginning or exposition (roughly Mark 1), the middle or complication (Mark 2–13), and the end, the climax (Mark 14–16). Along the way, other literary features of the text will be revealed.

Understanding the Plot of the Gospel of Mark

The Gospel of Mark opens with this line: "The beginning of the good news of Jesus Christ, the Son of God." With this announcement, the author of the Gospel is introducing his main character, Jesus, and establishing his identity. He is the "Christ," a word meaning "anointed one." In ancient Judaism, persons were anointed with oil when they were chosen for some significant leadership position. Jesus is also identified as "the Son of God." Introducing the main characters and establishing their identities is the proper function of a plot's exposition. Therefore, those studying the Gospel of Mark through the lens of literary criticism should read its opening chapter in this light.

The Exposition

The characters introduced in the first part of the story include Jesus, John the Baptist, God, Satan, the first disciples, the Jewish people of Galilee (some of whom are possessed by demons or afflicted with various ailments), and the Jewish authorities. Of these characters, the most important by far is Jesus. Consequently, a literary analysis of the exposition should begin with Jesus, and then move on to the other minor characters.

Introducing Jesus

Having identified Jesus as the Christ (or "Messiah," see chapter 4) and the Son of God, the author of Mark gradually reveals what he means by these terms and supplies evidence to support each claim. This evidence can be grouped into two categories: the words and deeds of Jesus himself, and the **testimony** offered on his behalf by others. The Gospel begins with the latter type of evidence by describing the testimony of (1) a prophet, who points to Jesus as the coming Messiah; (2) God, who identifies Jesus as his Son; and (3) Satan and his demons, who acknowledge Jesus as the "Holy One of God."

Testimony in Support of Jesus' Identity. The testimony of John the Baptist (Mark 1:2–8) merits close analysis. John never directly identifies Jesus as the Messiah, but John's appearance, words, and actions strongly imply as much.

The author establishes John's reliability as a witness by presenting him as a holy man whose preaching was foretold by the prophet Isaiah

(Mark 1:2–3). John preaches a baptism of repentance for the forgiveness of sins, and the whole Judean countryside and all the people of Jerusalem went out to him and were baptized in the Jordan River, confessing their sins (vv. 4–5). Although the author of the Gospel of Mark does not use the word *prophet* to describe John, it is clear John fits into the mold of holy men from Israel's past. The plot detail about the overwhelming popular response to John suggests he was widely acknowledged as a prophet. Hence if John were to testify to Jesus' identity, his words should, the author implies, carry a certain weight.

Mark then states John "was clothed with camel's hair, with a leather belt around his waist, and he ate locusts and wild honey" (Mark 1:6). At first these details seem unnecessary. But Mark's description recalls the prophet **Elijah** (see 2 Kings 1:8). Many Jews believed that Elijah, who did not die but was taken up to heaven in a fiery chariot (see 2 Kings 2:11), would return to earth and prepare people for the coming of the Messiah: "Lo, I will send you the prophet Elijah before the great and terrible day of the LORD comes. He will turn the hearts of parents to their children and the hearts of children to their parents" (Mal. 4:5–6).

Clearly, Mark 1:6 is an **allusion**, a literary technique in which an author refers to something found in a previous book so that readers will recall the earlier text and connect it with the present one. In this case, Mark encourages readers to recall how Elijah dressed and conducted himself, that he did not die as other mortals do, and that it was predicted that he would return just prior to the "great and terrible day of the LORD" to warn people and prepare them. If one understands the allusion, it becomes clear what Mark is saying: John the Baptist *is* Elijah. Just as prophecy foretold regarding the return of Elijah, John warns people someone far greater than himself is coming. He prepares people by calling them to repent of their sins and be baptized, so

The Meaning of the Title "Son of God"

The term *Son of God* was familiar to both Jews and Gentiles of the first century CE. In the Gentile world, the Roman emperors sometimes referred to themselves as sons of God. Caesar Augustus, in particular, capitalized on the popularity of his uncle and adoptive father Julius Caesar, who had been divinized by the Senate following his death, by referring to himself as *divi filius*. Among Jews, the phrase "son of God" would have been known to readers of the Hebrew Bible. In Genesis 6:1–6, the "sons of God" are subordinate divine beings, apparently akin to angels, who engage in sexual intercourse with human women, producing a race of giants. In Psalm 2:7, the speaker reports that God said to him, "You are my son; today I have begotten you." In 2 Samuel 7:14-15, God promises David that he will raise up his offspring and establish an everlasting kingdom for him. "I will be a father to him," God says, "and he shall be a son to me." Throughout the Old Testament, there is also a sense that all human beings are children of God.

While early Christians, including the author of Mark, may have drawn upon these Roman and Jewish concepts, it is clear the Gospel does not view Jesus as *a* son of God but insists instead that Jesus had a *unique* relationship with God. Twice God's voice identifies Jesus as his "Beloved" Son (Mark 1:11; 9:7), and in each case it is implied this distinction is given to Jesus alone. Jesus prays to God using the intimate Aramaic term for father, *Abba* (14:36), a practice with no precedent in Judaism. In some ways, then, this term places Jesus on a par with God. Jesus' sonship enables him to do things only God can do, such as forgive sins (2:1-12).

However, one must be cautious in assuming that Mark uses this term to mean what later, explicitly Trinitarian, Christians would mean when they refer to Jesus as "God the Son." Mark includes no infancy narrative in which Jesus is born to a virgin, which leaves open the possibility that God was *making* Jesus his son at his baptism, as the adoptionists held (or as Psalm 2:7 suggests in the phrase "Today I have begotten you"). In Mark 10:18 Jesus seems to deny he could be "good" in the same way God is good, and in 13:32 Jesus confesses there are things known to the Father that are hidden from the Son. So, while the Gospel suggests that "Son of God" is a unique and highly significant designation, use of the phrase does not necessarily mean that the author believed Jesus was fully divine.

they can face messianic judgment with a clean slate. If John the Baptist is not just any prophet but is Elijah himself, his testimony about Jesus becomes much more powerful.

Next, in the baptism of Jesus (Mark 1:9–11), the testimony of Jesus' divine sonship comes not from a prophet, but from God. In Mark's recounting, a voice comes from the clouds (that is, the voice of God) and says, "You are my Son, the Beloved, with you I am well pleased." In other words, Mark depicts God identifying Jesus as his Son. This pattern of testimony continues throughout the exposition, with the demons indicating they too recognize Jesus as God's Son. "I know who you are, the Holy One of God," says the unclean spirit that Jesus casts out of a man during Jesus' first public appearance at the synagogue in Capernaum (1:20–28). Later the narrator notes Jesus would not permit demons to speak "because they knew him" (1:35).

The presentation of testimony in support of Jesus' identity continues beyond the exposition. In Mark 8:29 Peter is the first human being to correctly identify Jesus as "the Messiah," although Mark hints that Peter might not fully understand the meaning of his own words. No human being attests to the other part of Jesus' identity—that he is the "Son of God"—until the end of the Gospel. After seeing how nobly Jesus died on the cross, a Roman centurion (officer) finally proclaims, "Truly this was God's Son" (15:39). Although supernatural beings, or people with special access to the divine (like prophets), seem to be able to grasp Jesus' identity rather easily, Mark suggests it is more difficult for ordinary human beings, and this difficulty forms the heart of the conflict around which the plot of the Gospel of Mark revolves.

The Words and Deeds of Jesus. The second type of evidence Mark uses to support his claims about Jesus' identity is Jesus' own words and actions. Mark portrays Jesus as proving he is the Son of God in part by his supernatural deeds, such as performing exorcisms and healings. He commands unclean spirits to depart the human bodies they possess, and the demons must comply (e.g., Mark 1:21–28). He is able to cure various illnesses, such as leprosy (1:40–45) and fever (1:29–31). These healings and exorcisms also demonstrate Jesus' compassion. Jesus helps these people because he knows their suffering and feels pity for them (1:41). Mark contrasts Jesus to some of the other religious authorities of his day; instead of scolding or denigrating the less fortunate, Jesus raises them up and treats them with human dignity. In return, the crowds respond enthusiastically to Jesus, who taught them "as one having authority, and not as the scribes" (1:22).

Introducing the Minor Characters

The many other characters in the Gospel of Mark pale in significance next to Jesus, but each has a crucial role to play in the plot. Broadly speaking, the conflict revolves around

Jesus' struggle to get people to "repent, and believe in the good news" (Mark 1:15). While some people respond to Jesus with faith, others resist, misunderstand, and reject him. Most of the individual scenes or episodes in the Gospel fall into one of three types: (1) controversy stories, (2) healings and exorcisms, and (3) teachings and nature miracles. Controversy stories portray Jesus interacting with characters who reject him and seek to discredit or destroy him, namely the Jewish authorities.[1] Healings and exorcisms depict Jesus interacting with characters who are sick or possessed. Teachings and nature miracles show Jesus interacting primarily with his followers, especially his inner circle of twelve disciples (3:13–19). Each of these groups of characters is introduced or alluded to in the exposition, the first chapter of Mark.

The first to appear are some of Jesus' disciples (Mark 1:16–20). In this episode, Jesus calls Simon, Andrew, James, and John to follow him and assist in his ministry, and they respond enthusiastically. They show great commitment to Jesus, despite barely knowing him, by their apparent willingness to quit their jobs and abandon their families to follow him. They are fishermen, and they leave behind the tools of their trade, their boats and nets. James and John even leave their father, Zebedee, alone in the boat to fend for himself. In another context, this quick decision might seem rash or imprudent, but the Gospel of Mark has already identified Jesus as the Messiah and the Son of God, so the disciples' response here is presented as praiseworthy rather than blameworthy. The disciples make a very positive first impression, showing a great deal of faith in Jesus "immediately" (1:18, 20). Unfortunately, they are not able to sustain this level of faith as the Gospel progresses.

---

1. Referring to the religious authorities as "Jewish" is not meant to suggest that Jesus is being opposed by persons of a religion different from his own. Mark's Jesus is clearly a Jewish prophet and reformer who was opposed by the religious establishment of his time. The best shorthand for that establishment is "the Jewish authorities."

The Jewish authorities make no direct appearance in Mark 1, although they are mentioned by others. When Jesus teaches in the synagogue (1:21–28), people respond positively to him and say he teaches "as one having authority, not as the scribes" (1:22). This plot detail anticipates that the scribes (along with other Jewish authorities, the Pharisees and the chief priests) will become Jesus' main opponents in the Gospel, and it also foreshadows the basis of their opposition. They are presented here as rivals to Jesus, as religious authorities upon whose "turf" Jesus appears to be encroaching. Jesus is doing their job, and by Mark's account he appears to be doing it better than them. Their response is to become jealous[2] of Jesus' popularity.

The third group of characters with whom Jesus interacts most regularly are people he heals. These are represented in the exposition by the leper (Mark 1:40–45). The leper may seem to be an unsympathetic character, because he disobeys Jesus' command to "say nothing to anyone" and instead proclaims openly what Jesus has done for him, with the result that Jesus becomes so well-known he can no longer travel freely. However, two countervailing pieces of evidence show him in a more positive light. First, the leper shows faith in Jesus by approaching him, kneeling before him (a sign of reverence), and expressing his trust in Jesus' ability to heal him. Second, Mark likely expects that his audience, knowing how miserable the life of a leper was, would attribute the leper's disobedience not to malice toward Jesus but rather to his enthusiasm and excitement getting the better of him. On balance, the leper is more likely intended as a sympathetic character than as an unsympathetic one. In fact, as the Gospel progresses, the people Jesus heals or cleanses of demons turn out to be the most consistently faithful group he encounters.

The Complication

The complication of a plot begins when an element of conflict appears in the story. This occurs in Mark 2:1–12, in which the scribes accuse Jesus of **blasphemy**. Blasphemy was a serious offense (punishable by death) in which one curses or slanders God, or puts oneself in God's place, claiming some divine prerogative for oneself. The scribes believe Jesus is guilty of blasphemy because of what he tells a paralytic in this story. After the paralyzed man's friends go to great lengths to bring him into Jesus' presence, Jesus declares, "Son, your sins are forgiven." The scribes reason that only God can forgive sins and conclude that Jesus' claim that he has authority to

José Luiz Bernardes Ribeiro / Wikimedia Commons / Jesus healing the paralytic in Cafarnaum - Sant'Apollinare Nuovo - Ravenna 2016. jpg / CC BY-SA 4.0

This mosaic from the Basilica of Saint Apollinare near Ravenna illustrates Mark 2:1–12, in which Jesus heals a paralytic after declaring his sins forgiven. The scribes accuse Jesus of blasphemy for claiming the authority to forgive sins.

---

2. The "jealousy" of the Jewish authorities toward Jesus is not stated explicitly in the early part of the Gospel, but it is implied at a number of points and then confirmed by Pilate's words in Mark 15:10.

forgive sins is blasphemous. Jesus has put himself in God's place. Jesus perceives their thinking and poses a challenge to them: "Which is easier, to say to the paralytic, 'Your sins are forgiven,' or to say, 'Stand up and take your mat and walk'?" Jesus is suggesting that if he is able to cure the man's paralysis, then this should demonstrate he has authority to forgive sins. Jesus then tells the man to pick up his mat and walk, and the man does, cured of his paralysis. After this, "All were amazed and glorified God, saying, 'We have never seen anything like this!'" (2:12).

Despite this demonstration of power, the scribes and Pharisees are not convinced that Jesus' miracle proves he has authority to forgive sins. They neither gain faith in Jesus nor retract their accusation of blasphemy. Instead, they oppose Jesus more vigorously. Thus the Jewish authorities suffer from what the Gospel will later term "hardness of heart" (see 3:5). This refers to a stubborn refusal to allow oneself to be affected by what should be clear and convincing

evidence—in this case, Jesus' words and actions. As the Gospel unfolds, Jesus repeatedly heals in the presence of the scribes and Pharisees, but this has no effect on them. This depiction of their staunch unbelief suggests that, in the author's telling, there is nothing Jesus could have done to persuade his opponents within the religious establishment. They have made up their minds against Jesus and cannot be moved.

From this point on the conflict between Jesus and the Jewish authorities only escalates. The scribes and Pharisees begin to stalk Jesus—following him and watching his every move—hoping he will make a mistake so they can pounce on him with an accusation that will discredit him with the crowds. They make three such attempts in Mark 2, but each time Jesus effectively refutes their accusations. The first accusation is that Jesus eats with tax collectors, a group so notorious at the time that the Jewish authorities apparently believed merely pointing out Jesus' association with them would be enough

Why Did People Hate Tax Collectors So Much?

The near universal hatred of tax collectors is comprehensible only if one understands (1) the nature of the Roman tax system and its propensity for corruption, and (2) Jewish resentment of Roman rule. Some taxes were collected directly by the Roman government, but others were contracted out to private citizens. These tax farmers would prepay the Romans a set amount for the right to collect taxes or tolls in a particular area, with the understanding they would keep as profit whatever they collected beyond the required sum. This gave tax collectors an incentive to overcharge people for their taxes, sometimes grossly so, to enrich

themselves. Tax collectors appeared to be lining their pockets at the expense of poor people struggling to make ends meet.[3]

In Jewish territories, it was often Jews who held the contracts to collect the taxes. These Jews were seen as traitors—selfish individuals who collaborated with the hated Romans in oppressing their own people. Moreover, their constant contact with their Gentile employers also made them unclean. It is not surprising, then, that tax collectors were among the most unpopular people in Jewish society, and people were shocked Jesus would associate with them.

3. See John R. Donahue, "Tax Collectors," in *The Anchor Bible Dictionary*, ed. David Noel Freedman (New York: Doubleday, 1992), 6:337–38.

to discredit him. Jesus' response is beautiful in its simplicity: "Those who are well have no need of a physician, but those who are sick; I have come to call not the righteous but sinners" (2:17). Jesus admits that tax collectors are sinners, but that is precisely why he needs to associate with them—in hopes of persuading them of their wrongdoing and calling them to repentance. The strategy of the Pharisees seems to have involved shunning or ostracizing notorious sinners. Jesus suggests that such a strategy is wrong-headed, like a doctor who claims he wants to improve the public health, but shuns sick people. By contrast, there is evidence that Jesus' approach is working. He has converted one tax collector (Levi) and made him a disciple (2:14). In Mark's telling, Jesus' defense silences the Pharisees; he wins the argument and retains his following.

The same pattern repeats itself in the remaining controversy stories in Mark 2. In 2:18, the Pharisees accuse Jesus of allowing his disciples to be lax in **piety**. Pious behavior involves acts thought to please God, such as praying, fasting, giving alms (donating money to the poor), and making pilgrimages. In this instance, the Pharisees complain Jesus' disciples are impious because they do not fast. In his reply, Jesus does not disdain religious observance but suggests the need for it depends on the circumstances. There is a time for fasting and a time for feasting, and either can be inappropriate if the circumstances do not call for it. It would be the height of rudeness to abstain from food and drink at a wedding feast, even if one claimed to be doing so out of religious conviction.

In Mark 2:23–28 the Pharisees observe Jesus' disciples plucking heads of grain on the Sabbath and accuse them of breaking the law.

Sabbath regulations prohibited any kind of work from sundown Friday to sundown Saturday, and harvesting (gathering grain, as the disciples are doing) counted as work. In response, Jesus first cites a biblical passage in which David and his men are in extreme need of food and end up entering the Temple and eating the "bread of the Presence," which is not lawful for anyone but priests to eat. David and his men break the law, but they are not punished by God for this, because they have a good excuse: they are famished. By implication, then, Jesus is suggesting his disciples should be allowed to pluck heads of grain on the Sabbath if they are hungry and in need of food. It would be difficult for the scribes and Pharisees, with their great reverence for the Torah, to deny that Jesus has a point.

Moreover, Jesus goes on to make a broader point about the Sabbath (and perhaps the law generally): "The sabbath was made for humankind, and not humankind for the sabbath" (Mark 2:27). God did not create human beings so they could observe the Sabbath. He created the Sabbath so it could serve human beings, giving them time to rest and to worship. It was not designed to harm people. Jesus is saying that if the Pharisees believe that God would rather people go hungry than violate the Sabbath, they are distorting the meaning and purpose of the Sabbath. A slavish adherence to law when circumstances clearly indicate the need for an exception is called **legalism**. Mark's story implies that the Pharisees' position on the Sabbath is legalistic.[4] Finding the time and gathering the resources needed to follow the many rules and regulations imposed by religious authorities was difficult for people who were poor and starving. In this episode and many that follow, Jesus seems to be a champion of the

---

4. Whether this characterization of the Pharisees as rigid and unbending is fair or accurate is a matter of considerable dispute. However, in a literary critical analysis of the Gospels the question is not whether the author's depiction of certain characters or events is historically accurate. It is only to determine how the author *portrays* things. Mark portrays the Pharisees as legalistic; whether they were so in reality is a completely separate issue.

common person, especially in his insistence that the elites who claim to speak for God are misrepresenting God's will in some of their more onerous demands (see also 7:1–20).

Once again Jesus' argument silences his opponents, and their attempts to observe him making a critical error seem to have been unsuccessful. After this failure, Mark hints that they manufacture a situation in which Jesus appears to have no choice but to make a mistake. The trap is sprung when Jesus enters a synagogue on the Sabbath and encounters a man with a withered hand (Mark 3:1–6). The Pharisees watch Jesus closely, "so that they might accuse him" (3:2). This language is telling, because it reveals the Pharisees are not open-minded about Jesus. They are not wondering if Jesus will do the right thing, and willing to praise him if he does; rather, they are looking for an excuse to accuse him of something. Jesus has two choices here. If he heals the man, the Pharisees can accuse him of "working" on the Sabbath. If Jesus does not heal the man, they can accuse him of lacking the power or compassion to do so.

That the man's affliction is a withered hand is significant. Although the Pharisees were strict about what was allowed on the Sabbath, they allowed some exceptions. One could perform religious duties (such as sacrifices or circumcisions) on the Sabbath, and one could heal on the Sabbath if it was a life-threatening situation.[5] A physician who was presented with a minor complaint on the Sabbath could reasonably tell the person to come back the next day for treatment. The man with the withered hand was not dying and could presumably wait until the next day. So if Jesus healed the man he would be doing a prohibited kind of work.

Jesus protests this interpretation by asking, "Is it lawful to do good or to do harm on the sabbath, to save life or to kill?" It was understood that it was permissible to save life on the Sabbath, and that it was not permissible to kill. By analogy, then, Jesus wonders whether it should not be permissible to do any kind of good deed on the Sabbath, and whether what should be prohibited is only doing "harm." Jesus proposes to expand the exceptions to the rule against working on the Sabbath, so that he can lawfully cure the man with the withered hand.

The scribes and Pharisees have nothing to say in response. This is surprising, given that they spent their time studying the Torah and arguing about its applicability to different situations. They lived for this kind of argument, but in Mark's telling of this story they do not seem to want any part of a debate with Jesus.

Presumably the author wants his readers to understand that the scribes and Pharisees fear losing another debate with Jesus. If Jesus won the debate, and then cured the man with a withered hand, their trap would backfire: Jesus' reputation would remain intact, and he would probably be more popular than ever. Jesus, angered by their silence and grieved at their "hardness of heart" (Mark 3:5), heals the man and awaits their verdict.

Their reaction is highly significant: "The Pharisees went out and immediately conspired with the Herodians against him, how to destroy him" (Mark 3:6). That the Pharisees were willing to ally themselves with the hated Herodians, the Jewish kings (and their supporters) who ruled on behalf of the Romans, reveals the depth of their desire to eliminate their rival. Moreover, their stated wish to "destroy" (i.e., kill) Jesus would strike even the strictest observers of the Torah as excessive. A single violation of the Sabbath did not ordinarily incur the death penalty. The punishment does not fit the crime. Mark depicts the Jewish authorities as simply looking for a pretext to rid themselves of Jesus. The opposition of the scribes and Pharisees to Jesus is not really about

---

5. Gerhard F. Hasel, "Sabbath," in *Anchor Bible Dictionary,* ed. Freedman, 5:852–56.

the observance of the law but rather stems from jealousy of Jesus and his popularity.

A final indication that Mark portrays their true motivation as something other than a sincere concern for the law is that the scribes and Pharisees went out to conspire with the Herodians "*immediately.*" This means they took this action on the Sabbath.[6] Now if healing a man counts as work, then certainly conspiring to kill a man also counts as work. In effect, the Pharisees themselves violate the Sabbath in this passage. This shows that, at least in Mark's depiction, they do not really care about the law. The law is simply a means to an end. It provides them with the grounds for eliminating Jesus, perceived as a threat to their positions of power and privilege.

In Mark's portrayal, Jesus staves off the Jewish authorities seeking his death for some time, in part by using the messianic secret, and in part by avoiding a direct confrontation with the most powerful group within Judaism—the Sadducees—until he arrives in Jerusalem in Mark 11. Prior to this point, there are additional skirmishes between Jesus and the scribes and Pharisees. At one point Jesus accuses them of "teaching human precepts as doctrines," that is, of inventing rules for their benefit that have no divine origin (Mark 7:1–20). This accusation undercuts the essence of the Pharisees' identity: their goal was the interpretation and application of the Law of Moses in accord with God's will. Not only does Jesus dispute their traditions involving the interpretation

The Messianic Secret

The "**messianic secret**" is a **motif** (i.e., a recurring literary pattern) in the Gospel of Mark, in which Jesus tells those he has healed and demons who know who he is not to say anything about him. This motif is repeated three times in Mark 1 (in verses 25, 34, and 44), and several times thereafter (3:12; 5:43; 8:30).

Why would Jesus not want the news of his identity and healing powers to spread? This seems counter-intuitive, and requires explanation. Many highly speculative theories have been offered as to why (or whether) the historical Jesus might have tried to keep his messianic identity a secret.[7] Literary critics, however, seek only to explain why it would

make sense *in Mark's story* for the character of Jesus to behave in this way, and hence would seek an explanation that is not speculative but has textual evidence behind it.

Almost invariably, Jesus' desire for secrecy is accompanied by some reference to the spread of his fame.[8] When the leper disobeys his command to keep silent, Jesus is mobbed so badly he can no longer enter a town openly (Mark 1:45). The crowds in Capernaum are such that the friends of the paralytic go to the extreme of taking the roof off of a house to lower him down to see Jesus (2:4). At one point Jesus has to tell his disciples to prepare an escape route (by sea) when

continued

---

6. See Mary Ann Tolbert, *Sowing the Gospel: Mark's World in Literary-Historical Perspective* (Minneapolis: Fortress, 1989), 135.

7. For example, William Wrede famously argued in his 1901 book *The Messianic Secret* that the author of the Gospel of Mark invented the messianic secret motif to explain the apparent dissonance created by early Christians' proclamation of Jesus as the Messiah after the resurrection, when neither Jesus nor his followers appear to have made such a claim during Jesus' earthly ministry. This theory involves some speculation on both ends, as it is not exactly certain (1) that Jesus was never identified as the Messiah during his ministry or (2) that later Christians like Mark were sufficiently bothered by the aforementioned dissonance that they would invent the sayings that comprise the messianic secret motif.

8. See Tolbert, *Sowing the Gospel*, 137–38.

The Messianic Secret *continued*

he is preaching, to escape being crushed to death by the crowds (3:9).

But a more significant motivation for keeping his fame from spreading out of control may have been the desire to ward off the murderous jealousy of the Jewish authorities, which appears to grow in lockstep with the rise in Jesus' popularity in the Gospel of Mark. Support for this theory can be found in the story of the Gerasene demoniac (Mark 5:1–20). After Jesus casts the "Legion" of demons out of this man and into a herd of pigs, the man begs Jesus that he might become one of his followers. But Jesus refuses him, and tells him instead to go home to his friends and tell them all that the Lord had done for him, and what mercy God had shown him. This is the opposite of the messianic secret; here Jesus tells the man to spread the word about him far and wide, instead of commanding silence and secrecy. Why lift the veil of secrecy here? In this episode Jesus is not in Jewish territory; he is in Gentile territory. Those in Mark's audience who were familiar with Palestinian geography and demography would have known this from the reference to the land of the Gerasenes or because the man spreads the

word about Jesus throughout the Decapolis, regions with a Gentile population.

There are many other theories about the messianic secret. Some say that Jesus did not want to become known primarily for his miracle-working, although this cannot account for Jesus' commands to secrecy that do not involve his miracles. Others argue that Jesus' identity as a *suffering* Messiah was so surprising and unexpected–especially among Jews whose messianic expectations tended toward a powerful and glorious figure–that Jesus could not expect to be understood as such during his lifetime. The disciples' confused reactions to Jesus' passion predictions seem to bear this out. Jesus' resurrection plays a critical part in affirming the concept of a suffering Messiah, because despite his ignominious and shameful death, Jesus is vindicated by God through the resurrection and exalted from the lowest status of crucified criminal to the highest position in heaven. If Jesus could not be truly seen as a suffering Messiah until after his resurrection, it might explain why he tells his disciples after the Transfiguration "to tell no one about what they had seen, until after the Son of Man had risen from the dead" (Mark 9:9).[9]

of the law, he even overturns part of the Law of Moses. Jesus says that divorce, which was permissible under Jewish law, is contrary to the will of God. He does not deny that God told Moses that divorce was acceptable, but he claims that God did so only because of Israel's "hardness of heart" (10:1–12).

The conflict between Jesus and the Jewish authorities takes a decisive turn in Jerusalem, when Jesus cleanses the Temple (Mark 11:15–19). Jesus enters the Temple and drives out the moneychangers and those who are buying and selling, and proclaims, "Is it not written, 'My house shall be called a house of prayer for all the nations'?

9. N. T. Wright writes, "It was a claim to a Messiahship which redefined itself around Jesus' own kingdom-agenda, picking up several strands available within popular messianic expectation but weaving them into a striking new pattern, corresponding to none of the options canvassed by others at the time. Jesus' style of Messiahship was sufficiently similar to those in the public mind to get him executed, and for his first followers to see his resurrection as a reaffirmation of him as Messiah, not as something quite different. But it was sufficiently dissimilar to mean that everyone, from his closest followers through to the chief priests, misinterpreted at least to some extent what he was really getting at; and that the movement which did come to birth after his resurrection, though calling itself messianic, cherished agendas and adopted lifestyles quite unlike those of other movements with the same label. If Jesus was a Messiah, he was a Messiah with great difference"; N. T. Wright, *Jesus and the Victory of God*, Christian Origins and the Question of God 2 (Minneapolis: Fortress, 1997), 539.

But you have made it a den of robbers" (11:17). These words and deeds of Jesus infuriate the chief priests, who immediately seek to arrest and kill Jesus and are prevented from doing so only by Jesus' popularity with the crowds. It is implied that these crowds would rally to Jesus' support if his opponents attempted to apprehend him. Nonetheless, Jesus' death is arranged within a week of the cleansing of the Temple.

A Subplot: Jesus' Conflict with the Disciples

Jesus' clash with Jewish authorities is not the only conflict in the Gospel of Mark. Jesus also struggles with his own disciples, who continually exhibit fear, misunderstanding, selfishness, and doubt. Readers today who are accustomed to think of Jesus' apostles as heroes of the faith may be surprised to find Mark depicts these characters negatively.

In Mark 4:35–41, the disciples grow frightened as a great windstorm arises, and their boat is swamped. Jesus calms the storm and then asks, "Why are you afraid? Have you still no faith?" (4:40). The present-tense verb indicates the disciples did not cease being afraid once the storm was calmed. Their fear is now oriented toward Jesus, and Jesus perceives this and regards it as a sign of their lack of faith. In some ways, Jesus' two questions in 4:40 represent a challenge as well as a rebuke. Jesus is asking his disciples to overcome their fear and believe in him. Their response to Jesus' questions is dismaying. A literal translation of this response is: "They feared a great fear" (4:41). Jesus has called them to show faith and not be afraid, and in response "they were terrified" (NIV), or "more afraid than ever" (CEV).

Subsequent events prove the disciples' lack of faith is chronic. In Mark 6 the disciples have difficulty with Jesus' ability to feed thousands of people with only a few loaves of bread and fish. When Jesus tells his disciples to feed the hungry crowds, they skeptically ask, "Are we to go and buy two hundred denarii worth of bread and give it to them to eat?" (Mark 6:37). Jesus takes the five loaves and two fish that they have and manages to feed five thousand people, with twelve baskets full of broken pieces left over.

While the disciples' inability to understand Jesus' ability to multiply loaves and fishes is understandable, given he had never done so before, that they continue to have trouble grasping this is harder to comprehend. When Jesus walks on water, the disciples are terrified, and the narrator reveals, "They did not understand about the loaves, but their hearts were hardened" (Mark 6:52). In Mark 8, there is once again a huge crowd with nothing to eat, and Jesus feels compassion for them. Again he asks his disciples to feed the people, and they respond, "How can one feed these people with bread here in the desert?" (8:4). That Jesus had previously fed five thousand people with five loaves and two fish apparently did not occur to the disciples. The disciples' apparent forgetfulness becomes even more astounding in the next episode (8:14–21), when the disciples and Jesus get into a boat. The disciples forget to bring bread, and have only one loaf with them. Jesus tells his disciples, "Beware of the yeast of the Pharisees and the yeast of Herod." The disciples respond, "It is because we have no bread." Jesus is obviously using yeast as a metaphor for the potential of the ideology of the Pharisees and Herod to grow and multiply, but the disciples take Jesus literally and think he is talking about real yeast, which is found in bread, and this prompts them to exclaim that they have forgotten to bring (sufficient) bread for all of them. When Jesus hears their response, he challenges them, asking, "Why are you talking about having no bread? Do you still not perceive or understand? Are your hearts hardened? Do you have eyes, and fail to see? Do you have ears, and fail to hear?" (8:17–18). He reminds them how he fed five thousand with five loaves and fed four thousand with seven loaves. Why then would they think he could not feed the handful of people in the boat with one loaf? Jesus concludes by asking his disciples, "Do you not yet understand?" The disciples are silent, giving the impression that they remain in the dark.

If the disciples lack faith in Jesus, why do they follow him? The Gospel of Mark suggests they are motivated by a desire for fame, power, greatness, and glory. After Peter correctly identifies Jesus as "the Messiah" (Mark 8:29), Jesus explains that he is going to suffer and die, and then rise again. Peter immediately rebukes Jesus. A messiah who suffers and dies is apparently not what Peter expected when he began following Jesus. Jesus replies that Peter is setting his mind "not on divine things but on human things" (8:33).

That these "human things" are fame, power, greatness, and glory is proven by the disciples' subsequent words and actions. At one point Jesus catches the disciples arguing with each other and demands to know the source of their disagreement. "But they were silent, for on the way they had argued with one another who was the greatest" (Mark 9:34). In 9:38–41, the disciple John tells Jesus he found someone casting out demons in Jesus' name, and so he told the man to stop, because "he was not following us." His disciples apparently feel casting out demons is *their* job, and they are entitled to all the glory that comes with this.

By the time James and John take Jesus aside and ask, "Grant us to sit, one at your right hand and one at your left, in your glory" (Mark 10:37), there is little question they are speaking of the

earthly kingdom they expect Jesus to claim and their hope to be appointed his top two lieutenants. Jesus has repeatedly told his disciples he is not a political messiah, and that he will not be raising an army and making himself king. His way is the way of the cross, of suffering and sacrifice, of service to others, and of laying down his life on behalf of others (8:34–35; 9:35; 10:42–45). However, in Mark's telling this message never seems to penetrate the hearts of the disciples, and as a result, they are unprepared for the persecution awaiting them in Jerusalem. When matters play out just as Jesus had predicted, the disciples crumble.

The subplot involving the disciples ends tragically when they fail Jesus in his hour of need. One disciple, Judas, betrays Jesus for money. Most of the others run away when Jesus is arrested: "All of them deserted him and fled" (Mark 14:50). Peter, who had sworn to remain true to Jesus even if it cost him his life, denies Jesus three times. When he realizes what he has done, Peter breaks down and weeps.

This is the last the reader sees of the disciples in the Gospel of Mark. As the section on textual criticism in chapter 7 indicates, most biblical scholars agree the Gospel of Mark originally ended with 16:8, where the women who discover the empty tomb "fled from the tomb, for terror and amazement had seized them, and they said nothing to anyone, for they were afraid." Jesus does not appear to his disciples after the resurrection, and there is no reconciliation between them.[10] In the other three Gospels (and in the

---

10. Some scholars, such as C. H. Turner and Rudolf Bultmann, have argued the Gospel did not originally end at 16:8 but went on to include resurrection appearances and a reconciliation between Jesus and the disciples. This ending, they believe, was somehow lost. Or perhaps the author was interrupted before completing his work. There are hints in the text that would lead one to anticipate a post-resurrection meeting between Jesus and his disciples (14:28; 16:7). Nevertheless, the arguments for a lost ending of Mark are not ultimately convincing. A number of scholars point out that the ambiguous, open-ended conclusion of the Gospel at 16:8 is both intelligible and quite in keeping with the author's sensibility. "Mark's story of Jesus becomes the story of his followers, and their story becomes the story of the readers. Whether they will follow or desert, believe or misunderstand, see him in Galilee or remain staring blindly into an empty tomb, depends on us. . . . Mark's narrative as we have it now ends as abruptly as it began. There was no introduction or background to Jesus' arrival, and none for his departure. No one knew where he came from; no one knows where he has gone; and not many understood him when he was here"; Richard Burridge, *Four Gospels, One Jesus? A Symbolic Reading* (Grand Rapids: Eerdmans, 2005), 64.

longer ending to Mark that was later added by scribes), Jesus does appear to his disciples, who show their faith in him and are entrusted with the leadership of the church. But this does not happen in Mark. The disciples fail Jesus and that is that.

The Climax

The endgame of the Gospel of Mark is revealed by Jesus in the parable of the Wicked Tenants (Mark 12:1–12). In this parable, a man plants a vineyard, provides it with a wall, a winepress, and a watchtower and then leaves the country and rents the vineyard to tenants. The tenants are supposed to give a share of the vineyard's produce to the owner as rent. However, the tenants refuse to pay their rent. The owner sends his servants to remind them of their obligation, but they ignore, beat up, and even kill these servants. The owner then sends his beloved son, thinking the tenants will respect him. However, the tenants recognize the son as the heir and resolve to kill him so that the vineyard will be theirs. They murder the son. Jesus then asks, "What then will the owner of the vineyard do? He will come and destroy the tenants and give the vineyard to others" (12:9).

This episode is an allegory, a kind of parable in which there are multiple points of comparison between the characters and events of the story and the reality of which the teller of the parable is truly speaking. The vineyard owner's "beloved son" compares to Jesus, who has been named with that phrase by God twice in the Gospel (Mark 1:9–11; 9:2–10). The owner symbolizes God, the vineyard signifies Israel, and the servants are the prophets. The wicked tenants represent the Jewish authorities. That the parable is directed at the leaders rather than the Jewish people as a whole is signaled by the fact that the Jewish authorities perceive that they are the target of Jesus' parable, but they cannot retaliate because the larger body of the Jewish people supports Jesus and will riot if Jesus is arrested (12:12).

Significantly, the tenants kill the beloved son knowing full well who he is. They do not mistake him for a servant or act out of ignorance. Given the symbolism of the parable, this suggests Jesus is telling the Jewish authorities he knows they are about to murder him, and they should know that when they do so it will be reckoned as the deliberate murder of the Son of God.

Now that the chief priests have joined the scribes and Pharisees in a conspiracy to kill Jesus,

Blaming the Jews for the Death of Jesus

Modern interpreters tend to shy away from the conclusion that the parable of the Wicked Tenants indicates that those Jews who conspired to kill Jesus did so in the full knowledge that he was the Messiah and Son of God. This conclusion, it is thought, would imply that "the Jews" (or some portion of them) are guilty of **deicide**, the murder of God. The accusation of deicide has motivated Christian persecution of Jews throughout history, including during the Holocaust, even though the historical truth is that the Romans

bore the primary responsibility for the death of Jesus (see chapter 21).

In the final analysis, it appears that Mark's narrative does blame the Jewish leaders for Jesus' death. Nevertheless, there is a huge and unjustifiable leap between Mark's condemnation of a specific group of first-century Jewish leaders and the centuries of Christian persecution of Jews that followed. Even if some Jews were involved in the way the Gospel of Mark suggests, that is no excuse for persecutions centuries later.

their only challenges are (1) to arrest Jesus without his supporters rioting in response (see Mark 14:1–2), and (2) getting the Romans to agree to kill Jesus for them, as the Jews in Judea did not ordinarily have the authority to execute criminals without Roman approval. The first problem is resolved by the corruption of one of Jesus' disciples, Judas. Judas reveals to the Jewish authorities Jesus' private place of prayer, the Garden of Gethsemane (14:10–11). The Temple police are able to arrest Jesus when there are no crowds present to cause an incident (14:43–52).

Jesus is then taken before the Sanhedrin, the Jewish court of law that the Romans allowed the Sadducees to maintain as part of their practice of giving conquered peoples a modicum of local control. The Gospel emphasizes that Jesus' trial (Mark 14:53–65) is a mockery of justice. The judges are biased against Jesus: they were "looking for testimony . . . to put him to death" (14:55). According to Jewish law (Deut. 19:15), they need two witnesses to testify to some wrongdoing on Jesus' part. The Jewish leaders compel people to testify falsely against Jesus, but their testimony does not agree. Apparently they cannot get their lies straight. Then the high priest, in desperation, switches tactics and seeks to get Jesus to implicate himself. At first Jesus refuses to answer his questions. Then the high priest asks Jesus, "Are you the Messiah, the Son of the Blessed One?" (14:61). Jesus answers, "I am." Immediately, the Sanhedrin convicts Jesus of blasphemy, of falsely claiming to be the Messiah and the Son of God, and they sentence him to death.

The Jewish authorities then face their second challenge, which is to get the Romans to agree to execute Jesus. The Romans, however, do not care about blasphemy against the Jewish God, so the Jewish authorities need to come up with a reason for killing Jesus that the Romans will take seriously. This is another sign from Mark that the accusations against Jesus are illegitimate. The new charge is that Jesus is advocating revolution against Rome (Mark 15:1–5). When they say Jesus claimed to be "the King of the Jews," they implicitly accuse him of treason or sedition, because the only way Jesus could become king is to throw off Roman rule. The Roman prefect of Judea, Pontius Pilate, is not fooled by this subterfuge. He sees that Jesus is innocent and that the Jewish authorities are only accusing him because they are jealous and fearful of his popularity (Mark 15:10). However, his attempt to have Jesus released backfires. Mark says that, at Passover time, the Romans had a practice of releasing one Jewish prisoner. The festival of Passover recalled the Exodus, in which the Jews' ancestors escaped bondage in Egypt; presumably the feast tended to awaken Jewish longing for freedom from the Romans, and the Romans resorted to the release of a prisoner as a way of calming Jewish resentment. Pilate seizes upon this already-scheduled grant of amnesty as an opportunity to release Jesus. So Pilate offers to release Jesus, but the people instead ask for the release of Barabbas, a man convicted of murder as part of an insurrection, and demand that Jesus be crucified. Pilate knows Jesus is innocent, but placates the crowd and consents to Jesus' execution.

Jesus is flogged and then forced to carry his cross to the place of execution. Apparently he needs assistance, because Simon of Cyrene is compelled to carry his cross for him part of the way. Jesus is nailed to the cross at nine o'clock in the morning on the Friday before Passover. Just before three o'clock Jesus cries out, "My God, my God! Why have you forsaken me?" (Mark 15:34). Then Jesus breathes his last. He is dead.

This appears to be an incontrovertible victory for the Jewish authorities. They have sought Jesus' death and now they have succeeded. However, things are not what they appear. The first sign of this is that the Roman centurion at the foot of the cross, impressed by Jesus' noble death, proclaims, "Truly this man was God's Son!" (Mark 15:39). In what follows, it becomes clear

Why Do the Crowds Call for Jesus' Death?

Up to Mark 15, the crowds have supported Jesus. What turns them against Jesus in his hour of need? Why do they call for his crucifixion when offered the choice between Jesus and the murderer Barabbas?

The literary answer is disappointment. Jesus does not turn out to be the messiah they hoped he would be. When Jesus enters Jerusalem, the people welcome him as a king. They cry, "Hosanna!" and lay palms in his path, a welcome used for none save the king (Mark 11:9). Jesus' disciples have earlier fallen prey to the false belief that Jesus is a political/military messiah, despite Jesus' protestations to the contrary. The common people seem to share this illusion.

By the time Jesus is presented to them alongside Barabbas, it is clear the people can no longer harbor such hopes. Jesus stands before them a beaten man, both literally and figuratively. Their support for Jesus turns to anger. Together with Jesus' longtime enemies, they mock him as he endures the crucifixion they called for so stridently (Mark 15:13-14). Indeed, their taunts reveal that they think anyone who claimed to be the messiah would not be suffering such an ignominious fate: "Those who passed by derided him, shaking their heads and saying, 'Aha! You who would destroy the temple and build it in three days, save yourself, and come down from the cross!' In the same way the chief priests, along with the scribes, were also mocking him among themselves and saying, 'He saved others; he cannot save himself. Let the Messiah, the King of Israel, come down from the cross now, so that we may see and believe'" (15:29-32).

that killing Jesus did not destroy him. On the third day after Jesus' death, several women go to visit the tomb where his body has been laid (16:1–8). They arrive to find the stone that sealed the tomb rolled away, and Jesus' body missing. A young man dressed in white tells the women that Jesus has risen from the dead, just as he had predicted. The women fail to deliver this message to the disciples as instructed, but the author of the Gospel clearly suggests Jesus' missing body, the testimony of the young man dressed in white, and Jesus' previous predictions are sufficient evidence that Jesus rose from the dead.

The news of Jesus' resurrection is only part of the reason the author of the Gospel of Mark can characterize his story as "good news" despite Jesus' being killed. The real promise of the Gospel is that justice will be done, that those who believe will be vindicated, and those who doubt will be punished. Jesus articulates this promise in Mark 13, known as the "apocalyptic discourse."

In this chapter Jesus proclaims that the Temple will be torn down and, at the disciples' prompting, proceeds to outline the other events that will accompany this destruction. Jesus speaks of wars, famines, earthquakes, and persecutions. After this suffering, Jesus predicts, the entire cosmos will collapse. "The sun will be darkened, and the moon will not give its light, and the stars will be falling from heaven, and the powers in the heavens will be shaken" (13:23). At this time Jesus will return from heaven with armies of angels to gather the "elect"—those who have remained faithful to him despite all their tribulations—and rescue them from all this destruction.

Jesus indicates "this generation will not pass away" (Mark 13:30) until all these things have happened. Earlier in the Gospel, he said, "There are some standing here who will not taste death until they see that the kingdom of God has come with power" (9:1). To many interpreters, these verses together suggest that Mark's Gospel shows

Jesus saying that the end of the world will take place within the lifetime of some of the people who heard his preaching. Jesus spoke these words in approximately 30 CE. By the time the Temple was destroyed in 70 CE, there were likely very few people still alive who had heard Jesus' preaching. The Gospel of Mark, which was written in 70 CE or just before it, seems to be telling its audience the end of the world is upon them. The initial words of Jesus, as presented by Mark, take on a new import: "The kingdom of God has come near; repent, and believe in the good news" (1:15). Throughout the Gospel the author of Mark is warning his audience that the end is near and they have very little time left before the judgment of God will fall upon them.

In Mark 13:2, Jesus predicts the destruction of the Jerusalem Temple. Fragments of the "Western Wall," essentially a retaining wall supporting the Temple courts, are all that remain of the Temple complex.

Understanding the Characters in the Gospel of Mark

One recent literary interpretation of Mark argues that the parable of the Sower (Mark 4:1–20) provides a framework for understanding the myriad characters in the Gospel.[11] In this parable, Jesus speaks of a farmer who scatters his seed on the ground. Some seed falls on the path, where the ground is hard-packed and unreceptive; birds come along and eat up the seed. Other seeds fall on rocky ground, where there is apparently a thin layer of soil above solid rock. Here the seed springs up quickly, but because of the poor soil quality it cannot develop a healthy root structure, and hence when the sun comes out it withers. Other seed falls among thorns. The thorns choke the seed, and it yields nothing. Finally, some seed falls on good soil, and produces an abundant yield of grain.

Jesus explains that the sower sows "the word." Since Jesus is the one in the Gospel who preaches "the word," the sower is Jesus himself, and the seed is the gospel. The four types of ground that the seed falls upon, Jesus further explains, correspond to the different types of responses people have to his preaching. Some respond to Jesus as the seeds on the path; the word never penetrates their hearts just as the seed never penetrates the ground. They reject the word immediately. Others respond to Jesus as the seeds on the rocky ground. When they hear the word, they immediately respond with joy. However, their faith is shallow and cannot hold up under pressure. Still others, like the seeds sown among thorns, do not immediately reject Jesus, but are led astray by "the cares of the world, and the lure of wealth, and the desire for other things"; ultimately they yield nothing. Last, those who listen to the word, accept it, and "bear fruit," are like the seeds sown

---

11. Tolbert, *Sowing the Gospel*, 151–72.

in good soil. These people have faith and live their faith in demonstrable ways.

With this parable and its explanation, Jesus has outlined how the characters of the Gospel should be understood. Jesus says people respond to him in one of four paradigmatic ways, and in the Gospel his words are borne out. The various characters Jesus encounters in the Gospel fit one of the four descriptions.

The ground "on the path" is illustrated by the scribes and Pharisees. Just as the seed that is sown on the hard path never grows an inch, so also the word that is sown on the "hardened" hearts of the Jewish authorities never has a chance. The scribes' and Pharisees' refusal to give Jesus a chance is their defining characteristic in the Gospel.

The "rocky ground" describes the disciples, especially Peter. The disciples "immediately receive [the word] with joy," when they respond to Jesus' call to become his followers with enthusiasm and commitment (Mark 1:16–20), and they also "endure . . . for a while," remaining by Jesus' side until the events in the Garden of Gethsemane. However, their faith is shallow and they fall away "when trouble or persecution arises on account of the word," as happens when Jesus is arrested (14:50).

Peter's fear and shallow faith are the most egregious, as he denies Jesus three times under the questioning of a mere servant girl. In fact, Peter's name is a clue that he is the single best representative of the "rocky ground." When he is first introduced, his name is not Peter but Simon. Jesus changes his name from Simon to Peter (*Petros*, Greek for "rock"). Peter was not a common name at the time. People actually knew this disciple as "Rock." When the Gospel speaks about the "rocky" ground, it uses a cognate of Peter's name (*petrōdes*). The connection is unmistakable in Greek.

Several different characters are symbolized by the seed that falls on "thorny ground." Judas Iscariot, unlike his fellow disciples who fail because of fear of persecution, fails because of greed. He betrays Jesus for money; the "lure of wealth" has choked his faith, and he "yields nothing." The rich man in Mark 10:17–22 is another example. He asks Jesus what he must do to inherit eternal life, and Jesus asks if he follows the commandments. The man replies that he does, and Jesus, "looking at him, loved him, and said, 'You lack one thing; go, sell what you own, and give the money to the poor . . . then come, follow me.'" The man is shocked and goes away grieving, because he cannot bring himself to part with his material goods; his faith is snuffed out and he does not "bear fruit."

Most surprising, in many ways, is the Gospel's presentation of the characters who are symbolized by seeds sown on "good soil." The most obvious group in this category are those whom Jesus heals. It is a consistent pattern in the Gospel that such people approach Jesus and show some sign of great faith *before* the performance of a miracle on their behalf. The leper in Mark 1:40–45 kneels before Jesus and says, "If you choose, you can make me clean." The woman with the hemorrhage in 5:24–34 thinks to herself, "If I but touch his clothes, I will be made well." Blind Bartimaeus (10:46–52) calls out, "Jesus, Son of David, have mercy on me!" The friends of the paralytic go to the extreme of removing the roof from a house so that they can lower the man down to see Jesus: "When Jesus saw their faith, he said to the paralytic, 'Son, your sins are forgiven'" (2:5). Jesus often attributes the miracle to the faith of the supplicant, rather than to himself. He says to both the woman with the hemorrhage and Blind Bartimaeus, "Your faith has made you well."

The stance of the Gospel of Mark is that miracles do not produce faith; they are the result of faith. People need to have faith in Jesus for them to receive the divine benefits he has to offer. When Jesus arrives where there is little or no faith, as he does in his hometown of Nazareth (Mark 6:1–6), miracles do not follow: "And he could do no deed of power there. . . . And he was amazed at their unbelief."

The people Jesus heals are not the only ones whose faith or good works is praised by Jesus in the Gospel. There is the widow who put two copper coins—"all she had to live on"—into the Temple treasury (Mark 12:41–44). There is also the woman who anointed Jesus' head with costly ointment (14:3–9), of whom Jesus says, "Truly I tell you, wherever the good news is proclaimed in the whole world, what she has done will be told in remembrance of her." What all of these "good soil" people have in common is that they are nobodies in the eyes of society. Almost all of them are poor. Many of them are women. Several are ritually unclean (the leper, the woman with the hemorrhage), according to the Jewish conception of purity. Some, like the Syrophoenician woman (Mark 7:24–30), are from despised ethnic groups. Many have conditions (like blindness or paralysis) that were thought to be the result of having been cursed by God for committing some sin. The author of the Gospel seems to have a marked preference for the outcast, the afflicted, and the untouchable.

What is the point of all this? Ultimately, a Gospel is persuasive literature with a missionary function. The author's goal is to make Christians, or if someone is already a believer, to make him or her a better Christian. The plot is crafted and the characters are portrayed in such a way as to have this kind of impact. Mark portrays characters as sympathetic or unsympathetic, thus encouraging his readers to adopt certain attitudes and behaviors and to discourage them from adopting others. The scribes and Pharisees, disciples, political rulers, and the like are all portrayed negatively at least in part so that readers will see their mistakes and wrongdoing and endeavor not to be like them. The heroes of the Gospel serve the opposite function; they are presented as role models and exemplars. The people Jesus heals are among the heroes of the Gospel. However, the ultimate hero of the Gospel cannot be a character who is introduced in a single episode and then disappears. The true hero of the Gospel is Jesus himself. Jesus is the one who offers the best example of compassion and courage in the face of adversity; his are the teachings the author of the Gospel wants his readers to follow.

Key Terms

literary criticism	Elijah	legalism
exposition	allusion	messianic secret
complication	blasphemy	motif
climax	piety	deicide
testimony		

Review Questions

1. Who are the main characters in the Gospel of Mark? How are their identities established in the exposition of the Gospel?

2. What is the main conflict that drives the plot of the Gospel of Mark? How is this conflict introduced and developed in the complication of the Gospel? How is it resolved in the climax of the Gospel?

3. Why in Mark does Jesus tend to tell those he has healed as well as demons who know who he is not to say anything about him?

4. How does the parable of the Sower provide a framework for understanding all of the characters Jesus encounters in the Gospel of Mark? What four types of responses to Jesus' preaching are described in it, and how are these responses illustrated in the Gospel by various characters?

Discussion Questions

1. This chapter suggests that a critical distinction should be made between how a Gospel *portrays* people and events and how they may have been in reality. Do you agree or disagree with this? Are there specific parts of the Gospel that you think support your position in this regard?

2. The introduction to this textbook argues that critical study of the Bible is marked in part by a consideration of both historical context and literary context in the process of interpretation. Are there particular stories from the Gospel of Mark that you think differently about after learning some things about the ancient world and studying the Gospel in its entirety?

3. The Gospel of Mark is in many ways the strangest of the four canonical Gospels, and it was the least-used and commented upon in early Christianity. What aspects of the Gospel do you think led to its being treated this way? Why do you think the Gospel made it into the canon of the New Testament despite its oddity?

Bibliography and Suggestions for Further Study

(Books and websites that are accessible for general undergraduates are marked with an asterisk; other sources listed are appropriate for advanced students.)

Anderson, Janice C., and Stephen D. Moore, eds. *Mark and Method: New Approaches in Biblical Studies*. Minneapolis: Fortress, 2008.

Fowler, Robert M. *Let the Reader Understand: Reader-Response Criticism and the Gospel of Mark*. Harrisburg, PA: Trinity, 2001.

*Kelber, Werner H. *Mark's Story of Jesus*. Philadelphia: Fortress, 1979.

Tolbert, Mary A. *Sowing the Gospel: Mark's World in Literary-Historical Perspective*. Minneapolis: Fortress, 1989.

Source Criticism and the Synoptic Problem

Mark is generally supposed to have been the first Gospel written. Such a claim should not be accepted without evidence, however. From at least the time of Saint Augustine (early fifth century), it was believed Matthew was the earliest Gospel, which justified its place as the first book in the New Testament canon. Scholars began to argue for **Markan priority**—the theory that Mark was the first of the Gospels to have been composed—in the nineteenth century. A new branch of biblical studies, **source criticism**, was responsible for this insight. Source criticism examines texts that appear to have some relationship of dependence and attempts to determine the nature and direction of that dependence. Biblical source critics concluded that three of the Gospels in the New Testament depend on one another: Matthew, Mark, and Luke.

The Synoptic Problem

Matthew, Mark, and Luke include many of the same stories and often tell them in the same order. However, this by itself is not necessarily indicative of dependence of one author on another. Three sportswriters reporting on the same game might easily focus on similar dominant storylines and include those elements in the same order. But the similarities between Matthew, Mark, and Luke go beyond content and structure. Consider the following example:

Mark 11:27-33[1]	Matt. 21:23-27	Luke 20:1-8
And they came again to Jerusalem. And as he was walking in the temple, the chief priests and the scribes and the elders came to him, and they said to him, "By what authority are you doing these things, or who gave you this authority to do them?"	And when he entered the temple, the chief priests and the elders of the people came up to him as he was teaching, and said, "By what authority are you doing these things, and who gave you this authority?"	One day, as he was teaching the people in the temple and preaching the gospel, the chief priests and the scribes with the elders came up and said to him, "Tell us by what authority you do these things, or who it is that gave you this authority."
Jesus said to them, "I will ask you a question: answer me, and I will tell you by what authority	Jesus answered them, "I also will ask you a question; and if you tell me the answer, then	He answered them, "I also will ask you a question; now tell me. Was the baptism of

continued

---

1. The RSV is used in this table.

Mark 11:27-33 *continued*	Matt. 21:23-27 *continued*	Luke 20:1-8 *continued*
I do these things. Was the baptism of John from heaven or from men? Answer me."	I also will tell you by what authority I do these things. The baptism of John, whence was it? From heaven or from men?"	John from heaven or from men?"
And they argued with one another, "If we say, 'From heaven,' he will say, 'Why then did you not believe him.' But shall we say, 'From men?'—they were afraid of the people, for all held that John was a real prophet.	And they argued with one another, "If we say, 'From heaven,' he will say to us, 'Why then did you not believe him?' But if we say, 'From men,' we are afraid of the people, for all hold that John was a prophet."	And they discussed it with one another, saying, "If we say, 'From heaven,' he will say, 'Why did you not believe him?' But if we say, 'From men,' all the people will stone us; for they are convinced that John was a prophet."
So they answered Jesus, "We do not know," And Jesus said to them, "Neither will I tell you by what authority I do these things."	So they answered Jesus, "We do not know." And he said to them, "Neither will I tell you by what authority I do these things."	So they answered that they did not know whence it was. And Jesus said to them, "Neither will I tell you by what authority I do these things."

The placement of these parallel texts in side-by-side columns is what is known as a **synopsis**. The term comes from two Greek roots: *syn*, which means "together," and *optic*, which means "seen." A synopsis allows these three Gospels—which are together known as the **Synoptic Gospels**—to be "seen together" and hence for their similarities to be more easily detected.

The high degree of word-for-word similarity in these passages is striking. Three writers covering the same event might include some of the same elements, but they would almost never compose entire sentences—let alone paragraphs—that are virtually the same. Nor is it conceivable that each evangelist got his version of the story from oral tradition. Empirical studies confirm that oral tradition is not so precise that a common oral source could account for three independent versions of the story with this high an incidence of verbal similarity. Some cultures are better at oral tradition than others, but none are this good. If a teacher received three papers from students that exhibited this degree of commonality, that

Digital image courtesy of the Getty's Open Content Program

A radiant Jesus is flanked by Moses and Elijah. The Transfiguration is an example of a story found in all three Synoptic Gospels.

teacher would conclude the students worked together and copied from one another. Similarly, this much overlap between Gospel texts suggests literary dependence; one author copied from another.

This pattern of verbal similarity appears in dozens and dozens of stories throughout the Gospels. Stories that are found in Matthew, Mark, and Luke with high percentages of word-for-word similarity are called **triple tradition** material. One task, then, of source criticism of the Gospels is to explain why these nearly identical versions appear in the three Synoptic Gospels. The task of explaining this and the other patterns of agreement and disagreement in wording and content in the Gospels of Matthew, Mark, and Luke is termed the **Synoptic Problem**.

There are also some two hundred verses of material found in Matthew and Luke with close verbal similarity, but not found in Mark. This is called **double tradition** material, and the first example in the Synoptic Gospels is the preaching of John the Baptist:

The Plagiarism Analogy

If a teacher receives two papers with a few paragraphs that share word-for-word similarities, it is not necessarily the case that one student copied from another. They might both have copied from the same website or from the same book in the library. If the teacher finds the common source on the web or in the library, then she might conclude the two students did not collaborate on their papers. However, it is also possible that student A copied from the web or library source, and student B copied from student A. How could a teacher determine which explanation is correct? The problem is difficult but perhaps not insoluble. A detailed comparison of the three texts might reveal some telltale signs of either dependence or independence.

The plagiarism analogy is not perfect, as the borrowing done by the evangelists is not a question of cheating or dishonesty but simply one of utilizing source material. Ancient authors had no conception of plagiarism and it was common for them to borrow material from earlier authors without attribution. But the question of whether one evangelist borrowed from another or if two Gospels each borrowed from an earlier source is hugely important. If two Gospel writers did copy from a previously unknown written source, that would indicate there was an earlier Gospel or collection of source material. Scholars might search for this source or attempt to reconstruct it from the quoted material in the Gospels. Evidence of such a source, whether found or reconstructed, would greatly benefit scholars' understanding of the development of early Christianity.

Matt. 3:7-10	Luke 3:7-9
But when he saw many Pharisees and Sadducees coming for baptism, he said to them, "You brood of vipers! Who warned you to flee from the wrath to come? Bear fruit worthy of repentance. Do not presume to say to yourselves, 'We have Abraham as our ancestor'; for I tell you, God is able from these stones to raise up children to Abraham. Even now the ax is lying at the root of the trees; every tree therefore that does not bear good fruit is cut down and thrown into the fire."	John said to the crowds that came out to be baptized by him, "You brood of vipers! Who warned you to flee from the wrath to come? Bear fruits worthy of repentance. Do not begin to say to yourselves, "We have Abraham as our ancestor'; for I tell you, God is able from these stones to raise up children to Abraham. Even now the ax is lying at the root of the trees; every tree therefore that does not bear good fruit is cut down and thrown into the fire."

The high incidence of verbal similarity between Matthew and Luke here indicates a literary relationship. Someone definitely copied from someone else. However, a variety of literary relationships could explain the similarity. It is possible that one author copied from the other or that both copied from a third source, one that may or may not be available to source critics.

Before turning to the principles of source criticism that might help determine which possibility is more likely, the problem is complicated even further by the recognition of some additional patterns of agreement and disagreement. In addition to triple-tradition and double-tradition materials, there are stories unique to each Gospel.

Material Unique to Each Synoptic Gospel

Mark	Matthew	Luke
• Jesus' family trying to restrain him (3:20–21) • Parable of the Seed Growing Secretly (4:26–29) • Healing of a deaf and mute man (7:31–37) • Healing of a blind man in two stages (8:22–26) • Naked young man running away (14:51–52)	• An angel speaks to Joseph about Jesus' birth (1:18–25) • Visit of the wise men (2:1–12) • Slaughter of children; flight to Egypt (2:13–23) • Sermon on the Mount elements: (1) exceeding righteousness (5:17–20); (2) teaching on anger, lustful thoughts, divorce, swearing oaths (5:21–37); (3) acceptable forms of almsgiving, fasting, and prayer (6:2–8, 16–18) • Disciples sent only to lost sheep of Israel (10:6–16) • Parables: (1) Weeds (13:24–30), (2) Hidden Treasure and Pearl (13:44–45), (3) Net (13:47–50), (4) Unmerciful Debtor (18:22–35), (5) Laborers in the Vineyard (20:1–16), (6) Two Sons (21:28–32), (7) Wise and Foolish Bridesmaids (25:1–13) • Peter walks on water (14:28–31) • Peter named "rock" on which the church is built (16:17–19) • Coin found in fish's mouth (17:24–27) • Eunuchs for the kingdom of heaven (19:10–12) • Judas' remorse and suicide (27:3–10) • Pilate washes his hands (27:24–25) • Guards posted at Jesus' tomb (27:62–64, 28:11–15) • Great commission (28:16–20)	• Preface to Theophilus (1:1–4) • Events surrounding the birth of John the Baptist (1:5–25, 39–45, 57–80) • Events surrounding the birth of Jesus (1:26–38, 46–56, 2:1–38) • Finding of twelve-year-old Jesus in the Temple (2:39–52) • Miracles: (1) great catch of fish (5:1–11); (2) raising of widow of Nain's son (7:11–17); (3) healing of a crippled woman (13:10–17); healing of a man with dropsy (14:1–6); cleansing of ten lepers (17:11–19) • Teachings: (1) woes against the rich (6:24–26); (2) true blessedness (11:27–28); (3) true cleansing (11:37–41); (4) repentance and destruction (13:1–5); (5) response to "that fox" Herod (13:31–33); (6) considering the cost (14:28–33); (7) worthless slaves (17:7–10); (8) kingdom of God is among you (17:20–21); (9) examples of judgment (17:28–32) • Parables: (1) Good Samaritan (10:25–37); (2) Persistent Friend's Request (11:5–8); (3) Rich Fool (12:15–21); (4) Barren Fig tree (13:6–9); (5) Places of Honor (14:7–14); (6) Lost Coin (15:8–10); (7) Prodigal Son (15:11–32); (8) Unjust Steward (16:1–8); (9) Rich Man and Lazarus (16:19–31); (10) Unjust Judge (18:1–8); (11) Pharisee and Tax Collector (18:9–14) • Inaugural sermon at Nazareth; attempt to kill Jesus (4:16–30) • Jesus' women followers (8:1–3) • Rejection by Samaritans (9:51–56) • Mission of the seventy (10:1–12, 17–20) • Lament over Jerusalem (19:41–44) • Trial before Herod Antipas (23:6–12) • Criminals crucified alongside Jesus (23:39–43) • Disciples disbelieve women's testimony of resurrection (24:10–11) • Jesus appears to two disciples on the road to Emmaus (24:13–49) • Ascension into heaven (24:50–53)

As the table shows, the list of material unique to Mark is short. The list of material unique to Matthew and unique to Luke is longer.[2] Fully one-fifth of Matthew's Gospel is unique, and one-third of Luke's.

All of this indicates that the Synoptic Problem presents tremendous complexities, because of the sheer variety of the patterns of agreement and disagreement, similarity and dissimilarity. One author having copied from another might explain the similarities between them, but for a theory to be persuasive it must also explain the differences. If Mark copied from Luke, that would explain why 88 percent of Mark's material is also found in Luke. But where did the other 12 percent of Mark come from? Since Mark is much shorter than Luke and includes only 47 percent of the material in Luke, why would Mark exclude the other 53 percent? In particular, why would he omit the story of Jesus' virgin birth,

his resurrection appearances, the Sermon on the Plain, and such noteworthy parables as the Good Samaritan and the Prodigal Son? These are difficult questions to answer, and a student might rightly perceive they make it unlikely that Mark copied from Luke. But, as will be shown, almost every proposal to solve the Synoptic Problem presents such difficulties.

The Principles of Source Criticism

Source critics often rely on common-sense principles to determine the relationship between texts with word-for-word similarity. Source criticism is based on calculating the probability of a scenario unfolding in one way or another. If two different Gospels contain word-for-word similarities but are not identical, then either the author of Gospel A copied from Gospel B, or the author of Gospel B copied from Gospel A.[3] The source critic looks at the differences between the two Gospels and imagines what would likely have happened to bring these differences about. If Gospel A came first, are there clues that suggest the author of Gospel B made the changes that produced his similar but not identical version? Or is it easier to account for the differences by assuming that Gospel B came first and Gospel A made slight changes to material he found there?

Some familiar stories occur in only one Gospel. The wise men who come from the East to worship the baby Jesus, depicted in this sixth-century mosaic from the Basilica of Saint Apollinare near Ravenna, appear only in Matthew.

---

2. Indeed, it is too long to fit into a manageable table. The list of passages unique to Matthew and Luke in the table is not comprehensive, but includes only the major items.

3. There is at least one other possibility, namely that the authors of Gospel A and Gospel B copied from a third source, Gospel C. That possibility is discussed later in this chapter.

Consider again an analogy from the college classroom. If a student mistakenly turns in two drafts of a paper, the teacher should be able to identify the final draft. The teacher would likely notice telltale signs: one version has misspellings and grammatical mistakes that are absent from the other version; one version has place holders for parenthetical citations and the other contains citations; one version uses slang terms or inappropriate language and the other uses formal, proper English; or one version is much shorter than the other. Whichever version is "rough" is the early draft. Whichever version is more complete, more refined, more reflective of editing and revision, is the final version.

This logic applies as well in biblical source criticism. To determine which of the Synoptic Gospels was written earliest, one should look to the version that appears to be most primitive, the "roughest" in its language, and the least theologically sophisticated. Consider first grammar and style. Whatever their other virtues might be, the Gospels were not written in the most elegant style. The quality of the Greek is generally rather low, reflective of the common "Koine" Greek used by less well-educated people in areas that had been Hellenized. All of the Gospels contain mistakes of language: grammatical errors, awkward constructions, ill-chosen words, and the like. Often these errors are lost in the process of translating from Greek into modern English, but some cases can still be detected. In Mark 5:9–10, for example, the author switches back and forth between singular and plural pronouns for the same referent: "Then Jesus asked him [sing.], 'What is your name?' He [sing.] replied, 'My name is Legion;

for we [plur.] are many.' And he [sing.] begged him earnestly not to send them [plur.] out of the country." While all of the Gospels contain some mistakes, some Gospels contain more than others. The more error-ridden Gospel is likely to be the earlier one, for it is more likely that a later writer would correct mistakes than introduce new ones.[4]

Another sign of a Gospel likely having been written earlier is length. It is more likely that the material in a later Gospel would expand rather than contract. Generally, when it comes to stories from the Gospels, it is harder to explain omissions than additions. If an evangelist knew of material (such as stories about Jesus or sayings of Jesus) in addition to the material in the source from which he was copying, it seems probable he would include it. The longer Gospel, then, would more likely be the later one. For the opposite to have occurred, one would have to explain convincingly why a later Gospel chose to omit certain materials from the earlier Gospel from which he was copying.

A third criterion for determining the chronology of the Synoptic Gospels is the texts' level of theological orthodoxy and sophistication. For example, Christian theology gradually came to understand Christ as fully human and fully divine.[5] The Gospel that has the highest Christology in the New Testament is John, which is not coincidentally usually regarded as the latest of the Gospels to have been written. Therefore, if scholars find one Gospel that includes stories suggesting Jesus was not fully divine but had human limitations, while another Gospel contains versions of those stories in which those human limitations are absent, the second Gospel is likely the later version. The theological

---

4. See Robert H. Stein, *The Synoptic Problem: An Introduction* (Grand Rapids: Baker, 1987), 54.

5. This movement can be traced within the manuscript tradition. So, for example, the early manuscripts of Matt. 24:36 read, "But about that day and hour no one knows, neither the angels of heaven, nor the Son, but only the Father." But later manuscripts omit "nor the Son" from this verse, to remove the implication that Jesus lacked omniscience and was not fully divine. See Bart Ehrman, *The Orthodox Corruption of Scripture: The Effect of Early Christological Controversies on the Text of the New Testament* (New York: Oxford University Press, 2011), and Bart Ehrman, *How Jesus Became God: The Exaltation of a Jewish Preacher from Galilee*, updated and with a new afterword (New York: HarperOne, 2014).

shortcomings of the earlier Gospel would have been addressed in the later Gospel.

The Easy Part: Which Gospel Came First?

As mentioned, the long-time favorite for earliest Synoptic Gospel was Matthew. Augustine, among the first to recognize a relationship of literary dependence between the Gospels, thought Matthew had been written first and Mark had copied from Matthew, producing a condensed version of the Gospel. Augustine believed Luke was written third and used both previous Gospels as sources.[6]

Griesbach Hypothesis

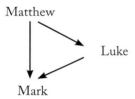

The theory of **Matthean priority** was also promoted by biblical scholar J. J. Griesbach in 1776, although he disagreed with Augustine about the order of the subsequent Gospels. According to the **Griesbach hypothesis**, Matthew came first, Luke was second and used Matthew as a source, and Mark came third and employed material from both prior Gospels. The modern champion of the Griesbach hypothesis (rechristened the Two Gospel Hypothesis) is biblical scholar William Farmer.[7] However, the overwhelming majority of scholars reject Matthean priority and instead favor the view that Mark was the first Gospel. This conclusion is based on the **argument from grammar** (Mark has the most grammatical and stylistic mistakes), the **argument from length** (Mark is the shortest Gospel), and the **argument from theological evolution** (Mark has the most passages that are theologically difficult, puzzling, or problematic).

The Argument from Grammar

It is difficult to illustrate errors of grammar, syntax, and usage found in Mark and corrected in Matthew and Luke without presuming a knowledge of ancient Greek. Those without linguistic training will have to take the word of the experts that in Mark 2:4 the author uses *krabatton*, a slang word for "mattress" or "pad" ("having dug through [the roof], they let down the mat on which the paralytic lay"), while Matthew 9:2 and Luke 5:18 substitute a more refined, acceptable word for mattress (*klinē*). Mark also alternates chaotically between past and present verb tense while Matthew and Luke tend to be consistent. In fact, Mark is full of "rude, harsh, obscure or unusual words or expressions,"[8] which Matthew and Luke regularly correct. It is much more difficult to conceive of the opposite, that Mark was copying the more refined and correct prose of either Matthew or Luke and carelessly inserting errors and clumsy words and expressions.[9]

The Argument from Length

The best way to measure the length of a Gospel is not by chapter or verse, which both vary in

---

6. Augustine, *Harmony of the Gospels* 1.2.4.

7. William L. Farmer, *The Synoptic Problem: A Critical Analysis* (New York: Macmillan, 1964).

8. John C. Hawkins, *Horae Synopticae* (Grand Rapids: Baker, 1968), 131.

9. A striking example of Matthew and Luke correcting Mark is found in their handling of the John the Baptist material. Mark 1:2–3 opens this section, "As it is written in the prophet Isaiah," and then offers a quotation that conflates material from Isaiah and Malachi. Matthew and Luke both eliminate the Malachi material from this quotation (Matt. 3:3; Luke 3:4–6).

length, but by the number of words. Mark's Gospel has 11,025 words, Matthew has 18,293 words, and Luke has 19,376. If Matthew and Luke copied from Mark, they included 97 percent and 88 percent of Mark respectively. By contrast, if Mark copied from Matthew, he included only 60 percent of his source. If Mark copied from Luke, he kept only 47 percent of that Gospel.

If one argues that Mark was copying from Matthew and Luke, one would have to explain why he felt the need to omit so many passages from his sources. However, these omissions are very difficult to explain, for they include such things as the birth of Jesus, the Sermon on the Mount, the Sermon on the Plain, the Lord's Prayer, numerous famous parables and other teachings, and Jesus' resurrection appearances. To most source critics, it seems improbable that Mark would have felt the need to dispense with such material. For example, it is very hard to envision Mark taking the endings of either Matthew and Luke and removing everything that provides closure, reassurance about the resurrection, and redemption for the disciples. On the other hand, it is easy to see why subsequent evangelists found Mark's abrupt ending unsatisfactory and altered it.

Moreover, to support Matthean priority instead of Markan priority, one must not only explain the sections that Mark would have had to omit from Matthew and Luke but also the additions he would have made. A supporter of Matthean priority would have to argue that a story found only in Mark was not copied from Matthew or Luke but was added by Mark. The material unique to Mark includes the story where people begin saying that Jesus is insane and his family goes out to restrain him (Mark 3:20–21), the healing of a blind man that requires two attempts on Jesus' part to accomplish (8:22–26), and the story of the young man who runs away naked when Jesus is arrested (14:51–52). Most source critics

argue that it is highly improbable Mark would have chosen to add this material at the same time he was deleting so much other material of greater interest. Does it make sense to say that Mark had no room in his Gospel for the Lord's Prayer, because he was saving space for passages such as rumors of Jesus' insanity, a semi-botched healing, and the naked escapee from Gethsemane? Most source critics find this impossible to accept.

Moreover, source critics dismiss the idea that Mark omitted material in the cause of brevity because in every other respect Mark does not abbreviate Matthew and Luke. "Whereas Mark is considerably shorter in total length than Matthew and Luke, when we compare the individual pericopes that they have in common, time and time again we find that Mark is the longest!"[10] If Mark was seeking to shorten the Gospel overall, why would he consistently expand those passages he chose to include?

The Argument from Theological Evolution

While both Matthew and Luke tend to rewrite Markan passages that, on the surface at least, appear to contradict some important point of Christian theology, some of the clearest examples are found in Matthew.

In Mark's version of the story of the woman with a hemorrhage, Jesus does not know who touched him. The woman sneaks up on him surreptitiously and is healed without Jesus being conscious of what has happened. He turns and asks, "Who touched my clothes?" The response of Jesus' disciples indicates that it is impossible to tell who is responsible, because the crowd is pressing around Jesus and many people are touching him. That Jesus "looked all around to see who had done it" also confirms Jesus simply

---

10. Stein, *The Synoptic Problem*, 49.

The Healing of the Woman with a Hemorrhage

Mark 5:24-34	Matt. 9:20-22
And a large crowd followed him and pressed in on him. Now there was a woman who had been suffering from hemorrhages for twelve years. She had endured much under many physicians, and had spent all that she had; and she was no better, but rather grew worse. She had heard about Jesus, and came up behind him in the crowd and touched his cloak, for she said, "If I but touch his clothes, I will be made well." Immediately her hemorrhage stopped; and she felt in her body that she was healed of her disease. Immediately aware that power had gone forth from him, Jesus turned about in the crowd and said, "Who touched my clothes?" And his disciples said to him, "You see the crowd pressing in on you; how can you say, 'Who touched me?'" He looked all round to see who had done it. But the woman, knowing what had happened to her, came in fear and trembling, fell down before him, and told him the whole truth. He said to her, "Daughter, your faith has made you well; go in peace, and be healed of your disease."	Then suddenly a woman who had been suffering from hemorrhages for twelve years came up behind him and touched the fringe of his cloak, for she said to herself, "If I only touch his cloak, I will be made well." Jesus turned, and seeing her he said, "Take heart, daughter; your faith has made you well." And instantly the woman was made well.

The Metropolitan Museum of Art, Gift of J. Pierpont Morgan, 1917

The ailing woman touches Jesus' hem and is healed in the scene carved in this sixth or seventh century Egyptian amulet. It seems that Matthew retells this story in such a way as to rule out the possibility that Jesus was truly ignorant of what had occurred.

does not know who caused the power to go forth from him. In this way Mark's version shows Jesus as something less than fully divine, because he lacks omniscience. He is capable of ignorance.

Matthew's version is shorter but, most scholars contend, more closely aligned with the proto-orthodox Christian belief in Jesus' full divinity. As a result, (1) Jesus has no need to ask who had touched his clothes, (2) the disciples have no need to respond that it is impossible to tell, and (3) Jesus has no need to look around to see who did it. In Matthew's version, Jesus simply looks around, sees the woman, and pronounces her healed. Matthew has eliminated elements from Mark's version that might suggest to his audience that Jesus was not omniscient, and thus not fully divine.

A similar example involves Jesus not performing "deeds of power" (i.e., miracles) in his hometown of Nazareth:

Mark 6:1-6	Matt. 13:54-58
He left that place and came to his hometown, and his disciples followed him. On the sabbath he began to teach in the synagogue, and many who heard him were astounded. They said, "Where did this man get all this? What is this wisdom that has been given to him? What deeds of power are being done by his hands! Is not this the carpenter, the son of Mary and brother of James and Joses and Judas and Simon, and are not his sisters here with us?" And they took offence at him. Then Jesus said to them, "Prophets are not without honor, except in their hometown, and among their own kin, and in their own house." And he could do no deed of power there, except that he laid his hands on a few sick people and cured them. And he was amazed at their unbelief.	He came to his hometown and began to teach the people in their synagogue, so that they were astounded and said, "Where did this man get this wisdom and these deeds of power? Is not this the carpenter's son? Is not his mother called Mary? And are not his brothers James and Joseph and Simon and Judas? And are not all his sisters with us? Where then did this man get all this?" And they took offence at him. But Jesus said to them, "Prophets are not without honor except in their own country and in their own house." And he did not do many deeds of power there, because of their unbelief.

Mark's version indicates that Jesus "*could*[11] do no deed of power there" (Mark 6:5). In other words, Jesus was unable to perform miracles in that location; he lacked the power or the ability to do so. Again, this depicts Jesus as not omnipotent and therefore less than fully divine.

In Matthew's version, the word "could" is omitted. Instead, Matthew writes that Jesus "*did* not do many deeds of power there" (Matt. 13:58). This implies Jesus *chose* not to perform many miracles in Nazareth rather than that he was *unable* to do so. Matthew's version captures emerging Christian beliefs about Jesus' divinity better than does Mark's version; in that sense, Matthew has improved Mark's version of the story. By contrast, it is much more difficult to explain why Mark would rewrite a story into which Jesus "did not" do many miracles to one that says he "could not."

The Hard Part: If Mark Came First, What Happened Next?

Markan priority goes a long way toward solving the Synoptic Problem. Triple-tradition material is explained by the theory that Matthew and Luke copied certain stories from Mark. The material unique to Matthew and Luke can be accounted for by each evangelist's having access to either oral traditions or perhaps a written source that the others did not have. That certain stories are common to Mark and Matthew but not Luke, or to Luke and Mark but not Matthew, could be explained by both Matthew and Luke having exercised judgment on what parts of Mark to preserve in their Gospels. Usually, they agreed and included the same stories from Mark. Occasionally, one chose to keep a Markan story while the other did not. The material unique to Mark is explicable on the theory that it contains odd and puzzling material that *both* Matthew and Luke chose to omit.

However, Markan priority cannot account for the double-tradition material. These are mostly

---

11. Greek, *edynato*, "to be able."

sayings of Jesus that are common to Matthew and Luke but not found in Mark at all. And because these stories, some two hundred verses in total, contain *verbatim* similarities, it is unlikely that they stem from common oral traditions. One can only account for two texts that contain word-for-word parallels by reference to some kind of *literary* relationship—that is, a written document.

When it comes to the double-tradition, there are three main possibilities. The first is the stories—at least in their written form—originated with Matthew, and Luke later copied them. The second is the stories originated with Luke, and Matthew later copied them. The third is both Matthew and Luke copied these stories from another source. How can source critics determine which explanation is most likely?

To return to the earlier plagiarism analogy, suppose a professor assigns a paper to students and receive two submissions with some word-for-word similarities. Let us further suppose these similarities are not found throughout both papers but only in a few paragraphs in a few different places in their papers, and these paragraphs are not identical but about 80 to 90 percent the same. Whenever there is such a high percentage of verbal similarity it is certain that copying has occurred. But did one student copy from the other, or did both of them use the same book or website as a source?

One way to find out would be to search the web and the library, locate the source they used, and examine the two student versions in comparison with it. The existence of such a source would not prove that one student did not copy from another; one of them could have done the research and the other could have plagiarized from the classmate's paper, at least in part. However, if both students' papers *departed from the source in the exact same way,* then it would be clear one had copied from the other. If two students used the same source independently, then one student might alter the source in one way, and

the other in another way. The chance that both students would alter the source in exactly the same way is almost nil. Such alterations therefore are known as "agreements against" one's source. Agreements against a source are the telltale sign that one author copied from another, rather than both of them copying independently from the same source. Two authors copying from the same source independently should never, or almost never, agree against their source.

Q and the Two Source Hypothesis

Most scholars who have considered the preceding criterion have concluded that Matthew and Luke are independent of each other, and hence they must have each copied (independently) from a common source. The name given to that source is "**Q**."[12] Q is a hypothetical "lost gospel," consisting mostly of sayings of Jesus, believed to have been used as a source by both Matthew and Luke before its unfortunate disappearance from the annals of history.

Two Source Hypothesis

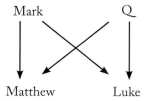

If one accepts Markan priority and accounts for the double-tradition material in Matthew and Luke with the theory that both relied on Q, then one arrives at the solution to the Synoptic Problem called the "**Two Source Hypothesis**." According to this theory, Mark and Q were used as sources by the authors of Matthew and Luke; Matthew and Luke independently adopted material from Mark and Q into their

---

12. The German word *quelle* means "source," and the late nineteenth and early twentieth-century German biblical scholars who first popularized this gospel's existence appear to have used the first letter of that word to name it.

Gospels. Also, Matthew and Luke each incorporated some source material that the other did not know, with the result that, as already noted, some material occurs only in Matthew, and some material occurs only in Luke.

The Q hypothesis rests on two pillars. One is the independence of Matthew and Luke. The other is the plausibility of the Q source.

The Independence of Matthew and Luke

The first pillar argues that neither Matthew nor Luke appears to have copied from the other Gospel. In lieu of such copying, a common source is the only way to account for the verbatim similarities between them.

Arguments for the independence of Matthew and Luke fall into two main groups. The first examines these two evangelists' use of their Markan source, and claims that neither evangelist seems to be familiar with the alterations made to Mark by the other writer. The second looks at the material that is unique to Matthew and Luke and argues for the improbability of either evangelist omitting so much good material from the other's Gospel had he been familiar with its contents.

Matthew and Luke's Use of Mark. Supporters of Q assert that Matthew and Luke seldom agree against Mark when all three Gospels include the same story. When Mark tells a story, sometimes

Matthew makes changes to it while Luke tells it the same way. And sometimes Luke makes changes to it while Matthew tells it the same way. Sometimes both Matthew and Luke make changes to Mark's version, but they seldom make the *same* changes. Agreements against one's source, as indicated above, signal that one copyist knew of another copyist's work, rather than their having worked independently.

One example involves the previously mentioned inconsistent use of pronouns in Mark's version of the story of the Gerasene demoniac (Mark 5:1–13). Matthew solves this problem by rewriting the story to include two demoniacs so that he can use plural pronouns throughout (Matt. 8:28–34). Luke provides an entirely different solution: after the man (singular) explains that many demons have entered him, the demons (plural) do the talking and the pronouns switch from singular to plural: "*They* begged [Jesus] not to order *them* to go back into the abyss" (Luke 8:31). Supporters of Q argue that if Luke copied from Matthew as well as Mark, why did he not simply adopt Matthew's improvements to Mark? Or if Matthew copied from Luke as well as Mark, why did he not adopt Luke's changes? Under the Two Source Hypothesis, this is because Matthew and Luke were unaware of each other's improvements of Mark's problem passages.

There are also numerous occasions in which Matthew appears to provide an improvement to Mark while Luke retains the Markan version. One example involves the rich young man who approaches Jesus to ask about eternal life:

Mark 10:17-18[13]	Matt. 19:16-17	Luke 18:18-19
And as he was setting out on his journey, a man ran up and knelt before him, and asked him, "Good Teacher, what must I do to inherit eternal life?" And Jesus said to him, *"Why do you call me good? No one is good but God alone."*	And behold, one came up to him, saying, "Teacher, what good deed must I do, to have eternal life?" And he said to him, **"Why do you ask me about what is good? One there is who is good."**	And a ruler asked him, "Good Teacher, what shall I do to inherit eternal life?" And Jesus said to him, *"Why do you call me good? No one is good but God alone."*

---

13. The RSV is used in this table.

Matthew appears to have noticed a problem with Mark's version, in which Jesus says, "*Why do you call me good?* No one is good but God alone." If goodness is a quality reserved for God and God alone, and Jesus will not tolerate being called "good" out of respect for God, then he is implying that he is not God, or that his goodness does not approach the level of God's. Matthew seems to fix this by changing both the question and the answer. The person who approaches Jesus does not refer to him as "Good Teacher" but asks instead, "What *good deed* must I do, to have eternal life?" Jesus can then respond, "Why do *ask me about what is good?* One there is who is good." If Luke copied from Matthew as well as Mark, he surely noticed the difference here. However, he sticks with Mark's version regardless, warts and all. Proponents of Matthew and Luke's independence argue that it is difficult to explain why—given a choice—Luke would have preferred Mark's seemingly inferior version to Matthew's evidently superior one.

Improbability of Major Omissions. Did Matthew copy from Luke, or Luke from Matthew? Of these two possibilities, it is more likely that Luke copied from Matthew because Luke is longer than Matthew, Luke's writing is superior to Matthew's, and Luke's theology is arguably more sophisticated.

The problem is that such a scenario requires Luke to have omitted a great deal of prime material from Matthew. For example, Luke must have chosen to omit almost everything Matthew has to say about the birth of Christ: the star, the wise men, the slaughter of the innocents, and the flight to Egypt. He also chose to omit numerous Matthean parables: the weeds, the treasure, the pearl, the net, the laborers in the vineyard, the two sons, and the bridesmaids. And, most improbably to many scholars, Luke would have taken Matthew's magnificent 111-verse long Sermon on the Mount and chopped it into the 29-verse long Sermon on the Plain, with the remaining verses being either omitted or scattered elsewhere in Luke's Gospel. Q supporters argue that these omissions and

alterations do not make sense. Therefore, Luke could not have been aware of Matthew's Gospel.

The Plausibility of Q

The Q theory posits that a written collection of sayings and stories of Jesus existed in the very early church, that Matthew and Luke both had access to a copy of it and used it in writing their Gospels, and that it subsequently disappeared without a trace. This theory involves some inherent improbabilities. But it is *plausible* that things happened this way.

Q supporters point out that most of the books written in the ancient world are now lost to us. The production of books was expensive and laborious, and the market was small, since few people could read. As a result, there were never many copies of any book in circulation. Moreover, books are fragile things, easily destroyed. Further, when a book lost its usefulness—when there was no longer a demand for it that led to new copies being made—then it tended to disappear as the few extant copies were lost, burned, or reused for other purposes.

Defenders of Q claim that when Matthew and Luke incorporated Q into their Gospels, this "source" became obsolete. Matthew and Luke took the contents of Q and presented them in a more appealing format—in a narrative Gospel with a beginning, middle, and end—and the result was that no one needed Q anymore.

The idea of a gospel consisting mostly of sayings received a boost with the discovery of the full text of the Coptic *Gospel of Thomas* in 1945. Thomas is not Q; very few of the sayings in the double tradition overlap with those in *Thomas*. But Q was supposedly like *Thomas* in form and structure. If the *Gospel of Thomas* could exist and have an audience, then so too Q could have existed and had its readers.

Strong arguments for the independence of Matthew and Luke have persuaded generations of biblical scholars, and for decades the Two

Source Hypothesis approached the status of a consensus in the field. Confident Q scholars have even reconstructed its text and published critical editions of it.[14] And yet, doubts remain.

Markan Priority without Q

The theory that the Synoptic Problem can be explained without Q, by simply positing Luke's dependence on Matthew, first came to prominence as a result of the work of Austin Farrer in 1955[15] and received fresh support from Michael Goulder in 1974 and 1989.[16] This theory is known as the **Farrer hypothesis** or the Farrer-Goulder hypothesis.

Farrer Hypothesis

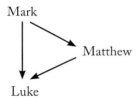

More recently the theory has found an energetic champion in New Testament scholar Mark Goodacre.[17]

Goodacre and his predecessors solve the Synoptic Problem by accepting Markan priority but rejecting Q as the explanation for the double-tradition material. This rejection is based on two mutually reinforcing arguments: Q is not plausible, and Luke did in fact rely on Matthew as a source.

Why are these scholars skeptical about Q?[18] To begin, no copies of Q have survived, not even a fragment. When Q supporters point out that many ancient books have not survived, Farrer hypothesis proponents counter that, in the case of many lost ancient books, there is at least indirect evidence that they once existed, for other ancient writers refer to them and sometimes quote them.[19] But no ancient author refers to or quotes from Q. The Q supporters claim this is a specious argument, because *Matthew and Luke* both quote from Q. But the real point Farrer supporters are making is that, if Q existed, *no one else* besides Matthew and Luke seems to have been aware of its existence, and this seems highly unlikely. For the Q theory to work, Q must have been sufficiently well-known and widely-distributed to have been discovered independently by both Matthew and Luke. Then, supposedly, Q suddenly disappeared without a trace. Books from antiquity do tend to disappear when they become obsolete. But this does not usually happen quite so abruptly.

The existence of agreements between Matthew and Luke against Mark also creates real

14. Among the most prominent Q scholars of recent years is John Kloppenborg, who published a critical edition of Q (along with James Robinson and Paul Hoffman) in 2000 and has also written works on the history and interpretation of the text, such as *Excavating Q: The History and Setting of the Sayings Gospel* (Minneapolis: Fortress, 2000).

15. Austin Farrer, "On Dispensing with Q," in *Studies in the Gospels: Essays in Memory of R. H. Lightfoot*, ed. Dennis Nineham (Oxford: Blackwell, 1955), 55–88.

16. Michael Goulder, *Midrash and Lection in Matthew* (London: SPCK, 1974), and *Luke: A New Paradigm*, JSNT Supp. 20 (Sheffield, UK: Sheffield Academic Press, 1989).

17. See especially, Mark Goodacre, *The Case against Q: Studies in Markan Priority and the Synoptic Problem* (Harrisburg, PA: Trinity, 2002).

18. The arguments that follow borrow heavily from Mark Goodacre's "Ten Reasons to Question Q," *www.markgoodacre.org/Q/ten.htm*. These arguments are also available in printed form in Goodacre's book, *The Case Against Q*.

19. For example, the Greek comic playwright Menander was famous enough to have been quoted or referenced in hundreds of ancient works, including Paul, but his works were not preserved. Modern scholars have discovered fragments of some of these plays, enough to reconstruct a nearly complete version of exactly one play. But there is no doubt that scores of other plays by Menander once existed.

doubt about Q. To review, if two authors used a source independently, it is unlikely they would make the exact same alteration to their source. Q skeptics assert that such agreements between Matthew and Luke occur more often than they should if these two works are independent of each other.

One example of agreement between Matthew and Luke against Mark involves the Parable of the Mustard Seed:

All of these agreements can be explained if Luke copied from Matthew as well as from Mark, sometimes using Matthew's wording instead of Mark's. Why do supporters of the Farrer hypothesis find the possibility that Luke copied from Matthew more plausible than proponents of Q? In some ways this is a matter of perspective. If one assumes Q existed, then it is easy to develop explanations for why Matthew and Luke used it independently in the ways

Mark 4:30-32	Matt. 13:31-32	Luke 13:18-19
He also said, "With what can we compare the kingdom of God, or what parable will we use for it? It is like a mustard seed, <u>which</u>, when sown upon the ground, is the smallest of all the seeds on earth; yet when it is sown it grows up and becomes the greatest of all shrubs, <u>and puts forth large branches</u>, so that the birds of the air can make nests <u>in its shade</u>."	He put before them another parable: "The kingdom of heaven is like a mustard seed *that someone took* and sowed in his field; it is the smallest of all the seeds, but when it has grown it is the greatest of shrubs and *becomes a tree*, so that the birds of the air come and make nests *in its branches*."	He said therefore, "What is the kingdom of God like? And to what should I compare it? It is like a mustard seed *that someone took* and sowed in the garden; it grew and *became a tree*, and the birds of the air made nests *in its branches*.

What the underlined and bold-faced italicized phrases show in these passages is that in three separate instances, Matthew and Luke agree against Mark. Both Matthew and Luke refer to the seed "that someone took" and sowed, but they were not getting this wording from their source, Mark. Moreover, where Mark refers to the shrub that "puts forth large branches," both Matthew and Luke substitute (in almost identical form) "became a tree." And where Mark refers to the ability of birds to nest in the "shade" of this tree, both Matthew and Luke say the birds nest "in its branches." When two authors are copying from the same source, it is possible that occasionally they will make the same alteration to that source, but for this to happen three times in the space of two verses strains credulity.

they did and to discount evidence that seems to suggest Luke used Matthew. On the other hand, if one assumes Luke copied from Matthew, then much of the evidence takes on a different hue. For example, defenders of Q say it is impossible Luke would have known Matthew and yet used so few of his "improvements" to Mark. However, on the Farrer theory, the entire double tradition consists of additions (i.e., improvements) that Matthew makes to Mark that Luke also incorporates into his Gospel. In other words, Luke copies a great deal of material from Matthew—mostly sayings, but some narrative material. One could hardly say he neglects Matthew's additional material.

Much of the debate about whether Luke borrowed from Matthew centers on highly subjective

Mark-Q Overlaps?

Defenders of Q have developed the concept of "**Mark-Q overlaps**" to account for the phenomenon of agreements between Matthew and Luke against Mark. They say, for example, that both Mark and Q had a version of the parable of the Mustard Seed, and in these cases Matthew and Luke sometimes borrowed their wording from Mark and sometimes from Q.

While this is possible, it is unclear whether Mark-Q overlaps could account for all of the agreements between Matthew and Luke against Mark. Goodacre estimates there are "about a thousand" minor agreements between Matthew and Luke against Mark. There is scarcely a pericope in the triple tradition, he points out, that does not feature at least one such agreement. It would seem,

then, that Q would have had to have parallel versions of most of the stories in Mark for such overlaps to account for all of these minor agreements.

However, there are also agreements between Matthew and Luke against Mark in passages where there could not have been a parallel Q version. Supporters of Q agree this gospel did not include a passion narrative. Rather, Q consisted mostly of sayings, with just a few narratives mixed in. Therefore, the one place scholars should not find agreements between Matthew and Luke against Mark is in the passion narrative. However, compare the following accounts after Jesus' conviction by the Sanhedrin on the charge of blasphemy:

Mark 14:64–65	Matt. 26:66–68	Luke 22:62–64
All of them condemned him as deserving death. Some began to spit on him, to blindfold him, and to strike him, saying to him, "Prophesy!"	They answered, "He deserves death." Then they spat in his face and struck him; and some slapped him, saying, "Prophesy to us, you Messiah! **Who is it that struck you?**"	Now the men who were holding Jesus began to mock him and beat him; they also blindfolded him and kept asking him, "Prophesy! **Who is it that struck you?**"

Both Matthew and Luke add, "Who is it that struck you?" The Mark-Q overlap theory cannot explain the phenomenon, nor is it plausible that Matthew and Luke coincidentally added the same phrase.

matters of aesthetics and theology. For example, some Two Source Hypothesis proponents look at Matthew's skillful arrangement of Jesus' teaching material into five discourses, the first of which is the Sermon on the Mount (Matt. 5–7) and cannot imagine how Luke, copying from it, would not choose to preserve it intact. If the Farrer theory is true, Luke chopped the Sermon on the Mount to bits, using some of the material in his Sermon on the Plain (Luke 6), omitting

some material, and scattering the rest throughout his Gospel. For Luke to have treated Matthew's masterpiece so poorly is inconceivable to some scholars, and proof enough that Luke could not have known Matthew.

However, the claim that Matthew's arrangement is more artistic and theologically correct is a judgment call. Luke may not have agreed. Perhaps Luke thought having Jesus preach for three consecutive chapters was too long, and that it would be better to alternate speech with action.

While the Farrer hypothesis has not become the majority view among scholars, it is gaining momentum. In fact, one might venture to say that the jury is still out, and that it would be a mistake to proceed as if the Two Source Hypothesis and Q's existence were matters of fact. In the following chapters, therefore, only the most assured conclusion of source criticism and Synoptic studies is assumed: Markan priority.

Key Terms

Markan priority
source criticism
synopsis
Synoptic Gospels
triple tradition
Synoptic Problem
double tradition

Matthean priority
Griesbach hypothesis
argument from grammar
argument from length
argument from theological
    evolution

Q
Two Source Hypothesis
Farrer hypothesis
Mark-Q overlap

Review Questions

1. Why do biblical scholars believe there is a literary relationship between the Synoptic Gospels? Why is it unlikely or impossible for the similarities between these three Gospels to have been due to eyewitness testimony or reliance on the same oral traditions?

2. What are the arguments for Markan priority? What specific features of Mark's Gospel suggest it was the first to appear, while Matthew and Luke represent later revisions of Mark?

3. Why do most scholars support the theory that a lost sayings gospel, which they term "Q," must have been the original source for the non-Markan material common to Matthew and Luke? Why do they believe that Matthew and Luke are independent?

4. Why does a minority of scholars reject the existence of Q and claim the double-tradition material is best explained by Luke's use of Matthew as a source?

Discussion Questions

1. Which theory (or theories) about the origin of the Synoptic Gospels do you believe? What arguments or evidence are the most persuasive to you?

2. The idea of an earlier Gospel being revised or rewritten by subsequent evangelists is jarring to some people at first. But are there analogies to this process in modern culture?

How many Hollywood scripts are revised and rewritten before the film is finally made? How many Hollywood films are in fact re-makes of earlier productions? Is it possible that the creative process behind the Gospels was in any way similar to that utilized in modern film-making or other media?

Bibliography and Suggestions for Further Study

(Books and websites that are accessible for general undergraduates are marked with an asterisk; other sources listed are appropriate for advanced students.)

Farmer, William L. *The Synoptic Problem: A Critical Analysis.* New York: Macmillan, 1964.

Goodacre, Mark. *The Case against Q: Studies in Markan Priority and the Synoptic Problem.* Harrisburg, PA: Trinity, 2002.

Goulder, Michael. *Luke: A New Paradigm.* JSNT Supp. 20. Sheffield, UK: Sheffield Academic Press, 1989.

Goulder, Michael. *Midrash and Lection in Matthew.* London: SPCK, 1974.

Nineham, Dennis, ed. *Studies in the Gospels: Essays in Memory of R. H. Lightfoot.* Oxford: Blackwell, 1955.

*Stein, Robert H. *The Synoptic Problem: An Introduction.* Grand Rapids: Baker, 1987.

10
CHAPTER

The Gospel of Matthew

The scholarly consensus is that Matthew was written ten to twenty years after Mark, between 80–90 CE. That a new Gospel was produced within a decade or two of the writing of Mark could mean that the author of Matthew thought Mark's Gospel was incomplete or incorrect in some respects. If Matthew felt that the Gospel of Mark was sufficient, there would have been no need to write a new Gospel that rather thoroughly revises its predecessor and adds so much to it. People accustomed to the coexistence of the canonical Gospels often assume each Gospel writer must have seen his work as complementary to that of the other evangelists (to the degree that he was aware of the others), but it is possible later Gospels were written to supplant their predecessors, or at least to eclipse them in significance and influence. As orthodox Christianity developed, Matthew did not supplant Mark, but Matthew's Gospel became far more influential.[1] The Gospel of Mark lived on, but only in the shadow of Matthew.

One reason for this imbalance in influence is that Matthew seems to render Mark superfluous.[2] Almost 60 percent of the Gospel of Matthew consists of stories drawn from Mark, and a full 97 percent of Mark's Gospel finds its way into Matthew.

So as Matthew copied from Mark, he deleted almost nothing from his source. He included additional material, perhaps from oral tradition or from a written source or sources, that accounts for the 40 percent of Matthew that has no parallel in Mark. Moreover, Matthew also altered the stories he inherited from Mark in striking and noteworthy ways. The realization that many of these alterations were motivated by theological considerations led to the development of **redaction criticism** (see chapter 7) as a method of biblical criticism. The word *redact* means "to edit." This method sees Matthew as an editor, as someone who revised the stories he found in Mark and added new ones to produce his own Gospel.

---

1. One of many indicators of this is the frequency with which the early Church Fathers produced commentaries on the respective Gospels. There are dozens of surviving commentaries on Matthew, but sustained commentary on Mark is extremely rare. "While Matthew, Luke, and John have all benefitted from being the subject of several line-by-line patristic commentaries, there are no complete commentaries of Mark that have survived the patristic period"; Thomas C. Oden and Christopher A. Hall, *Mark*, Ancient Christian Commentary on Scripture 2 (Downers Grove, IL: InterVarsity, 1998), xxxi.

2. If Matthew's incorporation of almost all of Mark into his Gospel rendered Mark's Gospel redundant, why did the latter not fall out of favor completely and disappear? Note that, as mentioned in chapter 9, Q supporters claim this is exactly what happened to Q: once incorporated into Matthew and Luke, Q disappeared without a trace. One possible reason why the Gospel of Mark did not suffer the same fate is that it came to be associated with the preaching of Peter as early as the second century. This may have won Mark's Gospel more respectful treatment.

Redaction criticism looks at the changes Matthew made to Mark as key to understanding his purpose(s) in writing. This method argues that Matthew omitted or altered material from Mark only when he disliked it for some reason, disagreed with its implicit teaching or portrayal of key figures, or found it confusing, misleading, or irrelevant. Likewise, he altered material in a particular direction or added new material only when the changes and additions reflected his theological point of view.

This reasoning provides justification for dividing the analysis of Matthew into two main sections. The first section will consider the stories Matthew inherited from Mark and altered in some significant way. The second will consider the stories Matthew added to his Gospel, stories that have no parallel in Mark. There is much from Mark that Matthew apparently liked and left intact. However, to understand what is distinctive to the Gospel of Matthew, one must study the differences between the two Gospels.

The focus in this chapter will be exclusively on redaction criticism because the goal is to introduce students to each major method of biblical criticism through the sustained analysis of a particular text, and Matthew is particularly well-suited to the redaction-critical approach. Redaction criticism, however, is by no means the only suitable method of studying Matthew, which might profitably be approached using literary criticism, New Testament theology, ideological criticism, or a host of other methods.

Matthew's Revision of Markan Traditions

As he copied and revised the stories he inherited from Mark, Matthew made literally thousands of changes. Many of these changes are merely stylistic: correcting Mark's grammar, revising a sentence to make it smoother, or changing a word here or there to provide a particular nuance or connotation. Such changes have little effect on the meaning of the text. However, some of Matthew's changes to Mark dramatically affect meaning, and very often the same types of changes are made consistently throughout the Gospel. Certain patterns emerge that allow one to conclude there were subjects about which Matthew had very different ideas than Mark.

Portrayal of the Disciples

One of the groundbreaking studies that introduced redaction criticism to the field of biblical studies was Günther Bornkamm's 1948 article comparing the Stilling of the Storm passage in Mark and Matthew.[3] The differences between the two accounts are best illustrated by placing them side-by-side as follows:

Mark 4:35-41[4]	Matt. 8:23-27
On that day, when evening had come, he said to them, "Let us go across to the other side." And leaving the crowd, they took him with them in the boat, just as he was. And other boats were with him. And a great storm of wind arose, and	And when he got into the boat, his disciples followed him. And behold, there arose a great storm on the sea, so that the boat was being swamped by the waves; but he was asleep. And they went and woke him, saying, "Save, Lord; we

continued

3. Günther Bornkamm, "Die Sturmstillung im Matthäusevangelium," *Wort und Dienst: Jahrbuch der Theologischen Schule Bethel* 1 (1948): 49–54.

4. The RSV is used in this table.

Mark 4:35–41 *continued*	Matt. 8:23–27 *continued*
the waves beat into the boat, so that the boat was already filling. But he was in the stern, asleep on the cushion; and they woke him and said to him, "Teacher, do you not care if we perish?" And he awoke and rebuked the wind, and said to the sea, "Peace! Be still!" And the wind ceased, and there was a great calm. He said to them, "Why are you afraid? Have you still no faith?" And [they feared a great fear],[5] and said to one another, "Who then is this, that even wind and sea obey him?"	are perishing." And he said to them, "Why are you afraid, O men of little faith?" Then he rose and rebuked the winds and the sea; and there was a great calm. And the men marveled, saying, "What sort of man is this, that even winds and sea obey him?"

Some of the changes made by Matthew are merely stylistic. However, many of the changes indicate a clear desire on Matthew's part to produce a different impression than that produced by Mark's account.

For example, in Matthew the disciples address Jesus as "Lord," which implies that they understand Jesus' essentially divine nature and have faith in him. In Mark the disciples address him as "Teacher," which shows respect but not necessarily *faith* in Jesus. In Matthew the disciples clearly ask Jesus to "save"; they awaken Jesus because they believe he can perform a miracle and rescue them. In contrast, Mark's wording—"Do you not care if we perish?"—gives no indication that the disciples are asking for a miracle or that they believe Jesus might perform one.

In Mark, Jesus asks the disciples, "Why are you afraid? Have you still no faith?" The second question is more obviously negative, as Jesus seems to question whether they believe in him at all. Matthew softens this to "O men of *little faith*," which implies that they may have slipped up, but Jesus has not lost confidence in them altogether.

In both Mark and Matthew, Jesus asks the disciples why they are afraid but, significantly, Matthew has changed the order of events. In Mark, Jesus calms the storm first, and then asks the disciples, "Why are you afraid?" In Matthew, Jesus asks the disciples why they are afraid and *then* calms the storm. This means that in Matthew, the object of the disciples' fear is the storm. This is understandable, as their boat is being swamped and they are afraid they will drown. In Mark, the storm is already over when Jesus asks, "Why are you afraid?" And the question does not refer to fear that has passed; Jesus does not ask, "Why *were* you afraid?" but, "Why *are* you afraid?" In Mark, then, the disciples' terror continues after the storm is calmed. The object of their fear is not the storm; it is Jesus. They are afraid of their master.

The most obvious difference between the two stories is the disciples' reaction to Jesus' questions. In Matthew, the disciples "marvel" at Jesus and comment that no sort of man could calm the wind and seas. This seems like a completely appropriate reaction; the disciples have recovered from their momentary lack of faith. But in Mark, if one translates literally, the disciples "feared a

---

5. The RSV (and NRSV) translates this phrase as "they were filled with great awe," which is misleading. The literal meaning of the Greek is "they feared a great fear," which is important in this case.

great fear." This is important because fear plays such a negative role in the Gospel of Mark. Jesus is constantly telling the disciples not to be afraid. Fear and faith are opposites. Being afraid is a sign that a person lacks faith. Having faith, by contrast, makes a person fearless. When Jesus asks his disciples, "Why are you afraid?" he is not just criticizing his disciples; he is *challenging* them to have faith and leave fear behind. Their response is to be more afraid than ever.

In this passage, Matthew makes four or five alterations to Mark's version of the story, all of which seem designed to portray the disciples in a more positive light. There are also many other passages in which Mark portrays the disciples negatively and Matthew rewrites the same story to provide a more positive portrayal.

One such passage is the episode in which Jesus walks on water (Mark 6:47–52; Matt. 14:22–33). The biggest change Matthew makes involves the conclusion to the story. Mark notes the disciples still "did not understand about the loaves" (that is, the earlier episode in which Jesus managed to feed five thousand people with five loaves and two fish), "but their hearts were hardened." Hardness of heart is a negative quality that links the disciples with villains like the Pharaoh in the book of Exodus and the scribes and Pharisees elsewhere in Mark's Gospel (see Mark 3:5). By contrast, Matthew ends his version of the episode with the disciples worshipping Jesus and saying, "Truly you are the Son of God." This is a common theme in Matthew's reshaping of the character of the disciples. They are not perfect and their faith sometimes falters, but most often they learn from their mistakes and end on a positive note. In Mark, this positive note is almost never found.

Other Markan episodes that Matthew significantly modifies to improve the portrayal of the disciples include the teaching about yeast (Mark 8:14–21; Matt. 16:5–12), Peter's confession and the first passion prediction (Mark 8:27–33;

Matt. 16:13–23), the second passion prediction and the dispute about greatness (Mark 9:30–35; Matt. 17:22–23; 18:1–5), the unknown exorcist (Mark 9:38–40; omitted in Matthew), and the third passion prediction and James's and John's request for positions of power (Mark 10:32–45; Matt. 20:17–28). In Mark, the disciples misunderstand Jesus' teachings, they are often afraid or terrified (frequently of Jesus himself), they lack faith in Jesus, and they are preoccupied with their own greatness, fame, power, and glory. In Matthew, the disciples sometimes misunderstand, but with Jesus' help they overcome their misunderstanding. They are less often afraid, and their faith eventually helps them overcome their fear. Their faith might falter at times, turning them into persons "of little faith," but their faith never disappears altogether.

Consequently, it comes as no great surprise when Matthew springs the biggest change of all: the disciples (minus Judas) find redemption after Jesus' resurrection. The disciples still betray, abandon, and deny Jesus in Matthew, but Jesus meets with them after his resurrection and entrusts to them the leadership of his church. "All authority in heaven and on earth" has been given to Jesus, and he in turn gives it to his disciples, telling them, "Go out and make" disciples of all nations, baptizing them in the name of the Father and of the Son and of the Holy Spirit, and teaching them to obey everything that I have commanded you" (Matt. 28:18–20).

Ecclesiology

Matthew's rehabilitation of the disciples is intimately related to his **ecclesiology** (teaching about the church) and his **eschatology** (teaching about the end of the world). Mark shows little interest in the ongoing life of the church, presumably because he thought the end of the world was imminent and the church, as an institution, would not be around very long before the end came. By contrast, Matthew clearly sought to lay a more solid foundation for the church as an institution,[6] presumably because he did not share Mark's view that the end of the world was imminent. If the church was to carry Christianity into the indefinite future, then its leaders and founders should be portrayed as men of faith and good character.

Mark's Gospel never uses the word "church" (Greek, *ekklēsia*), and nowhere does it evince concern about how Christianity will survive and prosper over the long term. Matthew's Gospel does use the word "church," and the significance he attaches to that term can be seen in his handling of a passage called Peter's confession and the first passion prediction.

The key passage is the insertion by Matthew into the middle of Mark's version of this story, in bold face in table below. Jesus praises Peter ("Blessed are you Simon son of Jonah"), and bestows authority upon him under a new name ("you are Peter, and on this rock I will build my church"). In the process Jesus lays a foundation for the church as an institution. He refers to "my church," making it clear that he approved of the creation of a church in his name. He also announces an important role for this church in the process of salvation, granting to it a great deal of authority. As leader of the church, Peter is given "the keys to the kingdom of heaven" and is told whatever he binds (prohibits) and looses (permits) on earth will

Peter's Confession and the First Passion Prediction

Mark 8:27-30[7]	Matt. 16:13-20
And Jesus went on with his disciples, to the villages of Caesarea Phillipi; and on the way he asked his disciples, "Who do men say that I am?" And they told him, "John the Baptist; and others say, Elijah; and others one of the prophets." And he asked them, "But who do you say that I am?" Peter answered him, "You are the Christ."	Now when Jesus came into the district of Caesarea Phillipi, he asked his disciples, "Who do men say that the Son of man is?" And they said, "Some say John the Baptist, others say Elijah, and others Jeremiah or one of the prophets." He said to them, "But who do you say that I am?" Simon Peter replied, "You are the Christ, the Son of the living God." **And Jesus answered him, "Blessed are you, Simon son of Jonah! For flesh and blood has not revealed this to you, but my Father who is in heaven. And I tell you, you are Peter, and on this rock I will build my church, and the powers of death shall not prevail against it. I will give you the keys to the kingdom of heaven, and whatever you bind on earth will be bound in heaven, and whatever you loose on earth shall be loosed in heaven."** Then he strictly charged the disciples to tell no one that he was the Christ.
And he charged them to tell no one about him.	

6. One must be cautious not to identify the church as Matthew conceived it with the church as it would develop in later centuries. There were no church buildings in Matthew's time, for example. All Christian services were conducted in private homes ("house churches"). Moreover, the hierarchy that would later be headed by bishops and popes was only just starting to develop in the late first century.

7. The RSV is used in this table.

Was Peter the First Pope?

The word "**pope**" (Greek, *pappas*, "father") was not coined until the third century CE, and at first it could be applied to anyone who held the office of bishop. "Pope" was not used as a title reserved for the bishop of Rome as the supreme leader of the Western Roman Catholic Church until the sixth century. Nonetheless, Catholic teaching maintains Peter was appointed by Jesus as the first pope,[8] even if he was never actually known as "Pope Peter."

The Catholic argument hinges on Matthew 16:17-19, which identifies Peter as the "rock" on which the church is built, grants him the power of binding and loosing, gives him "the keys to the kingdom of heaven," and suggests that Peter is a conduit for revelation ("flesh and blood has not revealed this to you, but my Father who is in heaven"). Consequently, the Catholic Church claims, Peter enjoyed supreme authority in early Christianity over the church, its members, and the other apostles.[9] Moreover, this authority was then handed on to the successors of Peter and the apostles: subsequent popes and bishops.[10] As a result, in the Catholic Church, the current pope is viewed as the successor to Peter and he can issue teachings (usually in the form of encyclical letters) that are binding on Catholics. An obvious example is the Catholic ban on the use of artificial methods of birth control, a teaching that has no scriptural backing.

Protestants, starting with Martin Luther, reject the authority of the pope. The primary Protestant argument against the papacy involves the *biblical* basis of the Catholic arguments.[11] Protestants note the scriptural evidence for Peter's papacy is slender and ambiguous. Only Matthew includes the idea that Peter was the "rock"[12] and held the "keys to the kingdom" (Matt. 16:19). No other New Testament text confirms this.[13] Moreover, other New Testament texts suggest the leaders of the early church were equal to each other (Acts 15; Eph. 2:19-20) or seem to undermine the claim that Peter held supreme authority in the early church. Paul does not seem to accept the idea that he owed obedience to Peter, and he writes scathingly of Peter's apparent hypocrisy in the incident at Antioch. At first Peter sat down and ate with Gentiles, but when "certain people . . . from James [the brother of the Lord]" arrived, Peter abandoned his earlier position and ceased to eat with Gentiles (Gal. 2:11-14). This episode suggests that—at least in Paul's view—Peter was hardly infallible and that he was afraid his behavior would be reported back to James. This should not have been the case if Peter held supreme authority.

---

8. See *Catechism of the Catholic Church* 424, 552.

9. Early Christian proponents of this view include Clement of Alexandria (*Salvation of the Rich* 21.3–5), Tertullian (*Antidote for the Scorpion's Sting* 10; *Modesty* 21.9–10), Cyprian (*The Unity of the Catholic Church* 4), and John Chrysostom (*De Eleemosyna* 3.4).

10. The earliest known testimony with respect to the doctrine of apostolic succession is in Irenaeus, *Against Heresies* 3.3, about 180 CE.

11. See Martin Luther, *Resolutiones Disputationum de Indulgetiarum*.

12. Many Protestants claim Peter is not the "rock" on which Jesus intends to build his church, pointing out two slightly different Greek words are used here: *petros* and *petra*. See, e.g., Keith Mathison, *The Shape of Sola Scriptura* (Moscow, ID: Canon, 2001), 184–85. However, other Protestant biblical scholars, such as Craig Blomberg and Donald Carson, admit the wordplay in the passage only works if Peter himself is the rock.

13. Many supporters of the papacy, both early and modern, argue the passage in John 21 in which Jesus tells Peter three times, "Feed my sheep" or "Feed my lambs" provides confirmation of Peter's primacy, but Protestants do not find this convincing.

In this mosaic from St. Peter's Basilica, the Vatican, Jesus gives Peter the keys to the kingdom of heaven and calls him the rock on which he would build the church. Matthew's Gospel expands the Markan account to include these details.

Eschatology

The textual basis for the claim that Mark expected the end of the world and the final judgment to occur in the near future is covered in chapter 8. In particular, Mark appears to have been written either in anticipation of the destruction of the Temple in 70 CE or in its immediate aftermath, and the author apparently took that catastrophic event as a sign the end was near. Matthew is writing, according to most estimates, ten to twenty years later, and it was by then clear to him and everyone else that the end had not occurred as early as Mark (and Paul) expected. This is known as the **delay of the parousia**, *parousia* being a technical term for Jesus' anticipated second coming.

determine the judgment of people in heaven. The passage as a whole implies membership in this church is essential for salvation, and Jesus entrusts the leadership of this church to his disciple Peter.

Later in the Gospel, in a passage known as the Great Commission (Matt. 28:16–20), Jesus states, "All authority in heaven and on earth has been given to me," and he in turn gives that authority to his remaining eleven disciples as a whole. Their task is to go out and "make disciples of all nations, baptizing them in the name of the Father and of the Son and of the Holy Spirit, and teaching them to obey everything that [Jesus] commanded." Carrying the message of Christianity to "all nations" is a huge undertaking that will require the concentrated effort of a major organization: that is, the church.

That Matthew was concerned about the delay of the parousia is evident from his inclusion of three parables not found in Mark, each of which includes such a delay and symbolically suggests the one being delayed is Jesus.[14] These parables are the Good and Wicked Slaves (Matt. 24:45–51), the Ten Bridesmaids (25:1–13), and the Talents (25:14–30). In the first, the wicked slave says to himself, "My master is delayed" (24:48), and uses this delay as an excuse for drunkenness and misbehavior. In the second, the ten bridesmaids are awaiting the groom's arrival with oil lamps to light his way to the wedding feast. Five of them are caught unprepared when "the bridegroom was delayed" (25:5); they run

14. See Gunther Bornkamm, "End-Expectation and Church in Matthew," in *Tradition and Interpretation in Matthew*, ed. G. Bornkamm, G. Barth, and H. J. Held (London: SCM, 1963), 23, and David C. Sim, *Apocalyptic Eschatology in the Gospel of Matthew* (Cambridge: Cambridge University Press, 1996). 151–52.

short of oil. It is easy to see Jesus as the "delayed" master and the bridegroom of these respective parables. The third parable is perhaps the most telling. The master entrusts each of his servants with talents (a large sum of cash) and goes away to leave them to make use of this money as they see fit. Then he does not return until "after a long time" (25:19). Many interpreters see this as Matthew's way of saying that not only has Jesus' second coming been delayed, it might not occur for some time to come.

The idea that Matthew thought there might be a significant amount of time prior to the second coming is also implied in the Great Commission (28:16–20). There Jesus promises he will be with his followers "to the end of the age" (28:20), but the enormity of the task he has laid before them—making disciples of "all nations"—would require an extended period of time to complete.

Christology

Several aspects of the analysis of the Gospel of Mark in chapter 8 can be used to demonstrate the claim that this Gospel has a relatively **low Christology**, meaning that Jesus is seen as more human and less divine. Indeed, that Mark begins with Jesus' baptism, in which God's voice declares, "You are my son, my beloved son, in whom I am well pleased," could be taken to mean that Jesus was not born as God's Son but that God was making Jesus his Son from this point forward. This is known as **adoptionism**, the idea that Jesus was born as an ordinary human being and was chosen to be the Messiah on the basis of his personal righteousness and was adopted as God's Son. It is not clear that Mark intended such an interpretation, but his account can be taken in that sense.

That Matthew begins his Gospel with the story of Jesus' birth to a virgin named Mary emphatically rules out adoptionism. According to Matthew, Jesus has no human father. He was not born as an ordinary human being: he was the Son of God from birth, and did not "become" the Son of God at some point in his adult life.

This is only the beginning of the Christological differences between Mark and Matthew. Repeatedly, Markan passages in which Jesus displays human limitations are reworked by Matthew to be more compatible with Jesus' divinity. One such episode is the healing of the woman with the hemorrhage:

Mark 5:29-34	Matt. 9:21-22
[The woman] said, "If I but touch his clothes, I will be made well." **Immediately her hemorrhage stopped; and she felt in her body that she was healed of her disease. Immediately aware that power had gone forth from him, Jesus turned about in the crowd and said, "Who touched my clothes?" And his disciples said to him, "You see the crowd pressing in on you; how can you say, 'Who touched me?'" He looked all around to see who had done it. But the woman, knowing what had happened to her, came in fear and trembling, fell down before him, and told him the whole truth.** He said to her, "Daughter, your faith has made you well; go in peace and be healed of your disease."	[The woman] said to herself, "If I only touch his cloak, I will be made well." Jesus turned, and seeing her he said, "Take heart, daughter; your faith has made you well."

Jesus' Rejection at Nazareth

Mark 6:4–6[15]	Matt. 13:57–58
Jesus said to them, "A prophet is not without honor, except in his own country, and among his own kin, and in his own house." **And he could do no mighty work there,** except that he laid his hands on a few sick people and healed them, and he was amazed at their unbelief.	And they took offense at him. But Jesus said to them, "A prophet is not without honor except in his own country and in his own house." **And he did not do many mighty works there,** because of their unbelief.

Matthew significantly omits parts of Mark's account. In Mark it is fairly clear Jesus does not know who touched him. The woman approaches Jesus surreptitiously and touches him without his knowledge. After perceiving that power has gone forth from him, he asks, "Who touched my clothes?" and then "he looked all around to see who had done it." Mark's Jesus is not omniscient; there are things he does not know. In Matthew, this is not the case. The woman approaches Jesus apparently without stealth, and Jesus heals her in full knowledge of who she is and what ails her.

Another such comparison can be made between Mark's version of Jesus' rejection at Nazareth and Matthew's account of the same event. Both stories begin with the crowds in Jesus' hometown mocking him and proclaiming there is nothing extraordinary about him. The stories diverge in their description of the aftermath of this rejection.

Again, one version clearly presents Jesus as subject to human limitation and the other does not. In Mark, Jesus is *unable* to perform miracles (except for a few) in his hometown, because his ability to work healings is dependent in part on the faith of the recipients. He is not omnipotent. In Matthew, Jesus merely *chose* not to perform many miracles in his hometown, because of their unbelief. There is no implication he lacked the power to do so.

In addition, in Mark the disciples tend to refer to Jesus simply as "teacher," while in Matthew they tend to use the more divine title "Lord." In Mark, when Peter confesses Jesus' identity, he says only that Jesus is "the Messiah" (Mark 8:29). In Matthew, Peter makes a stronger confession, calling Jesus "the Messiah, the Son of the living God" (Matt. 16:16). Jesus' resurrection is much more impressive in Matthew as well. There is ample evidence throughout the Gospel that Matthew sought to turn Mark's more human Jesus into a more powerful and divine figure, worthy of the kind of worship Christians were giving to him.

Matthew's Additions

There are large sections of Matthew's Gospel that have no parallel in Mark and hence deserve separate consideration. Foremost among these are Matthew 1–2 (the genealogy and birth of Christ) and Matthew 5–7 (the Sermon on the Mount).

Matthew's Infancy Narrative and Proof from Prophecy

In Matthew 1–2, the author indicates the events surrounding Jesus' birth fulfill various Old Testament prophecies that would supposedly signal the identity of the Messiah when he came. There are five separate places in Matthew 1–2 where Matthew pauses to show how a fulfillment of prophecy has occurred (Matt. 1:22–23; 2:5–6, 15, 17–18, 23). This kind

---

15. The RSV is used in this table.

of argument is called **proof from prophecy**, and Matthew was one of early Christianity's most ardent practitioners of it. More than half of the New Testament's explicit claims that Jesus fulfilled prophecy are found in Matthew.

In most cases, the fulfillment of a single prophecy was not enough to prove a given person was the Messiah. For example, the main purpose of Matthew's genealogy is to prove Jesus is a descendant of King David, because it was believed on the basis of the prophecy in 2 Samuel 7 that the Messiah had to be of David's

bloodline. However, many people at the time of Jesus could claim descent from King David. Consequently, being able to trace one's lineage back to David was a necessary but not sufficient condition for a messianic claimant. Matthew's purpose in the birth narrative and throughout the rest of the Gospel is to show that Jesus fulfills *all* of the messianic prophecies and therefore must be the Messiah.

The aforementioned prophecy in 2 Samuel 7 provides a good example of how this works, as well as illustrating some of the attendant difficulties. In

Was Jesus a Descendant of King David?

Like Luke, Matthew traces Jesus' genealogy through Joseph. The problem is—if the story of the virginal conception of Jesus is to be believed—Jesus does not have any of Joseph's blood flowing through his veins.

This problem can be resolved by claiming Mary is also a descendant of King David (as Tertullian[16] and other early Church Fathers did), but this was not satisfactory to most ancient audiences. One's genealogy was always traced through the father.

Instead, the problem is resolved by a common ancient understanding of paternity. Joseph does not need to be Jesus' biological father for Jesus to be considered of Joseph's blood. It is sufficient if Joseph agrees to be Jesus' legal father. That is, if Joseph claims Jesus as his son and accepts him as such, then

Jesus gets to claim Joseph's ancestors as his own, regardless of the biology of the situation.[17]

Dramatic tension in this regard is created in Matthew 2:18-25 when Joseph nearly decides against claiming Jesus as his son. Mary, his betrothed, turns up pregnant and he knows he is not the father. As a result, he resolves to dismiss (divorce) her quietly and to deny his paternity of this child. However, an angel appears to Joseph in a dream and tells him to proceed with his marriage to Mary and to claim Jesus as his son. The way that one did so was by naming the child.[18] The angel instructs Joseph to name the child "Jesus," and Joseph does so, thereby claiming Jesus as his own son, bestowing legitimacy upon him, and giving Jesus the right to be considered a "son of David."

---

16. See *On the Flesh of the Lord* 21.

17. John Meier writes, "The Jewish milieu out of which the Infancy Narratives came regularly traced a child's genealogy through his or her father, whether or not the 'father' was actually the biological parent. . . . In the eyes of the Old Testament, the legal father is the real father, whether or not he physically procreated the child"; John Meier, *A Marginal Jew: Rethinking the Historical Jesus*, Anchor Bible Reference Library (New Haven: Yale University Press, 1994–2009), 1:217. Yigal Levin argues, though, that there is scant evidence for such an adoption law or custom in ancient Judaism, and that it is the Roman law and practice with respect to adoption that Matthew is assuming when he asserts that Jesus can claim descent from the ancestors of his legal, adoptive father. See Yigal Levin, "Jesus, 'Son of God' and 'Son of David,'" *Journal for the Study of the New Testament* 28, no. 4 (2006): 422–28.

18. See Jane Schaberg, *The Illegitimacy of Jesus: A Feminist Theological Interpretation of the Infancy Narratives* (New York: Crossroad, 1990).

In Matthew's Gospel, the angel Gabriel convinces Joseph to accept Jesus as his son, although Jesus has no human father. The scene is portrayed in this painting by nineteenth-century artist James Tissot.

2 Samuel 7:12–14, the prophecy reads, "When your days are fulfilled and you lie down with your ancestors, I will raise up your offspring after you, who shall come forth from your body, and I will establish his kingdom. He shall build a house for my name, and I will establish the throne of his kingdom forever. I will be a father to him, and he shall be a son to me." The word *messiah* does not appear in this passage (and indeed rarely occurs in the Old Testament), but it is not hard to see how many Jews came to see this as a messianic prophecy. On its basis, it was expected that the messiah would be David's "offspring," having come forth from his body.

This is why Matthew includes Jesus' genealogy. Being a descendant of Abraham makes Jesus a Jew. Being a descendant of David makes Jesus eligible to be the Messiah (Matt. 1:1). Matthew further argues God has been planning the generations of Abraham's descendants carefully, to further point to Jesus' messianic identity. Matthew notes there are exactly fourteen generations between Abraham and David, fourteen generations between David and the exile, and fourteen generations between the exile and Jesus (1:17). This is significant not only because it suggests God's plan for the salvation of the Jews is coming to fruition and Jesus' arrival is right on time but also because the number fourteen had a special significance to Jews in Matthew's era. Each Hebrew letter had a numerical value, and the numerical value of the three Hebrew letters of the name "David" (*daleth*=four, *waw*=six, *daleth*=four) added up to fourteen. This further suggests that the time is ripe for the advent of the Davidic messiah.

Another proof from prophecy is given when the Magi (wise men, or astrologers) arrive at Jerusalem and ask where to find the newborn king of the Jews whose star they had observed. The chief priests and scribes of Herod's court explain that the Messiah will be born in Bethlehem, citing a prophecy: "But you, O Bethlehem of Ephrathah, who are one of the little clans of Judah, from you shall come forth for me one who is to rule in Israel, whose origin is from old, from ancient days" (Mic. 5:2; Matt. 2:5–6). Again the word *messiah* does not appear, but the reference to a future ruler was enough for many Jews to give this prophecy a messianic interpretation. When Matthew recounts how Jesus is born in Bethlehem, the hometown of his parents Mary and Joseph, he claims the prophecy is fulfilled.

A controversial case of Matthew's use of proof from prophecy is found in 1:22–23; Matthew claims that Jesus' virginal conception fulfills a prophecy from Isaiah 7:14, which he quotes as follows: "Look, the virgin shall conceive and bear a son, and they shall name him Emmanuel." The New Revised Standard Version's more accurate translation of Isaiah 7:14 reads, "Look, the young woman is with child and shall bear a son, and shall name him Immanuel." That is to say, Isaiah 7:14 speaks of a "young woman" being with child, not a "virgin."[19] Moreover, Isaiah speaks of a woman who "is with child," which means she is already pregnant. Matthew speaks of a woman who "shall conceive," indicating that the statement refers to a future pregnancy rather than a contemporary one.

Some Problems with Proof from Prophecy

Matthew's use of Isaiah 7:14 is one example of his taking a prophecy out of context and giving it a messianic spin. Another example is his citation of Jeremiah 31:15 as a foretelling of the "slaughter of the innocents." Jeremiah 31:15 does not even appear to be a prophecy, and its words have a very tenuous con-

Matthew's Gospel claims that prophecy was fulfilled by Jesus growing up in the city of Nazareth, shown here. No such prophecy has been identified.

nection with the events Matthew describes. But taking quotes out of context is only one of the problems critics have identified with Matthew's use of proof from prophecy.

For example, Matthew also cites a nonexistent prophecy in Matthew 2:23. He claims that Jesus grew up in the town of Nazareth "so that what had been spoken through the prophets might be fulfilled, 'He will be called a Nazorean.'" However, there is no trace of such a prophecy outside of Matthew's Gospel.

Another kind of problem is that sometimes Matthew and Luke both claim that Jesus fulfilled prophecy, but in different and contradictory ways. For example, both Matthew and Luke contain a genealogy, but their genealogies are wildly contradictory. Both Matthew and Luke also claim Jesus was born in Bethlehem, but Matthew implies this was Mary and Joseph's hometown, while Luke explains Mary and Joseph were from Nazareth, and were only visiting Bethlehem because of a census.

To some, these inconsistencies raise questions about whether the evangelists may have been tailoring their stories to make it appear as though Jesus fulfilled various prophecies. This suspicion is heightened by Matthew's revision of Jesus' triumphal entry into Jerusalem. Matthew alters the account he inherited from Mark so that instead of riding on a single animal, Jesus rides into the city on two animals, a donkey and a colt (Matt. 21:1–6). Matthew then asserts that this episode fulfills the prophecy in Zechariah 9:9, which he (mistakenly) believes refers to two beasts. His (mis)interpretation of the prophetic text seems to guide his version of the event, which is not how proof from prophecy is supposed to work.

© Ivan Vasylyev / Shutterstock.com

---

19. This objection was being made by Jews as early as about 160; see Justin Martyr, *Dialogue with Trypho* 43.

Matthew's mistaken reference to a "virgin" rather than a "young woman" is easily explained. The common Greek translation of the Hebrew Scriptures in Matthew's day was the **Septuagint** (abbreviated "LXX," the Roman numeral for seventy, which was the number of translators who supposedly worked on the Septuagint). The Septuagint rather clumsily translated the Hebrew word for "young woman" in Isaiah 7:14 using the Greek word for "virgin." Matthew was simply relying on the faulty LXX translation of the Hebrew text of Isaiah. Although this was not Matthew's mistake, it nevertheless deflates the import of his use of Isaiah 7:14 as a proof from prophecy. The virgin birth that Matthew reports did not fulfill any prophecy.

The other problem with Matthew's citation of this prophecy is that, when read in context, it is clear that the author of Isaiah 7 is not referring to the birth of a messiah hundreds of years in the future. The chapter is about how King Ahaz of Judah is feeling threatened by two rival kings. Ahaz's court prophet Isaiah reassures his king these threats will not materialize but will go away on their own. The "sign" given in 7:14–16 merely gives a time frame within which King Ahaz's problems will resolve themselves: A young woman is with child. By the time she gives birth to her son and the boy reaches the age at which he eats solid food and can distinguish between right and wrong, Ahaz can trust that the "land before whose two kings you are in dread will be deserted" (Isa. 7:16). Matthew has taken out of context a prophecy about the near-term political problems of an eighth-century BCE king of Judah.[20]

Jesus as the Suffering Servant from Isaiah

The most important debate over prophecy between ancient Jews and Christians concerned whether the Messiah's suffering and death are foretold in the scriptures. Many ancient Jews rejected the claim that Jesus is the Messiah precisely because of his ignominious death on the cross. They expected the Messiah to accomplish great things, not to be captured and tortured to death by his enemies.[21] Christians, however, claimed that the **Suffering Servant** passages in Isaiah 52-53 were the proof that it was God's plan for the Messiah to come and take upon himself the sins of the people, with his sacrificial death providing the atonement for those sins and making salvation possible. Jews had been examining those same passages for centuries and never saw in them a portent of a suffering Messiah. Instead, they claimed the messianic interpretation of Isaiah 52-53 was an *ex post facto* rationalization on the part of Christians to account for Jesus' unexpected death at the hands of the Romans.

---

20. The author of Matthew may not have been as bothered by this criticism as much as many modern readers are. In his era Matthew was not alone in thinking verses like Isa. 7:14 might have had hidden significance that would not have been apparent to their original author or audience. The Dead Sea Scrolls reveal that the Essenes articulated and often used a method of scriptural interpretation called *pesher*, whereby commentary was made on texts from the Hebrew Bible in which the historical context of the original writing was irrelevant, and it was assumed God had inserted some secret meaning behind the plain sense of the text. Christians would later develop an allegorical method of interpretation that held scripture had four possible levels of meaning, only one of which was the plain, literal sense. The difficulty with such methods, many critics have pointed out, is that if one is not bound by the literal meaning of words in their original context one can get the Bible to say almost anything.

21. Justin Martyr attributes these words to the Jew Trypho: "These and suchlike passages of scripture compel us to await One who is great and glorious and takes over the everlasting kingdom from the Ancient of days as Son of man. But this your so-called Christ is without honor and glory, so that He has even fallen into the uttermost curse that is in the law of God, for He was crucified" (*Dialogue with Trypho*, 32.1); translation from Justin Martyr, *Dialogue with Trypho*, in *The Ante-Nicene Fathers*, vol. 1, *Apostolic Fathers, Justin Martyr, Irenaeus*, ed. Alexander Roberts and James Donaldson (repr., Peabody, MA: Hendrickson, 1994).

Matthew offers an early example of the many Christian attempts to use Old Testament prophecy to prove Jesus is the Messiah. These attempts sparked a lively and sometimes bitter debate between Christians, who saw proof that Jesus was the promised Messiah everywhere in the Hebrew Scriptures, and others (especially Jews), who looked at the same texts and drew entirely different conclusions.

The Sermon on the Mount (Matthew 5–7) and Early Christian Ethics

Mark's Gospel does not contain a great deal of Jesus' ethical teaching, placing more emphasis on the urgent need to repent in the short time before Judgment Day. Matthew, by contrast, both

The Five Discourses of Jesus in Matthew

1. The Sermon on the Mount (Matthew 5-7)
2. The Missionary Discourse (Matthew 10)
3. The Parables of the Kingdom (Matthew 13)
4. The Discourse on the Church (Matthew 18)
5. The Eschatological Discourse (Matthew 24-25)

emphasizes the importance of ethical behavior for Christians to gain salvation and provides numerous examples of Jesus' ethical teachings, many of them concentrated in the Sermon on the Mount (Matthew 5–7).

Numerous scholars have noted the Sermon on the Mount is one of five discourses by Jesus in the Gospel of Matthew. The number five is symbolic of the five books of the Torah (or Pentateuch, which means "five scrolls"), which were traditionally thought to have been written by Moses. Possible parallels between Jesus and Moses are found in the infancy narrative as well. Both Jesus and Moses as infants survive attempts to kill them by tyrants, and both come out of Egypt to the Promised Land. Matthew's portrayal of Jesus as a kind of new Moses shows that he understood Jesus' role as the Messiah to include the functions of lawgiver and authoritative interpreter of the law.

© jorisvo / Shutterstock.com

Matthew's Gospel arranges Jesus' teachings into five discourses, possibly in imitation of the five books of the Torah. The first discourse is the Sermon on the Mount, depicted in this stained-glass window in the cathedral of Brussels, Belgium.

The importance of obeying the Law of Moses (as supplemented and reinterpreted by Christ) is seen in a number of passages Matthew adds to Mark. In the Sermon on the Mount, Jesus clearly teaches that professions of faith are not sufficient for salvation; they must be accompanied by deeds worthy of that faith. "Not everyone who says to me 'Lord, Lord' will enter the kingdom of heaven, but only the one who does the will of my Father in heaven. On that day many will say to me, 'Lord, Lord, did we not prophesy in your name, and cast out demons in your name, and do many deeds of power in your name?' Then I will declare to them, 'I never knew you; go away from me, you evildoers'" (Matt. 7:21–23).

Similar passages are found throughout Matthew's Gospel. In the Great Judgment (Matt. 25:31–46), Jesus preaches that on the day of reckoning he will separate the saved from the damned like a shepherd separates the sheep from the goats. The saved, Jesus says, are those who fought for social justice by feeding the hungry, clothing the naked, comforting the sick, giving hospitality to strangers, and visiting the imprisoned. The damned are those who neglected to care for the neediest among them. Finally, in the Great Commission (28:16–20), Jesus tells his apostles not only to convert and baptize people, but to "make disciples . . . teaching them to obey everything that [Jesus] commanded." Matthew consistently stresses that good behavior, which he terms "righteousness," is an essential part of leading a life pleasing to God.

In the field of ethics, Christianity had been given a considerable head start by its mother religion, Judaism. No other ancient religion had anything comparable to the 613 commandments found in the Law of Moses and the developing system of rabbinic teachings that extended and clarified the Torah. If Christianity was going to follow Judaism in making morality central to the religion, it would need to clarify the relationship of its new ethical system to the Torah.

In the Sermon on the Mount, Jesus explains that his vision of the law does not contradict the Torah, but intensifies it:

> Do not think that I have come to abolish the law or the prophets; I have come not to abolish but to fulfill. For truly I tell you, until heaven and earth pass away, not one letter, not one stroke of a letter, will pass from the law until all is accomplished. Therefore, whoever breaks one of the least of these commandments, and teaches others to do the same, will be called least in the kingdom of heaven; but whoever does them and teaches them will be called great in the kingdom of heaven. For I tell you, unless your righteousness exceeds that of the scribes and Pharisees, you will never enter the kingdom of heaven. (Matt. 5:17–20)

Matthew's Jesus goes on to clarify what he means by righteousness that "exceeds" in a series of examples, both positive and negative. These examples have a consistent linguistic pattern. Jesus begins by citing the Law of Moses: "You have heard that it was said to those of ancient times. . . ." Then he offers his new command: "But I say to you. . . ." Probably the most famous example involves violence and retaliation: "You have heard that it said, 'An eye for an eye and a tooth for a tooth.' But I say to you, Do not resist an evildoer. But if anyone strikes you on the right cheek, turn the other also" (Matt. 5:38–39). These teachings are known as **antitheses**, because they each provide a contrast. In addition to the issue of nonviolence, the antitheses cover murder, anger, adultery, divorce, the swearing of oaths, and the treatment of friends and enemies.

In Matthew 6, the antitheses are extended to pious deeds such as prayer, fasting, and giving alms. Jesus agrees these are good activities, but insists Christians do them "in secret." This will ensure that pious deeds are done for God rather than to earn the praise of others.

The Antitheses in Matthew's Sermon on the Mount

The Law of Moses	The Law of Jesus
You shall not murder . . . Whoever murders shall be liable to judgment. (5:21)	If you are angry with a brother or sister, you will be liable to judgment; and if you insult a brother or sister, you will be liable to the council; and if you say, "You fool" you will be liable to the hell of fire. (5:22)
You shall not commit adultery. (5:27)	Everyone who looks at a woman with lust has already committed adultery with her in his heart. (5:28)
Whoever divorces his wife, let him give her a certificate of divorce. (5:31)	Anyone who divorces his wife, except on the ground of unchastity, causes her to commit adultery; and whoever marries a divorced woman commits adultery. (5:32)
You shall not swear falsely, but carry out the vows you have made to the Lord. (5:33)	Do not swear at all, either by heaven, for it is the throne of God, or by the earth, for it is his footstool, or by Jerusalem, for it is the city of the great King. (5:34–35)
An eye for an eye, and a tooth for a tooth. (5:38)	Do not resist an evildoer. But if someone strikes you on the right cheek, turn the other also. (5:39)
You shall love your neighbor and hate your enemy. (5:43)	Love your enemies and pray for those who persecute you, so that you may be children of your Father in heaven. (5:44–45)

The overall theme of the Sermon is that Christians will be held to a higher standard. It is not enough to obey the letter of the law, one must adhere to its spirit as well. A person's interior orientation is as important as external compliance with the Torah. Although Jesus has a good deal to say elsewhere about mercy and forgiveness for sinners, the emphasis in the Sermon on the Mount is on God's demand for moral righteousness.

Is the Sermon on the Mount Too Strict?

Christians throughout the centuries have struggled with Jesus' difficult demands in the Sermon on the Mount. If people can never get angry, can never think a lustful thought, and must always love their enemies, then who can be saved?

A variety of strategies have been proposed for dealing with the uncompromising rigor of Jesus' ethical demands. One approach suggests that Jesus was asking people to *strive* for perfection, even though he knew fallible humans could never fully

continued

Is the Sermon on the Mount Too Strict? *continued*

attain it. The standards Jesus sets are aspirational rather than uncrossable boundaries. Jesus sets the bar high simply because doing so will lead to the best possible levels of performance. For example, a husband who tries to discipline his mind not to engage in sexual fantasies about other women is more likely to be faithful than one who indulges freely in such activity.

Another strategy (set forth by Martin Luther) is that Jesus sets impossible standards precisely to show that human beings cannot gain salvation by their own efforts, but must rely on the grace of God.

Others have argued that Jesus' most difficult teachings are to be applied to smaller, select groups of people than the human race generally. A traditional Catholic teaching is that some of Jesus' teachings are "precepts" (rules that apply to everyone) and others are "counsels of perfection" (rules that apply only to those who have taken sacred vows, such as the clergy and religious). Among the vows that priests, monks, and nuns often take are vows of poverty, chastity, obedience, and silence. Lay people are not expected to do the same.

Others have maintained a more uncompromising vision. The "historic peace churches" (the Quakers, Amish, and Mennonites) take Jesus' command to "turn the other cheek" literally and practice a strict pacifism. Jesus does say in the Sermon on the Mount that he is demanding nothing less than perfection: "Be perfect, therefore, as your heavenly Father is perfect" (Matt. 5:48). A literal interpretation of Jesus' ethical demands might lead to the conclusion that salvation is for the few, a conclusion that the Sermon on the Mount seems to encourage: "Enter through the narrow gate; for the gate is wide and the road is easy that leads to destruction, and there are many who take it. For the gate is narrow and the road is hard that leads to life, and there are few who find it" (7:13-14).

Key Terms

redaction criticism
ecclesiology
eschatology
pope

delay of the parousia
low Christology
adoptionism
proof from prophecy

Septuagint (LXX)
Suffering Servant
antitheses

Review Questions

1. In what specific ways does Matthew revise Mark's negative depiction of the disciples? Are there certain editorial moves that Matthew employs on a regular basis?

2. What passages show that the Christology of the Gospel of Matthew is "higher" than that of the Gospel of Mark? How exactly do these passages hint at a more divine Jesus?

3. How does Matthew attempt to lay a more solid foundation for the church as an institution? What does his Gospel contain that Mark's does not in this regard?

4. How does the Catholic interpretation of the passage in which Jesus names Peter as the "rock" on which the church will be built differ from Protestant interpretations? What is the significance of those differences?

5. How does Matthew's eschatology differ from Mark's?

6. How does Matthew use proof from prophecy to argue that Jesus is the Messiah? What problems have various critics noted in Matthew's use of Isaiah 7:14 and other Old Testament prophecies?

7. How does Matthew outline Jesus' ethical demands in the Sermon on the Mount? How do these demands relate to the Law of Moses? How have Christians through the ages attempted to cope with the extreme difficulty of Jesus' ethical demands?

Discussion Questions

1. Many people assume that the Gospel of Mark is the more accurate and reliable account, because it was written earlier than Matthew. But is that always the case? In your experience, has it ever been true that the early reports of a major event have turned out to be false or misleading, and the later accounts were better-informed and more accurate? One could argue that Matthew is trying to "spin" Mark in a direction more favorable to Christianity, but one could just as easily argue that he merely wanted to "set the record straight." Which possibility seems more plausible to you?

2. Redaction criticism has been discounted in some quarters because it seems to place all of its emphasis on the *changes* that Matthew made to Mark and seems to ignore all of the things from Mark that Matthew *left intact*. Do you think there is validity to this criticism? If so, how might it be addressed?

Bibliography and Suggestions for Further Study

(Books and websites that are accessible for general undergraduates are marked with an asterisk; other sources listed are appropriate for advanced students.)

Betz, Hans Dieter, and Adela Yarbro Collins. *The Sermon on the Mount: A Commentary on the Sermon on the Mount, including the Sermon on the Plain (Matthew 5:3–7:27 and Luke 6:20–49).* Minneapolis: Fortress, 1995.

Bornkamm, Gunther. "End-Expectation and Church in Matthew." In *Tradition and Interpretation in Matthew,* edited by G. Bornkamm, G. Barth, and H. J. Held, 15–51. London: SCM, 1963.

Bornkamm, Gunther. "The Stilling of the Storm in Matthew." In *Tradition and Interpretation in Matthew,* edited by G. Bornkamm, G. Barth, and H. J. Heid, 52–57. London: SCM, 1963.

*Edwards, Richard Alan. *Matthew's Story of Jesus.* Philadelphia: Fortress, 1985.

*Perrin, Norman. *The Resurrection according to Matthew, Mark, and Luke.* Philadelphia: Fortress, 1977.

Stanton, Graham. *The Interpretation of Matthew.* Philadelphia: Fortress, 1983.

Luke's First Volume: The Gospel of Luke

The previous chapters have applied a single method of biblical criticism per Gospel: literary criticism was applied to Mark and redaction criticism to Matthew. Each method highlights a particular aspect of the text's meaning. Literary criticism examines the text as a whole, while redaction criticism dissects it into its parts. Literary criticism sees the evangelists as creative authors, while redaction criticism envisions them less as authors and more as theologically motivated editors. At times these methods yield conflicting results, forcing interpreters to choose between them. In other cases, the methods complement one another and produce a fuller picture of the meaning of the text than either could alone.

To demonstrate the complementarity of the methods, this chapter examines the Gospel of Luke using both literary and redaction criticism and introduces two additional branches of biblical studies: New Testament theology and feminist biblical criticism. As described in chapter 7, feminist biblical criticism is attentive to the portrayal of women in the text, critiques the construction of gender and sexuality in the text (as it applies to both God and humans), and examines the relationship between the text and the broader culture with respect to issues of concern to women. Luke-Acts is unusually rich in female characters, so it provides a good opportunity for the application of feminist biblical criticism.

The Unity of Luke and Acts

Scholars have long argued that the same (anonymous) author wrote both the Gospel of Luke and the Acts of the Apostles,[1] and that these should be read as two parts of the same work, rather than as two separate works. The general agreement about this is shown in the common substitution of the epithet "**Luke-Acts**" for the titles of the two works individually. The concept of the unity of Luke-Acts is based on the following observations: (a) each volume is introduced by a preface (Luke 1:1-4 and Acts 1:1-2) dedicated to the same individual (Theophilus), and in the second preface the author refers to the "first volume"; (b) Acts begins almost exactly where the Gospel of Luke ends; and (c) there are

continued

---

1. Scholar Henry J. Cadbury convinced most of the biblical academy of the unity of Luke and Acts in his seminal work, *The Making of Luke-Acts* (New York: Macmillan, 1927; London: SPCK, 1968).

The Unity of Luke and Acts *continued*

numerous stylistic, literary, and theological similarities between Luke and Acts that suggest a single author.[2]

In recent years, however, some scholars have begun to cast doubt on the claim that the Gospel and Acts are two parts of the same work and need to be read together.[3] One reason is that many of these scholars believe the two books belong to different genres (Luke to biography, Acts to history) and therefore they may not represent a single, unified work. Other arguments claim the theological affinities between Luke and Acts have been overstated, and there is no evidence the earliest

readers of Luke and Acts saw them as a unity or made any connection between them. It is also possible the Gospel of Luke (and perhaps Acts as well) underwent several revisions and the prefaces that seem to unite the two works were added at a late stage by a final redactor.

Because the work of these scholars questions the unity of Luke and Acts, it is no longer acceptable to claim this unity without demonstration. However, most scholars remain convinced the books are two parts of the same work and most continue to use the term Luke-Acts to refer to them, an approach followed in this text.

Chapter 7 also defined New Testament theology as a method that seeks to derive from a Gospel (or from the several works of a given New Testament author) at least an outline of an orderly, rational, coherent account of Christian faith. Such an account would include a doctrine of God as well as a Christology, pneumatology (teaching about the Holy Spirit), ethics, eschatology (teaching about the end of the world), **ecclesiology** (teaching about the church), theodicy (theory of the cause of human suffering), and so on. Although the Gospels are narratives rather than theologies in the strict sense, the stories they tell and the words and deeds they ascribe to Jesus have theological implications. That Matthew's implicit Christology and eschatology differ from Mark's, and that Matthew adds to Mark several passages suggestive of his ethics and ecclesiology, has already been discussed. In analyzing the Third Gospel here, the focus will be on several distinctive Lukan

teachings and themes that move beyond the theological conversation started by Mark and Matthew into new areas and will stake out some new positions, especially in the areas of ecclesiology and ethics.

Luke's Inclusive View of the Church

The previous chapter explored how Matthew reaches beyond his Markan source by using the word *church* (Greek, *ekklēsia*) and showing how Jesus authorized the creation of a church in his name, arranged for its leadership, and endowed it with a great deal of authority. Luke does not use the word *church* in the Gospel (although it is used frequently in his second volume, the Acts of the Apostles), but it is clear that the concept is very much on his mind in both books.

---

2. For an outstanding analysis of the cohesion between the two books, see Robert Tannehill, *The Narrative Unity of Luke-Acts: A Literary Interpretation*, 2 vols. (Philadelphia: Fortress, 1986; 1990).

3. See, especially, Mikael Parsons and Richard I. Pervo, *Rethinking the Unity of Luke and Acts* (Minneapolis: Fortress, 1993), and Andrew F. Gregory and Christopher K. Rowe, *Rethinking the Unity and Reception of Luke and Acts* (Columbia: University of South Carolina Press, 2010).

The Preface to the Gospel (Luke 1:1–4) and Luke's Attitude toward His Predecessors

The Gospel of Luke begins with a formal preface that extends for four verses and comprises a single, complex sentence (although it is not always translated that way).

> Inasmuch as many have attempted to compile a narrative of the events that have come to fulfillment in our midst, just as those who were eyewitnesses and ministers of the word passed them down to us, it seemed good to me also, having investigated everything thoroughly from the beginning, to write for you an orderly account, most excellent Theophilus, so that you might receive assurance about the things of which you have been informed. (author's translation)

Unlike the other Gospels, and indeed the remainder of the Gospel of Luke as well, the preface to Luke is not written in the common Koine Greek of the Hellenistic world, but in the elevated Attic Greek of the sophisticated philosophers and playwrights of the golden age of Athens. It is almost without question the best-written sentence in the New Testament, although it is followed by a brief stretch of some very rough Greek similar to the language of the Septuagint, and then proceeds in a common Greek style that is only marginally better than that of the other Gospels.

One reason the author might begin in this fashion, and then imitate the style of the Septuagint in his birth narrative (Luke 1:5–2:52), and then return to the Koine Greek (Luke 3:1) found in Mark and Matthew, is to show his mastery of several styles of writing.[4] Indeed, Luke seems to be making a claim in his preface that he is a professional writer. The "Theophilus" to whom the preface is dedicated is probably Luke's publisher, the patron who commissioned the book he is writing.[5]

In the preface, Luke acknowledges predecessors who also narrated the life of Jesus, referring to Mark and perhaps also to Matthew, Q, John, or L: "Inasmuch as many have attempted to compile a narrative of the events that have come to fulfillment in our midst" (1:1).[6] Luke then attempts to distinguish his work by claiming he has investigated "everything thoroughly from the beginning" and stating that this will enable him to compile an "orderly account" (1:3). An interesting question here is whether Luke is implicitly criticizing his predecessors and is in essence claiming the superior work he is about to present should *replace* previous Gospels, rather than exist alongside them.

Most Christians, and indeed many biblical scholars, assume that later Gospel writers intended their work to complement that of earlier Gospels. New Testament scholar Mary Ann Tolbert observes, "Many current New Testament scholars appear to assume without much argument or analysis that Matthew and Luke simply intended to extend and clarify Mark's vision for their own communities."[7] However, it is possible some Gospel writers saw the others not as partners but as competitors, and that they perceived their predecessors' work as

continued

---

4. Another possibility is that the diverse styles within the Gospel reflect Luke's sources more than conscious decisions on the part of the author.

5. See E. J. Goodspeed, "Some Greek Notes: I. Was Theophilus Luke's Publisher?" *Journal of Biblical Literature 73* (1954): 84.

6. Supporters of the Two Source Hypothesis would argue that Luke is referring to Mark and Q, but this seems unlikely in the latter case because Q—if it existed—would not have been a "narrative" but a list of sayings.

7. Mary Ann Tolbert, *Sowing the Gospel: Mark's World in Literary-Historical Perspective* (Minneapolis: Fortress, 1989), 28.

The Preface to the Gospel (Luke 1:1–4) *continued*

somehow inadequate and in need of replacement with something better. If one accepts the traditional dating of Mark at around 70 CE and of Matthew and Luke at between 80 and 90 CE, then the mere fact that within ten to twenty years of the appearance of Mark not one but two authors felt the need to rewrite Mark suggests there were at least parts of this text that people found unsatisfactory. Jewish biblical scholar Samuel Sandmel points this out: "Plural gospels should alert us to the probable existence of plural views; plural views run the gamut from mild divergency through direct antithesis."[8]

Unless one rejects this possibility on theological grounds, it can become a useful lens through which to view the development of multiple Gospels. Tolbert points out that there are good literary and historical grounds for thinking that later Gospels were an attempt to supplant their predecessors: "Suppose Matthew and Luke, for different reasons and in different ways, were attempting not to clarify and extend Mark's vision but to refute and undermine it. In the rhetorical fashion of the first century one very effective way of refuting one's opponents was to incorporate their arguments in one's own presentation and then demonstrate how faulty their conclusions were. . . . That Matthew and Luke intended to refute and supplant Mark rather than clarify and extend it is a less often voiced but equally likely possibility."[9] This possibility is all the more intriguing if one accepts a later date for Luke and posits that he was aware not only of Mark but also of Matthew. Sandmel sums up this view, saying, "Matthew wrote because he disapproved of Mark; and Luke, because he disapproved of Mark and Matthew."[10]

The early Christian church did not have many of the external signs and indicators—church buildings, clergy with distinctive clothing and credentials, and so on[11]—it would have in later centuries, but it was an organization, or better, an *association*. Associations were common in the Roman Empire. One example was the burial society, in which a group of people agreed to an arrangement whereby each member would pay dues or a subscription fee so that, in the event of a family member's death, the dead person's survivors would have some money for funeral expenses and household maintenance. Sometimes these were simply groups of friends; in other cases what brought them together was a common occupation (these associations were known as *collegia* or guilds) or similar political views or a common religion. These associations would meet regularly, often for meals, and would use the occasion for socializing, or for conversation about business, politics, or religion. Each association adopted rules and principles that established (1) its purpose or mission, (2) criteria for membership, (3) costs and associated benefits, and (4) the repercussions for breaking the group's rules.

---

8. Samuel Sandmel, "Myths, Genealogies, and Jewish Myths and the Writing of Gospels," in *Two Living Traditions: Essays on Religion and the Bible* (Detroit: Wayne State University Press, 1972), 163–64.

9. Tolbert, *Sowing the Gospel*, 28–29.

10. Sandmel, "Myths, Genealogies, and Jewish Myths," 152.

11. Another characteristic the early church lacked was a *unity* that would allow it to be referred to in the singular. As noted in chapter 1, a variety of rival groups existed within early Christianity. Thus, when the word *church* in this text is used in the singular, it refers specifically to the *proto-orthodox* branch of early Christianity that eventually gained dominance and selected the books that became the canon of the New Testament.

In the Roman world, associations often had the responsibility of paying the costs of members' funerals. The memorial inscription here commemorates a member of an association of carpenters.

Kleuske / Wikimedia Commons / M Licinius Privatus, dec.jpg / CC BY-SA 3.0

Whether early Christianity thought of itself as an association (it is clear that Romans like Pliny[12] saw it as such), it faced the same basic questions. While Matthew concerns himself mainly with the *mission* of the church (Matt. 16:17–19; 28:16–20) and with questions of *internal discipline* (18:10–35), Luke is far more concerned with the question of *membership*. Who was eligible for membership in the Christian church?

It may seem obvious to many today that the answer to this question is simply that *everyone* should be eligible to join. However, considering a really difficult case—for example, a confessed and unrepentant child molester—causes most people to rethink the idea of including just anyone.

Some associations are deliberately exclusive. Country clubs are notoriously selective about their membership. Many fraternities and sororities go to great lengths to make sure they attract the "right" sort of pledges, however they define that. It seems clear to some that religious groups should not behave like elitist golf clubs, sororities, or fraternities, but this does not mean that an organization is not entitled to have standards.

In this respect Christianity needed to decide whether to follow the lead of its mother religion, Judaism. Ancient Judaism was a somewhat exclusive religion. Indeed, it was a way of life. Compulsory circumcision alone indicates not just anyone could join the group. The group to which Jews belonged was defined by the covenant relationship with Yahweh. If a person held a covenant relationship with Yahweh, then he was a part of "Israel," the people of God. Ancient Jews knew this accounted for a small minority of the human race, and most were comfortable with the notion that they held a unique relationship with God that others did not enjoy, at least not yet. Non-Jews could *convert* to Judaism and become part of the covenant people, but—depending on the time period—this avenue was more open to some than others. In fact, at the time of Jesus, there were a number of groups whose members were regarded as unlikely candidates to join the covenant people, or who were eligible only for partial membership, or who were excluded from consideration altogether. These groups included Samaritans, Gentiles, women, and sinners. Of all the Gospel writers, Luke is the most concerned about differentiating the Christian approach toward these groups from that of Judaism. This distinction may not always have been fair to Judaism,[13] but

---

12. Pliny the Younger, *Letters* 10.96.

13. Early Christians who wanted to present their religion as more inclusive had reason to portray Judaism as perhaps more exclusive than it really was. It is also true that attitudes on the question of who could be included within the covenant people varied considerably within the Judaism of this time period.

it demonstrated Luke's determination to present a Christianity that was as inclusive as possible.

Samaritans

Samaritans were an ethnic group whose ancestry is traced (at least by Jewish sources) to the conquest of the northern kingdom of Israel/Ephraim by Assyria in 721 BCE. Hostility between the southern and northern tribes of Israel was already present prior to this time, as is indicated by the rebellion of the northern tribes that led to the creation of two separate kingdoms (see 1 Kings 12). This enmity only increased as the northern tribes responded to their conquest. According to 2 Kings, Ezra, and Nehemiah, the Israelites who remained in the northern kingdom began to worship Assyrian gods alongside the God of Israel (2 Kings 17:29–41) and to intermarry with Assyrian settlers (Ezra 9:1–10:44; Neh. 13:23–28). The term *Samaritan* applies to this mixed-race (Assyrian and Israelite) group. Israelites from the southern kingdom of Judah (Jews) apparently regarded their northern cousins as apostates who had allowed their blood and their religion to be contaminated by Assyrian elements,[14] and the two groups became bitter enemies. When the Jews who had been exiled to Babylon returned and sought to rebuild the Temple in Jerusalem, the Samaritans opposed them (see Ezra 4). After the Maccabean Revolt (167–164 BCE), the victorious Jews eventually attacked the Samaritans and destroyed their temple on Mount Gerazim in Samaria (Josephus, *Jewish Antiquities* 13.255ff.).

Relations had not improved by New Testament times. Josephus reports that a group of Jewish pilgrims from Galilee was allegedly massacred by hostile Samaritans in 52 CE, which led to bloody reprisals by militant Judeans (Josephus, *Jewish Antiquities* 20.118; *Jewish War* 2.234–35). Stories like this led some Galilean Jews to avoid traveling through Samaria on their way to Jerusalem—they would cross to the east side of the Jordan River and go all the way around Samaria, crossing the river again near Jericho and proceeding to Jerusalem from there.[15] Jews feared Samaritan violence and adopted a policy whereby they would have nothing whatsoever to do with them. "Jews have no dealings with Samaritans," the Gospel of John reports (4:9). Samaritans were prohibited from entering the inner courts of the Jerusalem Temple, an exclusion they protested in 6 CE by attempting to desecrate the Temple by scattering human bones on sacred ground (Josephus, *Jewish Antiquities* 18.29–30).

Given this history of animosity, it is surprising that most references to Samaritans in the Gospel of Luke are positive. Luke writes that Jesus traveled through Samaria when he made the journey to Jerusalem that culminated in his death. He did not find a welcome reception in Samaria (Luke 9:53), but he rebuked his disciples for suggesting the Samaritan village should be destroyed in response.

Shortly thereafter, Luke's Jesus tells one of his most extraordinary parables, the **parable of the Good Samaritan** (Luke 10:25–37). Jesus himself was a Jew, and in Luke he tells this parable to a Jewish audience that likely held the usual

---

14. The Jewish claims about the extent of intermarriage are almost certainly overstated, and the claims about the acceptance of foreign religious ideas might be exaggerated as well. Samaritans always denied these accusations, and suggested that the Jews were the ones who had strayed from the path of true Israelite religion. But the questionable veracity of the accusations does not gainsay the fact that they were widely believed and accepted in Jesus' time.

15. Although it is widely reported in less scholarly sources that it was a strict and general policy for Jews to avoid traveling through Samaria, no ancient sources confirm this. Stories exist that tell of Jews following a route from Galilee to Judea that passes to the east of the Jordan River and then crosses over at Jericho, thus avoiding Samaria, but Josephus indicates that Jews did commonly travel through Samaria (*Jewish Antiquities* 20.118).

prejudices against Samaritans and considered themselves morally superior. In the parable, a man is going down from Jerusalem to Jericho (two cities in Judea, a region with a predominantly Jewish population), when he is beaten, robbed, and left half–dead. Although the victim is the only character in the parable whose ethnic identity is not specified, he is clearly a Jew. He is in dire need of help, and when a priest comes along, most Jews hearing this story probably expected that this well-respected, holy figure would aid his brother. But the priest ignores the man, passing by on the other side. This reprehensible callousness (or cowardice) would probably create discomfort for a Jewish audience, but they were likely reassured that a Levite comes along shortly thereafter. When the Levite too passes by on the other side, it becomes clear these supposed paragons of Jewish virtue are the villains in this particular drama. But Luke's Jesus is not finished undercutting any remaining feelings of moral superiority his Jewish audience might have had.

The next person to approach is a Samaritan, the sworn enemy of the Jews. Most Jews hearing this story would probably expect the Samaritan to behave in the violent, inhuman way that was, in their view, characteristic of this people. But the Samaritan shows compassion to the Jew in need, and not just a little compassion, but an extraordinary amount. He is "moved with pity" despite the fact the man is his enemy. He treats the man's wounds, puts him on his animal, takes him to an inn, pays for his stay, and promises to return and provide whatever more is necessary for the man's convalescence. Jesus had previously taught his followers, "Love your enemies, do good to those who hate you" (Luke 6:27). The Samaritan provides the best single illustration of this principle in action.

That Luke's Jesus did not share the allegedly common Jewish prejudice against Samaritans is further illustrated in a passage in Luke 17.

Jesus is beginning his journey to Jerusalem and is passing between the border of Galilee and Samaria when he encounters ten lepers. Despite the negative reception he had received from one Samaritan village (9:51–56), Luke's Jesus is still willing to travel into Samaria. He apparently did not fear violence from Samaritans. His faith is rewarded after he cleanses the ten lepers. Only one of them returns to thank Jesus and praise God for his cleansing, and he is a Samaritan. Jesus asks, "Were not ten made clean? But the other nine, where are they? Was none of them found to return and give praise to God except this foreigner?" (17:17–18). As in the parable of the Good Samaritan, the Samaritan leper is more upright than his Jewish counterparts. These two passages—both unique to Luke—suggest the author thought that Samaritans should be welcome in the people of God and that their reputation for immorality and irreligion was undeserved. The first-century Jewish exclusion of Samaritans was based, Luke suggests, on a myth.

In the Acts of the Apostles, Luke presents the church's decision to follow Jesus' lead and to develop a welcoming attitude toward Samaritans as beneficial to Christianity. In Acts 8, after a severe persecution forces all but the apostles to flee Jerusalem, a Christian convert named Philip finds himself in Samaria. He preaches the word to the Samaritans and receives a tremendous welcome. "The crowds with one accord listened eagerly to what was said by Philip" (Acts 8:6), and "there was great joy in that city" (8:8). Eventually, Peter and John join Philip in Samaria and the new Samaritan converts receive the gift of the Holy Spirit. Peter and John then preach the word to many other villages of the Samaritans (8:25). The Christian mission to the Samaritans is a success, unlike the mission to the Jews, which experienced some initial successes (Acts 2:41; 4:4) but ended in rejection and persecution.

Gentiles

First-century Jewish attitudes toward **Gentiles** (non-Jews) were more complex than the straight hostility shown to Samaritans. The Hebrew Bible strictly forbids Jews from marrying Gentiles (Deut. 7:3) and prohibits Jews from imitating Gentile manners in their dress or immoral sexual practices (Lev. 20:10–23). But the Torah also enjoins Jews to exhibit kindness to strangers (Lev. 19:33–34) and to extend compassion and support to widows and orphans who were foreigners as well as needy Jews (Deut. 14:28–29; 26:11). The mixture of positive and negative Jewish attitudes toward Gentiles continued through the time of Jesus. The second-century CE Rabbi Simon ben Yohai went so far as to say that even the best of the Gentiles did not deserve to live, although his views were known to be extreme on this issue. Many Jews, especially in the Diaspora, interacted with Gentiles regularly and were on friendly terms with them. Some even sought to bring their Gentile neighbors into the covenant.

Unlike modern Judaism, which does not have a strongly evangelistic orientation, ancient Judaism was an expansionary-minded, missionary religion.[16] Jewish evangelists, such as Paul prior to his "conversion" to Christianity, targeted Gentiles for conversion. Some Gentiles were attracted to Judaism because of its monotheism and highly sophisticated set of ethical principles and would attend synagogue services to listen and observe. The term that Jews developed for Gentiles who were admirers of Judaism but not full converts was "**God-fearers**" (see Ps. 115:11; Acts 13:16).

Although Judaism made inroads with Gentiles, there was never a mass influx of converts, and Judaism never came close to becoming the dominant religion in the Mediterranean world as Christianity eventually did. The reluctance of Gentiles to convert can partially be attributed to the terror of adult circumcision and the difficulty of maintaining ritual purity, two requirements that did not make much sense to Gentiles.[17] However, Jews often explained the relative failure of their mission to the Gentiles in terms of Gentile intransigence, a hard-hearted stubbornness that resulted from their sheer love of sin (see Rom. 1:16–32).[18] It often seems as if Jewish and Jewish-Christian literature from the time of Jesus cannot refer to Gentiles without adding the descriptor "sinners." Even Paul, who was a great champion of the inclusion of Gentiles in Christianity, cannot help using this terminology: "We ourselves are Jews by birth and not Gentile sinners" (Gal. 2:15).[19] Matthew's phrasing of Jesus' teaching about love of enemies seems to reflect this same sense of Jewish moral superiority: "And if you greet only your brothers and sisters, what

---

16. See chapter 14 for documentation of these claims.

17. On the Greek and Roman hostility toward circumcision, see F. M. Hodges, "The Ideal Prepuce in Ancient Greece and Rome: Male Genital Aesthetics and Their Relation to Lipodermos, Circumcision, Foreskin Restoration, and the Kynodesme," *The Bulletin of the History of Medicine* 75, no. 3 (2001): 375–405. With respect to ritual purity, the best-known aspect of this was the Jewish refusal to eat pork, which the Romans could not begin to comprehend. The Romans loved their pork; the Roman writer Varro (thirties BCE) attests that every Roman farm had its swine (*On Agriculture* 2.4.3). The Roman satirists Petronius, Juvenal, and Macrobius all mocked Jews' strange refusal to partake of such a tasty food; see Jordan D. Rosenblum, "'Why Do You Refuse to Eat Pork?' Jews, Food, and Identity in Roman Palestine," in *The Jewish Quarterly Review* 100 (2010): 99.

18. One must be cautious about citing Christian (or even Jewish-Christian) sources to document ancient Jewish attitudes about Gentiles, but the views articulated by Paul in this passage are not unrepresentative of non-Christian Jews of this era. To cite just one example, the Babylonian Talmud cautions Jews against buying cattle from Gentiles, or allowing their livestock to be under Gentile supervision, because Gentiles are suspected of engaging in lewd and immoral acts with beasts (*'Abodah Zarah* 22a).

19. Granted Paul may be using this term somewhat tongue-in-cheek, but the fact that the phrase is so close at hand suggests it was a common view among Jews. See also Ps. 9:17; Tob. 13:6; *Jub.* 23.23–24, among others.

more are you doing than others? Do not even the Gentiles do the same?" (Matt. 5:47).

The Gospel of Luke, however, shows an openness to Gentiles from the very beginning and suggests that one of God's major purposes in sending Jesus is to make the offer of salvation available to all people, not just the Jews. This is not to say that most Jews of Jesus' time thought that salvation was exclusive to them, or that it would always be.[20] Genesis 12:3 shows God telling Abraham that he and his kin will be specially blessed, but also that in him "all the families of the earth shall be blessed." Hence the idea that the Gentiles would eventually be included in God's plan of salvation was not foreign to Judaism nor unique to Christianity. But Jews and Christians of Luke's day probably disagreed about whether the Gentiles would receive the promised blessing now or later.

Luke clearly believed that the time was now, and that Jesus was the means by which God intended to extend the covenant promises to the Gentiles. While Matthew's genealogy traces Jesus' ancestry only as far back as Abraham, the father of the Jewish people, Luke traces it all the way back to Adam, the father of the entire human race (Luke 3:23–38). When the prophet Simeon sees and recognizes the baby Jesus as the Messiah, he proclaims, "Master, now you are dismissing your servant in peace, according to your word; for my eyes have seen your salvation, which you have prepared in the presence of all peoples, a light for revelation to the Gentiles and for glory to your people Israel" (2:29–32). This prophecy is fulfilled in the Acts of the Apostles, as the second half of the book shows Gentiles converting to Christianity in large numbers. The book concludes with its hero Paul excoriating the Jews for their predominantly unfaithful response, and saying to them, "Let it be known to you then that this salvation of God has been sent to the Gentiles; they will listen" (Acts 28:28).

For the Gentiles to be included in the people of God, however, their sinful past had to be reckoned with. The sins that Jews often associated with Gentiles were idolatry (worship of many deities, all of whom were false gods from the Jewish perspective), ritual impurity[21] (owing largely to their failure to keep kosher), and sexual immorality (again, see Rom. 1:16–32). It is certainly true that Greek and Roman society tolerated a much broader spectrum of sexual behavior than did Judaism. Many of these prototypically Gentile sinful behaviors come together in a single character in the Gospel of Luke, namely the younger son in the famous parable of Luke 15:11–32.

Best-known as the **parable of the Prodigal Son**, the story Luke's Jesus tells speaks of a man and his two sons. The younger son approaches his father and demands his share of the inheritance.[22] The younger son then takes his share of the inheritance and squanders it on "dissolute living." Before long he finds himself out of money and in desperate need. He is forced to take a

---

20. Some rabbis did feel this way, however. Eliezar b. Hyrcanus argued that Gentiles have no share in the life to come (*t. Sanhedrin* 13.2; *Sanhedrin* 105a).

21. It should be remembered that ritual impurity is not technically a sin, but it was seen as an obstacle to Gentiles being fully incorporated into the covenant people.

22. Amy-Jill Levine insists that "to ask, as the younger son does, for his share of an inheritance indicates a potential lack of wisdom, but it is not a sin"; Amy-Jill Levine, "A Parable and Its Baggage: What the Prodigal Son Story Doesn't Mean," *The Christian Century* 131, no. 18 (Sept. 3, 2014): 21. But it is noteworthy that she misrepresents the mood of the verb used in Luke 15:12, suggesting that it is interrogative (asking a question) rather than imperative (issuing a command, or making a demand). He does not ask; he demands his share of the inheritance. Levine is correct in saying that such a demand is not illegal, but it is not normal. It is arrogant, disrespectful behavior. Carol LaHurd's analysis of this same parable tends to confirm this view; see Carol LaHurd, "Reviewing Luke 15 with Arab-Christian Women," in *A Feminist Companion to Luke*, ed. Amy-Jill Levine (Cleveland: Pilgrim Press, 2004), 246–68.

menial job feeding pigs and is so hungry that he envies the swine their food. He thinks to himself that even his father's hired men eat better than he does, so he resolves to return to his father's house and beg to be taken in as a hired hand.

Two features of the text support the idea that the younger son symbolizes the Gentiles. First, the older son eventually reveals that the "dissolute living" in which the younger son squandered his inheritance consisted of the kind of sexually immoral behavior that Jews often associated with Gentiles: "[He] has devoured your property with prostitutes" (Luke 15:30). Second, the fact that the younger son works with pigs means he has become ritually unclean.[23] The presence of pigs and of people who are involved with them always brought to mind the Gentiles (see, for example, Mark 5:1–20 and parallels, where the Gentile region of Decapolis is populated by a herd of pigs into which Jesus can cast the "Legion" of demons).

If the younger son does symbolize the Gentiles, then the point of the parable is clearly that Gentiles are welcome in the Christian church, the people of God. When the younger son returns, his father is filled with compassion and rushes to greet him, embraces him, and kisses him. His father could have rejected him outright or granted him only partial acceptance by demoting him from the status of family member to that of hired hand. But his reaction shows that he is willing to overlook this child's past transgressions. He welcomes the boy not as a hired hand but *as a son*. He is fully restored to his former status, and the father orders a feast to celebrate his return.

Several of Jesus' best-known parables are found only in Luke's Gospel, including the Prodigal Son, depicted in Rembrandt's painting. Christians through the ages have found comfort in the image of God as a loving father who freely welcomes back a wayward child.

One could argue that his return is merely self-serving,[24] but that would overlook several features of the story, most important among them this son's reaction to his father's warm welcome. Before his return the younger son practiced the speech he would give to his father upon seeing him: "Father, I have sinned against heaven and before you; I am no longer worthy to be called your son; treat me like one of your hired hands"

---

23. Again, Levine misses the mark in arguing that "the Prodigal's problem is that he's hungry, not that he's 'unclean'"; Levine, "A Parable and Its Baggage: What the Prodigal Son Story Doesn't Mean," 20–21. Hunger and uncleanness are not mutually exclusive, and the character's perception of his problem might not correspond with the perception of early Christian readers.

24. Levine is a champion of this view, arguing that "first-century listeners may have heard not contrition but conniving. Junior recalls that Daddy still has money, and he might be able to get more" (ibid., 22). Levine's overall goal is to demonstrate that all Christian interpretations that see this parable as the story of a repentant sinner are misguided and ill-informed, owing largely to overt or inadvertent anti-Judaism. While she is unquestionably correct in arguing that some interpretations of this parable (and many other New Testament texts) fabricate negative images of Judaism in order to make Jesus' opposing views seem original or countercultural, in this case she protests too much.

(Luke 15:18–19). But when his father rushes out to greet him, it is clear that he has been forgiven and he no longer needs to make this speech. Indeed, by voicing it he would run a considerable risk: he might remind his father of just how bad his past behavior has been, and prompt him toward a milder welcome and a more conditional forgiveness. But the younger son, disregarding this danger, proceeds to give his speech, and this can only be because he is sincerely repentant and wishes to express his remorse.[25]

Hence the "moral" of the story seems clear: Gentiles would be welcome in Christianity[26] despite their sinful pasts as long as they sincerely repent of their transgressions. There are no misdeeds beyond God's mercy and forgiveness. The theme of the forgiveness of sin is dominant in Luke's Gospel and indeed throughout the New Testament; it became a hallmark of the Christian religion.[27]

Tax Collectors and Other Sinners

The same dynamic of sin and redemption is found in the Gospel of Luke in reference to individuals and groups regarded as "sinners" by Judaism. There appear to be two main categories of such people. The first consists of those whose *occupations* were inextricably entwined with sinful behavior. This would include criminals, certainly, but also prostitutes (whose behavior was considered shameful in the Roman Empire but certainly not illegal) and tax collectors. The other category consisted

of those who suffered from a serious physical or mental disability (usually understood as demonic possession). It was generally understood in Judaism that such maladies could only have resulted from the afflicted person being cursed by God as punishment for committing a serious sin.[28] One sees this attitude reflected in John 9:2, for example, when the disciples see a man blind from birth and ask Jesus, "Rabbi, who sinned, this man or his parents, that he was born blind?"

The Gospels, taken together, suggest the strategy of the Pharisees and scribes toward such people was to shun them.[29] In other words, they showed their social disapproval by having nothing whatsoever to do with a member of an offending group. The Gospels also agree that Jesus' strategy was different. On the one hand, the Gospels depict Jesus as not sharing the view that those afflicted with blindness, deafness, paralysis, epilepsy, and so on, were being punished for sin. Jesus is shown displaying nothing but compassion for such people, and he never turns down an opportunity to help them.

Chapter 8's analysis of the Gospel of Mark notes that Jesus seems to have rejected the strategy of shunning sinners in favor of engagement. This strategy is presented as preferable because it is more effective in leading sinners to repentance and because it avoids tendencies toward pride, arrogance, and contempt, which are often connected with shunning. Luke emphasizes these points in a series of passages unique to his Gospel. In Luke

---

25. Levine is confident that the younger son's words of repentance are insincere, because (she argues) they are so similar to the insincere words of Pharaoh in Exodus 10:16. However, it does not follow that because one person (or literary character) once used an expression insincerely that every subsequent use is equally disingenuous.

26. To be clear, Luke seldom uses the terms *Christian* or *Christianity* (see Acts 11:26 for an exception). Luke's term for the distinctive religion of Jesus' followers is "the Way" (Acts 9:2; 19:9, 23; 22:4).

27. Again, one must be careful not to assume that ancient Judaism said nothing of forgiveness or claimed that God's mercy was somehow finite. Not all of the key features of Christianity exist only in contradistinction to a Jewish "other." Luke argues that Christianity is in fundamental continuity with Judaism even as he critiques some elements of contemporary Jewish thought and behavior.

28. Deuteronomy lists the illnesses with which God will curse those who disobey his commandments and ordinances (Deut. 28:27–28).

29. Again, this characterization may not be historically accurate, but it is how the Gospels *portray* the Pharisees.

7:36–51, Jesus is invited to the house of Simon the Pharisee, and when he enters the house, there is a **woman who was a sinner** who showers him with love and affection. She washes his feet with her tears, dries them with her hair, and anoints them with ointment. Simon sees this and thinks that Jesus cannot possibly be a prophet, because if he was he would surely know "who and what kind of woman this is" and would not be allowing her to touch him and attend to him in this way. Simon's view is that a prophet would shun such a person. Jesus then tells Simon a parable that reveals he knows full well the woman is a sinner, and that he is allowing her to treat him so lovingly because she is merely expressing her gratitude for the forgiveness of her sins.

In the parable, two men owe money to a lender. One owes five hundred denarii, and the other owes fifty. When neither of them can pay, the creditor forgives the debt of each. Which of them, Jesus asks Simon, will love the lender more? Simon answers that the one who owed more will be more grateful. Jesus then indicates that the one who owed five hundred denarii is analogous to the woman who was a sinner. Her sins "were many," Jesus says, but having been the recipient of mercy she shows tremendous gratitude. Simon, by contrast, shows Jesus none of the respect or kindness the woman does. Luke's Jesus is suggesting that Simon is like the man who owed fifty denarii. He may not have committed as many sins as the woman, but he is still a sinner, and his sins create a debt toward God he cannot repay. He should not begrudge the woman her forgiveness because he himself stands in need of mercy, though his comparatively superior behavior has led him to overlook this fact.

The idea that overconfidence in one's righteousness can be a fatal flaw surfaces again in another uniquely Lukan parable, the **Pharisee and the Tax Collector** (Luke 18:9–14). This parable is explicitly directed toward "some who trusted in themselves that they were righteous and regarded others with contempt." In the parable, two men go to the Temple to pray. One, a Pharisee, prays, "God, I thank you that I am not like other people: thieves, rogues, adulterers, or even like this tax collector. I fast twice a week; I give a tenth of all my income." The other, a tax collector, prays quite differently. He beats his breast (a sign of repentance) and cannot even bring himself to look up to heaven. He prays, "God, be merciful to me, a sinner." Jesus concludes that only one man went back to his home "justified" (in a right relationship with God): the tax collector. This is true despite the fact that by any objective measure the behavior of the Pharisee is superior to that of the tax collector. Not only does the Pharisee avoid sins, he is fastidious in his piety—fasting and giving alms. However, there is a more important difference between the two men. The tax collector *acknowledges* he is a sinner and *asks for forgiveness.* The Pharisee is so busy congratulating himself for his righteousness that he fails to acknowledge his sinfulness. He cannot receive forgiveness he does not ask for, and apparently does not think he needs. The Gospel has a clear bias against the sanctimonious, holier-than-thou attitude of the super-religious individual. This attitude, in its own way, is more dangerous and harmful than simple moral weakness.

There are many other stories like those of the woman who was a sinner and the parable of the Pharisee and the Tax Collector. The story of the redemption of the tax collector Zacchaeus (Luke 19:1–10) is a prominent one that will be taken up in the next section. Each story emphasizes that one's past is not an insurmountable obstacle to full participation in the people of God. There is always a chance for a new beginning.

Women

As with other groups that were to some degree excluded or marginalized in Judaism, women are treated with a high degree of respect by the Lukan Jesus and allowed considerably more freedom and opportunity than the culture of the time generally gave them.[30] Furthermore, Luke seems concerned to show that women, in turn, responded positively to Jesus.

Luke 8:1–3, a passage unique to Luke, speaks of Jesus' women followers. The Gospel of Mark mentions, near the end, only three women who followed Jesus: **Mary Magdalene**, Mary the mother of James, and Salome (Mark 16:1). Luke indicates Jesus had a much larger contingent of female disciples and suggests they accompanied him *throughout* his ministry, not just toward the end.[31] Luke 8:1–3 mentions Mary Magdalene as well as Joanna and Susanna by name, but states there were "many" other women following Jesus, and they "provided for them [or him] out of their resources."

Luke's assertion that Jesus has female followers at all is significant and unusual. These women are apparently allowed to follow their own course. They seem to have a degree of freedom and independence uncommon for the time. Most women in traditional Jewish homes were not allowed to work outside the home. Nor were they usually permitted to travel freely, especially without a male family member as chaperone. There are other figures in both Jewish and Greco-Roman literature like Jesus—itinerant preachers, healers, philosophers, and so on—who had disciples, but in no other known case do these figures have female disciples.[32] The suggestion that Jesus had female followers is therefore remarkable.

Moreover, it seems clear these women played a crucial role in Jesus' ministry. The "resources" they used to provide for the needs of Jesus' ministry are almost certainly *financial*.[33] In other words, these women bankrolled Jesus' ministry. Not only is this a hugely important function, but it is one most women would not have been able to fulfill even if they wanted.

Women had very limited property rights under Jewish law, and seldom had access to money. Indeed, for the ancient Hebrews, women *were* property.[34] Attitudes toward women in Judaism progressed significantly in the Second Temple period, and one sign of that progress was that a woman usually brought a certain amount of property—a kind of dowry—with her into a marriage (an arrangement written into a document called a *ketubah*). This property would remain hers in the event of a divorce or the death of her husband, but *only* in the event of divorce or death—she could not sell the assets and spend the proceeds freely while her husband lived or the marriage endured. Hence control of the purse strings within a marriage usually rested entirely with the husband as head of household. This included any money a

---

30. This general judgment once enjoyed the support of the majority of Lukan scholars. However, in recent years a number of biblical critics (including many self-identified feminist biblical critics) have cautioned that the "liberating" aspects of Luke's portrayal of women have been overstated, and the Gospel has more problematic attitudes toward women than a surface reading of the text suggests. See, for example, Stevan Davies, "Women in the Third Gospel and the New Testament Apocrypha," in *'Women Like This': New Perspectives on Jewish Women in the Greco-Roman World*, ed. Amy-Jill Levine, SBL Early Judaism and Its Literature 1 (Atlanta: Scholars Press, 1991), 185–97. The present study accepts the generally favorable portrayal of women in Luke-Acts, while acknowledging the dissenting views of other scholars.

31. See Esther A. de Boer, "The Lukan Mary Magdalene and the Other Women Following Jesus," in *A Feminist Companion to Luke*, ed. Levine, 141.

32. See Ben Witherington III, "On the Road with Mary Magdalene, Joanna, Susanna, and Other Disciples—Luke 8:1–3," in *A Feminist Companion to Luke*, ed. Levine, 134–35.

33. Witherington agrees, pointing out that the Greek term used here "literally means 'substance' as in one's belongings (money, property)"; ibid., 137.

34. "From birth until the end of her life, [a female] was dependent on, and continually under, someone else's ownership: her father, her guardian, or her husband. Marriage symbolized a business transaction, in which the groom purchased the bride from the father much like the purchasing of a slave"; Alina Kemo Kofsky, "A Comparative Analysis of Women's Property Rights in Jewish Law and Anglo-American Law," *Journal of Law and Religion* 6 (1988): 323–24.

wife earned after the marriage began. Jewish legal scholar Alino Semo Kofsky writes, "Jewish law gave the husband many rights in the use and enjoyment to his wife's property. The husband was entitled to his wife's earnings and services."[35] Usually women could not inherit: daughters could be heirs only if there were no sons, and wives never inherited their dead husbands' estates. Provision was made for the support of widows (and divorcees), as indicated above. However, these provisions remained in place only as long as the women remained unmarried. More than a few widows chose not to remarry, and it is probably from this pool that Jesus drew many of his female followers.[36] By presenting Jesus as one who allowed such women to finance his ministry, Luke suggests, if only indirectly, that Jesus was comfortable with women controlling property and with widows and divorcees not remarrying but living more independently.

Another key passage is the story of **Mary and Martha of Bethany** (Luke 10:38–42). In this episode Jesus visits the house of these two sisters and begins teaching his disciples within. Listening to the teacher was understood as a male prerogative in Jewish society. Women were usually not allowed to receive an education.[37] The Talmud indicates that one of the key responsibilities of a wife was "to allow her husband and sons to engage in the study of Torah while she tended to the household and raising of the family."[38] In Jewish scholar Judith Hauptman's judgment, the Talmud tends to portray women as "lightheaded, emotional, prone to gossip, and incapable of serious study."[39] But Luke depicts Mary as defying this gender restriction and

This painting by the seventeenth-century Dutch master Johannes Vermeer shows Mary of Bethany listening to Jesus' teaching while her sister Martha attends to the table. Jesus seems to be explaining to Martha that he will not deny Mary the right to sit and learn, despite the apparent violation of social norms this created.

sitting at Jesus' feet, listening to his teaching. Her sister Martha, meanwhile, is busying herself with many tasks, apparently acceding to her traditional gender role by engaging in the household chores of cooking, cleaning, and serving. Martha is doing the "women's work," while Mary is acting like a male disciple. When Martha objects to being left to do this work all by herself and asks Jesus to command Mary to help her, Jesus refuses to do so. He tells Martha that "Mary has chosen the better part, *which will not be taken away from her*" (emphasis

---

35. Ibid., 328.

36. One of the named women in Luke 8:1–3 is "Joanna, the wife of Herod's steward Chuza," but she is the only woman whose husband is mentioned, and it is not clear whether Chuza is still alive at this point.

37. There were, of course, rare exceptions, but they almost always involved a woman who learned the Torah from her husband or father.

38. This is Kofsky's characterization of *Shabbat* 118b in "A Comparative Analysis of Women's Property Rights in Jewish Law and Anglo-American Law," 321.

39. Judith Hauptman, "Women in the Talmud," in *The Jewish Woman: An Anthology*, ed. Liz Koltun, *Response: A Contemporary Jewish Review* (Summer 1973), 162.

Women in Luke	Women in Acts
Elizabeth, the mother of John the Baptist (Luke 1:5-25, 39-45, 57-63)	Sapphira (Acts 5:1-11)
Mary, the mother of Jesus (1:26-56; 2:1-51; 8:19; also Acts 1:14)	The widows among the Hellenists (6:1)
Anna, a prophetess (2:36-38)	Tabitha/Dorcas (9:36-42)
The woman who was a "sinner" (7:36-53)	Mary and Rhoda (12:12-17)
Mary Magdalene, Joanna, Susanna, and the other female followers of Jesus (8:1-3)	Lydia (16:11-15, 40)
Mary and Martha of Bethany (10:38-42)	The slave girl with a spirit of divination (16:16-18)
Women healed by Jesus (4:38-39; 8:41-56; 13:10-17)	The Greek women of Beroea (17:12)
Women in Jesus' parables (15:8-10; 18:1-5)	Damaris (17:34)
The widow who gave two coins to the Temple (21:1-4)	Priscilla (18:1-3, 18-21, 26)
The women who observed Jesus' crucifixion, visited the empty tomb, and testified to Jesus' resurrection (23:27, 49, 55-56; 24:1-11)	

added). Thus Luke's story indicates that, despite her gender, Mary is capable of receiving an education and (in Jesus' mind) has every right to do so.[40] Moreover, when Jesus suggests that Martha too could pursue this option ("Martha, Martha, you are worried and distracted by many things; there is need of only one thing"), he indicates that Mary is not an exception in this regard. Thus Luke portrays Jesus as someone who believed that all women should be able to learn and study.[41]

Luke, like the other Gospel writers, also includes stories that portray women in a less affirming manner, or that reinforce structures of oppression in ways sometimes obvious and

---

40. Some feminist and Jewish scholars (Schüssler Fiorenza, Adele Reinhartz, Levine) have argued that to interpret Jesus' attitude toward women's education as somehow more progressive or enlightened than that of the Judaism of his era is in some way necessarily "anti-Jewish." But others, such as Turid Karlsen Seim, disagree. As Veronica Kopereski points out, Seim regards it as incontestable that "women within Judaism did not have the right or the duty to be taught, and in the strictest cases were prohibited from doing so, as *b. Kid* 29b indicates." Kopereski goes on to say that "Seim questions whether the type of argument she brings forth here should *eo ipso* be rejected as 'apologetically determined and comparatively anti-Jewish,'" although Kopereski herself definitively rejects Seim's position. See Veronica Kopereski, "Women and Discipleship in Luke 10.38–42 and Acts 6.1–7: The Literary Context of Luke-Acts" in *A Feminist Companion to Luke*, ed. Levine, 178.

41. One way to invert this reading and claim that the text is more oppressive than liberating would be to argue, as the esteemed Elisabeth Schüssler Fiorenza does, that Martha is acting as host and is treating Jesus as her guest. The host-guest relationship was one of equality. By contrast, Mary's role is more passive and—as a student sitting at the feet of the master—she is clearly subordinate to Jesus. So, by taking Mary's side, Luke's Jesus is pushing women toward more passive and subordinate roles. See Elisabeth Schüssler Fiorenza, "A Feminist Critical Interpretation for Liberation: Mary and Martha (Lk. 10:38–42)," *Religion and Intellectual Life* 3 (1986): 21–36. Schüssler Fiorenza establishes beyond question that this text has often been used in the history of Christian interpretation to encourage women to be quiet and listen passively to their male superiors, but whether that is a misreading of the text or a fair interpretation is a separate question.

sometimes subtle. But in general, when compared to the standards of the day, Luke attests to a surprisingly positive attitude toward women. The fact that at least some early Christian writings reflected relatively positive attitudes toward women might explain why Christianity became (at least reputedly) especially popular with women as it struggled to gain a foothold in the religious milieu of the Greco-Roman world. Some later New Testament works (e.g., 1 and 2 Timothy and Titus), clearly document Christianity's shift toward social conservatism and even misogyny. But the Gospel of Luke attests to an earlier Christian stance that is liberating for women and should be celebrated as such.

The Ethics of Wealth and Poverty in Lukan Perspective

Any attempt to craft a New Testament theology from the Gospel of Luke must acknowledge that, like Matthew but unlike Mark, this author is deeply concerned with ethics. But within the realm of ethics, Luke shows far greater interest than Matthew in economic justice. Each Gospel shows Jesus expressing compassion for the poor, but none of the others go as far as the Gospel of Luke.

This can be demonstrated with a redaction-critical analysis comparing Matthew's Sermon on the Mount (Matt. 5–7) with Luke's Sermon on the Plain (Luke 6:20–49). Both sermons begin with "beatitudes," sayings that proclaim God's favor toward certain groups and wish them well. But whereas Matthew pronounces blessings on "the poor *in spirit*" and "those who hunger and thirst *for righteousness*," Jesus' blessings in Luke are directed toward those who are literally poor and starving: "Blessed are you who are poor, for yours is the kingdom of God. Blessed are you who are hungry now, for you will be filled" (Luke 6:20–21).

Even more stark in comparison is that Luke includes not only blessings by Jesus, but *curses*, often referred to as "woes." These woes pronounce God's disapproval of certain groups and seemingly wish them ill. Who are the recipients of these condemnations? The targets of Jesus' wrath are those who are affluent and comfortable: "Woe to you who are rich, for you have received your consolation. Woe to you who are full now, for you will be hungry" (Luke 6:24–25). Many scholars argue that the translation "Woe to you" is a rather weak rendering of the meaning of the Greek in Luke, and that something like "Damn you" is far more accurate.[42] Thus in Luke Jesus actually condemns those who are rich and comfortable, a phenomenon that has no counterpart in the Gospel of Matthew or any other Gospel.

That there would be a degree of hostility toward wealthy people in the Gospels, or any literature not written by the elite themselves, should not be surprising given the economic realities of ancient Rome. Chapter 5 noted that Roman society was characterized by a huge gap between rich and poor. A small percentage of people were fabulously wealthy, while the vast majority of people were desperately poor. There was very little economic opportunity as well. People who were born poor were almost certain to die poor, no matter how hard they worked or how talented they might be. Most wealth was inherited, so there was not a strong sense that the wealthy had earned their fortunes and were thus entitled to them. These fortunes were often gained and augmented by conquest, land theft, and the exploitation of labor. Slavery is the ultimate form of exploitation, but even those who were not enslaved received low wages, worked long hours, and endured dangerous working conditions. Moreover, despite their hard work the common people wrestled with food scarcity, indebtedness, high taxation, and the threat of displacement.

---

42. See Robert J. Miller, ed., *The Complete Gospels*: Annotated Scholars Version, rev. and exp. ed. (Santa Rosa, CA: Polebridge, 1994), 420.

The Gospel of Luke includes a series of unique passages in which the author depicts Jesus articulating his criticisms of the rich and his hopes for their salvation. One example is the **parable of the Rich Fool** (Luke 12:15–21). Jesus prefaces the parable by saying, "Be on your guard against all kinds of greed; for one's life does not consist in the abundance of possessions." He then proceeds to tell of a wealthy man whose land produces abundantly. The man has so much grain he has nowhere to store it, for his barns are full. He decides to tear down his barns and build larger ones, and thus keep everything he has gained for himself. He congratulates himself on his wisdom: "Soul, you have ample good laid up for many years; relax, eat, drink, be merry." But God's voice intervenes and proclaims, "You fool! This very night your life is being demanded of you. And the things you have prepared, whose will they be?" Jesus then concludes, "So it is with those who store up treasures for themselves but are not rich toward God."

What is foolish about the rich man's behavior? On the one hand, he appears supremely confident that his life will go on for a long time, if not indefinitely. He appears unaware of his mortality and is taken by surprise when he dies sooner than he expected. Though he is well-situated for a long life, when death comes suddenly he is ill-prepared. He has focused on the material dimension of life (storing up "treasures" for himself) but has neglected the spiritual dimension of life (he is "not rich toward God"). His confusion about these two dimensions is perhaps suggested by the fact that he addresses his "soul" and tells it to "eat, drink, be merry." The body, not the soul, needs to eat and drink. The spirit needs a different kind of nourishment.

His neglect of the spiritual dimension of life is also manifested in his selfishness and greed. The parable emphasizes that he already has far more than he could ever need. He is a rich man, and his barns are full of grain. Despite this, when he receives an additional windfall, he thinks only of keeping it all for himself, not of sharing it with the needy. In every part of the Roman Empire there were people who were starving. But he hoards his grain, accumulating it for its own sake, rather than from a reasonable sense of need.

The lack of compassion toward the needy is implicit in the parable of the Rich Fool, but in the **parable of the Rich Man and Lazarus** (16:19–31) it becomes explicit. This uniquely Lukan parable begins by emphasizing how the rich man lives a life of incredible luxury. He wears the finest clothing and feasts sumptuously every day. This luxury is contrasted with the abject poverty of Lazarus, who lies sick and starving at the rich man's gate. Lazarus longs to eat even the crumbs that fall from the rich man's table, but the rich man apparently gives him nothing. Then both men die, and Lazarus finds himself in heaven, in the bosom of father Abraham, while the rich man is tormented in hell. In an ironic twist, the rich man asks father Abraham to send down Lazarus—to whom he had never shown an ounce of concern in life—to dip the tip of his finger in some cool water and place it on his tongue, because he is in agony in the flames. He seems to have a strong sense of entitlement, in that he still expects to receive the kindness he never was willing to give when he had the opportunity. Father Abraham reminds him of this and then tells him that fulfilling his request is impossible: "Between you and us a great chasm has been fixed, so that those who might want to pass from here to you cannot do so, and no one can cross from there to us." In this parable Luke's Jesus teaches that greed and a lack of compassion for the less fortunate are grave sins, misdeeds meriting damnation. One might think Jesus would save his harshest condemnation for murderers, rapists, and the like, but the only parable he tells in which a man ends up in hell is about a selfish rich man. Moreover, he warns that once a person has faced the final judgment, there is no longer a chance for repentance or redemption.

The story of the **Rich Ruler** in Luke 18:18–30 is also found in Matthew 19:16–30 and Mark 10:17–31, but it certainly fits in well with Luke's other warnings about the danger of riches. The story is simple. A rich man approaches Jesus and asks him what he must do to attain eternal life. Jesus tells him to follow the commandments, and the man tells him that he has kept them from his youth. Jesus tells him that he lacks one thing: he must sell all of his possessions and give the money to the poor, and then "come, follow" Jesus. The man leaves disheartened and sorrowful. He is unable to submit to Jesus' demand, because he has many possessions and is quite attached to them. The story suggests that riches have a corrupting influence on people. Once something is gained, it is difficult to part with it. The Jesus of the Gospels consistently teaches that great wealth does not make people more generous, but less so. The more people have, the more they think they need. Jesus concludes by proclaiming, "How hard it is for those who have wealth to enter the kingdom of God! Indeed, it is easier for a camel to go through the eye of a needle than for someone who is rich to enter the kingdom of God" (Luke 18:24–25).

That salvation for the rich is not impossible is illustrated by the inclusion in the Gospel of Luke of the story of **Zacchaeus** (Luke 19:1–10).

Can a Camel Pass through the Eye of a Needle?

Throughout history many people have been shocked, alarmed, or offended by Jesus' statement that it is easier for a camel to pass through the eye of a needle than for a rich man to enter the kingdom of God, and two basic interpretations have been developed to soften this saying. One solution is to make the camel smaller, so that it can fit through the literal eye of a needle. This solution proposes that somewhere along the line the word for "camel" (kamēlos, with an eta) was confused with the word for "rope" or "string" (kamilos, with an iota rather than an eta). The supporters of this view claim that Jesus actually spoke of a kamilos—thus his teaching was that it is easier for a thick string to pass through the eye of a needle than for a rich man to enter the kingdom of heaven. But he was misheard or mistranslated to have said kamēlos, and the thick string became a huge animal. There are even a few ancient biblical manuscripts that have kamilos rather than kamēlos at this point in the text. Now it is not easy to get a rope or a string through the eye of a needle, but it is a lot easier than getting a camel through one.

The problem with this solution is that there are no instances of the word kamilos being used to refer to a rope or string prior to the third century CE, and the manuscripts that include the kamilos reading are all late and probably owe something to the rising popularity of this particular attempt to soften Jesus' saying in contemporary sermons and scholarship. The earliest and most reliable manuscripts (including Codex Vaticanus, Codex Sinaiticus, and Codex Bezae) all support the kamēlos reading. There are variations on this solution in which Jesus' original Aramaic saying used a word that could mean either "camel" or "rope," but not only is this linguistically questionable,[43] the context of the passage makes any such interpretation pure folly. When Jesus addresses his disciples' objection to the saying, he speaks of something *impossible* being *possible* for God. It makes no sense for Jesus to speak subsequently of something

continued

---

43. The expression "the eye of a needle"—combined with the notion that it would be impossible for a large animal to pass through it—is used commonly in early rabbinic literature as well. The rabbis never speak of the difficulty of passing a rope through the eye of a needle.

Can a Camel Pass through the Eye of a Needle? *continued*

impossible if his original analogy referred only to something that was merely difficult.

The "thick string" theory goes back as far as Origen (third century CE). There is also an early commentary by Cyril of Alexandria (fifth century CE) in which he refers to it in a sermon. But already in the eleventh century the solution had been disproved by Ibn al-Tayyib, and almost every scholar who mentions it in recent scholarship does so only to repeat the fact that it is clearly false.

The other approach is to make the "eye of the needle" larger, so that a literal camel can get through it. This solution goes back at least as far as 1876, when a scholar named F. W. Farrar wrote that he had read some private letters from a traveler in the Middle East, dating from 1835, in which the traveler claims to have found a door in Jerusalem called the needle's eye.[44] But a few years later a scholar named Scherer (a longtime resident of the Middle East) refuted this claim emphatically: "There is not the slightest shred of evidence for this identification. This door has not in any language been called the needle's eye, and is not so called today."[45] Somehow the seed had been planted, though, and ever since then it has become increasingly popular. In fact it is common now for Jerusalem tour guides to point out to gullible tourists the precise location of the "needle's eye" gate. There are dozens of websites that testify to the existence of the gate, despite the complete lack of documentation for it.

The stubborn character of this myth and its resistance to debunking owes something to people's strong desire to soften Jesus' saying, and something to its own semi-plausibility. It is apparently true that there were main gates in the cities of ancient and medieval times that were extremely heavy and that would only be opened during the day when necessary, and that there were smaller, narrower doors nearby or connected that would allow a single person to enter, but not a fully loaded pack animal. The problem is that none of these gates in Jerusalem was ever called "the eye of the needle," certainly not in Jesus' time and not for centuries thereafter. There is no account prior to the modern period that refers to Jerusalem having a gate called "the eye of the needle" or anything like it.

All of this is not to say that Jesus taught that it was impossible for a rich man to enter the kingdom of heaven. Jesus was known for issuing some teachings that were so stark that they can only be understood as involving a kind of "**rhetorical exaggeration**" in which a speaker overemphasizes a point for effect. When a busy person begs off an engagement because he or she has "a million things to do," both parties know the number of tasks on the person's agenda is not actually in seven figures. People use this expression to indicate as vividly as possible just how hectic their schedules are and how impossible it would be to add to them. Similarly, when Jesus teaches in Matthew 5:29 (and parallels), "If your right eye causes you to sin, tear it out and throw it away," no one should take this literally. It is understood that Jesus is using an over-the-top metaphor to make his point about avoiding situations that tend to lead a person into temptation as vividly and as effectively as possible. Another likely example of exaggeration is the saying, "Whoever comes to me and does not hate father and mother, wife and children, brothers and sisters, yes, and even life itself, cannot be my disciple" (Luke 14:26). Just as Jesus was not here actually advocating hatred of one's family but rather using a figure of speech, so too might he have been using the "eye of a needle" metaphor to make his point more vividly, rather than describing a literal state of affairs.

---

44. F. W. Farrar, "Brief Notes on Passages of the Gospels. II. The Camel and the Needle's Eye," in *The Expositor* 3 (1876): 369–80.

45. George H. Scherer, *The Eastern Colour of the Bible* (London: National Sunday School Union, 1900), 37; see also Kenneth Bailey, *Poet and Peasant, and Through Peasant Eyes: A Literary Cultural Approach to the Parables in Luke* (Grand Rapids: Eerdmans, 1976), 2:166.

Zacchaeus was a chief tax collector, and very rich. When Jesus came to his town and was swarmed by the crowds, Zacchaeus showed his interest by climbing a tree to get a glimpse of him. When Jesus saw him, he told Zacchaeus that he wished to stay at his house that night. Knowing that Zacchaeus was a tax collector, people began to grumble: "He has gone to be the guest of one who is a sinner." But without a word from Jesus, Zacchaeus redeems himself: "Look, half of my possessions, Lord, I will give to the poor; and if I have defrauded anyone of anything, I will pay back four times as much." After this, Jesus proclaims that "salvation has come to this house" and that Zacchaeus too is a "son of Abraham" (that is, a member in good standing of the people of God). Despite his riches and his sinful occupation, Zacchaeus is saved.

To gain this status, Zacchaeus depends on the mercy and grace of God, but he also demonstrates four qualities that Luke's Gospel seems to suggest many of his rich brethren lack. The first is *compassion*. When Zacchaeus declares his willingness to donate money to the poor and to repay the poor wretches he defrauded (most likely by overcharging them on their taxes), he shows that he feels pity for the less fortunate. His empathy has been awakened, and it leads him to the feeling of solidarity with other human beings that is the basis of compassion.

The second essential quality is *generosity*. Zacchaeus does not give a small percentage of his wealth to the less fortunate, leaving a huge sum for himself. He gives fully half of his fortune to the poor and repays those he has defrauded four times over. This repayment goes above and beyond the call of duty, because the Torah only requires a double repayment in cases of defrauding. Given how much of a tax collector's profits came from overcharging, it is likely that this repayment will consume most of the remaining half of Zacchaeus's fortune. Unlike the rich people in Luke 21:1–4, who put their gifts into the treasury "out of their abundance" (that is, apparently still leaving themselves with large fortunes), Zacchaeus is

more like the poor widow who put in two copper coins, which represented "all she had to live on." Zacchaeus "gives 'til it hurts," as the saying goes, and his generosity does not go unnoticed.

Zacchaeus also implicitly promises that he will no longer defraud people as a tax collector. It would not make much sense for him to promise to repay anyone he defrauded four times over and then to persist in that behavior. In so doing, Zacchaeus demonstrates the third quality the Gospel of Luke suggests can lead to salvation for the rich: *a commitment to earning an honest living*. Similarly, in Luke 3:10–14, John the Baptist gives advice to sinners wanting to turn their lives around. His advice to tax collectors is not to quit their jobs, but to do them honestly: "Collect no more than the amount prescribed for you" (3:13). When soldiers appeal to him as well he does not tell them they cannot serve in the military but commands them not to resort to immoral means of making more money: "Do not extort money from anyone by threats or false accusation, and be satisfied with your wages" (3:14).

Lastly, and perhaps most unusually, Zacchaeus demonstrates the quality of *nonattachment*. The Rich Ruler is unable to part with his possessions because he has grown attached to them. Jesus' teaching about it being easier for a camel to pass through the eye of a needle than for a rich person to enter the kingdom of heaven seems to be based on the great difficulty the wealthy have giving away very much of their fortunes. Zacchaeus, by contrast, is that rare bird who is not excessively attached to his wealth. He gives away the overwhelming majority of his fortune at the drop of a hat. What is most interesting about this is that—unlike with the Rich Ruler—Jesus does not even have to ask Zacchaeus to do this. He offers all this without prompting.

In the end, the Gospel of Luke does not seem to argue that wealth itself is evil. Jesus' female benefactors in 8:3 were arguably somewhat wealthy. Rather, Luke's attitude seems to be similar to that of the author of 1 Timothy, who did not write (as is often mistakenly assumed) that money itself is the root of all evil but rather that *"the love of* money is the root of all kinds of evil"* (1 Tim. 6:10, emphasis added). The Gospel of Luke suggests there are two good purposes for money: to spend it[46] and to give it away. Only accumulating money for its own sake and denying others the benefits that might be gained from it is sinful and earns Jesus' strongest disapproval.

Many other theological themes and teachings of the Gospel of Luke can be uncovered using literary criticism and redaction criticism, and the Gospel is also explicable by means of the other methods of biblical criticism introduced in chapter 7. None of these chapters exhausts the meaning of a given New Testament text, but rather illustrates the application of certain methods and highlights some of the most important themes and teachings it contains.

Key Terms

Luke-Acts
ecclesiology
Samaritans
parable of the Good Samaritan
Gentiles
God-fearers

parable of the Prodigal Son
the woman who was a sinner
parable of the Pharisee and the Tax Collector
Mary Magdalene
Mary and Martha of Bethany

parable of the Rich Fool
parable of the Rich Man and Lazarus
the Rich Ruler
rhetorical exaggeration
Zacchaeus

Review Questions

1. What are the main reasons for believing the Gospel of Luke and Acts of the Apostles were written by the same author and form two volumes of a single work?

2. How does the preface to the Gospel of Luke (1:1–4) suggest that its author is a professional writer? What are some of the possible implications of this claim, especially with respect to Luke's attitude toward his predecessors?

3. What reasons did ancient Jews give for their negative attitudes toward Samaritans? How does the Gospel of Luke show Jesus rejecting negative stereotypes about Samaritans and indicating they should be welcome in the people of God?

4. Why did Jews tend to think of Gentiles as "sinners"? According to the Gospels, what kind of stance did the Pharisees advocate with respect to Gentiles and other sinners (such as tax collectors)? How does the stance of Jesus differ from that of the Pharisees in the Gospel of Luke?

5. In what ways were women excluded from full participation in the covenant in ancient Judaism? What are some of the ways in which Jesus granted women a higher status in his ministry than was typical of ancient Judaism?

6. What is the general attitude of the Gospel of Luke toward the rich and the poor? What features of ancient economic life may have contributed toward a generalized hostility toward the rich? What specific

46. Not that Jesus would necessarily approve of any kind of spending, but there is a story common to all four Gospels in which he defends a woman who anoints his feet or body with very expensive perfume or ointment (Matt. 26:6–13; Mark 14:3–9; Luke 7:36–50; John 12:1–8). Thus even extravagant spending is apparently sometimes justified.

criticisms of the rich are revealed by passages such as the parable of the Rich Fool (12:15–21), the parable of the Rich Man and Lazarus (16:19–31), and the story of the Rich Ruler (18:18–30)?

7. How does the story of Zacchaeus (19:1–10) show that salvation is not impossible for the wealthy? What qualities does Zacchaeus demonstrate that help lead to his salvation?

Discussion Questions

1. Some have argued that Jesus' stance toward Samaritans (including his praise of the Good Samaritan's compassion toward an enemy and stranger) is relevant to the modern debate over immigration and the treatment of resident aliens. Do you see a connection here? Are there other passages that are perhaps more relevant, such as Jesus' teaching in the Great Judgment (Matt. 25:31–46) that salvation is dependent in part upon whether one welcomes and shows hospitality toward strangers?

2. As the references to the diverse views of modern scholars in this chapter show, scholars are divided on the question of whether the Gospel of Luke portrays Jesus as an advocate of equality for women. Is the concept of "Jesus as feminist" a product of wishful thinking, or is there enough evidence in the Gospel of Luke to indicate that this concept has some legitimacy?

3. Jesus' teachings on wealth and poverty are at least in some ways a response to the prevailing economic conditions in the Roman Empire, including massive inequality, widespread poverty, slave labor or low wages, limited economic opportunity, and the near-total absence of a social "safety net." In what ways are economic conditions today very different from those of Jesus' time, and in what ways are they still very similar? What effect does such a comparison have on your understanding of how relevant Jesus' teachings are in the modern world?

Bibliography and Suggestions for Further Study

(Books and websites that are accessible for general undergraduates are marked with an asterisk; other sources listed are appropriate for advanced students.)

Cadbury, Henry J. *The Making of Luke-Acts*. New York: Macmillan, 1927; London: SPCK, 1968.

*Edwards, O. C. *Luke's Story of Jesus*. Philadelphia: Fortress, 1981.

Gregory, Andrew F., and Christopher Kavin Rowe. *Rethinking the Unity and Reception of Luke and Acts*. Columbia: University of South Carolina Press, 2010.

Johnson, Luke T. *The Literary Function of Possessions in Luke-Acts*. Missoula, MT: Scholars Press for the Society of Biblical Literature, 1977.

Levine, Amy-Jill, with Marianne Blickenstaff, eds. *A Feminist Companion to Luke*. Cleveland: Pilgrim Press, 2004.

Parsons, Mikeal Carl, and Richard I. Pervo. *Rethinking the Unity of Luke and Acts*. Minneapolis: Fortress, 1993.

Tannehill, Robert C. *The Narrative Unity of Luke-Acts: A Literary Interpretation*. 2 vols. Philadelphia: Fortress, 1986; 1990.

Tiede, David. *Prophecy and History in Luke-Acts*. Philadelphia: Fortress, 1980.

Luke's Second Volume: The Acts of the Apostles

The previous chapter dealt with particular features of the Gospel of Luke, especially in comparison to Mark and Matthew, but did not focus on the Gospel as a whole. The main reason for this is that the Gospel of Luke does not stand alone: it is one part of a two-volume work that includes the Acts of the Apostles. This is why scholars refer to these books as "Luke-Acts." Thus it is impossible to consider the purpose of Luke without including Acts. One could devote a single chapter to both books simultaneously; however, not only would this produce a dauntingly long chapter, it would not reflect the usual treatment of these texts in the history of Christianity. In the canon, Luke and Acts are separated from each other by the Gospel of John, and there is little evidence that early Christians ever worked with these texts in tandem.

Nonetheless, examining the two books together allows the interpretation of each book to inform the interpretation of the other. Certainly, this would honor the apparent intention of the author. Therefore, although this chapter is ostensibly devoted to the Acts of the Apostles, it also serves the function of addressing the purpose of the two-volume work as a whole.

The book of Acts sets out to recount the early history of the movement that became the Christian church, from its beginnings in Jerusalem after Jesus' resurrection and ascension to its spread to other parts of the world. The expansion of Christianity is made possible by the preaching of the **apostles**, people chosen by Jesus to serve as his representatives (or "witnesses") and specially empowered for this task. Many scholars have recognized that Acts 1:8 serves as a programmatic statement that provides the organizing framework for the book of Acts as a whole. This framework is geographical in nature. Jesus tells his apostles (minus Judas), "You will receive power when the Holy Spirit has come upon you; and you will be my witnesses *in Jerusalem, in all Judea and Samaria, and to the ends of the earth*" (emphasis added). Acts 1 then tells how on the day of Pentecost, a Jewish festival that took place in the late spring, the apostles were filled with the Holy Spirit and began speaking in tongues. After this, they begin to proclaim God's word and to make converts first in Jerusalem (Acts 2–7), then in Judea and Samaria (Acts 8), and then throughout the rest of the Greco-Roman world (Acts 9–28).

In telling the story of the spread of Christianity, Luke had to face a number of unpleasant realities.[1] One was that the relationship between Judaism and Christianity, which had been fraying

---

1. As discussed in chapter 6, scholars disagree over whether Luke-Acts was written in the late first century or the early to mid-second century. But the problems were similar in either case, and would only become more pressing as time passed.

Why Does Acts End Where It Does?

Many readers find the ending of Acts surprising and unsatisfying, mostly because it does not narrate the death of Paul. Both Peter and Paul were probably killed by the Roman emperor Nero in the mid-sixties CE, perhaps as part of the general persecution of Christians, who were blamed for the Great Fire that destroyed much of Rome in 64 CE. If Peter and Paul suffered a glorious martyrdom in Rome so close to the time at which Luke brings the book of Acts to a close, why did he not continue the story a little longer, tell of Paul's (and perhaps Peter's) final days, and end with a bang rather than a whimper?

Some scholars claim that if Luke had known of Paul's martyrdom, there is no way he would not have included it. Therefore, he must have written prior to that event in the mid-sixties. However, such an early date for Acts seems highly unlikely since, as discussed in chapter 6, there are no quotations of the book until the mid-second century.

Other scholars have suggested that Luke simply ran out of room. The papyrus scrolls on which first-century books were written had a maximum length, because the strength of the medium was such that longer scrolls were always in danger of bending or cracking in the middle. This is one reason why longer ancient works such as the epic poetry of Virgil and the histories of Thucydides were always broken up into "books." Acts comes close to pressing the limit of that maximum length, so some theorize that Luke discovered he was nearing the end of his scroll and had to wrap things up quickly, leaving him no space to include the death of Paul. But it is uncertain whether Luke was running out of room for Acts, as both the Gospel of Luke and the Gospel of Matthew are longer than Acts and neither seems to have had problems with length. Moreover, Luke would have been a very poor planner if he ran out of space before wrapping up his story.

The most likely explanation is that Acts ends exactly where the author intended. The plot of Acts is governed by God's plan for the spread of the word to "the ends of the earth" (Acts 1:8). Once the Gospel has reached Rome, the largest city in the world and the center of power and learning, at least the first phase of this purpose is accomplished and the story is over. Moreover, to have included the execution of Paul by the emperor would have undermined Luke's case regarding the innocence of Jesus and Paul of the criminal charges brought against them (see sidebar below).

since at least the mid-first century, was now unraveling completely. People had to choose sides between what had become two separate religions. Judaism was reeling from the crippling blow of the failed rebellion against the Romans in the First Jewish-Roman War of 66–70 CE, culminating in the near-razing of Jerusalem and the destruction of the Temple. As Judaism reorganized after the loss of the Temple, most Jews remained loyal to Judaism and rejected Christianity. There is evidence that a small sect of Jewish-Christians with an adoptionist Christology survived into the second century; but by that time it was clear to most Christian groups that the mission to the Jews had failed. Thereafter, any Jews who converted to Christianity were simply absorbed into the predominantly Gentile church. There was no longer an overtly Jewish branch of the church.

A second problem that Luke faced was that Christianity was internally divided and under tremendous pressure as a result of Roman persecution. Chapter 1 noted the many rival groups within early Christianity, and their bitter

Why Was the Rupture with Judaism a Problem for Christianity?

That Christianity eventually separated from Judaism, or to put it differently, that Christians were eventually disowned by the Jews, created practical and theological problems for Christians. On the practical side, from the Roman perspective Christians appeared to be Jewish apostates; Christianity began as a Jewish sect but was subsequently repudiated by its parent faith. This status made Christians seem more disreputable to many Roman critics and contributed to their persecution (see chapter 3). More important in the long run, however, was a theological difficulty. Christians claimed that God had now made a new covenant, through Christ, that took precedence over the covenant he had made with Israel; this raised questions about the consistency, or even the trustworthiness, of the Christian God.

The existence of a new covenant implies the old one was flawed, or that it was somehow no longer in effect. One way of looking at the situation was that the Jewish people had proved unfaithful and so God canceled that covenant and formed a new one with a new group of people, Gentile converts to Christianity. But would such a transfer of affections, however justified it may have been, make God appear to be fickle, or perhaps even unreliable? If God had summarily abrogated his agreement with the Jewish people and abandoned them for a different people altogether, what confidence could this new people have that God would not do the same thing to them at some point?

Early Christians tended to make two kinds of arguments in response to this problem. The first was that God did not *summarily* abandon his covenant with the Jewish people, but only after a long and troubled history in which the Jews *continually* broke faith with him and failed to repent despite being given chance after chance to do so. The second was that God did not completely cancel this covenant but remained faithful to it and continued to fulfill the promises of the covenant *to those Jews who remained faithful to God*. In Christian thinking, of course, "faithfulness to God" included accepting Jesus as the Messiah and Son of God. The existence of a "**faithful remnant**" of Jewish people who believed in Christ and as a result still enjoyed God's blessings was a crucial part of this argument. It proved that God was not fickle, nor was God an untrustworthy covenant partner. God could be relied upon to fulfill God's end of an agreement forever, as long as God's covenant partners fulfilled theirs.

disputes about whose version of Jesus was true. Jewish-Christian adoptionists, who looked to James the brother of the Lord as the apostle who provided the truest guide to the teachings and significance of Jesus, were on the wane, but other groups were on the rise. Gnostics, many of whom identified Thomas or Mary Magdalene as Jesus' best and most faithful disciple (see chapter 2), grew in power and influence until they were defeated by the proto-orthodox camp during the fourth and fifth centuries. But perhaps the most defining struggle of the second century was between Marcionite Christians, who claimed Paul was the only true guide to Christian doctrine, and proto-orthodox Christians, who looked to Peter (without, however, rejecting Paul).[2] Marcionites

---

2. The case for this understanding of the context of Luke-Acts is persuasively made, in these exact terms, by Joseph Tyson in *Marcion and Luke-Acts: A Defining Struggle* (Columbia: University of South Carolina Press, 2006).

argued for a complete separation between Christianity and Judaism; they not only believed these religions were based on two separate covenants but also that these covenants were formed with two distinct gods. By contrast, proto-orthodox Christians saw both continuity and discontinuity in their relationship to Judaism. Marcion and his followers showed such hostility to Judaism that the disagreement between the Marcionites and the proto-orthodox appeared to be irreconcilable. Perhaps the resulting division and infighting would prove fatal to nascent Christianity. On the other hand, if the enmity between the champions of Paul and the champions of Peter could be overcome, then Christianity would become stronger and more united moving forward.

The Purpose of Luke-Acts

Christians faced persecution from the Roman Empire and obstacles in the conversion of loyal Roman citizens, based partly on the charge that Christianity was founded and led by men who were convicted criminals, executed by the Roman state (Jesus, Peter, and Paul). Hence some scholars see Luke-Acts as an **apology** that seeks to exonerate Jesus, Peter, and Paul and demonstrate their innocence with respect to the charges brought against them. "Apology" (Greek, *apologia*) is here used in the technical sense, as an extended defense or refutation of charges. There is considerable evidence supporting the theory that Luke-Acts is an extended apology, and few doubt this was one of the author's purposes in writing. However, defending the founders of Christianity was almost certainly not Luke's only purpose, nor perhaps even the most important.

The debate over the purpose of Luke-Acts was dominated by a few major scholars for most of the twentieth century. However, in recent decades a variety of new theories have surfaced.

The Innocence of Jesus and Paul in Luke-Acts

All of the Gospels attempt to demonstrate that Jesus was not guilty of any crime deserving death, and that his crucifixion was a tragic miscarriage of justice resulting from a conspiracy hatched by his jealous enemies. But the author of the Gospel of Luke goes above and beyond his fellow evangelists in making this case and proceeds to do the same with respect to the hero of his second volume, Paul.

The basic elements of the defense of Jesus are the same in all four Gospels: (1) his trial before the Jewish Sanhedrin was manifestly unfair because of false testimony and biased judges, and neither the guilty verdict on the charge of blasphemy nor the death sentence was warranted; (2) the charge of treason leading to Jesus' crucifixion was trumped-up and unproven; and (3) the Roman prefect Pontius Pilate believed in Jesus' innocence, testified to that fact, tried to release Jesus, and assented to his execution only under duress.

Luke's preoccupation with Jesus' innocence can be seen in a number of alterations he makes to his Markan source. In Mark, Jesus eventually answers the high priest's direct question "Are you the Messiah, the Son of the Blessed One?" by saying, "I am." In Mark's view, this should not count as blasphemy, because it is a true statement. But it could be taken as an admission of guilt, in some respect, and so Luke's Jesus says only, "You say so," to the

continued

high priest's accusations. Consequently, in Luke's telling, Jesus' conviction of blasphemy is preposterous not only because there is no solid testimony against him but because he does not make a confession.

Later Luke adds to Mark's account of Jesus' trial before the Roman authorities by indicating that Pilate sent Jesus to Herod Antipas to be examined and that Herod also did not find him guilty. Luke also shows that Pilate proclaimed Jesus' innocence not once but three separate times (Luke 23:4, 14-16, 22) with increasing vehemence. In one instance, Pilate exclaims, "You brought me this man as one who was perverting the people; and here I have examined him in your presence and have not found this man guilty of any of your charges against him. Neither has Herod, for he sent him back to us. Indeed, he has done nothing to deserve death" (23:14-16).

The emphasis on Jesus' innocence persists in Luke's account of Jesus' crucifixion. Only in Luke's version of this story do the two criminals crucified to either side of Jesus

speak. One of them mocks Jesus, but the other rebukes his fellow criminal and acknowledges Jesus' innocence: "We indeed have been condemned justly, for we are getting what we deserve for our deeds, but this man has done nothing wrong" (Luke 23:41). In Mark's Gospel, after Jesus breathes his last the Roman centurion proclaims, "Truly this man was God's Son" (Mark 15:39). Luke's Gospel edits the proclamation of the centurion to read, "Certainly this man was innocent" (Luke 23:47).

In Acts, Paul too is accused of crimes and undergoes several trials. Unlike Jesus, Paul testifies extensively in his own defense, vigorously disputing the charges against him (Acts 22:1-21; 23:1, 6; 24:10-21; 25:8; 26:2-23). But in other ways their cases are similar. Charges are made against Paul that are demonstrably false (21:27-29; 24:2-9), and various authorities proclaim his innocence (21:38; 23:9, 29; 25:25; 26:30-32). It is only because of a legal technicality, Luke writes, that Paul is sent to Rome for trial. Otherwise, he would have been freed and exonerated.

Luke-Acts as a Multi-Purpose Work: The Theory of Henry J. Cadbury

Henry J. Cadbury, a scholar who specialized in Luke-Acts, believed that Luke-Acts had no single, overarching purpose, but was designed to achieve a variety of goals. Cadbury organized some of Luke's various aims under the categories of theology and social issues. The first category reflects Cadbury's belief that Luke entered into the debate over the dominant theological issues of the day, namely messianism and apocalypticism. Luke defines his notion of the Messiah, attempts to demonstrate that Jesus fulfills this role, and outlines a vision of salvation history that includes an account of when and how the

end of the world would come. The second category of purposes involve Luke's desire to address certain social issues, a purpose discernable in his concern with the huge gap between rich and poor and his keen sympathy and understanding toward women[3] (see chapter 11).

All of these elements form part of Luke's message, but none indicate Luke's overarching purpose or motives. For example, many scholars agree that Luke portrays women in a (mostly) positive and sympathetic light, but it would be difficult to argue this was his purpose in writing. Similarly, a particular theological message and conception of Jesus is indubitably present; Luke presents Jesus as the Messiah and argues implicitly for this identification in a variety of

---

3. See Henry J. Cadbury, *The Making of Luke-Acts* (New York: Macmillan, 1927; London: SPCK, 1961), 127–39.

ways. But proving that Jesus is the Messiah does not seem to have formed one of Luke's main, conscious purposes.

Instead, Cadbury attributes Luke's larger purpose in writing to three primary motives, one historical and the other two apologetic. The historical motive is seen in the evidence of divine guidance and control that pervade this work. The narrative suggests it is **God's plan** for Christianity to spread from Jerusalem to the rest of the world, and that God intervenes in this process to ensure the success of the religion and its leaders. When the apostles are arrested and locked up, God sends an angel to open the prison doors (Acts 5:17–21) so that Jesus' witnesses can continue their preaching.[4] When Saul's persecution of Christians causes them to scatter and grow afraid, God steps in with a vision that prompts Saul to abandon this persecution and to embrace the new "way" that he had previously regarded as heretical. In Acts, Luke writes that the conversion of Saul (also known as Paul) and his commissioning as an apostle is part of God's stated plan: "He is an instrument whom I have chosen to bring my name before Gentiles and kings and before the people of Israel" (Acts 9:15). When Paul's life or freedom is threatened, he is often alerted to the plot beforehand and is thus able to stay one step ahead of the law (9:23–25; 14:5–7). When the enemies of God succeed in arresting Paul and his companions, God sends an earthquake that results in the prison walls falling and the prisoners' chains being broken (16:25–26). For Luke, this divine intervention is one of the credentials of the Christian movement. The motif of the fulfillment of Scripture in his first volume's description of Jesus' life, ministry, and death is also designed for this end. Acts shows that the apostolic age also lies under the guiding hand of God.

One of Luke's two apologetic purposes, in Cadbury's interpretation, was the aforementioned goal of defending Christianity from charges that its heroes had broken the law. The second apologetic motive seen by Cadbury as providing Luke's justification for his two-volume work involves his desire to show the legitimacy of Christianity as a religion rooted in antiquity, rather than an upstart cult of recent vintage. To accomplish this Luke needed to show that Christianity had strong roots in Judaism and was not a splinter sect. Evidence of this motive is seen in the many fulfillments of scripture Luke documents in the two-volume work and in his drawing attention to his protagonists' consistent observance of Jewish law and practice. Luke omits the passage from Mark (retained by Matthew) in which Jesus overturns the kosher laws and disparages the Oral Torah (Mark 7:1–23). Luke is also careful to say that Paul was scrupulous in his observation of the law. The Jerusalem apostles relate that the Jewish believers in Jerusalem had been told that Paul was teaching all the Jews living among the Gentiles to abandon the Law of Moses (Acts 21:21). At their suggestion, Paul agrees to observe the purification rites for the upcoming festival so that all would know that such rumors were baseless, and that Paul himself observed the law (Acts 21:24). The birth stories in the Gospel also clearly reflect this purpose, as they are full of references to the fulfillment of Scripture and the characters are all portrayed as pious Jews.

Luke-Acts as an Answer to the Delay of the Parousia: The Theory of Hans Conzelmann

Cadbury's theories were eclipsed, at least temporarily, by the work of the redaction critic Hans Conzelmann. Conzelmann proposed that

---

4. Peter is the beneficiary of another angelic jailbreak in Acts 12:6–11.

Luke-Acts was written to address the problem of the **delay of the parousia**—that is, the realization that Christ's second coming (known as the "parousia") had not occurred as soon as many early Christians had expected. Luke addressed this problem by outlining a three-stage understanding of "**salvation history**." Conzelmann pointed to a few key verses that he regarded as programmatic. One is Luke 16:16, which reads, "The law and the prophets were in effect until John came; since then the good news of the kingdom of God is proclaimed." According to Conzelmann, this verse shows that Luke thought of history as divided between a first stage, the period of Israel, (the time of "the law and the prophets"), a second stage, the period of Jesus' ministry, and a third stage, the period since the ascension of Jesus (the period of the church). In Conzelmann's understanding, the Old Testament documents the first stage of redemptive history, the Gospel of Luke describes the second period, and the book of Acts is devoted to the third. Such sharp distinctions between each of the three phases, however, would imply that Luke saw a basic discontinuity between Judaism and Christianity, and another discontinuity between the period of Jesus and the period of the church.[5]

After initial widespread acceptance, Conzelmann's theory was subjected to various criticisms and eventually rejected by most scholars. Conzelmann relies heavily on a questionable interpretation of a few key verses. Nowhere does Luke mention the three phases of salvation history that Conzelmann claims provide the framework for the work. Only in one quote (Luke 16:16) does Luke seem to divide salvation history into the phases of which Conzelmann speaks, and only with regard to two phases. Moreover, the text of Luke-Acts offers little support for Conzelmann's claim that the main problem Luke faced was the delay of the parousia. And Luke's account does not support the idea that Luke saw a fundamental discontinuity between Conzelmann's first and second phases of salvation history. The birth stories (Luke 1–2), which Conzelmann denies were originally part of the Gospel, create serious problems for his theory, for they show clearly that Luke saw a fundamental continuity between the time of Israel and the time of Jesus, not a sharp distinction.[6] Indeed, the evidence throughout Luke-Acts suggests that Luke views all three periods as united in the single plan of God.

Recent Scholarship

In Conzelmann's wake there has been no agreement among scholars as to Luke's master plan, although many of Cadbury's ideas have returned to prominence. Earl Richard summarizes the consensus of modern biblical scholarship on the purpose of Luke-Acts as a whole: "Luke has a unique understanding of the Christian experience: it is God's plan for man's salvation *foretold* by the prophets of old, *realized* by the divine visitation of Jesus' son, and *actualized* through intermediaries."[7] This is a rather broad statement, though, and fleshing it out leads to many areas of scholarly disagreement. Nevertheless, there is agreement about some of the features of Luke-Acts. First, it is imbued with *Old Testament*

---

5. Conzelmann and some of his German Protestant colleagues made it clear that they saw the church as a poor substitute for Jesus. They tended to denigrate Luke as a representative of "early Catholicism," which they saw as a betrayal of the authentic message of Christ, preserved (in their minds) in the teaching of Paul.

6. See Paul Minear, "Luke's Use of the Birth Stories," in *Studies in Luke-Acts*, ed. Leander E. Keck and J. Louis Martyn (Nashville: Abingdon, 1966), 111–30.

7. Earl Richard, "Luke—Writer, Theologian, Historian: Research and Orientation of the 1970s," *Biblical Theology Bulletin* 13 (1983): 8. Richard's analysis preserves something of the three-phase scheme of Conzelmann without drawing such sharp lines between periods.

themes, inspiration, and language. Second, the work is consumed by the *divine plan* and its realization. Third, whatever were the root problems of the church in Luke's day, the effects of those problems were discontinuity, lack of unity, and threat to orthodoxy. Luke sought to resolve these problems in the theme of *continuity*. Luke uses numerous techniques to underscore the theme of continuity. For example, the second volume is a continuation of the first. There are numerous parallels between characters and events in Luke and Acts. The theme of promise and fulfillment pervades the narrative. Christianity is presented as the true heir to Judaism, and Luke's narrative is clearly a continuation of biblical history. That he appears to have written the birth stories (Luke 1:4–2:52) in conscious imitation of the style of the Septuagint suggests that he wanted his readers to see he was picking up where the Old Testament left off.

Is it possible to pull all of these insights together and devise a single, unifying theory about the purpose of Luke-Acts? Two scholars whose work provides the framework for such a theory are David Tiede and Luke Johnson.

The Historical Context of Luke-Acts

David Tiede argues that the historical event to which Luke most prominently responds is not the delay of the parousia but the sacking of Jerusalem and destruction of the Temple in 70 CE. These tragic events engendered radical questions about the faithfulness of Israel and the fulfillment of God's promises. But this was not the first time the Jews had faced defeat and disaster. For centuries, the Jewish people had learned to deal with catastrophe by appealing to their ancient scriptural heritage and its prophecies. The dominant message of these texts maintained Israel's fortunes were directly correlated to its obedience

and faithfulness to God; Israel's suffering should thus be viewed as a consequence of failure or refusal to heed the prophets sent to it.

Consequently, in interpreting the plight of Israel post-70 CE, most Jewish groups likely agreed this disaster was caused by the sin of the Jewish people. But the precise diagnosis of this sin was a matter of considerable disagreement. Some Jews, such as Josephus, attributed it to the lack of faith in God demonstrated by the taking up of arms against Rome. Others saw the problem as capitulation to Hellenism, or the wickedness inherent in humanity. Luke steps into this intra-Jewish hermeneutical debate, addressing the same situation with a common hope that God had not abandoned his people or his redemptive purpose. But Luke's Christian faith led him to a different interpretation than that of Josephus or other Jews. Luke's specific diagnosis of Israel's sin was that it involved the rejection by most Jews of "the king who comes in the name of the Lord" (Luke 19:38). This is seen clearly in a uniquely Lukan passage, the Lament over Jerusalem (19:41–44), in which Jesus looks over Jerusalem and begins to weep as he contemplates the city's future. He refers specifically to the coming siege of Jerusalem by the Romans, slaughter of its population, and destruction of the Temple. All this will happen, Luke's Jesus tells the Jewish people of Jerusalem, "because you did not recognize the time of your visitation from God."

Thus Tiede situates Luke as part of an essentially Jewish debate over the cause of the catastrophic events of 70 CE. The polemics, scriptural arguments, and proofs that are rehearsed in Luke-Acts are part of an *intrafamily* struggle that was deteriorating, in the wake of the destruction of Jerusalem, into a fight over who was really the faithful Israel. Luke claims the true Israel consists of those Jews who accept Jesus as the Messiah and those Gentiles who subsequently come to faith through the preaching of the faithful Jewish remnant. His view is that

God's promises to Israel are not in vain, but have found their fulfillment, *including* their reception by repentant Jews, in the Christian church as it is presently constituted. There was division, Luke admits, and those who rejected Jesus are not among the beneficiaries of the fulfillment. But Luke does emphasize the faith of many in Israel[8] as well as the rejection by some.[9]

The Men of the Spirit in Luke-Acts

Luke T. Johnson is one of many scholars who claim the purpose of Luke-Acts is more apparent in the second volume than in the first and that once the purpose of Acts is grasped, the structure and contents of the Gospel make a lot more sense. One phenomenon, for example, that requires knowledge of the complete, two-volume narrative is the remarkable degree of *parallelism* between the main characters. One first notices this with respect to the main characters of Acts, Peter and Paul, and upon reflection it appears to be the case that all of the apostles who receive significant attention in Acts (including Stephen, Philip, John, and Barnabas) are similarly portrayed. The shared feature is the role of the Holy Spirit in enabling these characters to function as figures of authority in Christianity.

Although Luke clearly indicates that all believers receive the Spirit, he portrays certain characters as possessing the Spirit in a special way, with the power to speak God's word and perform signs and wonders. Luke Johnson calls these figures "**men of the Spirit**" and discerns three distinctive characteristics: (1) when they

© Prado, Madrid, Spain / Bridgeman Images

Only Luke describes the descent of the Holy Spirit upon the apostles at Pentecost, depicted in this El Greco painting. Luke emphasizes the empowering action of the Spirit throughout the Acts of the Apostles.

receive the Holy Spirit they also receive the gift of *prophecy*, (2) they proceed to speak God's word

---

8. In addition to characters like Elizabeth, Zechariah, Simeon, and Anna in the birth stories (Luke 1–2) and the Jews who became followers of Jesus during his ministry, there are also the Jews who convert after hearing the preaching of Peter. Acts 2:41 mentions three thousand converts, to whom Peter says, "For the promise is for you, for your children, and for all who are far away, everyone whom the Lord our God calls to him" (2:39). Acts 4:4 speaks of another five thousand Jewish converts.

9. The preceding paragraphs are a summary of David Tiede's argument in chapter 1 of *Prophecy and History in Luke-Acts* (Philadelphia: Fortress, 1980), 1–18.

with "boldness" and are able to work *signs and wonders*, and (3) they elicit a response of *acceptance or rejection*. In this way, Luke presents the central characters in Acts as prophetic figures. Not only do these characters act like prophets, the people respond to them as prophets, by accepting or rejecting their message. Acts is, in many ways, a story that is well-known to Jewish audiences: the story of "the Prophet(s) and the People."[10] The Old Testament is full of stories of prophets warning the people of Israel of impending judgment because of their sinful ways. In some cases, the people accept the prophet and change their ways, and their repentance staves off disaster. But often the people reject the prophets and feel the full measure of God's wrath.

Seeing this, one realizes this plot line not only governs the book of Acts but also the Gospel of Luke. The Spirit that empowers the apostles in Acts *comes from* Jesus (see Acts 1), and the description of men of the Spirit in Acts finds its basis in the description of Jesus in the Gospel. What makes this especially clear is how Jesus is described in speeches made by the apostles in Acts. In Peter's speeches in Acts 2 and 10, for example, Jesus too is described as a prophet: being filled with the Holy Spirit, proclaiming God's word with boldness, and performing signs and wonders. Johnson explains,

> An essential element in the description of the Men of the Spirit was the divided response of acceptance and rejection their word stimulated. The same pattern forms the very core, the essential element of the discourses about Jesus. In the case of Jesus, this pattern goes: He who was rejected by the people has been accepted by God

(that is, raised by God from the dead). The formulation is very consistent.[11]

Thus Jesus too is understood by Luke as part of the pattern of the acceptance and rejection of a prophet by the people. Of course, Jesus is no ordinary prophet, as his resurrection from the dead and ascension into heaven make clear.

In Peter's speech in Acts 3, several aspects of Luke's understanding of Jesus and the key to the plot of Luke-Acts is revealed. Peter begins by describing Jesus again as a rejected prophet, but one whose rejection by the Jews is exposed as folly by the resurrection. This rejection does not appear to be final, however. In Acts 2 and 3, Peter is giving the Jews who rejected Jesus during his lifetime a *second chance* to accept him. Peter preaches, "And now, friends, I know that you acted in ignorance, as did also your rulers. In this way God fulfilled what he had foretold through the prophets, that his Messiah would suffer. Repent therefore, and turn to God so that your sins may be wiped out, so that times of refreshing may come from the presence of the Lord" (Acts 3:17–20). Peter's speech reveals that the death of Jesus is understood as *necessary* by Luke for the fulfillment of God's plan. Thus the culpability of those responsible for rejecting and killing Jesus is lessened by three factors: (1) their leaders led them astray, (2) they acted out of ignorance,[12] and (3) their rejection brought to fulfillment God's plan.

For these reasons, Luke suggests, the Jews are offered an opportunity to repent. The motivation for repentance is twofold: positively, repentance will lead to days of refreshment that will culminate in the restoration of all things; negatively, those who do not repent will be cut off from the people.

---

10. For Johnson's arguments on the "men of the Spirit," see Luke T. Johnson, *The Literary Function of Possessions in Luke-Acts* (Missoula, MT: Scholars Press for the Society of Biblical Literature, 1977), 38–60.

11. Ibid., 62.

12. On this point it is significant that only Luke shows Jesus saying of his tormentors as he heads for execution, "Father forgive them, for they do not know what they are doing" (Luke 23:34). The authenticity of this verse is uncertain on textual grounds, but it certainly fits with what Peter says in Acts 3.

Acts 3:22–23 is especially important to this theory. Here Peter announces,

> Moses said, "The Lord God will raise up for you from your own people a prophet like me. You must listen to whatever he tells you. And it will be that everyone who does not listen to that prophet will be utterly rooted out of the people."

Through Peter, Luke here presents Jesus as the promised "**prophet like Moses**" (Deut. 18:18–19) and adds the threat from Leviticus 23:29 that whoever does not listen to him will be cut off from the people.[13] In Luke's telling, God has fulfilled his promises to the prophets of old by sending the Messiah to Israel. If the people of Israel listen to him, all things will be restored to them. If they reject him, they will be cut off from the people, no longer considered part of the nation of Israel. The promises of God are then null and void as regards these people. They have failed to live up to the covenant or to heed the warnings of Moses and the prophets.

The picture that Luke paints is complicated by the fact that, when Peter declares in Acts 3 that Jesus is the messianic "prophet like Moses" promised in the scriptures, and that those who do not accept him and heed his words will be cut off from the people, Jesus has *already* been rejected. Nevertheless, those who rejected Jesus have not been cut off, but are being offered the chance for repentance. In effect, the "prophet like Moses" is being presented to the people *again* for the possibility of acceptance and rejection, and their response *now* will result in inclusion or definite exclusion from the people of God. Because there were extenuating circumstances in their first rejection of Jesus (Acts 3:17–18), the people are given another chance. But how can the "prophet like Moses" be accepted or rejected when he has

departed from the earth? How is Jesus present in this way? He is present in the power of the Spirit at work in his witnesses, the apostles, in their signs and wonders, and in their word about Jesus. The possibilities of acceptance or rejection are still alive for the people, because Jesus is alive and at work through the deeds of his witnesses. This is why the prophetic portrayal of the apostles is modeled after the portrayal of Jesus: they too serve the purpose of presenting Jesus for acceptance or rejection. The difference is that those who reject Jesus now reject him definitively and are as radically rejected themselves.

From this one may easily summarize the plot of Luke-Acts: God sends the "prophet like Moses" in fulfillment of his ancient promises to the Jews. This prophet is rejected by the people and their leaders, and killed. However, God raises him from the dead, confirming his status as a prophet and exalting him to an even higher position. Through a gift of the Spirit, the apostles are then able to present Jesus to the people again for acceptance or rejection, this time with the added proof of the resurrection that Jesus is the promised Messiah. Acts then plays out the drama of the re-presentation of Jesus by the apostles and the response by Jews (first), Samaritans, and then Gentiles.

At first the response of the Jews to the preaching of the apostles is quite positive. They are "cut to the heart" by the realization of their role in the murder of the Messiah (Acts 2:37). They repent, accept Jesus as the Messiah, and are forgiven. The numbers of the converted are large: three thousand after the initial speech of Acts 2, and five thousand more after Peter's second speech in Acts 3. However, after this, the positive response of the Jews to the preaching of the apostles fades and then reverses. The Jewish leaders continue to resist God's will by arresting and threatening the apostles. No more is heard of mass conversions.

---

13. On the presentation of Jesus as the "prophet like Moses" and the combination of Old Testament expectations in this regard, see Johnson, *The Literary Function of Possessions in Luke-Acts*, 65–66.

The stoning of Stephen stands prominently in the façade of the Convento do San Estaban in Salamanca, Spain. In Acts, Stephen's speech recounts Israel's rejection of God's messengers in the past, and concludes with his own rejection and death.

Luke's understanding of the response of the Jews in general to this second chance is revealed in the speech of **Stephen** in Acts 7. Stephen's speech is basically a summary of the history of Israel, with special emphasis on Israel's rejection of the prophets sent to it by God. Moses receives considerable attention in this regard. Luke structures the story of Moses in this speech so that it takes place in two stages, with an initial rejection of Moses (Acts 7:23–29) followed by a second rejection (7:35–43). The purpose of this representation of the career of Moses as a double rejection is plain. Just as Moses was rejected twice as the leader of the Jews, so too will the "prophet like Moses" (Jesus) be doubly spurned by the people.[14] The reader knows that in spite of the "faithful remnant" of Israel established in Jerusalem who have accepted Jesus (consisting of the disciples and the Jews converted in the first chapters of Acts), most Jews will reject Jesus a second time and will be cut off from the people.

Peter, Paul, and Early Christianity

While the mission to the Jews fizzles out in Acts, the mission to the Gentiles led by Paul is a resounding success. Luke is well aware that, in late first- and early second-century Christianity, what started out as a prophetic reform movement within Judaism that consisted exclusively of Jews had become an independent Christian church consisting predominantly of Gentiles. Luke's account reflects this transformation. Crucially, however, Luke does not present the Jewish Christianity of the Jerusalem community led by Peter and the Twelve and the Gentile Christianity of the Hellenistic world led by Paul as being in conflict with each other. For Luke, this transition was smooth, characterized by cooperation and compromise on all sides.

One does not need to look far in the other books of the New Testament to find evidence that Luke's account is at least partly idealized, for these books speak often of the kind of conflict between leaders and factions that Luke downplays or ignores. For example, in his letter to the Galatians, Paul speaks of the historic **Jerusalem Council** (also sometimes called the Apostolic Conference, which took place approximately 49 CE) rather differently than Luke does in Acts 15. This meeting was called to address the status of Gentile converts. The two opposing sides were the "progressive" representatives of Gentile Christianity (Barnabas and Paul) and the "conservative"

---

14. On the question of Moses as the model for the prophet (Jesus), see Ibid., 70–76.

representatives of Jewish Christianity. In the Acts account, the leading apostles (Peter, John, and James) serve apparently as the arbiters. Peter takes the lead in establishing the principle that Gentile converts should not be required to follow Jewish law, although in a compromise it is determined that certain minimum standards with respect to ritual purity remain in effect for them. The council wraps up the matter smoothly and amicably.

Paul, however, in his own account of this meeting, speaks somewhat disparagingly of the Jerusalem apostles, saying, "And from those who were supposed to be acknowledged leaders (what they actually were makes no difference to me; God shows no partiality)—those leaders contributed nothing to me" (Gal. 2:6). He characterizes the conservative Jewish-Christian faction, which apparently insisted Gentile converts be circumcised and assume all of the covenantal obligations of Jews, as "false believers secretly brought in, who slipped in to spy on the freedom we have in Christ Jesus, so that they might enslave us" (2:4). And he speaks of the outcome not as a compromise but as a complete vindication for his position: "We did not submit to them even for a moment" (2:5). The Jerusalem apostles "saw that I had been entrusted with the Gospel for the uncircumcised" (2:7), and "when James and Cephas and John, who were acknowledged pillars, recognized the grace that had been given to me, they gave to Barnabas and me the right hand of fellowship, agreeing that we should go to the Gentiles and they to the circumcised" (2:9).

Later, when Cephas (Peter) appeared to have abrogated this agreement, Paul calls him a hypocrite to his face.

> But when Cephas came to Antioch, I opposed him to his face, because he stood self-condemned; for until certain people came from James, he used to eat with the Gentiles. But after they came, he drew back and kept himself separate for fear of the circumcision faction. And the other Jews joined him in this hypocrisy, so that even Barnabas was led astray by their hypocrisy. But when I saw that they were not acting consistently with the truth of the Gospel, I said to Cephas before them all, "If you, though a Jew, live like a Gentile and not like a Jew, how can you compel the Gentiles to live like Jews?" (Gal. 2:11–14)

By contrast, Acts speaks of Peter not as a hypocrite who humiliated Gentile converts by suggesting they were not worthy of table fellowship, but as the first to advocate the inclusion of Gentiles. In Acts 10, Peter receives a baffling vision in which his refusal to eat food that he regards as profane and unclean is countermanded by the voice of God. He is told, "What God has made clean, you must not call profane" (Acts 10:15). He then meets a Gentile named Cornelius, whom God had directed to find him. Peter then recognizes the point of his strange vision; he says to Cornelius and his associates, "You yourselves know that it is unlawful for a Jew to associate with or to visit a Gentile; but God has shown me that I should not call anyone profane or unclean" (Acts 10:28). Peter converts Cornelius, and the Holy Spirit falls upon him. "The circumcised believers who had come with Peter were astounded that the gift of the Holy Spirit had been poured out even on the Gentiles" (10:45), but Peter is now a committed advocate of Gentile inclusion. When he returns to Jerusalem and faces criticism from the "circumcised believers," he simply recounts his vision, offering the proof that God had given the gift of the Holy Spirit to Gentile converts. "When they heard this, they were silenced. And they praised God, saying, 'Then God has given even to the Gentiles the repentance that leads to life'" (11:18). This is far from the account in Paul's letter to the Galatians, in which "circumcised believers" vigorously press their opposition to the presence of uncircumcised Gentile converts in their community to the Jerusalem Council and beyond.

To be fair, Luke does indicate in his version of the Jerusalem Council (Acts 15) that not all conservative Jewish Christians were swayed by Peter's arguments in Acts 11, and that Paul and Barnabas continued to face opposition from that group. At the Council, however, Peter and James each speak strongly for not imposing circumcision on Gentile converts. Peter identifies himself as the one chosen by God to preach the good news to the Gentiles and claims that they should not be regarded as unclean because God has cleansed their hearts by faith (15:9).

He concludes by asking the conservative faction, "Why are you putting God to the test by placing on the neck of the disciples a yoke that neither our ancestors nor we have been able to bear? On the contrary, we believe that we will be saved through the grace of the Lord Jesus, just as they will" (15:10–11). In Luke's account Peter and Paul share similar views about Gentiles, circumcision, and salvation by faith through grace.

The Historical Reliability of Acts

Like most of the books of the Bible, the historical reliability of Acts was not seriously questioned until the eighteenth and nineteenth centuries. The close examination of texts that came to characterize critical biblical scholarship, however, raised a number of doubts. Many of these doubts stem from discrepancies between Paul's letters and Luke's account in Acts. When these two sources disagree, scholars tend to give Paul the benefit of the doubt. Paul's letters were written earlier and consist of firsthand testimony from one who participated in many of the key events in question. Paul is certainly more likely to have better information than Luke, who wrote thirty to seventy-five years later. One must also reckon with Luke's apparent desire to present an idealized version of early Christian history that painted over some of the blemishes, egotism, jealousies, and rivalries of Christianity's founders.

Others point out that Paul's accounts might not be completely objective and unbiased either, and suggest that credence should not be given automatically to his version of events. Nonetheless, there remains a tendency among scholars to prefer Paul to Acts whenever the two sources conflict.[15]

Luke's history also occasionally comes into conflict with that of the Jewish historian Josephus. For example, the story of Theudas in Acts 5:33-39 is incompatible with Josephus's account in *Jewish Antiquities*. Acts' historical accuracy has been questioned on the basis of Luke's use of incorrect terms for Roman provinces (see 6:9), incorrect descriptions of the deployment of Roman troops (see 10:1), and a lack of confirmation in the inscriptional or literary record of certain facts asserted by Luke. Luke is also thought to have exaggerated some of his figures. He claims that Peter's speech in Acts 2 converted three thousand Jews, and that his speech in Acts 3 resulted in five thousand converts, but it was virtually impossible in that day and age to address so many people at once.

Others assert Luke's mistakes are relatively minor and that not all of the criticisms scholars have made are fully persuasive. Certainly, ancient historiography was not expected to maintain the standard of precise accuracy demanded of historians today. Very few ancient histories contained accurate quotations or verified every important fact. Moreover, any errors found in Acts could have been the fault of Luke's sources rather than the author himself, as good, reliable sources would have been few and far between. The paucity of surviving sources is exactly what frustrates modern historians of early Christianity. Perhaps Luke experienced some of this frustration as well.

---

15. See, for example, Walter F. Taylor, *Paul, Apostle to the Nations: An Introduction* (Minneapolis: Fortress, 2012), 21–31.

James is similarly progressive in Luke's account. He agrees, "We should not trouble those Gentiles who are turning to God" (by demanding circumcision) and suggests that Gentile converts follow only a bare minimum of Jewish ritual purity: "We should write to them to abstain only from things polluted by idols and from fornication and from whatever has been strangled and from blood" (Acts 15:20). This compromise is acceptable to everyone (Acts 15:30–34). Paul's letter to the Galatians, however, does not betray any willingness to compromise on this issue and does not suggest he agreed to impose any Jewish practice on Gentile converts. When issues like fornication or eating meat from animals sacrificed to idols comes up in his letters elsewhere, Paul offers his own views, which sometimes agree with and sometimes conflict with the dictum of Acts 15:20. For example, in 1 Corinthians 10:14–30, Paul addresses the question of whether it is wrong to eat food that had been offered to idols. Paul tells the Corinthians they are free to eat such food but that it is not advisable to do so when they have been specifically informed the food was a sacrificial offering, because some believers in the community will be offended. In this he never appeals to or mentions the ruling of the Jerusalem Council, which certainly predates the letter.

So the level of conflict is minimized in Luke's account and the Christian movement is presented as more unified and harmonious than other contemporary accounts indicate. By following this route, Luke is probably trying to address the problem of internal divisions mentioned earlier in this chapter and in chapter 1. Marcionite Christianity sprang up and became fairly popular in the early second century CE. To many, this strongly anti-Jewish approach and insistence that Paul was the only true apostle of Christ threatened to tear Christianity apart. Advocates of Petrine Christianity naturally recoiled at the Marcionites' rejection of Peter and at their claim that Judaism and Christianity lacked all continuity. Luke apparently did not choose sides in this battle, but constructed a vision of Christianity that could include *both* Peter and Paul, appealing to reasonable people on either side of the debate. Eventually, Marcionite Christianity was quashed, and Luke's insistence that Jesus had more than one true apostle carried the day.

Key Terms

apostles
faithful remnant of Israel
apology/apologetic
God's plan

delay of the parousia
salvation history
men of the Spirit

prophet like Moses
Stephen
Jerusalem Council

Review Questions

1. Why is it preferable to complete an examination of Acts before trying to determine the purpose of the Gospel of Luke?

2. What proposals have scholars made for the overarching purpose of Luke-Acts? What criticisms have been leveled at these proposals, and what features of the various proposals have garnered some kind of consensus?

3. According to David Tiede, what is the historical event to which Luke responds? What problems did this event create for Christianity?

4. Luke Johnson asserts that Luke-Acts exhibits a strong parallelism between the characters of Jesus, Peter, Paul, and Stephen, among others. What are the elements of this parallelism? What is its significance?

5. On what basis have some scholars questioned the historical reliability of Acts? What points have been made in Luke's defense in this regard?

6. Luke's account of a unified early Christianity with a minimum of factions and rivalries differs somewhat from the picture that one can derive from other New Testament texts. What might be Luke's purpose in presenting early Christianity as he does?

Discussion Questions

1. The book of Acts recounts the triumph of Christianity, arguing that the superiority of the Christian religion was demonstrated by the remarkable successes it achieved and the divine guidance it received. Is there anything about this narrative that is problematic, either with respect to Christian confidence in the correctness of their views or with respect to the way in which such a narrative tends to regard people of other faiths?

2. Who is the hero of Acts? Is it Peter? Paul? Stephen? The Holy Spirit?

3. To what degree do you think Acts is a historically accurate account of early Christianity? What specific things lead you to have confidence or doubts about its reliability?

Bibliography and Suggestions for Further Study

(Books and websites that are accessible for general undergraduates are marked with an asterisk; other sources listed are appropriate for advanced students.)

Cadbury, Henry J. *The Making of Luke-Acts*. New York: Macmillan Company, 1927; London: SPCK, 1968.

Johnson, Luke T. *The Literary Function of Possessions in Luke-Acts*. Missoula, MT: Scholars Press for the Society of Biblical Literature, 1977.

Levine, Amy-Jill, with Marianne Blickenstaff, eds. *A Feminist Companion to Acts*. Cleveland: T&T Clark, 2004.

*Pervo, Richard I. *Luke's Story of Paul*. Minneapolis: Fortress, 1990.

Tannehill, Robert C. *The Narrative Unity of Luke-Acts: A Literary Interpretation*. 2 vols. Philadelphia: Fortress, 1986; 1990.

*Tiede, David. *Prophecy and History in Luke-Acts*. Philadelphia: Fortress, 1980.

Tyson, Joseph B. *Marcion and Luke-Acts: A Defining Struggle*. Columbia: University of South Carolina Press, 2006.

13
CHAPTER

The Johannine Literature: The Gospel of John and the Three Letters of John

The preceding chapters have taken the Gospels of Mark, Matthew, and Luke as expressions of each evangelist's particular vision and beliefs, intended for a broad audience. The alternative approach—that differences between Gospels are best explained by their having been aimed at particular communities or audiences—has not been emphasized. These alternatives, however, need not be mutually exclusive. It is possible that a Gospel (or another New Testament text) was shaped by the experiences and concerns of the community from which it emerged or to which it was originally addressed, *depending on the evidence* found in the Gospel or text. With that said, discussion of the so-called "Johannine literature"—the Gospel of John and the three letters of John—can begin.

Of the canonical Gospels, the Gospel of John has the clearest signs of (1) having been produced by a procession of authors rather than a single author, (2) having gone through many stages of development and revision, and (3) reflecting the experiences of a particular faith community, to whom the Gospel was originally addressed. Additionally, the three letters of John seem clearly to have emerged from the same community and

these epistles address problems unique to this church and its nearby compatriots. This is why these four texts are often grouped together and referred to as the **Johannine literature**.[1]

In this chapter, the Gospel of John is considered first and then the three letters of John. Each of these texts bears witness to an early Christian community whose apparently unique experiences led them to produce a Gospel that is worlds apart from its canonical brethren. John is sometimes called "the maverick Gospel," precisely because it charts a course so different from the other Gospels. Huge swaths of John's narrative have no corresponding account in any of the Synoptic Gospels. There is little overlap between John and the Synoptics except for the passion narrative. Thus the first questions addressed here are how and why John differs from the other Gospels.

John and the Synoptic Gospels: A Comparison

One of the best ways to grasp the unique status of the Gospel of John is to compare it side-by-side with the three Synoptic Gospels. Mark, Matthew,

---

1. Although the book of Revelation has traditionally been grouped with the Gospel of John and the three letters of John, this is due only to the mistaken belief that its author, "John of Patmos," was the same person as John the apostle, the son of Zebedee and brother of James (see chapter 1). In truth, there are no stylistic or theological similarities between the book of Revelation (see chapter 20) and the other four Johannine books that would lead scholars to group them together.

and Luke all have important differences, but they also have much in common. They have a similar narrative progression and include many of the same stories—eighty-three pericopes (episodes, or narrative units) are found in all three Synoptic Gospels. Of the dozens of stories in the Triple Tradition, however, only a few are found in John. The cleansing of the Temple (John 2:14–22), the feeding of the five thousand (6:1–15), Jesus walking on water (6:16–21), and the anointing of Jesus at Bethany (12:1–8) are among the few stories from Jesus' ministry that readers of the Synoptic Gospels would recognize in John, apart from a few other stories with superficial resemblances. Most of John, then, is unique. The key differences between John and the Synoptics can be organized into seven major categories.

First, there is the category of *beginnings*. The Gospel of John starts differently from the Synoptics. Matthew and Luke begin with the birth of Jesus and quickly proceed to Jesus' baptism, while Mark opens with Jesus' baptism (his first *public* appearance). Both of these starting points are appropriate to the genre of biography. Many ancient biographies began with their subjects' birth or with their first public appearance. However, the Gospel of John opens with a poetic hymn called the Prologue (John 1:1–18), which does not begin at a point in human history but traces the origins of Jesus back to the beginning of time, to a divine being called the **Logos**, who partook in the creation of the universe and eventually took on a human form.

> In the beginning was the Word (Greek, *Logos*), and the Word was with God, and the Word was God. He was in the beginning with God. All things came into being through him, and without him not one thing came into being. What has come into being in him was life, and the life was the light of all people. The light shines in the darkness, and the darkness did not overcome it. (John 1:1–5)

Readers are alerted that the Gospel of John concerns a being who is too great to be introduced with the story of his human birth, however miraculous, or his first public appearance, even if it is accompanied by divine signs. The Prologue is clearly mythic and theological, rather than strictly biographical or historical. John narrates events extending back to the beginning of time, which its author could not possibly have witnessed. Jesus is not a "great man" of local or even international repute. Jesus was sent from heaven, and his appearance is a matter of cosmic significance.

The second category of difference between the Gospel of John and the Synoptic Gospels is *geography and chronology*. In the Synoptic Gospels, Jesus spends most of his ministry in and around Galilee. He ventures into Judea but once—at the end of the story when he makes a journey to Jerusalem, cleanses the Temple, and is killed within a week of having done so. In the Gospel of John, Jesus makes four trips to Jerusalem (usually for one of the Jewish pilgrimage festivals) and spends substantial time in Judea. Indeed, the Gospel of John suggests that Jesus' Judean ministry was as substantial as his Galilean ministry. The timing of events also appears to be different in John. The Synoptic Gospels are notoriously vague about the passage of time between events, but many scholars suggest the Synoptics envision a ministry of twelve months or less. The Gospel of John's temporal references suggest Jesus' ministry could not have been less than three years.

Moreover, even when John overlaps with the Synoptic Gospels in the telling of a story, the chronology is not always the same. The Synoptic Gospels place the cleansing of the Temple at the end of Jesus' life and ministry—indeed, it functions as the trigger that leads to his execution. In the Gospel of John, the cleansing of the Temple is one of the first things Jesus does. In John, the Jews are clearly angry about the Temple incident, but it does not lead to Jesus' crucifixion. Rather,

Contradictions between Gospels and the Cleansing of the Temple

This text approaches the Gospels by emphasizing the differences between them. In most cases these differences do not present a major hurdle to those wanting to believe the Gospels present an accurate, reliable, or even inerrant portrayal of the life and ministry of Jesus. That the Gospel of John tells many stories not found in the Synoptics is easily dealt with by harmonizing John's account with a similarly harmonized framework provided by the Synoptics: one simply inserts the stories found in John at some likely or appropriate place in the time line.

This becomes challenging where the Gospels apparently disagree. It is easy enough to reconcile differing accounts of visitors to baby Jesus in Matthew and Luke; one simply places both wise men *and* shepherds in the Nativity scene, perhaps sequentially. However, it is not so easy to explain whether Mary and Joseph were from Nazareth and merely visiting Bethlehem at the time of Jesus' birth (as per Luke), or were from Bethlehem and relocated to Nazareth after Jesus' birth (as per Matthew).

The question of whether the Gospels conflict with each other, or even contradict each other, is most problematic for those who claim the Bible is inerrant. One need not be a philosopher to realize that Joseph and Mary cannot have had *both* Nazareth and Bethlehem as a hometown at the same point in their lives.

Biblical literalists, however, devise many clever explanations for these apparent conflicts.

For example, many people examining the genealogies in Matthew and Luke would find them so plainly different as to be irreconcilable: working backward from Jesus' grandfather, none of his ancestors for the previous nine hundred years or so have the same names. But the biblical fundamentalist simply explains that Jesus' grandfather, and a great many of his other ancestors, went by two different names. Some people called Jesus' grandfather Jacob (as per Matthew), while others knew him as Heli (as per Luke). It is not unheard of for people to be known by two different names, but is it plausible that this unusual phenomenon happened in Jesus' family generation after generation for nine hundred years?

The cleansing of the Temple presents a different problem. On the one hand, that it is spoken of in all four Gospels speaks to the historicity of this event. But the timing of the event in John (at the beginning of Jesus' ministry) and the Synoptics (at the end of his ministry) seems blatantly contradictory. Biblical literalists resolve the problem by concluding that Jesus cleansed the Temple *twice*, once at the beginning of his ministry and once at the end of his ministry. Again, whether this is likely is debatable, but it is difficult not to appreciate the ingenuity.

the raising of Lazarus in John 11, a story not found in the Synoptics, is the event that leads to Jesus' crucifixion in the Fourth Gospel.

A third category of difference between John and the Synoptics involves *language and style*. The

Synoptic Gospels involve mostly straightforward storytelling in which the author plainly says what he means. Jesus' parables in the Synoptics require interpretation, and some of his teachings[2] and deeds[3] can be puzzling, but readers are not

---

2. Examples of notoriously difficult Synoptic sayings include Jesus' demand that his followers hate their mothers and fathers (Luke 14:26), his denial that he has come to bring peace (Matt. 10:34), and his cry of derelicision from the cross (Mark 15:34).

3. For example, why does Jesus curse a fig tree for not bearing fruit, even when it was not the season for figs (Mark 11:12–14, 20–25)? Almost certainly the fig tree is a symbol for the Temple, but this is not obvious at first glance.

How Old Was Jesus?

Jesus' age is less a matter of strong concern to the Gospel writers than to many readers. One often hears Jesus was thirty-three years of age when he was crucified. This figure is arrived at by combining information in multiple Gospels, in a sort of Gospel harmonizing that is characteristic of less critical biblical study. The Gospel of Luke indicates Jesus was "about thirty years old when he began his work" (Luke 3:23). So one adds the three-year ministry envisioned by John to the starting point of thirty approximated by Luke and one arrives at the age of 33. Naturally, both figures are estimates—one by scholars about the length of Jesus' ministry, and one by an evangelist about Jesus' age at the outset of his ministry; in neither case, then, can one place too much weight on the data. In the only other reference to Jesus' age, Jewish people who are arguing with Jesus speculate that he is "not yet fifty years old" (John 8:57). This is not inconsistent with Jesus being in his early thirties, but it could suggest he was older.

This question becomes more acute for filmmakers who make movies of the life of Jesus, who must decide how youthful or elderly Jesus should be before casting his part. In general, films with a more conservative outlook (like Cecil B. DeMille's *The King of Kings* from 1928) portray Jesus as a graybeard, older and presumably wiser, while films with a more radical orientation (like Martin Scorsese's 1988 *The Last Temptation of Christ*) envision a more youthful and vigorous Christ. Either choice is defensible on the evidence from the Gospels.

© United Archives GmbH / Alamy Stock Photo

© Album / Alamy Stock Photo

Jesus is a man of mature years in *King of Kings* but youthful in *Last Temptation of Christ*. It is impossible to say which depiction is more accurate, as there is no record of Jesus' age at the time of his death.

constantly required to dig beneath the words to uncover hidden meaning. By contrast, in John the author or Jesus frequently says things that need to be deciphered. The Gospel of John is filled with symbols, metaphors, and other kinds of figurative language. Jesus' interlocutors are constantly confused or uncertain of his meaning. Nicodemus is baffled about how a person can be "born again" (John 3:3–4) and the Samaritan woman misunderstands Jesus' offer of "living water" (4:10–15). Jesus refers to himself in such metaphors as the "bread of life" (6:35), the "light of the world" (9:5), the "good shepherd" (10:11), and the "true vine" (15:1), among others. Frequently his disciples have no idea what he is talking about. After Jesus refers to himself as the "good shepherd," the narrator comments: "Jesus used this figure of speech with them, but they did not understand what he was saying to them" (10:6). When his disciples finally understand one of Jesus' teachings, they rejoice at his clarity: "Yes, now you are speaking plainly, not in any figure of speech!" (16:29).

Not only is Jesus' speech in John sometimes opaque, it is also voluminous. The Synoptic Gospels frequently alternate between Jesus' speech and action. Mark and Luke, in particular, seldom show Jesus speaking for any length of time before the narrative reverts to actions. Matthew presents a more verbose Jesus, with its three-chapter Sermon on the Mount and four additional chapter-length discourses. But Matthew has nothing on John, which consists mostly of monologues by Jesus[4] or dialogues dominated

© Bridgeman Images

Only in John's Gospel is Jesus described as the Good Shepherd. The Good Shepherd has proved to be one of the most beloved motifs in Christian art; this fourth-century example comes from the Roman catacombs.

by Jesus (John 3; 4; 8; 10; 13–17; and at least half of John 5; 6; and 7), interrupted occasionally with narration of one of Jesus' deeds.[5]

A fourth category in which one finds substantial differences between John and the Synoptic Gospels involves the performance of *miracles*. Jesus does fewer miracles in John (only seven) than in the Synoptic Gospels. John refers to these miracles

---

4. It should be noted that there is sometimes considerable controversy over where Jesus' speeches end and where the narrator's comments begin, because quotation marks did not exist when the early manuscripts were written. A notoriously difficult example involves Jesus' dialogue with Nicodemus in John 3. It is clear that Jesus begins his concluding words to Nicodemus in 3:11 ("Very truly, I tell you, we speak of what we know"), but starting with verse 16 ("For God so loved the world that he gave his only Son, so that everyone who believes in him may not perish but may have eternal life"), it is no longer clear whether Jesus is still speaking to Nicodemus or whether Jesus' speech has ended and now the narrator is speaking directly to the reader. Jesus does sometimes speak of himself in the third person, so the use of the third person in 3:16–21 is not proof that Jesus is not speaking. But the voice of 3:16–21 seems very much like that of the Prologue to the Gospel (1:1–18), which is clearly that of the narrator.

5. A common technique in Bible printing involves presenting the words of Jesus in red ink, with the surrounding narration and descriptions in black ink. In these "red-letter Bibles," one generally sees short bursts of black and red in the Synoptic Gospels. John, by contrast, is a sea of red.

as "signs" (Greek, *sēmeia*) and they are sometimes *enumerated* in the text: "Jesus did this, the first of his signs" (2:11), "Now this was the second sign that Jesus did" (4:54). This has led to speculation that there was a written list of Jesus' miracles that was used by the author(s) of John, often referred to as the "Signs Source," that existed prior to the writing of the Gospel. These signs include healings and nature miracles, but no exorcisms. Jesus casts out many demons in the Synoptic Gospels, but none in John.

The absence of exorcisms is consistent with other aspects of John's contents. A prominent story in each of the Synoptic Gospels (especially in Matthew and Luke) is the temptation of Jesus by the devil in the wilderness. The Gospel of John does not include this story, and indeed Satan makes only a single appearance in the text, when he enters into Judas Iscariot prior to his betrayal of Jesus (John 13:27). One explanation for the relative absence of Satan and the demonic in John is that the Gospel conceives of Jesus as so powerful and divine that Satan would be no

match for him. The event in the Synoptic Gospels in which Jesus' divinity becomes manifest is the Transfiguration (Mark 9:2–9 and parallels). The Gospel of John does not include the Transfiguration, but it hardly seems to matter; Jesus is "transfigured" throughout the Gospel.

A fifth category of comparison is that of *friends, acquaintances, and associates.* Jesus interacts with people in John that are not familiar from the Synoptic Gospels, as well as some whose roles are expanded.[6] In addition to Nicodemus and the Samaritan woman, with whom he has long conversations, Jesus has a disciple named Nathanael (1:43–51) and another whose identity is kept a secret. This male character is known only as "the disciple whom Jesus loved" or "the **Beloved Disciple**." He makes his first appearance in John 13:23, where he reclines next to Jesus at the Last Supper, laying his head on Jesus' breast. From this point forward he is clearly Jesus' best and most faithful disciple. He is the only male disciple to be seen at the foot of the cross, offering support to Jesus.[7] Jesus entrusts to him the care

The Identity of the Beloved Disciple and the Authorship of the Gospel of John

The mysterious identity of "the disciple whom Jesus loved" in the Gospel of John has been a source of frustration for scholars and readers for centuries. The early Christian bishop and theologian Irenaeus (180 CE) names John as the author of the Fourth Gospel, and

Eusebius's *Church History* claims that earlier sources also identified John the apostle as the evangelist. But the earliest possible source Eusebius quotes is Papias (125-140 CE), and scholars have long been skeptical of the accuracy of Eusebius's quotations of Papias,

continued

---

6. Jesus and Pontius Pilate have a much more extended conversation in John (18:28–38) than in the Synoptics, and Jesus' mother makes two supportive appearances during Jesus' ministry: at the wedding at Cana (2:1–12) and at the foot of the cross (19:25–27). In the Synoptic Gospels, the only time Jesus' mother appears during his ministry is when she and his brothers and sisters call for Jesus to come out of the house in which he is teaching and speak to them, a request that Jesus refuses (Mark 3:31–35 and parallels). In Mark this takes place shortly after Jesus' family sided with those who were saying that Jesus was insane (Mark 3:21).

7. He is probably also the unnamed disciple who, with Peter, follows Jesus after his arrest, gains entrance to the courtyard where Jesus is being interrogated, and lets Peter in (John 18:15–16). Although this disciple is not specifically identified as the one Jesus loved, the designation of him as the "other disciple" is also used elsewhere to refer to the Beloved Disciple.

The Identity of the Beloved Disciple *continued*

or dismissive of the idea that Papias had any reliable information about the authorship of the Gospels, which were originally written anonymously.

Apart from this testimony the case for identifying John the apostle as the Beloved Disciple is based mostly on a process of elimination that involves information gleaned from other Gospels. The Synoptic Gospels identify Jesus' inner circle as consisting of two pairs of brothers, Simon Peter and Andrew, and James and John the sons of Zebedee, although Andrew is sometimes left out of the group. If one assumes that the Beloved Disciple must have been an apostle (based on his presence at the Last Supper) and further assumes that he is likely to have been a member of this inner circle, then John is the only viable candidate. Peter and Andrew are identified by name in the Fourth Gospel, and they are clearly distinct from the "disciple whom Jesus loved." James the son of Zebedee is thought to have been killed relatively early, in the first decades of early Christianity (see Acts 12:2), so it is unlikely that he could have written the Gospel or that it would be attributed to him. **John the son of Zebedee** is the only one left standing.

Skeptics point out this identification rests upon questionable deductions based upon questionable sources. Moreover, one must ask why John the apostle would write a Gospel that leaves out so many key incidents—such as the Transfiguration—that John is said to have witnessed in the other Gospels.

Some biblical critics suggest that if one turns to evidence found in the Gospel itself, a case can be made on behalf of **Lazarus**, the brother of Mary and Martha of Bethany, whom Jesus raises from the dead in John 11. Apart from the Beloved Disciple, Lazarus is the only male character who is specifically identified as being "loved" by Jesus (John 11:3, 5). It may be significant that the Beloved Disciple does not make his first appearance in the Gospel until John 12. Is it possible the Gospel is implying that, having been raised from the dead, Lazarus became intensely devoted to Jesus and turned into his best and most faithful disciple? One of the clearest characteristics of the Beloved Disciple is courage: he fearlessly enters the courtyard where Jesus' trial is taking place and is the only male disciple brave enough to show up at Jesus' crucifixion. The other disciples apparently regard both places as too dangerous for them. Is the reader to conclude that the Beloved Disciple does not fear death because he has already experienced it?

A few scholars have tried to make a case for Mary Magdalene as the Beloved Disciple (some noncanonical gospels—such as the *Gospel of Philip*—identify her as the disciple Jesus loved best) or James, the brother of the Lord, but many other scholars think the evidence is so slender that it is impossible to identify the Beloved Disciple.

One reason for ongoing interest in this question is that the authorship of the Gospel is explicitly connected to the Beloved Disciple: "This is the disciple who is testifying to these things and has written them, and we know that his testimony is true" (John 21:24) Most scholars take this third-person reference to the Beloved Disciple as indicative that the Gospel is *based on* his testimony, not that he wrote the Gospel. Richard Bauckham, however, has provided new arguments for the claim that John the apostle is the Beloved Disciple and that he personally wrote the Gospel.[8] However, Bauckham's arguments have not gained widespread acceptance. In any case, this is the only Gospel that claims to be based on firsthand testimony. Could this mean the Gospel of John—despite its many differences from the earlier Synoptic Gospels—is the most historically reliable Gospel? This question will be taken up in chapter 19.

8. Richard Bauckham, *Jesus and the Eyewitnesses: The Gospels as Eyewitness Testimony* (Grand Rapids: Eerdmans, 2006).

of his mother (19:25–27). Later, he and Peter race to the empty tomb after hearing Mary Magdalene's testimony, and he "outran Peter and reached the tomb first" (20:4). Seeing the linen wrappings inside the tomb, "he . . . believed" (20:8). The risen Jesus later appears to him and the other disciples involved in the miraculous catch of fish (21:1–15). This disciple's eventual death is a matter of concern to the author and his readership (21:20–23), and he is said to be the ultimate source of the material in the Gospel (21:24).

The *teachings* of Jesus form the sixth category of comparison between John and the Synoptic Gospels. Even when the events of John roughly correspond to those of the Synoptic Gospels, frequently their details differ. In all four Gospels there is a Last Supper, but in the Synoptics Jesus uses this occasion to distribute bread and wine to his followers, telling them they are his body and blood. In John there is no mention of bread and wine or body and blood at the Last Supper.[9] Instead, Jesus washes the feet of his disciples (John 13:1–20) to model the kind of service and humility he hopes they will emulate.

In the Synoptic Gospels, Jesus often teaches through parables, and indeed Jesus is famous as a teller of parables. However, Jesus does not tell a single parable in John, at least not one that is in any way similar to the narrative parables found in the Synoptic Gospels. Instead of speaking of the kingdom of God, or the end of the world and the second coming (about which Jesus says almost nothing in John), Jesus' teaching is entirely oriented toward his own *identity*. In particular, Jesus emphasizes that the key to understanding who he is involves knowing *where he comes from* and *where he is going*. These two subjects are sometimes referred to as the "whence" and "whither" of Jesus. The Jews are consistently portrayed as misunderstanding Jesus and rejecting him because they profess ignorance of his origins and destiny. "As for this man, we do not know where he comes from" (9:29).

This brings up the seventh and final category of comparison: the level of conflict between Jesus and "the Jews." Jesus faces more *hatred and rejection from the Jews* in the Gospel of John than in any other Gospel. The Prologue starts things off by indicating that Jesus' "own people did not accept him" (John 1:11). But the typical response of the Jews to Jesus in John goes beyond misunderstanding and rejection and veers into anger, hostility, and violence. Unlike Mark, for example, where there is a *single* (successful) attempt to arrest and kill Jesus and a minimum of discussion about killing him prior to this (Mark 3:6 stands alone in this regard), in the Gospel of John there are *many* attempts to detain or murder Jesus, and this is a matter of *constant* discussion among the Jews. For example, 5:18 indicates that "the Jews were seeking all the more to kill him." Later Jesus avoids Judea for a while "because the Jews were looking for an opportunity to kill him" (7:1). An attempt is made to stone Jesus to death in 8:59 and again in 10:31. References to attempts to arrest Jesus are made in 7:30, 32, 44–45; 10:39; and 11:57.

The Jews also frequently insult Jesus, as in John 8:48 ("Are we not right in saying that you are a Samaritan and have a demon?"); 9:24 ("We know that this man is a sinner"); 7:52 ("Surely you are not also from Galilee, are you? Search and you will see that no prophet is to arise from Galilee"); and 7:20 ("You have a demon!"). Even his followers are targeted for killing. There is a plot to kill Lazarus because his existence was proof of Jesus' greatest miracle and the spur for many conversions (12:9–11). Jesus also tells his followers that after he is gone they will be persecuted by the Jews, even unto death: "They will put you out of the synagogues. Indeed, an hour is coming when those who kill you will think that

---

9. There are, however, other passages with Eucharistic overtones in the Gospel of John: Jesus refers to himself as the "bread of life" in John 6, tells people that those who eat this bread will live forever, and declares, "The bread that I will give for the life of the world is my flesh" (6:51).

by doing so they are offering worship to God" (16:2). The language of hatred is used to describe both the reception that Jesus receives and that which his followers can expect: "If the world hates you, be aware that it hated me before it hated you" (15:18; cf. 7:7; 15:23–25; and 17:14).

Anti-Judaism, Anti-Semitism, and the Gospels

Hatred and misunderstanding have characterized the relationship between Judaism and Christianity from the start. It is true that the early centuries of Christianity saw some persecution of Christians by Jews, but once Christianity gained the upper hand in the fourth century CE, the persecution began flowing in the other direction. Any student of modern history knows of the Holocaust, or *Shoah*, in which more than six million Jews were systematically murdered by German Nazis and their collaborators. But this is only the most horrific example of the persecution of Jews. There were many earlier outbreaks of widespread violence and hatred against Jews, such as the pogroms in Russia in the nineteenth and twentieth centuries and the expulsion of Jews from Spain in the late fifteenth century. Throughout medieval and modern Europe, the rights of Jews to live where they wanted or to travel, emigrate, own property, and enter certain professions were restricted. In some places, Jews were legally forced to attend Christian services at least once a year to listen to a sermon haranguing them for killing Christ and failing to convert. In other places, Jews even had baptism forced on them and then were persecuted as heretics if they returned to their Jewish religious practices. There is a famous nineteenth-century story about a Christian servant in Italy who secretly baptized the young son of a Jewish couple for whom she was (illegally) keeping house. When she revealed this to Church authorities, they took the boy away from his parents on the grounds that a Jewish couple could not be entrusted with raising a Christian child. The boy, Edgardo Mortara, was taken in by Pope Pius IX, and despite a worldwide outcry against his kidnapping, the Pope refused all entreaties to return the boy to his parents and raised him as his adopted son in the papal household.[10]

In explaining this hatred and persecution, scholars distinguish between **anti-Semitism** and **anti-Judaism**. The former involves hatred of Jews based on their supposedly inferior *racial* characteristics. This form of bigotry gained momentum when modern science began placing people in racial categories in the late nineteenth century. Racial hatred became a leading factor in the Nazis' persecution of the Jews. Anti-Judaism is based, not on the race or ethnicity of Jewish people, but on their religion. This religious hatred is based largely on two related claims. The first claim is that Jewish people should have recognized Jesus as the Messiah and accepted him but, instead, they hated him and schemed to kill him. This claim requires exaggerating the responsibility of the Jewish authorities for Jesus' crucifixion and minimizing that of Pontius Pilate and the Roman government. The second claim is that after Jesus' resurrection the Jews should have repented for their sinful mistreatment of him and converted to Christianity. Instead, most Jews continued to reject Christian claims, persecuted Christian leaders, and made trouble for Christian believers, often by informing on them to the Romans. These two claims have led to labeling later generations of Jewish people as "Christ-killers" or murderers for their ancestors' treatment of Jesus and as stubborn or stiff-necked for their refusal to convert.

Certainly, other factors have also contributed to the historical persecution of the Jewish people.

---

10. See Garry Wills, *Papal Sin: Structures of Deceit* (New York: Image Books; Doubleday, 2001), ch. 2.

For example, in addition to xenophobia (hatred of foreigners/outsiders), Jews have been victimized by negative stereotypes that have become deeply rooted in the popular imagination of non-Jews. Jewish people have been portrayed in literature as rich, greedy, money-grubbing, heartless, and power-mad. One example of this sort of reprehensible anti-Judaism is the false rumor that around Easter-time Jews would engage in the ritual murder of Christian children and use their blood to make Passover matzoh bread, which they would then consume in an act of cannibalism. Another example of hateful ignorance and fear-mongering is the myth that Jews secretly control various world governments and industries—such as the media—and intend to achieve world domination and enslave the world's peoples. The forged document "The Protocols of the Elders of Zion" is alleged to provide proof of this claim, and many famous anti-Semites like Henry Ford and Father Charles Coughlin have used the "Protocols" to fan the flames of hatred toward Jews.

There are many aspects of the persecution of Jews for which Christianity has no direct responsibility and in which Christians may participate but are not doing so *as* Christians. However, there is no question that a great deal of Jewish persecution has been motivated by Christian anti-Judaism, and because of this it is not only fair but morally obligatory to ask whether the writings of the New Testament, and the Gospels in particular, have contributed to this tragic history of persecution.

All of the Gospels blame the Jewish authorities for Jesus' crucifixion and try to absolve Pontius Pilate. All of them show that throughout his ministry, Jesus faced rejection and hostility from Jewish quarters, especially the religious authorities. But two Gospels go beyond the others in this respect. One is Matthew, in which Pontius Pilate washes his hands of the death of Jesus and disclaims any responsibility for the death of this innocent man. The *people as a whole* then respond, "His blood be on us and on our children!" (Matt.

Christians committed many acts of violence against Jews in the Middle Ages. A plaque on Clifford's Tower, the only portion of York Castle still standing, remembers the hundred and fifty Jews martyred there by a Christian mob in 1190.

27:25). This verse has probably been the cause of more suffering than any other in the Bible, because it has been used throughout history to claim that the Jews are subject to an *eternal curse* as a result of their role in Jesus' death. The inclusion of "our children" among those taking responsibility has resulted in a common Christian belief that later generations of Jews are just as guilty as their ancestors in the killing of Christ. It was only in the 1960s with the Second Vatican Council that the Catholic Church, for one, officially began teaching that Jews of the present cannot be held accountable for the actions of their ancestors in the matter of Christ's death (see *Nostra Aetate*). Some other Christian denominations abandoned this calumny earlier than the Catholic Church, but there are also those that have yet to do so.

Although there is no single line in the Gospel of John as damaging as Matthew 27:25, John's pervasive anti-Jewish rhetoric should be a matter of concern for modern Christians seeking to forge a more positive relationship with their Jewish brethren and to come to terms with Christianity's past sins. As will be argued in this chapter, the tense relationship between the Johannine community and the synagogue from which it sprang played a key role in the Gospel's use of anti-Jewish rhetoric. But does that excuse the author(s) for passages in which Jesus speaks in harsh and insulting terms to the Jews? Consider the following:

> Jesus said to them [the Jews], "If God were your Father, you would love me, for I came from God and now I am here. I did not come on my own, but he sent me. Why do you not understand what I say? It is because you cannot accept my word. You are from your father the devil, and you choose to do your father's desires. He was a murderer from the beginning and does not stand in the truth, because there is no truth in him. When he lies, he speaks according to his own nature, for he is a liar and the father of lies. . . . It is my father who glorifies me, he of whom you say, 'He is our God,' though you do not know him. But I know him; if I would say that I do not know him, I would be a liar like you." (John 8:42–44, 54–55)

Some would argue that a passage such as this is beyond redemption, and that it needs to be repudiated by any Christian seeking genuine understanding and friendship with people of the Jewish faith. Others claim this passage must be understood in context and used with caution and sensitivity to its inflammatory character. Either way, the values of religious tolerance and freedom of religion can only be served by seriously reexamining historic Christian statements about and attitudes toward Jewish people.

The High Christology of the Gospel of John

Orthodox Christianity would eventually define Jesus' nature as "fully human and fully divine" at the Council of Chalcedon in 451 CE. While all of the Gospels speak of Jesus as having human and divine characteristics, the Gospel of John most clearly affirms Jesus' full divinity. None of the Synoptic Gospels identify Jesus as "God," at least not directly, but the Gospel of John does not hesitate to make this claim.

As mentioned previously, the Prologue to the Gospel of John (1:1–18) speaks of a divine being called the Logos, who existed in heaven from the beginning of time and participated in the creation of the universe before being sent to earth in the form of Jesus of Nazareth. The Prologue speaks of the relationship between God and the Logos, the Father and the Son, as one of not only *differentiation* but also *identity*. "In the beginning was the Word, and the Word was with God and the Word was God" (John 1:1). The statement "the Word was with God" seems to imply two different beings, but "the Word was God" implies they are the *same* being. The Gospel does seem to be of two minds on this question, as Jesus is later heard saying both "The Father is greater than I" (14:28) and "The Father and I are one" (10:30). However, the main thrust of the Gospel is to insist that Jesus is God and that he has all of the attributes of God.

Many divine attributes were well understood and clearly defined by the time of Jesus. For example, it was generally agreed among ancient Babylonians and Greeks that the primordial gods, by their nature, are *eternal*.[11] Their emergence marks the beginning of time. These gods are timeless and never die. This is why foundational Greek texts such as Hesiod's *Theogony* often refer to the gods as "immortals."[12] Judaism came to share this view: Genesis 1:2 indicates that when the universe was as yet nothing but chaos ("the earth was a formless void, and darkness covered the face of the deep"), God already existed ("a wind from God swept over the face of the waters"). Moreover, monotheistic Judaism had come to believe that the one God had

---

11. In Greek mythology, for example, the deathless primordial gods—who precede even the Titans—are Gaia (earth), Tartaros (underworld), and Eros (sexual desire), according to Hesiod's *Theogony* (116–22).

12. Hesiod, *Theogony* 116–22.

also to be the *creator* of the universe, *benevolent*, *omnipotent*, and *omniscient*.[13]

All of these qualities are attributed to Jesus (or the Logos) in the Prologue and throughout the Gospel. Jesus' *eternal* status is emphasized twice in the first two verses of the Gospel: "*In the beginning* was the Word, and the Word was with God, and the Word was God. He was *in the beginning* with God" (John 1:1–2). The idea that the Logos did not come into being with the birth of Jesus of Nazareth nor at any point between creation and

that birth is known as **preexistence**. John the Baptist is quoted as saying, "This was he of whom I said, 'He who comes after me ranks ahead of me, because *he was* before me" (1:15). The sentence is grammatically difficult, but the gist is that people should not mistakenly believe that John the Baptist has seniority over Jesus because of his more advanced human age; Jesus, as the Logos, has existed for eons longer than John. The aforementioned quote from Jesus, "Before Abraham was, I AM" (8:58), also indicates Jesus' preexistence.

The "I AM" Statements in the Gospel of John

In Exodus 3:14, God reveals his name to Moses in Hebrew as *'eyeh 'asher 'eyeh*. This name is usually translated as "I am" or "I am who I am" or even "I am the One who is." In the Gospel of John, Jesus has a curious way of saying "I am" that is designed to invoke the meaning of the name of God and hence to claim equality (or identity) with God. The ordinary way to say "I am" in Greek requires only that one use the first person singular form of the verb "to be" (*eimi*). No pronoun is required, as the verb form indicates the person and number. However, pronouns do exist in Greek and are sometimes added to the verb form for emphasis. The Greek word for "I" is *egō*, so if one were to add this to the first person singular form of the verb "to be" then the result would be *egō eimi*, which might be rendered something like "I AM!"

Now when the Hebrew book of Exodus was translated into Greek in the Septuagint, the first part of "I am the One who is" was understandably rendered as *egō eimi*, and not simply as *eimi*. Exodus 3:14 reads, "And God spoke to Moses, saying 'I AM the one who is' (*egō eimi ho ōn*)'" Many scholars, from the patristic period forward, have noticed that

Jesus consistently uses the formulation *egō eimi* when he speaks of himself in the Gospel of John. Examples include "I am the bread of life" (John 6:35), "I am the good shepherd" (10:11), "I am the true vine" (15:1), and "It is I, do not be afraid" (6:20). Perhaps the most obvious instance is in John 8. The Jews ask Jesus if he thinks he is greater than their ancestor Abraham. Jesus answers that Abraham himself acknowledged Jesus' superiority over him. When the Jews wonder how Abraham, who lived some 1,700 years previously, could have acknowledged Jesus' superiority to him, Jesus answers, "Very truly, I tell you, before Abraham was, I AM" (8:58). This is interesting in part because it is not grammatically correct. If Jesus only meant to claim that his preexistence in heaven as the Logos allowed Abraham to see him, then he should have said, "Before Abraham was, I was." But Jesus does not say "I was" but "I AM." That the Jews understand Jesus to have thus placed himself on God's level is apparent because they immediately pick up stones to kill him for his "blasphemy." If he had not invoked the name of God and applied it to himself, no blasphemy would have occurred.

---

13. Most of these qualities are on display in Genesis 1. God "created the heavens and the earth" (Gen. 1:1). His benevolence is reflected in the goodness of creation: "And God saw that it was good" (1:10, 12, 18, 25, 31). His omnipotence is shown in his superiority to the forces of nature, which he makes and controls (such as the sun and the moon in 1:14–18).

Divine beings are understood as creators and not as created beings, or creatures. Of the Logos it is said, "All things came into being through him, and without him not one thing came into being" (John 1:3). This is followed by a statement about the *benevolence* (or "goodness") of the Logos: "In him was *life*, and the life was the *light* of all people. The light shines in the darkness, and the darkness did not overcome it" (1:4–5). These verses call upon an opposition between good and evil, with the good being associated with life and light, and the evil being associated with death and darkness. The Logos, of course, is good and brings good things like light and life to people. It is not unlikely that these two terms foreshadow two of Jesus' greatest miracles in the Gospel of John: the healing of the man born blind in John 9 and the raising of Lazaraus in John 11. The two miracles demonstrate concretely how the benevolent Logos imparts goodness: Jesus brings "light" to the blind man and "life" to Lazarus.

The *omniscience* of the Logos is reflected in such passages as John 6:64: "For Jesus knew from the first who were the ones that did not believe, and who was the one that would betray him." The remarkably powerful miracles that Jesus performs in John show his *omnipotence*. Jesus changes about 150 gallons of water into wine at the wedding at Cana (2:1–12). Jesus heals a royal official's son from a distance in John 4:46–54. In the Gospel of Mark, Jesus does not raise anyone from the dead. In Mark 5:21–43, Jesus raises a little girl who is said to be dead, but he insists she is merely "sleeping." In John 11, however, Lazarus is clearly dead. After four days, he has even started to decompose. Martha warns Jesus there will be a stench if they roll away the stone from her brother's tomb: "Lord, by this time he stinketh!" (KJV). But Jesus is still able to bring

him back to life. This shows that there is nothing beyond Jesus' power.

The mechanism by which the Logos came down from heaven and revealed his glory to human beings is called the **Incarnation**, and its biblical basis is John 1:14. The word "incarnation" comes from the Latin word *carne*, which means "flesh"; John 1:14 explains, "And the Word *became flesh* and lived among us." The Incarnation—the idea that God became man, that God took on a human form—is one of the signature doctrines of Christianity, one that sets it apart from the other great monotheistic religions of the world. With its expression in the Gospel of John, one could argue that the early Christian wrestling with the nature of Christ reached its maturity. The high Christology of the Gospel of John was adopted as the orthodox position on the matter. One can see the progression of the major Christological options in the following set of diagrams.[14]

Adoption Christology

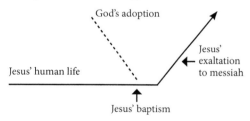

Agency Christology

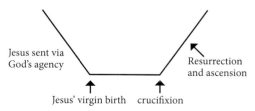

---

14. The following diagrams are based upon those of Robert Kysar, *John: The Maverick Gospel* (Louisville: Westminster John Knox, 2007), 29–30. Kysar, in turn, draws upon Reginald Fuller.

Incarnational Christology

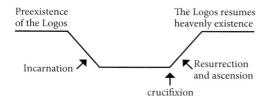

The Gospel of John is placed last among the canonical Gospels and hence it is given the last word. From the perspective of orthodox Christianity, John's Christology does not contradict that of the other Gospels, but extends and clarifies their visions of Jesus to reveal his full significance.

Sociohistorical Analysis of the Johannine Community: Conflict with the Synagogue

More than any other canonical Gospel, John shows signs of having been a group production; it had multiple authors over several stages of development. At one point the authors speak of themselves in the plural: "This is the disciple who is testifying to these things . . . and *we know* that his testimony is true" (John 21:24). There are numerous contradictions between different parts of the Gospel that suggest the contributions of different authors were combined in the final text. For example, 3:22 reads, "After this Jesus and his disciples went into the Judean country-side, and he spent some time there with them and baptized." But 4:1–3 says, "Now when Jesus learned that the Pharisees had heard, 'Jesus is making and baptizing more disciples than John'—although it was not Jesus himself but his disciples who baptized—he left Judea and started back to Galilee." It seems unlikely that the same person wrote 3:22 and 4:1–3.

Not only does the Gospel of John show more signs than the other Gospels of being the product of a particular community rather than a single author, it also shows more signs of having been addressed to the unique needs and problems of that community. The other Gospels seem to have a more general audience in mind. **Sociohistorical criticism** is a method of biblical criticism that attempts to determine, from clues in a text about its authors and intended audience, the circumstances that led to the writing of this particular text with its unique themes and idiosyncrasies. The "social history" of the **Johannine community** (the community that produced the Gospel of John and the three letters of John, and to whom this literature was originally directed) concerns the unique events and experiences of this group. This method assumes that a Gospel would be shaped by such events and experiences. If, for example, a particular church community experiences great persecution and suffering, and that community then produces a Gospel, it is probable this community will select for inclusion in its Gospel as many stories about Jesus as possible that deal with him being persecuted and tormented by his enemies. Those kinds of stories would speak to such a community in a special way and would resonate with their experiences. Sociohistorical criticism attempts to work "backward," as it were, from the stories selected and the details emphasized to the kind of experiences the community may have undergone that would lead to these selections and emphases.

In this respect, it has already been noted that the Gospel of John shows Jesus being rejected by Jewish people more harshly than in other Gospels, and that John has a higher Christology than any other Gospel. Could this be because the community that produced the Gospel of John had a tense and hostile relationship with the local Jewish community? Could that tension have stemmed from the Johannine community's claims that Jesus was fully divine? Many sociohistorical critics, influenced by the pioneering work of the Johannine scholar J. Louis Martyn, have answered these questions affirmatively.

Martyn proposed that the social history of the Johannine community unfolded in three phases, and that these phases can be detected in various passages in the Gospel, especially in the story of the healing of the man born blind in John 9.

In the first phase, a group of Jews in a particular city converted to Christianity. However, the Christian group originally remained within the Jewish synagogue. The Christian Jews and the non-Christian Jews originally worshipped side-by-side in an atmosphere of mutual toleration. Initially, the non-Christian Jews did not regard the Christian Jews' claims as blasphemous or heretical. But it seems that the Christians gradually elevated Jesus above the status of a prophet and even above the status of the Messiah, eventually regarding him as a divine being on the same level as God. Non-Christian Jews in the synagogue became increasingly concerned about these claims. They began to feel that Christianity was threatening the essence of Judaism, that these new Christians were no longer really Jews, and that they were trying to get others in the synagogue to abandon Judaism as well. At this point outright hostility developed in this synagogue between those Jews who believed in Jesus and those who did not, to the point where peaceful coexistence became impossible.

In the second phase, the Christian Jews were cast out of the synagogue—"excommunicated"—an event that appears to have been extremely traumatic for this group. Moreover, it seems that many Christian sympathizers within the synagogue were not willing to confess their belief in Jesus and face expulsion and the loss of their position in the community and the synagogue, so they hid their faith and remained in the synagogue. These are called "**crypto-Christians**."

The third phase was characterized by continuing hostility and resentment from the synagogue toward its now-excluded former brethren. Not only were these Christians thrown out of the synagogue, but there appears to have been further persecution as well: beatings, imprisonment, and even executions. As a result of the expulsion and persecution, the Christian group became a small and isolated minority, fearful and suspicious of outsiders and hostile toward the non-Christian Jews.

According to Martyn, the first two phases are documented in John 9. In that healing story, the man born blind starts off with a low level of faith in Jesus, but his faith grows until he proclaims Jesus' divinity. As he undertakes this faith journey, he experiences increasing hostility from Jewish people, who move from a more divided and tolerant attitude toward Jesus and his followers to one of united opposition. This culminates in the decision of the Jews to excommunicate anyone who professes faith in Christ from their synagogue. At the end of John 9, they apply this decision to the man born blind, casting him out of their community.

There is no doubt that the story in John 9 shows the progression of faith that Martyn identifies. When asked how he regained his sight, the healed man replies simply that the "man" called Jesus rubbed mud on his eyes, after which he could see (9:11). When he is questioned further by the Pharisees, he proclaims that Jesus is a "prophet" (9:17). When he is hauled in for questioning a third time and ordered to condemn Jesus as a sinner—because he performed this healing on the Sabbath—the man refuses: "Never since the world began has it been heard that anyone opened the eyes of a person born blind. If this man were not *from God*, he could do nothing" (9:32–33). Later, Jesus tells him that he is the Son of Man and the man responds, "'Lord, I believe.' And he worshiped him" (9:38). That the man's faith rises as the story progresses is indisputable.

The hostility of the Jews toward Jesus and his followers rises in a parallel fashion in the course of the episode. At first the Jews are merely curious as to how the man regained his sight. Later, some Jews express concern that Jesus must be a sinner because he performed this healing on the Sabbath, while others defend Jesus (John 9:16). Then the Jews are united in their opposition to Jesus. They even summon the man's parents for questioning, hoping to disprove Jesus' miracle by raising doubt as to whether the man who now sees was the same man who was born blind. The parents confirm the man is their son but claim not to know how he regained his sight. The parents avoid the question because "they were afraid of the Jews; for the Jews had already agreed that anyone who confessed Jesus to be the Messiah would be put out of the synagogue" (9:22). They do not want to be expelled, and in their cowardice turn the spotlight back onto their son: "Ask him; he is of age. He will speak for himself" (9:21). The parents, then, represent the crypto-Christians. They have some faith in Jesus, for they believe that Jesus healed their son, but they keep their faith a secret because they fear persecution.

The concept of being cast out of the synagogue is not mentioned in any other Gospel. Within a few decades of the death of Jesus, most Christian converts were Gentiles. They did not attend synagogue but formed simple house churches at the homes of their wealthier brothers and sisters in Christ. But for Jews who came to believe in Jesus it was not at all clear that their new faith meant they would have to leave the synagogue and form a separate church. They could hope their fellow Jews would come to agree with them that Jesus was the Messiah, or at least that their evolving beliefs would not require their departure from the faith community in which

they were raised. Synagogues were far more than places of worship; they were community centers where family, friends, and business associates came together. To be excluded would be a devastating blow, resulting in social isolation. The evidence suggests some Jewish communities expelled their Christian members sooner than others. It seems that in the Johannine community this did not occur until much later than usual, however, as the Gospel, written circa 90–100 CE, speaks of this rupture as if it were a recent wound.[15]

The separation of the Jewish-Christians from the non-Christian Jews in this particular community might well be described as a kind of divorce, and divorces are sometimes particularly bitter when the partners have been together a long time. The man born blind plays the part of the scorned spouse in this scenario, as his continued defense of Jesus leads to his expulsion from the community: "They drove him out" (John 9:34).

Thus Martyn suggests that John 9 is a two-level drama: the literal level tells the story of a healing by Jesus and its aftermath, and the symbolic level tells the story of the Johannine community and the synagogue that cast them out. The three phases of Martyn's social history of the Johannine community would all be represented if the man born blind had been further persecuted after his expulsion from the synagogue, but the text says nothing of this. Other passages in the Gospel, however, speak of persecution of Christians *by the Jews*, and when these passages are combined with John 9 the full picture emerges. In John 16:2, Jesus tells his disciples, "[the Jews] will put you out of the synagogues. Indeed an hour is coming when those who kill you will think that by doing so they are offering worship to God." It would be surprising if the Gospel included this

---

15. While Jewish Christianity was languishing by the end of the first century, its death throes took centuries. A small number of Christians continued to attend synagogues long after the rabbis first prohibited this; John Chrysostom complained as late as the fourth century CE that members of his congregation in Antioch also worshiped at the local synagogue; see *Against the Jews*, Homily 1.4.6ff.

prediction by Jesus if it had not come true. Indeed, Martyn argues that the mistreatment Jesus suffers from the Jews in the Gospel of John—mocking, insults, death threats, attempted arrests, attempted stonings—mirrors the persecution faced by Christian preachers of the Johannine community.

If Martyn is right, then the community that produced the Gospel of John was in crisis. They had lost the home where they had worshiped for decades and where their families, friends, and associates flourished. Some of these friends and associates were themselves believers in Christ but had decided the cost of confessing their faith was too high. This meant the confessed Christians were deprived of badly needed allies and were a smaller and more isolated group because of their fellow-believers' cowardice. In addition, the Jews inflicted further persecution on these Christians, even unto death. John 5:1–18 and 7:10–31 symbolically hint that the Jews had criminalized Christian proselytizing, making those who spoke to synagogue Jews about Jesus liable to arrest. Similarly, when Jesus' Jewish opponents express anger and bewilderment over Jesus' ongoing ability to attract audiences in 10:20 ("Why listen to him?"), despite the warnings they have issued about his status as a deceiver and a beguiler, it suggests that the Jewish community with which the Gospel author(s) was interacting had made it a sin for a Jew to even *listen* to a Christian evangelist. By this account, the Johannine community was under siege. That kind of pressure is enough to make most people crack and, as will be seen in the examination of the letters of John below, the Johannine community did eventually collapse.

Some scholars have challenged Martyn's three-phase reconstruction of the social history of the Johannine community, suggesting that the evidence is slender and susceptible to many interpretations. But there is no question that Martyn's theory would explain a great deal about the Gospel of John. Indeed, it would explain a great deal about the letters of John as well.

Succumbing to Persecution from Without and Division from Within: The Johannine Epistles

Whether the three letters of John should be considered separately or together, and whether they should be considered in conjunction with the Gospel or apart from it, are questions to which biblical scholars do not give a unanimous response. In some ways 1 John is quite different from 2 and 3 John. The latter two are short and rather personal letters from a church leader who calls himself the **presbyter** (or "elder"), while 1 John is more of a tractate, a longer address for a broader audience and more general application.

However, important features link the three letters. For example, 2 and 3 John both speak of the same problem—the acceptance or rejection of traveling Christian teachers—and claim to be written by the same person, the presbyter. In addition, 1 and 2 John speak of the same major doctrinal and moral issues—whether Jesus came "in the flesh" and whether Christians are bound by the commandments—and in much the same terms. Stylistic similarities suggest the letters were written by the same author, or by authors who were closely associated with one another and used the same style and vocabulary.

Similarly, one could point to major differences between the three letters and the Gospel of John and suggest that they should be treated separately. Largely absent from the Gospel are certain issues raised in 1 and 2 John: whether Jesus came "in the flesh," whether Christians are bound by the commandments, the end of the world, and the sacrificial nature of Jesus' death. Indeed, these latter two issues are thought to reflect an *early* stage of first-century Christianity and raise the question of whether the letters of John might predate the Gospel.

Most of the evidence, however, indicates that the Gospel and the letters emerged from the same "school"[16] and were addressed to the same community, and that the Gospel was mostly completed before the letters. Although there are differences between the Gospels and the letters, there are no outright contradictions or major points of tension. The documents speak of different theological matters because

"love" seven times. The Gospel of John uses it thirty-eight times, and 1 John uses it twenty-seven times in only five chapters.

Moreover, the teaching with respect to love, and the phrasing of that teaching, is so similar that it is difficult not to see the texts as closely related. The following table shows some of these similarities:

Gospel of John	First Letter of John
"For God so loved the world that he gave *his only Son*, so that everyone who believes in him may not perish but may have eternal life." (John 3:16)	"God's love was revealed among us in this way: God sent *his only Son* into the world so that we might live through him." (1 John 4:9)
"For this reason the Father loves me, because I *lay down my life* in order to take it up again." (John 10:17)	"We know love by this, that he laid down his life for us—and we ought to *lay down our lives* for one another." (1 John 3:16)
"I give you a new commandment, that you *love one another*. Just as I have loved you, you also should *love one another*." (John 13:34)	"For this is the message you have heard from the beginning, that we should *love one another*." (1 John 3:11)
"If you love me, you will *keep my commandments*." (John 14:15)	"By this we know that we love the children of God, when we love God and *obey his commandments*. For the love of God is this, that we *obey his commandments*." (1 John 5:2-3)

the occasion for each writing varied. Moreover, there are some overarching theological similarities, such as the emphasis on love as the key to the relationship of God to the world, of Jesus to his followers, and of believers to their "brothers and sisters." The Gospel of Mark uses the word

The letters of John were most likely written after the Gospel. The best argument in this regard is that the Johannine churches[17] were facing a serious internal schism in the letters, a theme absent from the Gospel. In the Gospel, opposition comes from unbelieving Jews. In the

---

16. The question of authorship is especially complex for the Johannine literature because evidence indicates the Gospel underwent several revisions and had several contributors. Many scholars refer to the author/editor of the final version of the Gospel as "the Redactor," and believe the Redactor is also the author of the three letters of John, identical to the "presbyter" of 2 and 3 John, all of which would account for their stylistic similarity. Other scholars believe the Redactor and the presbyter are two different people, and the differences between the Gospel and the letters outweigh the similarities. Still other scholars speak of a larger group of contributors, several for the Gospel and at least two for the letters, again based on differences found in the writings. Raymond Brown speaks of a "Johannine *school*" of students who were once close to the Beloved Disciple; see Raymond Edward Brown, *The Community of the Beloved Disciple* (New York: Paulist, 1979), 101–2. This school produced a number of author-theologians who shared a similar outlook and style and who contributed variously to the Johannine literature.

17. By the time the letters were written, and probably even during the period of the composition of the Gospel, the Johannine community appears to have expanded beyond the original church founded by the Beloved Disciple to a number of other nearby cities and towns. The second and third letters of John are written by a leader of one church—probably the original one—to another church within its sphere of influence, and to its leaders. Consequently, one may speak of Johannine churches in the plural.

letters, opposition comes from differently believing Christians. The first problem is likely to precede the second. A once-unified community faced Jewish persecution together, and that unity is reflected in the Gospel. However, under the pressure of arrest, execution, abandonment, and social isolation, the members of the Johannine churches began to turn on each other. Whenever the members of a small, isolated group are faced with tremendous opposition from the outside world, their only hope is to stick together. The author of the three letters of John understood that and preached it to his readers. Unfortunately, it seems they did not listen. The letters document the gradual disintegration of the Johannine community.

Although the letters seem to postdate the Gospel, they may not have been written in their canonical order. Third John logically seems to come last, but 2 John may well have preceded 1 John. The letters will be considered in that order.

Second John

In 2 John, the presbyter writes to a church he refers to as "the elect lady" and to its members as "her children" (2 John 1), to warn them not to receive or welcome traveling preachers who are spreading ideas that go "beyond" the teaching of Christ and that would foster dissension amid the Johannine churches (v. 9). The only specific feature of this false teaching identified by the presbyter is the idea that Jesus Christ did not come "in the flesh" (v. 7).

This phrase appears to be shorthand for those who thought that Jesus' divinity was so total that he could not have been truly human. The idea that Jesus could not have had a corruptible body, and thus could not have experienced pain or death, would later become characteristic of Marcionite Christianity and of some forms of Gnostic

Christianity (see chapter 1). This view, known as **Docetism** (from the Greek word *dokeō*, "to appear"), asserts that Jesus merely "appeared" (or pretended) to be human. In reality he was pure spirit.

The author does not elaborate on this idea except to say that it goes "beyond" the teaching of Christ, and that anyone who does not confess that Jesus came in the flesh "does not have God" (2 John 9) and is guilty of "evil deeds" (v. 11). Any proponent of this idea is called a "deceiver and the antichrist" (v. 7). He concludes by indicating that he has a great deal more to say on the matter but would prefer to do it in person rather than by letter. Later evidence suggests, however, that the author was subsequently barred from airing his full views to the church community in question by people who had adopted the very position that he warns against in 2 John. The tables are turned on the author: instead of shunning his opponents, the "elect lady" decides to shun him. As a consequence, he is forced to make his full argument in writing rather than in person, and he does so in a letter that turns out to be 1 John.

First John

First John seems to envision a situation in which a group with theological and ethical views contrary to those of the author and his school has already infiltrated some of the Johannine churches, causing a **schism** to erupt. Some individuals and churches remained loyal to the presbyter and his teaching, while others cast their allegiance with his opponents. The differences between these two groups apparently became irreconcilable, and the resulting conflict turned into a death struggle.

Raymond Brown refers to the opponents of the author of 1 John as the "secessionists," although he is cognizant that their perspective on this matter—if a version of it survived—would have reversed the roles of hero and villain.[18] Assuming

---

18. Raymond E. Brown, *Community of the Beloved Disciple* (New York: Paulist Press, 1979), 103–4.

the author of 1 John is characterizing their views accurately, scholars are able to reconstruct their major positions and determine that the areas of disagreement involved Christology, ethics, and eschatology, with a strong emphasis on the former. Brown argues that these secessionists were most likely members of the Johannine community who interpreted the teachings of the **Fourth Gospel**[19] in a way that differed from the author of 1 John and his allies.[20] It is, therefore, not a question of outsiders coming in and preaching ideas that have no relationship to the Johannine tradition, but of an intra-family squabble over the proper interpretation of shared traditions.

Clearly the Johannine community eventually developed a high Christology. Two key parts of this Christology are the idea of the preexistent Logos and the Incarnation. It appears the secessionists came to believe (a) that the preexistence of the Logos means that Jesus' earthly career is not the be-all and end-all of his importance, (b) that the process of Incarnation did not require the Logos to become truly human, but merely to take on a human form, and (c) that salvation is not made possible by Jesus' death on the cross but simply by the Logos coming down from heaven. Jesus, they claimed, is a *revealer*, not a *redeemer*.

This interpretation cannot be described as a complete distortion of the Gospel of John. There are features of the Gospel that appear to *minimize* Jesus' humanity, *deemphasize* the sacrificial nature of Jesus' death, and *highlight* Jesus' function as a revealer. As to the first point, it must be admitted that most of the stories from the Synoptics in which Jesus exhibits characteristically human limitations are missing from John. In the Synoptics, Jesus needs help from Simon of Cyrene to carry his cross to Golgotha. In John,

Jesus' strength never fails him; he needs no help carrying the cross. In the Synoptics, Jesus is in agony in the garden of Gethsemane and begs God for "the cup" (of crucifixion) to be removed from him. Jesus seems to be in genuine distress, perhaps even afraid. But in John Jesus does not pray to be relieved of the obligation to endure a torturous, humiliating death. In fact, Jesus seems to mock this idea: "What should I say—'Father save me from this hour'? No, it is for this reason that I have come to this hour" (John 12:27–28). In Mark and Matthew, Jesus cries out in seeming despair on the cross: "My God, my God! Why have you forsaken me?" (Mark 15:34; Matt. 27:46). But in John, Jesus never utters this cry of dereliction. He is perfectly calm and in control on the cross. He arranges for his mother to be taken care of and then gives up his spirit after announcing, "It is finished!" (John 19:30).

However, the author of 1 John believes the secessionists are misinterpreting the Gospel and developing docetic beliefs that go beyond what the Gospel explicitly authorizes and what the Johannine Christians have traditionally believed. For the author, the fact that the idea that Jesus did not come "in the flesh" has not been around since "the beginning" is one key sign that its proponents are wrong. Second John had already raised this point—"this is the commandment just as you have heard it *from the beginning*" (2 John 6)—and 1 John uses it as the opening line of the letter: "We declare to you what was *from the beginning*" (1 John 1:1).

Another key sign that the secessionists are wrong is the divisions they have caused. The presbyter speaks frequently of the importance of "fellowship" (1 John 1:7) and of believers loving one another. He suggests his opponents

---

19. Biblical scholars often refer to the Gospels by the order in which they appear in the canon, usually to remove any implication that they agree with the traditional identification of the authors of those Gospels. Hence John may be referred to as the "Fourth Gospel."

20. Brown, *Community of the Beloved Disciple*, 106–8.

have been arrogant, exclusive, and demeaning of those who disagree with them. Their contemptuous attitude, to him, indicates they are in error: "Whoever says, 'I am in the light,' while hating a brother or sister, is still in the darkness" (2:9). The presbyter claims his opponents are the cause of the schism, not his faction: "They went out from us, but they did not belong to us; for if they had belonged to us, they would have remained with us" (2:19) His opponents' failure to recognize that unity is more important than anything is proof they do not understand the Johannine tradition and never have.

To the presbyter, that the secessionists deny the salvific importance of Jesus' death on the cross is a sign they have not read the Gospel carefully. While the Gospel of John does not emphasize the atoning nature of the death of Christ to the degree that some other New Testament texts do, the motif is not completely absent from the Gospel. John the Baptist speaks of Jesus as the "Lamb of God who takes away the sin of the world" (John 1:29), a clear hint that Jesus did not save humanity simply by coming into the world, but by shedding his blood on its behalf as the Paschal Lamb.[21] Similarly, in John 10:15 Jesus says, "I lay down my life for the sheep." So also the presbyter affirms that "the blood of Jesus . . . cleanses us from all sin" (1 John 1:7).

From what the presbyter says, it seems as if his opponents did not feel the need to be cleansed of sin by the blood of Jesus, because they saw themselves as having such a close communion with God that they were perfect. He quotes them as saying, "We have no sin" (1 John 1:8) and "We have not sinned" (1:10). Therefore, the secessionists do not emphasize the need to keep commandments (2:3; 3:22–24; 5:2–3). It is likely that this faction did not claim perfection in the sense of having never committed a bad act, but rather in the sense that—unlike infidels who are still enslaved to sin—they have been set free by Christ and are no longer slaves to sin (see John 8:31–34). Jesus tells the Pharisees who cast out the man born blind in John 9, "If you were blind, you would not have sin. But now that you say, 'We see,' your sin remains" (John 9:41). Conversely, the blind man who has gained his sight, both physical and spiritual, is not guilty of sin, and his sin does not remain.[22]

There is no evidence that the presbyter thought of his opponents as sinners. Rather, he suggests they simply thought ethical behavior was irrelevant to their salvation. They gained eternal life simply by knowing God, through his only begotten Son. "Sin" is redefined as rejection of Jesus, not the commission of immoral deeds. This is the sense in which Jesus can say to the Pharisees of John 9, "If you were blind, you would not have sin." More explicitly, Jesus later says, "If I had not come and spoken to them, they would not have sin" (John 15:22).

In refuting these claims, the presbyter cannot appeal to any major body of ethical teaching in the Gospel of John. There is no Johannine equivalent to the Sermon on the Mount, and no emphasis on repentance in the sense urged by Jesus and John the Baptist in the Synoptic Gospels. But he does say it is imperative for Christians to follow the example of the earthly Christ, and this includes living in a manner that is above reproach. True believers must "walk just as

---

21. The "paschal" (or Passover) lamb was sacrificed on the eve of Passover and consumed on the following day. The authors of the Gospel of John saw Jesus' death as a substitute for the sacrifice of the paschal lamb. This is indicated in part by John presenting the timing of the death of Jesus differently from the Synoptics. In Matthew, Mark, and Luke, Jesus is killed on the day following the Day of Preparation. The Last Supper is a Passover meal, and takes place on a Thursday evening, with Jesus' execution following on Friday, the day *after* the Passover lambs were sacrificed. In John, the Last Supper is not a Passover meal, and Jesus is executed *on* the Day of Preparation, *at the same time* as the Passover lambs.

22. See Brown, *Community of the Beloved Disciple*, 125.

[Christ] walked" (1 John 2:6) and act righteously "just as [Christ] is righteous" (3:7).

Although Jesus does not issue a great many ethical commands in the Gospel of John, he does make one clarion demand: that his followers love one another (John 13:34–35; 15:12, 17). The presbyter argues that this is the ultimate proof his opponents do not "abide" in truth: they hate those who were once their brethren. To the presbyter, this betrayal is akin to murder. He likens them to Cain, who killed his brother Abel (1 John 3:12–15; cf. Gen. 4:8)

In the face of these bitter divisions, the author of 1 John pleads for love and unity. The evidence suggests, unfortunately, that his pleas went unheeded. The next missive in the Johannine correspondence indicates that the situation has grown worse, not better.

Third John

Third John is not addressed to a church (as is 2 John), or to a general audience (as is 1 John), but to an individual: Gaius. This in itself seems to indicate the presbyter is running out of friends. He indicates that his particular enemy in the church to which Gaius belongs is a man named Diotrephes. He denigrates Diotrephes as someone who "likes to put himself first," does not acknowledge the authority of the presbyter, and spreads "false charges" against him (3 John 9–10). Moreover, he prevents any representatives from the camp of the presbyter from even addressing his church. The presbyter places his hope in

a man named Demetrius, who may have been a rival of Diotrephes, and recommends that Gaius support him.

After this, no more is heard from the Johannine community. The letters of John suggest that the secessionists were the larger of the rival groups, and it seems likely they triumphed in the end. Their Christology is docetic (seeing Jesus as a pure divine spirit who merely pretended to be human), and it is likely that what remained of the Johannine churches eventually embraced full-blown Gnosticism.

It seems the proto-orthodox Christians viewed the Gospel of John with suspicion in the early to mid-second century, presumably because the Gospel was susceptible to a Gnostic interpretation. However, the proto-orthodox eventually claimed the Gospel for themselves. Moreover, the three letters of John offered a way to interpret the Gospel in an orthodox, non-Gnostic fashion. In the end, the proto-orthodox group embraced the high Christology of the Gospel of John. More than any other Gospel, John provided the foundation for the creed articulated at the Council of Nicea in 325 CE. The language about Jesus in that creed—"God from God, light from light, true God from true God, one in being with the Father, begotten not made, being of one substance with the Father"—can only have been inspired by the Gospel of John. No other Gospel embraces the full divinity of Christ so explicitly. The Johannine community may have lost the battle, but they won the war.

Key Terms

Johannine literature	anti-Judaism	crypto-Christians
Logos	preexistence	the presbyter
Beloved Disciple	Incarnation	Docetism
John the son of Zebedee	sociohistorical criticism	schism
Lazarus	Johannine community	Fourth Gospel
anti-Semitism		

Review Questions

1. What are the major differences between John and the Synoptic Gospels regarding (a) beginnings, (b) geography and chronology, (c) language and style, (d) friends, acquaintances, and associates of Jesus, (d) miracles, (e) teachings of Jesus, and (f) Jesus' relationship with the Jews?

2. What are the main theories on the identity of the "disciple whom Jesus loved"? What arguments are used to support each theory? Why is it considered important to know who the Beloved Disciple is?

3. What are the main sources of the historical persecution of the Jews? What are the main pillars of Christian hostility toward Judaism? How do the Gospels of Matthew and John each contribute in a unique way to the historic persecution of Jews by Christians?

4. What are the features of the high Christology of the Gospel of John? How do particular passages or details in the Gospel support the Logos as omniscient, omnipotent, benevolent, eternal, and creative? How does an incarnational Christology differ from an adoption or agency Christology? In what ways does the Gospel of John assert the identity of Jesus (the Logos) and God?

5. What is sociohistorical criticism? According to one application of this method, what are the three phases of the history of the Johannine community? What passages in the Gospel of John are used to support this reconstruction?

6. What are the main differences between the faction of the presbyter and that of the secessionists as revealed in 1 John? How could each group justify their positions by citing aspects of the Gospel of John?

7. How do 1, 2, and 3 John document the growing rupture within the Johannine community that eventually led to its disintegration?

Discussion Questions

1. The high Christology of the Johannine literature became part of Christian orthodoxy as the religion developed, and canonical books with a lower Christology (such as Mark) were either marginalized or reinterpreted in light of this understanding of Jesus. Was this, in your view, the "right" decision for Christianity? What is gained and what is lost when more emphasis is placed on Jesus' divinity?

2. Is it fair to paint the Gospel of John as anti-Jewish? Does the historical context in which the Gospel was produced justify or excuse its statements about Jews and Judaism? Is it only in light of subsequent historical developments that some people raise this charge against John?

3. Why do you think the Johannine community collapsed? Was this avoidable, or inevitable? Christianity today is fractured into hundreds or even thousands of denominations; do the disputes that led to the Johannine community's disintegration foreshadow later Christian sectarian divisions? Is there something about Christianity that lends itself, more than other religions, to bitter disagreements?

Bibliography and Suggestions for Further Study

(Books and websites that are accessible for general undergraduates are marked with an asterisk; other sources listed are appropriate for advanced students.)

Bauckham, Richard. *Jesus and the Eyewitnesses: The Gospels as Eyewitness Testimony*. Grand Rapids: Eerdmans, 2006.

*Brown, Raymond Edward. *The Community of the Beloved Disciple*. New York: Paulist, 1979.

Culpepper, R. Alan. *Anatomy of the Fourth Gospel: A Study in Literary Design*. Philadelphia: Fortress, 1987.

*Kysar, Robert. *John's Story of Jesus*. Philadelphia: Fortress, 1984.

*Kysar, Robert. *John: The Maverick Gospel*. Louisville: Westminster John Knox, 2007.

Martyn, J. Louis. *History and Theology in the Fourth Gospel*. Louisville: Westminster John Knox, 2003.

Introduction to Paul

The apostle Paul's importance to early Christianity is second only to that of Jesus. More than half of the books of the New Testament—fourteen out of the twenty-seven—were believed to have been written by him. In addition, more than half of the Acts of the Apostles narrates Paul's activities.

Paul's prominence was not easily secured, however. His career was filled with controversy and there was a time when his writings were all but forgotten. During his lifetime, Paul's enemies rejected his claim to be an apostle and liked to remind people that, unlike Peter, John, and others among the Twelve, Paul had not been among Jesus' followers and had never met Jesus while he was alive. Jewish-Christians in particular tended to revile Paul because he is thought to bear the primary responsibility for dropping the requirement that Gentile converts continue to adhere to the Torah, observe ritual purity, and submit to circumcision. In the second century CE, when Paul's popularity rebounded and his letters were being collected and disseminated, he was still tainted in the eyes of many orthodox Christians because the arch-heretic **Marcion** claimed his teachings were supported by Paul's writings (see chapter 1).

Fortunately for Paul and his legacy, however, Marcion was not his only defender, and Marcion's anti-Jewish version of Paul and his message did not prevail. Paul's supporters among the proto-orthodox convincingly argued that Marcion distorted Paul's message to reflect his own hatred of Judaism. Paul's champions eventually convinced proto-orthodox Christianity to embrace him as a true apostle and to grant him and his ideas an exalted place in the story of the founding of Christianity. As a result, Paul emerged from the controversies of the first and second centuries as a towering figure, a "second founder" of Christianity.

© Image courtesy of www.HolyLandPhotos.org

By convention, the apostle Paul is usually depicted as lean, dark-haired, and balding, as in this sixth-century fresco from Ephesus. There is no way of knowing whether this convention is accurate, as no record survives of Paul's actual appearance.

Was Paul the Inventor of Christianity?

One legacy of the so-called Quest for the Historical Jesus (see chapter 21) is the claim that Jesus' teachings were transformed and even distorted by the oral and written traditions that formed after his death. Some historical critics envision a Jesus who preached a simple message of radical egalitarianism, apocalyptic hope, political resistance, or something else, but who never claimed to be the Son of God and did not hold himself out as an object of worship. Such critics believe the **religion of Jesus** was transformed into the **religion about Jesus**, and many of them blame Paul for this. Paul, they say, corrupted the message of Christ and turned Christianity into something that Jesus would never have imagined or approved. In the words of the great playwright George Bernard Shaw, Paul's theology was a "monstrous imposition upon Jesus."[1]

This claim is not baseless. Certainly Paul makes very few explicit references to the historical Jesus. In his letters, Paul says nothing about Jesus' alleged miracle-working, includes none of his parables, and cites only a few of his earthly teachings.[2] To Paul, the most important things about Christ—almost to the exclusion of anything else—were his death, resurrection, and imminent return, and he ascribed to them a cosmic significance that clearly indicates that Jesus was far more than a role model and teacher, however wise.

There is no question that Paul advocated the worship of a divine Christ, but whether he was the first to do so, or whether this was somehow contrary to the wishes of Jesus himself, is not so clear. On the one hand, the more skeptical historical Jesus scholars voice good reasons for doubting the authenticity of those Gospel passages that reflect an understanding of Jesus as fully divine. However, many other scholars find it difficult to believe that Paul could have radically transformed the message of the historical Jesus so soon after his death without creating an uproar. Whether Paul is to be credited or blamed, he undoubtedly turned Christianity in a new direction, and this new direction contributed hugely to the tremendous popularity that Christianity would eventually enjoy.

This chapter examines what is known of Paul's life and career, while the following chapters discuss Paul's letters and the theological messages they convey. Our sources for a biography of Paul consist of Paul's genuine letters and the Acts of the Apostles. These writings suggest that Paul's career can be broken down into three main phases, with the dividing lines determined by whether Paul was preaching and practicing (1) Judaism, (2) Jewish Christianity, or (3) Gentile Christianity.

Overview of the Life of Paul

First Phase: Paul as Zealous Pharisee, Jewish Missionary, and Persecutor of Christians

Paul was born in Tarsus, in the Roman province of Cilicia in the region of Asia Minor (modern-day Turkey), probably around the same time as Jesus.[3] Given the Hebrew name of **Saul**, he was

---

1. George Bernard Shaw, "The Monstrous Imposition on Jesus," in *The Writings of St. Paul*, ed. Wayne Meeks (New York: Norton, 2006), 296–302.

2. Paul cites Jesus' teaching only twice, once about divorce (1 Cor. 7:10–11) and once about Jesus' return (1 Thess. 4:15–18). See E. P. Sanders, *Paul* (New York: Oxford University Press, 1991), 23. It is possible that there are echoes of Jesus' teaching in a few other passages (e.g., 1 Cor. 6:1–6; Phil. 2:8).

3. Paul says nothing in his letters that would allow us to estimate the date of his birth. It is known that he was already an adult in the first years following the crucifixion of Christ (early thirties CE), since he was leading an independent life that

part of a strict Jewish family who belonged to the party of the Pharisees, known for devotion to the Torah, personal piety, and a religious life centered on the synagogue and led by scholars known as rabbis. Paul writes that he was "circumcised on the eighth day, a member of the people of Israel, of the tribe of Benjamin, a Hebrew born of Hebrews; as to the law, a Pharisee; as to zeal, a persecutor of the church;

as to righteousness under the law, blameless" (Phil. 3:5–6). Given this upbringing, it is not surprising that Paul's writings display expertise in Judaism generally and an intimate familiarity with its scriptures in particular. Acts 22:2 describes Paul speaking in Hebrew and claiming he was raised in Jerusalem and taught by the famous rabbi Gamaliel, although that cannot be confirmed by Paul's writings.[4]

Sources for the Life of Paul

Paul's letters and the Acts of the Apostles supply information about Paul's biography, but there is an inverse relationship between the amount of information supplied and the likely reliability of that data. Paul's letters are first-hand accounts; Paul might have embellished some aspects of his biography, but in most cases there is no reason for Paul to lie and hence no reason to doubt his veracity. Unfortunately, in his letters Paul seldom has cause to reveal much about his personal history. Hence one can build only a bare-bones version of Paul's life based on this source.

On the other hand, Paul's history is of considerable interest to the author of the Acts of the Apostles, and hence Acts contains a great deal of information about the key events of his life and career. Unfortunately, as discussed in chapter 12 (see "The Historical Reliability of Acts"), the author of Acts wrote long after Paul's death and was not guided by modern historians' standards

for objectivity and accuracy. In particular, Paul's speeches in Acts are likely to be the author's compositions rather than anything based on notes or recollections of what Paul said on these occasions. Such invention was expected of ancient historians, who seldom had any choice given their usual lack of sources for things such as speeches. Other aspects of Paul's life and message may be heavily colored by Luke's desire to portray the founders of Christianity as forming a united, harmonious movement smoothly guided by God from one triumph to the next. Hence Paul's account of his career—in which there is a good deal of tension, conflict, and controversy—often does not suit the purposes of the author of Acts. Similarly, Luke wants to emphasize the continuity between Judaism and Christianity, and thus presents Paul as maintaining his status as an observant Pharisee even after his conversion (Acts 21:24; 23:6), while Paul's letters suggest he

continued

---

allowed him to pursue the persecution of Christians. In his letter to Philemon, written probably in the mid-fifties CE, he refers to himself as an "old man" (Philem. 9). In the Roman Empire, a man in his fifties would be considered old, so Paul was likely born in the first decade of the first century CE or slightly earlier.

4. E. P. Sanders points out that the author of Acts may simply have assumed Paul studied under Gamaliel because Paul was an outstanding Pharisee and Gamaliel was the leader of that sect. Acts suggests, though, that Gamaliel advocated tolerance of Christians (Acts 5:33–39), while the younger Paul insisted on persecution and harsh punishment for them. See Sanders, *Paul*, 8–9. This apparent contradiction raises doubts that Paul was trained by Gamaliel, especially when combined with the fact that Gamaliel was based in Jerusalem, while Paul claims in his letters to have spent so little time in Jerusalem that the Christians there did not know him (Gal. 1:22).

Sources for the Life of Paul *continued*

cast off the basic principles of Pharisaic Judaism after becoming a Christian (Phil. 3:5-9).[5] As a result, most scholars grant that claims about Paul based on Acts must be taken with a grain of salt, and that when Paul's letters and Acts conflict, the benefit of the doubt is usually given to Paul's writings. When there is no conflicting evidence or particular reason to doubt claims about Paul in Acts, however, they are usually accepted with caution.[6]

What distinguished Paul from most of his early Christian contemporaries was not his Jewish upbringing but that he came from the Hellenistic world and had assimilated much of its worldview. "In the Asia Minor of Paul's youth, the Jews had already accommodated themselves to their Greek environment. They attended the theater, took part in sports, gave their children Greek or Latin names, and decorated their tombs with Greek art."[7] **Paul** (*Paulus*)[8] was not a new name that he took when he converted to Christianity, it was simply the Roman name he used when among Gentiles.[9] Paul not only came from the Hellenistic world but had also received a formal education and could speak, read, and write in Greek. Most of Jesus' earliest followers spoke Aramaic and were likely illiterate. Paul had the ability to preach to Gentiles in their own "common tongue," to translate Jewish religious concepts into Hellenistic categories, and to guide and communicate with his converts using Hellenistic rhetoric.[10]

The combination of Judaism and Hellenism in Paul's background made him uniquely qualified to oversee the transformation of Christianity from a small, Palestinian sect to a world religion that would eventually control the Roman Empire.

By Paul's time, Judaism had already achieved the status of a well-established, respected world religion. Indeed, before the disastrous revolts against Rome of the later first and early second centuries, Judaism was thriving in the Roman Empire, and not just in Palestine. Estimates vary, but most scholars believe the number of Jews in the first century CE was somewhere between four and eight million, which would be 7–10 percent of the total population of the Empire.[11] Many of these Hellenistic Jews lived outside of Palestine in the **Diaspora**. Some had migrated at some point in the past from Palestine and established communities large and small throughout the Western world, but a substantial number were converts to Judaism.

---

5. See Günther Bornkamm, *Paul, Paulus* (New York: Harper & Row, 1971), xviii.

6. Walter F. Taylor outlines the three main approaches to sources about Paul's life: (1) "Acts as chief source," (2) "Letters as sole source," and (3) "Letters as chief source." The third approach is the one taken here, as well as the one Taylor recommends. "When Paul's letters contain no evidence, we may gingerly cite Acts, having made historical judgments about the veracity of what it says. When Paul's letters and Acts conflict, we will choose Paul"; Walter Taylor, *Paul: Apostle to the Nations: An Introduction* (Minneapolis: Fortress, 2011), 31.

7. Calvin Roetzel, *The Letters of Paul: Conversations in Context* (Atlanta: John Knox, 1975), 7.

8. *Paulus* is the Latin form of the name. The Greek spelling was *Paulos*; the name is of Latin origin, not Greek.

9. See Acts 13:9.

10. Bultmann was the first to recognize that Paul frequently uses a Greek rhetorical method called the "diatribe" popularized by the Stoics. See Rudolf Bultmann, *Der Stil der paulinischen Predigt und die kynisch-stoische Diatribe* (Gottingen: Vandenhoeck und Ruprecht, 1910).

11. Bornkamm, *Paul, Paulus*, 4. See also Louis Feldman, "The Omnipresence of the God-Fearers," *Biblical Archeology Review* 12, no. 5 (Sept–Oct 1986): 58–69.

While Judaism today is not a missionary religion and spends little energy seeking new converts, most scholars believe that at the time of Paul Judaism was highly expansionary-minded.[12] Given the tumultuous nature of the times, many people were dissatisfied with traditional Greco-Roman religions and were looking for new answers. Some found those answers in Judaism. Several ancient sources reveal that Gentiles found Judaism attractive in part because of the Sabbath, a weekly day of rest that had no parallel in Greco-Roman society.[13] Another distinctive feature of Judaism that attracted converts was its monotheism. Jews coined a name for Gentiles who were attracted to Judaism but reluctant to become **proselytes**, or full members of the Jewish people; they called them "**God-fearers**." In the Diaspora, God-fearers were accepted as long as they observed certain minimum requirements: confessing belief in the one God, keeping the Sabbath holy, and abstaining from unclean foods. They were not required to be circumcised. This was not a matter of settled policy, however, as there were factions in Judaism that thought of the exemption from circumcision and full observance of the law as too lenient. The leading Pharisees in Jerusalem in particular disapproved of this and insisted on circumcision for all male converts, sometimes even to the point of chasing down these partial converts and attempting to convince them their salvation was uncertain unless they submitted to circumcision.

One theory suggests Paul probably spent his young-adult years in the effort to spread Judaism among Gentiles. In other words, this theory contends, prior to his conversion to Christianity Paul was a *Jewish missionary*.[14] To be sure, this would not have been full-time work. It is widely acknowledged that Paul had a day job; even as a Christian he worked for a living so as not to be a financial burden to the communities he served (1 Cor. 4:12; 2 Cor. 11:27; 1 Thess. 2:9).

---

12. Shaye Cohen writes, "While Judaism did not sponsor missionary journeys, various individuals tried to teach Judaism to outsiders and Jewish authors wrote literary works in order to attract gentiles to Judaism. It is in this sense that, according to the most widely accepted scholarship, Judaism in this period was a missionary religion"; Shaye J. D. Cohen, "Did Ancient Jews Missionize?" *Bible Review* 19, no. 4 (2003): 41.

13. The Roman philosopher Seneca derided Jews and Sabbath-observant Gentiles for their laziness in wasting one-seventh of their lives, according to Augustine, *The City of God* 6.11.

14. This is not a consensus position. Some scholars argue there was no Jewish missionary effort in which Paul could have participated. Dunn argues, "Judaism was not a missionary religion. . . . [Jews] were not in the business of trying to win *non-*Jews to adopt their praxis. Judaism was, after all, the national religion of the Jews; it was not a matter of going out to convert non-Jews to a non-ethnic religion"; James D. G. Dunn, *Beginning from Jerusalem* (Grand Rapids: Eerdmans, 2009), 299–300. However, Louis Feldman (in "The Omnipresence of the God-fearers") and Shaye J. D. Cohen (in "Did Ancient Jews Missionize?") make a stronger argument that Second Temple Judaism did engage in missionary work. Bornkamm summarizes the arguments for the majority view of the existence of a thriving Jewish mission in the first century CE and concludes that Paul was part of it: "We have good grounds for believing that when the Diaspora Jew Paul chose to become a Pharisee, he also decided to be a Jewish missionary to the Gentiles along the lines taken by orthodoxy, and was actually such before becoming a Christian"; Bornkamm, *Paul, Paulus*, 12.

Among the arguments for a non-missionary Judaism is the claim that earlier scholars, influenced by their own Christian convictions, tended to force ancient Judaism into the shape of a kind of proto-Christianity: "The theory that diaspora Judaism was characterized by missionary activity . . . is an integral part of a larger and decidedly Christian conception of ancient Judaism, in which Judaism is viewed not only as a preparation for the church but also as Christianity *manqué*. Such a conception may have a place in Christian theology but not in Jewish history"; Shaye J. D. Cohen, "Adolph Harnack's 'The Mission and Expansion of Judaism': Christianity Succeeds Where Judaism Fails," in *The Future of Early Christianity*, ed. B. A. Pearson (Minneapolis: Fortress, 1991), 169. On the other hand, it is just as likely that recent scholars, influenced by their own Christian convictions, would rather see Christianity as having invented missionary work than credit that to Judaism.

Acts describes his occupation as tent-making (Acts 18:3), a skill whose products were in high demand among soldiers and travelers seeking to avoid the often squalid and crime-ridden inns of the time.[15] Such an occupation would be highly portable, enabling Paul to set up shop in a variety of locations throughout the Greco-Roman world. But Paul's true passion, his vocation, was preaching. As already noted, prior to his conversion Paul may have been a Jewish missionary, seeking to impress upon the God-fearers the need for circumcision. Paul himself hints at this: "But if I, brethren, *still preach circumcision*, why am I still persecuted?" (Gal. 5:11, RSV).[16] The language suggests that Paul had, at one point, preached circumcision.

One characteristic that could have led Paul to this missionary activity was his apparently boundless enthusiasm for his first religion. Paul was a proud Jew. Speaking of opponents who "boasted" of their Jewish heritage, Paul says that he shares their pride: "Are they Hebrews? So am I. Are the Israelites? So am I. Are they descendants of Abraham? So am I" (2 Cor. 11:21–22). In fact, Paul attributes his persecution of followers of Jesus to his great zeal for Judaism.

> You have heard, no doubt, of my earlier life in Judaism. I was violently persecuting the church of God and was trying to destroy it. I advanced in Judaism beyond many among my people of the same age, for I was far more zealous for the traditions of my ancestors. (Gal. 1:13–14)

Paul's self-description in the letter to the Philippians is similar: "As to zeal, a persecutor of the church; as to righteousness under the law, blameless" (Phil. 3:6). Paul was, by his own admission, a religious extremist whose certainty in the correctness of his views led him down the dark path of intolerance.

Paul's persecution of Christians was probably aimed at the Hellenistic faction within Jewish Christianity that subscribed to a minimalist approach to Jewish law.[17] The more liberal strategy for the inclusion of God-fearers was condemned by the strict Pharisees of Jerusalem. Acts 6:1–6 mentions a conflict in the Jerusalem church between "**Hebrews**" and "**Hellenists**," with the former probably describing Aramaic-speaking Jewish Christians who were fully orthodox, Temple-worshipping, and pro-circumcision, while the latter were Greek-speaking Jewish Christians who were far more liberal with respect to the Torah.

While the author of Acts minimizes the conflict and presents both groups as faithful Jews, one faction aroused the hostility and opposition of Jewish authorities far more than the other. **Stephen**, the leading spokesman for the Hellenists, is accused of speaking against the Temple and the Torah: "This man never stops saying things against this holy place [the Temple] and the law; for we have heard him say that this Jesus of Nazareth will destroy this place and will change the customs that Moses handed on to us" (Acts 6:13–14). Acts describes these as false charges, but there probably was at least some

---

15. See Sanders, *Paul*, 10. The Greek term used for Paul's occupation actually refers to leather-working generally, of which tent-making was one variety; Bart Ehrman, *The New Testament: A Historical Introduction to the Early Christian Writings*, 6th ed. (New York; Oxford: Oxford University Press, 2016), 326. Some scholars have connected Paul's work to the claim (made several times in Acts) that Paul was a Roman citizen and had been from birth. Romans sometimes rewarded those who served the empire, especially in its military, with citizenship. If Paul learned his trade from his father and inherited his citizenship from him, tent-making would fit well as their shared work because it was a service often used by the military and one for which a person might be rewarded with citizenship.

16. On Paul as a Jewish missionary who insisted on circumcision for Gentile converts, see Bornkamm, *Paul, Paulus*, 12.

17. Another prominent theory is that Paul objected to the idea that a *crucified* Jesus could be the Messiah, given that the Torah insists that a person who dies "hung on a tree" (as in crucifixion) is *ipso facto* accursed by God (Deut. 21:23).

basis for them. If the Hellenists had not taken such a stance toward the law, Paul would have had no reason to persecute them. It is unlikely the persecution was caused simply by their proclamation of Jesus as the Messiah. Other Jewish groups before and after the advent of Christianity proclaimed one or another prophet as the Messiah, and there is no mention of their being persecuted for this.[18] Acts indicates that the Twelve were not accused and persecuted as Stephen was; they were allowed to remain in Jerusalem while the Hellenists were forced to flee (Acts 8:1). It would make no sense for the Jerusalem authorities to expel certain Christians but not others unless the latter were practicing a more Torah-friendly brand of Christianity that was more acceptable to the Jewish authorities.

The precise nature of Paul's persecution of Christians is murky. Acts describes a single killing—that of Stephen—and indicates that Saul observed his stoning approvingly but did not participate (Acts 8:1). Later Saul is described as "breathing threats and murder against the disciples" (9:1). But when he seeks official approval for the persecution of Christians, he asks only to bring them "bound" to Jerusalem (9:2), and the initial mention of a church-wide persecution similarly speaks of arrests rather than killings: "But Saul was ravaging the church by entering house after house; dragging off both men and women, he committed them to prison" (8:3). Some scholars contend that Acts is mistaken in speaking of imprisonment, a punishment that Jews were unlikely to be able to impose in most

places, and that it is more likely Paul simply urged Jewish communities infested with Hellenist Jewish Christians to respond with corporal punishment. Paul would encourage Jewish communities to give these Christians "the severest punishment a synagogue could mete out,"[19] namely, thirty-nine lashes of the whip. One might think such a severe flogging would discourage all but the most committed Christians, but Paul himself eventually experienced thirty-nine lashes on five separate occasions for his advocacy of Christianity (see 2 Cor. 11:24) and never learned his lesson. Plainly, Paul had become a committed Christian, a remarkable about-face for a man who had previously been Christianity's most notorious foe.

Second Phase: Paul's Conversion and Career as a Jewish-Christian Missionary

Paul never speaks of his conversion[20] in detail. The Acts of the Apostles, however, provides three accounts of Paul's conversion (Acts 9:1–19; 22:3–16; 26:9–23). Acts indicates Paul was on his way to Damascus to continue his persecution of Christians when he was blinded by a bright light and heard the voice of the resurrected Jesus. "Saul, Saul," the voice said to him, "Why do you persecute me?" Paul replied, "Who are you, Lord?" And Jesus responded, "I am Jesus, whom you are persecuting" (9:4–5). Jesus then tells Paul to get up and enter the city

---

18. See Bornkamm, *Paul, Paulus*, 15.

19. Sanders, *Paul*, 9.

20. Krister Stendahl argues that "call" rather than "conversion" is the correct term for what Paul undergoes on the road to Damascus; see Krister Stendahl, "Paul among Jews and Gentiles," in *Paul among Jews and Gentiles, and Other Essays* (Philadelphia: Fortress, 1976). To some, "conversion" implies that a sinner has repented of his past life (which is not at all the case for Paul), or that one has *changed* religions. To be sure, at the time of Paul's revelatory experience, Christianity was not yet a religion separate from Judaism, and Paul certainly felt he was serving the same God he served as a Jew. Others believe that "conversion" is the better term because of the enormity of the transformation Paul undergoes. It is a complete change of direction for Paul to become a passionate advocate for that which he had previously persecuted.

of Damascus and to await further instructions.

As the account in Acts continues, in Damascus Paul is met by a disciple named **Ananias,** to whom it had been revealed that Paul had been chosen by God to be the "instrument" through whom the name of the Lord would be brought to "Gentiles and kings" (Acts 9:15). After meeting Paul, Ananias cures his blindness and baptizes him as a Christian. Paul then begins preaching that Jesus is the Son of God, and his former friends and enemies are shocked at his transformation: "In the synagogues immediately he proclaimed Jesus, saying, 'He is the Son of God.' And all who heard him were amazed, and said, 'Is not this the man who made havoc in Jerusalem of those who called on this name?'" (9:20–21, RSV). When Paul travels to Jerusalem, the disciples "were all afraid of him, for they did not believe he was a disciple" (9:26, RSV). Paul is not welcomed as a brother by the Jerusalem church until Barnabas—a leader of the Christian church in Antioch—vouches for Paul. Barnabas testifies that Paul is a sincere convert and not a spy seeking to infiltrate the church and then arrest the believers (9:27).

While few of these details are confirmed in Paul's letters, it is clear from what Paul writes that (1) he believed he had seen and spoken to the risen Jesus, and he considered his experience to be as much a "resurrection appearance" as were Jesus' appearances to Peter, James, and the other disciples in the immediate aftermath of his crucifixion (see 1 Cor. 15:5–8), and (2) he was convinced God had called him to be an apostle, and

The Metropolitan Museum of Art, Robert Lehman Collection, 1975

Paul's Damascus road experience, depicted in this painting by Spinello Aretino, is traditionally termed his "conversion." Paul himself, however, describes the event as a *revelation:* "God . . . was pleased to reveal his Son to me" (Gal. 1:15-16)."

commissioned him to bring the gospel of Christ to the Gentiles (Gal. 1:16; 2:7–9).

Paul indicates his earliest Christian missionary work took place in Arabia, where he toiled for three years apparently with little or no success.[21] Paul says nothing in his letters about making converts there or founding Christian churches, and Acts is silent about this period as well. Given the spectacular success of Paul's later missionary work, it is possible the gospel Paul was preaching in this early phase of his career was a less-popular version of Christianity than the one he later championed. In other words, Paul—the former Pharisee and defender of circumcision—did not immediately advocate a Gentile Christianity that dispensed with the

---

21. See Bornkamm, *Paul, Paulus,* 27.

requirements of Judaism but rather preached the more conservative Jewish Christianity that was the standard of orthodoxy set by the mother church in Jerusalem. Acts states that, as a new convert, Paul "disputed against the Hellenists" (Acts 9:29, RSV), indicating he initially took the side of the "Hebrews." This stance would account for both Paul's apparently undistinguished missionary record—Jewish Christianity was a notoriously tough sell—and for the absence of any disapproval of Paul from the Jerusalem apostles at this point in his career. Paul indicates he then visited Cephas (Peter) in Jerusalem for two weeks, and they parted amicably (Gal. 1:18–24).[22]

Paul insists in his letters that he had almost no contact with the apostles in Jerusalem. He preached the gospel for three years before his first meeting with any of them, and when he finally went to Jerusalem it was for a short visit where he met only with Peter and James the brother of the Lord. According to Paul, it would be another fourteen years before he again encountered the apostles of Jerusalem, this time for a momentous meeting of Christian leaders that would determine the future direction of the religion: the Jerusalem Council.

Time Line of Paul's Life and Career

32 CE	Crucifixion of Jesus
34 CE	Call/Conversion of Paul
34–36 CE	Paul's early missionary activity in Arabia
36 CE	Paul's first visit to Jerusalem; meeting with Peter and James
36–49 CE	Missionary activity in Cilicia; Paul is brought to Antioch by Barnabas and becomes one of the leaders of the increasingly Gentile-oriented Christian church there
49 CE	Jerusalem Council; Paul and Barnabas meet with Peter, James, and John, advocate for Gentile Christianity, and are opposed by conservative Jewish Christians
49–52 CE	Missionary activity in Asia Minor and Greece; 1 Thessalonians written
52–55 CE	Missionary activity centered in Ephesus; Galatians, 1 Corinthians, parts of 2 Corinthians, Philemon, and Philippians written
55–58 CE	Final missionary activity in Greece; parts of 2 Corinthians and Romans written
58 CE	Final journey to Jerusalem; arrest and imprisonment
59–60 CE	Journey to Rome as a prisoner
62 CE	Paul executed in Rome

22. See ibid., 24.

During that fourteen-year interval, Paul initially preached the gospel in his home region of Cilicia—again with no apparent success—before being summoned to Antioch in Syria by **Barnabas**, the leader of the Christian church there. After fleeing from Jerusalem, many of the Hellenists had taken up residence in Antioch and continued to practice and develop their liberal version of Jewish Christianity. At some point it was decided Gentile converts did not need to follow any of the requirements of Judaism, and their salvation was dependent solely on faith in Christ. This became known as **Gentile Christianity**. Whether Paul initiated this move, was one of several architects, or joined in a process that was already underway is unclear, but it is plain that Paul became a vocal champion of Gentile Christianity and eventually assumed the leadership of the church in Antioch along with Barnabas. These events set the stage for the most significant phase of Paul's career.

Third Phase: The Jerusalem Council and Paul's Career as Gentile Christian Missionary

There were two major turning points in Paul's career. The first was his conversion experience in approximately 34 CE. The second was the apostolic council that took place probably in 49 CE in Jerusalem. Two accounts survive of the gathering scholars call the **Jerusalem Council**: one in Paul's letter to the Galatians and the other in Acts. Acts presents the council as a calm affair in which the various sides compromised and came to a lasting agreement. Paul describes a more tense meeting in which he refused to yield and emerged triumphant—although subsequent events proved that the matter had not been fully settled.

In Acts, the council is needed because of the controversy created by a conservative Jewish Christian faction with roots in the Pharisees.

This faction insisted Gentile converts must be circumcised and follow the Torah strictly. Paul and Barnabas, sent by the church in Antioch to represent their position, disagree and testify that many signs and wonders have been accomplished among the Gentile converts in Antioch despite their nonfulfillment of the full requirements of Judaism. Then Peter and James speak and the matter is resolved: Gentiles do not need to be circumcised or submit to the "yoke" of the law, but need to meet certain minimum requirements related to ritual purity and sexual morality. They must not eat meat that comes from animals sacrificed to idols or that have been "strangled," nor can they consume blood. They are also prohibited from engaging in fornication (Acts 15:20, 29). This decree is sent "with the consent of the whole church" in a letter by the Jerusalem apostles and elders and is met with rejoicing (15:22–31). After this, fellow Christians no longer question the legitimacy of Paul's gospel.

In Galatians, Paul is writing to Gentile converts in Asia Minor who have been told by conservative Jewish Christian emissaries that their salvation is in doubt because Paul had misinformed them about circumcision. These emissaries have also told the Galatians that Paul is not a real apostle, and further seem to be claiming that the genuine apostles in Jerusalem all agree Gentile converts must submit to all the requirements of Judaism, including circumcision. Paul gives his version of the outcome of the Jerusalem Council to persuade the Galatians that his opponents are wrong, both about Paul's status as an apostle and the necessity of circumcision.

In Galatians, Paul is at pains to indicate first that he was not summoned to the council but rather was sent to Jerusalem by God through a revelation (Gal. 2:2). His stance indicates he did not see himself as subordinate to any other apostle or subject to anyone's orders other than God. He also reveals he was accompanied at the meeting by not only Barnabas but also Titus, an uncircumcised Gentile convert whose admission to the council is cited by Paul as proof that circumcision is not necessary. He describes the pro-circumcision faction in starkly negative terms: they were "false believers secretly brought in, who slipped in to spy on the freedom we have in Christ Jesus, so that they might enslave us" (2:4). Paul proudly proclaims that he "did not submit to them even for a moment" (2:5). His uncompromising stance met with the approval of

the Jerusalem apostles: "They saw that I had been entrusted with the gospel for the uncircumcised, just as Peter had been entrusted with the gospel for the circumcised" (2:7). Hence, Paul claims, Peter and James and John "recognized the grace that had been given to me" and "gave to Barnabas and me the right hand of fellowship, agreeing that we should go to the Gentiles and they to the circumcised" (2:9).

Subsequent events would prove that Paul's supposed victory at the Jerusalem Council did not end the controversy. Conservative Jewish Christian opponents went on trying to persuade Pauline converts like the Galatians of the necessity of circumcision. Even the Jerusalem apostles seem to have had second thoughts. Paul describes an incident in Antioch in which Peter visited and initially was willing to eat with Gentiles, an indication that he felt the Jewish requirements for ritual purity were no longer in force for Gentile converts or even circumcised Jews like himself. But when representatives from James arrived, Peter did not want to be seen eating with Gentiles and withdrew from table fellowship with them (Gal. 2:11–14). Paul is furious at what he calls Peter's hypocrisy and condemns him to his face.

Nonetheless, such ongoing opposition and hostility from Jews and conservative Jewish Christians did not slow Paul down. He emerged from the Jerusalem Council energized, and his missionary work began to take off when he began spreading the gospel of Gentile Christianity to new territories. He undertook several ambitious journeys to Asia Minor, northern Greece (Macedonia), and southern Greece (Achaia), and began making converts at a rate that far surpassed all of his contemporaries.

Although this phase of his missionary work was brief (48–58 CE), the spectacular success Paul achieved in this period would eventually make him the most famous Christian missionary in history. He made his way through cities and towns founding church after church, and after he left a place where he had established a Christian community, he would continue to communicate with his converts by letters. Several of Paul's letters to these churches survive, and these documents were eventually given canonical status and came to comprise the largest portion of the New Testament.

The record of Paul's written communications with his churches trails off around 58 CE. Paul indicates in one of his later letters (Romans) that he planned a journey to Jerusalem to deliver a monetary donation that he had long been collecting for the struggling and impoverished Christian community there. Acts indicates Paul was arrested in Jerusalem, as he had often been in the latter part of his career, for disturbing the peace.[23] Paul had become so notorious for his perceived betrayal of Judaism that his presence in a city with a significant Jewish or Jewish Christian population often resulted in a riot.

Following his arrest in Acts 21, Paul successfully pleads his case to the Roman authorities in Palestine, but due to a technicality he is sent to Rome for a final disposition of his case despite his captors' belief in his innocence. At the end of Acts, Paul has reached Rome and is preaching the word there. Later Christian tradition indicates that Paul was killed in Rome by the emperor Nero as part of a general persecution of Christians in the early to mid-sixties. Some other traditions claim Paul survived Nero's persecution and went on to proclaim the gospel in Spain, but most scholars are inclined to accept the dominant tradition of Paul's execution in Rome.

---

23. The author of Acts claims that Paul, following his arrival in Jerusalem, was falsely accused of illegally sneaking a Gentile into one of the inner courts of the Temple (Acts 21:28–29).

Paul's Apostolic Mission

How did Paul go about making converts during the most successful phase of his career? The book of Acts and Paul's letters diverge on this point. Acts indicates that Paul would go to the local synagogue and use that as a base of operations, arguing from scripture that Jesus was the Messiah and persuading Jews and Gentile God-fearers. Paul's letters, however, paint a different picture. In Thessalonica Paul's converts were neither Jews nor synagogue-attending Gentiles with monotheistic leanings, but pagans: Paul reminds them that they had "turned to God *from idols*, to serve a living and true God" (1 Thess. 1:9). Paul also indicates his base of operations was not the synagogue but his place of business. As noted, Paul was a skilled manual laborer (a leather-worker, perhaps a tent-maker) and he continued to ply his trade throughout his missionary career. Other Christian missionaries devoted themselves full-time to the ministry and accepted the financial support of their congregations, but Paul apparently did not wish to accept money, food, or housing from believers. Moreover, practicing his trade gave Paul the opportunity to interact socially with those who patronized his business, and apparently he spent much of this time speaking to them about the benefits of the Christian faith: "You remember our labor and toil, brothers and sisters; we worked night and day, so that we might not burden any of you while we proclaimed to you the gospel of God" (1 Thess. 2:9).

The "we" in 1 Thess. 2:9 refers to Paul and his coworkers. Acts and the genuine Pauline letters agree that Paul usually worked with a team of associates. In Thessalonica, Paul's coworkers were Silvanus and Timothy. Others who worked with Paul at one point or another include Titus, Barnabas, Mark, Aristarchus, Demas, and Luke. Although Paul refers to these associates as "brothers" and addresses his letters as if they are authored by the whole entourage, in truth the content of the letters is determined by Paul, and he is clearly the leader of the missionary effort. The Pauline letters often use the first-person plural "we" to address readers, but Paul sometimes reverts to using first-person (e.g., Philem. 19), revealing that he is the one writing (or dictating) the letter.

These associates also engaged in manual labor and used their workplace as an opportunity to do missionary work. Paul also used them as stenographers (dictating his letters to them), emissaries, and messengers. Paul sent Timothy to check on believers in Thessalonica who were facing persecution (1 Thess. 3:2, 6), and sent Titus to the rebellious church in Corinth in an attempt to win them back (2 Cor. 7:6–7; 12:18).

Paul's coworkers proved especially helpful when he was imprisoned, which apparently happened frequently. Paul wrote several of his letters from prison (Phil. 1:12–14; Philem. 1, 9, 23). While Paul was often punished at the hands of local synagogue officials, this usually involved corporal punishment (2 Cor. 11:24). Paul's imprisonments are more likely to have resulted from running afoul of Roman authorities, as Acts suggests, probably on charges of inciting a riot or disturbing the peace (Acts 16:20; 19:40). It was on such a charge that Paul was arrested for the final time in Jerusalem (Acts 21:27–34). Another reason for Paul's reliance on coworkers was his advancing age (he describes himself as an "old man" in Philem. 9) and there are hints in his letters that Paul was sickly. He refers to his opponents' claim that his "bodily presence is weak" without challenging it (2 Cor. 10:10). He reminds the Galatian believers that "it was because of a bodily ailment that I preached the gospel to you at first" (Gal. 4:13) and acknowledged that his care was a trial for them (4:14). In 2 Corinthians, Paul may speak of a specific illness: "And to keep me from being too elated by the abundance of revelations, a thorn was given me in the flesh, a messenger of Satan, to harass me, to keep me from being too elated" (2 Cor. 12:7, RSV). Some scholars have speculated that this "thorn" was a nonphysical affliction such as lust or spiritual doubts, while others claim that Paul had epilepsy or malaria. Speculation that Paul suffered from an eye condition rests on a passage in Galatians, where Paul recalls that their concern for him when he was ill there was so great that they would have "plucked out [their] eyes" and given them to him (Gal. 4:15). Others have suggested that the term "thorn in the flesh" would be especially appropriate if Paul suffered from kidney stones.

At any rate, Paul needed help and, unlike the other apostles (see 1 Cor. 9:5), he did not have a wife to help take care of him (1 Cor. 7:8).[24]

The apostle Paul writes an epistle in this seventeenth-century painting. Each letter of Paul represents a snippet of an ongoing conversation with a Christian congregation; the rest of the conversation is often difficult to reconstruct.

He was fortunate to have a variety of loyal associates who assisted him with his personal needs, his ministry, and his correspondence and also carried on his work after he died, continuing to write letters in his name. Paul's genuine letters—which were preserved in the New Testament canon—are the subject of the next chapter. Here, however, a few things about these letters are noted in reflecting on Paul's typical missionary work. First, all of Paul's letters except one (Romans) were written to churches he had established. Paul was writing to an audience that was familiar with him and his gospel; as a result he does not always spell out the basic teachings that his readers already know. Second, Paul is engaged in a dialogue with these churches. He has previously spoken to them, and they have responded to Paul. Now he is writing to them, but often in response to a letter they have sent him, or an emissary from their community carrying a message, or a report from one of Paul's associates. Hence Paul's letters are part of a conversation, but one in which only one side survives. To understand Paul's letters, one must attempt to reconstruct this conversation. Sometimes this is relatively easy and other times it is maddeningly frustrating and likely to lead to errors. One cannot be sure one is hearing all of Paul's side of the dialogue either, since it is clear in some cases that Paul wrote many letters to a community and sometimes only one letter survives, or in other cases several letters were later combined into a single document. Finally, Paul had a fiery personality and wrote with great passion, emotion, and excitement. However, he is not always clear or consistent. Thus reading Paul's letters presents challenges, and it is to these challenges the next chapter turns.

---

24. 1 Cor. 7 clearly shows that Paul was unmarried and celibate, but it is possible that Paul was married at some prior point and that his wife had died; see Taylor, *Paul: Apostle to the Nations*, 86. Paul makes it clear that his apocalyptic views contributed strongly to his feeling that marriage was an unnecessary distraction: "Those who marry will have worldly troubles, and I would spare you that. I mean, brethren, the appointed time has grown very short" (1 Cor. 7:28–29). As a Pharisee prior to his conversion, Paul would likely have had apocalyptic leanings, but there is no evidence that such beliefs led other Pharisees to remain celibate.

Key Terms

Marcion
religion of Jesus
religion about Jesus
Saul
Paul

Diaspora
proselyte
God-fearer
Hebrews
Hellenists

Stephen
Ananias
Barnabas
Gentile Christianity
Jerusalem Council

Review Questions

1. How and why did Paul persecute Christians prior to his conversion?

2. What was the nature of Paul's conversion experience, and what changes in his life and career resulted from it?

3. Why was Paul rather unsuccessful during the early part of his career and spectacularly successful in the later part?

4. Who were Paul's main associates and how did they assist him in his ministry?

5. Given the circumstances in which Paul's letters were usually written, what challenges does a reader face in understanding them?

Discussion Questions

1. At one point, this chapter describes Paul as "a religious extremist whose certainty in the correctness of his views led him down the dark path of intolerance." Paul himself admits this, although he suggests that it was true only of the period prior to his turn to Christ. Is there any sense in which he continued to be a religious extremist even after becoming a Christian?

2. If you had to guess at what really happened at the Jerusalem Council, how would you respond? What reasons would you give for preferring one version over another for each of the major points that are in dispute?

Bibliography and Suggestions for Further Study

(Books and websites that are accessible for general undergraduates are marked with an asterisk; other sources listed are appropriate for advanced students.)

Bornkamm, Günther. *Paul, Paulus*. New York: Harper & Row, 1971.

Dunn, James D. G. *Beginning from Jerusalem*. Grand Rapids: Eerdmans, 2009.

Koester, Helmut. *Paul and His World: Interpreting the New Testament in Its Context*. Minneapolis: Fortress, 2007.

*Roetzel, Calvin J. *The Letters of Paul: Conversations in Context*. Atlanta: John Knox, 1975.

Sanders, E. P. *Paul*. New York: Oxford University Press, 1991.

Stendahl, Krister. *Paul among Jews and Gentiles, and Other Essays*. Philadelphia: Fortress, 1976.

*Taylor, Walter F. *Paul, Apostle to the Nations: An Introduction*. Minneapolis: Fortress, 2012.

The Genuine Letters of Paul: Rhetorical Criticism and the Letter to Philemon

Scholars broadly agree that not all of the thirteen New Testament letters that now bear Paul's name were actually written by him. Among mainstream scholars, the only controversy is whether the number of **deutero-Pauline**[1] letters— those written not by Paul himself but by his associates writing in his name in the generation after his death—is three, four, five, or six. Almost always identified as deutero-Pauline are 1 Timothy, 2 Timothy, and Titus, known collectively as the Pastoral Epistles because they are addressed to church leaders (pastors) rather than to churches. Most scholars also regard Ephesians as deutero-Pauline.

A substantial majority doubt the authenticity of 2 Thessalonians and Colossians as well, although there are more dissenters in these cases who continue to regard one or both as genuine letters of Paul.

The next few chapters follow the majority view that six letters are deutero-Pauline, leaving seven letters that were written by Paul himself. The reasons for the exclusion of each of the six deutero-Paulines from the list of genuine letters are covered in chapter 18. The seven undisputed letters exhibit a uniformity of style and thought that indicate they were written by a single author. These letters can be reliably dated to the period in which Paul was alive and engaged in active ministry, and there is no reason to doubt their authenticity. It is likely that, in their present form, some of the letters were edited and (in some cases) stitched together, but virtually all of the words and sentences are Paul's.

A medieval scribe copies a manuscript in this engraving. Modern textual critics suspect that the notorious misogynistic passage 1 Cor. 14:33b-35 may have originated as a marginal note that a later copyist mistakenly assumed was part of the text.

---

1. This term as it is used here refers to any pseudonymous letter attributed to Paul, although in some scholarly discussions only Ephesians, Colossians, and 2 Thessalonians are eligible for inclusion under the heading "deutero-Pauline," while 1 Timothy, 2 Timothy, and Titus are categorized as Pastoral Epistles but not deutero-Pauline.

If Not Paul's Words, Then Whose?

Occasionally, scribes who copied the manuscripts of Paul's letters would make small insertions called **interpolations**. Sometimes this resulted from a previous scribe having made a marginal note, called a **gloss**, which was then mistaken by a subsequent scribe as part of the text of the letter and inserted therein. One famous example, according to some scholars,[2] is the notorious passage about women: "As in all the churches of the saints, the women should keep silence in the churches. For they are not permitted to speak, but should be subordinate, as even the law says. If there is anything they desire to know, let them ask their husbands at home. For it is shameful for a woman to speak in church" (1 Cor. 14:33b–35).[3] Paul is often vilified for sexism and misogyny here, but he may not have written these words. Reasons for thinking the passage is not Pauline include the bald contradiction between this statement and what Paul says in 1 Corinthians 11:5–where it is clear that women *can* speak in church–and the invocation of "the law" in a way that is very unlike Paul. Furthermore, in different manuscripts the location of this passage varies.[4] This is seen as proof by some that it was not part of the original letter but rather was a marginal gloss, probably by a scribe who was thinking of a similar passage in 1 Timothy 2:11-12. This scribe apparently did not realize Paul was not the author of 1 Timothy or that the attitudes toward women expressed there are much harsher than those of Paul himself. According to the interpolation theory, later copyists understood this gloss as Pauline and eventually incorporated it into the body of the letter.

Rhetorical Criticism of the Letters of Paul and the Hellenistic Letter Form

Six of the seven undisputed letters of Paul are addressed to people or communities with whom Paul is closely familiar. Paul is writing to churches that he had founded, and his communication cultivates an ongoing dialogue. The only exception is the letter to the Romans, which is written to a church Paul did not found and had not yet visited, but which he intended to visit in the future. Further investigation reveals the six letters (and even Romans, to some degree) are *occasional* in nature. That is, each letter is written to address a specific set of circumstances unique to the church Paul is addressing. The letters are not general proclamations that Paul would make regardless of his audience and that would apply always and everywhere. In other words, Paul writes usually in response to a problem that has arisen in one of his churches, and the letter is designed to provide a solution to a specific problem.

---

2. An example of a scholar who argues that 1 Cor. 14:33b–35 is a non-Pauline gloss is Hans Conzelmann, in *1 Corinthians* (Philadelphia: Fortress, 1975), 246. More recently Gordon Fee, Philip Payne, and Raymond F. Collins have advanced the argument. Many other scholars, on the other hand, are convinced that 14:33b–35 are Pauline and that these verses were always part of the letter, largely because there are no manuscripts that do not include these verses. For a summary of this argument, see Ben Witherington III, *Conflict and Community in Corinth: A Socio-Rhetorical Commentary on 1 and 2 Corinthians* (Grand Rapids: Eerdmans, 1995), 288.

3. The RSV is the default version used in this chapter.

4. Most manuscripts locate this passage after 1 Cor. 14:33a, but in other manuscripts it follows 1 Cor. 14:40. Some of the manuscripts also include scribal markings that indicate the scribe was uncertain about the authenticity of the text.

Rhetorical Criticism

Paul's solutions tend to argue that his readers adopt a certain point of view or change their behavior in some way. That is to say, Paul's letters are aimed at the *persuasion* of his audience. Therefore, one can understand them as a species of **rhetoric**. Broadly defined, rhetoric is the art of persuasion, the attempt to use language skillfully to move audiences in the direction the speaker or author would like them to go.[5] Rhetorical criticism, then, looks at a piece of writing and asks two basic questions: (1) *what* is the author trying to persuade his audience to do, think, feel, and so on, and (2) *how* is the author using the rhetorical tools at his disposal (logical arguments, emotional appeals, authoritative commands, etc.) to do so.

The first question involves what critics refer to as the **rhetorical situation**.[6] This involves understanding the author's relationship to his audience and the circumstances that have led to writing the persuasive discourse. This is best understood as determining the *problem* faced by the writer. The second involves the author's **rhetorical strategy**—the use of persuasive arguments and devices designed to address this problem and lead to a desired result within the limits imposed by the situation. The rhetorical strategy outlines the author's proposed *solution* to the problem.

Rhetorical criticism is a useful analytical tool when one seeks to understand any speech or text designed to influence an audience, but it is especially helpful when it comes to analyzing *ancient* texts from the Greco-Roman period, and even more so texts produced by writers who were educated in a school that followed the standard Greco-Roman curriculum.

The study of rhetoric was a major and explicit part of what came to be called *liberal* education (later "liberal arts") in the classical period. The word "liberal" has its roots in the Latin *liber*, which means "free." It was believed that a free man (i.e., a person who was male and not a slave) would need to be able to make speeches of various kinds to function properly as a citizen of the *polis*. Hence, after learning the rudiments of the Greek or Latin language (grammar), a student would advance to rhetoric,[7] studying great speeches of past orators and practicing speechmaking in a variety of contexts that might arise in his lifetime. If a man was on the city council, he would need to be able to argue persuasively for the government to take certain actions, such as engaging in war or making a treaty. If he was wronged, or accused of wrongdoing, he would need to be able to argue his case in the courts of law. If his father died, he would need to be able to deliver a proper eulogy. Aristotle defined the three branches of rhetoric[8] in line with these examples. The first branch is **deliberative** (or legislative) rhetoric, and involves cases where a speaker (or writer) seeks to exhort his audience to follow a particular course of action in the *future*, or to dissuade them from following a particular course. The second branch is **judicial** (or "forensic") rhetoric, and involves circumstances in which the speaker tries to get his audience (perhaps a judge or jury) to take a certain view of *past* actions, seeing them as just or unjust, harmless or tortious. The third is **epideictic** (or "ceremonial") rhetoric, which involves

---

5. Paul's letters are written, so he will be referred to henceforth as an author rather than a speaker.

6. See, for example, George A. Kennedy, *New Testament Interpretation through Rhetorical Criticism* (Chapel Hill: University of North Carolina Press, 1984), 34–37.

7. "Rhetoric was a systematic academic discipline universally taught throughout the Roman empire. It represented approximately the level of high-school education today and was, indeed, the exclusive subject of secondary education"; ibid., 9.

8. See Aristotle, *Rhetoric* 1.3.

speech or writing that praises or blames and thus seeks to hold or reaffirm some point of view in the *present*. Some modern occasions for praise include funeral eulogies, obituaries, graduation or retirement celebrations, nominating speeches at conventions, wedding toasts, and the like. Occasions for blame would be, for example, the death of a tyrant, or a retrospective look at the career of a corrupt politician or disgraced general.

For each type of speech, ancient students would practice forming persuasive discourses by focusing on five areas: invention, arrangement, style, memorization, and delivery.[9] The last two pertain to spoken discourse, so only the first three apply to Paul's writings. The foundational and highest aspect of rhetoric is **invention**, which involves the creation of arguments rather than how these arguments are framed (style) or the order in which they appear (arrangement).

Invention is based either on external proofs, which the author uses but does not create (for example, the evidence of witnesses, or documents), or on internal or "artistic" proof, which the author is said to invent himself.[10] When Paul argues for Jesus' resurrection in 1 Corinthians 15, he uses the evidence of witnesses. He also often cites documents (books of the Old Testament) whose authority he takes for granted and assumes his audience will accept.

With respect to artistic proof, invented by the author, Aristotle speaks of three general types of arguments, differentiated from each other by whether they are based on ethos, pathos, and logos.[11] **Ethos** involves character, and "may be defined as the credibility that the author or speaker is able to establish in his work. The audience is

induced to trust what he says because they trust him, as a good man or an expert on the subject."[12] The author must present himself as wise, virtuous, and benevolent to engender the good will of his audience and by this effort make them more amenable to persuasion. When the author of the Gospel of Luke opens his narrative with a long, complex, and beautifully written sentence that uses a number of elegant words and expressions (see chapter 11), he is trying to persuade his audience that he is a well-trained, professional writer, and as such deserves their attention.

Pathos has to do with emotion. As part of training in rhetoric, ancient orators and authors studied a sort of psychology to enable them to manipulate their audiences' emotions. For example, they learned how to influence an audience's sense of compassion, because arousing their pity would make them more sympathetic to a speaker's or author's situation and more inclined to see things as he wished. Instilling fear, another common emotion, would make audiences more alert to danger and more inclined to take precautions, if the discourse recommends such a course of action. A common New Testament form of this sort of argument occurs when an author invokes the threat of damnation.[13]

Logos refers to the logical arguments—both inductive and deductive—made by the author in his attempt to persuade readers. Inductive arguments, which move from the specific to the general, work by citing particular examples of a phenomenon that the author is claiming is a broad truth. In the Gospels, when Jesus proclaims, "The Sabbath was made for humankind and not humankind for the Sabbath" (Mark 2:27, NRSV), this is a broad

---

9. See Kennedy, *New Testament Interpretation*, 13–14.

10. Ibid., 12.

11. Aristotle, *Rhetoric* 1.2.

12. Kennedy, *New Testament Interpretation*, 15.

13. A good example is Matt. 5:29: "If your right eye causes you to sin, pluck it out and throw it away; it is better that you lose one of your members than that your whole body be thrown into hell."

truth for which examples are provided, such as the disciples plucking heads of grain because they are hungry (2:23–27) and Jesus proclaiming the evident superiority of healing a man with a withered hand on the Sabbath rather than forcing him to continue suffering (3:1–6). These examples are inductive arguments for Jesus' claim in Mark 2:27.

Deductive arguments employ premises and conclusions. If each of these is spelled out, then the resulting argument is known as a syllogism. The premises are the building blocks of the argument, and the conclusion is based on inferences that follow from the premises. A commonly cited example is the following, where P stands for "premise" and the three-dot symbol "∴" stands for "therefore":

P^1 All men are mortal.

P^2 Socrates is a man.

∴ Socrates is mortal.

Most speakers and authors do not make their arguments in complete syllogistic form. One common variety of deductive argument is the **enthymeme**, which is a syllogism with at least one of its usual components—two premises and a conclusion—unstated. An example is found in Peter's speech in Acts 2, where the disciples receive the gift of the Holy Spirit and begin speaking in tongues. Those who hear them are amazed, and some mock them, claiming they are inebriated (Acts 2:13). To this Peter responds, "These men are not drunk, as you suppose, since it is only the third hour of the day" (2:15). The underlying syllogism is easy enough to decipher:

Premise 1: People tend to get drunk at night, or in the afternoon, not in the early morning. (Restated, this might be "All drunkenness is nocturnal.")

Premise 2: It is early in the morning—"the third hour of the day" means 9 a.m. (Restated, "It is not nighttime.")

Conclusion: The disciples are not drunk.[14]

However, the first premise of the argument is unstated. It is simply assumed by Peter (and the author of Acts) that his audience knows and believes that drunkenness is uncommon in the early morning and unlikely to account for odd behavior displayed by Jesus' disciples at that time. It is possible to dispute this premise and claim that early morning drunkenness is not impossible—and that may be the reason this assumption is left unstated. Voicing it might make its weakness apparent to the audience and create doubt in their minds as to the soundness of the conclusion, which is the last thing the speaker wants to do.

Indeed, the arguments used in a discourse are not always valid or sound. Well-trained readers will spot logical fallacies such as denying the antecedent,[15] affirming the consequent,[16] appeal to majority,[17] *ad hominem* (personal attack),[18]

---

14. In symbolic logic, this would be represented thus:

P^1 All X is Y

P^2 ~Y

Therefore ~X

15. "If it rained outside recently, then the grass will be wet. It did not rain, so the grass cannot be wet." This is true unless, of course, someone turned the sprinklers on.

16. "If it rained outside recently, then the grass will be wet. The grass is wet, so it must have rained." Again, the sprinklers could have come into play.

17. Everyone thinks X, so it must be true: "I'm a Pepper, he's a Pepper, she's a Pepper. Wouldn't you like to be a Pepper too?" or "Fifty million Elvis fans can't be wrong."

18. This kind of argument attacks the characteristics of a speaker or a subject of an argument in a way that is irrelevant. An example of this fallacy would be if two people were arguing over whether Abraham Lincoln was a great president, and one debater was losing and said to the other, "Oh yeah? Well, you're ugly." The personal appearance of one's opponent is not relevant to the validity of the argument he is making.

appeal to authority,[19] begging the question,[20] false equivalence,[21] and false dilemma,[22] among others. However, not all readers will spot these fallacies, and even those who do might not entirely discount their evidentiary value. So analyzing logos in a discourse is not restricted to identifying "good" arguments but applies to all arguments.

The Hellenistic Letter Form

Another thing Paul would have learned as part of his Greek education is how to write a letter (*epistle*, from the Greek, *epistolē*) according to the conventions of the time. Just as American schoolchildren were once taught[23] to begin letters with the date and then a greeting such as "Dear Aunt Sally" and to conclude them with "Sincerely, Joe" or "Love, Katie," so young students receiving a Greek education were taught to construct their letters according to a particular pattern. Paul's shortest letter, Philemon, can be used as an example to illustrate the various parts of the epistle.

The introduction to a Hellenistic letter consisted of three parts: the **sender**, **addressee**, and **greeting**. The first three verses of Philemon include all three parts: "Paul, a prisoner for Christ Jesus, and Timothy our brother" identifies the *senders* of the letter; "To Philemon our beloved fellow worker and Ap'phia our sister and Archip'pus our fellow soldier, and the church in your house" specifies the letter's intended recipients, its *addressees*; and "Grace to you and peace" is the initial *greeting* Paul typically uses in his letter.

The second essential part of a Hellenistic letter is called the **thanksgiving**. In the thanksgiving the letter writer brings into view the situation of the recipients and gives thanks for any positive aspects of it. Paul writes, "I thank my God always when I remember you in my prayers, because I hear of your love and of the faith which you have toward the Lord Jesus and all the saints, and I pray that the sharing of your faith may promote the knowledge of all the good that is ours in Christ. For I have derived much joy and comfort from your love, my brother, because the hearts of the saints have been refreshed through you" (Philem. 4–7). The thanksgiving is a formal element of the letter, and its conclusion signals the reader that the real reason for the author's writing is about to become clear.

The **body** of the letter follows the thanksgiving and reveals the letter's true purpose and function, in this case identifying the problem at hand and outlining Paul's solution to it. Most of the arguments Paul uses to move readers toward a certain perspective or particular course of action are contained herein; the following analyses of Paul's letter will focus largely on the body. Paul often signals that the body of the letter is coming to a close by discussing his upcoming travel plans.

The next component of the letter form is called **parenesis**. Parenesis refers to the issuing of commands, instruction, or exhortation, usually ethical in character. Paul will sometimes speak of specific actions that he wants his readers to undertake or avoid—for example, "Contribute to the needs of the saints, [and] practice hospitality" (Rom. 12:13). At other times the exhortation is

---

19. "It must be true because my teacher said so." But even experts can be wrong.

20. Assumes without evidence the truth of the very matter under discussion: "The belief in God is universal; after all, everyone believes in God."

21. "You know who else supported gun control? Hitler."

22. "You're either with us or against us." This ignores other possibilities, such as neutrality.

23. The advent of e-mail and the near-disappearance of personal letters has obviated the necessity of this kind of education, although it still takes place in many quarters.

more general: "Hold fast to what is good; abstain from every form of evil" (1 Thess. 5:21–22). The parenesis in Paul's letter to Philemon is found in verse 22: "Prepare a guest room for me, for I am hoping through your prayers to be granted to you." Here Paul is able to combine his typical way of ending the body of his letter (an indication of his near-term travel plans, as seen in his hint that he is hoping to be released from prison and plans to go from jail to Philemon's house for a visit) with parenesis (the command to prepare a guest room).

The conclusion to a Hellenistic letter usually consisted of last requests as well as final greetings and well-wishes for its recipients. Paul typically uses one or more of the following: (1) a benediction or final blessing, such as "The grace of our Lord Jesus Christ be with you" (1 Thess. 5:28), (2) greetings from others in Paul's entourage who are known to the church community to whom he is writing, as in Philemon 23–24, "Epaphras, my fellow prisoner in Christ Jesus, sends greetings to you, and so do Mark, Aristarchus, Demas, and Luke, my fellow workers," (3) a final command, such as an order to pray for Paul and his ministry ("Brethren, pray for us," in 1 Thess. 5:25), or to maintain friendship and intimacy among themselves ("Greet one another with a holy kiss," in 1 Cor. 16:20; cf. 1 Thess. 5:26), or to make sure that Paul's letter is read out aloud to the entire community ("I adjure you by the Lord that this letter be read to all the brethren," in 1 Thess. 5:27).

Paul's Letter to Philemon

The New Testament canon arranges the letters of Paul from longest (Romans) to shortest (Philemon). Here and in the next chapters that order is reversed: Philemon's brevity and simplicity make it an ideal candidate for illustrating the principles of rhetorical criticism, and the unique status of Romans (the only letter Paul wrote to a church he had not founded and had never visited) makes it an outlier and thus best saved for last.

Paul's letter to Philemon consists of only twenty-five verses, making it the third-shortest book in the Bible (after 2 and 3 John). It is also the most personal and idiosyncratic of Paul's letters, dealing with a unique situation from which it is hard to draw any general lessons. Probably the only reason the letter was included in the canon is that it was unquestionably written by Paul.[24]

Rhetorical Situation of Philemon

While Paul is in prison, perhaps in Ephesus or Rome, he receives a visit from, or runs into, a man named **Onesimus** with whom he was previously acquainted. Onesimus had been a slave (Philem. 16), and Philemon was his owner. **Philemon** is a wealthy Christian—rich enough to host the local church in his house (vs. 2)—whom Paul had previously converted and with whom he remained friends. Other hints in the letter reveal that Onesimus ran away from his master Philemon, after getting into some kind of trouble. Paul indicates that Onesimus might have "wronged" Philemon, or perhaps "owes" him some money (vs. 18). Some household servants or slaves were entrusted with money or handled their masters' financial transactions (see Luke 16:1–9). Perhaps, then, Onesimus misappropriated funds and fled when this was discovered. It is unlikely that Onesimus then simply bumped into Paul,[25] since Paul, in prison, was not likely to be running into many people. Onesimus probably sought Paul out and asked him to intervene with his master,

---

24. Many scholarly books on Paul do not mention Philemon at all, for example, Gunther Bornkamm, *Paul, Paulus* (New York: Harper & Row, 1971), and E. P. Sanders, *Paul* (New York: Oxford University Press, 1991).

25. Calvin J. Roetzel, for example, suggests that Onesimus met Paul "by coincidence"; Calvin Roetzel, *The Letters of Paul: Conversations in Context*, 4th ed. (Louisville: Westminster John Knox Press, 1998), 117.

This ancient Roman bas relief depicts a domestic slave bringing a tablet to his master. While most slaves in the Roman world were illiterate laborers, some were given an education and placed in positions of trust and responsibility.

knowing that Paul was respected by Philemon and that Paul had authority in Philemon's eyes. He begged Paul to smooth over the hard feelings his misdeeds and escape had created with Philemon. Onesimus runs away *from* Philemon and *to* Paul because he thinks Paul may be the only one who can get him out of the trouble he is in.

After meeting Paul in jail, Onesimus is converted by Paul. When Paul says he became Onesimus's "father" during his imprisonment (Philem. 10), he means that he baptized him as a Christian. Onesimus then begins to serve Paul in his ministry, apparently in much the same way that Paul's other associates did. Paul apparently found Onesimus very helpful. He tells Philemon that Onesimus has finally fulfilled the meaning of his name (*Onesimus* means "useful" or "beneficial"): "Formerly he was useless to you, but now he is indeed *useful* to you and to me" (vs. 11). Later Paul redeploys the pun: "Yes, brother, I want some

benefit from you in the Lord" (vs. 20). Paul clearly wants Onesimus to continue in his service (vs. 13) but he has a legal and moral hurdle. Onesimus is Philemon's property, and technically Paul cannot retain him without Philemon's consent and approval. In fact, Philemon has every right to expect Paul to return his property to him and to require Onesimus (1) to make restitution for the damages Philemon incurred at his hands and (2) to face punishment for those actions. Hence Paul faces a delicate situation, and the letter he writes to Philemon is his attempt at solving this problem. He writes to Philemon and sends Onesimus to deliver the letter—thus returning the runaway slave to his master—but in the letter he asks Philemon to forgive Onesimus's transgressions and return him voluntarily to Paul's service.

Rhetorical Strategy of Philemon

To persuade Philemon to grant Paul (and Onesimus) this huge favor, Paul employs a variety of rhetorical techniques. The type of rhetoric used is *deliberative*, in that Paul seeks to convince Philemon to take some action in the future. According to scholar Walter Taylor, "The letter exhibits the three major divisions of deliberative rhetoric as found in Aristotle, Cicero, and Quintilian: the exordium, which praises the recipients with the goal of winning their approval (vv. 4–7); the body or proof, which tries to persuade the recipients about a future course of action (vv. 8–16); and the peroration, which is a summary and emotional appeal (vv. 17–22)."[26]

---

26. Walter F. Taylor, *Paul: Apostle to the Nations* (Minneapolis: Fortress, 2012), 280.

The *invention* in the letter consists primarily of artistic rather than external proofs; Paul does not employ any witnesses or cite any authoritative documents but rather creates his own arguments. These arguments make use of all three sources: ethos, pathos, and logos. In terms of *ethos* (arguments based on the good character of the speaker), Paul continually reminds Philemon of his status as an apostle of Christ who is dedicating his life and sacrificing his freedom on behalf of the gospel. When he makes the crucial request for Philemon to release Onesimus from his service and transfer his allegiance to Paul, he asserts that he would be a worthy recipient of such a favor. He speaks of his imprisonment four separate times in the space of twenty-three verses (Philem. 1, 10, 13, 23), apparently to remind Philemon of both his need and his unquestionable integrity.

The letter is rich in its use of *pathos*, as Paul calls upon the emotions of Philemon in a number of ways. Paul appeals to Philemon's *pity*, not only in speaking so often of his imprisonment but also in suggesting that his advanced age puts him in special need of assistance (Philem. 9). He also makes it clear to Philemon that he very much needs Onesimus: "I am sending him back to you, sending my very heart" (vs. 12).[27]

In the thanksgiving, Paul *flatters* Philemon and speaks in particular of his reputation for love: "I thank my God always when I remember you in my prayers, because I hear of *your love* and of the faith which you have toward the Lord Jesus and all the saints. . . . For I have derived much joy and comfort from *your love*, my brother" (Philem. 4–7). When he gets around to requesting the favor he desires, Paul again refers to love: "Accordingly, though I am bold enough in Christ to command you to do what is required, yet *for love's sake* I prefer to appeal to you" (vv. 8–9).

Paul also appeals to Philemon's *loyalty* and *gratitude*. He repeatedly refers to Philemon as his "brother" (Philem. 7, 20). He implies that he and Philemon are engaged in the same effort—winning the world for Christ—and because of this any request he makes should automatically find Philemon inclined to comply: "So *if you consider me your partner*, receive him [Onesimus] as you would receive me" (vs. 17). He reminds Philemon that he owes Paul far more than Paul is requesting of him now, for Paul, by his conversion of Philemon, has made possible his very salvation: "I . . . say nothing of your owing me even your own self" (vs. 19). Given how much Paul has done for Philemon, he suggests, the favor he is asking now is of the most trivial sort, and there should be no question of Philemon's willingness to grant it: "Confident of your obedience, I write to you, knowing that you will do even more than I say" (vs. 21).

Finally, Paul appeals to Philemon's sense of *decency*. To forgive Onesimus, to release him from his service, and to allow him to return to the imprisoned Paul and be helpful to him is obviously (to Paul) something that is deep-down *good*. Paul apparently feels he is almost doing Philemon a favor by giving him such a golden opportunity to demonstrate his munificence and generosity, and to receive full credit for it: "I preferred to do nothing without your consent, in order that *your goodness* might not be by compulsion but of your own free will" (Philem. 14).

In terms of *logos*, Paul employs a number of logical arguments. He insists that Philemon's financial condition will not be harmed by his

---

27. The Greek word here means "bowels" (the same word is used in vs. 7: literally, "The bowels of the saints have been refreshed through you"). The bowels or intestines were used as a metaphor for the inner person, because they were thought to be the location of strong emotions; Taylor, *Paul: Apostle to the Nations*, 284. Modern people tend to refer to the emotional seat of the body as the heart, and hence translators often prefer that term for rendering Paul's meaning in Philem. 7 and 12.

forgiveness of Onesimus's debt, for Paul promises to compensate Philemon: "If he has wronged you at all, or owes you anything, charge that to my account. I, Paul, write this with my own hand, I will repay it" (Philem. 18–19). Of course, Paul goes on to say that Philemon owes him everything, implying that it would be rather bad form for Philemon to actually demand money from Paul. Nonetheless, Paul insists that if Philemon chooses to be so petty, he stands ready to make good on his promise.

Paul also strongly suggests it is God's will that Onesimus be allowed to continue in his service. There is something about Onesimus finally becoming "useful" that suggests it was his destiny to leave Philemon's service and enter Paul's: "Perhaps this is why he was parted from you for a while, that you might have him back for ever, no longer as a slave but more than a slave, as a beloved brother, especially to me but how much more to you, both in the flesh and in the Lord" (Philem. 15–16).

Paul, the Bible, and Slavery

As harmless as it seems, Paul's letter to Philemon was destined to play a key role in the most divisive moral issue of the nineteenth century in the United States: slavery. After the Second Great Awakening, a religious revival between 1790 and 1850, the United States was full of zealous Christians seeking to purge the nation of sin and reform society along biblical lines. For many, America's most heinous, ungodly crimes were the slave trade, the holding of human beings in bondage, and the inhumane treatment of slaves by their masters. To abolitionists, it could not be more obvious that a good and loving God would never approve of owning another person, depriving people of liberty and dignity on account of the color of their skin, selling children away from their mothers and fathers, or inflicting terrible punishments on slaves who were insolent, disobedient, or runaways.

On the other hand, slave owners and other defenders of the institution of slavery were comforted that the Bible seemed to approve of keeping people in bondage. There are no explicit condemnations of slavery in the Bible. In the Old Testament, the existence of slavery seems to be virtually taken for granted, and God himself is frequently quoted as speaking of slavery as if he approved of it (Exod. 21:2–6;

Lev. 25:44–46). United States court rulings favoring slavery frequently invoked Genesis 9:25 where descendants of Ham (who are conveniently identified with dark-skinned people) are subject to a perpetual curse of slavery. Jesus never condemns slavery in the Gospels, and he tells several parables involving slaves without any hint of disapproval (e.g., Matt. 24:45–51). The deutero-Pauline letter to Titus is rather explicit in its acceptance of slavery: "Bid slaves to be submissive to their masters and to give satisfaction in every respect; they are not to be refractory, nor to pilfer, but to show entire and true fidelity, so that in everything they may adorn the doctrine of God our Savior" (Titus 2:9–10).

The letter to Philemon could be seen as either a singular exception or another in the long list of slavery-supporting passages. Abolitionists stressed that Paul apparently asks Philemon to release Onesimus from slavery and claimed this showed his disapproval of the practice. That Paul speaks of the enslaved Onesimus as "useless" and the potentially liberated Onesimus as "useful" seemed to abolitionists to confirm their view.

By contrast, slaveholders took comfort in that (1) when Paul discovers a runaway slave, he returns him to his owner, and (2) in asking

continued

Paul, the Bible, and Slavery *continued*

Philemon for his approval with respect to what to do next with Onesimus, he accepts the fact that Onesimus is Philemon's property and Philemon has the final say on his future. Moreover, even if Paul was asking for Onesimus's emancipation, slavery supporters insisted, that does not necessarily mean he felt *all* slaves should be released.

However, it is not certain that Paul was encouraging Philemon to free Onesimus from slavery; Paul might be asking Philemon to transfer ownership of Onesimus to him. Paul does not explicitly refer to setting Onesimus free; readers simply assume this meaning from the phrase "no longer a slave." Modern scholars point out that Paul's phrasing—"that you might have him back forever, no longer as a slave but more than a slave, as a beloved brother" (Philem. 15-16)—does not necessarily mean that Onesimus should be set free.[28] Paul might be telling Philemon that Onesimus will no longer be *merely* a slave, but will now be a slave *and* a "beloved brother." In fact, when Paul concludes by asking Philemon to let him have "some benefit" (vs. 20), the word "some" is not actually present in the Greek, and the word for "benefit" is *onaimen*, the word from which the name Onesimus is derived. So, Paul might actually mean, "Let me have Onesimus, the slave."[29]

Even without this complication, the two sides in the slavery debate both claimed Philemon as their biblical support. Ultimately, the antislavery side prevailed, but it was not because they convinced Southerners the Bible disapproved of owning slaves. In truth, supporters of slavery probably had the stronger claim in terms of biblical support,[30] unless one claimed (as abolitionists did) that the "love command" of Jesus was (1) incompatible with slavery, and (2) so basic to Christianity that it trumped any apparent support for slavery elsewhere.[31]

At the least, the eighteenth-century debate over slavery showed that it was not easy to reform American society along biblical lines. For one thing, people disagreed about what a "biblical" society would look like. Moreover, because such disagreements could grow divisive and violent, the realization that a harsh, nomadic society such as that of ancient Israel might not be the best model for a modern, liberal, democratic state, led many Americans to conclude that perhaps religion and politics did not mix well. Those who supported separation between church and state began to battle biblical reformers in courts of law and in public opinion, with first one side (separation advocates in the early to mid-twentieth century) and then the other (conservative evangelicals in the latter half of the twentieth century) alternately holding the upper hand.[32]

---

28. Bart Ehrman proposes the following analogy: "If I were to say to a female acquaintance, 'I love you not as a woman but as a friend,' this would not be to deny her gender!"; Bart Ehrman, *The New Testament: A Historical Introduction to the New Testament Writings*, 6th ed. (New York: Oxford University Press, 2016), 369.

29. Ibid.

30. The earliest and strongest supporters of abolition, the Quakers, were a distinctive sect because they did not rely only on the Bible for revealed truth. Instead, they claimed each person has an "Inner Light" through which God might speak. Not only did this allow for new (antislavery) revelations, it also suggested all people were equal before God regardless of race, because everyone possessed the same Inner Light. See David Sehat, *The Myth of American Religious Freedom* (New York: Oxford University Press, 2011), 74, 85.

31. Abolitionists also commonly argued that biblical slavery was not nearly as cruel as what resulted from the African slave trade but was a different kind of slavery altogether. See, e.g., Willard M. Swartley, *Slavery, Sabbath, War, and Women: Case Issues in Biblical Interpretation* (Scottdale, PA: Herald, 1983), 41–43. However, whatever differences there might have been, the premise of owning another human being remains the same.

32. See Sehat, *The Myth of American Religious Freedom, passim.*

Finally, Paul makes several appeals to his *authority*. Paul indicates that as an apostle he could simply command Philemon to do what he wants him to do (Philem. 8) and that he is only phrasing this as a request so Philemon can gain the credit for having done the right thing of his own free will rather than by "compulsion" (vs. 14). All this makes it clear that even though Philemon seems to be free to make his own choice about Onesimus, he really has no choice at all. If he resists Paul's will, Paul can simply order him to comply. By the end of the letter, Paul has made this so clear that he (perhaps unconsciously) slips back into the language of compulsion rather than free choice: "Confident of your *obedience*, I write to you, knowing you will do even more than I say" (vs. 21). In addition, it is perhaps intentional that Paul addresses this letter not only to Philemon but also to two other named individuals and to the "church in your [Philemon's] house" (vs. 2). Paul apparently intends this letter, like the others he wrote to his churches, to be read aloud to the entire congregation. Therefore, if Philemon were to defy Paul's will, everyone would know it. Such disobedience would probably result in strong public disapproval, and Paul's raising of this fear in Philemon might be intended as a final way to secure his compliance. Paul seems to leave nothing to chance.

The preceding rhetorical analysis is rather exhaustive, something that is only permitted by the brevity of the letter to Philemon. But such a thorough analysis of at least one letter is useful. It illustrates the practice of rhetorical criticism and shows that Paul's letters are especially suited to this kind of examination. Paul was a most persuasive fellow. No one could have been as successful a street-corner preacher as Paul was without superior rhetorical skills. But clearly Paul was a master of argumentation not only in person, but in print. His letters are full of arguments, more of which are considered in the next chapter.

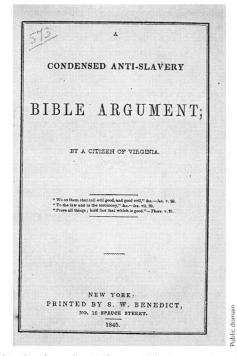

In his *Condensed Anti-Slavery Bible Argument* (1845), George Bourne (1780-1845) pointed out that the Bible counts "menstealers" among the "ungodly and . . . sinners" (1 Tim. 1:9-10, KJV). The passage, however, does not unambiguously condemn slavery per se.

Key Terms

deutero-Pauline	deliberative rhetoric	logos	thanksgiving
interpolation	judicial rhetoric	enthymeme	body
gloss	epideictic rhetoric	epistle	parenesis
rhetoric	invention	sender	Onesimus
rhetorical situation	ethos	addressee	Philemon
rhetorical strategy	pathos	greeting	

Review Questions

1. What are the arguments for and against the authenticity of 1 Corinthians 14:33b–35?

2. What are the three main branches of rhetoric? How do they correspond to particular rhetorical situations?

3. What is the difference between external proofs and artistic proofs? Give examples of each.

4. What are the three sorts of arguments available to an author or speaker when constructing artistic proofs as part of the invention of a discourse?

5. What are the components of the Hellenistic letter (epistle)? How does Paul's letter to Philemon illustrate each part?

6. What is the rhetorical situation of Paul's letter to Philemon?

7. What arguments does Paul use in his effort to persuade Philemon to follow the course of action he recommends?

Discussion Questions

1. Can you think of good examples of the use of ethos, pathos, and logos in modern public discourse? What are some of the most egregious examples of the various logical fallacies you have heard?

2. Do you think that Paul wanted to free Onesimus? Or do you think he wanted a slave of his own?

3. The slavery issue is settled, for the most part, but there are many other modern political and moral issues where the Bible is invoked on one side or another. What are some examples of this? Think of one example; on which side of this issue do people make the better case that their position is supported by the Bible? Explain your choice. How important are such arguments in determining your own position on issues? Why is it important to so many people? Should it be?

Bibliography and Suggestions for Further Study

(Books and websites that are accessible for general undergraduates are marked with an asterisk; other sources listed are appropriate for advanced students.)

Bornkamm, Günther. *Paul, Paulus.* New York: Harper & Row, 1971.

*Kennedy, George A. *New Testament Interpretation through Rhetorical Criticism.* Chapel Hill: University of North Carolina Press, 1984.

*Roetzel, Calvin J. *The Letters of Paul: Conversations in Context.* Louisville: Westminster John Knox, 1998.

Sanders, E. P. *Paul.* New York: Oxford University Press, 1991.

*Sehat, David. *The Myth of American Religious Freedom.* New York: Oxford University Press, 2011.

Stendahl, Krister. *Paul among Jews and Gentiles, and Other Essays.* Philadelphia: Fortress, 1976.

Swartley, Willard M. *Slavery, Sabbath, War, and Women: Case Issues in Biblical Interpretation.* Scottdale, PA: Herald, 1983.

*Taylor, Walter F. *Paul, Apostle to the Nations: An Introduction.* Minneapolis: Fortress, 2012.

16
CHAPTER

Paul's Correspondence with the Thessalonians, Philippians, and Galatians

Like the letter to Philemon, each of Paul's genuine letters is *occasional*—written to meet the concrete needs of discrete, first-century Christian communities, most of which Paul had founded and whose unique history, character, and challenges Paul knew well. Small inconsistencies between the letters indicate that Paul tailored his message somewhat to the particular audience he was addressing. For example, he speaks more negatively of Judaism in letters where his converts are being tempted to adopt Jewish beliefs and practices that Paul thought inappropriate, but he speaks positively of Judaism in other letters where his audience seems to believe that Judaism had no place in God's plan of salvation or that the Jews had been utterly forsaken by God.

When Paul was alive he probably would not have approved if someone had read one of his letters to a community to whom Paul did not address it, but after his death this is exactly what happened. Some of his letters were preserved and collected, and they began to be cited as scripture. There is no question that Paul could not have anticipated the remarkable afterlife that his letters had after his passing, wherein they became the guideposts for millions of Christian communities beyond the six fledgling churches that Paul's genuine letters were originally intended to guide. Surely Paul would have been surprised to learn these letters would serve as a main blueprint

for the next two thousand years of Christianity. It is perfectly legitimate to read Paul's letters today and apply them to modern situations, as Christian communities do. But the question here is this: What purpose did each letter serve in its *original* context?

Paul's Letter to the Thessalonians

First Thessalonians is widely believed to be the first of Paul's genuine letters, which makes it the earliest surviving piece of Christian literature. Written probably around 51 CE, the letter is addressed to a community of Greeks that Paul and his coworkers Timothy and Silvanus had recently converted to Christianity. After founding the church in Thessalonica, Paul left for southern Greece to engage in further missionary work, but he worried terribly about the Thessalonians' fragile new faith and was anxious for news about them.

Greece at the time was divided into two Roman provinces: Macedonia (north) and Achaia (south). Achaia was home to the raucous seaport of Corinth and Athens, the city-state remembered for democracy, philosophers, playwrights, and orators. Paul is said to have visited these cities and founded churches in them. In the north,

Paul's journeys took him along the northeast coast of Greece, where the district capital of Thessalonica was found. Paul came to Thessalonica after being driven out of Philippi, another Macedonian city (Acts 16:11–17:1; 1 Thess. 2:2).

Rhetorical Situation

One can generally deduce the kinds of challenges a Pauline church was experiencing from Paul's letters. So, if Paul writes to a congregation that he wishes they would stop suing each other (1 Cor. 6:1–8), it is safe to say that Paul has heard that litigation is plaguing that church. One must be careful about this, however, because not every statement by Paul is necessarily directed at a particular problem that the community is experiencing. If one overhears a man saying to his college freshman daughter on the phone, "Please stay away from those wild fraternity parties," one might conclude that this father has heard his daughter is partying heavily and that he is gravely concerned. On the other hand, this could just be a piece of fatherly advice based on a general concern that this sort of behavior is common on college campuses, and not something prompted by hard information about the daughter's wayward behavior. It is easy to misinterpret when one hears only one side of a conversation.

Readers of 1 Thessalonians face a similar dilemma. Certain aspects of the situation in Thessalonica are quite clear from Paul's letter, while others are ambiguous. To begin with, it is clear that Paul worried especially about the faith of the Thessalonians because they were experiencing persecution. He speaks frequently of the affliction that the Thessalonians are undergoing (1 Thess. 1:6; 2:14; 3:3–4, 7), but does not specify the precise nature of the persecution. Acts suggests that the source of this persecution was the synagogue (Acts 17:5–10), but Paul makes it clear that the Thessalonians suffered at the hands of their own "countrymen" (1 Thess. 2:14), that is, from Gentiles.[1] Paul feared that these recent converts would be "moved by these afflictions" (3:3) to abandon their Christian faith.

Despite a strong desire to visit the Thessalonians in person, Paul was unable to do so: "We endeavored the more eagerly and with great desire to see you face to face, because we wanted to come to you—I, Paul, again and again—but Satan hindered us" (1 Thess. 2:17–18).[2] The hindrance of Satan most likely refers to Paul being in prison and unable to travel. Thus detained, Paul sent one of his associates in his place, his coworker **Timothy** (3:5–6).

Timothy returned with a glowing report about how the Thessalonians were standing firm in the face of persecution and remained as loyal to Christ (and to Paul) as ever (1 Thess. 3:6–8). Paul was overjoyed at Timothy's report, and this joy helps account for the generally pleasant tone of the letter and the ebullient thanksgiving (1:2–10) with which it begins.

Timothy apparently brought Paul a full report along with certain theological questions from the Thessalonians; 1 Thessalonians provides Paul's answer to these questions. This much is clear. What is less clear is whether Timothy also related to Paul that there was murmuring against Paul or that the Thessalonians were exhibiting unethical behavior.

---

1. The full statement by Paul makes this clearer: "For you, brethren, became imitators of the churches of God in Christ Jesus which are in Judea; for you suffered the same things from your own countrymen as they did from the Jews" (1 Thess. 2:14). It is possible, of course, that local Roman authorities were *informed* by Jews about trouble-making Christians, but Jews were clearly not the source of the actual persecution. The RSV is the default version used in this chapter.

2. Here we see another example of Paul lapsing into first-person address in a letter that is ostensibly from three persons (Paul, Silvanus, and Timothy; see 1 Thess. 1:1).

The theory that Paul is responding to murmuring against him stems from some defensive-sounding remarks Paul makes. In chapter 2, Paul rehearses his initial encounter with the Thessalonians, but distinctly emphasizes his integrity as an apostle. He notes the courage that it required for him and his companions to preach the word in Thessalonica, given that they had been "shamefully treated" (1 Thess. 2:2) and driven out of the nearby city of Philippi. He reminds his readers that he never asked for or accepted money from them, but instead worked for his keep (2:9). He insists that he did not win their conversion by trickery or flattery (2:5), but simply by preaching the truth. Paul did not seek personal glory or make demands on the people of Thessalonica, although his authority as an apostle might have entitled him to do so (2:6). When Paul mentions that his behavior, and that of his companions, was "holy and righteous and blameless" (2:10), he may be implying that there was never any hint of sexual immorality attached to himself or his team.

Did Paul say all of these things because segments of the Thessalonian church were claiming that he was a greedy, deceitful, opportunistic charlatan who took advantage of his flock and fled at the first sign of trouble? Many scholars believe that is the case, and argue that the body of the letter begins with 1 Thessalonians 2:1 and that Paul's first purpose is **apologetic**, that is, that he seeks to defend himself against charges made against him.[3] However, other scholars believe that all of chapters 2–3 is part of an extended *thanksgiving*, and that the body of the letter does not in fact begin until 4:1. In this case Paul's purpose in chapter 2 is not apologetic, and no accusations may have been made against him.

The latter view has certain advantages. First, although Paul adopts a somewhat defensive tone in 1 Thessalonians 2, it is nowhere near as defensive as his tone in Galatians, where most certainly strong accusations were being made against him. Galatians shows that Paul did not respond to these kinds of charges in such calm and measured tones as one finds in 1 Thessalonians. Second, Paul probably would not have exhibited such a generally favorable attitude toward the Thessalonians had they been saying such terrible things about him. And finally, there are alternate explanations for Paul's statements in chapter 2. In this part of the letter, Paul is preparing his readers to listen to and hopefully accept his advice about ethical matters and trust his answers to their theological questions. In order to prepare them, he needs to remind his audience that he is a man of wisdom, integrity, and character. In other words, Paul's arguments in this portion of the letter fall into the category of *ethos*. As described in chapter 15, *ethos* involves character, and "may be defined as the credibility that the author or speaker is able to establish in his work. The audience is induced to trust what he says because they trust him, as a good man or an expert on the subject."[4] The author must present himself as wise, virtuous, and benevolent in order to engender the good will of his audience and make them more amenable to persuasion.

---

3. As noted in chapter 12, an "apology" in this sense is not a statement of remorse and contrition, but rather an argumentative self-defense such as the one given by Socrates in Athens when he is accused of corrupting the young, preserved in Plato's *Apology*. Calvin Roetzel, for example, argues that Paul is engaged in apologetic in 1 Thessalonians 2. "In spite of his best efforts, Paul had not escaped the charge that his preaching was for personal gain. His sudden departure confirmed the suspicions of some that he, like the wandering preachers of pagan cults, had breezed into town, covered his greed with false pretenses, lined his pockets with money from the church, and then abandoned his converts when he came under fire from Gentile officials"; Calvin Roetzel, *The Letters of Paul: Conversations in Context* (Louisville: Westminster John Knox, 1998), 81.

4. George A. Kennedy, *New Testament Interpretation through Rhetorical Criticism* (Chapel Hill: University of North Carolina Press, 1984), 15.

This was especially important for Paul because he was part of a most disreputable profession. He is essentially the equivalent of a modern televangelist—a scandal-ridden occupation widely assumed to be populated by scoundrels.[5] The reputation of the traveling evangelist was not much better in Paul's time. Many of them peddled bogus cures, took advantage of desperate people, and demanded substantial fees for their services. These negative stereotypes were always in the air, and Paul needed constantly to distinguish himself from the frauds and charlatans that travelled many of the same roads that he did. Paul reminds his readers that they trusted him earlier precisely because he *refused* to flatter them or take money from them. Thus Paul's defensiveness in 1 Thessalonians 2 is probably preemptive and perhaps even a bit unconscious, rather than reflecting a report by Timothy to Paul of a hostile attitude toward him.

Similarly, when Paul urges the Thessalonians to abstain from sexual immorality (1 Thess. 4:3–8), to cultivate love for their fellow Christians (4:9–10), to live quietly and mind their own affairs, and to work hard and gain the respect of outsiders (4:11–12), one could take this as a sign that Timothy had reported to Paul that the church in Thessalonica was a hotbed of fornication, adultery, hatred, and sloth—and some scholars believe that something like this was the case.[6]

Again, though, a bit of caution is probably warranted. All of Paul's letters contain *parenesis* (commands, usually of an ethical nature), and Paul need not have heard definite reports about fornication or laziness to remind his congregations to be diligent and to avoid sexual immorality. Indeed, Paul's phrasing suggests that the Thessalonians' behavior is already excellent, and that he writes about ethical matters only to urge them to even greater heights of righteousness: "Finally, brethren, we beseech and exhort you in the Lord Jesus, that as you learned from us how you ought to live and to please God, *just as you are doing*, you do so more and more" (1 Thess. 4:1); "But concerning love of the brethren you have no need to have any one write to you, for you yourselves have been taught by God to love one another; and *indeed you do love all the brethren* throughout Macedonia. But we exhort you, brethren, to do so more and more" (4:9–10).

If Paul is not writing to defend himself against scurrilous accusations or to chastise the Thessalonians for bad behavior, why does he pen this letter? The answer is found in 1

---

5. One could cite hundreds of examples, but among the more prominent recent cases are the following. (1) Jim Bakker (1987): Bakker was jailed for fraud after misappropriating millions of dollars of donations and deposits for his Christian "Disneyland," the Heritage USA theme park in Charlotte, N.C. Prosecutors showed that Bakker conned thousands of people into paying for the lavish lifestyle of himself and his wife Tammy Faye Bakker and financing a bribe for a church secretary he had allegedly sexually assaulted. (2) Robert Tilton (1991): Tilton promised to intercede with the Lord on behalf of viewers who sent in prayer requests along with their money donations. Hidden TV cameras later showed that, while the donations went immediately to the bank, the prayer requests were consigned to the trash without Tilton's having ever seen them. (3) Jimmy Swaggart (1988, 1992): Swaggart was a conservative moralist who railed against the sexual immorality of others—especially homosexuals—but was then found in the company of prostitutes whom he asked to replicate with him the sex acts he had seen in pornographic material. (4) Benny Hinn (2004): Hinn claimed to be a genuine faith healer with "documented" miracles. Even today he routinely sells out huge arenas and has millions of television viewers. But all his miraculous claims were debunked by a carefully reported, hour-long Canadian documentary that later aired on *Dateline NBC*.

6. Again, Roetzel is typical of those who take this position: "Timothy also brought word about tensions within the church itself over the idle, the fainthearted, and the weak (5:14). . . . Some were so engrossed with the things of the spirit that they refused to work. They demanded support from others in the congregation (4:11–12; 5:14, 19–22) and rejected the need for instruction (5:12). Thus, the leisure of some was bought at the cost of added toil for others. Resentments flared up, tensions mounted, and disorder threatened the very existence of the church"; *The Letters of Paul*, 81–82. However, there does not appear to be enough evidence in the letter to justify these conclusions.

Thessalonians 4:13–5:11, where it is revealed that Timothy has brought back to Paul a request that he answer two questions they have about the end of the world and the second coming. When he was first among them, Paul apparently preached to them that they were living in the last days. Jesus Christ, who was crucified and then raised from the dead, would soon return to judge the world and collect all of his people. Sinners and worshipers of false gods would be punished, while mercy and peace would be granted to the faithful. People must repent and watch for Jesus' imminent **advent**.[7]

Given the apparent passage of time since Paul's conversion of the Thessalonians, they have begun to wonder about two things. First, what happens to those believers who die prior to Jesus' second coming? Will they miss out on the kingdom of God because of their untimely deaths? Second, why was it taking so long for Jesus to return? How soon exactly should they expect the end to occur?

Rhetorical Strategy

Given the simplicity of the rhetorical situation, Paul's strategy is just to answer the questions and hope that his pleasant demeanor, his reminders to the Thessalonians of their strong previous relationship of love and trust with him, and his authority as an apostle will lead them to agree. With respect to the first question, Paul reassures his readers that those who have died will not miss out on salvation, because when Jesus returns there will be a massive resurrection of the dead, and those people will face judgment along with the living. In fact, Paul writes, the dead in Christ will *precede* living believers on the way to heaven.

But we would not have you ignorant, brethren, concerning those who are asleep, that you may not grieve as others do who have no hope. For since we believe that Jesus died and rose again, even so, through Jesus, God will bring with him those who have fallen asleep. For this we declare to you by the word of the Lord, that we who are alive, who are left until the coming of the Lord, shall not precede those who have fallen asleep. For the Lord himself will descend from heaven with a cry of command, with the archangel's call, and with the sound of the trumpet of God. And the dead in Christ will rise first; then we who are alive, who are left, shall be caught up together with them in the clouds to meet the Lord in the air; and so we shall always be with the Lord. Therefore comfort one another with these words. (1 Thess. 4:13–18)

The Thessalonians' other question to Paul concerns "the times and the seasons," a reference to the timing of the end of the world and the final judgment (1 Thess. 5:1). Paul has apparently told them that Jesus will be returning *soon*, and his language in 1 Thessalonians 4 reinforces this message. Paul twice says he expects that the second coming of Christ will occur within his lifetime (1 Thess. 4:15, 17). But how soon *exactly* will all this happen?

It is difficult to live in a state of feverish anticipation for a long time. A firm belief in the imminence of the end of the world led many early Christians to extremes of repentance and piety, and this kind of intense preparation cannot be sustained indefinitely. Nonetheless, Paul proceeds to tell the Thessalonians they have no choice but to do exactly that. Paul does not provide any specific hints as to how much longer

---

7. Advent means "coming," which is why it is used in some Christian liturgical calendars to refer to the four weeks prior to Christmas, in which the faithful anticipate the arrival or "coming" of Jesus on the day of his birth, December 25. This is also why Christian denominations that preach the nearness of the end of the world are known as "Adventist." Such denominations include the Jehovah's Witnesses (founded by Charles Taze Russell in the 1870s) and the Seventh Day Adventists (which sprang from the "Millerite" movement started in the 1840s by William Miller).

To Meet the Lord in the Air: The Rapture

The film *Left Behind* (originally made in 2000, remade in 2014) begins with scenes from the everyday lives of ordinary people. A flight attendant ponders her relationship with a married pilot. A skeptical reporter plans his next big story. Suddenly the world is thrown into chaos when millions of people simply disappear into thin air. Planes crash when their pilot seats are found empty, occupied only by their flight uniforms. Cars collide when their drivers vanish. All of the children are gone, also leaving behind only their clothing. The reporter and the flight attendant are still there, though, with millions of others who have been "left behind," wondering what in the world has just happened. One thing they realize quickly is that—besides the children—all the people who are missing were devout, conservative Christians.

This film is based on the bestselling book *Left Behind*, by Timothy LaHaye and Jerry Jenkins, from a sixteen-part series that has sold more than sixty-five million copies. The disappearance of the faithful in the narrative represents the authors' view of an end-times event that has come to be called the **rapture**. In the books, the rapture is followed by an upheaval in which a Romanian politician connives to become secretary-general of the United Nations and uses that position to create an oppressive one-world government. In reality this politician is the Antichrist, and

he comes to be opposed in his efforts by the members of the Tribulation Force—"left behind" people who have realized the error of their ways and become born-again Christians. After seven years of tribulation, the second coming of Christ occurs and Christ leads the forces of God to final victory in the battle of Armageddon, which is followed by the millennial ("thousand-year") reign of Christ.

Although the *Left Behind* series purports to be based on biblical prophecy, the biblical exegesis on which it is founded is highly suspect and does not represent the majority opinion of biblical scholars or the official teachings of most Christian denominations. Critics charge that Lahaye and Jenkins, as well as other authors in the same tradition, such as Hal Lindsey, are biased by their **premillennial** and **dispensationalist**[8] theology to read the Bible in ways contrary to sound scholarship. These authors take disparate passages from a variety of books (especially Ezekiel, Daniel, Isaiah, and Revelation) and then combine them to produce a single vision of the end-times that was probably not held by any of the authors of these books. They then proceed to interpret their selected verses as if the events referred to in the prophecies are all clearly being fulfilled in the present day, rather than referring to events that were anticipated in the near future[9] at the time of the books' writing.

continued

---

8. Dispensationalism, developed by J. N. Darby in the nineteenth-century, is the idea that God has dealt differently with humans over the course of several epochs in human history, called "dispensations." The most popular schema posits seven dispensations: (1) the time of innocence in the garden of Eden; (2) the "antediluvian" (pre-flood) period, in which people were guided by conscience; (3) the dispensation of civil government; (4) the patriarchal dispensation beginning with Abraham; (5) the Mosiac period, in which people were guided by the law; (6) the period of the church, in which people are granted God's grace through Christ; and (7) the millennial kingdom. "Premillennialism" is the belief that Jesus' return (and the rapture) will take place before his millennial reign.

9. Apocalyptic literature often includes predictions of events that have, in fact, already taken place at the time of writing; typically the author backdates the time of the book's composition to make it look as though the future was correctly foreseen by the prophet. See chapter 20.

To Meet the Lord in the Air: The Rapture *continued*

Premillennial Dispensationalism: The Seven "Dispensations"

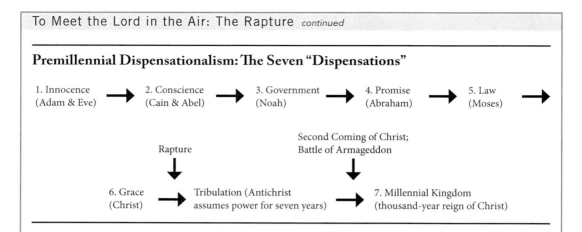

1. Innocence (Adam & Eve) → 2. Conscience (Cain & Abel) → 3. Government (Noah) → 4. Promise (Abraham) → 5. Law (Moses) →

Rapture ↓

Second Coming of Christ; Battle of Armageddon ↓

6. Grace (Christ) → Tribulation (Antichrist assumes power for seven years) → 7. Millennial Kingdom (thousand-year reign of Christ)

For example, in Daniel 7 the prophet sees a vision of four beasts, which represent four great kingdoms. In the author's mind, these kingdoms were almost certainly those of the Babylonians, Medes, Persians, and Greeks. The fourth kingdom is divided among ten kings, just as the Greek empire was divided up by his generals after the death of Alexander the Great. One king then arises who is different from the others, and he defeats three of the other kings. This is almost certainly a reference to the Seleucid king Antioches IV Epiphanes, a mortal enemy of the Jews whose rule was ended by the Maccabean revolt of 167–164 BCE. However, Hal Lindsey has claimed that the one "different" king is in fact the Antichrist,[10] and that the "ten kings" refers to an alliance of nations that supports the Antichrist. Lindsey writes that this ten-nation alliance is to be identified with the European Union, and that the formation of this coalition is a sign that the Antichrist is coming and that the rapture is at hand. Never mind that the European Union originally had six members, not ten. It

did have ten members later (1981–1986), but as of 2018 included twenty-eight nations.

Of course there are many Christians who believe Lindsey is barking up the wrong tree altogether. Some Christian groups do not believe in a literal thousand-year reign of Christ following the second coming. These groups are called **amillennial**. Premillennial groups are further divided between those who believe that the rapture will precede the seven years of tribulation that will culminate in the battle of Armageddon ("pre-trib rapture") and those that hold that even believers will have to suffer through the tribulation prior to Christ's final victory ("post-trib rapture"). Obviously, Lahaye, Jenkins, and Lindsey are in the pre-trib rapture camp.

The rapture actually has very little biblical support. In fact, the *only* reference to such an event in the entire Bible is 1 Thessalonians 4:17, where Paul speaks of being "caught up" to meet the Lord in the air. In none of the genuine letters does Paul refer to the Antichrist, a period of tribulation, the battle of Armageddon, or a thousand-year reign of Christ.

his readers will have to wait for Jesus to return. He says only that, inasmuch as Christ will come again at a most *unexpected* time, they must *always*

be ready. To warn the Thessalonians not to be caught unawares, Paul compares the coming of Christ to that of a "thief in the night" (1 Thess.

---

10. The concept of the Antichrist in the *Left Behind* books has little to do with the Antichrist—or *Antichrists* (plural)—in the New Testament (1 John 2:18, 22; 4:3; 2 John 1:7).

Paul states that, at Christ's return, "we . . . will be caught up (Latin, *rapiemur*) . . . to meet the Lord in the air" (1 Thess. 4:17). The rapture has become a central belief for many fundamentalist Christians.

5:2) who does not come when the homeowners are awake and aware but waits until they have fallen asleep to break into the house. He also compares the waiting to the anticipation of the onset of labor for a pregnant woman (5:3). No one can tell exactly when labor pains will begin, but a woman in the final stages of pregnancy will always try to avoid putting herself into a position where she does not have access to the help she will need to deliver her child. Paul's advice is quite consistent with other New Testament texts that stress the unpredictability of the onset of the end-times (see Mark 13:32–33).

Paul's Letter to the Philippians

In 1 Thessalonians, Paul refers to having been "shamefully treated" in Philippi (1 Thess. 2:2). A number of problems beset the Philippian church, but Paul maintained a warm and mutually affectionate relationship with its members. Paul wrote the letter to the Philippians from prison, either from Ephesus (perhaps 55–56 CE) or Rome (ca. 58–60). When word

of his imprisonment and possible condemnation (Phil. 1:20; 2:17) reached Philippi, the Philippians sent help to Paul through Epaphroditus (2:25), who brought money and a willingness to attend to Paul's well-being. Unfortunately, he was unable to be of much service to Paul because he fell critically ill (2:26). It was after Epaphroditus's arrival and subsequent health problems that Paul wrote this letter.

Rhetorical Situation

After Epaphroditus arrived, Paul seems to have written a letter of thanks to the faithful in Philippi. Either Paul or the bearer of this letter apparently apprised the Philippians of Epaphroditus's poor health. The Philippians then wrote to Paul, raising a number of issues to which Paul responds in this letter.

First, the Philippians express their concern over Epaphroditus and request his return. Paul indicates that he is more than willing to comply and speaks glowingly and appreciatively of the risks Epaphroditus faced for his sake (Phil. 2:25–30). But more significantly, the letter of the Philippians revealed that they were facing a number of problems that required Paul's advice and attention.

It seems a quarrel had erupted between two women in the congregation, Euodia and Syntyche (Phil. 4:2–3). In addition, some local Jews were pressuring the Philippians, who may formerly have been God-fearers, to accept circumcision (3:2–11) and perhaps to forsake their new Christian faith for a more orthodox form of Judaism. Moreover, some Philippians were proclaiming Christ out of envy and rivalry, with their partisanship apparently directed against

Paul himself (1:15–17).[11] Finally, some members of the congregation minimized the importance of the cross of Christ (3:18), apparently emphasizing instead the glory of the resurrection, the salvation it made a reality, and the freedom that its promise granted to believers to act as they pleased.

These problems seem to bear little relation to each other and Paul's response to them appears to be all over the map, skipping from one topic to another. Indeed, Philippians is one of the least internally coherent letters in the Pauline corpus. Perhaps Paul is simply responding to a letter from the Philippians that similarly lacked cohesion.[12] Or Paul may have had only sketchy information about the problems in Philippi, leading him—at least at times—to flail about for answers. Many scholars have noted the unusually vague nature of Paul's responses in the first part of the letter.[13]

Another possibility, however, is that the document that now survives as a single letter to the Philippians may actually be a combination of two or more letters that Paul had written to the church at different times, addressing different problems. It is almost certain that this practice of combining letter fragments resulted in 2 Corinthians, which may contain portions of as many as four different letters (see chapter 17). The case of Philippians is less clear-cut, but some tell-tale signs are present. These include the following:[14]

- *Literary seams.* These are abrupt or awkward transitions between one part of the letter and the next, such as between Philippians 3:1 and 3:2.
- *False stops.* These occur when a letter appears to build to a conclusion and seems about to draw to a close ("Finally, my brothers and sisters . . ." in 3:1), only to continue for long stretches.
- *Odd sequencing.* These are elements not in logical order, as when Paul waits until the end of the letter to thank the Philippians for their financial support (Phil. 4:14–20), a gesture of gratitude that would normally be found in the beginning of such a letter.
- *Varying levels of specificity and concern about opponents.* In a single, unified letter it would not make much sense for Paul to speak of his opponents vaguely and without alarm in one portion of the letter, only to identify them specifically and with alarm in another portion.

Some scholars[15] defend the unity of Philippians, but for most the real question is whether the current text contains parts of two earlier letters[16] or three.[17] The three-letter hypothesis is the more popular; the usual division[18] is that the first letter was a letter of thanks Paul sent after the arrival of Epaphroditus (Phil. 4:10–20); the second was written to report on Paul's present status as a prisoner and address apparent Philippian

---

11. One possible explanation for the development of an anti-Paul faction is that his arrest and imprisonment by Rome, a polity of which the Macedonian city of Philippi was an especially proud member, had become a source of embarrassment and shame. See Walter F. Taylor, *Paul, Apostle to the Nations* (Minneapolis: Fortress, 2012), 255–56, 266.

12. Roetzel (*The Letters of Paul*, 115) notes that this view essentially suggests that "Paul addresses several types of opponents in this letter: Jews bent on winning back Gentile God-fearers, those who had slipped into morally lax habits, and believers critical of the gospel."

13. Roetzel mentions that scholars have suggested "Paul was slow to recognize the character of the opposition and is thus somewhat confused" (Ibid.).

14. This list is drawn from Taylor, *Paul, Apostle to the Nations*, 258.

15. For example, Walter Taylor, David Aune, Howard Clark Kee, Luke T. Johnson, Gordon Fee, and Werner Kümmel.

16. E. J. Goodspeed and Leander Keck are among the scholars who support the two-letter hypothesis.

17. Proponents of the three-letter hypothesis include F. W. Beare, Günther Bornkamm, Reginald H. Fuller, Helmut Koester, Ernst Lohse, and Willi Marxsen.

18. See Taylor, *Paul, Apostle to the Nations*, 258.

concerns about it (1:1–3:1; 4:4–7, 21–23); and the third was written to warn about opponents and to correct bad behavior (3:2–4:3, 8–9). One need not follow this division in order to read Philippians and understand Paul's rhetoric, but it can provide a helpful framework for understanding how the different parts of the letter might fit into a sensible schema overall.

After 40 BCE, Philippi was re-founded as a Roman colony; the Roman forum, shown here, dates to this period. The Philippians were proud that their city was a Roman colony, but Paul reminds believers there, "Our citizenship is in heaven" (Phil. 3:20).

Rhetorical Strategy

Some elements of Paul's rhetorical strategy in Philippians are too obvious to require much elaboration. Where thanks are required for gifts given by the Philippians to Paul in his imprisonment, Paul expresses gratitude (Phil. 4:14).[19] Where quarrels have erupted between fellow believers, Paul tells them to stop fighting (4:2). When some claim to have already obtained salvation in the present (3:12), Paul insists that salvation has both a present and a future dimension (resurrection from the dead). When some urge Gentile converts to receive circumcision, Paul condemns them as "dogs" (3:2). He insists that, as an especially devout and observant Jew, he once had as much reason as any preacher of circumcision to be confident "in the flesh" (3:4–6), but now, because of Christ, Paul has come to regard these landmarks of Jewish devotion

as of no avail (3:7–10).[20] When some imply that Paul's chains are a mark of shame and dishonor, he responds that Jesus endured the ultimate dishonor when he was crucified and was nonetheless exalted through resurrection. Hence Paul's suffering and imprisonment are in fact a badge of honor.[21] He even claims that people have been so impressed by his demeanor as a prisoner that it has actually "served to advance the gospel" (1:12–13). The proud Roman citizens among the Philippians should not worry about Paul appearing to be a criminal in the eyes of Rome, because their true citizenship "is in heaven" (3:20).

Other elements of the letter are less clear and have become hugely controversial. The most

---

19. Paul stresses that he did not ask for this help and could have gotten by without it, perhaps because he does not want the Philippians to think of him as a client and themselves as his patrons or benefactors. The patron/client relationship, fundamental to Roman society, conferred a superior status on the patron and a subordinate status on the client. Paul clearly wants to avoid this inference. See Ibid., 273–75.

20. These comments about Judaism might seem to suggest that Paul had come to see his former religious tradition as having no value whatsoever, but this was certainly not Paul's view, as his comments elsewhere make clear (see, for example, Rom. 9:1–5). See Roetzel, *The Letters of Paul*, 115–16. Here again one must remember the *occasional* character of Paul's letters; the unique circumstances of the opposition Paul faces in Philippi lead him to speak in such a seemingly negative fashion about his Jewish heritage.

21. See Taylor, *Paul, Apostle to the Nations*, 266.

contested part involves Paul's apparent quotation of a preexisting[22] hymn to Christ in Philippians 2:6–11. In the passage that precedes the hymn, Paul is urging the Philippians to behave selflessly, to humbly regard others as better than themselves, and to look not to their own interests but to the interests of others (2:1–4). In this, they should have the same mind as Christ Jesus:

> Who, though he was in the form of God
>   did not count equality with God
>   a thing to be grasped,
> but emptied himself,
>   taking the form of a servant,
>   being born in the likeness of men.
> And being found in human form
>   he humbled himself
>   and became obedient unto death,
>   even death on a cross.
>
> Therefore God has highly exalted him
>   and bestowed on him the name
>   which is above every name,
> that at the name of Jesus
>   every knee should bow,
>   in heaven and on earth and under
>   the earth,
> and every tongue confess
>   that Jesus Christ is Lord,
>   to the glory of God the Father.[23]

The poem is divided into two halves. The first half describes the condescension of Christ, whereby he lowered himself from a divine, heavenly status by taking on a human form, by being *incarnated* (literally, "becoming flesh"). The second half of the poem describes the exaltation or raising up of Christ, according to which his obedience to God leads to God granting him an even higher divine status than he held before his Incarnation. The first half of the poem serves Paul's rhetorical purpose: providing the Philippians with a model of the kind of humility and selflessness he hopes they will learn to exhibit. However, the part about exaltation seems to run counter to Paul's rhetorical strategy, suggesting that one's motivation for acting with humility should be the desire to receive a greater reward for oneself—that is, to behave selflessly for selfish reasons.

But the poem as a whole is important for more than rhetorical reasons. It provides a lens for viewing Pauline and pre-Pauline Christology. It is worth taking a short respite from rhetorical criticism and focusing on the underlying *theology* of this passage. Scholars debate whether the poem reflects an **exaltation Christology** or an **incarnation Christology**.[24] Exaltation Christology sees Jesus as originally an ordinary human who was exalted to divine status as a result of his exemplary behavior and obedience to God. Incarnation Christology sees Jesus as originally a divine being who lowered himself and took on a human form—becoming "incarnated"—before being exalted by God to the highest rank in heaven.

Those who see exaltation Christology here rely heavily on two arguments. One is that the mid-fifties when this letter was written, or the

---

22. There are several reasons for believing that the hymn predates Paul and was not composed by him but quoted. First, the passage has the form and structure of a poem, and Paul was no poet. Second, the passage contains a number of words that are not used elsewhere in Paul's letters—words like *form* and *grasped*. Finally, the passage does not fit its rhetorical context very well. As will be seen, Paul only really needs the first half of the poem to make his point about selflessness to the Philippians. The second half of the poem does not help this argument; indeed, it is somewhat counter-productive. Given this, the probable reason for Paul quoting the final three stanzas is that he did not feel free to quote only part of a hymn that was perhaps well-known and widely used by his readers. For a fuller account of these reasons, see Bart Ehrman, *How Jesus Became God: The Exaltation of a Jewish Preacher from Galilee* (New York: HarperCollins, 2014), 255–56.

23. This quotation is formatted to show the three-part poetic structure of the stanzas.

24. The following draws upon Ehrman, *How Jesus Became God*, 247–66.

thirties or forties when the hymn was originally composed, are simply *too early* for an incarnational Christology to appear. An incarnation Christology is a *high* Christology, and the general trend in first-century Christianity seems to have been a movement from low to high. Mark, the earliest Gospel, has the lowest Christology, while John, probably the latest, has the highest. Only in John does one find the language of incarnation. The second argument for an exaltation Christology is that there are hints here and elsewhere in Paul's writing that he thought of Jesus as a **second Adam**. The first Adam brought sin and death into the world through his disobedience, while the second Adam, Jesus, brought salvation and eternal life through obedience to God: "Just as one man's trespass led to condemnation for all, so one man's act of righteousness leads to justification and life for all. For just as by the one man's disobedience the many were made sinners, so by the one man's obedience the many will be made righteous" (Rom. 5:18–19, NRSV). The first Adam was fully human, and so presumably the second Adam must have been fully human as well and not a preexistent divine being.

Two elements of the Christ-hymn in Philippians seem to fit this interpretation. First, its description of Christ as being "in the form of God" is reminiscent of Adam being created "in the image of God" (Gen. 1:26–27). Second, the suggestion that Christ as the second Adam did not find equality with God something to be "grasped" contrasts him to the first Adam whose motivation for eating the forbidden fruit is apparently to become "like God, knowing good and evil" (Gen. 3:5).

However, these arguments are not foolproof. For one, Paul does not specifically invoke the name of Adam here as he likely would have done if this was the association he wanted his readers to make. Moreover, Paul speaks of Christ being in the "form" of God rather than being in the "image" of God; the supposed allusion to Genesis 1:26–27 is imperfect in a way that could easily have been rectified if that was the intention. But most importantly, passages in other Pauline letters clearly indicate that Paul thought of Christ as a preexistent divine being.[25]

The argument for an incarnational interpretation of the Christ-hymn in Philippians has been made by many scholars, most persuasively by Bart Ehrman in his 2014 book, *How Jesus Became God*. Ehrman solves the chronological problem of Philippians and its sources being too early for the appearance of an incarnational Christology in part by suggesting that the hymn does not imply that Jesus was *fully* divine or equal to God, at least originally. It is true that the concept of a fully divine, preexistent Logos would not enter into Christian thought until the Gospel of John, written long after Paul's time. But it was possible for earlier Christians to have thought of Christ as a preexistent divine being of *subordinate* status to God. In fact, Ehrman argues that Paul thought of the preexistent Christ as an *angel* or an angel-like being.[26] A crucial text in this regard is Galatians 4:14, where Paul writes that the Galatians received him "as an angel of God, as Christ Jesus."

In the Jewish tradition, angels[27] were seen as divine beings, as members of the heavenly

---

25. In particular, Ehrman cites the passage in which Paul speaks about the miraculous rock that provided water for Moses and the Israelites during their sojourn in the desert and concludes that "the Rock was Christ" (1 Cor. 10:4). Ehrman rightly points out that this would not have been possible for Christ "unless he existed at the time"; Ehrman, *How Jesus Became God*, 262.

26. In this regard, Ehrman is relying especially on the scholarship of Charles Gieschen and Susan Garrett (see references below).

27. In the Hebrew Bible, these beings are referred to by various (but related) terms. The Greek word *angelos*, from which the English word "angel" derives, means "messenger."

council (Gen. 1:26; Job 1:6; 2:1), as messengers for God (Gen. 22:11–18), and as intermediaries between the earthly and heavenly realms. They can be called "God," and in some passages they are indistinguishable from God[28] (Gen. 16:7–14), but they can manifest themselves as human beings (Gen. 6:2; 19:1–22).

If Paul understood Christ as having been an angel prior to his earthly manifestation as Jesus of Nazareth, then the movement in the hymn that he approvingly quotes in Philippians begins to make a great deal of sense. If the preexistent Christ were an angel, even the "chief angel" as Susan Garrett argues,[29] then he would have been a divine being ("in the form of God") but would not have been equal to God. The key part of the poem is this: "Did not count equality with God a thing to be grasped" (Phil. 2:6). The word translated by the RSV as "grasped" and by Ehrman as "grasped after" is rare and can be used in multiple senses, but Ehrman argues persuasively that usually it refers to something a person does not have but is seeking to attain.[30] Such a divine being, even if not equal to God, would need to lower himself in order to take on a human form: "But emptied himself //Taking the form of a servant//Being born in the likeness of men//And being found in human form//He humbled himself."

The hymn goes on to suggest that because the angel-become-human Christ proved to be obedient to God even unto death, God exalted him to a status above that which he formerly held in heaven, indeed a status that made him God's equal. It would not be possible for God to have exalted him *more highly* (Phil. 2:9) if he already

Why Was It So Important to Paul that Jesus Died on a Cross?

Scholars believe that the one part of the Christ-hymn in Philippians 2:6-11 that was not part of the pre-Pauline version is found in the final line of the third stanza, where the poem reads, "Became obedient unto death, even death on a cross." The phrase "even death on a cross," which disrupts the poetic balance of the hymn, is believed to be a Pauline insertion. For Paul it was crucial not just that Jesus died, and not just that he was executed, but that he was executed in a particular manner, namely crucifixion. Jesus' death would not have worked for Paul if he had died by other means, such as beheading, stoning, or natural causes. The book of Deuteronomy indicates that anyone who hangs on a tree is accursed by God (Deut. 21:23). Being killed on a cross of wood, being hung from a tree and left to rot there is seen as a clear sign of God's disapproval and hatred of a person. Paul argues that, by dying on a cross, Christ bore the curse of sin that other people deserved; in this way the death of Christ can serve a sacrificial or substitutionary function on behalf of others (Gal. 3:10-13).

But Paul believes that the same Jesus who was crucified was raised from the dead by God, a clear sign of God's approval and love. To Paul, the resurrection proves that Jesus did not deserve the curse of being hung from a tree; therefore he must have been bearing the curse that was owed to others.[31] And because Jesus bore the curse and punishment for the sin of others, their transgressions are understood to have been forgiven, and they are restored to a right relationship with God (see below) and can gain salvation.

---

28. See Charles Gieschen, *Angelomorphic Christology: Antecedents and Early Evidence* (Leiden; Boston: Brill, 1998), 57–58.

29. Susan Garrett, *No Ordinary Angel: Celestial Spirits and Christian Claims about Jesus* (New Haven: Yale University Press, 2008), 11.

30. Ehrman, *How Jesus Became God*, 263.

31. See ibid., 258.

had the highest possible status, equality with God. The final two stanzas of the hymn ("that at the name of Jesus every knee should bow, in heaven and on earth and under the earth, and every tongue confess that Jesus Christ is Lord to the glory of God the Father") echo Isaiah 45:22–23, where Yahweh says, "To me every knee shall bow, every tongue shall swear." While the passage in Isaiah insists that there is only one God and no other ("For I am God, and there is no other"), the hymn in Philippians indicates that there is another: Christ. It is only *after* his exaltation that Christ is raised to the

Depictions of the crucifixion were rare in the first centuries of the church, when crucifixion was still a common mode of execution. One of the earliest examples is this fifth-century carving from the doors of Santa Sabina, Rome.

status of God's equal, when God "bestowed on him the name which is above every name" (Phil. 2:9). This name is not Christ's by nature, but it is *bestowed upon* him by God.

This interpretation is controversial for a number of reasons. First, Galatians 4:14 has not traditionally been understood to be identifying Christ as an angel, although some recent scholars have pointed out good reasons for this interpretation.[32] Second, this interpretation runs counter to a number of later Christian theological conclusions. Later Christian tradition rules out the notion that Christ was somewhat divine prior to his Incarnation and only later came to be fully divine. Christian theology would come to think of human and divine as mutually exclusive alternatives. But Greco-Roman society viewed human and divine as two ends of a spectrum. A god could be more or less divine, and could exhibit human characteristics, and a human could be somewhat divine, or more or less so.[33]

Students of Christian history know that the idea that Christ was not always fully God, that he did not share the divine nature but had been made God by the Father, is the Arian heresy condemned at the Council of Nicea in 325. The Arians insisted that Jesus had been made God, but the council fathers insisted that Christ was "begotten, not made" and that he was "true God from true God." The position ascribed to Paul in the preceding interpretation is not *exactly* Arian—the Arian controversy was based on an understanding of a gulf between the created and the uncreated that was unknown to Paul—but there are similarities. What must be remembered here is that the Christology implicit in Paul's letters—and in the preexisting traditions he cited—represents a very early attempt to come to grips with the divinity of Christ. One cannot expect that all of the conclusions reached by the Nicene fathers almost three centuries after the death of Christ will be perfectly represented in earliest Christianity.

---

32. Ibid., 252–53.

33. Ehrman cites an inscription in the city of Mytilene that indicates that the deified Emperor Augustus could be further deified if he achieved anything more glorious than that which he had already accomplished (ibid., 39).

In the end, the opposition to an "incarnational" interpretation of the Christ-hymn along the lines proposed by Ehrman seems to rest more on theological presuppositions than exegetical arguments. The evidence for the Christ-hymn in Philippians reflecting an incarnational Christology, according to which an angel condescended to take a human form and then was exalted to a status equal to God, is quite substantial. Given how recently this theory has surfaced, however, it will take some years to determine whether it will become the scholarly consensus.

Paul's Letter to the Galatians

Galatians is an angry letter. The signs of Paul's fury are everywhere. Galatians is the only letter in the New Testament without a thanksgiving; Paul apparently feels there is nothing about the situation in Galatia worth giving thanks to God. Instead Paul immediately expresses his shock and outrage over what he sees as a personal betrayal: "I am astonished that you are so quickly deserting him who called you in the grace of Christ and are turning to a different gospel" (Gal. 1:6). Paul then curses those who have led the Galatians astray, damning them to hell twice in consecutive

verses (1:8–9).[34] He also wishes castration upon his opponents: "I wish those who unsettle you would castrate themselves" (Gal. 5:12, NRSV). As he writes, Paul is evidently feeling a variety of strong emotions; not just rage but disappointment and bewilderment over the astonishing turn of affairs: "O foolish Galatians! Who has bewitched you . . . ?" (Gal. 3:1).

What led to this outburst? The letter suggests that Paul had no reason to expect that things would turn sour in Galatia, a Roman province located in Asia Minor (modern-day Turkey). Paul had apparently fallen ill when he was travelling through Galatia, and the local people graciously took him in and nursed him back to health (Gal. 4:13–16). When Paul returned their hospitality by offering them the joy of salvation through Jesus Christ, a bond of great and lasting affection seemed to have been formed between the new converts and the apostle who had become their spiritual father. Paul goes so far as to suggest that the Galatians would have given him their eyes if necessary (4:15).

Everything seems to have changed when the Galatians were told—or determined for themselves—that Paul had not told them the entire truth.[35] They came to believe that a crucial

---

34. "As we have said before, so now I say again, if anyone is preaching to you a gospel contrary to that which you received, let him be accursed" (Gal. 1:9). The Greek word translated as "accursed" is *anathema*, the same word that church councils like Nicea (325) would later use to condemn heretics to everlasting hellfire.

35. Whether Paul's opponents in Galatia were outsiders or insiders is a matter of considerable controversy in biblical scholarship. The traditional view is that certain persons (literally "Judaizers"; Gal. 2:14), perhaps from Jerusalem and perhaps under the influence of Peter or James, followed Paul from place to place and attempted to correct his gospel by insisting that adherence to the Jewish law was necessary for salvation. This view is complicated by Paul's own account of the Jerusalem Council in Galatians 2, where he suggests that Peter and James approved of both his gospel and his apostleship, and by Paul's reference to his tormenters as "those who are being circumcised," which would not have been the case for Jewish-Christians whose circumcisions would have taken place long ago. Moreover, Paul suggests that the Galatians have gone astray not only by embracing circumcision but by continuing the pagan practice of engaging with the "elemental spirits" (4:9), observing pagan festivals (4:10), and engaging in sexual immorality (5:13), all of which was alien to conservative Jewish Christianity. This has led Johannes Munck and other scholars to speculate that Paul's opponents were not "outsiders," a word that Paul uses in other letters to describe his opponents but not in Galatians, but consisted of a faction of the Galatian community who were introduced to the Jewish scriptures by Paul and then proceeded to read passages like Gen. 17:11–14 for themselves, after which they concluded that circumcision was necessary for salvation. One problem with this view is that Paul speaks vividly of a pro-circumcision faction of "false" believers who attended the Jerusalem Council (Gal. 2:4) and who seem to have advocated much the same stance as Paul's opponents in Galatia. Still others believe that the Galatians were *syncretists*, who sought to combine what they saw as the best elements of Judaism, Christianity, and paganism into an eclectic blend uniquely suited to their needs and desires. For a complete discussion of the major views about Paul's opponents in Galatia, see Roetzel, *The Letters of Paul*, 98–100.

missing element in Paul's gospel was circumcision. Some Galatian converts submitted to circumcision and advocated that others do the same. When Paul heard about this, he became very upset.

Rhetorical Situation

Paul's response suggests that one of the problems he faced in Galatia is that his congregation had come to believe that he was not a *real* apostle and hence could not be trusted. The main basis of the challenge to Paul's authority as an apostle seems to have been the fact that Paul never knew Jesus when he was alive and was not among his earthly followers.[36] Men such as Peter and John, leaders of the church in Jerusalem, had much better apostolic credentials. They were among "the Twelve" that had formed Jesus' inner circle during his ministry and had witnessed Jesus' miracles and heard his teachings firsthand. Paul, on the other hand, could be accused of having picked up what he knew of Christianity secondhand, learning Christian teachings at the feet of others rather than receiving it directly from Christ. The fact that the "real" apostles in Jerusalem apparently all practiced and preached circumcision, combined with the Genesis 17 passage that insists on circumcision, suggested to the Galatians that Paul had misinformed them on this crucial topic.

If Paul was wrong about circumcision, the Galatians seem to have concluded, perhaps he was generally unreliable. At the time of Paul's writing, the Galatians seem to be convinced that Paul's gospel—his version of Christianity—is "from man" (or "of human origin," Gal. 1:12) rather than from God, and that Paul simply concocted his distinctive take on the significance of

Jesus Christ. Thus, to regain the loyalty of the Galatians, Paul needs to defend the legitimacy of both his apostleship and his gospel, a gospel that claimed faith in Christ was sufficient for salvation and that the grace of God had abrogated the necessity of circumcision.

Rhetorical Strategy

Despite the fact that Paul is engaged in a defense of himself and his gospel, the species of rhetoric he employs is not judicial but deliberative.[37] Paul is less concerned about the Galatians having a certain view of the past and more concerned with their future course of action: they need to be convinced that Paul's gospel is from God rather than of human origin so that they will not rely on circumcision and works of the law for their salvation. Of course, in order to persuade them that his gospel is true, Paul will need to restore his credibility as an apostle, and he begins the letter by arguing this point.

Paul begins with a simple assertion of his apostolic authority, in the very first line of the letter: "Paul, an apostle—sent neither by human commission nor from human authorities, but through Jesus Christ and God the Father" (Gal. 1:1, NRSV). He then supports this assertion with a series of arguments, each of which is designed to address particular perceived weaknesses in his claim to apostleship. The three main points Paul makes are (1) that he was once a persecutor of the Christian church; (2) that he has spent relatively little time in the company of the Jerusalem apostles such as Peter, James, and John; and (3) that at the Jerusalem Council his views prevailed and he was acknowledged as an apostle by the

---

36. There is no hint in Paul's genuine letters that he ever denied this, but whether he advertised the fact is not as certain.

37. Kennedy makes this argument in *New Testament Interpretation*, 144–46, against Hans Dieter Betz, *Galatians: A Commentary on Paul's Letter to the Churches in Galatia* (Philadelphia: Fortress, 1979). Kennedy believes Betz was misled by the presence of an "apologetic" narrative of the past in Galatians 2, where Paul seeks to recast his personal history in a way that reveals the legitimacy of his apostleship. While Galatians 2 is "defensive" in nature and would seem to suggest that the letter is thus employing judicial rhetoric, the other parts of the letter suggest otherwise. In particular, Paul's *exhortation* of the Galatians (5:1–6:10) to adopt a different course of action in the future is incompatible with judicial rhetoric but is very characteristic of deliberative rhetoric.

recognized leaders of the church. Each of these points requires some unpacking.

Paul's reference to his past as a persecutor of the Christian church seems counterintuitive. He writes, "For you have heard of my former life in Judaism, how I persecuted the church of God violently and tried to destroy it" (Gal. 1:13). How does reminding the Galatians of his vicious opposition to the followers of Christ serve his interests here? One must remember that Paul's claim to apostleship is based not on personal experience with Christ during his earthly ministry but on his allegedly having received revelation(s) from the *risen* Christ. Such revelations would naturally be of a private nature; there would be no witnesses to verify the authenticity of Paul's experiences. Consequently, Paul must appeal to indirect proof. He refers to his past as a persecutor only to contrast it with his present stance. His motivation for persecuting Christians had been his exceptional zeal for Judaism (1:14). Of course the Galatians knew that at some point Paul had forsaken these traditions and turned to Christ. The man who had once been the most notorious persecutor of Christians became one of Christ's most ardent defenders and champions. Paul's point appears to be that only *something dramatic* could account for his complete reversal regarding Christianity, something like a genuine revelation from Christ.

His second point about being relatively unknown to the apostles in Jerusalem serves that same basic purpose. Paul claims that he received his gospel directly from Christ through personal revelation. The alternative explanation would be that Paul simply learned his gospel from some human source, picking it up secondhand from others who actually knew Jesus. The most likely candidates to have taught Paul his gospel were obviously the acknowledged apostles of Jerusalem, especially Peter (Cephas), James, and John. Paul believes that if he can *rule out* the possibility that he learned his gospel at the feet of these apostles, then the Galatians will be forced to admit that

Paul's own explanation—a direct revelation—is more likely to be the truth. For this reason, Paul insists that after his initial call experience, he did not have any contact with people from whom he could have absorbed the teachings of Christianity: "But when he who had set me apart before I was born, and had called me through his grace, was pleased to reveal his Son to me, in order that I might preach him among the Gentiles, I did not confer with flesh and blood, nor did I go up to Jerusalem to those who were apostles before me, but I went away into Arabia; and again I returned to Damascus" (Gal. 1:15–17). This solitary sojourn apparently lasted for three years. Implicitly, then, Paul is asking the Galatians how he could have functioned as a missionary for Christ for this length of time without having had contact with any other apostles unless he was armed with knowledge gained in a supernatural fashion.

Then Paul relates that he did go up to Jerusalem after this three-year period. But when he did so, he met only a few of the apostles and spent very little time with them. His point is that he could not have learned his entire gospel in such a brief period. The encounter was so fleeting, Paul insists, that the members of the Jerusalem church would not afterwards even be able to recognize him by looking upon his face.

> Then after three years I went up to Jerusalem to visit Cephas, and remained with him fifteen days. But I saw none of the other apostles except James the Lord's brother. (In what I am writing to you, before God, I do not lie!) Then I went into the regions of Syria and Cilicia. And I was still not known by sight to the churches of Christ in Judea; they only heard it said, "He who once persecuted us is now preaching the faith he once tried to destroy." (Gal. 1:18–24)

The fact that Paul vehemently insists that he is not lying about this point indicates clearly that his opponents are saying the exact opposite. They have told the Galatians that Paul spent considerable time with the main Jerusalem apostles and learned his gospel at their feet.

Paul goes on to say that he spent the next fourteen years (Gal. 2:1) working as a Christian missionary without again encountering these other apostles. When he finally did meet them again, at the summit later to become known as the Jerusalem Council (49 CE), Paul insists that

Paul's Confrontation with Peter at Antioch

After the Jerusalem Council, Paul and Barnabas returned to the church at Antioch where they had apparently been working as the leaders of an increasingly Gentile congregation. Peter visited the church, and at first he and Paul seem to have gotten along fine. Both Peter and Paul engaged in table fellowship with Gentile converts who had not apparently been circumcised and did not keep kosher. Eating with Gentiles is prohibited under Jewish law, and so the willingness of Peter and Paul to share meals with these Gentile converts in Antioch seems to signal that both are agreeing that the Jewish kosher restrictions are no longer binding on any Christian, whether Jew or Gentile. However, when certain representatives of James appeared, Peter withdrew from the table, apparently not wanting to be *seen* violating the rules about table fellowship by those who were more conservative in this regard and still believed that all the kosher laws were still in effect. Paul then accused Peter of both cowardice and hypocrisy. Paul claims that Peter was motivated by "fear of the circumcision faction" (Gal. 2:12, NRSV). Paul's accusation of hypocrisy is devastating: "If you, though a Jew, live like a Gentile and not like a Jew, how can you compel the Gentiles to live like Jews?" (2:14).

Paul's description of this incident suggests that not everyone at the Jerusalem Council was fully on board with the decision to permit the spreading of the gospel to Gentiles without requiring them to submit to circumcision and the Jewish law. It is not clear whether the circumcision faction apparently led by James simply had second thoughts after the council or had been outvoted on this point, but there is little question that there was lingering tension between conservative Jewish Christians and Christians like Paul who proclaimed that Gentile converts were free from the yoke of the Torah.

This passage also indicates that in Paul's view, whatever any Jerusalem apostle might be saying *now* about the necessity of Torah observance, the fact is that the matter was settled at the Jerusalem Council, and any backsliding on this issue by James, Peter, or anyone else was simply illegitimate and unacceptable. If they now disputed the very points they had previously agreed to, then this only showed their hypocrisy and weakness. By contrast, Paul describes himself as utterly consistent in this respect, and he suggests that this consistency is the hallmark of a real apostle. His willingness to call Peter out for his misbehavior also shows that Paul did not regard himself as inferior or subordinate to the Jerusalem apostles.

Finally, it is noteworthy that in Paul's description Peter appears to have been afraid of James, the Lord's brother. According to tradition, Peter was the supreme leader of the early church (see chapter 10). "Petrine supremacy" is one of the foundations of the Catholic theory of the papacy. However, this passage suggests James, not Peter, had the upper hand in Jerusalem. This might just have been Paul's perception, but it finds support in other early sources, including the *Gospel of Thomas*, where Jesus explicitly instructs his disciples to look to James as their leader.[38]

---

38. *Gospel of Thomas* 12.

he was acknowledged as an equal by the very apostles to whom he is now being negatively compared. It is clear Paul suffered from no inferiority complex in relation to the Jerusalem apostles, despite their reputation. He insists that he was not summoned to this meeting by them, but rather that he went to Jerusalem in response to a revelation (2:2). He speaks of these apostles in less than reverent terms: "And from those who were reputed to be something (what they were makes no difference to me; God shows no partiality)—those, I say, who were of repute added nothing to me" (2:6). Paul was not advised by them to make a single change in his preaching—not that he would have—but instead they gave both his gospel and his apostleship the seal of approval, the "right hand of fellowship," agreeing that Paul had been given a mission to preach to the Gentiles (2:7–9). Paul's point is that if the so-called "real" apostles in Jerusalem accepted Paul's apostolic authority and acknowledged him as their equal, then Paul's opponents in Galatia are in no position to claim otherwise. The Galatians, therefore, should not believe anything of the sort.

Having defended his apostleship, Paul turns to his larger purpose, the defense of his "gospel," that is, his version of Christianity. The initial broadside announcing the cause of his angry letter bemoans the fact that the Galatians are turning to a "different gospel" (Gal. 1:6). Actually, Paul says, there cannot be more than one correct version of the gospel; what the Galatians are embracing is a perversion of the gospel (1:7). He is certain that he received the full truth about Christ during his direct revelation: "The gospel that was proclaimed by me is not of human origin; for I did not receive it from a human source, nor was I taught it, but I received

it through a revelation of Jesus Christ" (1:11–12, NRSV). From this it follows that any deviation from Paul's gospel is necessarily false and would jeopardize the salvation of those who strayed. And woe be unto those who are responsible for misleading Paul's converts: "But even if we, or an angel from heaven, should preach to you a gospel contrary to that which we preached to you, let them be accursed!" (1:8).

The sign that the Galatians have strayed from Paul's gospel involves their acceptance of the necessity of circumcision, which Paul had apparently already told them had been annulled by the coming of Christ. To Paul, the Galatians who became circumcised or who were considering circumcision were not only showing a lack of trust in this one area of Paul's teaching; they were in fact betraying everything he had proclaimed to them. Paul clearly believes that circumcision is unnecessary[39] and does not help a person get to heaven. But beyond that he is convinced that becoming circumcised is actually harmful to one's chances of salvation. Why is circumcision such a big deal to Paul? And why would the Galatians even consider undergoing such a procedure, especially given Paul's prior assurances of its uselessness?

Paul gets to the heart of his argument in this regard in the latter half of Galatians 2, beginning with this general statement: "We ourselves, who are Jews by birth and not Gentile sinners, yet who know that a man is not justified by works of the law but through faith in Jesus Christ, even we have believed in Christ Jesus, in order to be justified by faith in Christ, and not by works of the law, because by works of the law shall no one be justified" (Gal. 2:15–16). To begin to understand how this argument shows that circumcision is unnecessary and harmful, one must examine the

---

39. One brief argument Paul makes in this regard slips into his narrative of the events of the Jerusalem Council, at which he was accompanied by his associates Barnabas and Titus (Gal. 2:1). Paul mentions that Titus, who was a Greek, was not compelled to be circumcised (2:3). Paul's point is that if Titus was not compelled to be circumcised by the undisputed apostles Peter and John, despite the apparent pleading of conservative, pro-circumcision Jewish Christians, then neither should the Galatians feel compelled to be circumcised.

meaning of the word "justified," and the concept of **justification** (Greek, *dikaiosynē*). The constellation of Greek words with the root *dikaio-* has legal overtones. To "justify" means to declare an accused person to be righteous, that is, to *acquit* the defendant on the charges leveled against him or her. A justified person is one who has been declared righteous by a judge, even if the accused is in fact guilty, and the just penalty for the crime is lifted.

In the theological sense in which Paul uses the term, justification maintains its legal connotations, but it is understood as *relational*. A person is "justified" in the sense that Paul is using the word if that person is in a *right relationship* with God. To avoid condemnation and punishment, a person needs to be righteous in the eyes of God, that is, in the court of divine judgment. In both ancient Judaism and early Christianity, it was understood that all humans are sinners who have fallen short of the glory of God: "God looks down from heaven upon the sons of men to see if there are any that are wise, that seek after God. They have all fallen away; they are all alike depraved; there is none that does good, no, not one" (Ps. 53:2–3). Hence human beings stand in a *wrong* relationship with God because of sin.

According to Paul, if human beings were judged on the basis of their deeds—their "works" in Paul's way of speaking—no one would be justified. The only way for the relationship between God and humans to be restored is for God to reach out and offer reconciliation, to overlook humans' unworthiness, and to forgive their sins. Paul preached that God had done exactly this by raising from the dead Jesus, who had offered his life as a sacrifice to atone for human sin. God, completely apart from human action, has made this reconciliation available. Humans need only have faith, that is, to believe and *trust* that God has in fact taken this step, in order to be justified, to be restored to a right relationship with God.

For Paul, then, justification is offered to humans as a free gift. The Greek word for "gift" is *charis*, and Paul uses this word often to describe God's action in Christ Jesus. It is usually translated as **grace**, the idea that God loves humans unconditionally even though they do not deserve his favor. Now if salvation is offered by God as a free gift, Paul believed, then it is not something *earned* by human beings through their own actions. This idea is expressed in Philippians as well, where Paul dismisses the idea of "having a righteousness *of my own*, based on law" (Phil. 3:9). The idea of gaining acquittal in the court of God by pleading "not guilty" and defending one's behavior as righteous struck Paul as absurd and impossible. One needed to throw oneself on the mercy of the court and trust that a gracious God—who had proven his trustworthiness by raising Jesus from the dead—would overlook one's obvious guilt and render a kindly verdict.

It is in this context that Paul's adamant opposition to circumcision for his Gentile converts begins to make sense. He has told them that faith alone is enough for salvation, and that their justification depends on grace and not on their own deeds or actions. By accepting the yoke of circumcision, the Galatians are seemingly violating this basic Pauline principle: there is nothing one can do to bring about one's own salvation. Justification depends entirely on the gracious activity of God through Christ. Paul understands well enough that the Galatians would only undergo circumcision—a painful and rather dangerous process—if they thought it would help them gain salvation. For Paul, this meant that instead of trusting in God, they were trusting in themselves. They were seeking to earn justification instead of accepting it as a free gift. Grace and works, in Paul's thinking, are an either-or proposition. "You who want to be justified by the law have cut yourselves off from Christ; you have fallen away from grace" (Gal. 5:4, NRSV). People either allow God to justify them or they seek to gain justification for themselves. And if a person can earn salvation by works of the law, then there was no need for

Christ to die on the cross. "I do not nullify the grace of God; for if justification were through the law, then Christ died to no purpose" (2:21).

Whether or not ancient Judaism could accurately be characterized as claiming that justification was obtained by works of the law,[40] it is clear that Paul's opponents were telling them that faith in Christ was not sufficient and that it had to be accompanied by circumcision, minimally.[41] It is also clear that the law they spoke of as binding on the Galatians was the Law of Moses. Since Paul's opponents were appealing to the resources of Judaism to persuade the Galatians to become circumcised, Paul attempts to use those same resources to convince them otherwise.

For example, the story of Abraham in Genesis 12–24—a passage that his opponents may have used to convince the Galatians of the necessity of circumcision—is used by Paul to make the opposite point. Paul's opponents could cite Genesis 17:10–14: "Every male among you shall be circumcised. You shall be circumcised in the flesh of your foreskins, and it shall be a sign of the covenant between me and you. . . . Any uncircumcised male who is not circumcised in the flesh of his foreskin shall be cut off from his people; he has broken my covenant." But Paul capitalizes on an earlier verse, in which God promises Abraham that he will have numerous descendants; Abraham has no children at this point and his wife is long past child-bearing age, so this would have been a difficult promise to believe. But Abraham "believed the LORD; and he [i.e., the LORD] reckoned it to him as righteousness" (Gen. 15:6). To be "reckoned as righteous" is exactly the same thing as being "justified." In this way Paul can argue that Abraham was justified by

Genesis 16–21 tells of Abraham's sons Ishmael, by Hagar, and Isaac, by his wife Sarah, shown in this statue from Florence. Paul's use of allegory to interpret Sarah and Hagar as referring, respectively, to the new and old covenants resembles the allegorical technique of the Jewish philosopher Philo (ca. 25 BCE–40 CE).

his faith and not by circumcision (which was not yet demanded by God), or by works of the law (which was not revealed until long after Abraham's time). "This is what I mean: the law, which came four hundred and thirty years afterward, does not annul a covenant previously ratified by God, so as to make the promise void" (Gal. 3:17). Paul further

---

40. Judaism certainly preached the importance of avoiding sin by obeying the Law of Moses and taught that one could atone for sins by a variety of means. But this does not mean that Judaism relied solely on human effort and had no place for faith or grace.

41. It is not clear whether Paul's opponents had told the Galatians that they had to follow the Torah as a whole. Paul says later in the letter that those who have undergone circumcision are in fact obliged to obey the entire law, and he says this as if it would be news to them. This has led some to question whether Paul's opponents were Jewish Christians from outside the community—who would certainly have known that following the Torah was an all-or-nothing proposition—or whether they were insiders who had acquired only a passing knowledge of Judaism and came to believe that Paul had simply misled them on the necessity of circumcision.

argues that it was foretold that the Gentiles would follow in Abraham's steps as far as being justified by faith: "So, you see, those who believe are the descendants of Abraham. And the scripture, foreseeing that God would justify the Gentiles by faith, declared the gospel beforehand to Abraham, saying, 'All the Gentiles shall be blessed in you.' For this reason, those who believe are blessed with Abraham who believed" (Gal. 3:7–9, NRSV).[42]

Paul's case against his opponents in Galatia includes many arguments, some of which are better than others, at least from a modern perspective. Paul claims that Genesis explicitly refers to the coming of Christ: "Now the promises were made to Abraham and to his offspring. It does not say, 'And to offsprings,' referring to many; but, referring to one, 'And to your offspring,' which is Christ" (Gal. 3:16). The author of Genesis is speaking of a group, not of a single individual, but the Hebrew word is singular and Paul takes full advantage of that fact.[43] Paul's biblical exegesis is even more fanciful when he interprets the story of Abraham's two sons (4:21–31). But such interpretive techniques[44] were quite common at the time, and Paul's arguments probably seemed much more persuasive to his contemporaries than they do to modern readers.

Paul concludes his angry letter with a plea to the Galatians to forsake their new teachers and return to his gospel, the gospel whose acceptance led them originally to receive the Holy Spirit (Gal. 3:2–5; 5:5, 16–6:1) and to experience freedom from the bondage of sin (5:1, 13–15). Everything depends, Paul argues, on the Galatians changing their minds: "He who sows to his own flesh will from the flesh reap corruption; but he who sows to the Spirit will from the Spirit reap eternal life" (6:8).

Key Terms

Timothy
advent
rapture
premillennial

dispensationalist
amillennial
exaltation Christology
incarnation Christology

second Adam
justification
grace

Review Questions

1. What rhetorical situation does Paul face in 1 Thessalonians? Why is the answer to this question somewhat uncertain?

2. What is Paul's personal history with the Thessalonian church? Why might he have felt the need to review this history as he does in 1 Thessalonians?

---

42. Kennedy rightly identifies this argument as an *enthymeme*; see *New Testament Interpretation*, 149. In syllogistic form, Paul's argument would be:

> P[1] Abraham was justified by faith.

> P[2] Through Abraham all the nations of the earth (i.e., the Gentiles) would be blessed.

> Conclusion: All nations of the earth (i.e., the Gentiles) will be justified by faith.

43. See Roetzel, *The Letters of Paul*, 101.

44. Paul speaks of the story of Hagar (the slave woman) and Sarah (the free woman) as an "allegory" (Gal. 4:24). Allegorical interpretation of scripture, which remained popular in Christianity for more than a millennium, is notorious for very creative interpretations that bear little relationship to the original meaning of a text. Allegorical interpretation assumes that there are various levels of hidden or secret meaning in the text, placed there by the Holy Spirit for discovery by later generations of believing readers. This method of biblical interpretation became discredited with the advent of critical biblical scholarship in the late eighteenth century.

3. What questions did the Thessalonians have about the end of the world, and how does Paul answer them?

4. What rhetorical situation does Paul face in Philippians? Why might the letter address such a wide variety of problems, and in such a disjointed fashion?

5. What are the arguments for seeing the Christ-hymn in Philippians 2:6–11 as reflecting an exaltation Christology? What are the arguments for seeing the hymn as reflecting an incarnational Christology? How do the advocates of an incarnational interpretation respond to objections?

6. What rhetorical situation does Paul face in Galatians? On what basis were Paul's apostleship and gospel under attack?

7. How does Paul try to convince the Galatians that he is a real apostle?

8. Why is Paul so opposed to the Galatians becoming circumcised?

Discussion Questions

1. For some, the fact that Christians have been expecting the second coming of Christ for almost two thousand years without this expectation being realized is a major obstacle to Christian faith. In particular, the fact that Paul believed Jesus would return within his lifetime, and the fact that many Christian preachers since then have made false predictions about the second coming, is a source of no small amount of mockery online and elsewhere. On the other hand, most Christians do not appear to be troubled by this fact at all, and remain generally hopeful about the return of Christ. Why do you think this is?

2. Do you think that Philippians expresses an exaltation Christology or an incarnation Christology? If you fall into the incarnational camp, are you more inclined to see Philippians envisioning the preexistent Christ as fully divine or as a subordinate divine being like an angel?

3. Does Paul make a persuasive case for his apostleship in Galatians? If someone you knew made similar arguments about having received a divine revelation, would be inclined to believe that person, or would you be skeptical? Why?

Bibliography and Suggestions for Further Study

(Books and websites that are accessible for general undergraduates are marked with an asterisk; other sources listed are appropriate for advanced students.)

Bornkamm, Günther. *Paul, Paulus*. New York: Harper & Row, 1971.

*Ehrman, Bart. *How Jesus Became God: The Exaltation of a Jewish Preacher from Galilee*. New York: HarperOne, 2014.

Garrett, Susan R. *No Ordinary Angel: Celestial Spirits and Christian Claims about Jesus*. New Haven: Yale University Press, 2008.

Gieschen, Charles A. *Angelomorphic Christology: Antecedents and Early Evidence*. Leiden: Brill, 1998.

*Kennedy, George A. *New Testament Interpretation through Rhetorical Criticism*. Chapel Hill: University of North Carolina Press, 1984.

*Roetzel, Calvin J. *The Letters of Paul: Conversations in Context*. 4th ed. Louisville: Westminster John Knox, 1998.

Sanders, E. P. *Paul*. New York: Oxford University Press, 1991.

*Taylor, Walter F. *Paul, Apostle to the Nations: An Introduction*. Minneapolis: Fortress, 2012.

Paul's Correspondence with the Corinthians and Romans

The remaining genuine letters of Paul— 1 and 2 Corinthians and Romans—present challenges beyond those of the letters previously discussed. First Corinthians (16 chapters), 2 Corinthians (13 chapters), and Romans (16 chapters), are all much longer than their Pauline siblings. Because of this, an introductory text must be highly selective in its consideration of topics. In what follows the primary focus will continue to be the rhetoric of these letters, with a secondary goal of uncovering the theology underlying them.

Paul's Letters to the Corinthians

With a resident population of as many as eighty thousand, Corinth was a major tourist and trade destination. The Isthmian Games, second in prestige only to the Olympics, were held nearby every two years, bringing thousands of visitors to Corinth. Corinth was also a trade center, located strategically between the eastern and western halves of the Roman Empire. Revenue from shipping, taxes, and tourists made Corinth wealthy.[1]

Corinth was also famous for sin—especially sexual sins. Some scholars have argued that this reputation is an exaggeration created by jealous Athenians seeking to denigrate a rival city-state. But it is certainly not impossible that sexual morality was lax in this cosmopolitan port city. The ancient writer Strabo (*Geography* 8.6.20) revealed that Corinthians worshipped a number of gods but were especially devoted to the goddess of love, Aphrodite. Strabo claimed that there were a thousand temple prostitutes in Corinth. Paul's letters certainly seem to confirm the willingness of Corinthians to experiment with unusual sexual arrangements (see 1 Cor. 5). This is just one of several behavioral problems that seemed to plague the Corinthian church, in addition to many doctrinal and ecclesiastical controversies. In essence, Corinth was a troubled Christian community. But it was also a vital Christian community, and as a result it received a great deal of attention from Paul.

Paul likely sent more than one letter to many of the churches he founded. But only with the Corinthian correspondence is it certain[2] that the surviving record includes more than one genuine letter. Multiple letters, especially ones as long as 1 and 2 Corinthians, afford a

---

1. Walter F. Taylor, *Paul, Apostle to the Nations: An Introduction* (Minneapolis: Fortress, 2012), 163.

2. As noted in chapter 16, many scholars believe that Philippians contains fragments of two or three separate letters, and there are scholars who defend the Pauline authorship of 2 Thessalonians.

Miguel Hermoso Cuesta / Wikimedia / Lupanar, Pompeya. 03.JPG / CC BY-SA 4.0

Prostitution was legal in the Roman world, and men incurred no stigma by visiting a brothel, such as this large example from Pompeii. The Corinthian Christians seem to have had some difficulty accepting Paul's argument that such activity was immoral.

fuller and richer picture of Paul's ministry than is available elsewhere. Unfortunately, that picture is more difficult to bring into focus than one might imagine, because 2 Corinthians probably consists of fragments of multiple letters edited together after Paul sent[3] them.

Timeline and Circumstances of Paul's Correspondence with the Corinthians

While the disagreements over how many letters Paul wrote and which of them are preserved in the canon result in some rather different portraits of Paul's evolving relationship with the Corinthians, there is also consensus on some points. Among these are the following:

Order and Content of the Early Correspondence. It is generally agreed that 1 Corinthians was written prior to any part of 2 Corinthians and that 1 Corinthians was not the first letter Paul wrote to the church at Corinth. 1 Corinthians 5:9 mentions a previous letter that does not survive. That first letter is often referred to as Letter A, while what is now called 1 Corinthians is generally termed Letter B.

Problems Addressed in Letter A. Letter A followed Paul's lengthy stay in Corinth. Paul came to Corinth after being driven out of both Philippi and Thessalonica, but he received a warm welcome in Corinth and ended up spending eighteen months there (sometime between 51 and 54 CE) before moving on to Ephesus for three years. While at Ephesus, Paul received reports of problems in Corinth. The nature and extent of these problems is not fully known, but they definitely included instances of sexual immorality (1 Cor. 5:9). Other problems seem to have involved (1) an over-emphasis on the importance of "speaking in tongues" (*glōssolalia*), according to which a person under the influence of the Holy Spirit would speak the language of the angels, and (2) Christian participation in pagan celebrations, particularly feasts at which the meat came from animals that had been sacrificed to pagan gods and goddesses. Paul wrote Letter A to respond to these problems, which can be summed up as **libertinism** (the belief that the freedom associated with the gospel enabled Christians to ignore previously-firm moral and religious boundaries) and **enthusiasm** (an over-emphasis on the display of spiritual gifts such as glossolalia).

---

3. The postal service in the Roman Empire was mostly reserved for official (government) communication. Private mail was usually carried by friends, associates, or even strangers known to be traveling in the right direction, or by private couriers (usually slaves).

Problems Addressed in Letter B (1 Corinthians). Sometime after he sent this first letter, Paul received further reports, both oral and written, about the emergence of more serious problems in the church. One of these involved the emergence of rival factions in the church, with different groups claiming allegiance to a particular Christian leader. One group was loyal to Paul, but other groups favored Peter, Apollos (an Alexandrian Jewish convert), or even Christ. Other problems included continuing sexual immorality, the pursuit of lawsuits that had the effect of exposing the Christians' dirty laundry to those outside the community (1 Cor. 6), and the adoption by some of extreme asceticism regarding sex (1 Cor. 7). Paul wrote Letter B (which consists of all or most of canonical 1 Corinthians) in response to these problems.

Continuing Strife in the Corinthian Church. Problems persisted in Corinth, some old and some new. Paul's apostleship came under attack and forced him to make a defense. Divisions persisted or reappeared between different groups loyal to certain local leaders dubbed "super-apostles" (2 Cor. 11:5); these apostles denigrated Paul and his message while boasting of their own charismatic gifts and wonder-working abilities.

Paul's Painful Visit and the Letter of Tears. After hearing of these lingering problems, Paul made a visit to Corinth that did not resolve the issues (perhaps 55 CE) and included some kind of public humiliation of Paul (2 Cor. 2:5–11); this is known as the "**painful visit**." Following this visit, Paul wrote a third letter (Letter C), which scholars term the "**Letter of Tears**" (see 2 Cor. 2:3–4; 7:8, 12). This letter harshly criticized the Corinthians and threatened them with the wrath of God. Later Paul sent Titus back to Corinth as his emissary. Titus returned to report that the Letter of Tears had been effective, at least in some measure, and the situation in the Corinthian churches had improved. Paul and the Corinthians appear to have reconciled. Whether that reconciliation lasted or subsequently fell apart and led to more angry correspondence is a matter of disagreement. Paul probably made a final visit to Corinth around 56–57 CE, before moving on to Jerusalem and his final arrest.[4]

These are the main points of agreement among scholars. On most other matters, there is considerable disagreement, much of which concerns 2 Corinthians. There are three main theories about the composition of 2 Corinthians.[5]

1. A Single, Unified Letter. Some scholars insist that 2 Corinthians represents a unified composition. They argue that the presence of literary seams (see sidebar) is overstated and the hypothesis of complex revisions by editors are mere speculation. Paul may simply have dictated a single letter over a period of several days, his mood changing between dictation sessions. Or perhaps Paul received news of additional developments halfway through the letter and, rather than start over, decided simply to add on to what he had already written. Most other scholars, however, view these explanations of the truly jarring inconsistencies within 2 Corinthians as unpersuasive.

2. Two Letters: 1–9 and 10–13. Separating 2 Corinthians into two letters is based mostly on the abrupt break between chapters 9 and 10 and the relative consistency of tone, style, and content in chapters 1–9 and 10–13, suggesting that each section represents all or most of a single letter written on a particular occasion. Scholars who

---

4. This account of the consensus regarding the chronology of Paul's dealings with the Corinthians relies in part on Taylor, *Paul, Apostle to the Nations*, 200–204, and Calvin Roetzel, *The Letters of Paul: Conversations in Context*, 4th ed. (Louisville: Westminster John Knox, 1998), 53–62.

5. What follows draws upon Taylor, *Paul, Apostle to the Nations*, 194–99.

Literary Seams and the Integrity of Paul's Letters to the Corinthians

No one knows exactly how Paul's letters came to be preserved or why some were saved while others were lost. It is widely believed that prior to reaching their final canonical form, Paul's letters were edited. In some cases it is likely that an editor combined several shorter letters to the same church into a single long letter. This theory was raised regarding the letter to the Philippians (see chapter 16), but it is also sometimes thought to apply to 1 Corinthians and even more often to 2 Corinthians.

The major evidence for these theories is the presence of **literary seams**. A literary seam is the literary equivalent of a seam in a garment: a sign (or signs) that shows two originally distinct documents have been stitched together. The most obvious kind of literary seam is an abrupt change of tone and topic. The material after the seam seems out of place with the material that precedes it.

One example involves the very different character of chapters 1-9 of 2 Corinthians compared to chapters 10-13. There are minor stylistic indications that the chapters were written on different occasions, such as Paul's use of the first-person plural ("we") in chapters 1-9 and first person singular ("I") in chapters 10-13. More serious differences involve tone and content. In chapters 1-9 Paul's tone is relatively positive, even joyful. Although he mentions that he has faced recent challenges in Corinth, he goes on to speak of reconciliation

and the dawning of a new day in his relationship with the Corinthians: "I rejoice, because I have complete confidence in you" (2 Cor. 7:16). But in chapters 10-13, Paul's tone is angry and disappointed, and he seems to be addressing a very different and darker period in his relationship with the Corinthians. He rips the "super-apostles" who are undermining him and boasting of their superiority, suggesting that his opponents are Satanic (11:14) and that the Corinthians who are falling for their tricks are like Eve being deceived by the serpent (11:3). In chapters 1-9, Paul speaks calmly and rationally, employing logical arguments. But in chapters 10-13, Paul speaks emotionally and authoritatively, eschewing arguments ("we destroy arguments"; 10:4) and even admitting that he is "talking like a madman" (11:23).

Second Corinthians also lacks any logical progression from chapters 1-9 to chapters 10-13. In chapters 8-9, Paul appeals to the Corinthians for money, which suggests that Paul is on good terms with them. But he then proceeds, in the very next section of the letter (chapters 10-13), to savagely criticize the very people to whom he was appealing for financial support. Paul, then, was either the world's worst fundraiser or, more likely, he wrote two separate letters on two different occasions. Theories about multiple letters being combined are a result of scholars wrestling with internal tensions such as these.

support this theory differ on whether these two letters are in the correct order.

Some argue that the harsh language and sharp criticism of chapters 10–13 fits exactly Paul's description of his Letter of Tears, following the Corinthians' rejection of him during his "painful visit." Paul refers to this letter in chapters

1–9 as having *preceded* the one he is presently writing. Therefore, if chapters 10–13 came from the Letter of Tears, then when 2 Corinthians was stitched together, the editor put the excerpts out of order: chapters 10–13 were written *before* 1–9 but were mistakenly appended *after* them. Chapters 10–13 speak of estrangement; chapters 1–9 speak of reconciliation. Reconciliation follows logically from estrangement, not the other way around. In this theory, chapters 10–13 become Letter C and chapters 1–9 become Letter D, with Letter A being the only one of the four not to survive.

The alternative argues that chapters 10–13 do not come from the Letter of Tears but from another harsh letter written later in Paul's stormy relationship with the Corinthians. Proponents of this theory point to inconsistencies between those chapters and what Paul says about the Letter of Tears in 2 Corinthians 2 and 7. This theory posits that after (1) the painful visit, (2) the Letter of Tears (Letter C, which in this theory does not survive), (3) Titus's visit to Corinth, and (4) Paul's reconciliation with the Corinthians (chapters 1–9, Letter D), Paul's relationship with the church in Corinth took *another* turn for the worse and led to (5) the sending of another letter consisting of a lengthy and harsh rebuke (chapters 10–13, Letter E).

3. Multiple Fragments. Some scholars posit that the breaks and ruptures within chapters 1–9 indicate that these chapters combine fragments from several letters. Possibilities include the theory that 2:14–6:13 and 7:2–4 once comprised a single letter written prior to the painful visit defending Paul's apostleship—unsuccessfully, as it turns out—from various attacks. Another common suggestion is that other parts of 2 Corinthians (1:1–2:13; 7:5–16; and perhaps even 13:11–13) formed a single letter written upon the happy occasion of the ultimate resolution of Paul's conflict with the Corinthians. The two chapters in which Paul asks for money (2 Cor. 8–9) are often supposed by "multiple fragments" theorists to be a separate letter, or even two separate appeals written at different times.[6]

The following analysis posits that 2 Corinthians consists of parts of two letters, and that these fragments are in the correct order. The first fragment consists of chapters 1–9, and these chapters were written before the second fragment, chapters 10–13. Chapters 10–13, then, are not part of the Letter of Tears but of a subsequent letter. While it is necessary to posit some such scenario in order to proceed, the evidence regarding 2 Corinthians is so divided that other possibilities cannot be ruled out, and conclusions based on a single reconstruction should be correspondingly tentative.

Rhetoric and Theological Themes in Paul's Correspondence with the Corinthians

Paul fashions his argument for unity in 1 Corinthians largely through **deliberative rhetoric**. In deliberative rhetoric (see chapter 15), a speaker or writer exhorts his audience to follow or not to follow a particular course of action in the *future*.[7] Paul has heard reports about infighting, immorality, and confusion within the Corinthian community, and he writes to urge them to modify their behavior and adjust their thinking. Paul's thesis appears in the first lines of the body of the letter: "Now I appeal to you, brothers and sisters, by the name of our Lord Jesus Christ, that all of you be in agreement and that there be no divisions among you, but that you be united in the same mind and the same purpose. For it has been reported to me by Chloe's people that there are quarrels among you" (1 Cor. 1:10–11).

One problem Paul seeks to correct involves the community's tolerance or indifference toward sexual immorality. People have told Paul that

---

6. 2 Cor. 8 appeals to the Corinthians in particular, while 2 Cor. 9 appeals more broadly to all the people of Achaia (the Greek region of which Corinth was a part).

7. Taylor argues that chapters 1–4 and 9 might be better classified as judicial rhetoric, and chapter 13 as epideictic, but agrees that most of the letter is deliberative. See Taylor, *Paul, Apostle to the Nations*, 169.

among the Corinthian Christians a man is living and sleeping with his stepmother. Many ancient cultures, including paganism and Judaism, would have seen this arrangement as incestuous. Paul is angry about this, but he directs his ire less at the man himself and more at his fellow Corinthians, who are condoning this.

Paul advises them to remove this man from their community and to have nothing whatsoever to do with him anymore (1 Cor. 5:13). In his argument, Paul does not explain why it is wrong for a man to have sex with his stepmother; he apparently regards the immorality of such behavior as self-evident, for even pagans recognized it as wrong (5:1). Instead, Paul makes two kinds of rhetorical moves to persuade the Corinthians of the danger this man poses to all of them and the necessity of his removal. The first rhetorical move is an **argument from analogy**, which readers of the Gospels will recognize from Jesus' use of parables. Paul likens the brazenly immoral man to a lump of yeast: "Do you not know that a little yeast leavens the whole batch of dough?" (5:6). When making bread, a small amount of yeast has a dramatic effect on a large batch of dough.[8] In the same way, Paul claims, a single instance of sexual immorality can have a corrupting effect on the entire church. The man is like a cancer in the collective body of the Corinthian community, and he needs to be removed before the disease spreads.

The second rhetorical move Paul uses is the **argument from authority**, in which a speaker asks his audience to accept a certain claim because the claimant has some special status, based perhaps on the speaker's wisdom, experience, expertise, or office.[9] Whenever a parent tells a child,

"Because I said so!" the parent is employing the argument from authority. Paul cites both his own authority and Christ's to justify his demand that the immoral man be banned from the church. He reminds them that he already wrote in a previous letter for them "not to associate with sexually immoral persons" (1 Cor. 5:9). Paul then proceeds to clarify that he was not referring only to nonbelievers here. He identifies the man sleeping with his stepmother as exactly the kind of "immoral person" with whom they should not associate, and clearly he expects this will be enough for them to realize they must remove the man from their presence. Paul's authority stems from Christ: "I have already pronounced judgment *in the name of the Lord Jesus* on the man who has done such a thing" (5:3–4).

Another example of Paul's deliberative rhetoric can be found in 1 Corinthians 6:1–11, in which Paul responds to reports that Christians are suing each other in secular courts of law. Paul believes Christians should settle their disputes internally, and not air their dirty laundry before outsiders. Paul urges them to appoint some wise Christian men to serve as arbitrators in their disputes and administer justice. If they cannot find anyone to do the job, then they should rather allow themselves to be wronged: "To have lawsuits at all with one another is already a defeat for you. Why not rather be wronged? Why not rather be defrauded?" (6:7).[10]

Paul further argues that secular authorities are unworthy to serve as judges in disputes among Christian believers. The faithful, he points out, "will judge the world" in the eschatological judgment. Why then would they consider themselves "incompetent to try trivial cases?" (6:2).

---

8. Jesus makes the same point in the Parable of the Leaven (Matt. 13:33; Luke 13:20–21). Paul may betray some knowledge of Jesus' parable here, although it is equally likely that this was a commonplace observation.

9. The argument from authority (or "appeal to authority") is often considered a logical fallacy, but it does carry weight if the authority claimed is real, legitimate, earned, or in some other way *accepted* by the audience.

10. Some scholars see in Paul's statement "Why not rather suffer wrong?" echoes of Jesus' teaching in Matthew and Luke to "turn the other cheek." As noted in chapter 15, Paul seldom refers explicitly to the teachings of Jesus. But some scholars think Paul was more interested in Jesus' teachings and knew more about them than is generally supposed, and point to 1 Cor. 6:7 as an example.

Paul, Sex, and Celibacy

THIS IS GOOD

"I want to marry the person of my choice."

THIS IS BETTER

"I choose Christ as my spouse."
(See 1 Corinthians 7, 32-34).

© Catholic Book Publishing Corp.

The *Baltimore Catechism* (1962) concedes that sexual activity in marriage is good but argues that the celibate life is better; note that the catechism cites Paul's Corinthian correspondence in support of this assertion (1 Cor. 7:32–34).

Paul is probably the most famous advocate of celibacy in Christian tradition. Jesus, John the Baptist, and Mary were all claimed by early Christian celibates as their inspiration, but none of these figures left any writings and, compared to Paul, there is less historical evidence that they were celibate. While it is not clear whether Paul had ever been married (he may have been a widower), there is no question that when he wrote his letters he was unmarried and sexually inactive. It is also certain that Paul encouraged others to adopt the celibate lifestyle. Paul states, "I wish that all were as I myself am" and advises those who are unmarried or widows "to remain unmarried" as he is (1 Cor. 7:7–8). He asks, "Are you free from a wife? Do not seek a wife. . . . Those who marry will experience distress in this life, and I would spare you that" (7:27–28). He explains further: "The unmarried man is anxious about the affairs of the Lord, how to please the Lord; but the married man is anxious about the affairs of the world, how to please his wife, and his interests are divided." He adds that married women have the same disadvantage (1 Cor 7:32–34).

For various reasons, some early Christians came to believe that all sex is bad and sinful,

even within the context of marriage, and that the celibate life is superior to the married life. First Corinthians 7:1 was often cited in support of this view: "Now concerning the matters about which you wrote: 'It is well for a man not to touch a woman.'" One reading of this verse is that Paul is *stating his own opinion* when he states that it would be best for a man never to "touch" (be sexually intimate with) a woman. However, one must remember that in first-century writing there were no quotation marks or other punctuation. It is in fact more likely that Paul was *quoting* the letter he received from the Corinthians in 7:1, and that this is not actually his view, but that of some Corinthians in the letter to which he is responding. In that case the translations should read something like this: "Now concerning the thing that you wrote, namely that, 'It is well for a man not to touch a woman,' [let me respond as follows . . .]." In this reading, Paul follows his quotation of the Corinthians' extreme position with his own more moderate view. What comes after 7:1 is Paul's *comment* on their written statement, in which he partially agrees with them and partially disagrees.

If Paul really believed that it would be best for a man never to touch a woman, it would follow that he would believe it best *even for married men and women* to abstain from sexual relations with their spouses. But Paul clearly does not believe this. To the contrary he argues that "the husband should give to his wife her conjugal rights, and likewise the wife to her husband" (1 Cor. 7:3). He allows that husbands and wives might consent to periods of abstinence for religious reasons but indicates that this should only occur by mutual consent and should always be for a limited time (7:5).

Ox, ram, and boar are readied as offerings to the gods in this first-century bas relief; surplus meat was sold in the marketplace. Early Christians wondered if eating such food meant that they were they engaging in pagan worship.

In this form of argument, known as a ***reductio ad absurdum***, a speaker attempts to discredit his opponent's position by following it to its logical conclusion and showing that it leads to a ridiculous and unacceptable outcome.

Some issues raised in the Corinthian correspondence resonate with modern audiences more than others. Few Christians today have faced the question of whether to eat the meat of animals offered as sacrifices to pagan gods (addressed in 1 Cor. 8:1–11:1). But early Christians were confronted by this issue all the time, because the meat available in the shops almost always consisted of the remnants of a sacrifice. Could the Corinthians, who knew that in reality these pagan gods did not exist and hence that the sacrifices to them were meaningless, partake of meals at which such meat was served? Paul's gospel told these Gentile Corinthian converts that they were free from the law and not subject to the demands of the kosher dietary restrictions, so it seemed to them that eating this meat was harmless. However, many people *thought* that eating the flesh of an animal sacrificed to a particular pagan god implied acknowledgement of the reality of that god and the legitimacy of the sacrifice. Realizing this, Paul urges them not to partake of such food knowingly (10:27–28). To do so, he says, is not strictly speaking prohibited, but it is inadvisable: "'All things are lawful,' but not all things are beneficial. 'All things are lawful,' but not all things build up" (10:23).

In making this argument, Paul makes an analogy to his rights as an apostle: he has the right to travel with a wife (as do the other apostles; 1 Cor. 9:5),[11] and he has the right to compensation for his work. But Paul chooses not to avail himself of these rights (9:12), apparently because he believes that being unmarried and celibate permits him to work unconstrained by the demands of a family (see 7:32–34) and earning his own living makes him more credible as an apostle. Paul has rights but chooses not to exercise them for the greater good; similarly, he tells the Corinthians, they have freedom from the law, but there are some cases where it would be better not to exercise that freedom. If exercising their freedom might lead to a harmful result, then love (concern for how their behavior might influence others) should win out over freedom.

---

11. This verse suggests that Peter and the other apostles were married. Some Catholic leaders have denied this, as in their minds it would undermine the argument that priests should be unmarried and celibate like Jesus' apostles. Many priests and bishops were married and had children in the first thousand years of the Catholic Church's existence, but eventually mandatory celibacy became the norm. Mark 1:29–31 and parallels refer to Simon's "mother-in-law," obviously implying Peter had a wife. One could respond that Peter was a widower when he became an apostle, but there is no evidence to support this and 1 Cor. 9:5 certainly suggests otherwise. Asked if a majority of the apostles were married, most biblical scholars would simply respond, "Yes."

The supremacy of love among the Christians virtues is beautifully articulated by Paul in 1 Corinthians 13, a passage well-known even to persons unfamiliar with the Bible because it is one of the surprisingly few scriptural passages suitable for reading at weddings.[12]

> If I speak in the tongues of mortals and of angels, but do not have love, I am a noisy gong or a clanging cymbal. And if I have prophetic powers, and understand all mysteries and all knowledge, and if I have all faith, so as to remove mountains, but do not have love, I am nothing. If I give away all my possessions, and if I hand over my body so that I may boast, but do not have love, I gain nothing. Love is patient; love is kind; love is not envious or boastful or arrogant or rude. It does not insist on its own way; it is not irritable or resentful; it does not rejoice in wrongdoing, but rejoices in the truth. It bears all things, believes all things, hopes all things, endures all things. (1 Cor. 13:1–7)

Interestingly, however, the beginning of this passage indicates that Paul is not exactly speaking of marriage but is trying to cure the Corinthians of an overemphasis on speaking in tongues and prophesying. There is no doubt that Paul spoke in tongues ("ecstatic speech" or *glōssolalia*) when he was originally among the Corinthians. Apparently he believed that the Holy Spirit could take possession of a person and speak through him or her. But it seems that the Corinthians began to see speaking in tongues as a necessary and sufficient condition of salvation, which Paul does not believe. Calvin Roetzel argues that Paul's position was that the Corinthians were confusing cause with effect:

speaking in tongues was one (possible) sign of a person's salvation, not the essential precondition.

Angel speech, as it was called (see 1 Cor. 13:1), indicated who was in tune with the divine, or as they put it, who had "knowledge." Those "in the know" felt so secure in Christ and so secure in their power to prevail over this world that they behaved in ways Paul would have found foolhardy. Since they knew that idols had no real existence, they freely attended pagan celebrations, participated in pagan cultic meals, and ate meat offered to idols. It is possible, if not likely that this "knowledge" led some to attempt to live above mere accidental distinctions, like sex, since in the kingdom of God by Paul's own admission there is neither male nor female.[13]

The emphasis Paul's opponents in Corinth placed on "knowledge" (Greek, *gnōsis*) has led many to identify them as Gnostics or proto-Gnostics. While it is known that Gnosticism challenged proto-orthodox Christianity from the second to at least the fifth century (see chapters 1 and 2), there is less certainty that there were Gnostic Christians as early as the sixth decade of the first century. In any case, there was a faction in Corinth that claimed superiority over other Christians by virtue of their "knowledge" or spiritual gifts, and their boastfulness was creating problems that Paul sought to address in his letter.

Paul's response to this boastfulness is that these Corinthians have misunderstood the entire message of the cross. The fact that a man who was crucified—tortured to death in the most humiliating fashion, accursed according to the

---

12. Some couples choose the story of the wedding at Cana in John 2, although it has little to do with conjugal love. Why is there so little in the Bible for the bride and groom to choose from? For one thing, marriages in the ancient world were very seldom if ever based on love. Most marriages were arranged by the fathers of the bride and groom; indeed a couple could not legally marry over the objections of a father, although under Roman law the consent of the marriage partners was required. Also, early Christianity did not perform marriages. Marriage was a private and secular affair, subject to the contract law of the state, but otherwise left to the families. Weddings were not commonly performed in Christian churches until the late medieval period.

13. Roetzel, *The Letters of Paul*, 55–56.

law—was nonetheless exalted by God and raised from the dead should indicate to them that it is not the wise, the strong, or the well-connected that God values, but those who are weak, outcast, vulnerable, and abused. Paul reminds them that the message of the cross is "foolishness" to Gentiles and a "stumbling block" to Jews, but to believers it is the true wisdom of God. Human wisdom means nothing in light of the reality of Christ's resurrection, because according to human wisdom such a thing should never have happened. "Has not God made foolish the wisdom of the world?" (1 Cor. 1:20).

Given all this, those who follow Christ should not be boastful but humble. Their leaders should not be "puffed up" (1 Cor. 4:6), bragging of their adherents and accomplishments, but should give the credit to God. Paul reminds them that he brought them salvation not with eloquence and lofty words, but humbly: "I came to you in weakness and in fear and in much trembling. My speech and my proclamation were not with plausible words of wisdom" (2:3–4). As an apostle, Paul has grown accustomed to suffering, humiliations, and poverty. But he responds with love, and by doing so proves that Christ is in him: "When reviled, we bless; when persecuted, we endure; when slandered, we speak kindly" (4:12–13). The Corinthian faction now think of themselves as kings and boast of their riches (4:8). They are not following the example of Christ and of Paul himself, but he wishes they would: "I appeal to you, then, be imitators of me" (4:16). Paul insists that his criticism is not meant to shame the Corinthians; rather, he is admonishing them as a loving parent (4:14).

Paul often uses himself as a positive example, as in his argument in 1 Corinthians 9 that he has rights and freedoms as an apostle that he chooses not to exercise, and that the Corinthians should do likewise when it comes to eating meat sacrificed to idols. But Paul also peppers his arguments with negative examples. Thus he cites the

ancient Israelites as another group who thought they had reached the pinnacle of godliness, but learned the hard way that salvation was not yet theirs. Like the newly-baptized Corinthians, the Israelites whom God delivered in the Exodus had been "baptized" in the cloud of God's presence and the water of the Red Sea (1 Cor. 10:1–2). But they complained and put God to the test by engaging in sexual immorality and idolatry (10:7–10). As a result they were destroyed. "Now these things occurred as examples for us" (10:6).

Invoking stories and sayings from the Hebrew scriptures is another kind of argument from authority that Paul uses liberally in 1 Corinthians. In one three-chapter stretch he quotes from Isaiah (twice), Psalms, Job, and even from an unknown Jewish text (perhaps the *Apocalypse of Elijah*) that he apparently regarded as canonical (see 1 Cor. 1:19; 2:16; 3:19, 20; and 2:9, respectively). In each case the quotation is appropriate to the situation. For example, the quotation from Isaiah 29:14 LXX in 1 Corinthians 1:19 ("I will destroy the wisdom of the wise, and the discernment of the discerning I will thwart") fits perfectly with Paul's argument against the proud and boastful and in favor of a new order in which the weak and outcast will be exalted. The authority of scripture—and hence the rhetorical impact of these quotations—is something that Paul seems to take for granted. Undoubtedly it formed part of the preaching Paul had done when he first converted the Corinthians and was something he thought he could rely upon.

Another kind of authority that Paul cites are the words of Christ himself. Paul frequently cites the example of Christ, especially the example provided by the crucifixion. Paul does not often quote Christ, but when he does he is careful to distinguish a command of Christ from his personal opinion (1 Cor. 7:10, 12).

Paul employs the words of Christ to rhetorical effect when he urges the Corinthians not to make a mockery of the Lord's Supper by making social distinctions. In Greco-Roman society some people at communal meals held places of honor at the table while others were excluded. It seems that in Corinth the converts were continuing this practice at the Lord's Supper, for it was reported to Paul that some early arrivals—probably wealthier converts who had the leisure to come sooner and the resources to supply more and better food at the potluck supper—ate and drank their fill before others could even arrive (1 Cor. 11:21). Lower-class Christians who had work obligations that detained them would arrive to find most of the food and drink gone. To jog their memories with regard to the solemn occasion of the sacred meal, Paul reminds the Corinthians of the traditions he "received" and "handed on" to them: "The Lord Jesus on the night when he was betrayed took a loaf of bread, and when he had given thanks, he broke it and said, 'This is my body that is for you. Do this in remembrance of me.' In the same way he took the cup also, after supper, saying, 'This cup is the new covenant in my blood. Do this, as often as you drink it, in remembrance of me'" (11:23–25). Paul warns them, therefore, that whoever "eats the bread or drinks the cup of the Lord *in an unworthy manner* will be answerable for the body and blood of the Lord" (11:27).

Was Paul a Misogynist?

Paul's reputation as a sexist and **misogynist** (hater of women) is based largely on quotes from the deutero-Pauline epistles (see chapter 18)—in other words, letters that Paul himself did not write. However, there are some seemingly harsh views toward women expressed in Paul's genuine letters as well.

One of the most controversial passages states, "As in all the churches of the saints, women should be silent in the churches. For they are not permitted to speak, but should be subordinate, as the law also says. If there is anything they desire to know, let them ask their husbands at home. For it is shameful for a woman to speak in church" (1 Cor. 14:33b-35). This passage has certainly played a role in the historical exclusion of women from the ordained ministry, an exclusion that persists to this day in some Christian denominations, most notably the Catholic Church. How can a woman preach a sermon if she is not even allowed to speak in church?

Many scholars think that Paul never penned these words, however. This possibility was introduced in chapter 15, but a fuller consideration is in order here. There are a number of suspicious aspects of 1 Corinthians 14:33b-35.

Internal contradictions. A blanket prohibition against women speaking in church contradicts what Paul writes in 1 Corinthians 11:5, where Paul has no problem with women praying and prophesying in the assembly, provided they wear a head covering.

Interruption of Paul's argument. These verses sharply disrupt the flow of Paul's argument in 1 Corinthians 14; removing them would considerably improve the continuity of the author's thought.

Presence of ideas foreign to Paul's thought. The text indicates that women should be subordinate *"as the law also says."* The appeal to the Jewish law is highly unusual for Paul, who was not a proponent of requiring Gentile converts to obey the Torah.

Possibility of influence from deutero-Pauline letters. The sentiments expressed here are much more closely aligned with the deutero-Pauline letters than with Paul's

continued

Was Paul a Misogynist? *continued*

genuine letters, indicating perhaps that someone with less progressive views about women inserted these lines into 1 Corinthians to make it look as though the apostle agreed with him.

Hints of confusion about the passage in the manuscript tradition. The fact that a few ancient manuscripts locate these verses in a different place (namely after verse 40) appears to confirm that there was some uncertainty about them. The theory is that a scribe copying 1 Corinthians made a marginal notation on a page containing 1 Corinthians 14, a notation that reflected the more conservative view of women found in the deutero-Pauline letters, and that this verse was mistaken by subsequent copyists for an actual part of the text that the earlier scribe had absent-mindedly left out and then scribbled in the margin.[14] The later scribes would then have thought that they were simply putting the verses *back in*, and their guesses about where best to locate the verses led to some differences in the order.

However, many scholars believe that the evidence is not strong enough to warrant the conclusion that these verses where not written by Paul.[15] Of those, some defend Paul from the charge of sexism by arguing that he was not addressing all women at all times. Instead, they claim, Paul had heard about some women who were excessively talkative or "chattering" in the church at Corinth. These women would talk about things unrelated to the matter at hand—the Lord's Supper—distracting the assembly. In this interpretation, Paul merely told *them* to be quiet, not *all* women always

and everywhere. Others respond to this claim by rejecting the idea that the women's speech being criticized is properly characterized as "chatter," as the Greek verb does not have that connotation. Moreover, the prohibition against women speaking appears to be general, not situational.

Indeed, some believe that Paul really did regard women as inferior beings who were suited only for subordinate roles in the church and society. If he did in fact think this way he was hardly alone in the ancient world. Almost all male writers from antiquity would have assumed male superiority. Is it expecting too much of Paul that he would be the exception to the rule, an advocate of women's equality in a world where such a claim was almost unthinkable?

Of course, there are those who say that Jesus was very much an advocate for women, and that he allowed them considerably more freedom than was customary in either Jewish or Roman society (see chapter 11).[16] If this is true, then one could accuse Paul of betraying Jesus by adopting a more retrograde stance with respect to women. But before one condemns Paul as a sexist who turned back the clock on women's rights in contravention to Jesus' teachings, one should consider the whole picture and not only 1 Corinthians 14:33b-35. There is little in Paul's other genuine letters that would lead one to categorize him as a misogynist, and in fact there are a number of passages that suggest the opposite. He speaks highly of a number of female colleagues, praising them for their hard work and leadership. One famous early Christian missionary team was a wife and husband,

continued

---

14. For a scribe to accidentally omit a line, phrase, or word was quite common, and the manuscripts are full of marginal corrections made either by the scribe himself or by a later editor.

15. While there are manuscripts that place 1 Cor. 14:33b–35 in a different location, there are none that omit the passage altogether. Hence, if an interpolation took place, it must have occurred very early in the process.

16. Of course, there are also scholars who claim that Jesus' "feminist" stance has been exaggerated by modern Christian readers engaged in wishful thinking.

Was Paul a Misogynist? *continued*

Priscilla (or Prisca) and Aquila. Paul speaks of them as if they are equal partners, and equally valuable to him and to the Christian church as fellow workers in Christ (Rom. 16:3-4). Paul refers to this couple as "Prisca and Aquila," rather than in the reverse order as was customary, leading many to conclude that Paul regarded her as the true head of household.

Paul also speaks highly of other women, such as Mary and "the beloved Persis," whom Paul compliments for their hard work, and a group of women who were active in the missionary field, sometimes paired with husbands or brothers, including Julia, Nereus's sister, Tryphena, Tryphosa, Euodia, Syntyche, and Rufus's mother (Rom. 16:6-15; Phil. 4:2-3). Paul refers to **Phoebe** as a "deacon" (literally "servant"), a title that is as close as the New Testament comes to the ordained ministry (Rom. 16:1-2). It is the same title that Paul uses

for Timothy, who is Paul's most trusted and prominent associate. In Romans 16:1-2 Paul makes it clear that he is entrusting the delivery of the letter to Phoebe, and she is recommended to the Romans in the strongest terms as a *prostatis*, the helper and patron of many (including Paul). Paul confers upon **Junia** an even higher distinction, declaring that she is "prominent among the apostles" and that she also suffered prison on behalf of Christ. As an "apostle," her rank was equal to Paul's (16:7).[17]

Paul speaks of Phoebe and Junia with the utmost respect. Are these the words of a misogynist? Perhaps Paul was a recent convert to the view that in Christ "there is no longer male and female" (Gal. 3:5) who occasionally lapsed into old ways of thinking. Or could the opposite be true—that Paul was fundamentally chauvinistic but occasionally entertained thoughts of equality? The debate rages on.

While there is a good deal of criticism of the audience in 1 Corinthians, and Paul is sometimes shocked at their shortcomings, at no point does Paul's emotional or rhetorical intensity rise to the level that it does in Galatians. However, things change as Paul's relationship with the Corinthians progresses. The gap between the "gentle persuasion" of 1 Corinthians and the harsh rebukes of some parts of 2 Corinthians is wide indeed. In some ways the change in tone is inevitable, as it is clear that 1 Corinthians (which is actually letter B, Paul's second letter to the church) did not have the intended effect.

Timothy had visited Corinth and reported back to Paul that the problems were not resolved and that, even worse, some of the Corinthians had lost respect for Paul. At this point Paul made a trip from Ephesus to Corinth in an attempt to straighten things out personally. However, this trip went badly; Paul describes it as a "painful visit" (2 Cor. 2:1). He was insulted publicly (2:5–8) and returned to Corinth shamed and humiliated (12:21). At this point he wrote a harsh and angry third letter to the Corinthian church, which has become known as the "Letter of Tears," because Paul says that he wrote it "out

---

17. The fact that Paul refers to a female apostle has rankled some, especially in the Catholic tradition, where the claim that Jesus' apostles were all male has been used to justify the all-male priesthood. Some have claimed that Paul referred in Rom. 16:7 not to a woman named Junia but to a man named Junias—due to the grammatical construction of this verse, the name could be either masculine or feminine. The problem with this is that "Junias" was not a name used by males in the first century. Some names have both a masculine and feminine form (think of Stephan and Stephanie, or George and Georgina), but other names are exclusively male (Greg, Mark) or exclusively female (Jill, Rhonda). In the first century CE, there were no men named Junias referenced in either Greek or Roman literature. There were only women named Junia (see "A Female Apostle?," CBMW.ORG: The Council on Biblical Manhood and Womanhood, *https://cbmw.org/uncategorized/a-female-apostle/*). So, unless we have the ancient equivalent to Johnny Cash's "A Boy Named Sue," Paul was almost certainly referring to a woman as an apostle in Rom. 16:7.

of much distress and anguish of heart and with many tears" (2:4).

Miraculously, this now-lost letter apparently moved the Corinthians, and they came to regret their shabby treatment of Paul. The unnamed person who insulted him was rebuked and punished, which was sufficient for Paul to forgive him (2 Cor. 2:5–11) and attempt to move forward with the rest of the Corinthians on the basis of renewed understanding and commitment. Paul begins his next letter to the church (Letter D, consisting mostly of 2 Cor. 1:1–7:1) by giving thanks for this unlikely reconciliation.

Whether there are lingering mistrust and ongoing divisions or whether Paul wishes merely to shore up the foundation of his newly reestablished apostolic authority over the Corinthians, in 2 Corinthians 2–6 he launches into a defense of his credentials over against those of his rivals in Corinth. These rivals have "letters of recommendation"; Paul argues that he does not need such letters because he has already proved himself to the Corinthians (3:1–3). The rivals preach themselves and brag about themselves, but Paul preaches Christ and is guided by love and humility before God rather than boastfulness (4:1–6; 5:11–6:2). The rivals claim their preaching is validated with manifestations of glory, but Paul's ministry is validated through suffering, in imitation of Christ (4:7–5:10). As the crucifixion of Christ showed, suffering and weakness are transformed by God into strength and power. So while Paul and his preaching might appear to be nothing, the plain wrapping of the man and his message does not invalidate the value within. "Treasure in clay jars" (4:7) is how Paul describes what he offers the Corinthians.

A Hollywood film would probably close the story here, because it appears that the Corinthians have returned to the fold and there is a happy ending. But in real life reconciliations do not always last. Apparently some Jewish-Christian preachers arrived in Corinth, claiming superiority to Paul and maligning his ministry. Paul is enraged to discover that they have persuaded many of his former supporters.

These Jewish-Christian preachers claim to be apostles (2 Cor. 11:5, 13) and servants of Christ (11:23); Paul derides them as "super-apostles." Their case against Paul is nicely summarized by Calvin Roetzel:

> They said Paul lacked charisma, that he was an ineffective preacher. He was frail and hypocritical—a bully in his letters but harmless in person (2 Cor. 10:10). When Paul was in Corinth he had refused money, these men alleged, either because he was insecure in his apostolate (2 Cor. 11:7, 9), or because he planned to cream off some of the Jerusalem offering for himself (12:17). For their part, these Jewish-Christian missionaries boasted of their exploits in service of the gospel. By signs and wonders they demonstrated the power of their message; through visions they gained access to heavenly secrets; and for these divine gifts they demanded support from the church and so undermined Paul's efforts to collect an offering for the poor in Jerusalem.[18]

In 2 Corinthians 10–13 (Letter E), an infuriated Paul lights into both his opponents and the Corinthians who appear to have betrayed him once again. However, he does not want to appear to be a bully, because this is precisely one of the accusations that have been made against him. So despite his anger, he needs to tread carefully. In this section, Paul's rhetoric often switches from *logos* (logical reasoning) to *ethos* (arguments based on the good character of the speaker) and *pathos* (appeals to the emotions of the audience). At times his tone is pleading. For example, when he appeals for the Corinthians to listen to him (10:1), he is almost begging: "I wish you would bear with

---

18. Roetzel, *The Letters of Paul*, 61.

me in a little foolishness. Do bear with me!" (11:1). He seems to be trying to show restraint when he says that his opponents "do not show good sense" (10:12), but at times this instinct leaves him and he gives full vent to his fury, as when he compares his opponents to the "cunning" serpent who deceived Eve (11:3) and to Satan himself (11:14).

Paul is put into the difficult position of having to defend himself without appearing to be defensive. This is a nearly impossible rhetorical challenge, but Paul rises to it, imploring his audience to remember who they know him to be: "Look at what is before your eyes" (2 Cor. 10:7). He asserts, "I think that I am not in the least inferior to these super-apostles. I may be untrained in speech, but not in knowledge; certainly in every way and in all things we have made this evident to you" (11:5–6). He employs a *reductio ad absurdum* argument to address his opponents' claim that his refusal to take money demonstrates his inferiority: "Did I commit a sin by humbling myself so that you might be exalted, because I proclaimed God's good news to you free of charge?" (11:7). How could Paul's earnest desire not to burden them with financial demands be regarded as wrongdoing? Better to look with suspicion, he suggests, upon those who demanded money from them.

In fact, Paul goes on to say that these so-called "super-apostles" are not even his equals. They claim to have Jewish roots. Well, so does Paul. But when it comes to their service for the gospel, how could Paul be counted inferior? A better example of an argument based on *ethos* can hardly be offered than the following: "Are they Israelites? So am I. Are they descendants of Abraham? So am I. Are they ministers of Christ? I am talking like a madman—I am a better one: with far greater labors, far more imprisonments, with countless floggings, and often near death. Five times I have received from the Jews the forty lashes minus one. Once I received a stoning. Three times I was shipwrecked; for a night and a day I was adrift at sea; on frequent journeys, in danger from rivers,

danger from bandits, danger from my own people, danger from Gentiles, danger in the city; danger in the wilderness, danger at sea, danger from false brothers and sisters; in toil and hardship, through many a sleepless night, hungry and thirsty, often without food, cold and naked" (11:22–27).

Paul goes through the catalogue of accusations his new opponents have made against him and demolishes them one by one. They have had visions? So has Paul (12:1–10). If they have performed signs and wonders, then the Corinthians should remember that Paul did as well: "The signs of a true apostle were performed among you with utmost patience, signs and wonders and mighty works. How have you been worse off than the other churches, except that I myself did not burden you? Forgive me this wrong!" (2 Cor. 12:12–13). Paul employs *pathos* with the obvious sarcasm of this final remark, attempting to appeal to the emotions of his audience. He is disappointed and suggests that they should feel guilty and ashamed.

Paul concludes the letter by warning the Corinthians that he is preparing for a third visit, and they should be sore afraid. Unless they repent of their errors, Paul will be "severe in using the authority that the Lord has given" him (2 Cor. 13:10). The Corinthian correspondence ends on this ominous note, and one might be tempted to believe that no matter what happened when and if Paul visited Corinth again, their stormy history would prove to be too much and there could be no final reconciliation. However, the fact that the Corinthians retained, preserved, and probably copied at least three of Paul's letters to them suggests that they did return to Paul in the end.

Rhetoric and Theology in Paul's Letter to the Romans

Romans is the one letter that Paul wrote to a church that he had not founded. Indeed he had never even visited Rome, so he is writing to what is essentially a community of strangers. Paul planned to visit Rome (see Rom. 1:15) after he had delivered the money offering he had laboriously collected for the poor in Jerusalem (15:26–28); he hoped to use Rome as a launching point for a mission to Spain (15:24–25). Rome was by far the largest and most important city in the Roman Empire, not only serving as its capital but as the home to some one million residents (probably no other city exceeded 300,000), including almost all of the empire's leading political and cultural figures. A missionary and Christian leader as prominent and accomplished as Paul may have felt that his career could not possibly have been complete without a stint in Rome.[19] Therefore he wanted to lay the groundwork for his ministry in Rome by sending a long letter introducing himself[20] and addressing some of the problems that he had heard were plaguing the church there.

One theory about the letter is that—as the Romans had not had the benefit of hearing Paul's preaching in person—Paul felt the need to introduce his message from beginning to end. This would account for the letter's unusual length and its less occasional and more general character. Paul's broad approach in the letter may also have served the particular needs of the Roman community as Paul understood them, because of the turbulent recent history of both the Jews and Christians who lived there. Both the Acts of the Apostles (see 18:2) and Roman sources (in particular Suetonius, *Divus Claudius* 25.4) indicate that the Emperor Claudius expelled the Jews from Rome sometime between 49 and 51 CE, because they were believed to be the source of some kind of "disturbances." Suetonius indicates that these disturbances were made at the instigation of a certain "Chrestus," which many believe to be a corrupted spelling of "Christus." What exactly this means is not clear, but it certainly points to tension between Jews and Christians. It is likely that the Christian community consisted of both Jewish and Gentile converts, but that Jewish Christians were in the majority and held most of the leadership positions.

One possibility, then, is that the non-Christian Jews in Rome were upset about Hellenistic Jews who had accepted Jesus as the Messiah and were advocating vigorously for more converts. The other possibility is that the Jews (and perhaps the Jewish Christians as well) were up in arms about a Gentile version of Christianity that abandoned the Torah and circumcision, as Paul's gospel did. Certainly Paul's other letters (and Acts) document a number of cases in which Paul's message caused riots elsewhere, so it would not be surprising if a similar message, even without Paul present personally, could cause violent conflict between Jews and Christians in Rome. In either event, the Romans did not distinguish between Jews and Christians until late in the first century. They would have put both Jews and Jewish-Christians into the same category as *Jews*, while Gentiles who may have converted to Christianity but had no historical connection to the Jews would not be categorized as Jews. As a result, any edict barring Jews from the city would also have applied to Jewish Christians. It would not, however, apply to Gentile Christians.[21]

As a result it appears that Claudius's expulsion of the Jews from Rome left the Gentile Roman Christians there to fend for themselves. A few years passed, and this Gentile-dominated

19. George Kennedy, *New Testament Interpretation through Rhetorical Criticism* (Chapel Hill: University of North Carolina Press, 1984), 152.

20. Paul's desire to "introduce" himself is signaled immediately by the fact that Paul spends seventy-two words (in Greek) identifying himself as the sender of the letter, when in his other letters usually four or five words suffice.

21. See Roetzel, *The Letters of Paul*, 70; Taylor, *Paul, Apostle to the Nations*, 225.

church began to flourish. Then when Jewish Christians (along with other Jews) were allowed to return to Rome following the death of Claudius in 54 CE, they found that they were now in the minority, and that Gentiles had taken all or most of the leadership positions. This new reality created a tension that Paul heard about and sought to address in his letter.

The letter's body begins with a statement of Paul's thesis: "For I am not ashamed of the gospel; it is the power of God for salvation to everyone who has faith, to the Jew first and also to the Greek" (Rom. 1:16). Happily, this single thesis would allow Paul both to introduce his basic message to an audience who had never heard it before and to address what Paul knew of the problems in Rome between Jews and Gentiles ("Greeks"). The idea that salvation was dependent on faith alone is not new for Paul, as it formed the heart of the letter to the Galatians and featured prominently in other letters as well. What is new in this letter is that Paul is speaking to a mixed audience of Jewish Christians and Gentile converts, rather than exclusively to former pagans as appears to have been the case in Galatians and his other letters to churches in Macedonia and Achaia. With these two different audiences in mind, Paul needs to shape his rhetoric accordingly. In particular, he must realize that those Jewish Christians who continue to adhere to the law might be hostile to his message, while those Gentiles who have found justification by faith through grace may have succumbed to the temptation toward libertinism as had some members of Paul's other congregations (especially in Corinth).

The letter can be divided into two main sections and several subsections. The first main section (chapters 1–11) discusses the possibility of salvation by faith through the power of God for Jews and Gentiles in general terms, while the second (chapters 12–15) appears to address specific issues within the church at Rome. Within the first section, Paul begins with the "power of God for salvation," and contrasts it to the power of God for damnation (Rom. 1:18–2:16). Then he alternately addresses the Jewish situation and the Gentile situation. However, each heading is of interest to both audiences. Gentiles need to know that Jews have not been excluded from the process of salvation. In chapters 9–11 Paul speaks of God's ongoing covenant with Israel and his faithfulness to the promises he made to the Jews; this section is likely addressed to Gentiles who thought that the church had *replaced* Israel as God's covenant partner. Similarly, chapters 6–8 reassure Jews who thought that Gentiles not under the discipline of the law would degenerate into immorality; Paul insists that freedom from the law does not mean permission to sin with impunity.

The general species of the rhetoric in Romans is **epideictic**.[22] While this is often thought of as the rhetoric of praise and blame, it is also the rhetoric of ceremonial occasions, such as anniversaries, festivals, Olympic games, state visits, and other openings and closings. The "speech" Paul presents in Romans is similar to one he might give upon his arrival in Rome, as a visiting dignitary on an official visit. He is simply giving this speech ahead of time, to predispose his audience to receive him gladly when he comes in person.

Paul's argument can be summarized as follows:

Sin is a reality that afflicts everyone. Paul believes that human history shows all people "have sinned and fall short of the glory of God" (Rom. 3:23). Jews were given the law but constantly disobeyed God's commands, as their own prophets acknowledged. Gentiles could have perceived the existence of the one God through creation but

---

22. Kennedy, *New Testament Interpretation*, 152.

instead worshiped false gods of nature, mistaking the creation for the Creator. The inevitability of human sin is connected to the sin of Adam, from whom all humans descend. Consequently, Paul argues that all humans, both Jews and Gentiles, are condemned by God and merit only damnation.

Sin and salvation both entered the world through a single man. Paul's main point in the letter is that salvation was made possible for all people, both Jews and Gentiles, by one man, Jesus Christ. But there is a symmetry, he claims, between the fall and the redemption of humankind. Just as sin, guilt, and death entered the world as a consequence of the actions of one man (Adam), so too has acquittal and life been made possible by the actions of one man (Christ).

Grace does not give humans license to sin. Although human sin elicited God's grace in the form of Christ, it does not follow, Paul insists, that humans should sin more in order that God's grace might be multiplied.[23] Sin was the dominating characteristic of people's lives before they were reborn by faith. Now that they have a new life, they cannot return to the old. For Paul, this would be like a freed slave wanting to return to bondage, or a woman whose husband had died continuing on as if she were still married to him.

The Jews have a place in God's plan of salvation. God has created a new covenant with all humans through Christ, but that does not mean that God has reneged on his promises to the Jews or abandoned the covenant he had with them. Paul is aware that many Jews had heard the gospel and rejected faith in Christ, and it would seem inevitable that they would be forsaken by God as a result. But Paul has confidence that in the final analysis—at the end of days—both Jews and Gentiles will be saved through Christ.

Peaceful co-existence between Jewish and Gentile converts to Christianity is crucial. Within the Roman church, Paul teaches, the different groups should seek unity, tolerance, and understanding: "Welcome one another . . . as Christ has welcomed you" (Rom. 15:7). Gentiles should respect the dietary scruples of their Jewish Christian brethren, and Jewish Christians should refrain from harsh criticism of Gentile converts' behavior.

Christians should seek cordial relations with outsiders. Paul insists that Roman Christians should also seek to get along as well as possible with outsiders. They should respect the civil authorities and pay taxes to persons to whom they are due. Paul maintains that the Roman Christians' primary allegiance should be to Christ, not to Rome, and in the world to come the masters of the empire will be subjects of God. However, Paul insists that for the time being the social order is ordained by God and the stability it provides gives Christians the opportunity for travel and witness.

Paul's agenda for the future. Paul reveals that he has big plans for a major new missionary effort in the western Mediterranean, if he can survive his visit to Jerusalem, and he hopes the Romans will play an important part in the fulfillment of these plans. He asks for their prayers and support. He concludes by greeting those Christians that he knows who are currently in Rome.

In this letter Paul seems to use as much of his rhetorical repertoire as he can, perhaps thinking that a Roman audience would be more learned and sophisticated than people from the provinces.

For example, Paul's thesis statement includes a **litotes**, which involves an understatement with ironic effect, often expressed as a double negative. To say that something is "not too shabby" is an

---

23. Roetzel (*The Letters of Paul*, 72) cites a wonderful illustration of this view from W. H. Auden's character Herod in *For the Time Being* (London: Faber & Faber, 1958): "I like committing crimes. God likes forgiving them. Really the world is admirably arranged" (116).

Paul and Politics

Romans 13:1–7 is often taken as Paul's definitive statement on politics and the relationship of church and state. Biblical scholar Walter Pilgrim finds three major political stances in the New Testament.[24] One is the "ethic of critical distancing," in which Christians stand apart from the government and criticize it based on Christian principles, but do not take action against the ruling regime. He finds this approach in the Gospels and Acts. The second is the "ethic of resistance," which he locates in the book of Revelation. This involves Christians actively opposing the corrupt and evil ruling authorities, cooperating with God to destroy secular governments. The third is the "ethic of submission," according to which Christians should accept the ruling authorities as ordained by God and do their civic duty as this is defined by the government. Pilgrim situates Paul firmly in the third camp, based largely on Romans 13.

Paul does counsel the Romans to submit to the rulers of the empire and bestows upon political leaders the stamp of divine approval (Rom. 13:1). The authorities exist to create and maintain order, Paul maintains, and as long as Christians behave lawfully they should have nothing to fear from the government. Paul seems to bestow upon the government a monopoly on the legitimate use of violence, arguing that the authorities employ the sword to inflict God's wrath on the wicked (13:4). So Christians should pay their taxes and give due respect and honor to their rulers.

Although the majority of Christians throughout history have followed Paul's advice, there have been exceptions. Some groups have withdrawn as much as possible from politics, seeing government as hopelessly corrupt and advocating a total separation of church and state. Other groups have cooperated so closely with the government that church and state were one and the same. But after the advent of modern secular nation-states, most Christians have seen church and state as separate but utterly compatible entities and have felt no conflict between their religion and their national citizenship. These Christians generally pride themselves on their patriotism as much as their piety, and often serve voluntarily in their country's military and otherwise support the preservation and furtherance of the nation.

Some noteworthy individuals and groups have, in Christ's name, resisted governments guilty of imperialism, colonialism, enslavement, or some other form of repression. Sometimes the dissenters have embraced violent resistance; certain Latin American liberation theologians have supported communist insurgencies against brutal authoritarian regimes. Often the resistance has been nonviolent, with violence viewed as incompatible with the teaching and example of Christ. A classic example is the civil rights movement led by the Rev. Dr. Martin Luther King Jr.

Would Paul have disapproved of Dr. King's conflicts with, for example, the state of Alabama? King himself did not believe so, and in his famous "Letter from Birmingham Jail" he even compares himself to Paul. Like Paul, who left his hometown of Tarsus and traveled throughout Greece and Asia Minor, King left his home in Atlanta and heeded the call of a distant city. According to Acts 16:9, Paul had a vision of a Macedonian man who begged him, "Come over to Macedonia and help us." King says that he too must constantly "respond to the Macedonian call for aid." However, King did not support the governing authorities in the

continued

---

24. See Walter E. Pilgrim, *Uneasy Neighbors: Church and State in the New Testament*, Overtures to Biblical Theology (Minneapolis: Fortress, 1999).

Paul and Politics *continued*

city of Birmingham and the state of Alabama. He clashed with them and condemned their policies of segregation and discrimination.

Was Paul's support for the governing authorities related to and contingent upon the relatively benign character of Roman rule during his lifetime? The empire of Paul's day was no paradise, but he lived during a long era of peace and stability; most citizens felt fairly secure if not prosperous. Perhaps Paul might have offered the Roman Christians different advice had he lived to see the persecutions of Nero.[25] But history has seen even worse regimes than Nero's. Perhaps a better question in the modern context is this: Was it acceptable for faithful Christians to give aid and support to the most evil regime of the twentieth century, that of Nazi Germany?

Some contemporary Christians might be embarrassed to learn that in Nazi Germany the overwhelming majority of Christian men of military age volunteered to serve in Hitler's armies or agreed to be conscripted, regardless of how they may have felt about National Socialism. Many other Christians either supported the Nazi regime enthusiastically or offered only the meekest resistance. In fact, only one Catholic is known to have refused to serve in Hitler's military: a courageous Austrian named Franz Jägerstätter. He was beheaded for his refusal. He did not enjoy the support of his priest or bishop, both of whom urged him to fight, citing Paul's advice in Romans 13 and Jesus' teaching to "render therefore unto Caesar the things

Christian Michelides / Wikimedia / Gedenktafel für Franz Jägerstätter.JPG / CC BY-SA 4.0

Franz Jägerstätter (1907-1943) was executed for refusing military service under the Nazi regime. At the time, local church authorities urged him to comply, only later recognizing his integrity and heroism. In 2007 he was declared a martyr and saint. This memorial plaque reads: "The young farmer Franz Jägerstätter from St. Radegund refused to fight in an unjust war. Therefore he was condemned to die on the scaffold on Aug. 9, 1943 in Brandenburg."

which are Caesar's" (Matt. 22:21, KJV). But Jägerstätter insisted that the Nazi war against Russia was aggressive and unjust, and he considered Hitler evil. His inspiration came (in part) from the Acts of the Apostles: "We must obey God rather than any human authority" (Acts 5:29).[26] Would Paul have supported Jägerstätter, or would he have urged or permitted him to fight for his country? Given the dilemma this question poses, one must wonder whether Romans 13:1-7 was perhaps appropriate in the limited historical context of Paul's world circa 55-56 CE but might not be the best basis for Christian political philosophy in all contexts.

example of litotes, as the speaker in fact means it is very good. Paul uses this device when he says that he is "not ashamed of the gospel" (Rom. 1:16). In truth Paul is proud of the gospel, despite the fact that the gospel had often been mocked and rejected and its messengers persecuted and

mistreated. Thus Paul's willingness to proclaim the gospel with pride and boldness creates a courageous persona within the letter, and this kind of argument (however implicit) falls under the category of *ethos*, arguments that will predispose an audience to look favorably on the character of the

---

25. Roetzel, *The Letters of Paul*, 75.

26. Jägerstätter's story is told in Gordon Zahn, *In Solitary Witness: The Life and Death of Franz Jägerstätter* (New York: Holt, Rinehart and Winston, 1965) and re-told in the 1971 German-language film *Die Verweigerung* ("*The Refusal*").

speaker. Paul had spoken often in his earlier letters of his courage or "boldness" in the face of opposition and the credibility he believed this bestowed upon him, and he returns to this theme later in the letter to the Romans as well (8:35–36; 15:15).

Romans 5 provides an excellent example of the rhetorical device called **climax**[27] (in Greek, "staircase" or "ladder"). Climax here involves arranging words, phrases, or clauses in increasing order of importance. A generic example would be "A is good, B is better, but C is best." After speaking of his suffering as an apostle, Paul argues that this suffering is salutary because of the good results that follow from it: "Suffering produces endurance, and endurance produces character, and character produces hope, and hope does not disappoint us, because God's love has been poured into our hearts through the Holy Spirit that has been given to us" (5:3–5).

Another device found in Romans is **pleonasm**, the use of more words than strictly necessary to make a point. This excess, or even redundancy, one finds in expressions like "black darkness" or "I saw it with my own eyes." Paul employs pleonasm when listing the historical sins of Gentile pagans: "They were filled with every kind of wickedness, evil, covetousness, malice. Full of envy, murder, strife, deceit, craftiness, they are gossips, slanderers, God-haters, insolent, haughty, boastful, inventors of evil, rebellious toward parents, foolish, faithless, heartless, ruthless" (Rom. 1:29–31).[28] If Paul wished to use litotes, he might simply have said that pagans are usually "not the greatest people," but in this instance pleonasm seemed to him to be the better way to go.

By far the most frequent figure of speech found in Romans is **hypophora**, which involves

a writer asking a question and then immediately providing an answer.[29] Hypophora is useful for heightening the importance of certain topics and showing that the author is clever enough to anticipate what his audience is probably thinking. For example, Paul asks, "Then what advantage has the Jew? Or what is the value of circumcision? Much, in every way. For in the first place the Jews were entrusted with the oracles of God" (Rom. 3:1–2; cf. 6:1–2; 7:7–8).

This device is so frequent that it has led some commentators to identify Romans as an example of a particular kind of discourse called a **diatribe**. In modernity this term has evolved to mean a violent and bitter written or verbal attack. But in antiquity a diatribe was a teaching technique that philosophers employed in which they addressed and rebuked their students and refuted logical objections to their doctrines that students had made or might make.[30] The teacher might be stern with his students, but this was only because he loved them and cared for their intellectual well-being.

This fits well with Paul's apparent attitude toward the Romans. If he wishes to visit them, be welcomed by them, and gain their support for his further missionary efforts, it hardly stands to reason that he would attack them. However, he does want them to avoid theological pitfalls that he had seen ensnare many other new converts. Even so, Romans as a whole cannot be classified as a diatribe, as a few scholars have maintained. There are too many sections in which Paul is doing something other than anticipating questions and refuting potential objections. But the letter does make frequent use of the techniques of a diatribe.

Paul also wished to explain to the Romans his plans for the future. As noted, these plans

---

27. Identified but not explained by Kennedy, *New Testament Interpretation*, 155.

28. Ibid., 155.

29. Hypophora is not quite the same as a "rhetorical question," for in the latter case no answer is provided or necessary.

30. Kennedy, *New Testament Interpretation*, 155. Kennedy draws on the work of Stanley K. Stowers, *The Diatribe and Paul's Letter to the Romans,* SBL Dissertation Series 57 (Chico, CA: Scholars Press, 1981).

involved (1) a trip to deliver contributions from the churches in Achaia and Macedonia for the needy Christians in Jerusalem (Rom. 15:24–28); (2) a journey from Jerusalem to Rome, where Paul hoped to sojourn for a while and receive support (15:24); and (3) a missionary trip to Spain (15:24, 28) and perhaps other points west, which were uncharted territory for Christian expansion (15:20–21). Paul senses that the first leg of this itinerary might be the most dangerous; he appeals for prayers that he may "be rescued from the unbelievers in Judea" and that his "ministry to Jerusalem may be acceptable to the saints" (15:31). Clearly Paul anticipates opposition in Jerusalem from the Jewish authorities, and perhaps also from the leaders of the Jerusalem church, with whom Paul had clashed in the past (see Gal. 2).

Paul's concern for his safety turned out to be prescient; according to Acts, Paul was arrested in Jerusalem and charged with capital crimes. Acts ends with Paul in Rome, facing trial but still alive. Many ancient traditions indicate that Paul (along with Peter) died there shortly thereafter, in Nero's persecution of Christians. Some other traditions, however, claim that Paul was acquitted and went on to found churches in Spain. Most scholars believe Paul was killed in Rome, never having reached Spain but having accomplished so much that he became a hero second only to Jesus in the annals of Christian history.

Key Terms

libertinism	deliberative rhetoric	*reductio ad absurdum*	litotes
enthusiasm	argument from	misogynist	climax
painful visit	analogy	Phoebe	pleonasm
Letter of Tears	argument from	Junia	hypophora
literary seams	authority	epideictic rhetoric	diatribe

Review Questions

1. What are the different kinds of literary seams, and how does each one suggest that two originally separate documents have been stitched together? What examples of these seams are found in Paul's Corinthian correspondence?

2. What parts of the chronology of Paul's relationship and correspondence with the Corinthians are generally agreed upon by scholars? What are the points of disagreement?

3. What are the main theories as to how many letters were combined to form 2 Corinthians?

4. What is the rhetorical situation in 1 Corinthians? What arguments does Paul use to address problems of libertinism, enthusiasm, and internal divisions?

5. What is the rhetorical situation in 2 Corinthians 1:1–7:1? What is the situation in 2 Corinthians 10–13? Why is Paul's tone so different in these two parts of the letter?

6. What rhetorical devices does Paul employ in 1 and 2 Corinthians? To what end is he arguing in each case?

7. Why is 1 Corinthians 7:1, "Now concerning the matters about which you wrote: 'It is well for a man not to touch a woman,'" so controversial regarding issues of sex and celibacy?

8. Why do some critics claim that Paul was a misogynist? How have others defended him on this charge? What role does 1 Corinthians 14:33b–35 play in this controversy?

9. In what ways does Paul's letter to the Romans function as an introduction to

himself, something akin to a ceremonial speech he would make after arriving as a visiting dignitary in a new city? What two main groups does Paul address in Romans, and what does he say to each of them?

10. What does Paul say about politics in Romans 13? How does his stance compare to that found in the Gospels and in the book of Revelation? Is it more likely that Paul's advice was confined to the political situation at the time he wrote it, or that he meant for Christians to always and everywhere submit to government authority?

11. What sophisticated rhetorical devices does Paul employ in the letter to the Romans?

Discussion Questions

1. What do you make of Paul's stance toward women? Would you agree that Christianity has a long history of sexism and misogyny? If so, how much blame do you think Paul (or, for that matter, the Bible generally) deserves for this? In your view, are a society's attitudes toward women attributable more to culture or to religion?

2. Paul saw a certain value in celibacy. Do you agree or disagree with his position? Do you think Paul's arguments are related to his expectation that the end of the world would occur soon, or do you think they are independent of that belief?

3. If you had been in Corinth and received some of the angrier correspondence sent by Paul (for example, 2 Corinthians 10–13), would you be more likely to be offended by his biting remarks or ashamed of your behavior and mistreatment of him? How effective is the rhetoric of anger? Are there times when this is the only appropriate response to a situation?

Bibliography and Suggestions for Further Study

(Books and websites that are accessible for general undergraduates are marked with an asterisk; other sources listed are appropriate for advanced students.)

Bornkamm, Günther. *Paul, Paulus.* New York: Harper & Row, 1971.

*Ehrman, Bart. *How Jesus Became God: The Exaltation of a Jewish Preacher from Galilee.* New York: HarperOne, 2014.

*Kennedy, George A. *New Testament Interpretation through Rhetorical Criticism.* Chapel Hill: University of North Carolina Press, 1984.

Osburn, Carroll D. *Essays on Women in Earliest Christianity.* Vol. 1. Eugene, OR: Wipf and Stock, 1993.

Pagels, Elaine. *The Gnostic Paul: Gnostic Exegesis of the Pauline Letters.* Philadelphia: Fortress, 1975.

Pilgrim, Walter. *Uneasy Neighbors: Church and State in the New Testament.* Overtures to Biblical Theology. Minneapolis: Fortress, 1999.

Ranke-Heinemann, Uta. *Eunuchs for the Kingdom of Heaven: Women, Sexuality, and the Catholic Church.* New York: Penguin, 1991.

*Roetzel, Calvin J. *The Letters of Paul: Conversations in Context.* 4th ed. Louisville: Westminster John Knox, 1998.

Sanders, E. P. *Paul.* New York: Oxford University Press, 1991.

*Taylor, Walter F. *Paul, Apostle to the Nations: An Introduction.* Minneapolis: Fortress, 2012.

The Deutero-Pauline and Pastoral Epistles

The letters discussed in this chapter are attributed to Paul by tradition and also within the letters themselves. Nevertheless, the Pauline authorship of these letters has been challenged since the beginning of historical-critical biblical scholarship. The bases for the challenge differs from letter to letter, but some common themes have emerged: (1) these letters tend to differ from Paul's genuine letters in vocabulary, theology, and literary style; (2) they reflect a historical situation or developments in church structure that do not fit Paul's known lifespan; or (3) early external attestation for these letters (references to or quotations from them in other literature) is lacking.

These letters are grouped under two categories: 2 Thessalonians, Ephesians, and Colossians are categorized as "**deutero-Pauline**," or "second-Pauline," and are considered closer in style and content to Paul's genuine epistles and generally closer historically to Paul as well. 1 and 2 Timothy and Titus are called the **Pastoral Epistles** and are considered later than the deutero-Pauline letters. They are also distinctive for their more personal nature, claiming to have been sent by Paul[1] to individual coworkers (hence "pastors") rather than churches, and including

content that focuses heavily on the institution and offices of the church.

Good reasons have been advanced both for and against Pauline authorship for the letters. Recently Luke Timothy Johnson, Michael Gorman, and other prominent scholars have reconsidered the Pauline authorship of some of these letters on the basis of a more fluid notion of authorship that relies on a secretary (*amanuensis*) doing most of the writing, or a coauthor taking an advanced role, or even an associate working from notes. Nonetheless, most scholars remain convinced that all of these letters are pseudonymous. The consensus is stronger for the Pastoral Epistles than for the deutero-Pauline letters.

Second Thessalonians

Readers of the New Testament know quite a bit about Paul's mission to Thessalonica from 1 Thessalonians and from Acts 17. First Thessalonians is sent from somewhere in Greece, probably Corinth, as Paul went there after his time in Athens. As indicated in chapter 16, 1 Thessalonians was probably written in 51 CE, although a slightly earlier date is possible.

---

1. In order to maintain consistency and avoid unnecessary complexity, the author of all of these letters will be referred to as Paul, even where Pauline authorship is doubtful.

While in Corinth, Paul was brought before Proconsul Gallio (Acts 18:12). This event can be dated with rare precision. The fragmentary inscription shown here identifies Gallio (ΓΑΛΛΙΩΝ) as proconsul of Achaia in 52CE.

Authorship

For the substantial minority of Pauline scholars who believe 2 Thessalonians was written by Paul and his coworkers, this history is important. In this view, 2 Thessalonians was written soon after 1 Thessalonians. Paul was probably still in Corinth, where he stayed for eighteen months, so the letter would be dated to 52 or 53 CE. Second Thessalonians suggests a worsening situation in the church not long after Paul had written to them, especially involving confused views of the second coming of Jesus. Michael Gorman proposes three developments that prompted Paul to write 2 Thessalonians: (1) continuing persecution (2 Thess. 1:6), (2) claims that the day of the Lord has arrived (2:2), and (3) a growing problem with idleness (3:6–15; cf. 1 Thess. 5:14).[2]

If the letter is pseudonymous, though, the chronology of Paul's historical mission to Thessalonica is not significant. There are a number of reasons for believing that 2 Thessalonians was not written by Paul and his coworkers,

not all of which cohere. Some scholars would say that 2 Thessalonians grapples with the delay of the parousia, given that 1 Thessalonians indicated that Jesus was going to return very shortly. Paul himself would not need to deal with disappointment over Jesus' failure to return in glory after only a few months or years, but Paul's surviving colleagues faced this issue in later decades. Other scholars note that in 2 Thessalonians Paul refers to a letter that was circulating at that time that falsely claims to have been authored by him (2 Thess. 2:1–2); this points to a date after Paul's death, since pseudonymous letters would probably not be circulating during Paul's lifetime.

Some scholars who assert the pseudonymity of 2 Thessalonians argue that the similarities in structure and language between the two letters addressed to the church at Thessalonica are superficial, and that the second letter is the work of a later writer who simply copied words and phrases from Paul's genuine letter to the Thessalonians. Perhaps the most common arguments for pseudonymity, however, rely on alleged differences in eschatology, theology, style, and tone between 1 and 2 Thessalonians.

Paul's tone in 1 Thessalonians is warm and comforting. He presents himself as the mother and father of his readers; they are his children whom he yearns to see. In 2 Thessalonians, however, the author seems distant and cold.

The theological content is also strikingly different. For instance, in 1 Thessalonians Paul asserts that no one knows when the end will come, but in 2 Thessalonians the author says that certain signs must occur before the end comes. Some scholars see this as contradictory to what Paul says in 1 Thessalonians. However, defenders of Pauline authorship of 2 Thessalonians argue that the Christian tradition, starting with Jesus in the Gospels, often maintains both

2. Michael Gorman, *Apostle of the Crucified Lord: A Theological Introduction to Paul and His Letters* (Grand Rapids: Eerdmans, 2004), 169–70.

that the timing of the end is unknown and that people should nonetheless watch for signs of the coming end. Thus 1 Thessalonians says, "we do not know," but 2 Thessalonians says "keep alert for the signs." Moreover, if some people in Thessalonica were arguing that the end had already come, Paul would be trying to disabuse them of this notion and so would adopt a more distant tone, perhaps due to anger or disappointment.

In dealing with the coming day of the Lord in chapter 2, though, Paul uses terminology that is not found elsewhere in his letters, or in the New Testament as a whole, such as "the lawless one," "the one who now restrains," and "the rebellion." While these terms seem to refer to end-time scenarios that are similar to those found in Paul's letters, the Gospels, the non-Pauline letters, and Revelation—scenarios that refer to an "Antichrist," or "beast," or false messiahs and the signs prior to the final eschatological events—2 Thessalonians does not use these terms or ideas but employs its own unique language. To many of those in the pseudonymity camp, this language makes authorship by Paul doubtful.

Outline

Like Paul's genuine epistles, this short letter begins with a salutation (2 Thess. 1:1–2) from Paul and the two coworkers named as co-senders of 1 Thessalonians, Silvanus and Timothy. The salutation has a typical grace, which is slightly longer than that in 1 Thessalonians. In fact, apart from the longer grace ("from God our father and the Lord Jesus Christ") the salutations are identical. Some scholars cite this as evidence that Paul wrote both letters, while others see this as evidence of pseudonymity; the author of 2 Thessalonians merely copied Paul's style.

The thanksgiving (2 Thess. 1:3–12) reflects some of the concerns of 1 Thessalonians, as he thanks them for their faith, love, and steadfastness while enduring persecutions and afflictions (1:3–4). Paul assures them this suffering makes them "worthy of the kingdom of God" (1:5). This section reflects some of the positive elements of 1 Thessalonians. Paul strongly condemns those who persecute the disciples of Jesus; when Jesus returns, God will "repay" them "with affliction" and they will be separated from God forever (1:6–10). Paul then prays that their faith might continue to grow through God's power (1:11–12), but it is the condemnation theme that sets the letter's tone.

The main theme of the body of the letter (2 Thess. 2:1–3:15) is the apocalyptic scenario briefly outlined above in the discussion of authorship. Paul warns his readers not to be deceived by people who claim that the day of the Lord has already arrived. Apparently some were circulating a letter, supposedly from Paul, saying that the resurrection had already occurred (2:2). To counter this false view, the author states that prior to the second coming a "rebellion" will occur, centered on **"the lawless one"** (2:3, 6, 8). Something is now "restraining" him (2:6–7). Paul defines none of these terms. Is the lawless one like the Antichrist mentioned in 1 John? Who or what is restraining him? Ultimately the restraint will be removed and "then the lawless one will be revealed, whom the Lord Jesus will destroy with the breath of his mouth, annihilating him by the manifestation of his coming" (2:8).[3] This scenario, Paul suggests, is unfolding now, seen in "the working of Satan" who turns people from the truth with deception. Because of Satan's trickery, people "refused to love the truth and so be saved" (2:9–10). Curiously, it is not Satan who sends the deception, but God: "God sends them a powerful delusion, leading

---

3. The "breath of his mouth" echoes earlier eschatological writings (see Isa. 11:4; *4 Ezra* 13:10).

them to believe what is false" (2:11). The idea of God as source of deception raises a theological problem not easily solved.

In the remainder of the body of the letter, Paul asks for prayers for him and Timothy and Silvanus so that the "word of the Lord" might be spread everywhere and that they might find relief from "wicked and evil" people (2 Thess. 3:1–2). Paul is confident that God will remain faithful with them and strengthen them to continue "doing the things that we command" (3:4). The tone changes after this. It seems that—due to the mistaken notion that the resurrection has already occurred—some believers have stopped working (3:6, 11–12). Paul insists that all who want to eat must work, following the example set down by the apostles themselves (3:7–10). Paul calls for imitation of himself, as he did in 1 Thessalonians (1 Thess. 2:14). There they were to imitate Paul (and the apostles and Jesus) by enduring suffering patiently; here they are to imitate Paul and his coworkers by working to earn a living. Paul orders that those who do not obey the commands of this letter be shunned so that they will be "ashamed" (3:14).

The closing of the letter begins with a peace wish (2 Thess. 3:16) and ends with a simple grace (3:18), but it is the verse between them that garners the most attention: "I, Paul, write this greeting with my own hand. This is the mark in every letter of mine; it is the way I write" (3:17). For proponents of Paul's authorship, this line is the quintessential proof, intended to counter the "supposed" letter of Paul mentioned in 2:2. However, for those who argue the letter is pseudonymous, this is one more aspect of the ruse intended to support Pauline authorship. The claim of genuine authorship is so adamant that it begins to look suspicious, a classic case of the old Shakespearean adage: "The lady doth protest too much" (*Hamlet*, 3.2.254).

Colossians

Colossae was a small city in the Lycus Valley, near Hierapolis and Laodicea, two other early Christian centers in Asia Minor (present-day Turkey). Colossae is about 200 km (120 miles) from Ephesus, the major Roman city of this region, located on the Aegean Sea, where Paul spent a number of years, according to Acts. Colossians asserts the church was founded by Epaphras, a coworker of Paul's, who was also a native of Colossae (Col. 1:7–8; 4:12–13; Philem. 23). The letter also presents a situation in which Paul is in prison (Col. 4:3, 10, 18), perhaps in Rome, though Caesarea and Ephesus have also been suggested.

Authorship

The question of the location of Paul's imprisonment, however, is moot if he was not the author. Reasons for disputing Paul's authorship include perceived differences in theology, vocabulary, and style between Colossians and Paul's undisputed letters. Key theological differences in Colossians from Paul's authentic epistles include Christ as "cosmic" ruler (Col. 1:15–20); the church as a "cosmic" body (1:18, 24–27); Christians already sharing in the resurrection (1:13); and a "household code" restricting the behavior of women, children, and slaves (3:18–4:1). Such a code represents the later thinking of the Pauline school and not that of the historical Paul.[4] Some scholars, however, dispute whether these theological differences with Paul's letters are sufficient to rule out Pauline authorship. Colossians also differs in vocabulary and sentence structure, though. For example, in Greek the sentences in Colossians are extremely long, much longer than those typically found in the undisputed letters of Paul.

---

4. Gorman, *Apostle of the Crucified Lord*, 476.

The question of authorship, as a result, is probably more evenly divided for Colossians than any other disputed Pauline letter except 2 Thessalonians. If Paul wrote the letter, he would probably have done so from Rome and the letter would date to around 60 CE. If Paul was not the author, the letter would probably have been written not long after his death, probably not later than about 80 CE.

Outline

According to Colossians, the church there is dealing with a theological threat seemingly combining elements of Jewish religion and Greco-Roman Gnostic philosophy (Col. 2:8, 16–18, 20–23). These ideas are seen to challenge the unique place of Jesus Christ as Savior, in whom "the whole fullness of deity dwells" (2:9). In this combination of beliefs and practices, which scholars term the "**Colossian heresy**," it appears that Jesus was just one of several spiritual beings to be worshipped.[5] The letter presents Jesus as the supreme and unique locus of God's power and diminishes other claimants for divine worship, whether angels or other beings.

The salutation presents the letter as from Paul and Timothy "to the saints and faithful . . . in Colossae" (Col. 1:1–2). The thanksgiving (1:3–14) speaks of the church's faith and love, which comes from "the hope" laid up for them in heaven, which must indicate Christ (1:4–6). Epaphras is identified as the one who taught them the faith and also brought information about them to Paul and Timothy (1:7–8). In the second half of the thanksgiving, Paul and Timothy pray for their continued spiritual growth

kristobalite / Flickr / Basilique Sant'Angelo in Formis à Capoue / CC BY-NC-ND 2.0

Christ sits enthroned in heaven in this eleventh-century fresco from Sant'Angelo in Formis. The author of Colossians insists that Christ's status is unique, far above that of angels.

and knowledge. The Colossians are told that they "share in the inheritance of the saints in the light," since they have been "rescued . . . from the power of darkness and transferred . . . into the kingdom of his beloved Son" (1:12–13). This seems to be at odds with Paul's genuine epistles, since Colossians presents salvation as something already accomplished.[6]

The body of the letter (Col. 1:15–4:1) opens with the heart of the theological teaching of Colossians (1:15–2:23): the cosmic reality of Christ, who is superior to all powers. Those who

---

5. Markus Barth, Helmut Blanke, and Astrid B. Beck, *Colossians: A New Translation with Introduction and Commentary*, Anchor Bible (New York: Doubleday, 1994), 21–39; Peter Thomas O'Brien, *Colossians, Philemon*, Word Biblical Commentary 44 (Waco, TX: Word, 1982), xxx–xli; Eduard Lohse, *Colossians and Philemon: A Commentary on the Epistles to the Colossians and to Philemon*, Hermeneia (Philadelphia: Fortress, 1971), 127–31.

6. Paul's genuine letters typically insist that salvation has a future element and is not fully realized in the present (see, e.g., Phil. 3:12–14).

have faith in Christ are made holy, blameless, and irreproachable. Believers gain reconciliation through the cross, if they "continue securely established and steadfast in the faith, without shifting from the hope promised by the gospel" they have heard, "which has been proclaimed to every creature under heaven" (1:23). Colossians 1:15–20, often called "The Christ Hymn," is thought to be a preexisting Christian hymn or poem (similar to Phil. 2:6–11). After citing the hymn, the letter then segues into a meditation on suffering and the hope of glory (Col. 1:24–2:7). In this section Paul claims that he is "completing" Christ's suffering (1:24). Two interpretations of this claim have been offered. One is that Paul is asserting that there are a series of apocalyptic sufferings that must be fulfilled before the end of time. The second is that Paul, as a part of the body of Christ, joins his sufferings to those of Christ in some mystical manner.[7] Paul would not have felt that there was something lacking in Christ's sacrifice, but instead is suggesting that the members of the body of Christ, the church, play a role in suffering for Christ. Paul sees this as a "mystery" that is now revealed to the saints, including Gentiles (1:26–27), in whom Christ now lives and who are to become "mature in Christ" (1:28).

Paul warns that Christians are to beware of "philosophy and empty deceit, according to human tradition, according to the elemental spirits of the universe, and not according to Christ" (Col. 2:8–23). What is meant by "human tradition" and "elemental spirits" (*stoicheia*)? The

point here seems to be to reject any sort of god or power or means of understanding the truth other than Christ. Since the "fullness of deity" is in Christ (2:9), nothing else is essential to salvation. As the Colossians were buried in baptism with Christ and raised with him in faith (2:12), their trespasses were "nail[ed] . . . to the cross" (2:13–15), and thus there is no reason to submit to the demands of other religious or philosophical traditions (2:16–23).

The last portion of the body of Colossians might be classified as ethical exhortation (Col. 3:1–4:1). Paul tells the Colossians that, since they have been raised with Christ, they must set their minds on things above (3:1–4). They are now in Christ, so they are to strip off their old selves and clothe themselves anew (3:9–11). There are to be no ethnic distinctions in Christ: "There is no longer Greek and Jew, circumcised and uncircumcised, barbarian, Scythian, slave and free; but Christ is all and in all!" (3:11; cf. Gal. 3:28)—so they should be clothed with compassion, humility, kindness, and love, not with ethnic identities or human status markers (3:12–17). Although this would seem to break down social barriers, the last portion of the letter focuses on how to maintain social distinctions based on a "**household code**"[8] that places each person in the hierarchical structure of the society.

The social implications of being "in Christ" (Col. 1:2, 4) do not seem to change one's status in the household (3:18–4:1). Three basic household pairs are defined: wives and husbands, children and parents, slaves and masters. The way these

---

7. Donald Senior and John J. Collins, "Commentary on Colossians," in *The Catholic Study Bible*, Oxford Biblical Studies Online, *http://www.oxfordbiblicalstudies.com/article/book/obso-9780195282801/obso-9780195282801-div1-7592*. For a complete list of possible answers to this "suffering," see Steven W. Spivey, "Colossians 1:24 and the Suffering Church," *Journal of Spiritual Formation & Soul Care* 4, no. 1 (2011): 43–62, especially 44.

8. This term refers to the rules governing social interactions in the household, especially those involving the husband/wife, father/child, and master/slave relationships. Fairly complete household codes occur in Eph. 5:21–6:9 and 1 Pet. 2:13–3:12 but in none of Paul's undisputed letters, nor do the Gospels suggest that Jesus ever issued such a code. Controlling social arrangements within the household seems to have been more a concern for the second generation of Christianity than the first, perhaps because of the delay of the parousia and the dawning realization that Christianity might need to settle in for the long haul.

roles are carried out might be modified by being in Christ, but the roles themselves remain intact.[9] Wives are to submit to their husbands, children are to obey their parents, and slaves are to follow their masters' commands. Does this indicate that equality in the church does not exist beyond the church doors? Perhaps at the time it did. Ancient society was very hierarchical. Slavery was an accepted social reality, legal throughout the Roman Empire. Marriage was patriarchal, with the *paterfamilias* assuming a dominant role in the family by both law and custom. The household codes in Colossians and elsewhere in the New Testament do not challenge the prevailing social structure. The codes simply reflect the household roles existing at the time. Most modern interpreters would say it is a mistake to simply assume that these ancient household codes necessarily establish the social order for all time. Slavery was accepted in New Testament times but is now abolished throughout the world, at least in theory, so it is fair to ask whether patriarchal marriage—in which wives must be obedient to their husbands—should also be discarded.

The closing of the body of the letter, with concluding admonitions (Col. 4:2–6) and greetings and instructions (4:7–17), is typical for a Pauline letter and one reason for positing a connection between this letter and the historical Paul. Here Paul mentions that he is in prison and refers to a large number of friends and associates by name. How does one account for the personal references within Colossians (4:7–17 especially), to people such as Tychicus, Aristarchus, Mark, Luke, and Nympha, all known acquaintances of the apostle Paul from other (genuine) letters? Do these references indicate that Paul himself wrote this letter? Or could it be that the pseudonymous author knew these individuals had been with Paul and simply used an existing list of his associates in a letter written long after Paul died? Could the entire imprisonment scenario be a creation of the deutero-Pauline author?

As noted, Paul claims to append a greeting written in his own hand (4:18). This verse, if not written by Paul, raises questions not just of pseudonymity but of flat-out deception.[10] Biblical scholars tend to downplay the element of deceit involved in pseudonymity, in part because there are so many examples of this practice in antiquity. But the word "pseudonymous" could be seen as a euphemism for "forgery." Are scholars too gentle about pseudonymity, excusing bald-faced lying simply because it was common in the ancient world? Because of considerations like this, many believers (and not a few scholars) recoil from identifying Colossians and other New Testament texts as pseudonymous.

Ephesians

Ephesus was a major Roman city on the Aegean Sea, in the province of Asia Minor (present-day Turkey), and a large commercial center in the eastern provinces of the Roman Empire. It was also the governmental city of the Roman province with a population of around 250,000, which placed it as the second or third largest city in the Roman Empire. Ephesus was noted for the Temple of Artemis, goddess of hunting and the moon, which stood for more than 1,200 years and was considered one of the seven wonders of the ancient world. Paul first went to Ephesus in the early fifties according to Acts 18:18–21. He returned a short time later and stayed for

---

9. Margaret Y. MacDonald, *Colossians and Ephesians*, Sacra Pagina (Collegeville, MN: Liturgical Press, 2000), 166–69; for the entire discussion see 152–69.

10. David Brakke, "Early Christian Lies and the Lying Liars Who Wrote Them: Bart Ehrman's *Forgery and Counterforgery*," *The Journal of Religion* 96, no. 3 (July 2016): 378–90.

Artemis as worshipped in Ephesus was a fertility goddess. Considered one of the seven wonders of the world, her temple was both a source of pride and income to the city, for it was a major tourist destination.

at least two years (19:10; 20:31). Acts 19 gives an account of his ministry there and a riot that broke out over Paul's impact on the trade in the Temple of Artemis.

Authorship

Though there is an extensive history of Paul's relationship with Ephesus, many more scholars consider Ephesians a pseudonymous letter than Colossians. For one thing, although Paul was close with the Ephesians according to Acts, his letter to them is presented in "a curiously impersonal tone."[11] Unlike Colossians, written to a church that Paul had never visited, Ephesians reflects little of the actual life or people of Ephesus. The letter is also closely related literarily and theologically to Colossians, which has led many scholars to reject its Pauline authorship, arguing it was written by a disciple or later follower of Paul around 80–100 CE.[12] Others identify Ephesians with the lost **letter to the Laodiceans** (Col. 4:16). Since some early manuscripts omit "in Ephesus" in 1:1, some scholars see Ephesians as a circular letter, which could have been sent to a number of cities. Those who maintain that the letter was written by Paul, whether as a circular letter or perhaps the letter to the Laodiceans, understand the similarities with Colossians as arising from it having been written at about the same time as Colossians, perhaps employing the same secretary. These scholars date Ephesians to the end of Paul's life, probably during his imprisonment in Rome in the sixties.

Outline

Ephesians focuses on the universal church. The author asserts that there is no greater power than Christ, an argument also made in Colossians, and that in Christ all peoples, Jew and Gentile, are brought together. This leads to reflections on the new life in Christ and how Christians are to live together. Though Ephesians is considered to be dependent upon Colossians (even by scholars who argue for its authenticity) it is a much longer letter.

The salutation is from Paul alone, unlike Colossians, which has Timothy as a co-sender. It is addressed "to the saints who are in Ephesus and are faithful in Christ Jesus" (Eph. 1:1–2). As noted above, the words "in Ephesus" are missing from some of the earliest and best manuscripts. This has led scholars to question the origin of the

---

11. Donald Senior and John J. Collins, "The Letter to the Ephesians," in *The Catholic Study Bible*, Oxford Biblical Studies Online, *http://www.oxfordbiblicalstudies.com/article/book/obso-9780195282801/obso-9780195282801-chapterFrontMatter-54*.

12. Ibid.

letter and its original purpose. The blessing that follows (1:3–14) echoes that of Colossians, especially in its references to the followers of Christ being blessed "in the heavenly places" (1:3) as they were chosen to be with Christ "before the foundation of the world" (1:4). They were, Paul says, "destined . . . for adoption as his children through Jesus Christ" (1:5; cf. 1:11). As in Colossians, Ephesians suggests a salvation that in many respects is already accomplished, though the blessing does note that they have been "marked with the seal of the promised Holy Spirit" (1:13) as "the pledge of our inheritance toward redemption" (1:14), which suggests that salvation is not yet fully realized.

The following section (Eph. 1:15–23) consists of a prayer. It has elements of a typical thanksgiving, namely a prayer on behalf of the recipients especially, but its placement so late in the letter is unusual. Paul prays that they "may know what is the hope to which he has called" them (1:18). This hope is the power of God for those who believe, which was active in Christ's resurrection and ascension (1:20). This power is above "all rule and authority and power and dominion, and above every name that is named, not only in this age but also in the age to come" (1:21), echoing the theme of Christ's superiority found in Colossians. Like Colossians, Ephesians presents Christ as the "head" of the body of Christ (1:22–23).

The body of the letter (Eph. 2:1–6:20) takes up the theological teaching of what Christ has accomplished on behalf of all humanity, which was dead through trespasses and sin because it followed the "course (Greek, *aeōn*) of this world" and the "ruler of the power of the air" (2:1–2). People were by nature children of wrath (2:3), dead in sin (2:5), but God "raised us up with him and seated us with him in the heavenly places in Christ Jesus" (2:6). "For by grace you have been saved through faith," Paul explains, "and this is not your own doing; it is the gift of God—not

the result of works, so that no one may boast" (2:8–9). No one merits salvation, but "we are what he has made us, created in Christ Jesus for good works, which God prepared beforehand to be our way of life" (2:10).

This new reality for humanity also leads to the unity of Jews and Gentiles, for "now in Christ Jesus you who once were far off have been brought near by the blood of Christ" (Eph. 2:13). Paul is clear that Christ created "one new humanity," reconciling "both groups to God in one body through the cross" (2:15–16). As a result, all people can now be "citizens" and "members of the household of God, built upon the foundation of the apostles and prophets, with Christ Jesus himself as the cornerstone" (2:19–20). The image of the church built on "the foundation of the apostles" suggests that the time of the apostles is in the past and is one of the reasons scholars see this letter as emerging from a time after Paul.

The author of Ephesians understands himself as a revealer of God's plan, offering divine knowledge (Eph. 3:1–13). The heart of the revelation is simply that Gentiles have joined the Jews as fellow heirs in God's plan (3:3–6), a mystery "hidden for ages in God," but now made known "to the rulers and authorities in the heavenly places" (3:9–10). Christian converts—both Jew and Gentile—have been freed from the bonds of the malevolent forces in the world and are now able to form a single community. In fact, the church, Paul says, is a *patria* (3:14–15), which could mean God's family (2:19) or even homeland. In this family, the love of Christ transcends all and Christ can accomplish "abundantly far more than all we can ask or imagine" (3:18–21).

The unity of humanity in the church leads to an extended ethical exhortation (Eph. 4:1–6:20). Paul makes an appeal for unity, to lead a life worthy of Christ's call, because there is one body and one Spirit, one Lord, one faith, one baptism, one God and Father "who is above all and through all and in all" (4:1–6). Having established the familial quality of the one church community, Paul insists on the need to grow to maturity (4:11–16).

Family members are told to strip off the old self and to be clothed with the new self (Eph. 4:22–24), as Christians are "members of one another" (4:25). It is essential to put away bitterness and wrath and malice, to be kind and tenderhearted (4:28–32), to be imitators of God, and to "live in love" (5:1–2). Certain forms of speech and behavior must be rejected, as these will not inherit "the kingdom of Christ and of God" (5:3–5).

Ephesians also provides hints at the content of early Christian worship: "As you sing psalms and hymns and spiritual songs among yourselves, singing and making melody to the Lord in your hearts" (Eph. 5:19). Many scholars believe that 5:14—"Sleeper, awake! Rise from the dead, and Christ will shine on you"—reflects an early baptismal liturgy.

Finally, as in Colossians, the social implications of being in Christ are outlined (Eph. 5:22—6:9). The metaphor of Christians as family is applied to the actual Christian household, with the three pairs of the household code represented again: wives and husbands, children and parents, slaves and masters. There is an even greater focus on the submission of wives, children, and slaves. Modern readers are quick to notice the lack of condemnation of the institution of slavery and the focus on wifely submission. In partial defense of the letter, Margaret Y. MacDonald notes that Ephesians differs from Colossians in the extended use of the marriage metaphor between Christ and the church and the mutual submission demanded of both husband and wife.[13] Even so, MacDonald concludes, "attempts by commentators to take the patriarchal sting out of Eph 5:22–6:9 have generally proved unconvincing."[14]

The closing of the body of the letter is more extensive than that of Colossians. In Ephesians 6:10–20 the author utilizes the image of two powers that are at war. So as to fend off attacks from the enemy, Christians need the whole armor of God. As in Colossians, Paul adds a personal ending, remarking that he is "an ambassador in chains" for the Gospel and that Tychicus is present with him and will be his messenger (6:20–22; cf. Col. 4:7). The letter closes with a short peace wish and grace (Eph. 6:23–24).

First and Second Timothy and Titus

The Pastoral Epistles, or letters, are addressed to Timothy in Ephesus (1 Tim. 1:2–3; 2 Tim. 1:2, 18) and Titus in Crete (Titus 1:4–5). Both of these men are known coworkers of Paul in his missionary journeys. **Timothy** is mentioned numerous times in Paul's letters and is often listed as a coauthor of his letters (e.g., 1 and 2 Thessalonians); he is also referred to in the Acts of the Apostles (see Acts 16–20). Though **Titus** is not mentioned in Acts, he appears as a major coworker of Paul's in 2 Corinthians (2:13; 7:6, 13–14; 8:6, 16, 23; 12:18) and Galatians (2:1, 3). These letters instruct Timothy and Titus as leaders in the church, with special attention to the proper ordering of the church.

These letters are called "**pastoral**" because they advise Timothy and Titus as to how they should fulfill their pastoral offices (i.e., their duties as church leaders) and how to appoint other men (and perhaps women) to leadership roles. In terms of content, they have been seen to form a group, although Michael Gorman points out that 2 Timothy stands apart from

---

13. MacDonald, *Colossians and Ephesians*, 336–41; for the entire discussion see 324–41.

14. Ibid., 341.

1 Timothy and Titus, for it does not deal with church offices at all.[15] All three letters, though, do share the same basic concern for the teaching of the church.

Authorship

Although these instructions are addressed in the form of letters to Paul's closest associates, many scholars do not believe they have the sense of private letters. Since the nineteenth century the authorship of the Pastoral Epistles has been contested, with most New Testament scholars doubting their authenticity. As a result, the scholarly discussion of the Pastorals has tended to revolve around the issue of Paul's authorship. There are five basic positions that will be outlined here, though others have been imagined.

1. The Pastorals are pseudonymous. Werner Kümmel, in his influential *Introduction to the New Testament,* claims that external attribution of these letters is less well attested in early church writers than the genuine letters of Paul, though he acknowledges that from the late second century on these letters are considered Paul's.[16] Kümmel contests Pauline authorship on the grounds that (a) the language and style are radically different than Paul's genuine letters; (b) the historical situation in the letters does not fit into the chronology of Paul's life as we know it; (c) the struggle against false teachers does not seem real but typological; (d) the community situation seems to indicate that the bearers of tradition, the apostles, have died,

and references to church leadership reflect a later, developed, institutional Christianity; and (e) the Christology of the Pastorals differs from that of Paul's undisputed letters.[17]

Kümmel does not believe these letters preserve any genuine fragments of Paul's writing, but thinks that one author wrote them all in the supposed style of Paul.[18] Who wrote them is not known, says Kümmel, though their origin is thought to be in Asia Minor at the beginning of the second century. Kümmel is expansive on the purpose of these letters, arguing that they are meant to defend "the living authority of Paul in churches which are threatened by false teaching and which must adjust to the world in view of the delay of the parousia."[19] In response, "a representative of these communities, as guarantor of the Pauline legacy," employs "the fiction of an apostolic writing to a recognized disciple of Paul" to combat false teaching.[20]

2. The Pastorals may be authentic. Luke Timothy Johnson states "emphatically the impossibility of *demonstrating* the authenticity of the Pastoral Letters," but goes on to say that "it is possible to state, however, that the grounds for declaring them inauthentic are so flawed as to seriously diminish the validity of the scholarly 'majority opinion.'"[21] So while the Pastoral Letters might evince a different style and vocabulary and, more significantly, a different theology, Johnson argues that (a) there is an "impossibility of systematizing Paul's 'thought'—even granting that there is anything systematic about it in

---

15. Gorman, *Apostle of the Crucified Lord,* 533–36.

16. Werner Georg Kümmel, Paul Feine, and Johannes Behm, *Introduction to the New Testament,* rev. ed. (Nashville: Abingdon, 1986), 370–71. For the entire discussion see 370–87.

17. Ibid., 370–84.

18. Ibid., 385–86.

19. Ibid., 386.

20. Ibid.

21. Luke Timothy Johnson, *The First and Second Letters to Timothy: A New Translation with Introduction and Commentary,* Anchor Bible (New York: Doubleday, 2008), 91. For the entire discussion see 55–99.

the first place"; (b) "there is no generic 'Pauline letter,' but only a collection of unique missives"; and (c) "there is no such thing as a 'Pauline theology' that stands outside these discrete compositions, but only the specific rhetoric of a pastor and teacher who responds in writing to situations presented by his churches."[22] Perhaps there was development in Paul's theology over time, or a new focus. If Paul's letters are "situational," why would the situation not influence their content and the form in which they are expressed?

Related to this is the supposed freedom of the *amanuensis* (or "secretary") in Paul's day, which means that Paul might have had less of a role in writing these letters if he was imprisoned, or that he might have had to rely more heavily on a secretary, or that he was employing a new secretary with a different style. There are numerous **hapax legomena** (words that appear nowhere else in a body of writing) in the Pastoral Epistles, which seems to set these letters apart from Paul's genuine epistles. However, most of these words occur in other writings prior to 50 CE and there are as many *hapax legomena* in Romans as in the three Pastorals, although Romans is much longer than the Pastorals. Johnson concludes by saying that "the possibility then emerges that these might be real letters, written by Paul in the manner of other types of letters in his diverse correspondence."[23]

3. Second Timothy alone is true to Paul. Michael Gorman has taken a modified position, recognizing, with both Kümmel and Johnson, that 2 Timothy differs significantly from 1 Timothy and Titus, especially on the ordering of church offices.[24] "A 'compromise' position," Gorman writes, "would be to hold that the basic contents of 2 Timothy come from the time of Paul and represent his thought accurately, while 1 Timothy and Titus are from a later time and represent a development from Paul himself."[25] Though Gorman is not certain whether this means 2 Timothy was written during Paul's life or compiled after his death, the letter "faithfully preserves the spirit, though not necessarily the letter, of the apostle Paul."[26]

4. The Pastorals contain fragments of genuine Pauline letters. C. K. Barrett believes that the vocabulary, style, and theology differ from Paul's genuine letters and that the historical situation is difficult to fit into Paul's career as we know it.[27] These factors suggest that Paul did not write these letters as they stand, but that some anonymous follower of Paul has taken fragments from genuine letters and inserted them in what became the Pastorals. Barrett cites with approval an earlier proposal that five fragments—(1) Titus 3:12–15; (2) 2 Tim. 4:13ff., 20, 21a; (3) 2 Tim. 4:16–18a; (4) 2 Tim. 4:9–12, 22b; and (5) 2 Tim. 1:16f, 3:10f, 4:1–6, and 4:18b–22a—are authentic pieces of Paul's letters that can be fitted into Paul's career.[28]

Why would the **pseudepigrapher** (literally, "false writer") take these fragments and build them into the Pastoral Letters? First, Barrett finds it difficult to believe that a pseudepigrapher himself would write such "artless—and in some ways pointless—scraps," and that while it is difficult to reconstruct the situation in which

---

22. Ibid., 93.

23. Ibid., 99.

24. Gorman, *Apostle of the Crucified Lord*, 534.

25. Ibid.

26. Ibid.

27. C. K. Barrett, *The Pastoral Epistles in the New English Bible* (Oxford: Clarendon, 1963), 5–10.

28. Ibid., 10–11.

someone would come upon such "scraps" of Paul's writing, "it seems more reasonable to suppose that fragments, whose original disposition cannot now be recovered, came into the hands of the author, and that he put them together in a way that made reasonable sense."[29]

Not many scholars have followed Barrett's lead, though many have agreed that it is curious that a pseudepigrapher would invent personal statements about Paul's colleagues who were probably all dead before the Pastoral Letters were even produced. These personal greetings have the strongest likelihood of being authentic Pauline fragments.

5. *The Pastorals were largely the work of an amanuensis.* Many scholars have wondered whether an *amanuensis* or secretary might be responsible for the Pastoral Letters, which has produced the divergences with Paul's genuine epistles. C. F. D. Moule even thought that he could be more specific and identified Luke as the *amanuensis*.[30] Moule stated that "there are many features, particularly evident in 1 Timothy but not absent from 2 Timothy and Titus, which make it intensely difficult to believe that these letters are fully Pauline."[31] Though Moule reckoned that one could explain the differences in vocabulary, style, and church order, he thought that the letters as a group "constituted a change in mentality" from what we know of the intellectually daring and powerful mind of Paul.[32] On the other hand,

Moule could not conjure up a situation in which these letters would be created by a pseudepigrapher either: "How [can one] explain the circumstantial references in the Pastorals to the apostle's movements and plans?"[33] That is, though Moule finds the Pastoral Letters unlike Paul's genuine epistles, he could not explain any good reason for a pseudonymous author to create these personal situations and incidents and embed them in a letter not written by the historical Paul.

Moule's suggestion is that "Luke wrote all three Pastoral epistles. But he wrote them during Paul's lifetime, at Paul's behest, and, in part (but only in part), at Paul's dictation."[34] In Moule's theory, Luke composed the letters just before Paul was released from prison in Rome, did the traveling implied by the Pastorals, and was imprisoned in Rome once again.[35] Moule suggests Luke as the scribe because he believes that the differences in style, vocabulary, and doctrine reflect Luke's writing from the Acts of the Apostles better than Paul's genuine epistles.

While most scholars still believe that the Pastorals are not written by Paul, arguments regarding the authorship of the Pastorals are being reassessed. It seems that the observation of the great German scholar Martin Dibelius remains true: "The judgment concerning the Pastoral Epistles depends less on a single argument than on the convergence of a whole series of arguments."[36]

---

29. Ibid., 11–12.

30. C. F. D. Moule, "The Problem of the Pastoral Epistles: A Reappraisal," in *Essays on New Testament Interpretation* (Cambridge: Cambridge University Press, 1982), 113–32.

31. Ibid., 114.

32. Ibid., 115.

33. Ibid., 115–16.

34. Ibid., 117.

35. Ibid., 130.

36. Martin Dibelius and Hans Conzelmann, *The Pastoral Epistles: A Commentary on the Pastoral Epistles*, Hermeneia (Philadelphia: Fortress, 1972), 1.

Outline

Three things should be kept in mind as one reads these letters. First, as noted, their style and vocabulary are noticeably different from Paul's other letters. Second, there are also some theological tensions between the Pastorals and Paul's other letters. For instance, in 1 Timothy the role of women in churches is severely restricted and their salvation is said to depend on childbearing (1 Tim. 2:8–15). Third, Paul seems more interested in the development of the structure of the church in 1 Timothy and Titus than in 2 Timothy. Does this interest reflect later ecclesiastical development in the church or could it have emerged in Paul's lifetime?

First Timothy

First Timothy begins with a salutation from Paul to Timothy (1 Tim. 1:1–2). Next, Paul urges Timothy to stay in Ephesus to combat false teachers of the law (1:3–11). Paul states that the law is not for the "innocent" but for lawbreakers, a sentiment which many scholars see as at odds with Paul's thought on the law in Galatians and Romans.

In the next section Paul reflects on the grace given him (1 Tim. 1:12–20) and the abandonment of the faith by others, as "certain persons have suffered shipwreck in the faith; among them are Hymenaeus and Alexander, whom I have turned over to Satan, so that they may learn not to blaspheme" (1:19–20). The remark about turning someone over to Satan resembles 1 Corinthians 5:5.

The following section (1 Tim. 2:1–15) raises more theological questions than any other passage in the Pastorals.

I desire then that in every place the men should pray, lifting holy hands without anger or quarreling; also that women should adorn themselves modestly and sensibly in seemly apparel, not with braided hair or gold or pearls or costly attire but by good deeds, as befits women who profess religion. Let a woman learn in silence with all submissiveness. I permit no woman to teach or to have authority over men; she is to keep silent. For Adam was formed first, then Eve; and Adam was not deceived, but the woman was deceived and became a transgressor. Yet woman will be saved through bearing children, if she continues in faith and love and holiness, with modesty. (1 Tim. 2:8–15, RSV)

There are several apparent inconsistencies between this passage and Paul's statements in his genuine letters. The roles of women in church outlined here differ from those in 1 Corinthians 11. Paul nowhere else speaks of women being saved through childbearing. The necessity of procreation does not seem to align with the superiority of celibacy

© Bridgeman Images

From the Catacombs of Priscilla, Rome, comes this third-century praying figure believed by many to be female, possibly serving as a priest. While 1 Timothy encourages men to "lift up their hands in prayer" in the assembly, women must remain silent.

outlined in 1 Corinthians 7 or what Paul says about salvation through Jesus Christ in general. Finally, we are told that "Adam was not deceived, but the woman was deceived and became a transgressor" (2:14), which is at odds not only with Genesis 3:6 but also with Paul's remarks in Romans 5:12–21: "Sin came into the world through one man."

In 1 Timothy 3:1–13 **overseers** (Greek, *episkopoi*, later to be known as **bishops**) and **deacons** (Greek, *diakonoi*, meaning "servants" or "ministers") are mentioned as well as the criteria for choosing them. A number of scholars also argue that 3:11 gives qualifications for female deacons, not simply the wives of deacons. This passage sheds light on early church offices, as does 5:1–22, which discusses the categories of widows and elders. It is entirely possible that **elders** (or "**presybters**"; Greek, *presbyteroi*) just describes old men, the equivalent of widows, who have a role in the order of the church but are not ordained clergy. In some later Christian traditions, *presbyteros* is the word for priest, while in others it refers to senior members of the laity who play a leadership role in a church or group of churches.

Where Are All the Priests and Bishops?

Priests play a huge role in the Catholic and Eastern Orthodox traditions. Protestant Christian churches mostly abandoned celibate priests in favor of marriage-eligible ministers, but most of these churches trace their ancestry to the priest-dominant Catholic Church. Members of all Christian denominations, then, might be surprised to learn that there are no Christian priests in the New Testament. The only priests mentioned in the New Testament are the Jewish priests who conducted sacrifices at the Temple in Jerusalem.

While some aspects of the celibate, all-male priesthood of Catholicism unquestionably developed over the course of centuries, defenders of the priestly institution believe they can trace the office to Christ and the New Testament. The word "priest" might not be used for Christian ministers in scripture, much as the word "pope" does not appear in the Bible itself, but that does not mean that priests are not present, the argument goes. Perhaps they are simply referred to by some other name.

Many Catholic authorities claim that the New Testament term *presbyteros* or "presbyter" refers at least sometimes to the priestly office. First Timothy 4:14 and 5:22 refers to "laying on of hands," a process that is often translated as "ordaining." The author of this epistle indicates that Timothy himself is ordained in this sense, and that he has the authority to ordain others. Although the text does not explicitly link this process to "presbyters," one could conclude that the "laying on of hands" was done particularly to them. First Timothy 5:17 does link *presbyteroi* to preaching and teaching, two functions that Catholics associate with priests, and James 5:14 shows that presbyters were tasked with anointing the sick with oil. Anointing of the Sick is eventually identified as one of the seven sacraments in Catholicism, and hence James 5:15 is taken as evidence that priests have the exclusive right to administer the sacraments. Thus in Catholicism only a priest can say Mass and consecrate the Host (turning the bread and wine into the body and blood of Christ).

Critics point out that, besides the anointing of the sick, only two or three of the rituals identified as sacraments in Catholicism (namely Eucharist, baptism, and perhaps confession) are even mentioned in the New Testament, while the others (Holy Orders,

continued

Where Are All the Priests and Bishops? *continued*

Matrimony, and Confirmation) are not. Moreover, nowhere in the New Testament does it say that only priests/presbyters can preside over the Eucharist or baptize new converts. The evidence for a New Testament basis for the Christian priesthood is not exactly clear cut.

The New Testament basis for the office of bishop is in some ways even less certain, although bishops are central to the leadership structure of the Catholic Church, the Eastern Orthodox Church, the Anglican (and Episcopal) Church, and some Lutheran denominations. The New Testament does mention bishops (*episkopoi* or "overseers") explicitly, which is not necessarily true of priests. But the responsibilities of the bishop are, if anything, even less well defined than those of presbyters. In fact, in Acts 20 bishops and presbyters are indistinguishable. All presbyters are also bishops, and there are several *episkopoi* in a single church, rather than the Catholic model of a single bishop overseeing numerous congregations in a diocese. The task of *episkopoi* is "shepherding," and it is not clear that they are called *episkopoi* because they engage

in this function or because they have been ordained to a distinctive office. First Timothy 3:1 does indicate that, for this author, *episkopos* refers to an office rather than a function. There are qualifications for this office, but very little is said about its rights and responsibilities. Among other things, a bishop should have only one wife, should have control of his children, and should not be a drunkard, arrogant, a lover of money, or quarrelsome (1 Tim. 3:2-5).

It was not until the early second century that Ignatius of Antioch (died 107) and other Church Fathers solidified the responsibilities of bishops and distinguished them clearly from presbyters and deacons. Eventually, based partly on *1 Clement* (written sometime between 90 and 140), it was claimed that the authority of the bishops derives from that of the apostles, who identified their successors, laid their hands upon them, and passed on their apostolic authority in a process that came to be called "apostolic succession." The first generation of bishops then identified their successors and passed on their apostolic authority to them—and so the process has continued to the present day.[37]

Timothy is also given instructions regarding false teachers and doctrines, though it is difficult to define what sort of group might lie behind these false teachings (1 Tim. 4:1–10). Scholars have proposed some form of Gnosticism, but this designation is imprecise and can refer to a wide range of communities and beliefs. Timothy is exhorted to retain sound teaching (4:11–16; 6:1–19). A short aside directs slaves to obey their masters (6:1–2a). The letter ends with an exhortation to guard the faith, and a short grace (6:20–21).

Second Timothy

Second Timothy opens with a short personal salutation (1:1–2) and a thanksgiving (1:3–7) for Timothy's faith. Paul urges him, "Hold to the standard of sound teaching that you have heard from me, in the faith and love that are in Christ Jesus. Guard the good treasure entrusted to you" (2:13–14). The letter presents Paul as a prisoner, deserted by everyone in Asia except Onesiphorus (1:8–18).

---

37. It should be noted that an episcopal structure (governance by bishops) can exist without the theory of apostolic succession. Those Lutheran denominations that have bishops would be examples of this phenomenon.

In light of all of this, Timothy is charged to "share in suffering like a good soldier of Christ Jesus" and to hold fast to the faith (2 Tim. 2:1–13). Paul describes Timothy as "a worker who has no need to be ashamed" (2:15). Apparently some believers, Hymenaeus and Philetus, think that the resurrection has already taken place, as in 2 Thessalonians, but Timothy is exhorted to have nothing to do with senseless controversies and to correct opponents with gentleness. Hymenaeus also appears in 1 Timothy 1:20, as an opponent of Paul. Throughout this section, Timothy is given strategies for dealing with false teachers (2 Tim. 2:14–26).

The whole of Paul's advice is set in the context of "the last days" when "distressing times will come" (2 Tim. 3:1). Most of 3:1–9 outlines the sins of these latter-day wrongdoers who "make their way into households and captivate silly women" (3:6). This derogatory reference to women seems to be a representation at odds with Paul's more respectful stance toward his many female coworkers elsewhere. Paul advises Timothy in 3:10–4:8 to expect persecution but to remain faithful and persevere in the truth. One of the most famous passages from the Pastorals follows: "All scripture is inspired by God and is useful for teaching, for reproof, for correction, and for training in righteousness, so that everyone who belongs to God may be proficient, equipped for every good work" (3:16–17). "Scripture" here refers to the Hebrew Bible. Paul also charges Timothy to preach the word—to be an evangelist when others are not preaching sound doctrine (4:1–5). Paul reflects on the end of his life, comparing himself to a libation, a type of liquid sacrifice (4:6). He famously adds, "I have fought the good fight, I have finished the race, I have kept the faith" (4:7).

The letter ends with a series of personal remarks in which Paul names the people who have abandoned him in his need (2 Tim. 4:9–18). He also issues greetings to many people, including the well-known wife and husband team of Prisca and Aquila, and adds a final grace for Timothy (4:19–22).

Titus

Titus is the shortest of the Pastorals but has the longest salutation, resembling those found in Paul's genuine letters (Titus 1:1–4). Titus is called "my loyal child in the faith we share" (1:4), which reflects language used by Paul elsewhere to describe Timothy (cf. Phil. 2:22). Titus is said to be on the island of Crete, carrying out work assigned him by Paul (Titus 1:5–16). Titus is to install overseers (bishops) and elders (*presbyteroi*) in Crete; Paul reviews the criteria for their selection (1:5–9). The criteria seem identical to those of the overseers in 1 Timothy. The letter switches from the term "elder" to "overseer," suggesting that both terms describe the same office. The confusing description of these offices may reflect an early stage in the development of the church or perhaps the localized nature of church offices.

The next section (Titus 1:10–16) deals with countering "rebellious people, idle talkers and deceivers, especially those of the circumcision" in Crete (1:10). Paul encourages Titus, in contrast, to teach sound doctrine (2:1–15). While the exhortation resembles those of 1 and 2 Timothy, it offers more specific instructions for various members of the community: older men (*presbyteros*, as in 1 Timothy and earlier in Titus), older women, young women, and slaves. Titus 3:1–11 concentrates on maintaining good deeds, such as obedience toward the established authorities and friendly treatment of everyone, and includes a warning about false teaching: "Avoid stupid controversies, genealogies, dissensions, and quarrels about the law, for they are unprofitable and worthless." Paul instructs Titus, "After a first and second admonition, have nothing more to do with anyone who causes divisions" (3:9–10).

The reference to the law connects this passage to the people "of the circumcision" in 1:10. The letter ends with personal greetings, some to people we have met before, such as Tychicus, and others we have not, such as Zenas the lawyer (3:12–15). Greetings are exchanged and a grace offered.

Key Terms

deutero-Pauline
Pastoral Epistles
amanuensis
"lawless one"
Colossae
"Colossian heresy"
stoicheia

household code
Ephesus
letter to the Laodiceans
patria
Timothy
Titus

pastoral
hapax legomena
pseudepigrapher
overseer/bishop
deacon
elder/presbyter

Review Questions

1. Is 2 Thessalonians "deutero-Pauline" or a genuine letter of Paul? What arguments can be advanced in support of either theory?
2. What is the "Colossian heresy"?
3. How might one explain the personal names at the end of Colossians if Paul did not write the letter?
4. There is a close relationship between Ephesians and Colossians. What is the nature of that relationship, and how might one explain it?
5. Do 1 Timothy and Titus reflect the same church organizational structure? Are bishops and presbyters separate orders at this time?
6. What are the most important theological concepts in the Pastoral Letters?
7. Why do some scholars believe one author wrote all three of the Pastoral Epistles while others do not?

Discussion Questions

1. Would you agree or disagree with those who characterize pseudonymous letters as "forgeries"? Why or why not?
2. Do you sense that the Pastoral Letters have a more negative view of women than other New Testament texts? How would you account for such a phenomenon? Did the Christian church simply become more conservative as it became older and better established?

Bibliography and Suggestions for Further Study

(Books and websites that are accessible for general undergraduates are marked with an asterisk; other sources listed are appropriate for advanced students.)

*Barrett, C. K. *The Pastoral Epistles in the New English Bible.* Oxford: Clarendon, 1963.

Barth, Markus, Helmut Blanke, and Astrid B. Beck. *Colossians: A New Translation with Introduction and Commentary.* Anchor Bible. New York: Doubleday, 1994.

*Brakke, David. "Early Christian Lies and the Lying Liars Who Wrote Them: Bart Ehrman's

Forgery and Counterforgery." *The Journal of Religion* 96, no. 3 (July 2016): 378–90.

Dibelius, Martin, and Hans Conzelmann. *The Pastoral Epistles: A Commentary on the Pastoral Epistles*. Hermeneia. Philadelphia: Fortress, 1972.

Fiore, Benjamin. *The Pastoral Epistles: First Timothy, Second Timothy, Titus*. Sacra Pagina. Collegeville, MN: Liturgical Press, 2007.

*Gorman, Michael J. *Apostle of the Crucified Lord: A Theological Introduction to Paul and His Letters*. Grand Rapids: Eerdmans, 2004.

Johnson, Lee A. "Paul's Letters Reheard: A Performance-Critical Examination of the Preparation, Transportation, and Delivery of Paul's Correspondence." *CBQ* 79, no. 1 (2017): 60–76.

Johnson, Luke Timothy. *The First and Second Letters to Timothy: A New Translation with Introduction and Commentary*. Anchor Bible. New York: Doubleday, 2008.

*Kümmel, Werner Georg, Paul Feine, and Johannes Behm. *Introduction to the New Testament*. Rev. ed. Nashville: Abingdon, 1986.

Lohse, Eduard. *Colossians and Philemon: A Commentary on the Epistles to the Colossians and to Philemon*. Hermeneia. Philadelphia: Fortress, 1971), 127–31.

MacDonald, Margaret Y. *Colossians and Ephesians*. Sacra Pagina. Collegeville, MN: Liturgical Press, 2000.

*Metzger, Bruce M. *The New Testament: Its Background, Growth, and Content*. Nashville: Abingdon, 2003.

Moule, C. F. D. "The Problem of the Pastoral Epistles: A Reappraisal." In *Essays on New Testament Interpretation*, 113–32. Cambridge: Cambridge University Press, 1982.

O'Brien, Peter Thomas. *Colossians, Philemon*. Word Biblical Commentary 44. Waco, TX: Word, 1982.

*Senior, Donald, and John J. Collins. "Commentary on Colossians." In *The Catholic Study Bible*. Oxford Biblical Studies Online. *http://www.oxfordbiblicalstudies.com/article/book/obso-9780195282801/obso-9780195282801-div1-7592*.

*Senior, Donald, and John J. Collins. "The Letter to the Ephesians." In *The Catholic Study Bible*. Oxford Biblical Studies Online. *http://www.oxfordbiblicalstudies.com/article/book/obso-9780195282801/obso-9780195282801-chapterFrontMatter-54*.

Spivey, Steven W. "Colossians 1:24 and the Suffering Church." *Journal of Spiritual Formation & Soul Care* 4, no. 1 (2011): 43–62.

Wilson, S. G. *Luke and the Pastoral Epistles*. London: SPCK, 1979.

The General Epistles: James, Jude, 1 and 2 Peter, and Hebrews

Previous chapters included analysis of the three letters of John and the thirteen letters with Paul's name attached. The other canonical letters found in the New Testament form a disparate set. Groupings of these letters have sometimes included the Johannine Epistles (see chapter 13), but most often only include 1 and 2 Peter, James, Jude, and Hebrews. The attempt to find a suitable name for these letters gives a sense of the difficulty in grouping them. They have been called **catholic epistles**[1] or **general epistles**, meaning that they were intended not for a particular Christian community, but "universally" for all of the emerging churches or at least a number of churches. As these terms suggest, most analysts see these as **circular letters**, meaning that they were not situational or occasional but intended for a broad audience and applicable to Christian communities regardless of their historical circumstances.[2]

It is best to examine these letters individually and determine on the basis of each letter its particular form and function. The question of function is, however, in some ways inseparable from the question of authorship. The vast majority of scholars regard all of these letters as pseudonymous, except for Hebrews, which is anonymous.[3] But this conclusion opens up another question: what purpose did it serve the real writers of these letters to attribute them to the particular apostles that are listed as their authors? Do the selections of Peter, James, and Jude as stand-ins for the real authors reveal anything important about the meaning of these texts?

The Letter of James

The Letter of James is traditionally attributed to James "the brother of the Lord." The letter famously appears to contradict Paul's teaching that a person is justified by faith, not works.

Authorship

The first surviving references to the letter of James are found in the work of the early third-century Christian writer Origen (*Commentary on John* 19.23; 20.10). However, it is not until the fourth century CE that a surviving work—that of

---

1. The non-capitalized term "catholic" means "universal" or "worldwide." These letters have been termed "catholic epistles" as early as the time of Eusebius (*Church History* 2.23.24).

2. Some scholars question whether this is true of Jude, 1 Peter, or Hebrews.

3. Though authorship is questioned for all of these letters, as a matter of convention and simplicity, this chapter will refer to the authors by the names traditionally associated with each letter, except for Hebrews, which is anonymous.

Eusebius—indicates that the James identified as the author of this letter is the "brother of the Lord" (as opposed, say, to James the brother of John and son of Zebedee, who was among the Twelve). Moreover, Eusebius views this identification as uncertain. Most scholars agree that the book was accepted into the canon largely on the basis of its alleged authorship by a close relative of Jesus. This James has been mentioned frequently (chapters 1, 2, 12, 14, and 16), but a brief review of his identity and the distinction between him and other figures also named James is in order here.

The name translated as **James** is actually derived from the Hebrew *Jacob*. The name Jacob/James is common and is found forty-two times in the New Testament. There are a number of men named James in the New Testament:

(a) James, "son of Zebedee," one of the twelve apostles (mentioned more than twenty times, including Acts 12:2)

(b) James, "son of Alphaeus," one of the twelve apostles (mentioned four times, including Mark 3:18)

(c) James, father of the apostle Judas (Luke 6:16; Acts 1:13)

(d) James the younger, son of Mary and brother of Joseph (mentioned four times, including Matt. 27:56)

(e) James the brother of Jesus, listed along with three other brothers—Joses, Judas, and Simon (Matt. 13:55; Mark 6:3)

(f) James, the brother of the Lord, identified singly (1 Cor. 15:7; Gal. 1:19; 2:9, 2:12)

(g) James, "a servant . . . of the Lord Jesus Christ" (James 1:1)

(h) James, brother of Jude (Jude 1)

(i) James, with no additional identification (e.g., Acts 12:17; 15:13; 21:18).

In seeking to identify the author of this letter, one can eliminate (a) through (d) quite easily since no one in the ancient church identifies the author of this text as an apostle (at least in the sense of being among the Twelve) or the father of an apostle.

James the brother of Jesus (e) and James the brother of the Lord (f) are probably the same person. This is most likely the same James who is called the brother of Jude (h) in Jude 1. This James was a major figure in the Jerusalem church and it is widely accepted that he is the James in Acts 15 at the Jerusalem Council (i); Paul terms him a "pillar" of the Jerusalem church in Galatians 1–2. This is most likely also (g), the James to whom this letter is attributed in James 1:1, a simple designation of a figure who needs no further introduction. He is sometimes referred to in early Christian literature as "James the Just" to distinguish him from other prominent early Christian leaders of the same name. Josephus indicates that this James was killed in Jerusalem sometime around 62 CE, although some later Christian sources, including Origin and Eusebius, suggest he was martyred in 69 CE and that his murder led to the siege of Jerusalem.[4]

The arguments for James's authorship depend in the first instance on the presence of several sayings of Jesus in the letter. These sayings reflect close contact with the Gospel tradition but not literary dependence. This evidence suggests the author is somebody close to the oral tradition, someone from the first generation of Christians, like James the brother of Jesus.

There are, however, a number of reasons for doubting that James is the author. First, while a simple designation of the author as "James" might be enough to imply to the letter's readers that the author is the brother of Jesus, in truth something more than this would probably be necessary (and desirable, from the author's standpoint) to assure

---

4. Still others dispute that he was martyred at all. Epiphanius, writing around 375, believed that James died at the age of ninety-six.

Scenes from the martyrdom of James overlap in this twelfth-century mosaic from St. Mark's, Venice. The captions read "The Jews," "He is pushed from behind," "St. James," "He is struck and dies," "The Pharisees," "He is buried," and "Jerusalem."

that this conclusion is drawn. And yet the letter contains no further identification of James. Second, the contents of the letter do not seem to fit what is known of the preaching of James the brother of the Lord and the Jerusalem church that he led. For example, the letter does not deal with Torah in any depth, a significant concern of the early Jerusalem church. Third, the text is written in cultured Greek not likely to come from the pen of a Galilean Jew of peasant origins. Finally, early Christians were slow to recognize this book as scripture, something that would not likely have happened if it were evident to all that it was written by James. While all this suggests that it is unlikely James is the author, it is possible that this epistle was sent as a circular letter on his behalf, either before or after his death.

Time and Place

The theory that the document is a circular letter sent on James's behalf opens up a broader range of dates for its composition. The letter was written after at least some of Paul's letters had circulated, since the letter demonstrates awareness of Paul's theology. It either opposes Paul's theology or seeks to correct some exaggerated interpretations of Paul's thought on law and works. Since Paul wrote circa 50–60 CE, this letter could potentially date as early as the sixties or seventies. Other scholars consider that the exhortation to steadfastness during persecution dates the letter to a period of empire-wide persecution, perhaps during the reign of Domitian (81–96 CE). On the basis of these two pieces of evidence, the letter could have been written any time between the sixties and about 100 CE, although most scholars place it in the latter half of this range.

Since the letter is sent to the "twelve tribes in the Dispersion" (James 1:1), and since James is always associated with the church in Jerusalem, the best hypothesis is that the letter was sent from Palestine.[5]

Occasion

The letter is definitely less occasional than Paul's (genuine) letters, but does address Christians

---

5. The cultured Greek style of James need not suggest a point of origin outside of Palestine. Parts of Judea, Jerusalem in particular, were strongly Hellenized, and there would have been no shortage of persons there capable of writing sophisticated Greek.

experiencing persecution, encouraging them to be patient and persevere. However, the letter makes numerous points that are not related to persecution but rather reflect the teachings of the Jerusalem church more broadly, such as the importance of practicing faith that is not empty, or the dangers of favoring the rich or depending too heavily on wealth.

The Literary Form

The absence of an occasion that would explain the letter as a whole is consistent with several aspects of the form of the letter of James. The obscurity of the letter's destination, the impersonal standpoint of the content, and the lack of any conclusion all seem to confirm that James is not a situational letter like most of Paul's letters, which are addressed to specific communities to deal with current theological and behavioral issues. James consists of a series of admonitions on different themes without any discernible plan. It appears to be an instructional document composed from strings of sayings and small essays. It may be, therefore, a collection of sayings, teachings, or short homilies—perhaps associated with the historical James—compiled as a circular letter to Christians scattered throughout the Roman Empire.

Theology

The letter of James famously argues that faith alone is insufficient for salvation and that belief must be accompanied by good works (James 2:24). This appears to contradict Paul, who insisted that salvation is by faith alone in Galatians and Romans. Werner Kümmel, like Martin Luther, argues that James and Paul are irreconcilable on this issue.[6] But Bo Reicke believes that

the letter was not written in strict opposition to Paul, but was part of a broad effort to affirm the communitarian aspect of salvation in opposition to an overly personalized faith that some might mistakenly interpret Paul to be advocating. Moreover, in Riecke's view James never asserts that a person is *not* justified by faith. He simply exhorts his readers to see that it is crucial for faith to *bear fruit* in works.[7]

Content

It is difficult to discern a logical progression in this letter. James begins with the usual introductory elements of a Hellenistic letter (James 1:1–8) but the body of the letter (1:9–5:20) offers, in no orderly sequence, a series of teachings, sayings, and admonitions without connections other than that they reflect general Christian doctrine and exhortations.

The letter opens with a short salutation (James 1:1) from James to the "twelve tribes in the Dispersion." This is followed by a thanksgiving (1:2–8) that centers on faith that rejoices in trials (*peirasmos*, which can also be translated as "temptations" or "tests"). The body of the letter (1:9–5:20) offers a small section on reversal of fortunes (1:9–11) and then states, "Blessed is anyone who endures temptation" (1:12–18), which could be a response to a misreading of the Lord's Prayer asserting that God leads people into temptation.

The author encourages readers not merely to listen to the word but to put the gospel into action by caring for orphans and widows (James 1:19–27). This point segues into a section that warns believers not to favor the rich over the poor (2:1–13). This theme is taken up again in 5:1–6. Apart from the focus on faith and works,

---

6. Werner Kümmel, Paul Feine, and Johannes Behm, *Introduction to the New Testament*, 17th ed. (Nashville: Abingdon, 1973), 414–16.

7. Bo Reicke, *The Epistles of James, Peter, and Jude* (Garden City, NY: Doubleday, 1964), 34.

care for the poor is the most significant theological theme of James.

In its comments on faith and works, James does respond, obliquely at least, to views associated with Paul. Whether he intended to refute Paul's point about justification by faith or merely to warn against an overemphasis on faith at the expense of works, James consistently claims that faith without works is "barren" (James 2:20) and fraudulent.

> What good is it . . . if you say you have faith but do not have works? Can faith save you? If a brother or sister is naked and lacks daily food, and one of you says to them, "Go in peace; keep warm and eat your fill," and yet you do not supply their bodily needs, what is the good of that? So faith by itself, if it has no works, is dead. But someone will say, "You have faith and I have works." Show me your faith apart from your works, and I by my works will show you my faith. (James 2:14–18)

James points out that even demons have faith of a sort: they know that God exists and "believe" in him to that extent (James 2:19), but this does not mean that they are saved or justified. Neither does James think that human beings are saved by faith alone. In an apparent refutation of Paul's claim that Abraham was justified by faith (Gal. 3:6–9), James insists that Abraham was justified by works, that is, by offering his son Isaac on the altar (James 2:21–23; cf. Gen. 22:1–19). Abraham had faith, to be sure, but his faith "was brought to completion by the works"

(James 2:22). James proposes that faith must be evidenced in a disciplined tongue (3:1–12). Just as immoral behavior reveals a lack of true faith, so also harsh words, boasts, curses, and lies reveal that a person does not have wisdom from God (3:13–18). Conflicts and disputes arise when Christians fail to resist the devil and submit to God (4:1–12). James sees complete dependence upon God as the key to the Christian life (4:13–17). This dependence includes a focus on eschatology, too, and especially the need to be "patient . . . until the coming of the Lord" and to display "the endurance of Job" (5:7–12).[8]

Finally, James offers concrete pastoral advice regarding swearing, anointing the sick with oil (a rite that Catholics will later come to list among the sacraments),[9] confessing of sins, praying, and bringing back a wandering sinner (James 5:13–20). The unit on swearing oaths resembles Jesus' teaching in Matthew 5:33–37.

There is no formal closing, which again suggests a circular letter, collected from sayings of James or from the early Christian tradition. No fellow Christians are addressed and the conclusion lacks a grace, special prayer, admonition to a holy kiss, or any indication of travel plans; the letter just ends.

The Letter of Jude

The letter of Jude is one of the least-studied books of the New Testament. At only twenty-five verses, it is tied for the third-shortest book in the

---

8. Job, in the Old Testament book of that name, was initially happy, prosperous, and devout, but later he experienced great loss and terrible suffering. Despite all this, he never lost his faith. As a result, Job became the example *par excellence* of undeserved suffering and the patient endurance of life's hardships.

9. Christian theology defines a sacrament as "an outward and visible sign of inward and spiritual divine grace." In other words, sacraments are a means of conferring grace—understood as a free gift from God that sanctifies a person and aids in salvation. Grace can be conferred by God in an infinite variety of ways, but sacraments carry with them a kind of guarantee that grace is received. Catholics (and most Orthodox churches) acknowledge seven sacraments: Baptism, Eucharist, Confirmation, Holy Matrimony (marriage), Holy Orders (the ordination of priests), Reconciliation (more commonly known as confession), and the Anointing of the Sick (sometimes called Last Rites or Extreme Unction). Most Protestant churches acknowledge only two sacraments—Baptism and Eucharist—arguing that only these two are explicitly grounded in scripture.

entire Bible (2 and 3 John are the only shorter books). Its obscurity in modern Christianity in some ways mirrors its treatment in early Christianity, although some in antiquity regarded the letter very highly.

Authorship

Although not considered of great importance today, Jude was sufficiently well-regarded in early Christianity to have been cited and used as a source by the author of 2 Peter (cf. 2 Pet. 2:1–18 and Jude 4–16).[10] The existence of the letter of Jude is otherwise attested in the second century only by Clement of Alexandria, Tertullian, and the Muratorian canon, but the letter must have carried some weight to have been copied and eventually included in the canon.[11]

Jude 1 says that the letter is written by "Jude, a servant of Jesus Christ and brother of James." **Jude** is actually the same name as Judas (from the Greek, *Ioudas*) and Judah (Hebrew). The name Judas/Jude appears thirty-six times in the New Testament:

(a) Judas Iscariot, more than twenty times in the New Testament

(b) Judas son of James, one of the twelve apostles (Luke 6:16; Acts 1:13)

(c) Judas Barsabbas (Acts 15:22)

(d) Judas the brother of Jesus, listed alongside three other brothers (Matt. 13:55; Mark 6:3)

(e) "Judas (not Iscariot)" (John 14:22)

(f) Judas, at whose house Paul stays (Acts 9:11)

(g) Judas the Galilean, who led a revolt (Acts 5:37)

It is probable that the Judas to whom this letter is attributed is not one of the twelve apostles or he

would have identified himself as such. This rules out (a), (b), and (e). One may rule out (f) and (g) because one is not a Christian and the other is mentioned only in passing. Judas Barsabbas (c) is sent out with Silas by the Jerusalem Council, so he is a major figure in the early church. But the best candidate is (d) because only this Judas is said to have a brother named James, which is how the author of the letter identifies himself. The author of this letter, then, like the author of the letter of James, claims to be a brother of Jesus.

Catholics, of course, do not identify James and Jude as full brothers of Jesus, an interpretation that is ruled out by belief in the perpetual virginity of Mary. The idea that James and Jude are brothers of Jesus only in a spiritual sense is untenable, because the same small group of individuals are always singled out as brothers of Jesus. Jesus would have had a great many brothers and sisters in the spiritual sense, but the fact that James, Joses, Judas, and Simon are the only people actually identified as his brothers indicates that the relation between them was familial and not spiritual. But it is possible to argue that they are close relatives of Jesus while not being children of Mary. Ancient tradition, based largely on the *Protoevangelium of James* (see chapter 2), identifies them as sons of Joseph by a previous marriage and so half-brothers of Jesus. Another common argument is that they are cousins of Jesus. Protestants, who do not ascribe to the perpetual virginity of Mary, have no problem identifying them as true siblings of Jesus, born to Mary and Joseph after the birth of Jesus.

But while the letter claims to be written by Jude, brother of James (and Jesus), much current scholarship regards the letter as pseudonymous. An argument in favor of the authorship of Jude is that the early church did accept Jude's authorship of this letter, although Eusebius noted

---

10. Harry Y. Gamble, *The New Testament Canon: Its Making and Meaning* (Philadelphia: Fortress, 1985), 48.

11. Ibid., 48.

that some disputed this.[12] The letter includes a direct allusion to the *Testament of Moses* and a direct citation from *1 Enoch*, Jewish texts that are not canonical, which suggests a Jewish author embedded in Jewish apocalyptic thought, a description that might well fit Jude. Modern commentators are almost unanimous in believing that 2 Peter has borrowed a passage from Jude, indicating the authority of Jude in at least some quarters in the early church, suggesting that the letter was accepted as genuine.

Against Jude's authorship, it has been noted that the letter is written in excellent Greek and includes twenty-two Greek words not found elsewhere in the New Testament.[13] Such literary skill is thought to exclude a lower-class Jewish peasant. Verses 17–18 are also viewed as problematic:

> But you, beloved, must remember the predictions of the apostles of our Lord Jesus Christ; for they said to you, "In the last time there will be scoffers, indulging their own ungodly lusts."

Many scholars conclude that this passage presupposes that the time of the apostles has ended, which would argue against Jude's authorship. Jude would have been about the same age as the apostles, so he, too, would surely have passed away if they had.

Occasion and Content

It is generally thought that the letter was occasioned by some "intruders" having entered one (or more) Christian communities (Jude 4). In the salutation (vv. 1–2), Jude states he is a brother to James and describes himself as a *doulos* of Jesus Christ, which is best translated as "slave" instead of "servant." The letter is sent "to those who are called," which could indicate a letter sent to many churches,[14] but it is more likely that the letter was sent to specific churches dealing with the particular theological problems that the letter addresses.[15] Typically the salutation would be followed by a thanksgiving, but what follows here is more of a statement of purpose due to a change of plan. He had intended to write about "the salvation we share," but now finds it necessary "to . . . appeal to you to contend for the faith that was once for all entrusted to the saints" (v. 3). This change of plan lends credence to the theory that this was an actual letter and not a contrived scenario.

The reason for the change of topic is that some "intruders" are perverting God's grace into "licentiousness" (*aselgeia*), a word suggesting sexual misbehavior (Jude 4). The identity of the intruders is mysterious. Are they outsiders who came into the community or insiders who have developed views that the author regards as dangerous? The letter does not provide enough information to answer this question.

The body of the letter opens with a reminder of what the addressees already know from scripture and tradition about the punishment that awaits the unrighteous and unbelievers (Jude 5–7). The first example concerns the Israelites who were saved by God out of Egypt but later rebelled and were destroyed (v. 5). The second example concerns the "angels who did not keep their own position, but left their proper dwelling," whom God "has kept in eternal chains in deepest darkness for the judgment of the great day" (v. 6). This verse concerns the angels of

---

12. See J. N. D. Kelly, *A Commentary on the Epistles of Peter and Jude* (London: Adam and Charles Black, 1969), 223–24.

13. Patrick J. Hartin, *James, 1 Peter, Jude, 2 Peter* (Collegeville, MN: Liturgical Press, 2006), 48.

14. Catherine Gunsales Gonzalez, *1 & 2 Peter and Jude: A Theological Commentary on the Bible*, Belief (Louisville: Westminster John Knox, 2011), 215; Daniel Keating, *First and Second Peter, Jude*, Catholic Commentary on Sacred Scripture (Grand Rapids: Baker Academic, 2011), 197.

15. Thomas Schreiner, *1, 2 Peter, Jude*, New American Commentary 37 (Nashville: Broadman & Holman, 2003), 429.

Genesis 6:1–4, whose violation of sexual boundaries by having sexual relations with women provoked God's displeasure and helped bring about the flood. In a later expansion of this story found in *1 Enoch* 10, a Jewish apocalyptic text cited later in this letter (vv. 14–15), these angels were punished by being cast into pits and chained to await the final judgment at the end of time. The final example concerns Sodom and Gomorrah and the surrounding cities, which "indulged in sexual immorality and pursued unnatural lust"

and so "serve as an example by undergoing a punishment of eternal fire" (v. 7).

Jude next outlines the behaviors of the intruders (Jude 8–13). He denigrates them as "dreamers," which suggests that they base their teachings on claims of divine revelations or visions.[16] Jude also accuses them of defiling the flesh, rejecting authority, and slandering "the glorious ones" (v. 8). These charges match exactly with the behaviors outlined in verses 5–7. Defiling the flesh jibes with the sexual immorality

Apocrypha and Pseudepigrapha

The author of the letter of Jude refers to two Jewish texts–*1 Enoch* and the *Testament of Moses*–as if they are scripture, but these books are not included in the Hebrew Bible or the Old Testament as they exist today. Several terms are used for the category of literature to which *1 Enoch* and the *Testament of Moses* belong. One term is **apocrypha**, a designation that refers to the *noncanonical* status of an ancient religious text. The seven books that are found in the Catholic Old Testament but not in the Protestant version of the Old Testament–books like 1 and 2 Maccabees, Judith, and Tobit–are often referred to as "the Apocrypha." Catholics refer to these books as "deuterocanonical." These seven books are not the only ones that can be called apocryphal, though, nor is this designation restricted to Jewish literature. Some of the books that were considered for inclusion in the New Testament but not ultimately included in the canon–books such as the *Apocalypse of Peter*, the letter of *Barnabas*, and the *Shepherd of Hermas*–are sometimes grouped together as the "New Testament Apocrypha."

A second term that is used for such literature, **pseudepigrapha** (literally "false writings"), refers to the fact that the books falsely identify their authors as figures such as Moses and

Enoch, who had been dead for centuries when the book was composed. A book could be both apocryphal and pseudepigraphical. This would be true of *1 Enoch*, for example, which is dated to the second century BCE at the earliest and cannot have been written by the great-grandfather of Noah, and which is not included in either the Christian Old Testament or the Hebrew Bible. But the noncanonical status of *1 Enoch* had not been finally determined in the first century CE when the book of Jude was written. Neither the Jewish nor Christian canon was closed at the time; the author of Jude obviously was in the camp that thought this book deserved to be included.

Although the term "pseudepigrapha" thus has a generic meaning and can be applied to any work that falsely claims to have been written by a famous historical religious figure, it can also be used as a proper noun rather than a common noun. When capitalized, the term "Pseudepigrapha" usually refers to a specific body of noncanonical Jewish literature written roughly between 300 BCE and 300 CE. The Pseudepigrapha includes *1 Enoch*, the *Testament of Moses*, 3 and 4 Maccabees, *Jubilees*, the *Ascension of Isaiah*, the *Testaments of the Twelve Patriarchs*, and many more.

16. Gonzalez, *1 & 2 Peter and Jude*, 218–19.

hinted at in the references to boundary-violating angels and the residents of Sodom and Gomorrah. But what is meant by slandering the glorious ones[17] is less clear.

Verse 9 is important for understanding this charge. A story about the archangel **Michael** contending with the devil for the body of Moses is believed to have been included[18] in an apocryphal Jewish text called the ***Testament of Moses*** (also known as the *Assumption of Moses*). In the story, Michael contends with the Devil for Moses' body; the Devil reviles Moses and calls him a murderer. In the letter of Jude, "the slanders of the false teachers are parallel to those of the devil, and the dignitaries reviled by them are comparable to Moses, here as elsewhere the representative of legally constituted authority."[19] Hence the intruders' slandering of the legitimate religious leaders in the Christian churches is comparable to the Devil's slandering of Moses. This places them in very bad company indeed.

Jude indicates that the slanders of the intruders are based on ignorance, for they slander what they do not understand (Jude 10). Verse 11 begins with a "woe" pronounced against them, which is like the "woes" (or curses) Jesus pronounces in the New Testament twenty-nine times. Jude excoriates his opponents with a series of comparisons to biblical villains like Cain (murderer of his brother Abel in Gen. 4:8) and to various unpleasant natural phenomena, like "clouds without water" and "autumn leaves without fruit" (v. 12).

The final verse in this section concentrates on the chaotic nature of their behavior and beliefs, casting the intruders as "wandering stars, for whom the deepest darkness has been reserved forever" (v. 13). The word "stars" is actually modified by the adjective *planētai*, which provides a clear sense of what Jude is getting at even in transliteration. Planets were "wandering stars," and in Second Temple Judaism stars and planets were often personified as angels or holy ones (see Dan. 12:3). But wandering stars could also refer to either fallen angels or to the fallen angels who controlled them. This assessment is confirmed with a citation from *1 Enoch* 1:9 (Jude 14–15). The reference involves a general warning regarding the coming apocalypse, which for Jude applies to these human intruders in the community.

Although *1 Enoch* does not appear in any biblical canon—with the exception of the Ethiopian Orthodox Church—certain texts that were not ultimately included in canonical lists were held in high esteem by many ancient Jews and Christians. Larry Hurtado, among others, has distinguished between scripture and canon in the ancient church, suggesting that some writings had the authority of scripture even though they were ultimately not canonized.[20] For Jude to cite this text so approvingly indicates the high regard in which he held *1 Enoch*. The use of *1 Enoch* also affirms the Jewish-Christian nature of the letter of Jude and its place in the earliest stratum of Christian literature. Christianity was becoming more and more dominated by Gentile converts as the first century CE drew to a close; it was the first generation of Jewish followers of Jesus who would have been familiar with *1 Enoch*.

---

17. Hartin, *James, 1 Peter, Jude, 2 Peter*, 52–53.

18. The story of Michael and the devil is missing from the one surviving ancient manuscript of the *Testament of Moses*, but scholars are certain the account was once included in the work because Clement of Alexandria, Origen, and others mention its presence there.

19. Reicke, *The Epistles of James, Peter and Jude*, 202.

20. Larry Hurtado, "'Scriptures' and 'Canon,'" Larry Hurtado's Blog, *https://larryhurtado.wordpress.com/2011/08/30/scriptures-and-canon/*.

© The Schøyen Collection, Oslo and London

Jude quotes the apocryphal book of *Enoch*, which survives complete only in Ethiopic translation, shown here. The Ethiopian Orthodox Church, unique among Christian denominations, regards *Enoch* as canonical scripture.

Jude proceeds to describe the intruders as "grumblers and malcontents" who are lustful, bombastic, and flattering (Jude 16). He encourages his readers to "remember the predictions of the apostles of our Lord Jesus Christ; for they said to you, 'In the last time there will be scoffers, indulging their own ungodly lusts'" (17–18). This passage places the community under the authoritative oral tradition of the same apostles.

Next Jude turns his attention to those recipients who have remained faithful, but in this exhortation Jude's attention also switches from denunciation of the intruders to a desire to reconcile with them and those they have influenced within the community (Jude 20–23). God's judgment on all members of the community is nigh, but mercy is possible through Christ even for those who have fallen into error.

Jude urges those who abide in the truth to do what they can to save the lost, "snatching them out of the fire" (23).

Jude does not fit in the genre of apocalyptic literature. However, it is imbued with the sense of the coming judgment that will occur in the last days. Many ancient Christians seem to have become almost preoccupied with thoughts of the nearness of the end. Jude fits in this camp.

The First Letter of Peter

The apostle Peter was, along with Paul, the foremost spokesperson for early Christianity after the death of Jesus. In all four Gospels he is the leader of Jesus' inner circle of twelve disciples. At times he fulfills this role admirably and is singled out for praise. In three Gospels he is the first to identify Jesus as the Messiah (see Mark 8:27–30 and parallels), and in one Gospel Jesus names him as the "rock" on which his church will be built and gives him the "keys of the kingdom" as well as the authority to bind and to loose (Matt. 16:18–19). At other times Peter is depicted as exhibiting the most egregious flaws, denying under questioning three times that he knows Jesus (Mark 14:66–72) and rebuking Jesus to the point that Jesus refers to him as "Satan" (Mark 8:33). The prevailing narrative in proto-orthodox literature, heavily influenced by the Acts of the Apostles, is that Peter overcame his fear and doubts to become a brave, fiercely loyal, and supremely competent leader of the early church.

As a consequence, one would expect that the writings of Peter would occupy a preeminent place in early Christianity. However, Peter is not thought to have authored a Gospel, although early tradition identified him as the source of the Gospel of Mark and this tradition likely contributed to Mark's survival and eventual inclusion in the canon. The only writings actually attributed to Peter are the two letters that bear his name. However, these letters did not come to occupy a central place in early Christianity and indeed made it into the canon only with some difficulty, in part because of doubts about Peter's authorship.

Authorship

As with so many of the New Testament letters, the question of the authorship of 1 Peter is tightly tied to the time the letter was written. The view that 1 Peter is pseudonymous is based on references to persecutions (1 Pet. 4:12–19; 5:6–9) that appear to reflect a time of more widespread persecution such as occurred during the reigns of Domitian (81–96 CE) and Trajan (98–110 CE), rather than the localized persecutions under Nero that took place in the sixties, during Peter's lifetime. Some scholars hypothesize that the letter, though produced after Peter's death, might be based on genuine teachings or writings of Peter, subsequently gathered together as a circular letter.

Time and Place

It is widely believed that the "sister church in Babylon" (1 Pet. 5:13), from which the letter is sent, is a reference to Rome. The majority of scholars accept that the letter, whether pseudonymous or not, emerged from Rome in a time of persecution, either under Nero or under Domitian or Trajan.

Occasion

The letter is sent as a comfort and admonition in the face of persecution (see 1 Pet. 1:6–9; 5:12). Peter desires to prevent suffering believers from abandoning the gospel. It is an exhortation to endure suffering. The author suggests that baptism (3:13–22) provides Christians with the strength to remain faithful despite persecution.

Recipients

The letter identifies the churches to which it is sent: "the exiles of the Dispersion in Pontus, Galatia, Cappadocia, Asia, and Bithynia" (1 Pet. 1:1), five Roman provinces in Asia Minor. It is likely that "dispersion" refers to all Christians in these regions, Gentile or Jewish, though the language of dispersion (literally "diaspora") emerged in the context of Judaism. Peter is anxious that the believers manifest loyalty to the local magistrates and to Rome (2:13–16) and not cause trouble in the broader culture at large, but accept suffering in this world since the end of the world and their redemption are at hand (3:1–5:11).

Outline

The letter begins with an ordinary salutation (1 Pet. 1:1–2), that is followed by a lengthy thanksgiving (1:3–12). The opening of the body of the letter (1:13–2:3) uses images, found also in Paul's letters and in Hebrews, of the Christians as children, "newborn infants" who "long for the pure, spiritual milk" (2:2). The next section of the body of the letter (2:4–4:19) encourages all Christians to "be built into a spiritual house . . . a holy priesthood" (2:5, 9). While these images emerge from the Jewish scriptures, here they include the Gentiles, who are now part of God's own people (2:9–10). The disciples of Jesus are now regarded as aliens and exiles surrounded on every side by unbelievers, but the author insists that they must nonetheless be submissive to the ruling temporal authorities (2:11–17).

Practical instructions, in the form of a household code like those found in the Pastoral and deutero-Pauline letters, take up the next major section of the letter. Slaves are told to "accept the authority of . . . masters with all deference, not only those who are kind and gentle but also those who are harsh" (1 Pet. 2:18). This might be the hardest advice offered to slaves in the whole New Testament, since slave-owners could beat their

First Peter 3:18-22 seems to refer to the "harrowing of hell," the idea that Christ, between his crucifixion and resurrection, descended to the underworld and freed all the righteous souls there, as depicted in this medieval psalter.

PD via Walters Museum

slaves almost to death and sexually abuse them without facing any repercussions. Peter encourages them to submit to their masters by using Jesus as an example, and certainly with eschatological deliverance in mind (2:18–25). But it is impossible to ignore the many forms of cruelty and injustice that Christian slaves are here advised to meekly accept.

The section on relationships between wives and husbands (1 Pet. 3:1–7) focuses on wives' behavior until the final verse. Wives are told to submit to the authority of their husbands and not to be overly adorned, both common tropes in Jewish, Roman, and Christian teaching. Husbands are told to "show consideration" for their wives since they are "the weaker sex" (2:7). This verse is the origin of the understanding that women are the "weaker sex." The word translated

as "sex" is actually *skeuos*, which means "vessel." It is not exactly clear what Peter is getting at with this phrase, whether it is intended to reflect female inferiority and, if so, whether this inferiority is intended in a physical, moral, or some other sense. A call for Christian unity, relying partly on what seems to be oral Jesus tradition ("do not repay evil for evil"), follows (3:8–12).

The last major section of the body of the letter (1 Pet. 3:13–4:19) is concerned with ethical exhortation. Peter encourages his hearers to suffer for what is good (3:13–17) as did Christ, who even "went and made a proclamation to the spirits in prison" (3:18–22), so that "the Gospel was proclaimed even to the dead" (4:1–6). Many see these two passages as the origin of the tradition that Christ, after his crucifixion, went and proclaimed the gospel to the dead, in what has become known as the "harrowing of hell."

As the letter closes, the letter's recipients are admonished regarding leadership in the church: "Do not Lord it over those in your charge" (1 Pet. 5:1–4). They must also accept authority and be faithful in suffering (5:5–11). Finally, Peter, "through Silvanus," with Mark and the church in Rome, greets the recipients and offers grace to them (5:12–14).

The Second Letter of Peter

In contrast to 1 Peter, very few scholars would argue that 2 Peter was authored or dictated by Peter, or based on his preaching, or authorized by him. Most estimates date 2 Peter to 110–115 CE. This late date, in turn, rests partly on the widespread belief that the author of 2 Peter drew upon the letter of Jude.

Authorship

The author presents himself as "Simeon Peter" (2 Pet. 1:1), but contemporary New Testament scholars generally agree that 2 Peter is pseudonymous.[21] The suggestion that the differences between 1 and 2 Peter are due to the use of a secretary (*amanuensis*) for one letter but not the other, or two different secretaries, was first made in antiquity.[22] Scholars, however, generally acknowledge that the differences between 1 and 2 Peter are so vast that they cannot both have been conceived by the same person, even if secretaries were involved. Another possibility is that Peter had a more direct role in one letter and a more indirect role in the other, which would have been written by an "agent" who had a completely free hand. According to this theory, Peter then approved the agent's work and allowed it to be sent out under his name.[23]

On the other hand, Bauckham notes, "the lack of resemblance between the two letters is such that, not only is common authorship very improbable and derivation from a common 'school' of Christian teaching equally improbable, but also the author of 2 Peter cannot, in his writing of 2 Peter, have been influenced by his reading of 1 Peter."[24] Despite the author's apparent ignorance of 1 Peter, Bauckham tries to maintain a connection between the writer of 2 Peter and the apostle, positing that the author of 2 Peter is "an erstwhile colleague of Peter's, who writes Peter's testament after his death, writing in his own way but able to be confident that he is being faithful to Peter's essential message. He would not have to study 1 Peter to be confident of this, and if 1 Peter itself was written not by Peter but by another colleague in the

Petrine circle, whether before or after Peter's death, he would know this and feel even less need to base his own work on it."[25] Whether or not the author was acquainted with Peter, it is almost certain that he was familiar with the contents of the letter of Jude.[26]

The author is a skilled writer, with a sophisticated vocabulary and a knowledge of Jewish, Greek, and Christian texts; his knowledge of Greek and Jewish tradition is seen in his reference to Hell as Tartarus rather than Gehenna. He also knows the Petrine tradition extremely well, alluding to the various revelations granted to Peter in the Gospels of Matthew and John.[27] For example, the author mentions that he was an "eyewitness" to the Transfiguration (Mark 9:2–9 and parallels) and heard the voice of God identify Jesus as his beloved Son (2 Pet. 1:16–18).

Time and Place

The author mentions no actual city or country to which he belongs, only mythical realms. Neyrey locates the author in a city in Asia Minor,[28] though others have suggested Rome. The apostle Paul certainly seems to be a figure of the past (2 Pet. 3:15–16), as his letters are discussed as if they have been distributed widely throughout the churches. The closest parallels to 2 Peter are a group of Christian writings that emerge from Rome, namely *1* and *2 Clement* and the *Shepherd of Hermas*. These texts share with 2 Peter a certain view of Christian traditions and language,

---

21. Jerome Neyrey, *2 Peter, Jude: A New Translation with Introduction and Commentary* (New York: Doubleday, 1993), 128.

22. Richard Bauckham, *Jude, 2 Peter* (Waco, TX: Word, 1983), 145. Daniel J. Harrington, SJ, *Jude and 2 Peter*, Sacra Pagina 15 (Collegeville, MN: Liturgical Press, 2003), 227.

23. Bauckham, *Jude, 2 Peter*, 145–46.

24. Ibid., 146.

25. Ibid., 147.

26. Neyrey, *2 Peter, Jude*, 121; Bauckham, *Jude, 2 Peter*, 141.

27. Neyrey, *2 Peter, Jude*, 132–33.

28. Ibid., 130.

locating 2 Peter in a Roman milieu.[29] Another reason for grouping these particular writings together is that all of them reflect a context in which the apostles are long deceased and can no longer be counted on for leadership and guidance. This was probably true by the end of the first century CE, and certainly true later.[30] This, together with its dependence on Jude, is thought to date 2 Peter to the early part of the second century CE.

Occasion

The author writes in response to "false teachers" (2 Pet. 2:1) and "scoffers" (3:3). Neyrey proposes that these opponents were Epicureans "who rejected traditional theodicy" (see chapter 3).[31] They attempted, Bauckham suggests, "to disencumber Christianity of its eschatology and its ethical rigorism."[32] The author's task is to "deliver the *apostolic* message in a *postapostolic* situation."[33] He must defend the Christian message against pagan skepticism and reaffirm the apocalyptic outlook of the early church. It is a polemical document, which means it employs denunciation of the opponents and apologetic arguments in favor of apocalyptic teaching.[34] While Ernst Käsemann criticizes the letter as an example of "early Catholicism" and increasing institutionalization, Bauckham disagrees, saying that 2 Peter highlights the primitive Christian belief in Jesus' coming parousia.[35]

The genre of 2 Peter is disputed. Neyrey says the letter form is a "literary fiction,"[36] while Daniel Harrington believes that it is "clearly a letter" but also a "testament," which is a farewell discourse by a departing, often dying, hero.[37] The author states in 1:12–15 that it is the farewell address of the author to his addressees. So, though 2 Peter is presented in the form of a letter, it is clearly a testament[38] and unique in the New Testament.

Outline

The letter opens with a simple salutation from Peter to "those who have received a faith as precious as ours" (2 Pet. 1:1–2). The thanksgiving concentrates on living a holy Christian life (1:3–11), especially since its author knows he is about to die, a commonplace of the Jewish testament genre (1:12–15).

The body of the letter (2 Pet. 1:16–3:13) begins with the personal witness of Peter regarding Jesus and the prophetic witness of scripture (1:16–21). These witnesses should suffice to warn the letter's readers to beware of false teachers who, like the false prophets mentioned in scripture, want to lead the people astray (2:1–3). Chapter 2 continues the denunciation of false prophets and outlines biblical accounts of destruction that such prophets occasioned (2:4–22). Most scholars argue

---

29. Bauckham, *Jude, 2 Peter*, 150.

30. Ibid., 150–51.

31. Neyrey, *2 Peter, Jude*, 122. Theodicy is the attempt to reconcile the existence of a perfectly good, all-powerful God with the reality of evil.

32. Bauckham, *Jude, 2 Peter*, 156.

33. Ibid., 153.

34. Ibid., 154.

35. That is, Jesus' triumphant return to earth. Ibid., 150–53.

36. Neyrey, *2 Peter, Jude*, 111.

37. Harrington, *Jude and 2 Peter*, 229.

38. Neyrey, *2 Peter, Jude*, 112.

that 2 Peter relies on Jude for much of this material, in some cases citing it directly.

Chapter 3 encourages the recipients to pay attention to the apostles and the true prophets from scripture and not to those who scoff about the delayed coming of Christ's parousia (2 Pet. 3:1–7). The end will come in due time, according to God's plan; the cosmos will be burned with fire and a new heaven and new earth will be established (3:8–13). While "waiting for these things," the addressees are to live holy lives (3:14–18). The letter ends without any formal closing, greeting, or acknowledgements, contributing to the sense that this is a general letter written long after Peter's death.

The Letter to the Hebrews

Hebrews is the longest and most influential of the general epistles. It contains some of the best writing and most innovative thought in the New Testament. Its presentation of Jesus as the eternal high priest who serves as the ultimate mediator between humanity and the divine is unique within early Christian literature. Hebrews also makes the most sustained and systematic argument for the claim that Christianity has eclipsed Judaism and rendered it obsolete. Unfortunately, the identity of the author of Hebrews is probably an insoluble mystery.

Authorship

As discussed in chapter 1, Hebrews was accepted into the canon based on the theory that it was written by Paul, although the letter itself makes no such claim; in fact, the letter is anonymous. Based on certain thematic similarities with Paul's letters, it was proposed sometime in the second century that the letter was Pauline. However, even in antiquity many observers noticed the huge difference in the rather rough Greek of Paul's genuine letters and the elevated style of Hebrews. Moreover, numerous theological ideas in Hebrews are completely foreign to Paul's thought, while key Pauline concepts are noticeably absent.

The New Testament canon reflects the nebulous status of Hebrews. After the Gospels and Acts of the Apostles, the thirteen letters with Paul's name on them are arranged in order by length, from longest (Romans) to shortest (Philemon). If Hebrews was considered unequivocally Pauline, it would have been included with the other thirteen, and should have been third in order, between 1 Corinthians and 2 Corinthians. Instead Hebrews is located after Philemon, apparently in a category of its own.

Early church leaders were divided on the question of Pauline authorship. Tertullian proposed Barnabas as the author. Origen opined that a disciple of Paul might have written the letter based upon Paul's notes. Other suggested authors include Apollos, Clement of Rome, and Priscilla. By the third century, though, the churches of Syria and Greece considered the letter canonical and Pauline. In the West, Hebrews was not considered Pauline until the fourth century. Clement of Alexandria suggested that Paul wrote the letter in Hebrew and that the present Greek text is Luke's translation. Most scholars reject Pauline authorship, though some subscribe to Origen's theory that the letter arose from a "Pauline school."[39] Origen said of Hebrews that he regarded it as "effectively Paul's" because "the thoughts are the apostle's" even though the text is written by a disciple of Paul.[40] Without good evidence to support a particular identification, the letter should be regarded as anonymous.

---

39. "Pauline school," though, is an amorphous concept. There are many parallels with Paul's letters, but do these indicate dependence on Paul or are they simply early Christian tropes?

40. Eusebius, *Church History* 6.25.13–14, as quoted by Bauckham, *Jude, 2 Peter*, 162.

Time and Place

Timothy, one of Paul's best-known associates, is said to be still alive when the letter is written (Heb. 13:23). If true, the letter was written during or shortly after Paul's lifetime. References to the Jerusalem Temple hint that it might still be standing. Indeed, it would be odd if the author did not mention the destruction of the Temple when one of his central themes is that Christ's priestly sacrifice has rendered the Levitical priesthood obsolete, as this would seem to prove his point. Since the Temple was destroyed in 70 CE, many scholars date this letter to the sixties. There is no reason this letter could not have been written in the fifties or sixties, when Paul's letters were written, although many scholars place it between 80–90 CE. Hebrews must predate Clement's letter to Rome (*1 Clement*, circa 96 CE), since Clement mentions it.

Hebrews was sent specifically to a Jewish Christian community; numerous passages indicate that the recipients, though embedded in Judaism, have been disciples of Jesus for some time (Heb. 2:1; 3:1, 14; 4:1–4, 14–15; 5:11–14; 6:1–6). But it is not possible to determine the actual community to which it was sent. The letter is sent from Italy (13:24), and so the likely point of origin is Rome.

Occasion and Recipients

The theological arguments in the letter suggest that, though the community being addressed consisted of Jewish disciples of Jesus, his role had been relativized by a syncretism that included worship of other divine figures such as angels. In addition, it is possible that some of the recipients argued that the animal sacrifices conducted by the Levitical priests were still necessary. The letter draws close connections between Jesus' activity and Old Testament prophecies, particularly pertaining to worship in the Temple and the sacrificial system. The Old Testament is cited thirty-five times in Hebrews (see especially Jer. 31:33; Ps. 2; 45:4–8; 110:1, 4; 2 Sam. 7:14). The author insists that the institutions of Judaism, though ordained by God, were not complete in themselves but would be fulfilled by Christ. In his view, the Old Testament prophecies point toward the Christian dispensation and truth as it exists eternally in the mind of God. In its stance toward Judaism, Hebrews is the most pronounced example of Christian **supersessionism** in the New Testament.

Supersessionism

When one religion emerges from another, as Christianity did from Judaism, there are two possible stances the new religion could take with respect to its predecessor. One stance is that the new religion "supersedes" the other, essentially replacing it and rendering it invalid. Since Christianity claims to represent a "new covenant," one could argue that the "old covenant" is null and void. Jews who do not convert to Christianity could be classified as unbelievers and excluded from salvation.

Hebrews clearly subscribes to this view: "In speaking of a 'new covenant,' [God] has made the first one obsolete. And what is obsolete and growing old will soon disappear" (Heb. 8:13). Supersessionism has been the default position of most Christian churches throughout history.

The other stance Christianity could take toward Judaism is that the old covenant remains in effect and both covenants are valid for their members. This is known as

continued

Supersessionism *continued*

"dual-covenant theology" and it has become more popular in the wake of the Holocaust. Increasingly Christian theologians and denominations are advocating the cessation of efforts to convert Jews to Christianity, on the theory that the covenant between God and Israel was never abrogated. There is little doubt that throughout history supersessionism has created tension and hostility between Jews and Christians, leading first to Jewish persecution of Christians and then later to even greater persecution of Jews when Christians gained the upper hand. Those who regret this history of persecution have attempted to find ways to develop a more tolerant and pluralistic attitude toward the other religion without compromising the essential claims of their own faith.

Christians would learn how it feels to have another religion claim to supersede their own when Islam came on the scene in the sixth century. Islam acknowledges Abraham, Moses, and Jesus as prophets, but teaches that the revelations given to them by God were altered and distorted by those who followed them and recorded their teachings. According to Islam, only the revelation to Muhammad was preserved perfectly, in the Qur'an. Naturally the Muslim belief that there is something lacking in Jewish and Christian sacred texts has caused some resentment, and has led to more conflict between the three great monotheistic world religions. This is a subject of ongoing concern and conversation.

Form

Hebrews differs from Paul's letters in structure, lacking a salutation, a thanksgiving, and a main body dealing with questions, problems, and controversial issues. In Hebrews, the instructional presentations are interrupted again and again by exhortations. Since Hebrews has no epistolary introduction, it should be regarded as a sort of homily or philosophical treatise that was sent as a "word of exhortation" (Heb. 13:22). While lacking many elements of a Hellenistic letter, it does end with a benediction and greetings.

Theology

The theology of Hebrews is not thoroughly Pauline, but there are a number of shared themes.

- Suffering (Heb. 2:10, 18; 5:8; 10:33; 13:12–13)
- Sanctification or holiness (2:11; 10:10)
- Faith (3:19; 4:2)
- Spiritual infancy and spiritual maturity (5:12–14; 6:1)

- Spiritual milk and spiritual solid food (5:12–14)
- Inability of the law to make perfect (7:19; 8:7–13; 9:15–20; 10:1–18)

These are only a few of the parallels, which might in some instances reflect general Christian teaching. But there are enough of them that the author's familiarity with Paul's teaching and letters seems likely.

There are certainly many differences as well, but one stands out. A major theme of Hebrews is Christ's role as the eternal high priest, something entirely absent from Paul's letters. This idea allows the author of Hebrews both to maintain the temporary validity of the Jewish sacrificial system but also to claim that it was intended to be superseded by the eternal high priest and victim, Jesus Christ. Christ is unique because he is both high priest (Heb. 3:1–10:39; esp. 7:1–28; 8:1–9:28) and atoning sacrifice (9:11–22; 10:1–9). As a priest he mediates between the earthly and heavenly realms and as a sacrifice he makes sinful humans acceptable to God by atoning for their transgressions. In his dual role he is thus able to represent humanity before the face of God. Because of his mediation, the saints who believe in him will gain everlasting rest (3:7–11) as they progress from the city of destruction to the celestial city (11:16; 13:14) and the holy place above (9:12, 23–28). The distinction between the earthly and heavenly cities presents a contrast between the copy/shadow world in which we live and the real world where Christ now dwells (1:3; 8:5; 9:23–24; 10:1). This treatise shows clear influence from Jewish-Hellenistic philosophy, particularly in the focus on the two worlds, one heavenly, one earthly, and the mediation of Christ between them. Although a direct link between Hebrews and the foremost Jewish-Hellenistic philosopher of the period, Philo of Alexandria, is unlikely, the presence of these theological-philosophical ideas in both authors leads some scholars to trace the letter to Alexandria.[41]

Outline

Stephen Harris divides the text into three major sections:

1. Christ, the image of God, is superior to all other heavenly and human beings (1:5–4:16).

2. The Torah's priestly regulations—including sanctuary, covenant, and sacrifice—foreshadow Jesus' role as a priest like Melchizedek (5:1–10:39).

3. Believers need faith in unseen realities, emulating biblical figures of old (11:1–13:6).[42]

The first section focuses on Christ as ranking higher than the angels and Moses (Heb. 1:1–4; 2:1–18; 3:1–6). The assertion that Christ is superior to Moses fits the letter's overarching theme of Christianity's superiority to Judaism. The assertion that Christ is superior to angels, however, does not fit that predominant theme. This lack of fit, along with the fact that 1:5–13 offers no fewer than seven quotations from the Old Testament regarding God's relationship to angels versus God's relationship to the Son, has led some scholars to wonder whether this reflects an actual problem, a Jewish or Jewish-Christian group that was worshiping angels. To this group the author of Hebrews directs a barrage of quotations that prove the Son is greater than the angels. The angels were made (1:7), while the Son was "begotten" (1:5). The angels are servants (1:7, 14), while the Son is a ruler with an everlasting throne (1:8). The Son is "the exact imprint of God's very being, and he sustains all things by his powerful word" (1:3). None of these things can be said of the angels (1:5).

The second section (Heb. 5:1–10:39) concentrates on the Old Testament priestly regulations, which were temporary and always intended to become obsolete. However, these priestly regulations are significant despite their obsolescence because they foreshadow Jesus' role as a priest like **Melchizedek** (5:10; 6:20; 7:1, 10–11, 15, 17). The author of Hebrews stresses Jesus' role as a mediator between the human and divine realms, a role that was occupied in Judaism by the **Levitical priests**. Now Jesus, the text explains, was from the tribe of Judah (7:14); he was not from the tribe of Levi and cannot have been a priest in this sense. However, the book of Genesis (14:18–20) briefly mentions a *non-Levitical* priest of the Most High God, namely Melchizedek. This reference is one of only two passages in the entire Old Testament that

---

41. Since the time of Martin Luther, Apollos, an early Christian from Alexandria noted for his rhetorical skill, has been suggested as the author of this letter.

42. Stephen L. Harris, *Understanding the Bible* (Mountain View, CA: Mayfield, 2000), 502.

Jesus was not of the priestly tribe (Levi); Hebrews asserts, however, that Jesus was high priest of a more ancient order, that of Melchizedek. Abraham meets Melchizedek (Gen. 14:17-24) in this bas-relief from a monastery in Moscow, Russia.

mention Melchizedek (cf. Ps. 110:4). Nonetheless these brief notices were enough to suggest to some interpreters—including the author of Hebrews—the existence of a superior priesthood predating the Jerusalem Temple and not involving descent from Levi or Aaron. The quote from Psalm 110:4, "You are a priest forever according to the order of Melchizedek" allows the author of Hebrews to suggest that this was a prophecy, fulfilled by Christ, who can then be seen as the eternal high priest. The text of Hebrews goes on to argue that the priestly order of Melchizedek is in fact superior to the Levitical priesthood. In Genesis 14, Melchizedek blesses Abraham and receives tithes from him. These details suggest to the author of Hebrews that (1) Melchizedek ranks above even Abraham, because "the inferior is blessed by the superior" (Heb 7:7), and (2) that a priest of the order of Melchizedek ranks above a Levitcal priest, because Abraham paid tithes to Melchizedek, and the tribe of Levi and its priests descend from Abraham. "One might even say that Levi himself, who receives tithes, paid tithes through Abraham, for he was still in the loins of his ancestor when Melchizedek met him" (Heb.

7:9–10). In all of this one can see the overarching purpose of the author of Hebrews, to demonstrate that Christianity has superseded Judaism and rendered it obsolete.

The author proceeds to argue that not only is Jesus' priesthood superior to that of the Jewish priests, but so also is his sacrifice. The problem with the animal sacrifices offered in the Temple is that they need to be made anew, year after year. By contrast, the sacrifice of Christ is perfect and therefore does not need to be repeated: "By a single offering he has perfected for all time those who are sanctified" (Heb. 10:14).

In the final section of the letter to the Hebrews, believers are called upon to act on their faith in unseen realities. Again the author begins with Judaism and then proceeds to Christianity, which compares favorably to its predecessor. The author lists the men and women of the Old Testament who showed faith: Abel, Enoch, Noah, Abraham, Moses, and more (Heb. 11:1–40). But he indicates that "although they were commended for their faith," they "did not receive what was promised" (11:39). The more perfect example of faith is provided by Jesus, "the pioneer and perfecter of our faith" (12:2).

Having argued for the superiority of Christianity to Judaism in every way, the author concludes his sermon. He issues some final exhortations and warnings (Heb. 12:14–29), admonishes his readers to demonstrate love and hospitality and to behave honorably within marriage (13:1–17), bestows a blessing (13:20–21), and conveys personal messages and greetings (13:18–25). Despite the great length of Hebrews, the author claims to have written "briefly" (13:22). Readers of this epistle might be inclined to disagree.

Key Terms

catholic epistles
general epistles
circular letter
James
Jude

1 Enoch
apocrypha
pseudepigrapha
Michael the archangel

The Testament of Moses
supersessionism
Melchizedek
Levitical priests

Review Questions

1. Does James contradict Paul regarding faith in Christ versus works of the law, or does he simply challenge a misreading of Paul's position? How does the author argue that faith alone is insufficient for salvation?

2. How does the author of Jude characterize the "intruders" who had penetrated the churches he addresses? What arguments does the author deploy against them?

3. How does the author of Jude use *1 Enoch* and the *Testament of Moses*? Where did this literature come from?

4. Is it likely that either 1 Peter or 2 Peter was written by Peter? If he did not actually compose the letters, could Peter have been involved indirectly?

5. In what ways does the author of 1 Peter prepare his readers to face persecution? Why does he believe that they should be able to overcome this challenge?

6. What danger did the author of 2 Peter believe was posed by "false teachers" and "scoffers"? How does the author attempt to discredit them?

7. How does the author of Hebrews argue for the superiority of Christianity to Judaism?

Discussion Questions

1. Teachers of the New Testament sometimes ask their students—as a thought experiment—to "vote" on whether certain books should or should not have made it into the canon. The most popular candidates for exclusion usually come from the letters covered in this chapter. Can you see why? Would you vote to remove any of them from the Bible?

2. How do you think faithful Jews might respond to the claims of the author of Hebrews that their religion is obsolete and fading away?

Bibliography and Suggestions for Further Study

(Books and websites that are accessible for general undergraduates are marked with an asterisk; other sources listed are appropriate for advanced students.)

Bauckham, Richard. *Jude, 2 Peter*. Waco, TX: Word, 1983.

Beavis, Mary Ann, and HyeRan Kim-Cragg. *Hebrews*. Wisdom Commentary 54. Collegeville, MN: Liturgical Press, 2015.

Brosend, William F. *James and Jude*. Cambridge, UK: Cambridge University Press, 2004.

Flusser, David. *Judaism and the Origins of Christianity*. Jerusalem: Magnes, Hebrew University, 1988.

*Gamble, Harry Y. *The New Testament Canon: Its Making and Meaning*. Philadelphia: Fortress, 1985.

Gonzalez, Catherine Gunsales. *1 & 2 Peter and Jude: A Theological Commentary on the Bible*. Louisville: Westminster John Knox, 2011.

Harrington, Daniel J. *Jude and 2 Peter*. Sacra Pagina 15. Collegeville, MN: Liturgical Press, 2003.

*Harris, Stephen L. *Understanding the Bible*. Mountain View, CA: Mayfield, 2000.

Hartin, Patrick J. *James, 1 Peter, Jude, 2 Peter*. Collegeville, MN: Liturgical Press, 2006.

Keating, Daniel. *First and Second Peter, Jude*. Catholic Commentary on Sacred Scripture. Grand Rapids: Baker Academic, 2011.

Kelly, J. N. D. *A Commentary on the Epistles of Peter and Jude*. London: Adam and Charles Black, 1969.

*Kümmel, Werner, Paul Feine, and Johannes Behm. *Introduction to the New Testament*. 17th ed. Nashville: Abingdon, 1973.

Neyrey, Jerome. *2 Peter, Jude: A New Translation with Introduction and Commentary*. New York: Doubleday, 1993.

Reicke, Bo. *The Epistles of James, Peter, and Jude*. Garden City, NY: Doubleday, 1964.

Schreiner, Thomas. *1, 2 Peter, Jude*. New American Commentary 37. Nashville: Broadman & Holman, 2003.

Yadin, Yigael. "The Dead Sea Scrolls and the Epistle to the Hebrews." In *Aspects of the Dead Sea Scrolls*, ed. Chaim Rabin and Yigael Yadin, 36–55. Jerusalem: Magnes, Hebrew University, 1965.

CHAPTER

The Book of Revelation

The final text in the New Testament is the book of Revelation, also known as the Apocalypse of John. The Greek title of this book is *Apokalypsis*, meaning a "revealing" or "uncovering," which accounts for the alternate names of this book. The English word "apocalypse" can refer to the *event* resulting in the end of the world, but it can also refer to a *genre of literature* involving visions revealed to a seer. Second Temple Judaism produced some notable examples of apocalyptic literature, such as chapters 7–12 of the canonical book of Daniel and the noncanonical but influential *1 Enoch* (see chapter 19). Early Christianity also generated a good deal of apocalyptic literature, which can be found both within the canon and beyond it. The *Apocalypse of Peter* and the *Shepherd* of Hermas are apocalyptic texts that were candidates for inclusion in the canon at one point. Parts of the Synoptic Gospels reflect apocalyptic thought as well, such as Mark 13, known as the Apocalyptic Discourse or Little Apocalypse. The purpose of this chapter is (1) to situate the book of Revelation within the genre of apocalyptic literature; (2) to summarize the historical situation in which Revelation was written, which in turn necessitates answering questions about the authorship, intended audience, and date of the book; and (3) to describe the basic purpose and main features of the book of Revelation, including major themes, symbolism, and use of the Old Testament.

The Genre of Apocalyptic

Scholars dispute the origin of **apocalyptic literature**, with various individuals arguing that the genre arose within Judaism as a result of one or more of the following:

- the development of eschatological themes in prophetic texts of the Hebrew Bible
- the hopes of oppressed Jews for the restoration of the Davidic monarchy, which had ended with the conquest of Judah by the Babylonians in 597 BCE
- the experience of ongoing persecution and foreign oppression
- the development of beliefs in resurrection, angelic battles, and a judgment at the end of time
- the influence of Persian Zoroastrianism, a religion based on a dualistic theology that featured cosmic warfare, heaven and hell, and the concept of a messiah

Probably all these and still other factors combined to produce this body of literature. Whatever the reasons, about three centuries prior to the Common Era, Jews living under Greek domination began to write texts about how God would take decisive action and radically transform the world in the near future.

What makes a book an **apocalypse**? The genre is defined by two types of characteristics:

those dealing with content (namely the presence of certain key theological ideas) and those concerned with form (that is, conventions of literary structure). Not all of these characteristics are necessarily present in one particular text, but Revelation reflects most of them.

Key Theological Ideas of Apocalyptic Literature

Seven theological ideas are commonly found in apocalyptic literature.

Dualism

First, apocalyptic texts reflect a *dualistic worldview*, in which people and institutions are divided into camps of evil or good. In this cosmic dualism, God leads the forces of goodness, while the supreme leader of forces of evil is usually called the Devil or Satan, sometimes Lucifer, Beliar, Mastemah, or some other name. The influence of good and evil is seen not only in our world, but in the spiritual realm of angels and demons. The current age is often presented as evil, but the world stands on the brink of the age to come, God's kingdom.

Imminence of the End

A second key theological theme is the *nearness of the end of time*. Eschatology (from Greek, *eschaton*, meaning "end") is teaching about "the last things." In apocalyptic texts a particular kind of eschatology prevails, in some ways following from the cosmic dualism mentioned above. Apocalyptic literature typically invokes the idea of the "end of the world," a final battle in which the forces of evil are destroyed and God triumphs over wickedness once and for all. Apocalyptic texts are usually wary of being too precise about when the end is coming, although some offer "coded" messages that suggest a definite time.

But they all agree that the end of time is coming soon, that it is imminent.

Pessimism

Apocalyptic texts are often permeated by a *pessimistic outlook*; the world is so filled with evil that only God's direct intervention can bring redemption. It is understood that most people are wicked and deserve damnation. At the same time, apocalyptic groups are optimistic, confident that, despite all appearances, God is in control of the world. The forces of evil are ascendant at present, but believers never doubt that soon God will intervene in history and make all things right.

Vindication

God's ultimate intervention in human history will *vindicate believers* for their faithfulness. Though persecuted now, the faithful will be rewarded in the (near) future. Moreover, God's justice cuts both ways. Some apocalypses, such as *1 Enoch*, expect many "woes" for unbelievers at the end of time; those who persecuted the faithful will receive the full measure of punishment.

The Coming of the Messiah

A fifth theological theme is that a *Messiah*—a king, a chosen one—will come and act as God's agent to bring about an everlasting kingdom.

The Climactic Battle

When the Messiah comes (or in Christian texts, comes again), there will be a *final battle* between the forces of good and evil. Most apocalypses personify evil in the form of a Satan figure, though some, like Daniel, personify evil in the human rulers of the empires that conquered and oppressed the Jewish people. Many apocalypses see human kingdoms as agents of the supreme leader of the forces of evil. The outcome of the final battle, waged by the forces of God against Satan and his allies, is foreordained: evil will be destroyed. Afterwards, both the wicked and the righteous will be raised from the dead.

The Final Judgment

Finally, after the arrival of the Messiah, the conquest of evil, and the resurrection of the dead, a *final judgment* will take place. In this judgment the righteous receive their reward, eternal life with God in a heavenly place of bliss. Likewise the wicked receive their reward, eternal punishment in a place of torment generally called Hell, Hades, or Gehenna.

Literary Features of Apocalyptic Literature

Three formal elements are common to apocalyptic literature. The first is *pseudonymity,* or writing under a false name. Apocalyptic texts are typically attributed to some famous person of the past, such as Ezra, Daniel, Abraham, Enoch, or Adam. The pretense of this literature is that an ancient figure received divine visions and wrote down the text, but those revelations were hidden by God until the end of time, which is now at hand. Claiming an ancient and highly esteemed author increased the authority of the text and confirmed its validity, while also shrouding it in a mysterious past.

Jewish apocalypses are invariably pseudonymous, but Christian apocalyptic literature includes examples of both pseudonymity and of authors writing in their own name. The book of Revelation is almost certainly not pseudonymous. Its author identifies himself as John and, as discussed in the section on authorship, there is no reason to doubt the truth of this statement.

A second common literary feature of apocalyptic literature is the centrality of *visionary experiences*, revelations of divine knowledge from angels, God, or the Messiah to a human recipient. Much like the prophets, but generally in a more direct fashion, apocalyptic visionaries receive divine information about the nature of reality and how history will unfold. The explicit claim of divine revelation speaks to the profound authority of the messages contained in the apocalyptic texts: God is the source of all the information provided and has verified its truth.

Third and finally, apocalyptic literature tends to be highly *symbolic*, couched in mysterious language that needs decoding. The author is passing on divine revelation in the form of enigmatic and complex visions that have been given to him. These visons include symbolic images and coded words and numbers, which are difficult or even impossible to interpret. This mysterious language and imagery supposedly reflects how these visions were revealed to the apocalyptic seer. Frequently the seer himself cannot understand them, but often an angelic interpreter explains the visions. Sometimes, however, the visions remain opaque even after explanation. Sometimes no interpretation is offered and readers are left in the dark.

Revelation features all of these characteristics, theological and literary, except for that of pseudonymity. The author identifies himself by name.

The Historical Situation, Authorship, and Date of Revelation

The writer, **John of Patmos**, reveals his current location on the island of Patmos, just off the western coast of modern Turkey (Rev. 1:9). Most scholars think that John was exiled to Patmos as punishment for his Christian faith and that he wrote Revelation as a response to this persecution after experiencing a series of visions while he was in exile. A series of messages addressed to seven early Christian churches provide glimpses into their situations (chapters 2–3). Some of the churches are rebuked for permitting false teaching to be circulated (e.g., 2:14–15, 20–23). Other problems include persecution (2:8–11, 13), lack of love (2:4–5), and carelessness (3:15–19). This section suggests that at this time Christian groups were having serious internal problems and were under considerable pressure from the Roman authorities. The author expected the situation to get worse.

The context of persecution suggests a date in the reign of either the Emperor Nero or the Emperor Domitian. Most scholars place the origin of Revelation in the reign of **Domitian** (81–96 CE), who, by some accounts,[1] precipitated a broad persecution of Christians in the nineties that was severe enough to explain the atmosphere of dread and terror that permeates the book of Revelation. However, some scholars argue that the circumstances reflected in the book fit better with the reign of **Nero**, which ended with his death in 68 CE. Nero engaged in a localized persecution of Christians, according to some sources, and the fact that Nero seems to be spoken of symbolically several times in Revelation argues in favor of the earlier date. However, there is strong external evidence for dating this text to the nineties rather than the sixties, in that the church father Irenaeus (who wrote circa 180) situated Revelation during Domitian's reign.[2]

The author of Revelation identifies himself as John four times (1:1, 4, 9; 22:8). But is this John the Apostle, the son of Zebedee and brother of James? Whether Revelation was written earlier or later in the first century, some scholars still maintain that John the Apostle could have been the author, as Christian legend says that he lived to an unusually old age and survived into the reign of Domitian.[3] The Muratorian Fragment[4] implies that John the Apostle wrote the Apocalypse, although the author simply identifies himself as John and never claims to be the apostle. Authorship was fiercely debated in the early church. The weight of evidence suggests that the author was not John the apostle but an otherwise unknown John, an itinerant prophet familiar with the churches of Asia Minor and knowledgeable about Palestine and the Old Testament. This John certainly had intimate information about the churches in Asia Minor and was accepted as an authority figure within them. He speaks knowingly of these churches and their situations and with the expectation that his words would be heard and accepted.

The Purpose of Revelation

In a time of great uncertainty and suffering, the author of Revelation felt himself directed by God to write this book to warn his fellow Christians to prepare for the worse tribulations to come and

---

1. The theory of widespread Roman persecution of Christians under Domitian rests primarily on reports by the fourth-century Christian historian Eusebius. There is, however, little evidence beyond Eusebius (and possibly Revelation) for such a persecution under Domitian. Nevertheless, the persecution need not have been official nor empire-wide to have prompted John to write Revelation. A fairly broad persecution could have escaped the notice of those few Roman writers whose work survives. Correspondence between Pliny the Younger to the Emperor Trajan (see chapter 3) in 112 CE discusses the capital punishment of Christians as if it is a standard, noncontroversial, and apparently longstanding practice.

2. *Against Heresies* 5.30.3. The Church Fathers were not known for their skepticism about the authorship and date of texts they regarded as canonical. They tended to support the earliest possible date. Hence Irenaeus's admission that Revelation was written as late as the nineties must carry some weight.

3. Such longevity would have allowed him to pen the Gospel of John also, widely assumed to be the last of the canonical Gospels. There is no early or reliable documentation of John's extraordinary lifespan, and the story could have been created precisely to allow Christians to attribute both the Gospel of John and the book of Revelation to an apostle.

4. This fragment, also called the Muratorian canon (see chapter 1), is traditionally dated to the late second century, although recently some scholars have argued for a much later date.

to encourage them to wait for God's final salvation (see, e.g., Rev. 1:1–3). Readers are apt to get lost in the dense symbolism and spectacular scenes in the book, but the author's main purpose was not simply to shock or amaze. He wrote with urgency to warn of impending events and to assert that God's plan was unfolding exactly as it should. His goal was to encourage his fellow Christians to "hang in there" no matter how much persecution came their way. He reiterates the importance of "endurance" through suffering and affliction (13:10; 14:12). Near the end of the book, readers are assured once again of eventual vindication and are urged to keep themselves free from sin in order to guarantee God will grant them the final reward of heavenly bliss (22:10–15). In other words, however complex the book may seem and however bizarre its form, the author had the clear purpose of urging his readers to keep the faith even though the world was falling apart around them.

John presents himself as the recipient of visions and prophecies from Jesus Christ or angels who are intermediaries for Jesus. He calls this book a "revelation" (Rev. 1:1) and claims to have been appointed by God to write it. The author considers the book a divinely-inspired prophecy (1:3; 22:10), and warns readers not to tamper with it (22:18–19).[5] But the book is also clearly related to and derivative of other apocalyptic and prophetic texts. This does not mean that the author was not basing his writing on genuine religious experiences, but there is no question that he interpreted his experiences in light of his familiarity with a large body of existing apocalyptic texts, engaging in conversation with the seers and prophets who preceded him. Specifically, the style and form of Revelation recall Daniel, *1 Enoch*, and *4 Ezra*. In addition, although Revelation does not feature any direct citations of the Old Testament, it contains more than eight hundred *allusions* to the Old Testament, more than any other New Testament book, drawing on Daniel, Ezekiel, Isaiah, and many others. Familiarity with such texts is necessary in order to understand this difficult book.

Major Themes of Revelation

The overarching themes apparent throughout Revelation provide the keys that unlock the author's purpose. The author is concerned to assure his readers that evil will ultimately be defeated. God is in control of history, despite the fact that the forces of evil are using the power of Rome to gain the upper hand at present. The author does not minimize the power of evil; it permeates the world and the churches to whom he writes. Indeed, his world is starkly divided between black and white. He shares the dualistic viewpoint common to apocalyptic literature. Ultimately, though, John believes that the strength of the forces of evil is only apparent; these forces are destined to fail. God permits evil to have its day for now. When the appointed time comes, the all-powerful God will finally destroy evil and punish its minions. Thus John's long-term optimism is borne of his confidence in the *sovereignty* of God, his certainty that God is more powerful than any other

---

5. The author's pleas in 22:18–19 that his words not be altered in the copying, and his condemnation of those who would do so, is often taken by Christian conservatives and fundamentalists as evidence that the text of the New Testament underwent few changes in the process of transmission. Most mainstream scholars take 22:18–19 in the exact opposite sense. The author would not have needed to issue dire warnings against scribes creatively altering manuscripts unless such creative alteration was fairly common. This warning also supports a relatively late date for the book of Revelation. In order for the author to complain about Christian scriptures being altered at the whim of copyists, there must have been a fairly extensive history of manuscript transmission, something one could not have reasonably expected to have occurred in the sixties or seventies CE.

spiritual force or human empire. No matter how mighty earthly kingdoms seem, they are nothing in the face of God's plan and can never conquer God's people.

Given the dire situation, but also the promise of God's deliverance, the readers of John's Revelation are asked in the midst of persecution and alienation to focus on endurance, steadfastness, and perseverance in their faith in Jesus Christ. In the midst of defeat, they should be confident of final victory. If there is one thing Christians can do to cultivate the necessary resilience within themselves and to assure God's intervention on their behalf, it is *praising God* as frequently and as effusively as possible, whether in personal prayer or communal liturgy. At several points in the text, John presents images of heaven in which God is continually praised and glorified, and he proceeds to call upon the disciples of Jesus to worship and praise God in a similar fashion (e.g., chapters 4–5; 7:9–12; 11:15–18; 15:2–4).

Literary Characteristics of Revelation

Revelation possesses many of the formal elements characteristic of the apocalyptic genre. Prominent among these elements are (1) the fundamental claim that a divine revelation has been given to a human being, who is instructed to write about what he has seen and heard; (2) the expression of this revelation in highly symbolic language and mythic narratives that both unveil the truth and cloak it in puzzling images; and (3) the presentation of a vision of the final end of evil and the establishment of

God's eternal kingdom. The first and third of these characteristics have already been noted; the second merits discussion, as do some of Revelation's atypical literary qualities. These include its frequent use of the Old Testament and its deployment of mythic narratives in highly repetitive fashion.

Symbolism

Revelation is full of symbols. In Revelation 5, the divine plan is pictured as a heavenly book with seven seals that have to be broken open (Rev. 5:1). Jesus Christ is often portrayed as a **lamb** (e.g., chapters 5–8, 12–15, 19, 21). The destructive forces of human history (conquest, war, famine, disease) are pictured as four horses of different colors (6:1–6). The sun-clothed woman of chapter 12 is thought to be a representation of Mary, or the church, or Israel.

The writer often uses contrasting pairs of symbols. For example, the lamb is contrasted with the beast (chapter 13) and the dragon (chapter 12). Likewise there is the contrast between God's throne in heaven (chapter 4 and numerous other places) and the throne of the beast on earth (16:10), and between the

A lamb symbolizes Jesus in this ninth-century mosaic from the Capella di San Zenone, Rome. Revelation and John's Gospel both depict Jesus as "Lamb of God" (John 1:29, 36), although the two works are not thought to come from the same author.

whorish city of evil ("Babylon," chapters 17–18) and the city of the righteous (the new Jerusalem, chapter 21).

Numbers are used symbolically. The number seven provides structure in many parts of Revelation. The number twelve and multiples of twelve are frequently related to the elect or righteous. For example, the new Jerusalem has twelve gates named after the Twelve Tribes of Israel, twelve foundations named after the apostles, and twelve jewels that adorn the city walls (Rev. 21:12–14, 18–21). Moreover, the city is 12,000 stadia in length, width, and height. The number of the righteous is 144,000, which is 12 x 12 x 1,000 (7:1–8). The number one thousand is used to describe the amount of time in years that Satan will be bound up in prison and the amount of time that the "saints" (holy ones) will reign with Christ before Satan has to be released (20:1–7). The use of one thousand in this passage has fueled speculation about the end of the world occurring at the turn of millennia, speculation that ran rampant before the year 1000 and again before the year 2000.

Probably the most famous symbolic number in Revelation is 666, "the number of the beast" (Rev. 13:18). This is a notorious puzzle, though it has often been thought to implicate Nero, the Caesar who was said to have persecuted Christians in Rome in the mid-sixties CE. Since ancient languages assigned a numerical value to the letters in their alphabet, all words had a numerical value.[6] It is difficult to work from the numerical value to a name, as the possibilities in theory are endless. But if the name "Neron Caesar" is rendered in Hebrew, the letters would be NRWN QSR: R = 200 (x2); Q = 100; S = 60; N=50 (x2); W = 6, which added together makes 666.[7]

The pervasive symbolism found in Revelation gives a sense of mystery to the text, but it also probably gave its first readers a sense of insider knowledge. At the same time, it allowed one to conceal messages that might have been politically and religiously dangerous. This elaborate symbolism opens the book of Revelation to a much wider range of interpretations than most other biblical books, and this openness is part of the reason why Revelation has always been a favorite of poets and novelists. Revelation spurs the imagination more than just about any other biblical text. Indeed, in recent decades the book of Revelation has provided inspiration not only for poets and novelists but for filmmakers, graphic artists, and other visual artists.

---

6. The idea that the numerical value of words has meaning, as well as particular attempts to interpret the meaning of these values, is known as *gematria*. A previous example of this was discussed in chapter 10, where the author of the Gospel of Matthew begins his Gospel with a genealogy of Jesus in which ancestors are grouped into three sets of fourteen generations. The significance of this is that it was believed that the Messiah would be a descendant of David, and the numerical value of the name of David is fourteen.

7. The form of the name Neron Caesar is attested in an Aramaic document from the Dead Sea; see J. T. Milik, Roland De Vaux, and Pierre Benoit, *Les Grottes de Murabba'ât: Par P. Benoit, J. T. Milik, et R. de Vaux; Avec des Contributions de G. M. Crowfoot, E. Crowfoot, A. Grohmann,* Discoveries in the Judaean Desert (Oxford: Clarendon, 1961), 2.18, plate 29. It should be noted that if 666 refers to Nero, this does not mean that the book of Revelation must have been written during Nero's reign. It was widely believed after Nero's reported death in 68 CE that either he had not in fact been killed or that he would come back from the dead. The description of the wounding and healing of the beast in Rev. 13:3 could be based on this belief. The notion that Nero would resurface is known as the *Nero Redivivus* legend, and on at least three occasions Nero imposters took advantage of its popularity to claim to be the former emperor, gain numerous followers, and lead significant, though ultimately unsuccessful, uprisings. Another variation on this legend was that the Emperor Domitian, who shared many characteristics with Nero, was in fact the "revived" Nero himself. This makes it possible, perhaps even likely, that Revelation was written during the reign of Domitian (81–96 CE).

Comic Books and the Bible

For many years academia ignored comic books. The medium of comics was deemed unworthy of serious academic study. The 1950s saw a genuine panic about the negative influence comics were thought to have on the youth of America. Bogus claims were made of a dramatic increase in juvenile delinquency and rebellion that could be linked directly to the rising popularity of comic books. These led to congressional hearings and the creation of a Comics Code whereby publishers had to submit their issues to the Comics Code Authority. These censors prevented the comics from engaging in any frank discussion or depiction of sex, any inclusion of violence that was deemed too graphic or lurid, or any storytelling that involved moral ambiguity or the questioning of authority. The fact that comics were not granted the same protections under the First Amendment as books, newspapers, and movies was a sign of the low esteem in which the medium was held.

Despite being hamstrung by the Comics Code, comics only grew in popularity through the sixties and seventies, eventually gaining a foothold as a respected and legitimate avenue of artistic expression. Although comics have traditionally focused on superheroes, horror, war, and romance, comics dealing with religion have consistently occupied a small segment of the market. Not surprisingly, many comics with a Christian perspective focused on Revelation.

Probably the most famous Christian comic artist was Jack Chick (1924–2016), creator of

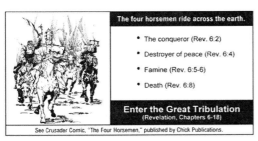

These images are part of Chick's end-time prophecy tract "The Beast."[8] They illustrate his literal interpretation of the book of Revelation and his premillennial dispensationalist theology (see chapter 17). *Copyright 1988 by Jack T. Chick. Used by permission of Chick Publications. Website - https://linkprotect.cudasvc.com/url?a=https%3a%2f%2fwww.chick.com&c=E,1,gTJWKLpOYIs-83xhe0tCkI2GeEh8WEi8WgU3NLo9ssN543gCG1bsvs6TYvASxavHT51f5pJyLwcfDf50ug5SOwMCKCGtpTAMvAokJosE12--G33d&typo=1*

continued

Comic Books and the Bible *continued*

dozens of "Chick comics" and hundreds of "Chick tracts." Chick publications claims to have sold over 750 million of the tracts, which are very small comic books, usually 3 x 5 inches. Chick got the idea of using these comics to spread his version of fundamentalist Christianity after hearing that the Chinese communists had successfully used small comics in the 1940s and 1950s to gain exposure and influence. Most of the millions of tracts in circulation were bought by amateur and professional Christian evangelists and distributed at street corners or in churches, or left in handfuls at bus depots and other public places or businesses where passersby might be tempted to pick one up and read it.

Chick has been criticized for his virulent anti-Catholicism[9] and for spreading conspiracy theories involving Catholics, Muslims, Jews, and Freemasons. He also engaged in fear-mongering against Satanic cults that appear not to exist. Nonetheless, he was a pioneer in his field and utilized the power of the comic form in a way that no one before or since has matched.

Another major figure in Christian comics was Al Hartley (1921-2003). Hartley was best-known for his work on the Archie comics, recounting the adventures of high school friends Archie, Betty, Veronica, Jughead, Reggie, and more in the fictional town of Riverdale. After his conversion to evangelical Christianity in 1967, Hartley began to infuse some Christian content into his works. After being told to cut back he did so, but he also began producing Christian comics for another publisher and eventually convinced the owner of Archie comics to let him license the Riverdale characters in an explicitly religious run of Archie books. An example of Hartley's Christian-themed work involving the Archie universe of characters can be found (along with biting commentary) at *http://www.misterkitty.org/extras/stupidcovers/stupidcomics141.html.*

Use of the Old Testament in Revelation

The author drew much of his symbolism from numerous passages in the Old Testament, particularly in Daniel, Isaiah, and Ezekiel. He was clearly immersed in the Old Testament, alluding to it more than eight hundred times by one estimate, though John never actually quotes the Old Testament.[10] Some of the most profound allusions to the Hebrew Bible are found in Revelation's use of the number forty-two (Rev. 11:2; 13:5), a number that is also found in coded language in Daniel to refer to three and a half years, that is, forty-two months (Dan.

7:25; 12:7). Similarly, John's allusion to the "beast" (Rev. 13) appears to rely on the image of human kingdoms as beasts found in Daniel 7:1–17. Finally, Revelation 4:1–11 presents an image of God's throne surrounded by living creatures or types of angelic beings. The complex symbolism seems to be derived from Ezekiel 1 and Isaiah 6.

Mythic Narrative in Revelation

Apocalypses present **mythic narratives**. The purpose of myth, according to Adela Yarbro Collins, is "to provide a logical model capable of overcoming a contradiction." According

---

9. See Michael Ian Borer and Adam Murphree, "Framing Catholicism: Jack Chick's Anti-Catholic Cartoons and the Flexible Boundaries of the Culture Wars," in *Religion and American Culture* 18, no. 1 (Winter, 2008): 95–112.

10. A list of these allusions can be found in Donal McIlraith, *Everyone's Apocalypse: A Reflection Guide* (Suva, Fiji: Pacific Regional Seminary, 1995), 114–17.

to Collins, in the case of Revelation the contradiction is between the belief that Jesus had conquered death and evil, and the reality that Christians were still persecuted and powerless. Why had not the triumph of Christ led to the end of death and suffering? Collins finds that Jewish apocalyptic texts also struggled with the tension between expectation and reality. Repetition of themes and images in Revelation stresses that the contradiction between what is (God triumphs over evil) and what seems to be (evil triumphs over Christians) is not ultimately real: Jesus will triumph. In fact, John says, Jesus has already triumphed.

A key element of mythic narratives is repetition. While some readers have seen Revelation as a linear text which proceeds through history in chronological order from a beginning to a preordained end, most scholars see the book as being composed of themes and narratives that are continually repeated. Each of these themes and narratives lead to "the end," but there are not multiple "ends." Rather, the same battle between good and evil is being retold in a number of different ways with different images. These cycles are not chronological, but overlapping. Part of their power comes from the continuous reaffirmation that in the end good will triumph over evil. The cycles will eventually be consummated and the universe will reach a final equilibrium. Like many other early Christians, the author of Revelation expected the parousia (second coming of Jesus) in short order.[11] At that time, not only would the inner, spiritual lives of Christians be transformed, but their external lives and the world as well. The cosmos itself would be remade, not just reimagined.

Basic Structure of the Text: Cycles of Seven

Adela Yarbro Collins suggests that Revelation's content is best grasped through the beauty and power of its form.[12] Much of the book's potency and appeal is due to the fact that the significance of many of the images and symbols is not immediately apparent. John's images do not necessarily have a single "correct" meaning or interpretation; they are polyvalent. The outline of Revelation that follows, based on one offered by Yarbro Collins and Craig Koester, represents only one of many scholarly constructions.

Groups of "sevens" form a major part of the book's structure. There are seven messages to churches (chapters 2–3). The "Lamb" (Christ) opens seven seals on the heavenly book (6:1–8:5). Seven angelic trumpets are sounded, causing momentous events on earth (8:6–11:19), and seven final bowls of divine wrath are poured out on the rebellious earth (chapters 15–16).

Both Yarbro Collins and Koester see the text as comprising six cycles of seven visions.[13] Yarbro Collins, for instance understands that after the prologue (Rev. 1:1–8) the first half of the book (1:9–11:19) contains three cycles of seven: the seven messages (1:9–3:22), seven seals (4:1–8:5), and seven trumpets (8:6–11:19). The second half (12:1–22:21) consists of seven unnumbered visions (12:1–15:1), seven bowls (15:1–16:20), a Babylon appendix (17:1–19:10), seven unnumbered visions (19:11–21:8), a Jerusalem appendix (21:9–22:5) and an epilogue (22:6–21). This half, then, also includes three cycles of seven, bringing the total to six. It is possible, though, to divide the Babylon appendix into another series of seven

11. See the sections on the eschatology of Mark (chapter 8) and 1 Thessalonians (chapter 16) for examples of other early Christian literature that anticipated the imminent return of Christ.

12. Adela Yarbro Collins, *Crisis and Catharsis: The Power of the Apocalypse* (Philadelphia: Westminster, 1984), 21.

13. Ibid., 111–34; Craig Koester, *Revelation*, Anchor Yale Bible 38A (New Haven: Yale University Press, 2014), 112.

visions and so get seven cycles of seven (49 total), with the Jerusalem appendix seen as the fiftieth cycle, the Jubilee year, the year of salvation, when in ancient Israel all debts were released and all slaves were freed.[14]

Each cycle expresses the whole message of the book: persecution of the righteous by the forces of evil; God's intervention to punish the persecutors, both human and demonic; and the final salvation of the persecuted. The repeated cycles drive home the importance of the basic apocalyptic message about Jesus Christ.

Outline of Revelation: The First Half (Chapters 1–11)

Prologue (Revelation 1:1–8)

The first half of Revelation begins with the prologue which stresses three things: the authenticity and authority of the message John receives from Jesus through God (Rev. 1:1–2); Jesus as the one "who is and who was and who is to come" (1:4, 8); and Jesus' imminent return (1:3, 7).

Vision of Christ and Commission (Revelation 1:9–20)

In this section John identifies himself and explains that he is on the island of Patmos "because of the word of God and the testimony of Jesus" (Rev. 1:9). This statement may suggest that Patmos was among the several islands the Romans used as places of punishment. In keeping with the key literary apocalyptic characteristics noted above, Jesus

appears to John in a vision and reveals to him what his task is to be (1:13). John is told that he is to write what he sees. The "seven lampstands," he is told, represent the seven churches of western Asia Minor to whom John is to write and the "seven stars" are the angels of these churches.

First Cycle of Visions—Seven Messages (Revelation 2:1–3:22)

Each message John receives focuses on specific problems in a church, though much of the relevance is lost today. Two churches are plagued by Christian heretics called Nicolaitans (Rev. 2:6, 15), while others are afflicted by Jews from "a synagogue of Satan" (2:9, 3:9), or bewitched by the teaching of "Balaam" (2:14) and "Jezebel" (2:20). Still other churches are spiritually "dead" (3:1) or "lukewarm" (3:16). While it is impossible to pinpoint the figures represented by names such as Balaam and Jezebel, the author is clearly concerned with general issues of sexual immorality and idolatry.[15] Moreover, the specific reference to the interference of the Jews and the ban against participation in pagan religious rites (eating "food sacrificed to idols," 2:14) suggest Christian exclusivism—the need for Christians to keep themselves separate from unbelievers. These messages argue against cultural assimilation, urging Christians to refrain from adopting the ways of either Jewish or Roman society.

The members of each church are told that, if they remain faithful, they will "conquer" and receive a reward. Some of the rewards are "permission to eat from the tree of life that is in the paradise of God," salvation from "the second

---

14. David E. Aune, *Revelation*, Word Biblical Commentary 52 (Dallas: Word, 1997), xciv, is critical of Yarbro Collins's attempt to create a series of seven unnumbered visions and would certainly also see as problematic the Babylon appendix divided as a series of seven. He writes, "The use of the designation 'unnumbered' is somewhat disquieting, since the author-editor is perfectly able to use the number seven explicitly when he wants to. Further, the two appendices in 17:1–19:10 and 21:9–22:5 are extensive sections of text that Yarbro Collins apparently cannot integrate into the overall structure of Revelation."

15. These two terms could refer to two separate activities or to one activity, as idolatry was often equated in Jewish thinking with "cheating on" Yahweh with other gods.

death," and "a place with [Christ] on [his] throne" (Rev. 2:7, 11, 17, 26–28; 3:5, 12, 21). The varied phrases all refer to the same essential reward: eternal life.

Second Cycle of Visions—Seven Seals (Revelation 4:1–8:5)

Chapter 4 of Revelation offers a vision of God's heavenly throne, similar to visions found in Ezekiel 1 and Isaiah 6. In John's vision twenty-four elders sit around God's throne. The elders represent the Twelve Tribes of Israel and the twelve apostles of Jesus.

As the vision of the throne room continues, a scroll is presented to "a Lamb standing as if it had been slaughtered" (Rev. 5:6). In the book of Revelation, the "Lamb" is coded language for Jesus. Only the Lamb is worthy to open this

The Metropolitan Museum of Art, Gift of Mrs. Felix M. Warburg, 1940

An engraving by Albrecht Dürer (1471–1528) depicts the four horsemen of the apocalypse (Rev. 6:1–8). Apocalyptic literature frequently includes highly symbolic descriptions of the trials and tribulations of the end times.

Public domain

William Blake (1757–1827) produced a series of engravings based upon scenes from the book of Revelation, including this representation of the twenty-four elders casting their crowns before the throne of God.

scroll, which represents judgment and salvation. The slaughtered Lamb, who appears weak and defeated, actually has power, in contrast to earthly empires, which appear powerful but will be defeated.

In chapter 6 the Lamb opens six of the seven seals on the scroll. The first four seals reveal the **four horsemen of the apocalypse** (cf. Zech. 6:1–8). They represent violence, famine, death, and pestilence, and are "given power over a fourth of the earth" (Rev. 6:8). The fifth seal reveals martyred Christians pleading for the Lord to finish his victory over the forces of evil (6:9–11). The sixth seal marks the time of the end, with nature run amok, for the "day of wrath" (6:17) has come. This vision illustrates Revelation's repetitive character: though the vision is of the end, there are still numerous cycles to go.

Chapter 7 represents an interlude between the sixth and the seventh seals, which some have interpreted as a sort of Sabbath rest. This interlude is full of powerful imagery, such as the symbolic number of 144,000 (12 x 12,000) people who are saved from among the Twelve Tribes of Israel. These have all been marked with a "seal" that grants them God's protection, resembling the protective mark God placed on Cain (Gen. 4:15) to prevent him from being killed after the murder of his brother Abel (cf. Ezek. 9:4–6; Exod. 12:1–24). The seal might also be related to the traditional apocalyptic idea of a book of life in which those who remain faithful are set apart for eternal life, or it could refer to a sign of the covenant, like circumcision or baptism. This interlude concludes with a vision of the salvation of the nations. John sees that the multitude who have suffered in the "great ordeal" (Rev. 7:14) are finally to worship before God's throne forever, no longer thirsting, hungering, or crying.

The opening of the seventh seal, which follows, leads to a mysterious silence in heaven "for about half an hour" (Rev. 8:1). This completes the visions of the seven seals, but it also segues to the next cycle of visions, the seven trumpets.

Third Cycle of Visions—Seven Trumpets (Revelation 8:6–11:19)

In the remainder of chapter 8, the first four angels blow their trumpets, the trumpet blast being a common sign announcing the end (cf. 1 Thess. 4:16). After these trumpet blasts, a third of the earth is burned up, a third of the sea becomes blood, a third of the waters turn to "wormwood" (wormwood is a bitter drug, see Jer. 9:15; 23:15), and a third of the light from the sun, moon, and stars is dimmed.

The whole of chapter 9 consists of horrible visions of the fifth and sixth trumpet blasts. The chapter begins with a vision of Satan as a falling star who opens up the pits of hell to release locusts (Rev. 9:1–3). These locusts torment all people who do not have God's seal for five months with a sting like scorpions, causing suffering but not death. The name of the locust king in Greek is *Apollyon*, which means "destroyer" (Rev. 9:11). Although this destroyer is identified with Satan, the name is most likely also a play on the name of the god **Apollo**, since the Roman emperor Domitian (reigned 80–96 CE) styled himself as an incarnation of Apollo and the locust was one of the many symbols of Apollo.

The sixth trumpet leads to the unleashing of four angels who will kill a third of humankind (Rev. 9:13–19). While killing seems like a terrible task for angels, it has biblical precedent: the angel of death kills all the firstborn in Egypt (Exod. 12). Despite the slaughter of a third of humanity, which recapitulates the earlier destructions (Rev. 8:7), the rest of humanity "did not repent" (Rev. 9:21). Their stubborn refusal to turn to God recalls Pharaoh, who did not repent in spite of the plagues (Exod. 8:15, 19).

Between trumpets six and seven, an interlude occurs (Rev. 10:1–11:13). A mighty angel appears and is given a "little scroll" (10:2), which John is told to eat (10:9). The scroll tastes sweet like honey in his mouth, but is bitter in his stomach. This episode is based on an Old Testament passage in which Ezekiel eats a bitter scroll (Ezek. 2:8; 3:1–3). John is then told that he will prophesy against many people and nations, so most likely the scroll symbolizes his prophecy.

During this interlude, John is told, God's two "witnesses" will prophesy for forty-two months or 1,260 days (Rev. 11:3). This period of time also equates to three and a half years, a span mentioned in the Old Testament book of Daniel (Dan. 7:25; 12:7). Much ink has been spilled trying to determine who these two witnesses represent, with some suggesting Elijah (2 Kings 1:10) and Moses (Exod. 7:17, 19) or Joshua and Zerubbabel (Zech. 3). There is no way to know with certainty who is intended, but these witnesses are given authority to "shut the sky" (Rev. 11:6) as Elijah did (1 Kings 17:1) and to turn water into blood as Moses and Aaron did (Exod. 7:17–21). These witnesses will be killed by the beast from the bottomless pit and will then lie dead in the street for three and a half days while people gloat over them. Then they will be brought up to heaven on a cloud, similar to Elijah's ascension (2 Kings 2:11). Only then does the seventh trumpet sound (Rev. 11:15–19), heralding the beginning of God's everlasting kingdom and prompting the twenty-four elders to praise and give thanks to God. The end of this cycle is not the end of the story, though, as more visions follow.

Outline of Revelation: The Second Half (Chapters 12–21)

The second half of the book maintains the mythic and symbolic language of the first, but presents the underlying message more clearly. The identity of the earthly persecutors, namely the Romans, is made explicit, as is the fact they are under the sway of the demonic forces of evil.

Fourth Cycle of Visions— Seven Unnumbered Visions (Revelation 12:1–15:1)

These visions begin with a "sign" or "portent" of a woman in birth pangs (Rev. 12:1). Interpreters have debated whether the woman represents the church, Mary, or Israel. The woman is certainly a heavenly representative, the antithesis of the "whore" who will soon appear in Revelation. The woman is in the throes of birth pangs, eventually giving birth to a male child—which might tilt the identification to Mary. But birth pangs can also be simply a symbol of the coming of the apocalypse (cf. Mark 13:8). In a second "portent,"

a dragon sweeps down a third of the stars from heaven (Rev. 12:3). The scene recalls themes of primeval chaos often found in ancient mythology (see also Jude 6; 2 Pet. 2:4). The dragon will soon be identified as Satan and the stars as the fallen angels who now comprise Satan's demonic forces. The story of the woman and the dragon, however, is also related to a particular pagan myth.

In the legend of Apollo—remembering that the Roman emperor Domitian styled himself an incarnation of Apollo—Apollo's mother, Leto, is impregnated by Zeus. Zeus' jealous wife, Hera, then persecutes Leto. The great dragon Python pursues Leto to devour her offspring. But Leto finds refuge from the dragon on the floating, barren island of Delos and gives birth to the sun-god Apollo (and his twin sister, the moon-goddess Artemis) on the seventh day of the seventh month.[16] In Revelation, the woman "clothed with the sun, with the moon under her feet" also escapes the clutches of a dragon intent on devouring her child. Instead the child is snatched away by God and the woman finds refuge in the wilderness and is nourished for 1,260 days (3½ years), a number earlier referenced in the vision of the trumpets.

The dragon reappears in the next scene, a vision of a war in heaven between **Michael**, the only angel named in Revelation, and the dragon, who symbolizes Satan and the fallen angels. The dragon, described also as a serpent, is defeated and thrown down to earth, where he again persecutes the woman unsuccessfully and then torments the woman's other children: those who believe in Christ.

The war in heaven and the dragon/serpent have many precedents and parallels in both Jewish and non-Jewish mythology. In Jewish literature, at the time of creation, God battles primeval forces of chaos such as land beasts (Behemoth, see *4 Ezra* 6:49–52; Job 40:15–24) and water

---

16. Plutarch, *Sept. sap. conv.* 8.

beasts (Leviathan, see Job 7:12; 41:1–34; Ps. 74:12–17; 104:26). The dragon (Satan) also has predecessors in other strains of ancient Near Eastern mythology. For instance, the Ugaritic sea serpent-god Lotan and the Babylonian sea-goddess Tiamat both have parallels to Satan. Each represents the forces of chaos in their respective mythologies; each is defeated to enable the emergence of a more orderly universe.

Revelation next turns to beasts who are more easily identified with the Roman Empire. The seven heads of the "beast rising out of the sea" (Rev. 13:1) must refer to the seven hills of Rome, while its ten horns refer to ten emperors, since horns refer to earthly kings in Daniel. In addition to the beast from the sea, there is a beast from the land (13:11). Scholars are confident the sea beast is Rome, but less certain how to identify the beast from the land. The "beast of the earth" has sometimes been identified with the Roman provincial elite of Asia Minor, who had a pronounced enthusiasm for the cult of the emperors. The second beast is later called the false prophet (16:13; 19:20); with the dragon and the beast from the sea, they seem to form an unholy Trinity. In order to buy and sell, the beast demands a "mark" (Greek, *charagma*), which can refer to the imperial stamp of Rome, also found on their coins (13:16–17). The **mark of the beast** is a parody of the seal of the Lamb (7:3), a bastardization of God's mark of protection.

Chapter 14 presents a vision of the Lamb with 144,000 people. When this number appeared earlier (Rev. 7:1–8), it was connected to the Twelve Tribes of Israel, but here it refers to those who have been celibate.[17] Arguments against sexual relations go hand in hand with an intense apocalyptic mentality and an expectation of the imminent end of the world. In the face of impending destruction, sex and childbearing lose the importance they have in normal times.

Fifth Cycle of Visions—Seven Bowls (Revelation 15:1-16:20)

In the next visions seven angels with seven plagues are given seven bowls full of God's wrath to pour out on the earth. The seven plagues resemble the ten plagues of Exodus 7–12, such as the sores (Rev. 16:2; Exod. 9:10–11), the bloody, dead sea (Rev. 16:3; Exod. 7:17–21), darkness (Rev. 16:10–11; Exod. 10:22), the dry river and the demonic frog spirits (Rev. 16:12–16; Exod. 8:3; 14:21–22), and the hailstones (Rev. 16:17–21; Exod. 9:24). However, the plague of drinking blood (Rev. 16:4–7) and the plague of fiery heat (Rev. 16:8–9) have no parallel in Exodus.

This section also provides another image of the unholy Trinity, as the demonic frog spirits come "from the mouth of the dragon, from the mouth of the beast, and from the mouth of the false prophet" (Rev. 16:13). They assemble the armies of the human kings in thrall to them at a place called **Armageddon** (or "Harmageddon"; 16:16). Armageddon, which has become shorthand for the end-time battle, holds an outsized place in popular culture. Mount Megiddo in Galilee (Hebrew, *Har Megiddo*) is most likely the location of the battle in John's mind.

Babylon Appendix (Revelation 17:1-19:10)

This next section begins with an image of the great whore, Rome. An angel explains to John that "the woman you saw is the great city that rules over the kings of the earth" (Rev. 17:18). She sits on a beast with seven heads, representing both the "seven mountains on which the woman is seated" (the seven hills of Rome) and also seven kings—seven Roman emperors, though exactly which seven is hard to say (17:9). On the great whore's forehead "was written a name, a mystery: 'Babylon

---

17. This celibacy could be literal or a metaphor for abstaining from the "adulterous" worship of false gods.

the great, mother of whores and of earth's abominations'" (17:5). **Babylon** was the capital of the empire that conquered Judea and destroyed the Jerusalem Temple hundreds of years earlier. As the nemesis of God's people, "Babylon" symbolizes Rome. The description of the sins of Rome as "fornication" might be literal or symbolic, referring to idolatry and sinfulness in general. The whore is "drunk with the blood of the saints and the blood of the witnesses to Jesus" (17:6), which might refer to Nero's persecution of Christians in Rome.

The beast "was and is not and is to come" (Rev. 17:8, 11). This probably represents Emperor Nero, who had lived ("was") and died ("is not"), but according to popular legend was prophesied to return ("is to come"). When he comes again (in the form of Domitian?), John is told, then the powers of the beast will be aligned against the forces of the Lamb, though the Lamb will ultimately be victorious. In fact, the martyr church is already triumphant in heaven, as mighty Rome is already judged and dead. Kings, merchants, and sailors mourn for Babylon because they have lost their power and wealth; saints, apostles and

The "whore of Babylon" sits upon the beast in this manuscript illumination. In the symbolic language of apocalyptic literature, "Babylon" represents Rome, for the Romans destroyed the Second Temple just as the Babylonians destroyed the original Temple in Jerusalem.

prophets rejoice at her downfall (18:20) and a heavenly multitude sing God's praise (19:1–10).

Sixth Cycle of Visions—Seven Unnumbered Visions (Revelation 19:11-21:8)

This group of unnumbered visions contains another white horse and rider, this time representing Jesus the conqueror. The rider has a "sharp sword" that comes from his mouth, and he will rule the nations with a "rod of iron" (Rev. 19:15). This leads to a great supper in which God calls on the birds of heaven to feast on the vanquished forces of Rome and the beast, a section with many parallels to Ezekiel 37–48. For instance, in Ezekiel 39 Gog and Magog—the apocalyptic enemies of God's people—are defeated and animals feast on the corpses of their fallen soldiers.

Then Satan is bound "until the thousand years were ended," after which he will be "let out for a little while" (Rev. 20:3). Interpreters have struggled to make sense of this thousand-year period, known as a **millennium**,[18] just as they have puzzled over Satan's subsequent release.

After the binding of Satan comes the first resurrection, when those who were martyred under Rome are raised and reign with Christ during the millennium. Many evangelical Christians believe in a literal thousand-year period during which those who are saved will reign with God, having been taken up at the Rapture—a term not found in Revelation but borrowed from Paul (see chapter 16). Catholic tradition

---

18. In book 20 of *The City of God*, Augustine suggests that Christians are already living in this millennial period.

interprets the length of time symbolically and sees the reign of believers with God as referring to the faithful who are with Christ in heaven.

Satan is then loosed and defeated along with the forces that he has gathered from Gog and Magog. The book of life is opened and everyone must stand before God's throne, where all are judged "according to their works" (Rev. 20:12). As the book nears its conclusion, John sees "a new heaven and a new earth" (21:1) and a vision of a new Jerusalem descending from heaven (21:2). The Lord, enthroned, proclaims, "It is done! I am the Alpha and the Omega"[19] (21:6). He dispenses the "water of life" to the faithful, but for those judged unworthy there is the "second death" (21:6–8).

Jerusalem Appendix (Revelation 21:9—22:5)

The penultimate section of the book develops the vision of "the holy city Jerusalem coming down out of heaven from God" (Rev. 21:10). The city is the bride, the wife of the Lamb, the true Israel (the church). On the city's gates appear "the names of the twelve tribes of the Israelites" (21:12) and "the wall of the city has twelve foundations, and on them are the twelve names of the twelve apostles of the Lamb" (21:14). The city is measured (cf. Ezek. 40–42): all measurements are multiples of twelve. In this city, in contrast to Ezekiel's vision, there is no Temple, because the Temple is God and the Lamb. The city is lighted by God's glory and flowing from God's throne is the water of life (Rev. 21:22–22:5).

Epilogue (Revelation 22:6–21)

The epilogue reassures readers that all these things "must soon take place" (Rev. 22:6). Jesus repeatedly asserts, "I am coming soon" (22:7, 12, 20), and the author responds "Come, Lord Jesus" (22:20; cf. 22:17). Revelation cloaks in symbols and visions the great hope of the early Christians: that Jesus would soon return and the triumph of God would be complete.

Key Terms

apocalyptic literature	lamb	Michael
apocalypse	mythic narrative	Mark of the Beast
John of Patmos	four horsemen of the apocalypse	Armageddon
Domitian	Apollyon	Babylon/Whore of Babylon
Nero	Apollo	millennium

Review Questions

1. What factors contributed to the development of the genre of apocalyptic literature? What are the differences between Jewish and Christian apocalypses?

2. Outline the major theological themes and literary characteristics of apocalyptic literature.

3. When was the book of Revelation probably written? Who was the "John" who wrote it?

4. List and define briefly some of the major theological themes and literary characteristics of Revelation.

---

19. Alpha and omega are the first and last letters of the Greek alphabet, and hence refer to the beginning and the end.

5. What are the major purposes of Revelation? How are these related to the original situation of the author and recipients?

6. What is the essence of the cycle of ideas that is repeated throughout the book of Revelation?

Discussion Questions

1. There appears to be a huge divide between those Christian groups that remain convinced the end of the world is coming soon and those that act as though the world will go on more or less in its current form indefinitely. Which group, in your view, has a better claim to being based on a reasonable interpretation of the Bible? Given past history and current events, does one group or another seem to have the upper hand in its expectations being met?

2. In 1993, a small religious sect called the Branch Davidians, led by a self-proclaimed messiah who called himself David Koresh, killed four government agents who were raiding the group's compound in Waco, Texas. The group had stockpiled huge numbers of (possibly illegal) weapons in anticipation of the battle of Armageddon. The FBI then laid siege to their compound for fifty-one days before a fire broke out and Koresh and seventy-five others were burned to death. Koresh's theology, and his insistence on not surrendering to the United States government, was based largely on his interpretation of the book of Revelation. This case provides one example of why some observers believe that the book of Revelation is the most dangerous book in the New Testament. Do you agree or disagree with that assessment?

Bibliography and Suggestions for Further Study

(Books and websites that are accessible for general undergraduates are marked with an asterisk; other sources listed are appropriate for advanced students.)

Aune, David E. *Revelation*. Word Biblical Commentary 52. Dallas: Word, 1997.

Beale, G. K. *The Book of Revelation*. NIGTC. Grand Rapids: Eerdmans, 1999.

*Collins, John J. *The Apocalyptic Imagination: An Introduction to Jewish Apocalyptic Literature*. Grand Rapids: Eerdmans, 1998.

Harrington, Wilfred J., OP. *Revelation*. Sacra Pagina 16. Collegeville, MN: Liturgical Press, 1993.

Koester, Craig. *Revelation*. Anchor Yale Bible 38A. New Haven: Yale University Press, 2014.

Laws, Sophie. *In the Light of the Lamb: Imagery, Parody, and Theology in the Apocalypse of John*. Good News Studies. Wilmington, DE: Glazier, 1988.

*McIlraith, Donal. *Everyone's Apocalypse: A Reflection Guide*. Suva, Fiji: Pacific Regional Seminary, 1995.

Schüssler Fiorenza, Elisabeth. *The Apocalypse*. Chicago: Franciscan Herald Press, 1976.

Weinrich, William C., ed. *Revelation*. Ancient Christian Commentary on Scripture: New Testament 12. Westmont, IL: IVP Academic, 2006.

*Yarbro Collins, Adela. *Crisis and Catharsis: The Power of the Apocalypse*. Philadelphia: Westminster, 1984.

21 CHAPTER

The Quest for the Historical Jesus

Many people, even if they know little else of biblical scholarship, have heard of the so-called "Quest for the Historical Jesus," if not from newspaper or magazine articles then perhaps from television. Occasionally some new discovery or theory emerges that the media then trumpet as the key piece of evidence that finally reveals who Jesus *really was*. The assumption behind these claims is that we do not already know who Jesus was—that his portrayal in the Gospels and the teachings of traditional Christianity is incorrect or misleading. But this assumption is not shared by millions of Christians, and the media stories usually do not explain exactly why it is that the traditional portraits of Jesus cannot be trusted. To understand fully how the Quest for the Historical Jesus developed, one must start at the point at which the reliability of the Gospels began to be seriously questioned.

The Development of Doubt about the Reliability of the Gospels

As chapter 3 explains, there was no shortage of doubters about the trustworthiness of the Gospels among pagan intellectuals in antiquity. Critics like Celsus and Porphyry insisted that the wondrous words and deeds of Jesus were recorded only by biased Christians, and never confirmed by contempory, objective observers. They noted with suspicion the stories that could have been verified by few if any witnesses (such as of Jesus' temptation), and hence could have been fabricated by Jesus or his overzealous followers. The story of Jesus' resurrection seemed especially suspect. Most of the testimony came from unreliable women, they argued, and could have been the result of hysteria, hallucination, wishful thinking, or outright fraud. Celsus identified contradictions between the various Gospel accounts of the resurrection, an early seed of doubt that would blossom into a major critique during the eighteenth century.

These early doubts were largely silenced by the triumph of Christianity over paganism in the Roman Empire after the late fourth century CE. Indeed, the works of Celsus and Porphyry were suppressed and destroyed; they survive today only in fragments or in reconstructions based on Christian responses to them. There may have been other accounts skeptical of the Christian claims for Jesus that vanished without a trace, but in truth very little is known about the early reaction of non-believers to the founder of Christianity. Almost no non-Christian works from anywhere near the time of Jesus mention him at all. He seems to have completely escaped the notice of Roman writers until the early second century, and Jesus is not mentioned in any first-century Jewish sources either, with the notable exception of Josephus. The curious silence of first-century non-Christian writers about the arrival of such a (supposedly) popular and significant religious figure troubled later historians, some of whom would even be moved to doubt that Jesus ever existed. But from late antiquity to the early modern period, the church dominated the political and intellectual landscape of Christian Europe; as a result, no one dared voice doubts about the utter reliability of the Gospels' portrait of Jesus.

To be sure, through the centuries many of Christianity's most acute thinkers, like Augustine of Hippo, recognized that there were parts of the Bible that contradicted other parts and that could not be literally true as written. But they were able to rescue the Bible's inerrancy by means of the **allegorical method** of biblical interpretation, which was eventually developed to the point of claiming that scripture had as many as four separate levels of meaning. In addition to the literal meaning of the text, a passage could have a moral significance, a Christological significance, and an anagogical (or eschatological) sense. If a passage could not be interpreted literally, it was only because the Holy Spirit had inspired within it some deeper meaning regarding morality, Christ, or the end of the world. In other words, Scripture might say one thing and mean something else entirely. A classic example of the allegorical method at work is Augustine's famous interpretation of the Parable of the Good Samaritan in the Gospel of Luke.

> *A man was going down from Jerusalem to Jericho;* Adam himself is meant.
>
> *Jerusalem* is the heavenly city of peace, from whose blessedness Adam fell.
>
> *Jericho* means the moon, and signifies our mortality, because it is born, waxes, wanes, and dies.

> *Robbers* are the devil and his angels.
>
> *Who stripped him,* namely, of his immortality; *and beat him,* by persuading him to sin; *leaving him half dead,* because in so far as man can understand and know God, he lives, but in so far as he is wasted and oppressed by sin, he is dead; he is therefore called *half-dead.*
>
> The *priest* and *Levite* who saw him and passed by, signify the priesthood and ministry of the Old Testament, which could profit nothing for salvation.
>
> *Samaritan* means Guardian, and therefore the Lord Jesus Himself is signified by this name.[1]

Augustine's commentary continues in the same vein for the whole of the parable. Now the idea that the Samaritan symbolizes Jesus, the robbers are Satan and his demons, and that the victim is Adam is not an indefensible interpretation, but it is clearly not a literal reading of the text; it is a Christological one.

It must be admitted that the allegorical method, though often applied to Jesus' teachings, was seldom applied to the stories about Jesus' deeds in the Gospels, which were generally assumed to be factual. Still, allegorical interpretation would have been available to resolve any problems that were identified and taken seriously. The advantage of the allegorical method is that it allows the interpreter to bypass problems created by contradictions between two or more biblical texts and obvious historical errors made by biblical authors. One simply claims that the passage is not meant to be taken literally but instead has some other significance. The disadvantage is that the method can be used to make a given passage mean more or less whatever an interpreter wants it to mean, free from any historical or literary constraint.[2]

---

1. Augustine, *Quaestionum evangelicarum* 2.19, as quoted in C. H. Dodd, *The Parables of the Kingdom* (New York: Scribner, 1978), 13.

2. In other words, the Bible did not mean what its original authors intended it to mean, what its earliest interpreters took it to mean, or what its words might mean in any other story or context.

During the Reformation, however, the allegorical method fell out of favor in Protestant Christian circles. The major Reformers looked with suspicion on allegorical interpretations that they regarded as fanciful and creative. They preferred to critique Catholicism using the "plain" sense of Scripture. But interpreting the Bible according to its plain sense would soon become problematic in all branches of Christianity. The Enlightenment saw the rise of four movements that created these problems: empiricism, rationalism, deism, and historical criticism. Each of these developments raised serious questions about the historical reliability of the Bible generally and the Gospels in particular.

Philosophical Doubts about Miracles

Although he had important philosophical predecessors,[3] the philosopher who did the most damage to the reputation of the Gospels was undoubtedly **David Hume** (1711–1776). The claim of Hume's philosophy important for biblical studies is that miracles have never happened. Hume is known as one of the founders of British *empiricism* (the claim that knowledge comes only or primarily from sensory experience) and *skepticism* (the claim that any assertion should be doubted until it is proven with good evidence). Hume had never seen a miracle, so he had no sense experience that confirmed their existence. He doubted all of the accounts he heard of miracles from his contemporaries. He was certain that those who testified to the reality of modern miracles were either lying, or misguided, or contradicted by other, more reliable witnesses.

If miracles did not occur in the modern world, Hume further argued, one should not believe that they occurred in biblical times either. Jesus' disciples supposedly were able to see all kinds of miracles. They in turn performed miracles that helped persuade the first generation of Christians to convert. As the centuries passed, however, credible reports of miracles became far more infrequent. Why, skeptics like Hume wondered, would the supply of miracles have dried up like this, especially in "civilized" societies where educated people were more aware of the natural causes of many extraordinary-seeming phenomena?

Hume also raised questions about the reproducibility of miracles. For Hume one of the key elements in justifying a belief was the *repeatability* of the phenomena on which it is based. One could run a hundred, a thousand, or a million experiments involving a lake and a pedestrian, Hume's argument held, and never once would one of them be able to walk on water. The absence of empirical evidence of miracles cast strong doubt, Hume maintained, upon the existence of such miracles in earlier times.

Hume defined a miracle as a "transgression of a law of nature by a particular volition of the Deity, or by the interposition of some invisible agent."[4] As a result, Hume did not categorize as miraculous certain events that others might call miracles, such as a person surviving unscathed a particularly horrific accident or recovering from an illness that doctors were sure would be fatal. Such events would fall into the category of "unlikely" or even "unexplained." But to say that humans do not understand the natural cause of an event is not to admit that it does not have one, Hume would argue.

Hume especially doubted the claims of religionists to have experienced miracles, because

3. In particular, Baruch Spinoza had expressed doubts about the possibility of miracles as early as 1670, in the *Tractatus Theologico-Politicus*.

4. David Hume and Peter Millican, *An Enquiry Concerning Human Understanding*, Oxford World's Classics (New York: Oxford University Press, 2007), 10.

they have an obvious reason to lie—namely to justify their beliefs to themselves and persuade others to join them. Hume noted that Christians are usually just as skeptical as he was about miracles when they consider miracles attributed to the Buddha, the Hindu god Ganesha, or the Greco-Roman demi-god Asclepius. Christians typically scoff at the flimsy supporting evidence for these miracles and marvel at the credulity and naïveté of those who accept such claims. But Hume thought that the quality of evidence for Christian miracles was no better than that for non-Christian miracles, and that the evidence for all of them was extremely weak.

Jesus walks on water in this drawing by Gustave Dore (1832-1883). With the rise of the scientific method, leading intellectuals found the Gospel accounts of miracles increasingly problematic.

Hume's skepticism about miracles did not immediately decimate the Christian religion. Most ordinary believers, few of whom were aware of Hume's critique in any event, continued to believe in miracles. Some of these believers might have restricted their acceptance of miracles to the era of Jesus and the apostles, but many of them insisted that miracles were still occurring. Such belief continues today: many Protestants accept the claims of faith healers like Benny Hinn and Peter Popoff, while many Catholics believe that the waters of Lourdes have healing powers or that the sun danced in the sky for the Catholic faithful at Fatima in 1917. An entire denomination—the Christian Scientists—advocates faith healing.

Hume and his allies had more influence among intellectuals than among the general populace. Thomas Jefferson, for example, famously took scissors to his Bible and excised the miracle stories. However, even among the elite there were Christians who claimed that Hume had failed to prove his central point about miracles. They might admit that many miracles are based on the unreliable, biased testimony of a few uneducated or highly superstitious people, but that does not mean that *all* miracles lack supporting evidence. Some miracles are attested by more people, by educated people, or by people who appear to have nothing to gain by lying. Hume himself could not possibly have investigated the case for every miracle story ever told, and given his stated principles about the necessity of empirical evidence, it seems that he could rule out the possibility of past miracles only by making an *a priori* determination that miracles were impossible. Others suggested that Hume had defined miracles and natural law in such a way that the possibility of miracles had been ruled out *by definition* rather than by scrupulous examination of the evidence.

Hume stands in a tradition of Enlightenment philosophers who trusted reason over revelation, and who were skeptical of tradition and authority as warrants for belief. Part of the Enlightenment ethos was that long-held traditional beliefs could be wrong, and deferring to authority—especially in matters of religion where the "authorities" have a vested interest in maintaining the status quo—could also lead to error. Despite the mixed reaction Hume received, his philosophy certainly made it more common for scholars to be skeptical about the miracles of Jesus, or at least to want to examine the underlying evidence for them. Moreover, when the examination of the supporting evidence was undertaken, some found it sorely wanting.

Pioneers of Historical Criticism

An enduring legacy of the Renaissance was the ascendance of the scientific method. Given its success, some scholars began to think that the scientific method should be applied not only in the "hard" or physical sciences (biology, chemistry, physics) but also in the social sciences (history, psychology, sociology, and economics). With respect to history, a more rigorous methodology was clearly needed; there is no question that a great deal of ancient and medieval history was false or misleading. Older historians too often (1) did not document their sources; (2) did not question the bias or trustworthiness of their sources; (3) made few attempts to verify the accuracy of the accounts they inherited and passed on; (4) had no qualms about inventing details (especially speeches) for which they had no sources, and, most importantly; (5) treated some sources and subjects differently from others. An example of the final point is the more favorable treatment given by Christian historians to Christian sources. When it came to general history and non-Christian religions, these historians could be as critical and skeptical as they wanted. But when it came to Christianity, special rules applied. Certain sources were privileged above others (canonical Gospels over noncanonical gospels, for example). When it came to the privileged

sources, doubts were not to be raised, for doubts were dangerous and sinful.

Modern historians discarded all of these tendencies as unscientific. Historians were taught to discover and compare as many sources as possible, to document their sources, to interrogate sources rigorously in search of bias and falsehood, to be skeptical of any individual account unless it could be verified by others, to approach all questions objectively, and to treat all historical subjects—even Christianity—equally. As these changes took effect, historians could no longer claim to offer versions of events with complete certainty. They could only conclude that one version was more probable than another, and although that probability could approach 100 percent, it could never actually achieve certainty.

Among the early scholars to apply the new historiography to the Gospels and the life of Jesus, two figures stand out: **Hermann Samuel Reimarus** (1694–1768) and **David Friedrich Strauss** (1808–1874). Reimarus was a **deist**, someone who believed in God and the immortality of the soul but denied the divinity of Christ and divine inspiration of the Bible. Deists maintained that God created the world but designed it to work according to reason and natural law. Consequently, God does not need to intervene in the course of the world's affairs, and in fact does not do so, contrary to the claims of miracle stories. Like other deists, Reimarus believed that an omnipotent God would not create a world that was in constant need of tinkering and interference.

Reimarus's most influential work, published anonymously after his death and only later sourced to him, was originally titled *Fragments by an Anonymous Author*. This work invented the Quest for the Historical Jesus.

Reimarus saw Jesus as a mortal, apocalyptic preacher who foresaw a radical transformation of the earthly affairs of humanity, much as many of his contemporary Jews did. He believed that Jesus' disciples then distorted Jesus' message and turned it into Christianity by claiming that Christ should be worshipped as divine. Reimarus suggested that the religion *of* Jesus had become the religion *about* Jesus. To document this claim, he pointed out many differences between what Jesus said in the Gospels and what the apostles said in other parts of the New Testament, most notably about the atonement. He accurately pointed out that Jesus seldom claimed divine status for himself, and despite advocating vigorously for the worship of *God* never plainly called for the worship of *himself*. The mechanism by which

the disappointed disciples turned Jesus into a god was the resurrection. Reimarus believed that the disciples stole Jesus' body and faked the resurrection to get their new religion off the ground (*Fragments* §53–55).[5]

Reimarus, like Celsus before him, pointed out multiple contradictions between the Gospel accounts of Jesus' resurrection. Reimarus identified ten contradictions (see *Fragments* §22–§32) between the different Gospels; subsequently, even more have been identified. The following chart illustrates some of the points raised by Reimarus and his allies.

	Original Gospel of Mark	Gospel of Matthew	Gospel of Luke	Gospel of John	Longer Ending of Mark[6]
Who went to the tomb	Mary Magdalene, Mary the mother of James, and Salome	Mary Magdalene and "the other Mary"	Mary Magdalene, Mary the mother of James, Joanna, and "other women"	Mary Magdalene, later joined by Peter and the "beloved disciple"	N/A
Why they went to the tomb	To anoint Jesus' body with spices	To see the tomb	To anoint Jesus' body with spices	No reason given; Jesus' body had *already* been anointed with spices	N/A
When the stone was rolled away	Before the women arrived	After the women arrived	Before the women arrived	Before the women arrived	N/A
Who testified to them about Jesus' resurrection	A "young man dressed in white"	An "angel of the Lord"	"Two men in dazzling apparel"	Two angels in white, plus Jesus himself	N/A
What they saw when they reached the tomb	A young man sitting inside the tomb	An angel sitting upon the stone outside the tomb	At first nothing except the empty tomb, but then two men appeared	The linen cloths that had wrapped Jesus, and (separately) the napkin that had covered his face	N/A

continued

---

5. Available in English as Hermann Samuel Reimarus, Charles H. Talbert, and David Friedrich Strauss, *Fragments* (Philadelphia: Fortress, 1970).

6. Reimarus, lacking the benefit of textual criticism, did not know that the long ending of Mark is a later addition to Mark's Gospel. Had Reimarus known this, he could have noted even more differences between Mark and the other Gospel accounts of the resurrection. Moreover, the longer ending of Mark provides a fifth version of certain parts of the resurrection story, with its own set of differences.

	Original Gospel of Mark *cont.*	Gospel of Matthew *cont.*	Gospel of Luke *cont.*	Gospel of John *cont.*	Longer Ending of Mark *cont.*
How they reacted to this news	They fled from the tomb in terror and amazement, and said nothing to anyone.	They departed quickly with fear and great joy, and ran to tell the disciples.	They returned from the tomb and told everything to the eleven and the rest.	Peter and the beloved disciple simply went home; Mary Magdalene stayed behind to weep.	N/A
The number of times the risen Jesus appeared to his followers	Zero	Two	Two	Four	Three
The persons to whom he appeared	No one	(1) The women leaving the tomb, (2) the eleven remaining disciples	(1) Two unidentified men, (2) those two men plus the eleven remaining disciples	(1) Mary Magdalene, (2) ten of the eleven disciples (minus Thomas), (3) the eleven remaining disciples, (4) seven disciples	(1) Mary Magdalene, (2) "two of them," (3) the eleven remaining disciples
Where Jesus appeared to them	N/A	(1) Jerusalem, (2) a mountain in Galilee	(1) on the road to Emmaus, (2) Jerusalem	(1) Jerusalem, (2) Jerusalem, (3) Jerusalem, (4) on the beach by the Sea of Tiberias	(1) unclear, (2) an unidentified location "in the country," (3) unclear
Proof that the risen Jesus was corporeal (had a body)	N/A	The women "take hold of his feet."	Jesus eats a piece of broiled fish.	Thomas puts his fingers in Jesus' wounds.	None provided
Proof that the body was not stolen	None provided	Guards are posted at Jesus' tomb to prevent such a theft.	None provided	None provided	N/A

Reimarus concludes, "Reader, you who are conscientious and honest: tell me before God, could you accept as unanimous and sincere this testimony concerning such an important matter that contradicts itself so often and so obviously in respect to person, time, place, manner, intent, word, story?" (*Fragments* §32). The contradictions, in many ways, speak for themselves. There are very few points of complete agreement, and significant differences in many details. In most areas of life, at a trial for example, such discrepancies and inconsistencies in testimony generally lead one to doubt the reliability of the witnesses.

Many critics responded that Reimarus had approached these accounts with a preexisting bias against miracles. He also failed to point out the large number of smaller points on which two or more Gospels *agree*, and the fact that the general tenor of the accounts exhibits an overall consistency. Still, beyond his work on the resurrection, Reimarus is credited with some lasting insights into the question of the historical Jesus. He pointed out (1) the degree to which Jesus' message is strongly eschatological, and the fact that the apocalyptic element cannot be ignored or marginalized; (2) the fact that the historical Jesus must be understood in the context of ancient Judaism, his preaching understood as likely in continuity with Jewish tradition on many points, and not a complete aberration; (3) the probability that there is, or at least might be, a significant difference between the Jesus of history and the Christ of faith; and (4) the importance of developing a historical framework into which one's individual biblical interpretations could be fitted. Reimarus advanced beyond the rationalists and deists who were mocking the supernatural elements in the New Testament by developing a comprehensive historical account of Christian origins that provided an alternative to the received account. Reimarus's specific conclusions are less important than his having opened the door to the use of historical biblical criticism to revisit and revise the origins of Christianity.

The work of D. F. Strauss was not quite as groundbreaking as that of Reimarus, but it did create a sensation. It is hard to overestimate the controversy that D. F. Strauss's work generated, published as it was while he was still alive. When one British noble opined that Strauss's work was "the most pestilential book ever vomited out of the jaws of hell,"[7] he was speaking for a great many Christians in Europe and America. But Strauss must be credited with refining Reimarus's techniques and developing a template that would be followed by many later historical

Jesus researchers: the creation of a "life of Jesus" that retold the story of Jesus, allegedly dispensing with historical inaccuracies and leaving only the pure core of historical truth.

Strauss's work, translated as *The Life of Jesus Critically Examined*, rejected the claims of rationalists like Reimarus, who argued that the miracle stories were either deliberate deceptions or credulous misinterpretations of non-supernatural phenomena. But neither did Strauss accept the miracle stories as factually accurate accounts of real events. Instead, Strauss interpreted the miracles through the category of **myth**. In the eyes of Strauss and his colleagues, a myth is not a factual story, but neither is it a simple lie. Myths are stories that people tell to express their deepest convictions, to assert primordial truths that often defy direct, literal description.

A classic example that illustrates this notion of biblical story as myth, at least in the eyes of some interpreters, is the story of Adam and Eve. This story, mythicists say, is not factually correct—that is, Adam and Eve were not historical people and the Garden of Eden was not a real geographic location. But the *story* of Adam and Eve was created to express certain beliefs about God and human beings, such as that humans are dependent upon God for their existence, that they have a natural tendency to rebel against God, and that this rebellion has tragic consequences. These beliefs can be true regardless of whether Adam or Eve ever existed. In a similar fashion, the parable of the Good Samaritan can express deep truths about love of neighbor even if there was never a Jewish victim of an attack who was overlooked by two fellow Jews and tended to by a compassionate Samaritan. In fact, the parable genre seems to assume that its readers or hearers understand that the story itself is fictional but meant to express deeper truths. Could that have been true not only

---

7. Quoted in, among other sources, Richard Walpole, *The History of Twenty Five Years*, vol. 4, (New York: Longmans, Green, and Co., 1908), 292. Walpole cites *Life of Lord Shaftesbury*, vol. 3, 164.

of some of the stories Jesus told, but the stories that his followers told *about him*?

Strauss believed that the miracle stories in the biography of Jesus were just such myths, stories created by the early Christian church to make sense of their experience of having gained salvation through Jesus. These early Christians sought to interpret that salvific experience in terms of the idea that Jesus was the Jewish Messiah foretold by the prophets in the scriptures, an identification that seemed to them to require verification through miracles like those performed by Moses, Elijah, and Elisha. Strauss picked away at the credibility of these tales much as Reimarus did the story of the resurrection, and in doing so he had plenty of company among the rationalists and deists of his day. But his employment of the category of myth allowed Strauss to avoid the extremes, as he saw it, of skeptical rationalism on the one hand, and naïve and credulous supernaturalism on the other.

Strauss thought that the influence of myth was so thoroughgoing in the Gospels that it was virtually impossible to identify enough historically accurate details to assemble a credible biographical outline of the historical Jesus. While later scholarship would agree with Strauss about the influence of mythic thinking in the Gospels, they tended to disagree about the possibility of looking behind the Gospels and other sources to reconstruct the life of Jesus as it really happened. Belief in the possibility of such a historical reconstruction led to what is now known as the "first quest" for the historical Jesus.

The First Quest for the Historical Jesus

The late nineteenth century saw a proliferation of "**lives of Jesus**." As it became more acceptable to view the Gospels as a mix of fact and fiction, both professional scholars and devout amateurs undertook with great enthusiasm to separate one from the other. Unfortunately, both professionals and amateurs often did this without any controls that would prevent their own biases from predetermining the outcome. Mark Alan Powell describes a three-stage process typical of these lives of Jesus. First, the author would develop some large-scale model for who Jesus really was, based on his personal preferences: Jesus as religious reformer, political revolutionary, moral puritan, or something else. Then the author would search the available sources for passages that could be made to fit this model, discarding any difficult or contradictory passages as later additions or distortions to the original message of Jesus. Finally, since there often was not enough supposedly authentic material to fully justify the scholar's model of Jesus, he would invent new details, psychologize (claiming to know what Jesus was thinking), and embellish until the gaps were filled and the model fleshed out.[8]

The result of this process was fairly predictable: scholar after scholar would conclude that all the parts of the New Testament that reflected the scholar's personal views were coincidentally the parts that were historically accurate. Conversely, all of the parts that did not reflect the scholar's religious opinions were later inventions or insertions that distorted the pure, authentic message of Jesus. These biblical scholars tended to produce pictures of the historical Jesus that looked remarkably like self-portraits, never noticing the unlikelihood of a first-century Jew so strongly resembling a nineteenth-century European liberal Protestant.

The man who sounded the death knell of this farce was a German biblical scholar named **Albert Schweitzer**, who would go on to even greater fame as a doctor working in Africa,

---

8. Mark Alan Powell, *Jesus as a Figure in History: How Modern Historians View the Man from Galilee* (Louisville: Westminster John Knox, 1998), 13–15.

winning the Nobel Peace Prize for his medical contributions and legacy. Schweitzer's 1906 book, translated (badly) as *The Quest of the Historical Jesus*, reviewed previous work on the life of Jesus and exposed how deeply compromised most accounts were by the biases and prejudgments of their producers. Schweitzer himself believed that the predominant element in Jesus' preaching was apocalyptic, a characteristic that Schweitzer observed Jesus shared with a great many other Jewish preachers in antiquity. He thought the evidence was strong that Jesus preached the imminent arrival of the kingdom of God, and that he believed that he would rise from the dead and return from heaven on clouds of glory with armies of angels to bring about this kingdom *within the lifetime* of his followers. Schweitzer found it incredible that the time periods Jesus projected for all this to be accomplished could possibly be interpreted as referring to hundreds or thousands of years in the future. Therefore, in Schweitzer's view, Jesus was not only an apocalyptic prophet, but a *failed* one at that. It was precisely the failure of Jesus' prophecies to be fulfilled that led to the proliferation of reinterpretations of the meaning of his preaching that one finds in the New Testament.[9]

While Schweitzer destroyed the credibility of the lives of Jesus movement, not all biblical scholarship from this period would need to be discarded. The better, more lasting work in New Testament studies in the late nineteenth century was done in the areas of textual criticism, philology (the study of biblical languages), and source criticism. Some of this work had implications for the study of the historical Jesus, and created brief hopes that were also sadly dashed in the early twentieth century. For example, when it was established by source critics that Mark was the earliest of the canonical Gospels and had served as a source for both Matthew and Luke, some came to believe that Mark provided the most accurate historical account of Jesus' ministry. Matthew and Luke were said to have added theological interpretations and additions to Mark's essentially historical account, and John to have provided a kind of spiritual meditation on the Jesus tradition even further removed from history.

But the project of relying on Mark for the historical facts ended with the publication of William Wrede's 1901 book, translated as *The Messianic Secret*, which revealed that the Gospel of Mark was every bit as theological as Matthew, Luke, or John. The author of Mark, Wrede proved, was not a mere transcriber of oral traditions but an independent thinker who had produced a portrait of Jesus that was deeply influenced by the author's own distinctive beliefs. The messianic secret motif itself, Wrede argued, was a Markan invention.

The Second Quest for the Historical Jesus

The "New Quest for the Historical Jesus," also known as the "second quest," is said to have been kicked off in 1953 by a German scholar named Ernst Käsemann, although the roots of this quest predate Käsemann by decades. A key figure in the redevelopment of the quest was **Rudolf Bultmann**, perhaps the most famous and influential New Testament scholar of the twentieth century. Bultmann's work had two trajectories, one of which involved New Testament theology, the other based in form criticism. In terms of New Testament theology, Bultmann was not convinced of the necessity of deriving authentic

---

9. None of this should be taken to mean that Albert Schweitzer lacked Christian conviction. He would launch a fifty-year second career as a doctor and hospital administrator in Gabon in part because of his desire to fulfill Jesus' command to become "fishers of men."

historical nuggets about Jesus beyond the fact that he existed and was crucified. Bultmann was heavily influenced by existentialist philosophy, especially that of Martin Heidegger. He thought that once the New Testament was stripped of what was, in his view, its primitive mythological language and framework it would show that Jesus was an existential hero who taught his followers how to live an "authentic" existence. This formed the basis of Bultmann's famous program of "demythologizing" the New Testament.

But Bultmann was also a prominent practitioner of form criticism on the New Testament. His massive *History of the Synoptic Tradition* (1921) took each pericope (individual unit) of the Gospels and classified it as belonging to a particular type of oral tradition: the parable, the apothegm (wisdom saying), the controversy story, and so on. Then, based on the assumption that each pericope was based on a combination of **tradition** (the oral version of the story inherited by the evangelists) and **redaction** (the editorial additions inserted by the evangelist to situate the story in his narrative and conform it to his theology), Bultmann separated tradition from redaction, showing which parts of each pericope were invented by the evangelist and which parts predated the author's modifications. Bultmann further determined the earliest form of the oral tradition based on the supposed laws of oral transmission affecting each form (or literary genre) of tradition, these laws having been determined by modern scholars who had studied folk stories and their oral history. Such an effort in separating tradition from redaction, as we have seen (see chapters 7 and 10), can be helpful in determining the theology of a particular evangelist if one focuses on the *redaction*; if one focuses on the *tradition* it can also reveal which parts of a Gospel predate the reworking of the evangelists and are thus more likely to go back to the historical Jesus.

Bultmann himself may not have thought there was much theological utility in such information, but his students—Käsemann among them—did.

But even if one could identify oral traditions behind the Gospels, there was no guarantee that those teachings emanated from the historical Jesus. Some of them could easily have been invented during the period of oral transmission by the early church. Other traditions could have been borrowed from ancient Judaism and improperly ascribed to Jesus. Even after stripping away the redaction to reveal the tradition, scientific *criteria* were needed for separating the authentic from the inauthentic teachings of Jesus, criteria that would avoid the pitfalls of personal preference and bias that had plagued the first quest.

Such a set of criteria was eventually cobbled together. Norman Perrin, a prominent American New Testament scholar, drew upon the work of Käsemann and others and eventually identified four **historical critical criteria** that he believed could be used to determine which parts of the Gospels are more likely to have come from the historical Jesus. These four are the criteria of dissimilarity, multiple attestation, coherence, and contextual credibility.

The **criterion of dissimilarity** claims that a given teaching or saying is probably authentic if it is dissimilar to the ideas characteristic of both early Christianity and ancient Judaism. This criterion is based on the idea that a teaching attributed to Jesus could have come from three possible sources: it could have been borrowed from Second Temple Judaism, it could have been invented by the early Christian church, or it could have been uttered by Jesus. If one can rule out the first two possibilities—by showing that the teaching or saying is *dissimilar* to the teachings of both Judaism and the early church—then the only logical possibility remaining is that the teaching emanates from the historical Jesus.

One example is Jesus' response to a prospective follower who claims that he has a prior obligation to bury his dead father: "Follow me and let the dead bury their own dead" (Matt. 8:22). This saying is unlikely to have been either borrowed from Judaism or invented by the early church. Both Jews and Christians of the time believed in respectful treatment of the deceased; neither of these groups are likely to have produced a teaching that seems to advise a son to neglect his father's burial. Therefore it is deemed highly probable that this teaching is authentic. For examples of events (rather than teachings) that pass the criterion of dissimilarity, one need think only of Judas's betrayal and Peter's denial. It is highly unlikely that early Christians invented stories in which Jesus inspired so little faith and loyalty among his closest followers.

The **criterion of multiple attestation** is based on the idea that a given saying of Jesus is more likely to be authentic if it is found in multiple independent sources or if it expresses an idea found in a variety of literary forms, such as the parable, apothegm, chreia (useful anecdote), and controversy story. Of course, the Synoptic Gospels are not independent of each other, so one cannot claim that a saying shared by Matthew, Mark, and Luke is multiply attested. But if a saying or story is found in both John and the Synoptics (such as the cleansing of the Temple), then it has more than one independent source backing it up.[10] Similarly, the fact that Jesus was sympathetic to sinners and tax collectors is found in a variety of literary forms—for example, both the parable of the Pharisee and the Tax Collector (Luke 18:9–14) and the saying in which Jesus notes his opponents' complaint that he is a "friend of tax collectors and sinners" (Matt. 11:19//Luke 7:34). Given this evidence from multiple literary forms (parable and saying), it seems safe to say that the historical Jesus was known for his fellowship with tax collectors and sinners.

The **criterion of coherence** essentially builds upon the previous two, suggesting that sayings,

parables, and stories that are consistent with material found authentic by the criteria of dissimilarity and multiple attestation are also more likely to be authentic. For example, if one knows for a relative certainty that Jesus preached the nearness of the end of the world, and there is a disputed saying that does not pass the criteria of multiple attestation or dissimilarity but reflects the imminent apocalyptic expectation of the historical Jesus, then that saying is deemed more likely to be authentic.

The **criterion of contextual credibility** differs from the other three in that it is only supposed to be used negatively, that is, it identifies sayings and stories as *inauthentic* rather than potentially authentic. What this criterion suggests is that if a given saying assumes an environment, linguistic background, or historical context that is completely foreign to that of the historical Jesus, then the saying cannot be authentic. The exclusively negative use of the criterion reversed a previous trend in biblical scholarship to affirm as historical those sayings that reflected a Galilean or Palestinian environment or an Aramaic linguistic background.[11] The problem with using this criterion positively is that Jesus' first followers also spoke Aramaic and lived in Palestine, so if they were to invent sayings and place them in Jesus' mouth, they would be indistinguishable from authentic teachings of Jesus.

An example of the negative use of this criterion involves Jesus' famously strict teaching against divorce. In Jewish Galilee and Judea, at the time of Jesus it was not permissible for a woman to divorce her husband. This was possible under Roman law, but not under Jewish law. As a result, when the Gospel of Mark quotes Jesus as saying, "Whoever divorces his wife and marries another commits adultery against her; and *if she*

---

10. The list of independent sources available to attest to a saying of Jesus varies from one scholar to another, but commonly includes Mark, Q, John, Paul, Thomas, Special Luke ("L"), and Special Matthew ("M").

11. This trend is associated most strongly with the work of Joachim Jeremias.

divorces her husband and marries another, she commits adultery" (Mark 10:11–12), then the second part of that saying is ruled out under the criterion of contextual credibility. It would not have made sense to a Palestinian Jewish audience to speak of a woman having the right to divorce her husband. Jesus might well have preached that husbands should not divorce their wives and remarry, but he almost certainly did not say anything about wives divorcing their husbands.

Note that these criteria apply largely to sayings and other teachings of Jesus, not to miracle stories. Some scholars have not bothered to apply criteria of authenticity to miracle stories because they believe no miracle stories reflect historical occurrences. Other scholars might be convinced that miracles can and do occur, but do not believe accounts of miracles can be verified by historical methods. Historical research makes judgments about the *probability* of events having occurred in a particular way, while miracles are by their nature *highly improbable* events. Thus accounts of miracles do not lend themselves readily to historical analysis.

Perrin's historical critical criteria drew both praise and criticism. Certainly it seemed as though the Quest for the Historical Jesus was on more solid intellectual ground with established criteria than it was with the relative free-for-all that prevailed during the first quest. However, there remained disputes about both the criteria and their application. Some criticized the criterion of dissimilarity as likely to produce both a small body of authentic sayings and a Jesus who was divorced from both his Jewish roots and his Christian followers. Surely *some* teachings of Jesus were in continuity with his Jewish heritage. Surely there were also *some* teachings that his Christian followers had faithfully inherited and transmitted. The criterion of dissimilarity, at least

by itself, was likely to produce a "weird" Jesus with nothing in common with either ancient Judaism or early Christianity. Others thought that the criterion of coherence was too soft, and that it allowed a large number of teachings to creep into the historical Jesus' repertoire that were more likely invented by his followers.

Still other scholars thought that there were additional criteria beyond those Perrin had developed. One was the criterion of **embarrassment**, which resembles the criterion of dissimilarity in some ways but also has important differences. The idea is that early Christians were mortified by certain details about Jesus' life, or by certain teachings of Jesus, some of which are harsh, shocking, impenetrable, or contradictory,[12] but that they held on to them precisely because they knew these sayings and stories were really spoken by Jesus or truly told about him. This criterion holds that any story that created difficulties for Christians or exposed weaknesses in their arguments with opponents would never have been invented by either the early church or the evangelists, and must have originated in authentic traditions about the historical Jesus.[13] A famous example is the story of Jesus being baptized by John the Baptist. There are two problems with this story from the standpoint of orthodox Christianity. One is that it seems to suggest that Jesus had at some point transgressed God's law, as the purpose of John's baptism was the forgiveness of sin. The other is that John baptizing Jesus seems to suggest that John was superior to Jesus, that he was the master and Jesus was the disciple. Either of these problems would have been enough to prevent early Christians from inventing a story about Jesus' baptism by John. Therefore, the story of Jesus' baptism is regarded as authentic by the criterion of embarrassment.

---

12. Examples include Jesus' requirement that his followers "hate" their family members (Luke 14:26) and his reference to Gentiles as "dogs" (Mark 7:27).

13. An account of the logic behind the criterion of embarrassment can be found in John P. Meier, *A Marginal Jew: Rethinking the Historical Jesus*, 5 vols., Anchor Bible Reference Library (New Haven: Yale University Press, 1994–2009), 1:168.

The results of the second quest were far more solid than those of the first. A significant number of Gospel sayings and events, at least in some form, gained wide acceptance as the authentic words and deeds of the historical Jesus. Despite this apparent progress, there remained major disagreements among scholars. First, the general reliability of the Gospels was disputed. Some scholars thought that a fairly high percentage of each Gospel's traditions were authentic, while others pegged the reliability rate at something more like 20–25 percent. Second, there was disagreement about which sayings beyond the core of obvious examples could be regarded as authentic. In many cases the application of the criteria was more art than science, and two different interpreters might not agree that a given saying is dissimilar to Jewish or early Christian thought, or that a particular story is embarrassing enough to meet that criterion, or that two sayings in independent sources are close enough in wording or content to be multiply attested. Lastly, the new quest was never able to divorce itself sufficiently from the existentialist philosophy that had animated the work of its founder, Rudolf Bultmann. When that philosophy went out of style in the 1960s–1970s, the second quest went out of style with it.

The Third Quest for the Historical Jesus

When prominent biblical scholar N. T. Wright became the first to refer to a "third quest" in 1992, he was not announcing a new project but acknowledging work that had been quietly under way for some years already. Although scholars had not fully succeeded in either the first or the second quest, the questions raised by the problem of the historical Jesus simply would not go away. All non-fundamentalist biblical scholars agreed that the Gospels contained a mix of authentic Jesus traditions and later accretions. Millions of lay people who had taken undergraduate courses in biblical studies were also well aware of this fact. But the question remained as to how to separate the historical Jesus from the early church's elaborations.

In some ways the third quest was simply a more dogged attempt to develop and apply the historical critical criteria utilized in the second quest. Some new criteria were developed, but many of the older ones remained. In addition, the body of sources to which these criteria could be applied was expanded.

Already during the second quest major use had been made of the reconstructed Q source to supplement the available streams of tradition that could provide multiple attestation: Mark/triple tradition, John, special Luke (material unique among the Synoptics to Luke, often called "L"), and special Matthew (material unique among the Synoptics to Matthew, often called "M"). Indeed, because Q is regarded by many of its supporters as the earliest available source of Jesus traditions, attempts at reconstructing the teaching of the historical Jesus often attach a great deal of importance to Q. The fact that Q also consists almost exclusively of sayings and does not contain any miracles means that its entire content is susceptible to historical analysis. Some Q scholars have gone further than simply identifying Q as an early source and have suggested that there was a community behind Q that shaped its development over a period of time, and that one could detect different strata of traditions within Q, and further identify some as early, others as middle, and others as late Q traditions. The earlier traditions would be closer to the teachings of Jesus.[14]

In addition to this heavier reliance on Q, another new development of the third quest was

---

14. A prominent example of this approach is Burton Mack; see his *The Myth of Innocence: Mark and Christian Origins* (Minneapolis: Fortress, 2006) and *The Lost Gospel: The Book of Q and Christian Origins* (San Francisco: HarperSanFrancisco, 1994).

a greater willingness to include one or more non-canonical gospels among the potential sources for authentic traditions about the historical Jesus. Almost every scholar now acknowledges that the *Gospel of Thomas* can be used to provide multiple attestation of Jesus' sayings, and a large number also agree that even *Thomas's* unique material has a chance of being authentic. Books that show Gospel passages in parallel columns—known as "Gospel parallels" or "Synopses of the Gospels"—now typically include five gospels: the four canonical Gospels plus *Thomas*. They often also include footnotes or glosses detailing parallels in yet other gospels, such as the *Gospel of Peter*. A number of third quest scholars believe that the *Gospel of Peter* was written earlier than had been previously believed, or that it is a revision of an earlier written source (the "Cross Gospel"); hence either *Peter* or its reconstructed source could also be used as a source in historical Jesus research.[15] *The Complete Gospels* (1994)[16] reflects the growing acceptance of noncanonical gospels by including infancy gospels, sayings gospels, Gnostic gospels, and more, alongside the canonical Gospels and reconstructions of their alleged sources, such as Q or the "Signs Source" supposedly used by the Gospel of John.

Among the new historical critical criteria proposed by third quest scholars, two are particularly noteworthy. The first is the **criterion of historical plausibility**. This criterion in some ways reacts against the criterion of dissimilarity's tendency to suggest that Jesus had nothing in common with first-century Judaism and that the early church proceeded to completely reinvent Jesus for their own purposes. The champion of this criterion, Gerd Theissen, believed that early Christianity was heavily influenced by Jesus. Early Christians might have invented some aspects of his teaching as their circumstances changed, but much of what they said about Jesus would be rooted in his actual teachings. Similarly, the idea that Jesus emerged from his Jewish upbringing completely untouched by it and created a religious movement that was absolutely divorced from Judaism is also quite unlikely, according to Theissen. On the basis of these arguments, he developed the criterion of historical plausibility, which regards as historically probable those teachings of Jesus that both explain the development of early Christianity in particular directions and could have emerged out of a Jewish context. "Whatever helps to explain the influence of Jesus and at the same time can only have come into being in a Jewish context is historical in its sources."[17] This criterion obviously allows a significantly larger body of material to pass the test of authenticity than, say, the criteria of dissimilarity or embarrassment.

Another third quest proposal draws conclusions from an indisputably accurate and hugely significant fact about Jesus' life: that he was crucified. This is called the **criterion of rejection and execution**. Jesus must have said and done things that prompted opposition from both Jewish and Roman authorities and led them to seek Jesus' death. Hence teachings of Jesus in which he challenges the authorities of his time are regarded as more likely to be historically accurate.[18] An obvious example would be the cleansing of the

---

15. John Dominic Crossan is a proponent of the "Cross Gospel" hypothesis and makes substantial use of it in his historical reconstruction of the life of Jesus. See John Dominic Crossan, *The Historical Jesus: The Life of a Mediterranean Jewish Peasant* (San Francisco: HarperSanFrancisco, 1991), 429.

16. Robert J. Miller, ed., *The Complete Gospels: Annotated Scholars Version*, rev. and exp. ed. (Santa Rosa, CA: Polebridge, 1994).

17. Gerd Theissen and Annette Merz, *The Historical Jesus: A Comprehensive Guide*, trans. John Bowden (London: SCM; Minneapolis: Fortress, 1998), 116.

18. John P. Meier, "Criteria: How Do We Decide What Comes from Jesus?," in *The Historical Jesus in Recent Research*, ed. James D. G. Dunn and Scot McKnight (Grand Rapids: Eisenbrauns, 2006), 126–42.

Temple, in which Jesus accuses the priests who ran it of corruption, turning it into a "den of robbers" (Mark 11:17).

Portraits of the Historical Jesus

There is basic agreement on certain facts of Jesus' life: he was baptized by John, debated Jewish authorities on various matters of law and theology, gathered a group of followers, taught in parables, gained a reputation as a healer and exorcist, and was crucified by Pontius Pilate. Such a bare-bones outline, however, leaves a tremendous amount of room for interpretation. It would be impossible to catalog all of the current theories about the historical Jesus, but it is fair to say that scholarly opinion has coalesced around certain major models. Included among these would be characterizations of Jesus as essentially (1) an apocalyptic prophet; (2) a political revolutionary; (3) a Jewish sage, prophet, and reformer; and (4) a Cynic philosopher. Despite some overlap between these models, for clarity each of them is treated separately in what follows.

Jesus as Apocalyptic Prophet

To many modern people, the most disconcerting part of Jesus' message in the Synoptic Gospels is the emphasis on the imminent end of the world. Much of this discomfort stems from the simple fact that the world did not end in the first century nor at any point since. Many modern Christian denominations remain undeterred by the delay in Jesus' second coming and place as much emphasis on the imminence of the apocalypse as any group in Christianity's past.[19] They simply reinterpret the temporal cues in Jesus' teachings

(and in other prophetic books) to refer to a final consummation of history near to the present moment, no matter how strained and unconvincing these reinterpretations might be to others.

There are several alternatives to this approach, however. One view, popularized by Rudolf Bultmann, is that the eschatological element in Jesus' message was personal rather than cosmic. Jesus' preaching shook the world of his hearers and caused a radical reorientation of their lives and perspective. The "end" was not the end of the world, but the end of the believer's inauthentic existence. While this view was common during the heyday of existentialist philosophy, it has since fallen from favor. Another strategy is to deny that the historical Jesus ever preached the nearness of the end of the world, and to attribute all of the eschatological parts of the early sources to Jesus' followers.

Others maintain that there is no escaping the conclusion that Jesus' message was that the world would literally be coming to an end in the near future, regardless of how many difficulties that might present to modern believers. Albert Schweitzer's theory that Jesus was a failed apocalyptic prophet has its modern proponents.[20] One of the strongest voices supporting this model is Bart Ehrman.

Ehrman begins by refuting the various attempts to explain away the apocalyptic traditions in Matthew, Mark, and Luke. He rightly observes that Q, if it existed at all, was loaded with teachings about the nearness of the end of the world. To dismiss all of these passages as later creations of the Q community strikes Ehrman as hugely speculative and unconvincing. He also doubts that the *Gospel of the Hebrews* and the alleged source behind the *Gospel of Peter*— two other favorites of the non-apocalyptic Jesus

---

19. Examples include Jehovah's Witnesses, Seventh Day Adventists, and Branch Davidians.

20. Among those in this camp are Meier, *A Marginal Jew*, especially vol. 2, and E. P. Sanders, *Jesus and Judaism* (Philadelphia: Fortress, 1985).

theory—can be relied upon as heavily as his opponents do. Neither document actually exists; both must be reconstructed based on references in other texts or by using source or form criticism on the late versions of the documents that do survive. Moreover, the theory that these hypothetical sources prove that the historical Jesus was non-apocalyptic only works if one assigns them an extremely early date (i.e., prior to Mark, Q, Matthew, and Luke). The evidence for such an early date is exceedingly slim: "In most cases, these texts are not quoted or even mentioned by Christian writers until many, many decades later."[21]

For Ehrman, the case for Jesus as an apocalyptic prophet rests on much more reliable testimony and is based on teachings and events that are more solidly established as historically accurate because they pass the criteria of dissimilarity, embarrassment, multiple-attestation, and contextual credibility.

- Jesus was baptized by John the Baptist, whose message was thoroughly apocalyptic. This suggests that Jesus was a disciple of John, and that he shared John's apocalyptic views.
- Jesus had twelve disciples. This number was symbolic of the renewal of Israel that would take place after the apocalypse occurred and the kingdom of God was established. Just as the old Israel had been established by twelve patriarchs, so too would the new Israel emerge with twelve leaders.
- Many of Jesus' best-attested teachings have a clear apocalyptic component. Mark introduces Jesus with a simple summary of his preaching: "The time is fulfilled, and the kingdom of God has come near; repent, and believe in the good news" (Mark 1:15). This saying and many others suggest that

Jesus had in mind an actual kingdom that one could "enter" (Matt. 7:21; Mark 10:15, 25) and that would arrive with unmistakable power (Mark 9:1) at some point in the very near future (Mark 13:30).

- Jesus associated with tax collectors, sinners, and women, while shunning and criticizing the more religiously-observant Pharisees and chief priests. One of the themes of apocalyptic thought involves the dramatic reversal of fortunes that will accompany the new kingdom. On many occasions Jesus preached that "many who are first will be last, and the last will be first" (Mark 10:31) and the humble "will be exalted" (Luke 14:11; 18:14; cf. 6:20–23) while the mighty and proud will be laid low (Luke 6:24–26). Participation in the kingdom required a radical repentance, which many sinners accepted, while those who thought themselves "righteous" believed they did not need to repent.
- Jesus had a reputation as an exorcist and healer. Laying aside the question of whether these miracles occurred, it can be affirmed that Jesus was *believed* to be able to cast out demons and cure the sick. Jewish apocalyptic thought held that in the coming kingdom, there would be no sickness or death, so Jesus' ability to cure illnesses and raise the dead anticipates the kingdom's nearness. Exorcisms fit neatly into an apocalyptic perspective, which maintains that the cosmic battle between God and the devil is played out in part by angels who help humans and demons who afflict them. In apocalyptic thinking, God would soon wage a final battle against the forces of evil and would prevail. Jesus' exorcisms indicate that the forces of God are more powerful than the forces of Satan and his allies, and his victory over the

---

21. Bart Ehrman, *The New Testament: A Historical Introduction to the Early Christian Writings*, 6th ed. (New York: Oxford University Press, 2016), 282.

demons prefigures the imminent cosmic victory of God.

- Jesus cleansed the Temple and predicted its destruction. The corruption and imminent destruction and renewal of the Temple is a common theme in Jewish apocalyptic thought at the time of Jesus. The literature of the Essenes (the Dead Sea Scrolls) provides the clearest evidence of this.

- Jesus was crucified. It is highly unlikely that either the Jewish or Roman authorities would have seen fit to kill Jesus if he was merely an advocate of nonconformity with a sharp wit. An apocalyptic preacher railing against the corruption and evil of the ruling authorities and predicting their imminent destruction would have made a much more likely target.

Ehrman is uncertain about the role Jesus saw himself playing in the apocalyptic drama. Was he thinking of himself when he foretold the coming of the Son of Man who would be the agent of destruction and judgment, or was he referring to someone else? Some sayings seem to suggest the former (Luke 12:8), while others imply the latter (Mark 8:38; 14:62). In any event, Ehrman doubts that Jesus claimed to be divine or saw his impending death as a sacrifice that would win forgiveness of sins for all humanity. Jesus may indeed have anticipated his death, but getting killed was a common enough way for a prophet to meet his end. In Ehrman's model, the saving event did not take place on Calvary. It would take place only when the Son of Man came from heaven on clouds of glory with armies of angels.

Jesus as Cynic Philosopher

This model of Jesus is most closely associated with the work of John Dominic Crossan and Burton Mack. **Cynicism**, Stoicism, and Epicureanism were the popular philosophies of the Hellenistic world (see chapter 4). Cynic philosophers were committed to radical freedom, self-sufficiency, and indifference to the affairs of the world.[22] They practiced a dogged asceticism, and flouted social conventions and mores. They also sought to awaken others from their pitiable, conventional lives by shameless public behavior[23] and offensively bold speech. They dressed badly, wore long hair, and begged for their food. They wandered from place to place and tried to make a scene wherever they went. Crossan describes them as the hippies of their day.[24]

There is no question that certain parallels exist between Jesus' teaching and Cynic philosophy. Jesus taught his followers not to be slaves to money (Luke 16:13), and not to worry about where their food or clothing might come from (Matt. 6:24–32). When Jesus sends out his followers, he tells them to carry "no purse, no bag, no sandals" (Luke 10:4), but to beg for provisions among those who welcome them into their homes (Luke 10:7). Jesus' teachings were often so nonconformist that they shocked his contemporaries as much as the Cynic philosophers did. The saying "Blessed is anyone who takes no offense at me" (Matt. 11:6) could easily have been uttered by a Cynic.

Proponents of the Jesus-as-Cynic theory point out that some recent archeological work suggests that the city of **Sepphoris**, of which Nazareth was a suburb, was thoroughly Hellenized. This raises the likelihood that a Hellenistic

---

22. Paul Rhodes Eddy, "Jesus as Diogenes? Reflections on the Cynic Jesus Thesis," *Journal of Biblical Literature* 115 (1996): 451.

23. The oft-cited example of this behavior is masturbating in public.

24. Crossan, *Historical Jesus*, 421.

philosophy like Cynicism might have reached Sepphoris and come to Jesus' attention. Moreover, Gerd Theissen's work on the sociology of early Palestinian Christianity concluded that Jesus did not so much found churches or communities as he called into being a group of wandering charismatics[25] who were in turn supported by local sympathizers. This is similar to the Cynic model, as the itinerant philosophers did not create "schools" or communities either. Finally, the scholars who claim that the Q source can be reconstructed and further divided

In Jesus' day, Sepphoris was a thriving Hellenistic city only 3.7 miles from Nazareth. As a "carpenter" (Mark 6:3), Jesus may have worked on construction projects in Sepphoris before beginning his ministry.

into early, middle, and late strata argue that the earliest stratum of Jesus sayings (Q-1)[26] closely parallels the teachings of Cynicism. Moreover, Q-1 and parts of the Gospel of Mark suggest that the earliest recollections of Jesus characterize him as a teacher of wisdom rather than an apocalyptic prophet or sacrificial lamb.

Critics of this theory argue that its proponents are both overstating its strengths and underestimating its weaknesses. There are parallels between Jesus' teachings and those of the Cynics, but do these teachings form the authentic *core* of Jesus' message? The heavy reliance on Q-1 as indicative of the authentic teaching of the historical Jesus is questionable. The mere existence of Q is a matter of considerable scholarly dispute. How much less probable, then, should one regard the claims that Q can be divided into early, middle, and late strata? Moreover, the same archeologists that Jesus-as-Cynic proponents cite for a thoroughly

Hellenized Sepphoris have cautioned against concluding that Cynics had a presence there or that Jesus is more likely to have been influenced by its urban setting than that of rural Nazareth.[27] The fact that the city of Sepphoris is mentioned *nowhere* in the New Testament is reason enough to doubt that it served as the primary crucible in which Jesus' ideas were forged.

The sources also reveal that Jesus was also known for some decidedly non-Cynic positions. First, one of the most distinctive characteristics of a wandering Cynic was his appearance, which included (among other things) a walking staff and a bag used for begging and carrying possessions. But when Jesus sends out his followers, he commands them to bring neither bag nor staff (Luke 9:3). He also tells them not to greet the people they encounter (Luke 10:4), which contrasts with the Cynic emphasis on "bold speech." Second, the message of Cynicism was decidedly individualistic

---

25. Gerd Theissen, *Sociology of Early Palestinian Christianity* (Philadelphia: Fortress, 1978), 8.

26. This claim is most strongly defended by John Kloppenborg, in such works as *The Formation of Q: Trajectories in Ancient Wisdom Collections* (Philadelphia: Fortress, 1987).

27. Eddy, "Jesus as Diogenes?," 463–67.

and antisocial. The same cannot be said of the Jesus movement, which relied on networks of local sympathizers. Third, Jesus was known for healing and exorcism, neither of which was part of the repertoire of the wandering Cynics. Finally, while Jesus did advocate flouting some aspects of Jewish law and convention, he did not do so in service of a complete freedom from such restraints.[28] He affirmed many parts of the Law of Moses, and even went beyond the Torah in advocating for the indissolubility of marriage, a conventional social relationship with which true Cynics would have no patience whatsoever.

Jesus as Political Revolutionary

The theory that Jesus was a Zealot, who saw himself as a Davidic political-military Messiah and sought to overthrow the Roman regime and become the king of an independent Israel, has recently resurfaced. This is due largely to the influence of a popular book by Reza Aslan, *Zealot: The Life and Times of Jesus of Nazareth.* Aslan's background is more in the field of sociology of religion than biblical scholarship, but his theory has supporters in the biblical guild.[29]

One of the central arguments in favor of the Jesus-as-Zealot model is the undisputed fact that Jesus was executed by Rome for alleged revolutionary activity: claiming to be the "king of the Jews." Biblical scholars tend simply to dismiss the possibility that this charge accurately reflects Jesus' activity and the Romans' reasons for killing him. They insist that Jesus advocated nonviolence, that his understanding of the role of the Messiah was spiritual or apocalyptic rather than political and military, and that the Romans who executed Jesus were misled by the Jewish authorities. But Occam's razor suggests that the Romans killed Jesus because they saw him as a genuine threat.

A growing number of scholars are recognizing that preaching the "kingdom of God" in an area under Roman occupation is a profoundly subversive thing to do. Every assertion by Jesus that the people of the world are suffering and in need of God's rule is an implicit challenge to the rule of Rome, which saw itself as the world's savior, the true provider of peace and prosperity. Aslan correctly points out that there was a great deal of revolutionary fervor in first-century Palestine, with a number of self-proclaimed prophets and messiahs fomenting resistance of various kinds against Rome, its Herodian representatives, and a priestly establishment that was seen as corrupt and complicit.

The only reason Jesus is not more widely recognized as a political revolutionary, Aslan argues, is that he hid it so well. Aslan sees the "messianic secret" motif of Mark's Gospel as a genuine strategy of the historical Jesus, deployed by the crafty Galilean peasant in order to keep his seditious intentions under wraps for as long as possible. Along the same line, Jesus' preaching of the kingdom of God was ambiguous enough—because it could pertain to spiritual as well as political matters—to provide him with plausible deniability.

In Aslan's telling, Jesus went to Jerusalem to start the revolution, but the uprising fizzled and Jesus was caught and executed for treason. Aslan suggests that subsequent claims for the divinity of Christ, for his atoning death, and for his imminent return were later reinterpretations of Jesus' identity, forged largely by Paul and furthered by the authors of the canonical Gospels.

Aslan's portrait of Jesus has been savaged by most of the biblical critics who responded to it. They pointed out that he makes a number of

---

28. On each of these four points, see ibid., 461–63.

29. See, for example, S. G. F. Brandon, *Jesus and the Zealots* (Manchester: Manchester University Press, 1967), and W. Buchanan, *Jesus: The King and His Kingdom* (Macon, GA: Mercer University Press, 1984).

basic historical errors that undermine his credibility. His contentions that Paul invented Christianity and that a high Christology was absent from the earliest sources have both been largely dismissed within biblical scholarship for many decades. His assertion of the historicity of the "messianic secret" is also dubious. Most scholars since at least 1901 have regarded this motif as an invention of the author of the Gospel of Mark. Aslan rejects this conclusion because he thinks Mark lacked the literary ability to craft such a clever device. It is true that the Greek of Mark's Gospel is rough and unsophisticated, but as noted in chapter 8, this does not mean that Mark was not a skilled storyteller.

In the end, Aslan's theory suffers from some of the same flaws as the Jesus-as-Cynic model. First, it requires one to look behind the plain statements of the earliest sources to detect a mostly hidden thread of political subversion. Second, it ignores a great deal of evidence to the contrary. There are many passages in the Gospels in which Jesus advocates peace, love, and nonviolence. Aslan is forced to argue that all of these passages are late and secondary, and his reasons for doing so are, if anything, even less apparent than the evidence provided for the Jesus-as-Cynic theory. Finally, Aslan's theory necessitates that the authors of the surviving first-century Christian literature got Jesus *completely wrong* and generally distorted his message beyond recognition. For many biblical scholars, not to mention most ordinary believers, that is a bridge too far.

Jesus as Jewish Sage, Prophet, Reformer, or Rabbi

Many scholars agree that Jesus is best understood within a Jewish—rather than Hellenistic—milieu but doubt that either the apocalyptic

prophet model or the revolutionary Zealot model adequately explains Jesus. Could Jesus have been a (non-apocalyptic) prophet? A Jewish sage? A learned rabbi? An advocate of a renewal movement within Judaism?

Among the pioneers of this view in modern scholarship is Geza Vermes, author of *Jesus the Jew*.[30] Vermes did extensive research on the kind of Judaism that flourished in Galilee (rather than, say, Judea or Alexandria) in the first half of the first century CE and found that most of Jesus' distinctive teachings reflected his Galilean Jewish upbringing and milieu. Vermes argues that Jesus did not reach out to Samaritans or Gentiles during his lifetime, but confined his message to his fellow Jews, whom he urged to repent and renew their covenant relationship with Yahweh. Vermes agrees with Ehrman that Jesus' preaching had an essential apocalyptic component, and that he saw his mission as instructing people on the religious duties they needed to perform to prepare themselves for the coming judgment. Many of these duties had to do with Jesus' interpretation of the Law of Moses, which was distinctive but also profoundly Jewish.

This last point places Vermes close to the Jesus-as-apocalyptic-prophet camp. Others, however, have followed his lead in emphasizing Jesus' Galilean Jewish orientation but differ from him in claiming that Jesus is better understood as a rabbi, sage, or non-apocalyptic prophet. The model of Jesus-as-rabbi is championed most notably by Bruce Chilton.[31] Chilton claims that Jesus grew up as a *mamzer* (a child of questionable parentage) and this resulted in his being ostracized and hence alienated from his local Jewish community. Eventually Jesus gravitated toward John the Baptist, where he discovered not only apocalypticism but more importantly an asceticism-aided mysticism. This mysticism allowed Jesus to commune directly with God

---

30. Geza Vermes, *Jesus the Jew: A Historian's Reading of the Gospels* (Minneapolis: Fortress, 1973).

31. Bruce Chilton, *Rabbi Jesus: An Intimate Biography* (New York: Image, 2002).

without the intermediary of the religious authorities, with whom he had become estranged as a result of his outcast status. Jesus returned to Galilee and gained a reputation as a rabbi, one who offered authoritative interpretations of the Torah and who emphasized table fellowship with all of God's children, regardless of their social status. He abandoned the asceticism of John and instead began "eating and drinking" (Luke 7:34). His apparent violation of the boundaries of ritual purity during meals brought him into even sharper conflict with the Jewish authorities.

In Chilton's telling, Jesus was indecisive and changed his strategy and tactics on numerous occasions. He hoped at one point to gain enough strength to organize active opposition to Rome, as did many of his followers, but Jesus eventually chose not to do this. Later Jesus saw an opportunity to create an uprising at the Temple, and along with Barabbas provoked an outburst of violence that left at least one person dead. But when the rebellion quickly stalled, Jesus melted into the crowds and hid in the countryside. He increasingly focused on the symbolic significance of the bread shared at communal meals and even came to see this as a substitute for Temple sacrifice, a "blasphemy" that led his disciple Judas to betray him. After being crucified, Jesus' angel appeared to his followers in their mystical visions, an angel that they mistook for a resurrected body.

Chilton's many critics have called him to task for wild speculation and psychologizing. It is by no means certain that Jesus was treated as a *mamzer*, or that it had a profound effect on his psyche. But his broader point about Jesus' identity as a rabbi is well-taken. Jesus is even called "rabbi" (often translated as "master" or "teacher") by his disciples (e.g., Mark 9:5; 11:21), by the Pharisees (John 3:2), by the disciples of John the Baptist (John 1:38), by the crowds (Mark 10:51; John 6:25), and by Mary Magdalene (John 20:16). There is no doubt that the Jesus of the Synoptic Gospels engaged in rabbinic arguments over the Torah and its interpretation and that he was intimately familiar with the Jewish legal tradition.[32] In Mark, Jesus debates the Pharisees and Sadducees over the Sabbath (2:23–28), ritual purity (7:1–8), divorce (10:1–12), resurrection (12:18–27), and the most important commandment (12:28–34) and in every case Jesus cites a passage from the Old Testament to support his opinion. This happens even more often in Matthew, in passages often sourced to Q or M. That Jesus presented himself as an authoritative interpreter of the Jewish legal tradition is definitely multiply attested.

Jesus was a prophet and a rabbi. But was he also, or even more fundamentally, a **sage** (that is, a teacher of wisdom and giver of advice)? Some scholars see Jesus as more reliant on the Jewish wisdom tradition than on its legal, prophetic, or apocalyptic strains. The model of Jesus as Jewish sage[33] has a great deal in common with the theory that Jesus was a Cynic, which is not surprising because sages and philosophers broadly overlap. Both models emphasize that the core of the authentic Jesus material consists of harsh or pithy **aphorisms** and biting wit for the purpose of social and cultural subversion. Some examples of shocking or comical sayings of Jesus include the following:

- "Do you not see that whatever goes into a person from outside cannot defile, since it enters, not the heart but the stomach, and goes out into the sewer? . . . It is what comes out of a person that defiles" (Mark 7:18–20). Jesus' main point in this passage

---

32. Moreover, even Paul indicates that he is familiar with some of Jesus' legal opinions (1 Cor. 7:10–11).

33. See Ben Witherington III, *Jesus the Sage: The Pilgrimage of Wisdom* (Minneapolis: Fortress, 1994), and Bernard Brandon Scott, "Jesus as Sage," in *The Sage in Israel and the Near East*, ed. J. Gammie and L. Perdue (Winona Lake, IN: Eisenbrauns, 1990), 399–415.

is that people's words and deeds matter to God, not their diets, but his reference to food passing through the stomach and eventually into the sewer shows that he is also engaging in a little bathroom humor here.

- In response to a Gentile woman who asks Jesus to heal her daughter, Jesus says, "Let the children first be fed, for it is not right to take the children's bread and throw it to the dogs" (Mark 7:27). Jesus' comparison of the Jewish people to children and Gentiles to *kynaria* (literally "puppies" or "little dogs") is rather shocking.
- "Can a blind person guide a blind person? Will not both fall into a pit?" (Luke 6:39). The image of the blind leading the blind is inherently ridiculous.

But those who see Jesus as a Jewish sage believe it is far more likely that Jesus drew the style and content of his message from Judaism's long and venerable sapiential (wisdom) tradition—including such biblical books as Job, Psalms, Proverbs, Ecclesiastes, Song of Songs, and the Wisdom of Solomon, as well as a great deal of intertestamental literature—than from a Hellenistic popular philosophy.

Nearly all[34] historical Jesus scholars agree that Jesus made heavy use of parables in his teaching. But there is no record of teaching in parables in the Cynic tradition.[35] By contrast, however, parables were commonly used in both the Jewish wisdom literature and rabbinic wittings.[36] Moreover, not only is the *form* of Jesus' teaching Jewish, but so is the *content*. The Cynic-like aspects of Jesus' aphoristic teaching—the warnings against the seduction of wealth and material possessions, for example—are also quite consonant with the Jewish wisdom tradition; no direct Cynic influence need be posited to account for them. When Jesus tells his disciples of the need to "hate" mother and father in order to be his follower, he is "not exemplifying anti-social Cynic values, but rather is making use of Semitic [Jewish]-style overstatement as a rhetorical ploy,"[37] much as he did when he encouraged his followers to tear out their right eye if it was causing them to sin (Matt. 5:29). Jesus' emphasis on honoring one's father and mother (Mark 7:9–12; 10:19) and the sanctity of marriage (Mark 10:1–12) reflect a characteristically Jewish emphasis on intact families and contain not a trace of Cynic individualism and antisocial tendencies.

The Jesus Seminar

Among the best-known recent efforts at reconstructing the life of Jesus, the **Jesus Seminar** attempted to combine the wisdom of some one hundred fifty professional biblical scholars and interested amateurs to produce a consensus version of the historical Jesus. The seminar was founded in 1985 by legendary biblical scholar Robert Funk under the auspices of the Westar Institute, Funk's biblical "think-tank." It included some of the most prominent historical Jesus scholars of its time, including John Dominic Crossan and

continued

---

34. A significant exception is Meier, who argues in vol. 5 of *A Marginal Jew* (see especially pp. 48–57) that only four of the Gospel parables are authentic.

35. Eddy, "Jesus as Diogenes?," 461.

36. See David Stern, "Rhetoric and Midrash: The Case of the *Mashal*," *Prooftexts* 1 (1981): 261–91.

37. Eddy, "Jesus as Diogenes?," 460, fn. 60.

The Jesus Seminar *continued*

Marcus Borg, and culminated in the production of three popular books: *The Five Gospels* (1993), *The Acts of Jesus* (1998), and *The Gospel of Jesus* (1999).

What made the Seminar the object of so much public curiosity was its unique method of determining which sayings and stories from the various sources about Jesus were authentic. Each scholar "voted" with a colored bead or marble. If he or she was fairly certain that a given saying reflected the actual words of Jesus, a red marble would be selected. Sayings that might not have been Jesus' actual words but represented something very similar merited a pink marble. Sayings that were probably inauthentic but reflected the *ideas* of Jesus would lead the scholar to cast a gray marble. Black marbles were used for those sayings that the seminar participants thought were almost certainly not said by Jesus and reflected only the later thoughts of early Christians. The marbles were given a numerical value, and an "average" for each unit was calculated. The same color scheme was then used in publications like *The Five Gospels*. The newly translated Gospels alternated between passages printed in red, pink, gray, or black, depending on the vote totals.

Many scholars outside of Funk's orbit viewed this as a publicity stunt designed to increase media coverage. If it was, it worked beautifully. Newspapers and magazines wrote incessantly about the seminar's latest findings, annual meetings, public lectures, and publications. Many reporters expressed shock at how few passages were printed in red and pink, and a great deal of the "balance" that journalists felt obliged to provide came from conservative scholars and pastors who decried the seminar's skepticism and liberal bias.

Some of the seminar's basic assumptions were surprising only to non-specialists, such as the priority of Mark, the existence of Q, the utility of noncanonical gospels, and the projection of a fairly long period of oral tradition in which short, pithy sayings and stories were more likely to be preserved—a likelihood sometimes known as the **criterion of orality**. However, even otherwise sympathetic biblical scholars sometimes thought that the seminar's process and results were flawed. One of the core findings (or assumptions, depending on one's perspective) of the seminar was that the eschatological aspects of the message of Jesus were all secondary accretions. Jesus was not a prophet of the apocalypse, the seminar avowed, but was presented as such by early Christians who confused or combined the teachings of John the Baptist with those of Jesus. A good number of scholars think that the seminar's rejection of apocalyptic—a dominant strain of Jesus' teaching in three of the four canonical Gospels—reflected wishful thinking and special pleading.

Another controversial aspect of the Jesus Seminar was its conclusion that Jesus had a distinctive teaching "style," one that involved irony, paradox, and reversal of expectations. This allowed them to classify, for example, the parable of the Good Samaritan (Luke 10:25-37) as preserving the authentic words of Jesus, even though this parable is not multiply attested and does not pass the criteria of embarrassment or orality. Simply put, critics thought that seminar members *liked* this parable—with its overtones of racial/ethnic and religious tolerance—and classified it as authentic simply for that reason, rather than on the basis of relevant criteria. It is certainly true that the seminar tended to produce a Jesus who was antiestablishment, countercultural, anti-materialist, and pro-social justice. Many observers could not help but think that the seminar members were crafting a Jesus in their own liberal and idealistic image.

Robert Funk died in 2005 and the Jesus Seminar ceased to function in 2006. Whether or not the seminar will have a lasting influence now that the headlines are gone remains to be seen. But there is no doubt that it brought the field of biblical studies unprecedented public attention.

Who Was Jesus?

Not every theologian or biblical scholar is enamored with the Quest for the Historical Jesus. Indeed, a great many systematic theologians, who like to argue that Jesus himself supported their dogmatic claims, find it exceedingly irritating to have to check to see if the passage or quotation they want to deploy in this service passes muster according to historical critics. They often complain that historical Jesus scholars are too skeptical, their methods are opaque, and their conclusions maddeningly inconsistent and subject to radical revision as new trends emerge.

This complaint is not unfounded. Many within the biblical guild feel the same way, although usually for different reasons. Some think that the historical Jesus cannot be recovered with any degree of certainty, given the fragmentary nature of the evidence and the infinite variety of interpretations it can engender. Does this mean that we can know nothing of the historical Jesus? Perhaps not. One of the things that tells us "who a person is" can and must be the impressions that the person made on others. Jesus made a tremendous impression on his followers, and this impression is recorded—imperfectly or otherwise—in the canonical Gospels, the letters of Paul, and other sources both within and outside of the canon. It may be that the only thing we can truly know about Jesus is the *portrait* of him painted by the authors of Mark, Luke, Thomas, and others. However inconsistent those portraits might be, they all probably reflect something true about Jesus.

This inconsistency should not be surprising. What prominent person in modern history has not engendered divergent interpretations? Take, for example, the thirty-seventh president of the United States. There are those who say that Richard Nixon was a crook, a liar, a war criminal, a race-baiter, an anti-Semite, and a dirty trickster. The fact that he was forced to resign in 1974 rather than face certain impeachment is taken by many as proof that he was among America's very worst presidents. There is plenty of data in the historical record to make a case to that effect. But there are also those who give Nixon credit for opening a relationship with China, achieving détente with the Soviet Union, negotiating genuinely effective arms limitation treaties, creating the Environmental Protection Agency, and proposing universal health care. His daughters Tricia and Julie would have defended their father as a man of impeccable character, who was laid low by the jealousy and false accusations of his political enemies. The "real" Richard Nixon, whom they might argue they knew better than any of his critics, was quite different in their experience than the portrayal of him they saw in the media.

Which version of Richard Nixon, the paranoid scofflaw or the respected statesman, represents the truth? Perhaps they both do. There's no reason to believe that Nixon—who, one must remember, was re-elected in 1972 by the largest electoral majority of all time—could not have stumbled into some genuine accomplishments even if he should also be blamed for illegally invading Laos and Cambodia, carpet-bombing North Vietnam, killing hundreds of thousands of innocent civilians, and taking revenge on his perceived political foes. And just as it was perhaps impossible for someone who had been the beneficiary of his sympathy for the "silent majority" of law-abiding, patriotic (mostly white) citizens to see that he was also capable of a complete lack of empathy for minorities and the poor, so also a victim of his divisive racial and cultural rhetoric might never be able to recognize that Nixon probably gave the environment its biggest boost in decades. Historians, however, would do well to include both versions of Nixon in their annals. Like most of history's most important figures, he was a complex character who defied easy categorization. If pinning down the real Richard Nixon is not so easy, with the wealth of information we have at our disposal, how much more difficult will it be to pin down the real Jesus?

Key Terms

allegorical method
David Hume
Hermann Samuel Reimarus
David Friedrich Strauss
deist
myth
lives of Jesus
Albert Schweitzer
Rudolf Bultmann
tradition

redaction
historical-critical criteria
criterion of dissimilarity
criterion of multiple attestation
criterion of coherence
criterion of contextual
    credibility
criterion of embarrassment
criterion of historical
    plausibility

criterion of rejection and
    execution
Cynicism
Sepphoris
sage
aphorisms
Jesus Seminar
criterion of orality

Review Questions

1. What arguments did David Hume deploy to claim that miracles never happened? How did the elite, educated class react to Hume?

2. How did Reimarus cast doubt on the Gospel accounts of Jesus' resurrection? What are the most important contradictions one finds between these various accounts?

3. How did D. F. Strauss use the category of myth to explain the miraculous parts of the Gospel accounts of the life of Jesus? How did the use of myth distinguish Strauss from both supernaturalists and the rationalists/deists of his day?

4. What dubious procedure did the authors of "lives of Jesus" employ in their reconstructions of the historical Jesus? How did Albert Schweitzer expose them and bring an end to the "first quest"?

5. How did the work of Rudolf Bultmann help inspire the "second" or "new" quest for the historical Jesus? How do the form-critical tasks of separating tradition from redaction and tracing the prehistory of the tradition contribute to historical Jesus research?

6. What are the four historical-critical criteria identified by Norman Perrin? Give

examples of each criterion and summarize the strengths and weaknesses of his general program, as identified by its critics and proponents.

7. What historical-critical criteria have been proposed in addition to Perrin's by scholars engaged in the second or third quests? How does each criterion work?

8. Besides the creation of some additional criteria, what other factors distinguish the third quest from the second quest?

9. What aspects of the use of reconstructed sources and noncanonical gospels in the third quest have been controversial?

10. What are the main features of the proposal that Jesus was an apocalyptic prophet? What evidence can be cited in support of this model? What criticisms have been made of it?

11. What are the main features of the proposal that Jesus was a Cynic philosopher? What evidence can be cited in support of this model? What criticisms have been made of it?

12. What are the main features of the proposal that Jesus was a political revolutionary? What evidence can be cited in support of

this model? What criticisms have been made of it?

13. What are the main features of the proposal that Jesus was a Jewish rabbi, non-apocalyptic prophet, or sage? What evidence can be cited in support of this model? What criticisms have been made of it?

Discussion Questions

1. Most Christians throughout history have never questioned the historical reliability of the Bible's portrait of Jesus. Have they been right to do this, or do the modern critics of the Bible's accuracy make a strong enough case to warrant serious examination of this issue by Christians?

2. Why do you think there is so much disagreement about who Jesus was? What factors account for the extremely wide variation in interpretations?

3. Which model of the historical Jesus seems most persuasive to you, or at least the closest to the person you imagine Jesus to have been? Why is this so?

4. Is there any genuine value to debating the historical Jesus? Can you conceive of individuals or groups forming or changing their views based on what they are persuaded Jesus really said and did?

Bibliography and Suggestions for Further Study

(Books and websites that are accessible for general undergraduates are marked with an asterisk; other sources listed are appropriate for advanced students.)

*Aslan, Reza. *Zealot: The Life and Times of Jesus of Nazareth*. 1st ed. New York: Random House, 2013.

Bultmann, Rudolf, and John Marsh. *The History of the Synoptic Tradition*. Rev. ed. New York: Harper & Row, 1976.

Chilton, Bruce. *Rabbi Jesus: An Intimate Biography*. New York: Image, 2002.

*Crossan, John Dominic. *The Historical Jesus: The Life of a Mediterranean Jewish Peasant*. San Francisco: HarperSanFrancisco, 1991.

Eddy, Paul Rhodes. "Jesus as Diogenes? Reflections on the Cynic Jesus Thesis." *Journal of Biblical Literature* 115 (1996): 449–69.

*Ehrman, Bart. *The New Testament: A Historical Introduction to the Early Christian Writings*. 6th ed. New York: Oxford University Press, 2016.

*Funk, Robert Walter, Roy W. Hoover, and the Jesus Seminar. *The Five Gospels: The Search for the Authentic Words of Jesus: New Translation and Commentary*. Paperback ed. San Francisco: HarperSanFrancisco, 1997.

*Hume, David, and Peter Millican. *An Enquiry Concerning Human Understanding*. Oxford World's Classics. New York: Oxford University Press, 2007.

Kloppenborg, John. *The Formation of Q: Trajectories in Ancient Wisdom Collections*. Philadelphia: Fortress, 1987.

*Mack, Burton. *The Lost Gospel: The Book of Q and Christian Origins*. San Francisco: HarperSanFrancisco, 1994.

*Mack, Burton. *The Myth of Innocence: Mark and Christian Origins*. Minneapolis: Fortress, 2006.

Meier, John. P. "Criteria: How Do We Decide What Comes from Jesus?" In *The Historical*

Jesus in Recent Research, ed. James D. G. Dunn and Scot McKnight, 126–42. Grand Rapids: Eisenbrauns, 2006.

Meier, John P. *A Marginal Jew: Rethinking the Historical Jesus.* 5 vols. Anchor Bible Reference Library. New Haven: Yale University Press, 1991–2016.

*Perrin, Norman. *Rediscovering the Teaching of Jesus.* New York: Harper & Row, 1976.

*Perrin, Norman, Dennis C. Duling, and Robert L. Ferm. *The New Testament: An Introduction; Proclamation and Parenesis, Myth and History.* 2nd ed. under the general editorship of Robert Ferm. New York: Harcourt Brace Jovanovich, 1982.

*Powell, Mark Alan. *Jesus as a Figure in History: How Modern Historians View the Man from Galilee.* Louisville: Westminster John Knox, 1998.

Reimarus, Hermann Samuel, and Charles H. Talbert. *Reimarus, Fragments.* Scholars Press Reprints and Translations. Chico, CA: Scholars Press, 1985.

Sanders, E. P. *Jesus and Judaism.* Philadelphia: Fortress, 1985.

Schweitzer, Albert. *The Quest of the Historical Jesus.* Edited by John Bowden. 1st complete ed. 1st Fortress Press ed. Minneapolis: Fortress, 2001.

Scott, Bernard Brandon. "Jesus as Sage." In *The Sage in Israel and the Near East*, ed. J. Gammie and L. Perdue, 399–415. Winona Lake, IN: Eisenbrauns, 1990.

Stern, David. "Rhetoric and Midrash: The Case of the *Mashal.*" *Prooftexts* 1 (1981): 261–91.

Strauss, David Friedrich. *The Life of Jesus Critically Examined.* Lives of Jesus Series. Philadelphia: Fortress, 1973.

Theissen, Gerd. *Sociology of Early Palestinian Christianity.* Philadelphia: Fortress, 1978.

Theissen, Gerd, and Annette Merz. *The Historical Jesus: A Comprehensive Guide.* Translated by John Bowden. London: SCM; Minneapolis: Fortress, 1998.

Vermes, Geza. *Jesus the Jew: A Historian's Reading of the Gospels.* Minneapolis: Fortress, 1973.

Witherington, Ben, III. *Jesus the Sage: The Pilgrimage of Wisdom.* Minneapolis: Fortress, 1994.

Wrede, William. *The Messianic Secret.* Library of Theological Translations. Cambridge, UK: J. Clarke, 1971.

22 CHAPTER

The New Testament in the Modern World

The primary focus of this book has been historical: to clarify how the books of the New Testament developed and functioned within the context of their first-century CE hearers and readers. But the interest of most modern readers of these books is not exclusively, or even primarily, historical. There are reasons why both scholars and lay people in the Western world have paid so much more attention to first-century Christianity and its literature than they have paid to other ancient religions or other historical periods and writings. One reason is the massive cultural impact the New Testament has had. Consequently, its study is useful even to those who do not profess the Christian faith, especially if they wish to be conversant with the 75 percent of Americans and 31 percent of people worldwide who identify themselves as Christians. The other reason is that the study of the New Testament is first and foremost of interest to people of faith. How does the New Testament function in their lives? What are the unique problems and opportunities presented by modernity to those who wish to not only *understand* the New Testament but to *apply* that understanding to their lives? These questions are explored in this final chapter.

Fundamentalism and the Christian Bible

Fundamentalism, as the term will be defined here, is not exclusive to Christianity. There are

Jewish, Hindu, and Muslim fundamentalists. Recent surveys suggest that between 26 and 42 percent of Americans identify themselves as "evangelical" or "born-again" Christians. Many, but not all, of these evangelical Christians are fundamentalists. Fundamentalism is defined by the following characteristics:

Literalism. Fundamentalists engage in a **literal interpretation** of the biblical text. Except for passages that clearly self-identify as fiction or metaphor (such as Jesus' parables), the Bible is understood to mean exactly what it says. When Genesis speaks of Adam and Eve as the first humans dwelling in the garden of Eden, this is understood as fact and not as a myth, allegory, or symbolic story.

Inerrancy. Christian fundamentalists believe that the Bible is the "word of God" in the sense that God is the actual author of the Old and New Testaments, even if human writers put the words to paper. Many fundamentalists believe that the Holy Spirit told the biblical authors what to write word-for-word (known as "verbal inspiration"). Since God is perfect and makes no errors, then the books of the Bible must also be mistake-free, or "**inerrant**."

All or nothing. Consistent with their belief that all of scripture was authored by God, fundamentalists insist that one cannot pick and choose some parts of the Bible as authoritative while ignoring other parts as outdated. Rather, one must obey *every single command* given by God in the revealed text. This argument is often deployed against Christians who would reject the authority of, for example, biblical passages that uphold patriarchy or condemn homosexuality. For fundamentalists, the Bible is either 100 percent true or 100 percent false.[1] When the debate is framed as if these were the only two options, people who see some value in the biblical text feel they must defend it in toto, since they do not want to discard it altogether.

One verse at a time. Fundamentalists do not typically attach great importance to a biblical passage's historical context, literary genre, or function within the larger book of which it is a part. Use of scripture usually takes the form of citing a single verse that is especially applicable to a particular problem or question, the meaning of which is assumed to be clear, universal, and transhistorical. Since the Bible is believed to be perfectly consistent, the viewpoint expressed in a single biblical verse may be taken as the viewpoint of the entire Bible.

Religious intolerance and faith sharing. Just as there is only one true revelation from God (the Bible), there is only one true religion and way of salvation. Other religions, or even other denominations of Christianity, are perceived as being in

error to the extent that they disagree with fundamentalist dogma. Since Christian fundamentalists believe that the consequence of unbelief is eternal torment in hell, they are highly motivated to share the virtues of the one, true religion with their nonbelieving friends and neighbors. This desire to preach, to "evangelize," is one of several reasons that this group has generally embraced the term "**evangelical**."[2]

Rejection of modernity. Fundamentalists generally believe the modern world is in serious political, economic, cultural, and moral decline. They prefer steady, authoritarian rule[3] to the chaos and unpredictability of democracy, and deplore the development of the welfare state and globalism. Fundamentalists tend to regard modern music, film, television, and literature as decadent. They complain about the rise of pornography, abortion, drug use, single motherhood, and sex before marriage as well as the decline of personal responsibility, deference toward elders, and church attendance.

Critique of science. A particular flaw of modernity, in the eyes of fundamentalism, is that science and technology have become dominated by unscrupulous individuals who are spreading lies and undermining traditional faith and morality. The dubious turn that modern

---

1. Fundamentalists often assert that the biblical writers themselves claimed that the scriptures were inerrant in their entirety, in passages such as "Every word of God proves true" (Prov. 30:5), "The words of the Lord are pure words: as silver tried in a furnace of earth, purified seven times" (Ps. 12:6, KJV), and "All scripture is inspired by God" (2 Tim. 3:16). This is circular logic: The Bible is mistake-free because its authors say that it is, and the authors cannot be wrong because the Bible is without error. Moreover, such passages don't always mean what fundamentalists claim; the 2 Timothy passage, for example, refers to the Jewish scriptures (the Old Testament), not to the New Testament, which did not yet exist.

2. It should be noted, however, that not every Christian individual or group that engages in *evangelization*, defined broadly as the attempt to spread the gospel of Christ, falls into the "evangelical" camp, defined narrowly as the conservative branch of Protestant Christianity. Failure to make this distinction can lead to some confusion. The Lutheran denomination in the United States has both liberal and conservative wings, but the Evangelical Lutheran Church in America (ELCA) is not—despite the name—the conservative branch. It is far more liberal than its counterparts, such as the Missouri Synod Lutheran and Wisconsin Synod Lutheran churches.

3. Peter Herriot observes, "The highly authoritarian individual is submissive to authority, aggressive toward out-groups, and holds tight to conventional values and norms of behavior. Psychometric measures of authoritarianism are found to be highly correlated with measures of religious fundamentalism." See Peter Herriot, *Religious Fundamentalism: Global, Local and Personal* (London; New York: Routledge, 2009), 149.

science has taken has resulted in the theory of evolution, birth control, and stem cell research on fetal tissue. The internet has made it possible for children to obtain sexually explicit material and for terrorists to network and learn how to make bombs.

Nostalgia for a supposedly ideal past. Everything would be better, fundamentalists typically believe, if we could turn the clock back to a time when children respected their parents, men worked hard and earned a decent living, and society in general embraced conservative Christian values. Of course, a closer look at history would raise doubts about whether the idealized golden age was really so wonderful for women, ethnic minorities, or a host of others; nevertheless, the fundamentalist worldview assumes that things were simpler and better long ago, before the onset of modernity.

Fundamentalism rejects the critical, historical, contextual, disciplined study of the Bible. Can fundamentalists and non-fundamentalists overcome that difference and coexist peacefully? It seems they cannot. Fundamentalism has been rejected by most mainstream Christian denominations, including the Roman Catholic Church and all of the mainline Protestant denominations, in no small part because maintaining a fundamentalist perspective requires a significant degree of intellectual dishonesty. The defender of fundamentalism must constantly employ special pleading, exhibit willful blindness to countervailing evidence, construct implausible scenarios, and develop tortured interpretations. Fundamentalism bases all of its conclusions on a preexisting set of beliefs, and does not allow the evidence to be weighed or even, in some cases, to be presented.

Can non-literalists convince fundamentalists to change their view of scripture? Probably not. Fundamentalists are sufficiently aware of weaknesses in their position to have developed defenses that they, at least, find convincing. For example, a fundamentalist will respond to someone pointing out the apparent contradictions between the genealogies in Matthew and Luke by simply claiming that many of Joseph's ancestors were known by two different names; some people called Jesus' grandfather Heli (Luke 3:23), and others called him Jacob (Matt. 1:15–16), and the same was true of Jesus' great-grandfather and many other ancestors.[4] Similarly, fundamentalists will argue that the timing of the cleansing of the Temple in the Synoptics (at the end of Jesus' ministry) and in John (at the beginning) is not a contradiction because Jesus really cleansed the Temple *twice*. However, some problems are especially difficult for fundamentalists to explain away. Particularly thorny problems include the following:

The translation problem. Fundamentalists tend to rely on a literal interpretation of the specific words of scripture. But the books of the Bible were originally written in ancient Hebrew and Greek, and since few fundamentalists learn to read these languages, they have to rely on a translation. Most fundamentalists recognize that this is a problem, since a translation is never quite the same as the original text. Some of them solve this problem by claiming that a particular English translation was guided by the Holy Spirit and hence produced a "perfect" translation with no loss of meaning or nuance. Those who embrace this view usually single out the **King James Bible** (completed in 1611) as

---

4. Ultimately this strategy does not work because (a) Matthew and Luke have different *numbers* of generations between various common points on the timeline and (b) Matthew and Luke trace Jesus' ancestry through a *different* son of David (Matthew uses Solomon, Luke uses Nathan), and these two are not the same individual.

the Spirit-guided translation. But the language of the KJV is archaic and often incomprehensible to modern English speakers. Another serious problem with it is that the translators of the KJV did not have access to the best Greek and Hebrew manuscripts of the Bible in the early 1600s. One must also deal with insoluble translation problems. When dealing with a long-dead ancient language, it is possible to encounter words and phrases whose meaning has simply been lost. The book of Job, for example, is notorious for its use of obscure, difficult, unknown, and unintelligible Hebrew words and phrases. It is a leap of faith indeed to believe that the translators of the KJV, or any other translation, correctly guessed the meaning of each and every such problem passage.

The textual problem. A New Testament in English is a translation of the Greek text of the New Testament; but which Greek text did the translators use? Many thousands of Greek manuscripts of parts of the New Testament have survived, and no two of them agree completely. Many of these disagreements are minor but hundreds of them are highly significant. Textual critics compare the various readings where manuscripts disagree and, using the established methodology of their discipline, make their best guess at what the original reading was in any given passage (see chapter 7). The conclusions of textual critics result in a single Greek text that combines readings from hundreds of individual manuscripts into a "consensus" version, a critical text that usually also contains an apparatus that documents the more significant variations in the manuscript record. Most modern English translations are based on these "critical texts" of the Greek New Testament. But this poses a problem for fundamentalists; how can one rely completely on a New Testament passage as God's word if the text underlying that passage is a scholarly reconstruction—in effect, a scholar's best guess? How can the scriptures give us the literal word of God if we cannot be sure what actual words were written by a biblical author for any single verse? The degree of uncertainty over the text of the Bible is simply inconsistent with the supreme confidence of fundamentalists that they can discern the will of God from scripture and that differences of opinion over the text, its translation, and its interpretation ultimately amount to nothing. Some fundamentalists avoid this problem by asserting that the reading preserved by the majority of manuscripts is the correct reading—and note that the "majority text" is (basically) the text used by the translators of the KJV. However, textual critics in both New Testament and secular literature[5] adamantly deny that the reading of the majority of manuscripts can be relied upon as preserving the original reading of a given text.[6] Therefore the "majority text" principle of fundamentalists again relies upon arbitrary belief—that the Holy Spirit made sure the word of God was preserved intact in the majority readings.

Obvious historical mistakes. A historian can neither confirm nor disprove that Jesus was tempted by Satan in the wilderness. But some biblical assertions can be tested, and some of them clearly fail that test. For example, both Matthew and Luke tell us that Jesus was conceived during

---

5. Textual problems exist not just for the Bible but for all ancient literature where the original text (the "autograph") does not survive and the existing copies exhibit variations. The text of some literature varies wildly, while in other cases the text remains relatively stable over time. The text of the New Testament is relatively stable as a whole, but there are many important exceptions to this general rule.

6. This is because a scribal alteration could be made relatively early in the transmission process and the altered text could be copied hundreds of times while the original reading might be copied infrequently or not at all.

the reign of King Herod the Great, who ruled from 37 BCE until his death in 4 BCE. Luke also tells us that Jesus was born when Quirinius was governor in Syria. Quirinius was appointed Imperial Legate (governor) in 6 CE, and conducted a census that same year, the one that presumably caused Joseph and the pregnant Mary to journey from Nazareth to his ancestral home in Bethlehem. However, unless Mary was pregnant for ten years these two claims cannot both be true. Another problem with this same passage is that there is no record of the Romans *ever* requiring people to journey from their place of residence to their ancestral homes in order to be counted. Not only would this create chaos, it would totally defeat the purpose of conducting a census, which is to find out how many people live and work in a particular area, in order to estimate how much tax revenue should be extracted. Most non-fundamentalists will point out that these are minor issues on which the truth of Christianity does not rise or fall, and simply admit that the evangelist made a mistake. But the fundamentalist cannot admit this.

Internal inconsistencies. Numerous previous chapters have pointed out that the Gospel writers do not always agree with each other, and that the deutero-Pauline letters sometimes contradict the genuine letters of Paul. Reimarus pointed out ten contradictions between the different accounts of the resurrection (see chapter 21). Luke's Gospel has Jesus and Mary's hometown as Nazareth, from which they strayed only temporarily in order to be counted in a census, while Matthew's Gospel states clearly that the hometown of Mary and Joseph was Bethlehem, and that the family only *relocated* to Nazareth (after a sojourn in Egypt) out of fear of Herod's

son in Judea. These contradictions may not be terribly significant, but they pose a problem for fundamentalism, which claims that the Bible is inerrant in all matters.

Picking and choosing. Fundamentalists loudly complain about people who accept the authority of the Bible with regard to some passages but reject the authority of other passages. But they are themselves guilty of such picking and choosing. There is a famous internet meme, often entitled "Why Can't I Own a Canadian," that makes this point in response to Jewish conservative talk show host and advice columnist Dr. Laura Schlesinger, who insisted that Bible believers must vigorously oppose homosexuality because Leviticus 18:22 says that God considers it an "abomination" when a man lies with another man. The meme takes the form of a letter to Dr. Laura asking for advice.[7] Among the questions the letter poses to her are the following:

When I burn a bull on the altar as a sacrifice, I know it creates a pleasing odor for the Lord—Leviticus 1:9. The problem is my neighbors. They claim the odor is not pleasing to them. Should I smite them?

I would like to sell my daughter into slavery, as sanctioned in Exodus 21:7. In this day and age, what do you think would be a fair price for her?

I know that I am allowed no contact with a woman while she is in her period of menstrual uncleanliness—Leviticus 15:19–24. The problem is, how do I tell? I have tried asking, but most women take offense.

Leviticus 25:44 states that I may indeed possess slaves, both male and female, provided they are purchased from neighboring nations. A

---

7. Although the letter is usually circulated without attribution, it was originally written by Kent Ashcraft, who sent it not to Dr. Laura herself but to a friend as a satirical comment on what he saw as Dr. Laura's hypocrisy. The friend passed along his email to several other friends, and within weeks the letter was a viral sensation. It was eventually published in several newspapers and formed the basis of part of an episode of the NBC drama *The West Wing*.

friend of mine claims that this applies to Mexicans, but not Canadians. Can you clarify? Why can't I own Canadians?

I have a neighbor who insists on working on the Sabbath. Exodus 35:2 clearly states he should be put to death. Am I morally obligated to kill him myself?

Most of my male friends get their hair trimmed, including the hair around their temples, even though this is expressly forbidden by Leviticus 19:27. How should they die?[8]

The point of this *reductio ad absurdum* argument is that fundamentalist Christians do not follow the *entirety* of the Bible's commands any more than their liberal opponents.

The intolerance and rigidity of fundamentalism mark it as a dark and dangerous development. But it should be noted that modern Christian fundamentalism is not, so to speak, native to Christianity but is a relatively recent development. It was only in the late 1800s that a segment of Christianity, in large measure because of the supposed threat of Darwinian evolution, began to rebel against modernity and insist on the inviolability of certain biblical beliefs. A series of tracts called "The Fundamentals" was published from 1910 to 1915 that sought to defend five essential Christian truths from the onslaught of liberalism and modernism: (1) the inerrancy of the Bible, (2) the literal truth of the stories of creation and Christ's miracles, (3) Christ's virgin birth, (4) the bodily resurrection and earthly return of Christ, and (5) the substitutionary atonement of Christ's death. The fact that this list was not formulated until the early twentieth century shows that fundamentalism is a recent development, not a constant feature of the Christian religion. While millions of Christians have gravitated toward this

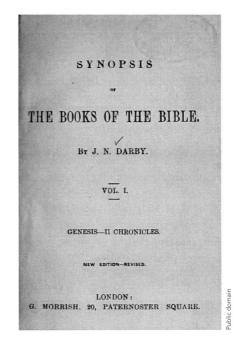

Some aspects of fundamentalism emerged in quite recent times, including *dispensationalism*, a kind of theology that divides different sections of the Bible into a series of discrete "dispensations" from God. This approach originated with John Nelson Darby (1800–1882).

reactionary, anti-intellectual, backward-looking phenomenon since its inception, millions more have not. The outcome of the struggle between modern liberal Christianity and rigid fundamentalism is far from certain, but modernity is gaining ground. A 2017 Gallup poll found that 24 percent of Americans believe that the Bible is the literal word of God, the lowest percentage in the forty-year history of the survey. By contrast, 47 percent of Americans affirmed that the Bible is inspired by God, but not to be taken literally. Young people in particular are less attracted to the fundamentalist understanding of the Bible.

---

8. For the complete version of one form of this letter, see "Why Can't I Own a Canadian," RationalWiki, at *http://rational wiki.org/wiki/Why_can%27t_I_own_a_Canadian%3F#The_text_of_the_letter*.

The Prosperity Gospel

Another controversial development in modern Christianity is the so-called **prosperity gospel**, also known as the gospel of health and wealth. This movement holds that financial success and physical health are always the will of God for Christian believers, and that faith (and cash donations to one's church) will increase a person's wealth and wellness. Leaders of the prosperity gospel argue that Jesus and his disciples were all personally wealthy as a result of their faith in God, and that every Christian can be similarly wealthy and comfortable if the correct path is followed. A prominent early advocate was Reverend Ike, who preached, in the 1970s, "It is the lack of money that is the root of all evil," and, "The best thing you can do for the poor is not to be one of them."[9] While this movement was once confined to the fringes of Christianity, in recent decades the prosperity gospel has gone mainstream. Many of the most prominent television preachers of the twenty-first century are advocates of the prosperity gospel, among them Joel Osteen, Kenneth Copeland, Joyce Meyer, Robert Tilton, Creflo Dollar, T. D. Jakes, and more.

While the prosperity gospel borrows heavily from the Old Testament idea that God rewards the righteous by showering his blessings on them in the here and now, there is a strong New Testament component as well. In particular, prosperity gospel preachers have argued strenuously, against the tide of tradition, that Jesus was rich and that he never preached against materialism, greed, or acquisitiveness. Among the arguments they make are the following:

- Jesus became wealthy when he was visited by kings at his birth. These kings supplied Jesus with a massive quantity of gold that he was able to draw upon for the rest of his life.

- Jesus used his wealth to support his disciples throughout a three-year ministry, as well as providing financial support to his mother Mary, after his father Joseph died many years before her.

- Jesus had so much money that he had a "treasurer" or an "accountant" to manage his wealth and keep track of it.

- Jesus must have built himself a fine home, because he was after all a carpenter.

- Jesus must have worn very fine clothing, because the soldiers at the foot of the cross saw fit to gamble over ownership of his garment. This would have only happened, prosperity gospel preachers insist, if Jesus' clothing were very valuable.

- Jesus must have had wealth in order to attract the kind of following that he did. "No one would follow a broke man," as one prosperity gospel preacher put it.

- When Jesus taught that it is "easier for a camel to pass through the eye of a needle than for a rich man to enter the kingdom of heaven," he was not referring to a literal (sewing) needle's eye, but to a gate in Jerusalem through which camels could squeeze only on their knees. Jesus' point was that a rich man needed to be humble (on his knees) in order to enter the kingdom, but that great wealth by itself presented no significant obstacle.[10]

Many critics have noted a strong element of self-interest in the message of prosperity gospel preachers. They encourage their followers to

---

9. Tony Norman, "The Wretched, Venal Life of Rev. Ike," in *The Pittsburgh Post-Gazette* (August 4, 2009).

10. All of these claims can be found in John Blake, "Was Jesus Rich? Swanky Messiah Not Far-Fetched in Prosperity Gospel," *Atlanta Journal-Constitution* (Oct. 22, 2006).

"sow a seed" in the form or a monetary donation to their ministries, after which they will "reap a harvest" in the form of heaven-sent riches and miraculous healings. The web pages and telecasts of prosperity gospel evangelists are filled with **testimonials** recounting the efficacy of "**seed faith**." A typical testimonial—ostensibly written by an average member of the flock—might explain how the donor gave, say, $1,000 to the ministry and shortly thereafter received a windfall—an inheritance, an unexpected tax return, a huge new promotion—that repaid the donor many times over. In some cases, the prosperity preachers specify that the amount "harvested" after sowing a seed will follow the pattern of Jesus' account in the Parable of the Sower of an abundant yield, and promise that donors will receive "thirty-, sixty-, and a hundred-fold" return on their investment. Hence the faithful are encouraged to give as much as possible to the ministry, so as to receive the greater reward. Many prosperity gospel preachers insist on their church's members donating a minimum of 10 percent of their income to the ministry, a practice in the Bible known as "**tithing**." A failure to tithe, they warn, could lead to God withholding the financial blessings received by those who are more generous.[11]

Prosperity gospel preachers flaunt their personal wealth—often gained through their ministry—to verify the legitimacy of their message. After his aging private jet was damaged in 2013, Pastor Creflo Dollar asked his huge megachurch and television audience to donate sixty-five million dollars so that he could purchase a new Gulfstream G650, the finest in private aircraft. He told his flock, "I knew it was time to start believing God for a new airplane." The board of his ministry later apologized for

his having made such an outlandish request, but Dollar himself was unapologetic and unrepentant. And in the end Dollar got his sixty-five million dollars and purchased the jet. Not to be outdone, prosperity televangelist Kenneth Copeland recently began raising funds so that he could purchase a *second* private jet and thus one-up his rival Pastor Dollar. Stories of minsters' lavish mansions, vacation homes, luxury yachts, and the like are rampant in the prosperity gospel narrative.

Their apparent greed has led many to question the credibility of the prosperity gospel preachers and their interpretation of the Bible, which is riddled with assumptions, distortions, conjectures, and quotes taken out of context. For example, only Matthew's Gospel indicates that Jesus receives a gift of gold at birth, and it never specifies the amount or the value. Prosperity gospel preachers maintain that because the givers were kings, and therefore wealthy, the gift must have been extravagant. But Matthew's Gospel says nothing about kings; that idea is based on a post-biblical legend. Those who provide gifts to the newborn Jesus are *magi*, best translated as "magicians" or "astrologers." There is no reason to think such individuals would be rich.[12]

There was also no gate in Jerusalem called the "eye of a needle" (see chapter 11). This theory appears to have been first proposed in the nineteenth century; there is no archeological or textual evidence that such a gate ever existed. Besides all this, the context of the story makes the prosperity gospel's interpretation impossible. Jesus has just seen a rich man decide not to become a follower because he cannot do what Jesus has asked of him: to give up his many possessions and give the money to the poor. Jesus then comments, "How hard it will be for those

---

11. And if a person does tithe and yet receives no divine compensation, one could still chalk that up to a lack of faith.

12. See Mark Allan Powell, "Neither Wise nor Powerful: Reconsidering Matthew's Magi in the Light of Reader Expectations," *Trinity Seminary Review* 20, no. 1 (1998): 19–31.

who have wealth to enter the kingdom of God" (Mark 10:23). He then proceeds to illustrate this principle by using the example of a camel passing through the eye of a needle. The analogy only makes sense if Jesus is speaking of something so difficult that it is almost impossible, rather than (as the prosperity gospel maintains) something rather easy. The story of the eye of a needle gate is a myth that was created precisely to blunt the clear meaning of Jesus' teaching: that it is extremely difficult for the wealthy to enter the kingdom of heaven.

The other prosperity gospel arguments are similarly flawed. The Gospels say nothing about Jesus having an "accountant" or a "treasurer." One passage indicates Judas "carried the common purse," but it requires a rather willful distortion of that single passage to conclude that he was an executive who oversaw Jesus' enormous fortune. Indeed, a "common" purse implies that Jesus and his followers *pooled* their limited resources in order to meet expenses. There are no passages that show Jesus paying the bills for either his disciples or his mother. The one passage that points to the source of the necessary funds indicates that a group of *women* financed Jesus' ministry. Luke 8:3 states that these women—probably wealthy widows whose number included Mary Magdalene, Joanna, and Susanna—"provided for them out of their resources." The Gospels say very little about how Jesus financed his ministry, but what they do say contradicts the prosperity gospel's claim that Jesus paid all the bills out of his great reservoir of wealth.

Similarly, there is not a single passage that suggests, as prosperity gospel preachers insist, Jesus built himself a "fine home." Throughout the Gospels, Jesus is always shown staying at someone else's house, never at his own. Indeed, the one comment Jesus makes in this regard suggests rather clearly that he was, in fact, *homeless*: "Foxes have holes, and birds of the air have nests, but the Son of Man has nowhere to lay his head" (Matt. 8:20//Luke 9:58). Prosperity gospel advocates insist that Jesus was speaking metaphorically here, and that his point was that he was "not of this world" because his true home was in heaven. But the quote about having "nowhere to lay his head" makes no sense as a statement about Jesus' heavenly home, because he is comparing himself precisely to creatures (foxes and birds) *who have an earthly dwelling*.

Most problematic, the prosperity gospel has to ignore a rather large body of teachings of Jesus and stories about him that run exactly counter to their general claim. Jesus preached, "Blessed are you who are poor" (Luke 6:20) and "Woe to you who are rich" (Luke 6:24). He warned his followers against "all kinds of greed" (Luke 12:15) and insisted that a person "cannot serve God and wealth" (Matt. 6:24//Luke 16:13). He told the parable of the Rich Fool (Luke 12:16–21) and the parable of the Rich Man and Lazarus (Luke 16:19–31). This list could easily be multiplied. All of this is why biblical scholars as a whole see the prosperity gospel as a gross distortion of the teachings of Jesus and centuries of Christian tradition.

The Bible and Politics

The Bible has always been used for political purposes, from the days of Christian resistance to imperial Rome to the height of Christendom during the Middle Ages. The Bible has been enlisted in support of holy wars against "infidels" (such as the Crusades), the colonization of the Americas, Africa, and Asia, the conduct of the African slave trade, and the enslavement and extermination of indigenous peoples. But the Bible has also served as the inspiration for the abolition of slavery and the civil rights movement. Some even say that the Bible forms the bedrock of American democracy.

The claim that the United States was founded on biblical principles is hugely controversial. Many liberals believe that the United States was deliberately founded as a secular nation, with a "wall of separation" between church and state. They point to the absence of any reference to God or Christ in the Constitution, the original version of which only mentions religion in an article proclaiming that there must be no religious test for public office. When the Bill of Rights was appended to the constitution, the First Amendment indicated that the free exercise of religion should not be abridged, but specified also that there would be no establishment of religion in the nation either. Despite many voices arguing for Christianity in general or Protestantism in particular as the official religion of the United States, the nation's founders—led by James Madison and Thomas Jefferson—declined to name it as such.[13]

While it is true that there is no institutional establishment in the United States, this does not mean that Christianity has not been central to the American experience. First of all, the *federal* prohibition against an established religion did not prohibit the *states* from endorsing and supporting Christianity. Many states had laws prohibiting atheists, Catholics, Quakers, Muslims, or Jews from holding public office, and the last of these laws was not struck down until the middle of the twentieth century. Some states built churches and paid the salaries of state-approved ministers from public funds.

One should also note that there is more than one type of "establishment" of religion. While there was no *institutional* establishment at the federal level, there was a degree of *ceremonial* establishment and a large dose of *moral* establishment. **Ceremonial establishment** refers to things like the use of the Bible in swearing-in ceremonies for officeholders, the observance of religious holidays, the appointment of chaplains to Congress, the use of prayer at invocations to open congressional sessions, the declaration of national days of prayer or fasting, the use of "In God We Trust" as a motto on currency, or the phrase "under God" in the Pledge of Allegiance. All of these practices belie the notion of a complete separation between church and state in the United States.[14]

But more importantly, the system of morality on which both state and federal law were based was largely that of Protestant Christianity. The fact that a person could be prosecuted for blasphemy against God or Christ in almost every state in the country for most of American history is a clear indication that there was (and is) a **moral establishment** of religion in the United States. There were also state laws, many of them still on the books today, prohibiting certain activities on the Christian sabbath, such as the sale of liquor. Christianity and its Bible explicitly influenced American law on questions of marriage and divorce, sodomy and homosexuality, abortion and birth control, the role of women in society, and many other subjects.

While the Bible's influence in America waned as the twentieth century gave way to the twenty-first, scripture remains a potent political force. Presidential candidates are virtually required to refer to the Bible during their campaigns, although a deep understanding of the text does not seem to be a necessary qualification for election. President George W. Bush had

---

13. Notorious pseudo-historian David Barton has argued that Jefferson and Madison were far more sympathetic to the concept of America as a Christian nation than is commonly supposed, but he was able to do this only by fabricating quotations, manipulating quotes through elision, and taking words grossly out of context. See "The Jefferson 'Lies,'" Harvard University Press Blog, *http://harvardpress.typepad.com/hup_publicity/2012/08/the-jefferson-lies-david-barton.html*.

14. On the general subject of the myth of separation of church and state in the United States, see David Sehat's excellent book, *The Myth of American Religious Freedom*, updated ed. (New York: Oxford University Press, 2015).

a semi-mandatory Bible study for senior members of his administration,[15] and sprinkled his speeches with biblical language and allusions in ways that endeared him to his evangelical base. Barack Obama had a vaunted "scripture game"[16] that suggested he was the most Bible-literate candidate in recent memory, although his intimate familiarity with the Christian scriptures did not insulate him from widespread (though demonstrably false) accusations that he was a secret Muslim. In 2016 Donald Trump was briefly ridiculed for referring to Paul's letter as "Two Corinthians" instead of "Second Corinthians." Despite an obvious lack of familiarity with its contents, Trump praised the Bible as the only book better than his own *The Art of the Deal*.

Depending on the electorate in their states or districts, members of Congress or state executives are more free to either ignore the Bible or embrace it unreservedly. Among the latter is Republican Tom DeLay of Texas, former House Majority Leader, who once claimed that he believed God was using him to impose a "biblical worldview" on America. Former congressional representative Michele Bachmann (R-Minn.) has argued publicly that America must support the state of Israel because Genesis 12:3 states that those who bless Israel will be blessed, while those who curse Israel will be cursed. She insisted for years that tragedies befalling the United States were God's punishment for Barack Obama's insufficient support for the Israeli regime and his occasional criticism of Israel's treatment of the Palestinians. Republican Governor John Kasich of Ohio bucked his own party by accepting the Medicaid expansion that was part of Barack

Obama's Affordable Care Act because it allowed 275,000 poor Ohioans to gain health coverage. When criticized for this decision, Kasich said that as a committed Christian he was compelled to act as he did by Jesus' words from Matthew 25, that he would be judged by whether he had fed the hungry, clothed the naked, and cared for the poor.

The political issues in which the Bible is cited on one side or the other are manifold as well. Opponents of abortion put Bible quotes on billboards, such as, "Before I formed you in the womb, I knew you" (Jer. 1:5). Those opposed to gay marriage cite the condemnations of homosexual activity in Leviticus 18–20 and Romans 1, while defenders of same-sex unions point out that Jesus said exactly nothing against homosexuality in the Gospels. The Bible plays a peripheral role in some of these debates, a central role in others. The following sections discuss a few of the debates with a significant New Testament component.[17]

Capital Punishment

The Bible is cited on the issue of capital punishment by both lay people and experts. Most devout Christians in the United States support the death penalty, and for them it is enough to remember the passage, "Show no pity; life for life, eye for eye, tooth for tooth, hand for hand, foot for foot" (Deut. 19:21). Without question, the ancient Israelites made liberal use of the death penalty. The Torah mandates execution not only for rape and murder but for such infractions as rebellion against parents and persistent drunkenness (Deut. 21:18–21), blasphemy (Lev. 24:10–16), Sabbath

---

15. Jeffrey S. Siker, "President Bush, Biblical Faith, and the Politics of Religion," SBL Forum Archive, Society of Biblical Literature, *https://www.sbl-site.org/publications/article.aspx?ArticleId=151.*

16. The phrase is that of Jacques Berlinerblau, who wrote of Obama's facility with scripture in *Thumpin' It: The Use and Abuse of the Bible in Today's Presidential Politics* (Louisville: Westminster John Knox, 2007).

17. Attempts by Christian conservatives to prevent the teaching of evolution in public schools and to replace it with biblical creationism will not be covered here, as the biblical passages invoked are almost exclusively from the Old Testament.

breaking (Exod. 31:14), adultery (Lev. 20:10), witchcraft (Exod. 22:18), and male sodomy (Lev. 18:22; 20:13). Moreover, when Christians gained political power after the fourth century CE they too enthusiastically executed offenders and usually saw no conflict between the practice of capital punishment and the teachings of Jesus. The late Supreme Court Justice Antonin Scalia published an article in which he traced his support for the death penalty back to Saint Paul's letter to the Romans, where the apostle preaches that the forces of government are ordained by God and must be obeyed. Scalia further argued that the more Christian a nation is, the more likely it is to support capital punishment.[18]

Scalia was well-known as a devout Catholic, but he was deviating from Catholic Church teaching in his advocacy of the death penalty. The Church has staunchly opposed capital punishment since at least Vatican II, although conservative American Catholics are prone to ignore the Church hierarchy on this issue. Death penalty opponents, whether Catholic or Protestant, tend to cite Jesus' teaching, in which he seems to explicitly overturn the "eye-for-an-eye" concept of equal retribution drawn from the Old Testament: "You have heard that it was said, 'An eye for an eye and a tooth for a tooth,' but I say to you, Do not resist an evildoer. But if anyone strikes you on the right cheek, turn the other also" (Matt. 5:38–39). As the U.S. Conference of Catholic Bishops put it, "While the Old Testament includes some passages about taking the life of one who kills, the Old Testament and the teaching of Christ in the New Testament call us to protect life, practice mercy, and reject vengeance."[19] Opponents of capital punishment also point out that Jesus himself was subjected to the death penalty, even though he had committed no wrongdoing. The prospect of executing an innocent person is one of the primary motivators for opposition to capital punishment, along with statistical evidence suggesting that it does not function as a deterrent to criminals.

The Environment

Many today cite climate change as the greatest current threat facing humankind. But even before global warming took center stage in the debate there was widespread concern about the despoiling of the environment that accompanied the industrial age. Deforestation, loss of habitat, decreasing biodiversity, smog and other kinds of air pollution, and the fouling of seas, lakes, rivers, and streams all caught the attention of environmentalists during the twentieth century. Their opponents tended to argue that these threats were overstated and that humankind would suffer more from industrial regulations, the economic consequences of blocking development, and limits on the exploitation of natural resources. Despite the fact that the environmental threats have only increased over time, these opponents have not changed their tune. They often express confidence that new solutions will present themselves if environmental problems ever reach a truly critical stage.

In many cases this confidence is borne of religious conviction. After President Donald Trump pulled the United States out of the Paris Climate Accord in 2017, Representative Tim Walburg (R-Mich.) endorsed the move and said, "I'm confident that, if there's a real problem, God can take care of that."[20] Walburg is part of a long tradition in conservative Christianity that argues

---

18. Antonin Scalia, "God's Justice and Ours," in *First Things: The Journal of Religion and Public Life* (May, 2002): 17.

19. USCCB, "A Culture of Life and the Penalty of Death" (2005), 11.

20. Mahita Gajanan, "Republican Congressman Says God Will 'Take Care of' Climate Change," Time, *http://time .com/4800000/tim-walberg-god-climate-change/*.

that God put the world and its resources at the disposal of human beings, to do with as they will. The biblical foundation of this view is the passage in Genesis 1 in which God gives humans "dominion" over the earth and its creatures.

> Then God said: Let us make human beings in our image, after our likeness. Let them have dominion over the fish of the sea, the birds of the air, the tame animals, all the wild animals, and all the creatures that crawl on the earth.
>
> God created mankind in his image;
>
> in the image of God he created them;
>
> male and female he created them.
>
> God blessed them and God said to them: Be fertile and multiply; fill the earth and subdue it. Have dominion over the fish of the sea, the birds of the air, and all the living things that crawl on the earth. (Gen. 1:26–28, NABRE)

There are even those who think that it is not until humans have fully "subdued" nature that history will be consummated. "God gave us these things to use. After the last tree is felled, Jesus Christ will return" is a quote famously attributed to James Watt, Secretary of the Interior under President Ronald Reagan. Although the quote is apocryphal, Watt did say that the imminent return of Christ made environmental concerns unimportant. "My responsibility is to follow the Scriptures which call upon us to occupy the land until Jesus returns," said Watt. "We will mine more, drill more, cut more timber."[21]

In 1967 Lynn White Jr. wrote a groundbreaking essay, "The Historical Roots of Our Ecological Crisis," in which he argued that the Christian ethos was largely responsible for environmental degradation, along with the alliance of science and technology that led to Western dominance of the modern world. White argues that Europeans developed a model of humans in relation to nature that emphasized ruthless exploitation of the land and other natural resources. This stance has its roots in the Judeo-Christian creation story, where "no item in the physical creation had any purpose save to serve man's purposes" and "although man's body is made of clay, he is not simply part of nature; he is made in God's image." Unlike pagan animism, which held that every tree, stream, and hill had its own guardian spirit and necessitated that nature be treated with respect and deference, Christianity held that only humans were imbued with spirits. As a result of Christianity's triumph over paganism, "the old inhibitions to the exploitation of nature crumbled." The idea of a sacred grove of trees became incoherent, and nature was devalued to the point where then-California Governor Ronald Reagan could say with no hint of irony, "When you've seen one redwood tree, you've seen them all."[22]

White argued that the ecological crisis could never be solved by science and technology alone. What is required is either a new religion or a new way of thinking about the old religion. He found hope in the spirituality of **Saint Francis of Assisi**.

> The key to an understanding of Francis is his belief in the virtue of humility—not merely for the individual but for man as a species. Francis tried to depose man from his monarchy over creation and set up a democracy of all God's creatures. With him the ant is no longer simply a homily for the lazy, flames a sign of the thrust of the soul toward union with God; now they are Brother Ant and Sister Fire, praising the Creator in their own ways as Brother Man does in his.

---

21. Bill Prochnau et al., "The Watt Controversy," The Washington Post, *https://www.washingtonpost.com/archive/politics/1981/06/30/the-watt-controversy/d591699b-3bc2-46d2-9059-fb5d2513c3da/?utm_term=.af6ab7fcef30.*

22. All quotes are from Lynn White, "The Historical Roots of Our Ecological Crisis," in *Science* 155 (March 10, 1967): 1203–7.

White noted that the "Franciscan doctrine of the animal soul" was quickly stamped out, but he wondered if the spirituality of Saint Francis might be resurrected in modern times.

White's hope has been fulfilled in many ways as there is now widespread support among both conservative and liberal Christians for protecting the environment. When the current pope was elected in 2013, he took the name Francis to honor the unofficial patron saint of ecology, Saint Francis of Assisi. Two years later he issued a major encyclical letter entitled *Laudato si': On Care for Our Common Home*, in which he argued that the world needs to recognize climate change as real and to act decisively to halt and reverse the damage being done to the atmosphere before devastating effects are felt, especially by the poor and disadvantaged. Some evangelical leaders have also converted to the cause of environmentalism—or "creation care," as some prefer to call it—forming the Evangelical Environmental Network in the 1990s and the Evangelical Climate Initiative in 2006. In 2002 the group launched a well-received campaign to bring attention to the need to decrease use of fossil fuels entitled "What Would Jesus Drive?"

These efforts have involved a significant reinterpretation of the Bible, especially Genesis. Instead of thinking that God gave the world to humans to use and exploit, scholars and preachers have suggested that God actually appoints humans as the "stewards" or "caretakers" of the earth. Because they are created in the image of God, humans are appointed to serve as God's regents or "viceroys" on earth, to act in God's stead. Since God created the world and its creatures and proclaimed them all "good," then it would clearly be contrary to God's will for humans to destroy or despoil their natural environment.

The New Testament says less about nature than the Old Testament, and not all of its passages can be interpreted as pro-environment,[23] but there have been attempts to build an environmentally-friendly version of Christianity based on the teachings of Jesus and his apostles. This would be an impossible task if the Gnostic view had prevailed, with its understanding of the world as a rotten, corrupt place created by an evil demi-god. But in orthodox Christianity, as reflected in the New Testament, the flesh is not inherently evil. Jesus is flesh and bone; he can feel hunger and pain, and even after his resurrection he is corporeal and can eat food and be held. Moreover, Jesus speaks about and interacts with the animal kingdom and the natural world in positive ways. During his temptation Jesus is "with the wild beasts" and no harm comes to him (Mark 1:13). He speaks positively of sowing seeds and abundant yields (Mark 4:1–20), he appreciates the mustard seed (Mark 4:30–32) and the grass and lilies of the field (Matt. 6:28–30). When seeds grow into plants, Jesus credits not the farmer but the earth itself (Mark 4:28). Jesus is compared to a shepherd who loves his sheep, watches over them (John 10:1–21), and retrieves them when they are lost (Luke 15:3–7).

One can also find a positive vision of creation in Paul's letters. In Romans Paul speaks of creation personified and longing eagerly for the redemption of humanity.

> For the creation waits with eager longing for the revealing of the sons of God; for the creation was subjected to futility, not of its own will but by the will of him who subjected it in hope; because the creation itself will be set free from its bondage to decay and obtain the glorious liberty of the children of God. We know that the whole creation has been groaning in travail together until now; and not only the creation, but we ourselves, who have the first fruits of the Spirit, groan inwardly as we wait for adoption as sons, the redemption of our bodies. (Rom 8:19–23, RSV)

---

23. For example, Matt. 6:26 speaks of humans as more valuable than the birds of the air.

According to this passage, as well as a similar one in Colossians 1:15–20, Jesus came not merely to save humanity but to redeem the entire world.[24]

The Bible and the Struggle for Social Justice

One of the most hopeful developments in the evolution of humanity is the increasing concern for social justice that has characterized the modern world. The eighteenth century saw the beginning of a campaign to end slavery, culminating in the eradication of (legal) slavery throughout the developed world by the late nineteenth century.[25] By that time the first grassroots, popular movement against the horrors of European colonial exploitation had emerged as well,[26] as had the women's suffrage movement. The twentieth century saw, among many other developments, (1) a worldwide labor movement advocating for better wages and safer working conditions; (2) Mohandes Gandhi's nonviolent campaign to win independence for colonial India from the British Empire; (3) a second wave of feminism focused on reproductive rights, sexual freedom, equality in the workplace, and an end to sexual violence and harassment; and (4) the American civil rights movement, famously led by the Reverend Doctor Martin Luther King Jr.

The Bible played a role in all of these movements (even the one led by Gandhi, himself a Hindu),[27] and it would be instructive to examine each of

The Martin Luther King Jr. memorial at the Southern Poverty Law Center prominently features a quotation from King's speech on August 28, 1963, "Until justice rolls down like waters." The phrase derives from the Bible (Amos 5:24).

---

24. Cf. also Col. 1:15–20. Most of this discussion is drawn from David Rhodes, "Reading the New Testament in the Environmental Age," *http://www.webofcreation.org/Articles/rhoads.html.*

25. See Adam Hochschild, *Bury the Chains: Prophets and Rebels in the Fight to Free an Empire's Slaves* (Boston: Houghton Mifflin, 2005).

26. See Adam Hochschild, *King Leopold's Ghost: A Story of Greed, Terror, and Heroism in Colonial Africa,* 1st Mariner Books ed. (Boston: Houghton Mifflin, 1999).

27. Gandhi was famous for drawing from a variety of religious traditions in addition to his own Hinduism. When it came to Christianity, he was an avid student of Jesus' Sermon on the Mount. He believed that Jesus' commands to "turn the other cheek" and "walk the extra mile" were not idealistic fantasies, but practical advice for resisting evil and injustice without using physical force. In the Oscar-winning film *Gandhi*, Ben Kingsley as Gandhi is seen interpreting Jesus' words as follows: "I suspect he [Jesus] meant you must show courage, be willing to take a blow, several blows, to show you won't strike back, nor will you be turned aside. And when you do that, it calls on something in human nature, something that makes [your enemy's] hatred for you decrease and his respect increase." Although the quote cannot be sourced to Gandhi, it is an accurate summary of Gandhi's view of "turning the other cheek."

them in detail. However, this section will focus on more *recent* history, which has seen steady activity on the social justice front for a variety of reasons. One such reason is that some of the gains made by workers, women, and racial and ethnic minorities in developed countries have not yet spread to other parts of the world, so there continue to be campaigns for basic rights and protections, usually led by locals and assisted by outside sympathizers and organizations. It is also true that in some places in the developed world progress on social justice issues has slowed, stopped, or even reversed. Finally, there are new frontiers in the campaign for social justice, such as movements for equal treatment and opportunities for the disabled, the mentally ill, members of the LGBTQ community, and religious minorities.

The Poor and Oppressed: Latin American Liberation Theology

The story of God liberating the Israelites from bondage in Egypt resonated deeply with antebellum African-American slaves. They saw themselves in the suffering of the Israelite slaves and hoped that God would also hear their "groaning" (Exod. 2:24) and deliver them. When Emancipation came, many freed slaves cast Abraham Lincoln in the role of Moses, and proclaimed the Year of Jubilee (Lev. 25:10) had arrived.

A century later the Exodus story swelled with meaning for the residents of Latin America, most of whom lived in searing poverty under brutal dictatorships. Their suffering was great, and they too hoped for liberation—not from slavery but from starvation, repression, and violence. Gustavo Gutierrez of Peru, Leonardo Boff of Brazil, and other early architects of Latin American **liberation theology** were Catholic

priests and theologians who thought that their Church's stances on political oppression and economic injustice were inconsistent with the Bible. They believed the Catholic Church in Latin America had been too supportive of the wealthy oligarchs who controlled the land and used paramilitary death squads to torture and kill those who protested for reform. They argued that the teaching of Jesus and the prophets required the Church to align itself with the poor, to take their side in any conflict with the powerful, and to advocate for political freedom and a more just distribution of wealth.

Both Vatican officials and American politicians were wary of liberation theology, largely because those fighting against the authoritarian political regimes in Latin America were usually communist insurgents. For decades the teaching of the Catholic Church had rejected Marxism as materialistic, atheistic, and violent. But liberation theologians believed that, despite its flaws, Marxist analysis of class structure hit the mark more often than it missed. They sometimes sympathized more with atheistic communist rebels or Marxist regimes than they did with the wealthy and powerful opponents of Marxism, who were nominally Christian but who viciously persecuted the poor. Liberation theologians who flirted too openly with Marxism, or who criticized the Church hierarchy too vigorously, found themselves being officially silenced by the Vatican.

However, these liberation theologians had struck a spark. One of their essential insights is that Jesus had identified with the poor and assailed the wealthy and powerful. Indeed, Catholic social teaching had been trending in favor of democracy, labor unions, and economic justice for decades prior to the rise of liberation theology.[28] Hence, despite its opposition to some

---

28. The beginning of Catholic social teaching is usually traced to Pope Leo XIII (1878–1903). Leo's encyclical *Rerum novarum* (1891) first outlined the modern Church's position in favor of just wages, safe working conditions, and the right of workers to organize labor unions and to strike.

aspects of liberation theology, the Church eventually agreed that authentic Christian teaching must be characterized by a "**preferential option for the poor**."[29]

Poverty was identified as an issue of central concern to the Christian gospel in *Gaudium et spes* (1965), the Pastoral Constitution on the Church in the Modern World, during the Second Vatican Council. The first line of the constitution reads, "The joys and hopes, the grief and anguish of the people of our time, especially of those who are poor or afflicted, are the joys and hopes, the grief and anguish of the followers of Christ as well." The document emphasizes Christ's concern for the poor, concluding, "The council, considering the immensity of the hardships which still afflict the greater part of mankind today, regards it as most opportune that an organism of the universal Church be set up in order that both the justice and love of Christ toward the poor might be developed everywhere."[30]

Many Gospel passages support the preferential option for the poor. Some of these have been previously considered (see chapter 11), such as the Beatitudes and Woes in the Sermon on the Plain (Luke 6:20–26), the parable of the Rich Fool (Luke 12:13–21), the parable of the Rich Man and Lazarus (Luke 16:19–31), and aphorisms such as "You cannot serve God and wealth" (Matt. 6:24//Luke 16:13) and "One's life does not consist in the abundance of possessions" (Luke 12:15). Gospel stories that show Jesus taking the side of the poor *against* that of the wealthy and powerful include his praise of the poor widow who put two copper coins into the Temple treasury and his dismissal

of those rich people who gave large sums because "they gave out of their wealth; but she, out of her poverty, put in everything—all she had to live on" (Mark 12:44, NIV). This parable of the Widow's Mite follows Jesus' warning against the scribes who "devour widows' houses" (Mark 12:40). This undoubtedly refers to the practice of loaning money to women whose husbands had died and whose source of income had disappeared, for the deliberate purpose of then evicting them from their homes when they could not repay the debt. Jesus preached that debts should be forgiven in circumstances such as this. And when Jesus sums up the criteria for salvation in the Great Judgment (Matt. 25:31–46), he emphasizes that those who will sit at his right hand and inherit the kingdom are the ones who cared for "the least of these who are members of my family" by providing food, drink, clothing, and comfort to those who are in need. Many similar passages could be cited, including passages that are highlighted in their respective Gospels as particularly important.

Christians, and Christian denominations, are still working out how to put in practice the preferential option for the poor. Increasing economic inequality will continue to present a challenge to those among the fortunate who wish to be faithful to Jesus' echoing concern for the dispossessed. Liberation theology as a political movement may or may not have a future, but liberation theologians have called attention to the problem of global poverty in such a way that no thinking, conscientious Christian can ignore it.

---

29. This may be defined as the idea that in any moral, political, social, or economic situation in which a choice must be made, preference should be given to the option that best contributes to the well-being of the poor and powerless in the community. Catholic canon law indicates that faithful Christians are "obliged to promote social justice and, mindful of the precept of the Lord, to assist the poor from their own resources" (1983 CIC, canon 222, §2).

30. Although *Gaudium et spes* did not employ the phrase "preferential option for the poor," this principle was developed by the conference of Latin American bishops at their 1968 conference in Medellin, Columbia.

The Oppression of Women: Feminist Biblical Interpretation

The Bible first became a target of women's rights supporters' ire during the "first wave" of feminism (mid nineteenth–early twentieth century), which fought to give women the right to vote, the right to an education, the ability to work outside the home, the right to own property, and legal authority to obtain a divorce and remarry. Many young people today find it difficult to believe that women did not possess all of these rights as recently as one hundred years ago, but it was only in 1920 that women gained the right to vote in the United States. Moreover, throughout the 1800s American marriage law utilized the legal doctrine of **coverture**, according to which the legal existence of a woman was suspended upon marriage, her rights and obligations being subsumed by those of her husband. This is based on the idea that the husband and wife had become one person, but that only the husband could own or buy property, or sign a contract on behalf of the union. A wife fell under the cover, influence, and protection of her husband, and hence was bound by his decisions and unable to act in her own interest.

First-wave feminists like the redoubtable Elizabeth Cady Stanton saw how deeply the Bible and Christianity were implicated in both the concept of coverture and in a variety of other practices inimical to women's happiness and fulfillment. Stanton advocated the then-radical notion of "free love"—the idea that men and women should be free to couple or uncouple as they saw fit, without requiring the approval of the church or the state. To help set women free, Stanton decided to expose the Bible—at least as it was then being translated and interpreted—as

a sexist and **patriarchal**[31] text, asserting that its claim to be the word of God was undermined by male authorship, abundant contradictions, centuries of revisions and scribal emendations, and its reliance on Bronze Age social and cultural values.

The vehicle for Stanton's crusade against the pernicious influence of scripture was *The Woman's Bible*, which selected passages involving women and then provided commentary from Stanton and a twenty-six-member "revising committee." Many on the committee were not as radical as Stanton and sought to defend scripture from her criticism, but Stanton's voice came through loud and clear. She argued that a liberating tradition for women in the Bible could be found, for example, in the creation story. Stanton, Lucretia Mott, and others in the project were familiar with the source-critical conclusion that Genesis contained not one but two different creation stories, one in Genesis 1:1–2:4a and the other in Genesis 2:4b–3:16, that had ultimately been woven together into a single narrative. The second creation story, the one involving Adam and Eve, was usually employed to women's detriment. Advocates of male superiority and domination would point out that, in this passage, (1) man was created first, then woman; (2) woman was made *from* man, which suggested to many subsequent interpreters that men were created in the image of God while women were created in the image of man; (3) woman was created to be man's "helper," as if he is the boss and she is his subordinate; (4) Eve talks to the serpent and is tempted, and is the first to eat the forbidden fruit; (5) Adam eats the fruit only after she gives it to him, suggesting that she has some responsibility for his misbehavior; and (6) Eve receives the greater punishment, including, it was claimed, a lifetime of domination by

---

31. Patriarchy (literally "the rule of the father") is defined as a mode of social organization in which males dominate at every level: family, clan, tribe, city, and nation. Fathers rule over their wives and children with an iron fist. Men control the overwhelming majority of the money and property, and have a monopoly on positions of leadership and power.

Adam and Eve are tempted by the serpent in this bas relief from Notre Dame, Paris. In medieval times, it was common to depict the serpent with female features, thus emphasizing woman's role in the origin of sin.

Adam: "Your desire will be for your husband, and he shall rule over you" (Gen. 3:16).

Stanton pointed out that the first creation story, in Genesis 1, presents a different view. Genesis 1:27 clearly implies that men and women are created at the same time, not one after the other, and that they are *both* created in the "image of God." The Hebrew word *'adam* here is often translated into English as "man" or "mankind," but the word does not refer specifically to males; Hebrew has other words for males specifically. *'Adam* is better translated as "humankind," so the text of Genesis 1:26–27 should read, "Then God said, 'Let us make humankind (*'adam*) in our image, according to our likeness. . . .' So God created humankind in his image, in the image of God he created them; male (*zaqar*) and female (*neqabah*) he created them."

Feminist biblical critics would go on to point out that the second creation story as well

is more sexist in the interpretation than in the actual text. Eve is created to be Adam's "helper," a word that has been taken—incorrectly—to imply subordination; the Old Testament repeatedly applies the same term to God (e.g., Ps. 33:20; 70:5; 115:9; 146:5). She is also identified as his "partner," a word that implies an equitable relationship. It is true that Eve gave the fruit to Adam, but she did not trick, deceive, or in any way lead him astray, as he was "with her" the entire time (see Gen. 3:6) and must have known what he was eating.[32]

Some rather sexist biblical exegesis of the Genesis stories can be found in the New Testament itself. For example:

> *A man has no need to cover his head, because he reflects the image and glory of God. But woman reflects the glory of man; for man was not created from woman, but woman from man. Nor was man created for woman's sake, but woman was created for man's sake.* On account of this, then, a woman should have a covering over her head to show that she is under her husband's authority. (1 Cor. 11:7–10, GNT, emphasis added)

> I also want the women to be modest and sensible about their clothes and to dress properly; not with fancy hair styles or with gold ornaments or pearls or expensive dresses, but with good deeds, as is proper for women who claim to be religious. Women should learn in silence and all humility. I do not allow them to teach or to have authority over men; they must keep quiet. *For Adam was created first, and then Eve. And it was not Adam who was deceived; it was the woman who was deceived and broke God's law. But a woman will be saved through having children,* if she perseveres in faith and love and holiness, with modesty. (1 Tim. 2:9–15, GNT, emphasis added)

---

32. For many of these points, see Phyllis Trible, "Eve and Adam: Genesis 2–3 Reread," in *Andover-Newton Quarterly* 13 (1973): 74–81.

Feminist biblical critics have pointed out how heavily the authors of these passages rely on the second creation story to the exclusion of the first, and how often the statements about Adam and Eve are based on biased misreadings of the text. Genesis 2–3 has some sexist content, but it is not as extreme as these New Testament interpretations suggest.

This discussion points out how feminist biblical scholarship both praises and criticizes the Bible. Feminist biblical scholarship highlights and celebrates oft-ignored parts of the Bible that portray women positively, that show women who are empowered, trustworthy, intelligent, and capable. Frequently the women in these stories are anonymous, such as the woman who anoints Jesus (Mark 14:3–9). Jesus says, "Wherever the gospel is preached in the whole world, what she has done will be told in memory of her" (Mark 14:9, RSV). The last phrase provided the title of Elizabeth Schüssler Fiorenza's landmark feminist study of the New Testament, *In Memory of Her*, which attempts to reconstruct the egalitarian character of earliest Christianity and to recover women's stories, which have often been erased, forgotten, or depersonalized.[33] A great deal of work has been done reconstructing the prominent role played in Jesus' ministry by Mary Magdalene, Mary and Martha of Bethany (Luke 10:38–42; John 11), and Joanna and Susanna (Luke 8:3). The role of Junia and Prisca in Paul's ministry has also garnered attention (Rom. 16).

Feminist biblical interpretation also takes a negative track, exposing texts (or interpreters) that support a patriarchal system contrary to the will of God. In the case of Genesis 2–3, as we have seen, the text itself has some sexist elements, but many of its interpretations have been far worse. Often such stories can be at least partially reclaimed; others appear to be irredeemably sexist. It is hard to imagine how to make something positive out of God giving permission for fathers to sell their daughters into slavery (Exod. 21:7), or a Levite who, when threatened by a hostile mob, throws his female concubine out the door to be raped to death (Judg. 19), or the insistence that women remain silent in church and submit themselves to their husbands at home, obeying them and calling them "Master" (1 Cor. 14:33b–36; Titus 2:5; 1 Pet. 3:1–5). Perhaps the only solution is for the texts themselves to be rejected as expressing sentiments that are contrary of the will of God, and reflective only of the desire of the human men who wrote them to dominate and subjugate women.

Indeed, many feminists have found the redemption of the Bible a hill too high to climb. In addition to the misogynistic texts mentioned above, the Bible presents us with an unmistakably male Savior and a presumptively male God. The Bible uses exclusively male pronouns to refer to God and the most commonly used metaphors for God are Father and King, both masculine terms. Led by Matilda Joslyn Gage in the 1890s and Mary Daly in the 1970s, the number of female scholars who have advocated abandoning Christianity for a more female-friendly religion or spirituality has steadily risen. Among the preferred alternatives are neopaganism (a religion often praised for its eco-friendly nature as well as its reverence for both male and female deities) and Wicca, which sees itself as a revival of traditional Anglo-Saxon witchcraft involving seasonally based festivals known as Sabbats and (sometimes) magic.

Those who have remained within the fold of Christianity have fought for changes, such as the introduction of ordained female ministers in those denominations that still prohibit them, the appointment of women to leadership

---

33. Elisabeth Schüssler Fiorenza, *In Memory of Her: A Feminist Theological Reconstruction of Christian Origins* (New York: Crossroad, 1983).

positions (such as bishops), and the transformation of the liturgy. More and more denominations use gender-inclusive language in their hymns and biblical translations, although this has been difficult for many traditionalists to accept and has created enormous controversy in many denominations. These battles are far from over. The ministry in the United States is still an extremely male-dominated profession. A recent Gallup survey found that 85 percent of all ministers were male, and the only major denomination that had achieved 50 percent female participation in the ministry was the Unitarian-Universalist Association, the most progressive and least traditionally Christian of all American sects.

In addition to the struggle for political liberation in Latin America and for gender equity, there are many other fronts in biblical scholarship on which the battle for social justice is proceeding. In the 1960s, scholar James Cone created Black Liberation Theology, and eventually developed a distinctively African-American biblical hermeneutics that many other scholars have since advanced. Another group of scholars in recent decades has begun looking at the Bible from the LGBTQ perspective. Still other scholars have examined the Bible from a postcolonial perspective, or from the standpoint of the disabled, or have studied the Bible's use in Asia or Africa, or in the immigrant communities from those places.

Despite the fact that the youngest parts of the Bible are almost two thousand years old, the amount of scholarship that is being produced about it continues to grow and to involve more diverse interpreters than ever before. One might suppose that with all the millions of words that have been written about the Bible, there is nothing more to say. But new perspectives on old texts, and new discoveries of texts and artifacts from the biblical period, as well as the value that a great many people continue to see in the Bible, together mean that the interpretation of the Bible is something that people will be arguing about for decades and centuries to come.

Key Terms

fundamentalism
literal interpretation
inerrant
evangelical
King James Bible
prosperity gospel

testimonials
seed faith
tithing
ceremonial establishment
moral establishment

Saint Francis of Assisi
liberation theology
preferential option for the poor
coverture
patriarchy

Review Questions

1. What are the key characteristics of biblical fundamentalism?

2. What problems are endemic to fundamentalism? Why do the issues of the text and translation of the New Testament create some of these problems? What are some examples of apparent historical errors and internal inconsistencies in the Bible?

3. What arguments have proponents of the prosperity gospel made to support their claim that Jesus was wealthy and that he never criticized the rich?

4. How have critics responded to the claims of prosperity gospel proponents? What are the key passages in dispute? What passages does the prosperity gospel seem to ignore?

5. Some claim that the United States is a Christian nation, founded on biblical principles, while others insist it is a purely secular nation; what legitimate arguments can each side muster in support of its position?

6. How has the Bible (and the New Testament specifically) played a role in the contemporary political debates over capital punishment and the environment?

7. What are some of the major areas in which campaigns for social justice have

transformed the modern world? How has the Bible (and the New Testament specifically) played a role in some of these campaigns?

8. What positive elements have feminist biblical scholars derived from the Bible in their attempt to promote the liberation of women? In what ways has the Bible contributed to the oppression of women throughout history?

Discussion Questions

1. In your experience, is fundamentalism on the decline, or does it remain a potent force in modern religious discourse, even among the younger generation?

2. Is capitalism fully compatible with a Christianity that is faithful to the teaching of Jesus? What are the points of conflict, if any?

3. Are there political issues beyond those mentioned in the chapter (death penalty, the environment) where you have seen the Bible being employed by one side or the other?

In your experience, has the Bible played any part in the debates over immigration, health care, war and military service, public assistance, or other contentious issues?

4. Christianity appears to be evolving to come to grips with popular modern notions of equality on issues such as race, gender, sexual orientation, and more. In your view, is it evolving fast enough? Are appeals made to the Bible generally more helpful or harmful in this regard? Are there areas in which this evolution has gone too far?

Bibliography and Suggestions for Further Study

(Books and websites that are accessible for general undergraduates are marked with an asterisk; other sources listed are appropriate for advanced students.)

*Berlinerblau, Jacques. *Thumpin' It: The Use and Abuse of the Bible in Today's Presidential Politics.* Louisville: Westminster John Knox, 2007.

*Blake, John. "Was Jesus Rich? Swanky Messiah Not Far-Fetched in Prosperity Gospel." *Atlanta Journal-Constitution* (Oct. 22, 2006).

*Cone, James H. *A Black Theology of Liberation.* 40th anniversary ed. Maryknoll, NY: Orbis, 2010.

*Daly, Mary. *Beyond God the Father: Toward a Philosophy of Women's Liberation.* Boston: Beacon, 1973.

*Gutierrez, Gustavo. *The Power of the Poor in History: Selected Writings.* Maryknoll, NY: Orbis, 1983.

Gutierrez, Gustavo. *A Theology of Liberation: History, Politics, and Salvation.* Maryknoll, NY: Orbis, 1988.

Herriot, Peter. *Religious Fundamentalism: Global, Local and Personal.* London; New York: Routledge, 2009.

*Hochschild, Adam. *Bury the Chains: Prophets and Rebels in the Fight to Free an Empire's Slaves.* Boston: Houghton Mifflin, 2005.

*Hochschild, Adam. *King Leopold's Ghost: A Story of Greed, Terror, and Heroism in Colonial Africa.* 1st Mariner Books ed. Boston: Houghton Mifflin, 1999.

*Pope Leo XIII. "Rerum novarum: Encyclical of Pope Leo XIII on Capital and Labor." 1891. *Http://w2.vatican.va/content/leo-xiii/en /encyclicals/documents/hf_l-xiii_enc_15051891 _rerum-novarum.html.*

*Powell, Mark Allan. "Neither Wise nor Powerful: Reconsidering Matthew's Magi in the Light of Reader Expectations." *Trinity Seminary Review* 20, no. 1 (1998): 19–31.

*Rhodes, David. "Reading the New Testament in the Environmental Age." Web of Creation. *Http://www.webofcreation.org/Articles/rhoads .html.*

*Scalia, Antonin. "God's Justice and Ours." *First Things: The Journal of Religion and Public Life* (May 2002): 17.

*Schüssler Fiorenza, Elisabeth. *In Memory of Her: A Feminist Theological Reconstruction of Christian Origins.* New York: Crossroad, 1983.

*Sehat, David. *The Myth of American Religious Freedom.* Updated ed. New York: Oxford University Press, 2015.

*Siker, Jeffrey S. "President Bush, Biblical Faith, and the Politics of Religion." SBL Forum Archive. Society of Biblical Literature. *Https://www.sbl-site.org/publications/article .aspx?ArticleId=151.*

*Stanton, Elizabeth Cady. *The Woman's Bible.* Salem, NH: Ayer, 1991.

*Trible, Phyllis. "Eve and Adam: Genesis 2–3 Reread." *Andover-Newton Quarterly* 13 (1973): 74–81.

*Trible, Phyllis. *God and the Rhetoric of Sexuality.* Philadelphia: Fortress, 1978.

*Vatican Council. *Pastoral Constitution on the Church in the Modern World: Gaudium et spes; Promulgated by His Holiness Pope Paul VI on December 7, 1965.* Boston: Pauline Books & Media, 1998.

*White, Lynn. "The Historical Roots of Our Ecological Crisis." *Science* 155 (March 10, 1967): 1203–7.

GLOSSARY OF SELECTED KEY TERMS

adoptionism The belief that Jesus was born an ordinary human but later chosen by God to be the Messiah and God's (adopted) Son.

advent The "coming" (Latin, *adventus*) of the Lord, usually in reference to the return of Christ at the end of the world, but sometimes also to the birth of Christ.

allegorical method Interpretation strategy whereby the biblical text is assumed to have multiple levels of hidden meaning in addition to the literal sense.

allegory A story with multiple points of comparison to the reality to which it refers, such that all or most of the events and characters of the story have a particular symbolic significance.

allusion Technique wherein a text makes reference to something in another, earlier text that the author expects readers will recognize.

amanuensis A secretary who takes dictation from an author or otherwise produces a written text at an author's behest.

amillenialism Rejection of the belief that Jesus will literally reign on earth for a thousand years as described in Revelation 20.

anonymity The situation in which the name of an author is not known or given in the text.

anti-Judaism Hatred of Jews on the basis of their faith and religious practices.

anti-Semitism Hatred of Jews on the basis of their race, specifically their supposed racial inferiority, or stereotypical ethnic characteristics.

aphorism A short, pithy saying, general principle, or piece of wisdom.

apocalypse (1) A literary genre in which seers write of the divine visions or revelations they have received, usually regarding the end of the world and typically featuring highly symbolic language. (2) The event at which the world comes to an end by God's decisive action.

apocrypha Books regarded as sacred literature but not officially included in a religion's canon of scripture.

apology An extended defense from someone accused of wrongdoing or someone speaking on behalf of an accused wrongdoer.

apostasy Renunciation of one's faith in the face of persecution.

apostle One who is "sent out" (Greek, *apostellein*) or commissioned as an authorized representative of Jesus to fulfill missionary and leadership functions within the Christian community.

Armageddon The location where the armies of the unbelieving kings will gather for a final battle with the forces of God, according to Revelation 16:16.

asceticism Religious practice involving strict control or disciplining of the body and its appetites for such things as food, sex, intoxicants, and physical comfort.

Asclepius Popular Greco-Roman hero and demi-god associated with health and healing, whose cult and health-related facilities were maintained at various locations throughout the Mediterranean world.

Barnabas Early Jewish convert to Christianity who assumed the leadership of the church at Antioch; one of the architects of the Gentile Christianity that emerged there, and, with Paul, a defender of Gentile Christianity at the Jerusalem Council.

Beloved Disciple An unnamed character in the Gospel of John described simply as "the disciple whom Jesus loved," portrayed as the best and most faithful of Jesus' disciples and as the ultimate source of the traditions in the Fourth Gospel.

bishop A leader and "overseer" (Greek, *episkopos*) of a church community in the proto-orthodox branch of Christianity, mentioned primarily in the later books of the New Testament.

blasphemy The act of insulting, reviling, or showing insufficient reverence for God.

Caesar Augustus Name adopted by Octavian after assuming power as the first emperor of Rome (reigned 27 BCE–14 CE), known for his military prowess, capable administration, deification by the Roman Senate, and founding of an imperial dynasty.

canon A list of books regarded as authoritative by a given religious community, officially recognized as the sacred scriptures of that community.

catholic Universal or worldwide (Greek, *katholikos*), one of the qualities that the proto-orthodox branch of Christianity claimed as characteristic of itself (along with "holy" and "apostolic").

Catholic Name adopted by the church (and its adherents) that claims descent from the Christian community founded by Jesus' apostles, distinguished from the other two major branches of Christianity (Protestant and Orthodox) by its being led by the pope of Rome and the bishops, and by its adherence to a set of beliefs and practices proclaimed by the pope or by the bishops acting together at ecumenical church councils up to and including the Second Vatican Council in the 1960s.

catholic epistles The New Testament letters of James, Jude, 1 and 2 Peter, and Hebrews, so called because these letters are not addressed to particular church communities but to the universal or worldwide (Greek, *katholikos*) church.

Celsus One of the foremost pagan critics of Christianity in antiquity; his major work *On the True Doctrine* (ca. 175–177 CE) does not survive, but much of its content is known through the Christian theologian Origen's response to his arguments, *Contra Celsum* (*Against Celsus*).

Christology Teaching about the status and significance of Christ; major topics include Christ's identity as human and/or divine and the way in which salvation can be found through him.

circumcision Surgical removal of the foreskin of the penis, a mandatory practice for inclusion in the people of Israel and the effectuation of the covenant with God originally made with Abraham.

client king A ruler appointed by Rome over one of its imperial possessions, usually chosen for his membership in the local ruling elite and his willingness to obey Rome's orders; also known as a "puppet king."

climax (1) In literary criticism, the part of the plot that resolves the conflict in some decisive fashion, signaling that the story has reached or neared its conclusion. (2) In ancient rhetoric, a technique in which words or phrases are arranged in order of increasing importance.

complication In literary criticism, the part of the plot in which an element of conflict is introduced into the story, creating dramatic tension that rises as the story progresses toward its climax.

Constantine The first Roman emperor (or co-emperor) to convert to Christianity, who ended persecution of Christians through the Edict of Milan in 313 CE and encouraged the bishops to resolve the Arian controversy at the Council of Nicaea in 325 CE.

covenant A binding agreement or contract between two parties, whereby each party has certain rights and responsibilities.

coveting An illicit desire to possess that which rightfully belongs to another, prohibited by one of the Ten Commandments and prosecutable only when accompanied by some kind of conspiracy to act upon that desire.

crucifixion Method of execution used by the Romans (among others), especially on slaves and foreigners, involving attaching the victim to a wooden cross using nails, rope, or both.

crypto-Christians Believers in Jesus who hid their faith to avoid being cast out of the synagogue they attended.

cult The process by which devotees "took care" (Latin, *cultus*) of a deity they worshipped through sacrifice, praise, and the erection of shrines and temples.

Cynicism One of the popular philosophies that spread from Greece throughout the Roman Empire, known for advocating nonconventional behavior and attitudes, including asceticism, voluntary poverty, and begging.

deacon Within early Christianity, a person who "served" (Greek, *diakonein*) the community in some way, such as presiding over and serving the communal meal known as the Eucharist or Lord's Supper.

Dead Sea Scrolls A trove of Jewish texts dating from the first century CE, discovered in 1947 on the coast of the Dead Sea near Qumran, containing the earliest surviving versions of the texts of the Hebrew Bible as well as some distinctive religious literature believed by most to stem from a Jewish sect called the Essenes.

deicide The murder of God, a charge raised by some within Christianity toward the Jews whom they hold responsible for the killing of Jesus.

deism A religious philosophy that flourished in the eighteenth and nineteenth centuries, according to which God exists and created the world, but does not interfere in its operation by means of miracles or other forms of divine intervention, conceiving of God as a "clockmaker."

delay of the parousia The religious problem created when the second coming of Christ (the parousia) did not occur quickly, as many early Christians expected.

deliberative rhetoric Speech or writing that seeks to persuade its audience to adopt some action or point of view in the future.

Demeter A popular Greek fertility goddess; according to myth her daughter Persephone, having been captured by Hades, must spend several months each year in the underworld, during which time Demeter's sadness leads to an end to the growing season.

denarius A silver coin that was the most popular Roman monetary unit at the time of early Christianity; it was the usual daily wage for a day laborer, which provided just enough money for the purchase of one's "daily bread" (four loaves).

deutero-Pauline letters (1) All New Testament letters that claim Pauline authorship but were not actually written by him. (2) A subset of non-Pauline letters, usually including Ephesians, Colossians, and 2 Thessalonians but excluding the Pastoral Epistles (1 and 2 Timothy and Titus).

Diaspora The community of Jews who lived outside the traditional homeland of Palestine, having been "dispersed" (Greek, *diaspora*, "dispersion") due to various political and economic causes.

diatribe A rhetorical technique or genre in which a speaker or author anticipates and voices questions and objections from the audience and attempts to answer them.

Dionysus Greek god of wine, religious ecstasy, and theatre, whose cult was famous for festivals that featured the unrestrained consumption of alcohol.

disciple A follower of a prominent teacher.

dispensationalism A modern variety of Christian theology that sees salvation history unfolding in distinct stages or "dispensations," originated by J. N. Darby and accepted by many conservative Protestant thinkers and denominations.

dissimilarity, criterion of Within historical Jesus research, a method of identifying sayings that are probably authentic by their dissimilarity from characteristic teachings of ancient Judaism and early Christianity, those being the major alternative sources of sayings attributed to Jesus.

divination Attempts to determine the will of the gods and the course of future events by either natural means (e.g., oracles) or artificial means (e.g., examining patterns found in the flight of birds, or the entrails of a slaughtered animal).

Docetism The belief that Jesus was not really human but was a divine spirit who merely "seemed" (Greek, *dokein*) to be human.

Domitian Roman emperor (reigned 81–96 CE) traditionally thought to have sponsored a persecution of Christians to which the book of Revelation was one response.

double tradition Stories and sayings found in the Gospels of Matthew and Luke but not in the third Synoptic Gospel, Mark; often theorized to have formed the backbone of the lost gospel now known as Q.

ecclesiology Teaching about the church (Greek, *ekklēsia*), covering such issues as criteria for membership, organizational structure and leadership, mission, and internal discipline.

Elijah Prominent Israelite prophet of the eighth century BCE, known especially for working miracles and for having been taken up to heaven rather than suffering physical death; the object of a prophecy that forecast his return just prior to the day of judgment.

enthymeme A syllogism in which one of the usual elements (two premises and a conclusion) is unstated and must be supplied by the audience.

Epicureanism Greek popular philosophy that saw worship of the gods as unnecessary and ineffective and advocated the pursuit of "happiness" (defined primarily as the absence of pain) through harmonious interaction with others and the enjoyment of life's simple pleasures.

epideictic rhetoric A form of speech or writing that seek to persuade the audience to adopt or maintain some point of view in the present, often directed toward the praise or blame of an individual or group.

epistle Derived from the Greek word for "letter," any communication sent from one person or group to another that is written in the ancient Greek style, the elements of which typically included sender, addressee, greeting, thanksgiving, body, parenesis, and closing.

eschatology Teaching about the end of the world, or the "last things" (Greek, *eschatos*).

Essenes A Jewish sect that flourished from approximately the second century BCE to the late first century CE; known for their monastic lifestyle and apocalyptic beliefs; founders of the Qumran community and probable authors of the Dead Sea Scrolls.

ethos An argument within a rhetorical discourse that derives its persuasive power from some appeal to the character of the speaker, such as his general trustworthiness or expertise in the matter at hand.

evangelical Broad term for modern conservative Protestant denominations and their members, deriving in part from these groups' strong belief that unbelievers will suffer eternal torment in hell and must therefore be "evangelized" (Greek, *euangelizein*, "proclaim good news") and converted in order to be saved.

exaltation Christology The idea that Jesus was "raised" by God from either a human status or that of a subordinate divine being (an angel) to a divine status (or a fully divine status) due to his obedience to God unto death on the cross.

exposition The beginning of a story, in which the story's setting is established and its characters are introduced prior to the development of the conflict around which the plot will revolve.

Farrer hypothesis One solution to the Synoptic Problem, according to which Mark was the first Gospel written, Matthew was written second and used Mark as a source, and Luke was written third and used both Mark and Matthew as sources.

feminist biblical criticism Interpretation of the Bible that is especially attentive to the portrayal of female characters in the text, the implicit or explicit understanding of gender roles in the text, the portrayal of God in traditionally masculine or feminine terms, and the role of sexism in the history of the text's interpretation.

form criticism Method of biblical interpretation that seeks to identify the oral traditions that lie behind the Gospels and attempts to reconstruct the history of the transmission and development of these traditions.

Fourth Gospel Alternative name for the Gospel of John, owing to its location in the New Testament canon.

Fourth Philosophy Umbrella term for Jewish groups of the Roman imperial period who sought the violent overthrow of the Roman regime and played a major role in the various Jewish rebellions against Rome.

fundamentalism An approach found in several modern religions that emphasizes the inerrancy and literal interpretation of the religion's scriptures, rejects modernity in favor of a restoration of traditional values and modes of social organization, and insists that all who do not subscribe to the religion's belief system are doomed to everlasting damnation.

general epistles One term for the letters of James, Jude, and Peter, and the letter to the Hebrews, owing to their being addressed to a "general" audience rather than to a particular church community.

Gentile Jewish term for a non-Jewish person.

Gnosticism A religious philosophy found in several ancient religions including Christianity, which sees the material world as an evil place that can only be escaped through the acquisition of special "knowledge" (Greek, *gnōsis*) given to humans by a divine revealer sent from the heavenly, spiritual realm.

God-fearers Jewish term for Gentiles who were attracted to the Jewish religion and who attended synagogue services but were reluctant to undergo circumcision and become full members of the covenant people of Israel.

Gospel (or gospel) From an Anglo-Saxon term meaning "good news." (1) A literary genre that encompasses books with accounts of the teachings and/or deeds of Jesus of Nazareth, or a book belonging to that genre. (2) The message of Christianity as a whole, or a particular version of that message.

grace In theological discourse, the concept of assistance toward one's salvation given by God as a free gift.

Griesbach hypothesis One solution to the Synoptic Problem, according to which Matthew was the first Gospel written, Luke was written second and used Matthew as a source, and Mark was written third and used both Matthew and Luke as sources; also known as the Two Gospel Hypothesis.

hapax legomena Term for a word that occurs once and only once within a body of literature; a high percentage of such terms is sometimes taken as a sign that a given text does not belong within that body of literature.

heresy Teachings or beliefs deemed false, dangerous, and unacceptable within a particular religious framework.

historical criticism (1) The effort to understand a given religious text as its first readers would have, by reference to its original context. (2) The attempt by modern biblical critics to determine the veracity of the historical claims made in particular religious texts.

household code A set of rules governing relations between husbands and wives, parents and children, and masters and slaves, usually understanding these relationships in sharply hierarchical terms.

hypophora A figure of speech or rhetorical technique in which a speaker or writer poses a question and then answers it.

ideological criticism Any method of biblical interpretation that poses questions to the text based on a certain ideology or perspective, such as feminism, Marxism, or anti-colonialism.

Incarnation The concept of God taking on a human form, as in the Christian belief—articulated in the Prologue to the Gospel of John and defined as orthodox at the Council of Nicea—that the pre-existent Logos "became flesh" (Latin, *incarnatus*) in the person of Jesus of Nazareth.

inerrancy The concept that a particular religious text is incapable of error, usually based on the belief that God is directly responsible for the contents of the text.

internal evidence In textual criticism, the arguments that a particular variant reading is more likely to reflect the original wording of a text based on factors that are "internal"—that is, not based on the manuscripts but on the actual reading, when compared to the readings found in other manuscripts that include the same passage.

interpolation The insertion of words, phrases, or entire passages by a scribe copying a manuscript into a text that did not originally contain them.

Isis The major goddess in ancient Egyptian religion, the husband of Osiris and mother of Horus, associated with fertility, the afterlife, healing, and magic.

James, the brother of Jesus One of four individuals identified within the New Testament as brothers of Jesus (along with Joses, Jude, and Simon), a leader of the Jerusalem Christian community, a champion of conservative Jewish Christianity, and traditionally believed to be the author of the letter of James.

James, the son of Zebedee Disciple and apostle, a prominent member of the Twelve; called by Jesus along with his brother, John; believed to have been martyred in the mid-forties.

Jerusalem Council A meeting of the leaders of Christianity in 49 or 50 CE, called to determine whether Gentiles who came to believe in Christ would be required to observe all the commandments and practices of Judaism.

Jewish-Christian A Christian of Jewish background who continued to observe all the ethical and ritual requirements of Judaism.

Johannine literature A body of texts, including the Gospel of John and the three letters of John, produced by and for a particular Christian community apparently founded by Jesus' "Beloved Disciple."

John of Patmos The self-identified author of the book of Revelation.

John, the son of Zebedee Disciple and apostle, a prominent member of the Twelve, called by Jesus along with his brother James, said to have become one of the leaders of the Jerusalem church, traditionally identified as the author of the Johannine literature and the book of Revelation.

Joseph The husband of Mary and father of Jesus; in some traditions Jesus' legal father but not his biological father.

Judas Iscariot Disciple of Jesus and member of the Twelve, according to the Gospels he betrayed Jesus to the Jewish authorities, leading to Jesus' crucifixion.

Jude Brother of Jesus, purported author of the letter of Jude.

judicial rhetoric Speech or writing designed to persuade an audience (perhaps a judge or jury) to adopt a particular stance with respect to some action in the past, such as whether the action was just or unjust, innocent or harmful.

Junia The only woman identified as an "apostle" in the New Testament (by Paul in Rom. 16:7).

justification In a theological context, the state of being in a right relationship with God, of not being estranged from God as a result of sin that has not been forgiven or atoned for.

King James Bible (KJV) Hugely influential English translation of the Bible completed in 1611 with the approval of King James I of England, widely used by Protestants in England and America.

kosher Hebrew term referring to the Jewish system of dietary laws and restrictions that disallows the consumption of animals and foods that are unclean and mandates that clean foods and animals be butchered and prepared in particular ways.

Lazarus In the Gospel of John, the brother of Mary and Martha of Bethany, who is raised from the dead in Jesus' greatest miracle.

legalism Slavish adherence to the letter of the law without regard for extenuating circumstances.

Levites Jews who were members of the tribe of Levi, a tribe set aside for religious service, usually distinguished from priests (who were also Levites) by not having descended from Aaron and not being eligible to conduct sacrifices.

liberation theology Modern theological movement that reads the Bible (especially the teachings of Jesus and the prophets) as reflecting God's preference for the poor and opposition to oppression, and seeks to orient the modern Christian church to work for economic and political justice.

libertine One who rejects behavioral constraints and acts in a licentious fashion, especially in sexual matters.

literalism In biblical interpretation, an insistence that all passages not clearly marked as figurative (such as poetry or parable) must be interpreted literally and as factual in a historic and scientific sense.

literary criticism Method of biblical interpretation that seeks to examine biblical narratives as communications from authors to readers by analyzing literary techniques such as plot, characterization, narration, allusion, symbolism, and foreshadowing.

literary seam A juncture within a text where an abrupt transition, change of tone or style, or other such break seems to indicate that two originally distinct writings have been stitched together to form a new unity.

litotes Rhetorical technique that utilizes understatement for ironic effect.

Logos (or logos) (1) A Greek word meaning word, book, speech, and reason. (2) name given by some early Christians to the divine being who became incarnated as Jesus Christ. (3) In rhetoric, arguments based on reason or logic, as opposed to appeals to emotion (pathos) or to the good character of the speaker (ethos).

Luke-Acts Title given by scholars to the Gospel of Luke and the Acts of the Apostles to indicate that these two books were written by the same author and were designed to be read as two volumes of the same work rather than as two independent books.

Marcion Christian leader of the early to mid-second century CE who developed a distinctive version of Christianity that was fiercely anti-Jewish and insisted that Paul was the only true and reliable interpreter of Jesus; Marcion and his followers were deemed heretics by the proto-orthodox group.

Markan priority The theory that Mark was the first of the Synoptic Gospels to have been written, a theory that gained prominence in the nineteenth century and remains the scholarly consensus today.

Martha of Bethany Sister of Mary and Lazarus, a follower of Jesus who is featured prominently in the Gospels of Luke and John.

martyr Someone who is killed for refusing to renounce religious beliefs, often regarded as a hero by the surviving religious community.

Mary Magdalene Jesus' most prominent female follower, mentioned in all four Gospels; provider of financial support to Jesus' ministry (Luke 8:3); witness to the crucifixion and the empty tomb; first to see the risen Jesus (in several accounts).

Mary of Bethany Sister of Martha and Lazarus, a follower of Jesus who is featured prominently in the Gospels of Luke and John.

Mary the mother of Jesus According to two Gospels (Matthew and Luke), she gave birth to Jesus as a virgin. In one Gospel (John) she accompanies Jesus for at least part of his ministry and is present at his crucifixion. In Acts she is part of the first Christian community in Jerusalem following Jesus' resurrection. She becomes an object of Christian devotion increasingly from the second century CE onward.

Matthean priority The theory that Matthew was the first of the Synoptic Gospels to have been written, a theory that held sway for most of Christian history until the nineteenth century, when the vast majority of scholars began to believe that Mark, not Matthew, was the first Gospel written.

Matthew Disciple of Jesus and member of the Twelve; a tax collector prior to becoming an apostle, possibly identical to the tax collector and disciple called Levi in the Gospels of Mark and Luke; purported author of the Gospel of Matthew.

Messiah A Hebrew term meaning "anointed one," translated into Greek as "Christ"; the object of a belief among some Jews in the Second Temple period that God would send a leader to rescue or deliver them in some way. Expectations about the timing and manner of this deliverance varied widely and often hinged on different interpretations of prophecy.

messianic secret A motif in the Gospel of Mark whereby Jesus insists that the people he has healed and demons who know who he is should not tell anyone about him.

miniscule A kind of New Testament manuscript that uses a lower-case cursive script developed around 800 CE to replace the less efficient uncial script.

misogyny Fear and hatred of women, often manifested in sexual violence, domestic abuse, laws and customs that restrict women's freedom and opportunities, and patriarchal forms of social organization.

motif A recurring pattern within a literary text.

multiple attestation Within historical Jesus research, a criterion for authenticity that suggests sayings attributed to Jesus are more likely to be authentic if they are found in multiple, independent sources.

mystery religions A group of Greco-Roman religions that did not reveal their beliefs and ritual practices to outsiders but introduced them gradually to initiates; prominent examples included the Eleusinian mysteries and the cults of Isis, Mithras, and Dionysus.

myth Stories within a particular religion or culture that express the group's deepest beliefs about the gods, the universe, and themselves.

Nag Hammadi library The trove of Gnostic Christian texts dating from the fourth century CE that were discovered near Nag Hammadi, Egypt, in 1945, including a complete copy of the *Gospel of Thomas*, the only surviving copy of the *Gospel of Philip*, and several copies of the *Gospel of Truth* and the *Apocryphon of John*.

Nero Roman emperor (reigned 54–68 CE) known for instigating a local but severe persecution of Christians, probably resulting in the deaths of Peter and Paul.

Onesimus A runaway slave on whose behalf Paul wrote the letter to Philemon, Onesimus's master.

oracle (1) A person who receives and transmits messages from the gods, such as the oracle at Delphi. (2) A prediction about the future, supposedly of divine origin.

Oral Torah In Second Temple Judaism, the teachings of the great rabbis on matters that were unclear or not covered in the written Torah or Law of Moses, which were remembered, passed along orally, and regarded as authoritative (especially among the Pharisees), also known as the "tradition of the elders"; eventually written down and collected in the Mishnah, and later expanded as the Talmud.

oral tradition Stories and sayings that are passed along orally from one community to another and from one generation to the next; the primary means by which the teachings and deeds of Jesus were preserved prior to the writing of Gospels some decades after his death.

Orthodoxy From the perspective of a particular church, denomination, or religion, those beliefs and opinions that are regarded as assuredly correct.

Osiris A major Egyptian deity associated with the underworld, the afterlife, and the cycle of life and death; husband and brother of Isis and father of Horus; said in myth to have been killed and dismembered by Set but reassembled and brought back to life by Isis.

Ossuary A box containing the bones of a deceased person.

paganism Umbrella term for a variety of religions united by (a) the worship of many gods, especially gods associated with the forces of nature; (b) an emphasis on agriculture and fertility generally; and (c) requiring devotees to sponsor regular sacrifices (usually of animals) during annual festivals overseen by the religion's priests and held at temples dedicated to each god.

paleography The study of ancient writing, often used to determine when a particular manuscript was written.

Palestine The Roman name for the region or province that included the traditional Jewish homelands known variously as Israel, Judah (or Judea), Samaria, and Galilee.

parable A short story or comparison used for teaching purposes, illuminating a difficult or obscure point by comparing it to something familiar and common in the lives of the audience; a teaching technique employed often by Jesus in the Synoptic Gospels.

parenesis Commands or exhortations, frequently ethical in nature, which formed one of the essential elements of a Hellenistic letter or epistle.

parousia In Christianity, the anticipated second coming of Christ at the final judgment.

Passover One of the major festivals in Judaism, celebrated in the early spring, consisting in part of a sacred meal in which the story of the Exodus is retold and participants feast on a lamb slaughtered for the occasion; part of a week-long celebration that beings with the Feast of Unleavened Bread.

Pastoral Epistles Collective name for 1 and 2 Timothy and Titus, a set of letters within the Pauline corpus distinguished by (a) almost certainly not having been written by Paul, (b) reflecting a period later than that of the genuine letters of Paul and the other deutero-Pauline letters, and (c) being addressed to individual church leaders (pastors) rather than church communities and dealing with matters pertaining to church structure and leadership.

pathos In rhetoric, arguments designed to appeal to the audience's emotions.

patriarchy A mode of social organization in which males rule over females both within the family and in the broader society, the male head of household (*paterfamilias*) has complete authority over his wife, children, and slaves.

Paul Apostle of Jesus Christ, author of at least seven letters included in the New Testament, and purported author of seven additional letters; hero of the second half of the Acts of the Apostles; converted to Christianity several years after the death of Jesus following a vision in which Jesus allegedly appeared and spoke to him; foremost champion of Gentile Christianity, the version of the religion that spread successfully throughout the Greco-Roman world; probably martyred under Nero in the sixties.

peasant A person who works the land in an agricultural capacity, either as a small landowner, tenant farmer, day laborer, or agricultural slave.

pericope An individual episode or unit within a literary work such as a gospel.

Persephone Greek fertility goddess, daughter of Demeter and part-time consort of Hades; worshipped within the Eleusian mysteries, among other cults.

Peter Also Simon Peter, Simon, and Cephas, disciple and apostle, the most prominent member of the Twelve; denied Jesus during his passion, but recovered his faith and courage to become one of the leaders of the post-resurrection Jerusalem Christian community. Christian tradition holds that Peter became the bishop of Rome toward the end of his life, and that he was killed by the Roman emperor Nero during an outbreak of persecution in the mid-sixties.

Pharisees One of several sects of Judaism that emerged in the Second Temple period. Known for their emphasis on knowledge and scrupulous observance of the Torah in daily life, their wisest members became the rabbis who ran the synagogues around which Jewish life centered, especially in the Diaspora. Rabbinic Judaism, which became the basis for all modern forms of Judaism, developed from the Pharisees.

Philemon An apparently wealthy Christian convert of Paul, whose house served as the location of church services in his city and whose runaway slave Onesimus became the subject of Paul's letter to Philemon.

piety Positive religious behaviors that are thought by a given religion to be pleasing to the divine. Such acts as praying, fasting, giving alms, and making pilgrimages to sacred sites are often considered pious.

pilgrimage A journey to a sacred place motivated by religious devotion and often culminating in a sacrifice or the performance of some other pious deed.

pleonasm A figure of speech involving the use of more words than are strictly necessary, for emphasis; for example, "I saw it with my own eyes."

polytheism Belief in and worship of multiple gods, as opposed to one god (monotheism) or no gods (atheism).

Pontius Pilate Roman governor (prefect or procurator) of the Province of Judea, on whose orders Jesus was crucified. The Gospels suggest that Pilate believed Jesus was innocent of wrong-doing and had no wish to see him killed, but that he succumbed to pressure from the Jewish authorities to approve Jesus' execution.

Porphyry Prominent pagan critic of Christianity. His major work in this area, *Adversus Christianos* (*Against the Christians*), does not survive but much is known of it from the works of Christian apologists who attempted to refute him.

preexistence In Christian theology, the belief that prior to the birth or appearance of Jesus of Nazareth, the being (known as the Logos) who was incarnated as Jesus existed in heaven from the beginning of time as a divine, spiritual being.

premillennialism In Christian theology, the belief that Christ's return to earth and all the events associated with it will occur before his literal thousand-year reign (the millennium), as opposed the belief that Christ's return will occur after the millennium (postmillennialism) or that there will not be a literal kingdom on earth (amillennialism).

presbyter An elder, either in the informal sense of a senior member of a church congregation or in the formal sense of an officer of a church with specific duties.

priest In many ancient religions, a person who was authorized to perform sacrifices and was expert in religious ritual.

proof from prophecy A form of argument in favor of Jesus' messianic identity based on his alleged fulfillment of prophecies about the Messiah in the Old Testament (Hebrew Bible).

proselyte A recent convert or a person in the process of converting to a new religion.

prosperity gospel A modern form of Christianity that insists that Jesus was personally wealthy and that God will bestow wealth upon true followers of Jesus.

proto-orthodox Term used for the group in early Christianity that eventually emerged as dominant and was able to define rival Christian groups as deviant and heretical.

provenance The place of origin of a writing or artifact, for example the city or region in which a Gospel was written.

Pseudepigrapha Noncanonical religious books classified as "false writings" (Greek, *pseudepigrapha*) because their authors employed pseudonyms, usually choosing the names of long-dead religious figures of some significance. When capitalized, the specific body of pseudonymous literature produced by ancient Judaism between 300 BCE and 300 CE.

pseudonymity The practice of writing a text under a false name.

Q A hypothetical lost gospel consisting mostly of sayings of Jesus, believed by many scholars to have been a source for the Gospels of Matthew and Luke.

rabbi From the Hebrew word for "master," a teacher who is expert in the Torah (Mosaic Law) and its application to daily life.

rapture Modern term for an apocalyptic event predicted in 1 Thessalonians 4:17, in which the faithful who are still alive at Christ's coming will be taken up "to meet the Lord in the air" during the events of the last days.

redaction In biblical criticism, parts of a text that do not derive from oral tradition or written sources, but are supplied by the author or editor.

redaction criticism A method of biblical criticism that compares the contents of later works to their written predecessors and notes how the later writer edited his sources, seeing these additions, deletions, and modifications as keys to revealing the author's purpose in writing and uncovering the meaning of the text.

resurrection In Christianity, a belief inherited from certain apocalyptic strains of Judaism that the dead will be raised and will receive rewards or punishment at the end of the age. Christians believe Jesus was raised from the dead and that his followers will be raised to eternal life as well.

rhetoric The art of persuasion in speech or writing, a major topic of study in Greco-Roman education.

rhetorical situation The specific set of challenges or problems faced by a speaker or writer in a persuasive discourse.

rhetorical strategy The plan formulated by a speaker or writer to persuade an audience by rhetorical means such as arrangement, delivery, arguments based on ethos, logos, and pathos, and the use of specific rhetorical devices or techniques.

ritual purity The state of being (ritually) clean in the eyes of God, achieved by avoiding contact with persons, things, or food that are deemed unclean in a particular religious framework, or by removing uncleanness (usually through washing with water in a prescribed manner).

Sabbath In Judaism, the seventh day of the week (understood as sundown Friday to sundown Saturday) on which no work could be done.

Sadducees A sect of Judaism that emerged in the Second Temple period, overseen and controlled by the priests of the Jerusalem Temple, their aristocratic allies, and the scribes and retainers within the governmental bureaucracy (most importantly within the Sanhedrin, a Jewish council that issued legal opinions and administered justice).

sage In Jewish tradition, a wise man whose wisdom was rooted in a religious perspective. Jewish sages were understood to be the primary authors of the Writings, the third set of books included in the Hebrew Bible (after the Law and the Prophets).

Samaritans People of Israelite ancestry who lived in Samaria, the territory north of Judea but south of Galilee, an area once controlled by the northern kingdom of Israel or Ephraim; seen by Jews (Israelites who lived in the southern kingdom of Judah) as enemies who had allowed their blood and their religion to be contaminated by foreigners, especially Assyrians.

Satan In Jewish tradition, a supernatural being (also known as Lucifer, Beelzebub, or the Devil) who evolved from an angel and member of the heavenly council whose task it was to "accuse" (Hebrew, *satan*) humans before God to a fallen angel who rebelled against God, was cast out of heaven, and ruled over the domain of hell with his army of demons, seeking to tempt human beings and capture their allegiance and their eternal souls.

schism A major split or rupture between two groups within a particular religion.

scribe In ancient Judaism, a person who earned a living by means of his ability to read and write, performing such functions as copying texts, drawing up contracts, reading and reciting for non-literate audiences, teaching, and serving as religious authorities.

Septuagint Second-century CE translation of the Hebrew scriptures into Greek, commonly abbreviated LXX (Roman numeral for seventy) because of the tradition that seventy translators produced the work. By the first century CE, this translation became the most commonly used version of the Hebrew Bible, especially in the Diaspora.

Sitz im Leben German for "situation in life," employed in biblical form criticism to describe a particular circumstance (such as preaching, ethical instruction, or apologetics) in the life of the early Christian community in which a specific oral tradition would have been preserved and utilized.

sociohistorical criticism Method of biblical criticism that seeks to reconstruct the social history of the community that produced and first used a sacred text and to understand how that history helped shape the kinds of stories that community remembered and how it led them to modify those stories in particular ways.

source criticism Method of biblical criticism that seeks to uncover the oral and written sources employed by a particular biblical writer through a careful study of the text and comparison of the text to other extant writings.

Stephen A hero of the Acts of the Apostles, a leader of the Hellenists within the Jerusalem church, martyred after delivering a fiery speech in which he criticizes the Jews for their unbelief.

Suffering Servant A figure mentioned in chapters 52–53 of Isaiah who takes on the sins of the people and suffers vicariously on their behalf, winning divine pardon in the process. These passages were cited frequently by early Christians to provide the biblical basis for their conception of a suffering Messiah (Jesus) who atones for the sins of many.

supersessionism The idea that a later religion emerging or evolving from an earlier one has replaced and invalidated its predecessor.

superstition (1) In general use, any unfounded, ignorant, or irrational belief. (2) Within Roman thought, any religion that lacked legitimacy because of its inability to provide an ancient pedigree.

synagogue A place where Jews gathered for worship, prayer, and the reading and study of the scriptures, found in every city or town with a significant Jewish population by the later part of the Second Temple period.

syncretism The combination of beliefs and practices from multiple religions into a single new system of belief and practice.

synopsis In biblical studies, a book that arranges similar texts in side-by-side columns for easy comparison.

Synoptic Gospels Collective term for the Gospels of Matthew, Mark, and Luke, so-called because their close similarities, which can be seen by arranging their texts side by side in a synopsis. Scholars believe these similarities result from literary dependence between these Gospels.

tax collector In the New Testament, a person of Jewish heritage who collected revenue on behalf of the Roman government. Tax collectors were despised because of their greed, corruption, and collaboration with foreigners in the oppression of their own people.

temple (1) A building or site where sacrifices to a particular deity took place. (2) When capitalized, the complex in Jerusalem at which sacrifices to YHWH were offered.

terminus a quo The earliest possible date for a text's composition.

terminus ad quem The latest possible date for a text's composition.

testament Archaic English word for covenant, used by Christians to divide the Bible into its two main parts: the Old Testament, which describes the covenant between God and the Jewish people, sealed by circumcision; and the New Testament, which describes the covenant between God and believers in Jesus Christ, sealed by baptism.

textual criticism A method of biblical criticism that examines the surviving ancient manuscripts of a given biblical text, compares the variations between them, and attempts to determine which variant probably reflects the wording of the original.

Timothy A prominent coworker of Paul, sent by him as his emissary to the Thessalonians (1 Thess. 3:5–8); purported addressee of 1 and 2 Timothy.

Titus A prominent coworker of Paul, sent by him as his emissary to the Corinthians (2 Cor. 7:6–7; 12:18); purported addressee of the letter to Titus.

Torah (1) Hebrew word meaning "law," used specifically for traditional Jewish instruction based upon the Law of Moses. (2) The five books (also termed the Pentateuch) in which the Law of Moses is found: Genesis, Exodus, Leviticus, Numbers, and Deuteronomy.

tradition In form and redaction criticism, the parts of a Gospel passage that the evangelist inherited from his oral or written source, as distinct from elements of the text that were added by the evangelist (which are called "redaction").

triple tradition Stories and sayings that are found in all three Synoptic Gospels: Matthew, Mark, and Luke.

Twelve, the In the Gospels, Jesus' inner circle of disciples, who were also appointed as apostles.

Two Source Hypothesis The most popular solution to the Synoptic Problem, which posits that the authors of Matthew and Luke each independently used the Gospel of Mark and the now-lost sayings collection Q as their primary sources.

uncial A style of Greek writing featuring unconnected capital letters and little or no punctuation, found in the earliest surviving New Testament manuscripts.

unclean In Judaism, a condition of ritual impurity displeasing to God and unacceptable in a holy place, endemic to certain animals such as pigs, shellfish, and snakes, and acquirable by humans by virtue of suffering certain conditions (such as bleeding or leprosy), eating unclean foods, or coming into contact with unclean persons.

variant reading Phenomenon wherein two or more surviving manuscripts of a particular ancient text have different wordings for a given passage, necessitating the application of textual criticism to attempt to determine which variant is more likely to reflect the wording of the original document.

YHWH The name of God (also known as the tetragrammaton) in the Hebrew Bible (Old Testament), related to the Hebrew verb "to be" and traditionally understood as a statement of God's self-existence ("I am"). It is usually pronounced "Yahweh" within Christianity, but observant Jews regard the name as too sacred to pronounce and utilize a substitute expression such as Adonai ("the Lord").

Zealots One of several revolutionary groups within Judaism during the period of Roman rule that together were called the "Fourth Philosophy" by Josephus; major participants in the First Jewish-Roman War of 66–70 CE.

INDEX

Note: The abbreviations *c, cap, d, f, i, m, s, t,* or *n* that follow page numbers indicate charts, captions, diagrams, figures, illustrations, maps, sidebars, tables, or footnotes, respectively.